ARBITRATION OF
THE STEEL WAGE STRUCTURE

ARBITRATION OF THE STEEL WAGE STRUCTURE

GUIDES, PRINCIPLES AND FRAMEWORK
FOR THE SETTLEMENT OF
JOB DESCRIPTION AND CLASSIFICATION
DISPUTES AND RELATED PROBLEMS

By HERBERT L. SHERMAN, Jr.

UNIVERSITY OF PITTSBURGH PRESS

DEDICATION

This book is dedicated as a monument to two great men—

R. CONRAD COOPER
United States Steel Corporation

and

ELMER J. MALOY
United Steelworkers of America

for their numerous invaluable contributions
to the field of collective bargaining.

Although their accomplishments are many,
they will be especially remembered in the
labor relations history of the United States
for their leading roles in the creation and
implementation of a unique and renowned
program to eliminate wage rate inequities in
some of the most basic areas of our entire
American economy.

CONTENTS

TABLE OF CASES

Following each docket number is a designation of an important function, piece of equipment, or area involved in that case.

INTRODUCTION

PURPOSE OF THE BOOK

The present collection of materials is designed to aid in the settlement of job description and classification disputes and related wage structure problems involving production, maintenance and non-confidential clerical employees. Since decisions of the Board of Arbitration for Untied States Steel Corporation and the United Steelworkers of America are so widely used as precedents throughout the United States and Canada, cited by both Union and Company, the publication of these guideposts in one document (in readily available form) will constitute a useful contribution to the steel industry and other segments of our American economy.

Industrial relations personnel, Union representatives, industrial engineers, lawyers, arbitrators and others who are concerned with the areas covered by this volume will find that these materials provide a most useful framework for the consideration of their problems. There is no other similar collection of materials readily available to the public.

Well over 200 arbitration cases involving job description and classification and related matters have been heard by the Board of Arbitration since installation of the standard hourly wage scale in the United States Steel Corporation in February 1947. These decisions have served as guides to both Management and Union representatives in the preparation and maintenance of new and changed job descriptions and classifications. The awards have also been used as interpretations of the basic manual and the contractually prescribed procedures set forth in the basic agreements between the parties. It is hoped that organization of the present materials in this volume will provide further enlightenment in these areas.

SOURCE MATERIAL

All the awards contained in this volume involve disputes between United States Steel Corporation and United Steelworkers of America, and all are decisions of the Board of Arbitration. The awards selected for publication were thus limited in order that the reader might become familiar with all the important precedents established through the arbitration process in this field in one important segment of the steel industry. In fact, the reader will find available in this volume every decision of the Board in which disputed classification ratings for production and maintenance jobs were resolved.

Several arbitrators have contributed to the development of this "body of law." Although the Board of Arbitration itself was established by the parties in 1945, the first significant decisions concerning the wage rate inequity program were issued by Ralph Seward—the second chairman of the Board. (Seward later became permanent arbitrator for Bethlehem Steel Company and United Steelworkers of America.) From the middle of 1949 to August 1, 1951, there was no permanent chairman of the Board. During this period, however, a number of arbitrators served the parties on an ad hoc basis. Included in this group were such nationally recognized arbitrators as Sidney Cahn (who later became chairman of the Board of Arbitration for Jones and Laughlin Steel Corporation and United Steelworkers of America), Jacob Blair, Ray Forrester, Charles Killingsworth, Frederic Harbison, Donald Crawford, Orvis Keller and Sylvester Garrett.

In August of 1951 Sylvester Garrett became permanent chairman of the Board. His qualifications for the job were impressive. With background experience as an attorney for the National Labor Relations Board and as chief counsel to the Office of Price Administration, he served as Chairman of the Third Regional War Labor Board from 1942 to 1945. After service as a Public Member of the National War Labor Board in 1945 and as Vice Chairman of the National Wage Stabilization Board in 1946, he was retained as Coordinator of Labor Relations for Libbey, Owens, Ford Glass Company and Pittsburgh Plate Glass Company. And from 1949 to 1951 he served as Professor of Law at Stanford University. Since 1951 operation of the Board has been the responsibility of Sylvester Garrett, except for a period of 1957-1958 when he was on leave of absence and the present writer served as Chairman.

1

In 1952 the provision for company and union arbitrators was deleted from the Basic Agreement of the parties, and Section 7-J was added. It reads:

> The Chairman of the Board, in consultation with the parties, may employ one assistant (or more, if agreed upon by the parties) to analyze cases, conduct hearings and recommend decisions, so that the Board's docket can be brought to a current status and maintained currently.

Pursuant to this Section the present writer served the Board as a full-time assistant in 1952-1953. And ever since 1952 various other arbitrators have also served the Board on an ad hoc basis. This group includes some of the ad hoc arbitrators from an earlier period, plus John Coleman and C. B. McDermott.

The present volume contains one or more awards of all the above-named arbitrators.

CONTRIBUTIONS OF THE EDITOR

The principal contribution of the editor of this book, in addition to the arrangement and organization of the material, will be found in the analyses contained in many of the printed awards themselves. Most of the awards are those of Sylvester Garrett or the editor of this book. And since 1952, the editor has assisted Sylvester Garrett in the drafting of a number of his awards in the field of job classification disputes.

Since the source materials were not available in readily organized form, selection of cases and breaking them down under appropriate headings were tasks obviously requiring a substantial amount of judgment. Although there may be differences of opinion as to the appropriateness of the headings under which given cases are inserted, the reader is provided with numerous cross references in order that he may find other cases relevant to his problem.

Moreover, it will be noted that the opinions are printed in full. It is true that excerpting remarks from the context in which they are made would have made the book much shorter. But it is also true that the usefulness of the book would have been reduced. Reference to principles removed from the context in which they are developed is of little value in the solution and disposition of actual problems. In its present form, the book is a much more practical tool.

HISTORICAL SKETCH OF WAGE RATE INEQUITY PROGRAM

Job evaluation is simply a tool to establish or measure the relative value of jobs. The primary purpose of a job evaluation program is to eliminate wage rate inequities—different rates for what are essentially the same jobs. In order to appreciate the tremendous contribution made by the present job evaluation program in the steel industry, some familiarity with the highlights of its background is essential.

Although wage rate inequities were known to exist in the steel industry prior to 1937, the advent of the United Steelworkers of America brought about a greater consciousness of the problem. With continued improvements in the fields of communication and transportation, and a national union in existence, comparison of wage rates between plants became possible. There resulted more and more allegations of wage rate inequities. Prior to the job evaluation program in the steel industry, the vast majority of all grievances came from disputes over wage rates.

With adjustment of wage rates on a local level and no mutually approved yardstick to use, it is easy to understand how wage rate inequity claims would multiply. Furthermore, there was always the danger that a wage rate determination might be influenced by such incongruous factors as race, color, religion, family relationship, or membership in a social club. And of course adjustment of some wage rates only tended to create even more inequities and more pressures. Adjustment of the rate for one job merely resulted in requests for adjustments of rates for similar or related jobs.

The United Steelworkers of America therefore joined the companies in seeking a solution to the problem. It also wanted to eliminate special rates for women, Southern differentials, and "Whispering Rates" (secret rate increases where the employees were told not to disclose the increases to others).

After various attempts had been made to solve the problem it came to a head in 1944 in the so-called "Steel Wage Case" before the National War Labor Board. In short, the Union was seeking "equal pay for similar work." Eighty-six steel companies with approximately 400,000 employees were involved in this dispute with the United Steelworkers of America. The existence of a serious problem was acknowledged by Management. Twelve of the steel companies had already formed the Cooperative Wage Study in Pittsburgh, Pennsylvania, to make a study of the relationship of pay and work. (This Study, which has grown to about 70 participating companies, has continued in existence as the Cooperative Wage Bureau in order to disseminate information to the participating companies about the application of the job description and classification procedures.)

On November 25, 1944, after a lengthy and detailed hearing, the National War Labor Board issued its famous order. This order in part directed the parties to ". . . negotiate the elimination of existing intra-plant wage rate inequities . . . in accordance with the following steps:

(1) Describe simply and concisely the content of each job.
(2) Place the jobs in their proper relationship.
(3) Reduce the job classifications to the smallest practical number by grouping those jobs having substantially equivalent content.
(4) Establish wage rates for the job classification. . . ."

To implement the Board's Directive, United States Steel proceeded first since it would have been awkward for all eighty-six companies to negotiate simultaneously with the Union. A Joint Wage Rate Inequity Committee was formed for United States Steel Corporation's steel producing subsidiaries. Elmer J. Maloy was chairman for the Union; R. Conrad Cooper was chairman for the Corporation. Meeting for the first time in February, 1945, the Joint Committee proceeded with its consideration of methods for describing and classifying jobs. The Union undertook joint responsibility with Management for the development of an acceptable and practical Manual.

3

Following mutually approved uniform procedures, the parties at top level then tested the Manual which they had developed by describing and classifying Benchmark and Specimen Example jobs. Almost 2,500 such jobs were eventually described and classified. The next step was to describe and classify the jobs at each plant. This was done by local Management and Union representatives who were guided by the Benchmark and Specimen Example job descriptions and classifications. If the local plant committees could not reach agreement, the dispute was referred to the Joint Wage Rate Inequity Committee. In the steel producing operations of the United States Steel Corporation about 25,000 jobs were described and classified at this time.

Craft and assigned maintenance jobs were given special treatment, and special conventions were developed for testing and inspection, spell hand, and groupleader jobs. The description and classification of hourly rated clerical and technical jobs, and instructor and learner jobs, about 10 per cent of the total, were held for later consideration. Classification of these jobs was completed in 1948 and 1949.

As previously planned, in late 1946, the parties proceeded with the problem of negotiating a standard hourly wage scale. Such a wage scale, progressing upward from job class to job class in uniform increments, was put into effect in February, 1947. All rates in effect lower than the Standard Hourly Wage Rates were raised. Wage rates in effect higher than the Standard Hourly Wage Rates were red-circled (personal out-of-line differentials were created, identified and applied to the individual employees while they remained on those jobs). Starting in May, 1947, all of the jobs described and classified were also reviewed for error under the guidance of the Joint Wage Rate Inequity Committee.

Since April 22, 1947, the Basic Labor Agreements between the United States Steel Corporation and the United Steelworkers of America have provided that no grievance alleging a wage rate inequity may be filed or processed. However, provision has been made for the handling of grievances which may result from disputes in the description and classification of new or changed jobs. And each new Basic Labor Agreement negotiated has included consideration of the standard hourly wage scale of rates, since such scale is the basis for the actual earnings of each employee represented by the Union.

In January, 1953, the various inequity agreements developed over the years by the Union and United States Steel Corporation were condensed and incorporated without change in substance into one document, the January 1, 1953 Job Description and Classification Manual for Hourly Rated Production, Maintenance and Non-Confidential Clerical Jobs.

All of the large basic steel companies except Inland Steel have adopted the Cooperative Wage Bureau's job description and classification Manual and its related procedures. In fact, this Manual has been applied to cover the description and classification of nearly 180,000 jobs covering some 600,000 employees in many different companies.

The job evaluation program in the steel industry has been hailed as a success by both Union and Management representatives alike. One of the outstanding reasons for its success is the fact that concrete Specimen Examples are employed in interpreting the abstract language used in describing the coding levels of the Manual. In fact, it is provided in the January 1, 1953 Manual that:

> The description and classification of each job shall be consistent with and
> properly related within the framework of the descriptions and classifica-
> tions of the appropriate "Benchmark" and "Specimen Example" jobs
> listed in Exhibit A of this manual which, by reference, are hereby made
> a part of the manual.

Several further developments should also be noted. In order to make as much information as possible on similar jobs readily available, the Cooperative Wage Bureau in 1952 developed a Handbook of Standard Titles and Codes with about 900 standard job titles. In 1955 all member companies completed the coding and titling of their job descriptions and classifications under this Handbook. This information is used by the companies in the correlation of new and changed jobs. In the United States Steel Corporation the Chief Industrial Engineer—Wage and Salary Evaluation uses this information in providing guidance to the various Divisions to insure policy compliance in matters relating to job descriptions and classifications. Joseph Molnar, whose efforts have contributed markedly to the success of the parties in handling these matters in recent years, was the incumbent of this position until late 1959.

Another development to be noted is the issuance of a new Specimen Example for a job of Electronic Repairman. The Specimen Example for that job was issued in 1958.

And finally, in the 1960 Basic Agreement, it was provided that a Human Relations Research Committee might consider, among other things, any mutual problems under the present job classification system.

For a more detailed history of the Wage Rate Inequity Program, reference may be made to *Stieber, The Steel Industry Wage Structure* (Harvard University Press, 1959).

PART I

STABILITY OF THE RATE STRUCTURE AND RELATED PROBLEMS

CHAPTER 1

CLAIM OF INITIAL CLASSIFICATION ERROR

This chapter presents cases in which either the Union or Company is claiming that an error was made in the initial description or classification of a job. They show an attempt *at some later time* to correct the alleged initial error, the job description and classification alleged to be improper having been in effect since their establishment. The last two cases involve a claim of oversight in failing to describe and classify certain work assignments as separate jobs in the initial wage rate inequities program.

Other relevant cases reported elsewhere in this volume are: USC-293 (page 232), A-716, -717 (page 151), T-274 (2 Awards) (pages 113 and 114), T-569 (page 152), G-105 (page 103).

T—265. Fairfield Steel Works. September 29, 1953

Herbert L. Sherman, Jr., *Assistant to the Chairman*

Approved by Sylvester Garrett, *Chairman*

BACKGROUND

1. This grievance requests that the job of Boiler Operator Gangleader in the Blast Furnace Steam Plant at Fairfield Steel Works be classified two job classes above the Boiler Operator. By agreement of the parties, both at local and top level, the job of Boiler Operator has been classified in Job Class 11 and the job in dispute at Class 12.

2. The Union argues that the undisputed job description characterizes grievants' job as Boiler Operator Gangleader under the standard title; that the job description requires direction of the Boiler Operating crew; and that the Gangleader Convention, agreed to by the parties in their Memorandum of Understanding dated February 14, 1947, should be applied to place the job in Class 13—two classes higher than the Boiler Operator which is the next highest rated job in the Boiler Operating crew. Conceding that the parties have agreed upon Class 12 for this job, the Union contends that an error was made which should be corrected under Section 9-I of the Agreement. That Section reads as follows:

"Notwithstanding any provisions of this Section, errors in application of rates of pay shall be corrected."

3. Management emphasizes that the present classification was jointly approved, based on Specimen 550 for Operator-Boilerhouse. Designation of the standard title of Boiler Operator Gangleader is explained as being for filing purposes only. The Company contends that grievants' request amounts to a claim of a wage-rate inequity which is barred by Section 9-H of the Agreement.

4. Under the initial Wage Rate Inequities Program the job in dispute was given the title of Head Boiler Operator and placed in Class 11 on November 11, 1946. The Boiler Operator job was placed in Class 9. During the 1947 Inequities Review Program the standard title was added to the job description for grievants' job. The local committee then negotiated the classification values for the Boiler Operator and Boiler Operator Gangleader jobs and sent its recommendations to a top level committee composed of representatives of both of the parties. The recommendations that the Boiler Operator be classified at 10.6 for Class 11 and that the Boiler Operator Gangleader be classified at 11.6 for Class 12 were approved. No change in the description or classification for these jobs has been made to the present time.

5. Although both these jobs were listed by the Union in the April, 1951 Review, they were withdrawn. The Company believes that the Union was motivated by the Company's contention that the Boiler Operator job was rated too high. The present grievance was not filed until September 24, 1952.

DISCUSSION AND FINDINGS

6. The Board has often stated that, in the absence of a change in a job, it will not disturb a mutually agreed upon classification

7

on the ground that a mistake of judgment was made in evaluating the content of the job. It is not necessary to determine whether the job in dispute warrants the assignment of Gangleader status. The standard title was inserted before the parties affixed their signatures of approval to the classification. If they saw fit to classify the job by reference to the Specimen Examples for Boiler House Operators, the Board will not now substitute its judgment.

7. It is agreed that there has been no change in the duties of the job since the description was mutually agreed upon. The Board is being asked to correct what is now alleged to be an error which the parties failed to correct even in their 1951 Review Program. The requested relief goes beyond the Board's authority.

8. This decision conforms to well-established Board policy. The only possible deviation from that policy which has been called to the Board's attention might be found in language in an opinion of Acting Chairman Morgan in Case T-117. There the Company discontinued paying the 17 grievants as "Gangleaders" on the ground that an error had been made in labeling and paying them as such. This was after Management came to realize that the 17 grievants never, at any time since 1941, had performed the actual duties of Gangleaders. The situation was confused in that the 17 grievants long had been called "Lead" *Ironworkers,* in Class 16, but were slotted into the *standard rate at Class 15 for Boilermakers* on May 2, 1948, after the parties on March 3, 1948, had agreed that "Ironworkers" (a position rated job) should be changed to the Boilermaker craft job at Class 15, whereas, as Ironworkers, they had been in Class 14. On March 3 or shortly thereafter the parties also had

agreed upon a classification of Gangleader-Boilermaker in Job Class 17, apparently to make possible continuance of the practice of paying Lead-Ironworkers at two job classes above the Ironworker job when it was set up as the craft job of Boilermaker. But by the time the new Boilermaker and Gangleader classifications went into effect on May 2, 1948, the Company had concluded that the former "Lead" Ironworkers were not—for the most part—truly Gangleaders.

9. Dr. Morgan's opinion in T-117 included language suggesting that it constituted an "inequity" to pay the grievants there a rate above the standard Boilermaker rate, while other men, doing the same work, got only the standard rate for Boilermakers. Elsewhere, however, he stated in effect that the situation presented was merely correction of an error in slotting employees into agreed classifications.

10. To avoid any doubt it should be made clear that where the parties have described and classified a specific job at a given job class, and one party or the other *later* feels that an "error" was made, no true error exists to be corrected by action unilaterally instituted under Section 9-I. As far as this Board is concerned the original agreed classification is correct. This is made clear in Cases CI-217, T-202, T-230, T-234, and A-406, among other decisions. Any inference which one party or the other might draw from language in Dr. Morgan's opinion to suggest a different result would be unjustified and, in any event, wrong. Any such possible inference therefore is repudiated here to avoid future misunderstanding.

AWARD

11. The grievance is denied.

T—202. Ensley Works. October 9, 1952
Sylvester Garrett, *Chairman*

1. This grievance involves a claim that three painters in the M & E Department at Ensley Works were improperly required to paint smokestacks on November 10, 1950. In essence, the grievants contend that the painting of smokestacks falls outside of their job description, and therefore should be compensated at a higher rate of pay than provided for painters (Job Class 11).

2. The job description of painters in the M & E Department at Ensley Works originally was signed by Company and Union representatives on June 28, 1946. Under Working Procedure, Item 4 stated:

"Paints smokestacks standing on ground, supplies paint and tools to painters

working above ground. Hoists painters up the stack or lowers painters down the stack."

3. This description was in effect at the time grievants were required to paint stacks on November 10, 1950. Subsequently, on September 1, 1951, the painters' job description at Ensley Works was revised by the parties to conform it precisely with the job description for painters which prevailed generally through basic steel producing subsidiaries of U. S. Steel. The revised job description does not contain any language similar to Item 4 in the earlier description.

4. The Union contends that the original job description was erroneous and should

not have included any language indicating that the painters properly could be required to paint smokestacks.

5. In effect, the Union now asks the Board to review action taken by the parties in describing the painters' job at Ensley Works under the Wage Rate Inequities Program in order to correct an error. This appears in the statements of the Union Representative as follows:

"MR. KESLER: I think we ought to show right here there is some factual information on this particular subject that we are discussing that is not in the realm of theory, it's factual, that the trade and craft jobs it describes, of those, *there isn't any plant in the United States Steel Corporation, United States Steel Company now, that had anything to do with writing their local plant craft job description.*

"When they became a part of the Inequity Program—those job descriptions of the craft do not represent necessarily any set of craft duties of that particular type of craft at any one plant. To the complete contrary, they represent what is known as comprehensive all inclusive description of the particular craft you are talking about, and if you found that particular craft at any one of the Company's plants that job description a benchmark trade and craft standard description was the description of that particular craft at any one of the plants. That is factual. No theory about that.

"So the Union's contention that the job description which was put into effect with a local Union grievance committeeman and local plant Management was completely in violation of the Inequity Program and one of the principal agreements, the trade and craft agreement, of the whole entire Inequity Program. That is factual" * * * (Tr. pp. 29-30) (Underscoring added.)

And again:

"MR. KESLER: As I have said to you, Mr.

Chairman, *we believe that this then falls, the request of these grievants, falls into the category of the error in Wage Rate payments.* The description part is behind us, because that has been changed, and the only reason that they were changed were that they were considered by all parties that they were standard. In the case of the craft there was just one description, a comprehensive, all inclusive job description of the craft, not of any particular job at any one plant, and therefore, we are asking the Board to give these people their just dues and their pay under the error section of the contract, errors in wage rate payments." * * * (Tr. p. 33) (Underscoring added.)

6. In regard to this case, of course, the Board operates under the authority conferred upon it by the parties in the Basic Agreement of April 22, 1947. Nothing in the Basic Agreement contains any general authority for the Board to interpret provisions of the May 8, 1946, Inequities Agreement between the parties, or to review the manner in which the Inequities Program has been applied in specific instances. Rather, the Board's authority in regard to the Inequities Program is limited to those instances in which the Basic Agreement makes specific reference to some portion of the May 8, 1946, Agreement as providing the basis for handling a given type of problem.

7. This was made clear in the Awards in Case A-372, and more recently in Case CI-217.

8. Here the Union asks the Board to correct an error of the parties in describing the position of painter at Ensley Works under the Inequities Program, and to rule in effect that the duty of painting stacks should have been included in the description of a higher rated position. Since the requested relief sought in this grievance lies beyond the Board's authority, the grievance will be dismissed.

AWARD

9. The grievance is dismissed.

T—230. Ensley Works. May 21, 1953
Sylvester Garrett, *Chairman*

FINDINGS

1. In this case grievant, a "Repairman-Tools" in the Rigger Shop at Ensley Works, asserts that he is required regularly to perform work falling outside his job description. The grievance requests that he either be relieved of these particular duties or that his job be classified at a higher rate.

2. Prior to 1946 grievant worked as a Rigger "A." By mutual agreement in the Inequities Program his job was described as Rigger "A" (Tool Man) and put in Job Class 8. In May, 1949, a grievance was filed requesting a change in this classification and urging that the job belonged in Job Class 14, at the standard rate for Rigger. During late 1949, while the grievance was pending, rep-

resentatives of the parties agreed upon a new job description and title of "Repairman-Mechanical," and placed the job in Class 11. As a result of this agreement, the grievance was allowed to die in the grievance procedure.

3. During the 1951 Review Program at T.C.I. grievant's job (he being the only incumbent) was one of many listed by the Union for review. According to the Union it was agreed in the course of the Review Program that Repairman-Mechanical jobs would be abolished and incumbents of such jobs assigned to other appropriate jobs, except where repair was limited to some specific single operation. In any event, most of the "Repairman-Mechanical" jobs at T.C.I. were eliminated in the Review Program and incumbents assigned to such jobs as Millwright, Motor Inspector, or Rigger. Some were retained but with special purpose titles as "Repairman-Ladle Cars." The title of the job in dispute was changed to Repairman-Tools, but there was no change in the description of the duties, or in the job class. The Union withdrew the job from further discussion in the Review Program, relying on a belief that thereafter the job would be confined to duties of the sort normally covered by a "Repairman-Tools" type of job.

4. Shortly thereafter grievant's Foreman directed him to look over the hoisting machinery on the Hot Bed for possible repair, and the latter protested that he would do so only if his job description was revised. Both men carried the difference of opinion before Assistant Shops Superintendent Hassell, who directed grievant to go ahead with the job or else take an "out card." Both the Foreman and Hassell regarded this work as essentially the same as other work grievant had been performing for years. Grievant did the work and filed the present grievance.

5. The working procedure of the disputed job originally provided:

"WORKING PROCEDURE:

"1. Repairs and maintains all chain hoists, tugger hoists, blocks, jacks, etc. used for hoisting or rigging work in Ensley and other Works.
"2. Repairs tarpaulins.
"3. Makes curtains for locomotives and locomotive cranes.
"4. Repairs aerial and hospital stretchers.
"5. Works as Rigger 'A' in rigging crew on outside when required."

6. In 1949 this was modified only by deletion of Item 5, at the time the job title was changed and the job put in Class 11. In support of the present grievance, the Union argues that the following duties have been added to the job:

"1. Makes all rope and snatch blocks used at Ensley and Bessemer Rolling Mill; blocks are not repaired but actually made by the grievant.
"2. Makes air ducts from canvas and according to specifications for diesel engines, such air ducts being used as a ventilator to keep particles of dust out of the generator.
"3. Takes measurements and makes tarpaulins for trucks throughout the Company.
"4. Makes and installs canopies on steel frames built on trucks; takes measurements for frames and gives it to Riggers who build the frames under the grievant's direction; performs drilling on the frames.
"5. Overhauls diesel machinery to the extent of taking machines apart for necessary replacement; writes up orders on any parts to be made and gives it to the Machine Shop; that such overhauling work is done on electric, steam and tugger hoists; that the tugger hoists are located in the field and the grievant goes to the field when working on them. (It was agreed at the hearing that the reference to diesel machinery under this item was an error.)
"6. Performs work on stiff-leg derricks reworking the blocks and shields and replacing repivot bushing; assisted in this work by the Riggers who are under his direction.
"7. Has overhauled hydraulic cable cutters repairing the cylinders and replacing washers.
"8. Maintains pipe benders which are brought to the shop.
"9. Orders and maintains large supply of material and parts used in his work."

7. The evidence is entirely clear that these are not new type duties imposed upon the grievant. He has performed substantially these duties during most of his 12 years of service in his present job, even though today he may be doing more work of some types, and less of others, than in earlier years. All of them can be related to language in the 4 items of the Working Procedure of the job, even though some go beyond the literal language of the description.

8. It is not uncommon, of course, that the parties fail to achieve perfection in de-

scribing the duties of a job. While this may give rise to troublesome problems for the parties, the Board is not authorized under the Basic Agreement to disturb the situation when it is clear that the job actually is being performed in the same manner as it was when described and classified. The Board has no standing to attempt to improve upon the results achieved by the parties under their Inequities Program.

9. Thus, unless some enforceable agreement as to this job resulted from the Review Program in 1951, the grievance must be denied.

10. The Union apparently believed in the 1951 Review Program that the existing written job description for the grievant described the extent of the job as actually performed, and its representatives therefore felt that the job was confined to repairing tools in the Rigger Shop. Some of the job descriptions involved in the Review Program were checked by the Union with the employees for accuracy, but this one was not. The Union contends that the present job description for grievant's job does not embrace all the duties actually performed by the grievant.

11. The Union further asserts that it would not have agreed to designate this job as Repairman-Tools had it known about these other duties which it believes are not covered by the description. Reference is made to the assignment of some of the former incumbents of "Repairman-Mechanical" jobs to a Millwright's position with an understanding that they would perform only the work of Millwrights (or whatever standard job it happened to be) and not the duties previously performed. Thus, the Union believes that the grievant should be relieved of the duties going beyond the precise language of the job description or that the job should be placed in a higher job class.

12. The Company agrees that an understanding was reached in the 1951 Review Program under which the word "Mechanical" was to be deleted from all Repairman-Mechanical jobs and the incumbents assigned to other jobs, or a specific label, as "Tools," also attached to the word "Repairman." Management points out, however, that the job in dispute was one of the last to be reviewed, that no particular or detailed discussion took place concerning it, and that the Union merely noted that Job Class 11 was assigned to this job. It was Management's impression then, as now, that the "Tools" repaired by grievant are "Rigger Tools" as indicated in the Primary Function of the job "to repair and maintain all rigging equipment for Ensley and other Works."

13. Under all the evidence, it is not shown that Management agreed in the Review Program that the duties performed in the disputed job thereafter would be limited to a narrower scope than had been the case up to that time. The Board cannot, therefore, undertake to accomplish a refinement in regard to this job which the parties did not agree upon definitely in the Review Program.

14. Accordingly, the grievance will be denied.

AWARD

15. The grievance is denied.

T—234. Fairfield Steel Works.   April 24, 1953
Sylvester Garrett, *Chairman*

BACKGROUND

1. This grievance presents the question of whether the Company properly eliminated the job of Rigger in the Machine Shop at Fairfield Steel Works.

2. Grievant Salter, a Rigger, was transferred to the Machine Shop in 1944. He held the position of Rigger in the Machine Shop both when the job was jointly described and classified in 1946, and when it was redescribed and reclassified under the Inequities Program. In 1951 the Company decided that Salter was not actually required to perform the full functions of a Rigger, and that he had not been performing such functions even when the job was described and classified in 1947. Grievant was therefore informed that his job was discontinued, and that he would either be laid off or transferred to the Rigger Shop. His former duties were then assigned to the Crane Hookers—Job Class 4. Grievant was transferred to the Rigger Shop, and requests that he be restored to the Rigger job in the Machine Shop.

3. In seeking to eliminate the Rigger job in the Machine Shop, the Company noted that grievant was the only Rigger in the Machine Shop, no Rigger being assigned to the 3 to 11 or 11 to 7 turns. The Union counters that 90% of the difficult loading and unloading was done on the 7 to 3 turn, when the Rigger was present to handle and direct the operation.

4. The Union contends that the Com-

pany violated an established practice under Section 2-B of the April 22, 1947, Agreement by eliminating the Rigger job. It denies that the Company can "discontinue" a job in these circumstances and reassign the duties to a lower job class. Reliance also is placed on Section 9-D, the Union asserting that a job cannot be terminated unless it is vacant for a year, the operation is not longer performed, or there is mutual agreement.

5. Primarily the Company argues that there is nothing in the Agreement which restricts Management's right to terminate a job. Great emphasis is placed on the fact that Salter in practice was not required to perform the full duties of a Rigger's job in the Machine Shop. The Company feels that the Crane Hookers are not being required to do anything which is not properly part of their job.

6. Though conceding that nothing was done between 1947 and 1951 which would have changed the work of the Rigger, the Company takes the position that it is entitled under Section 3 of the Agreement to discontinue the job and assign the duties to the Crane Hookers. In essence, it holds that a mistake was made when the parties described and classified the work done by Salter as that of a Rigger, Job Class 14.

DISCUSSION

7. Craft jobs have been treated differently from production jobs by the parties in that it is recognized that there are varying degrees of duties which may be required of a craftsman. Indeed, three job class rates have been established to take into account differences in the skills of individuals in this type of job. Uniformity is achieved, however, by employing a standard job description and classification for that which a fully qualified craftsman may be required to perform at a given work station. Qualifications and ability are credited in classification of the craft job whether or not the duties actually performed in any given instance, as a Rigger in the Machine Shop,

call for full utilization of such qualification and ability. The parties thus decided that where the existence of a craft job was clear, they would not concern themselves with the question as to whether or not the full duties of the craft job were being performed.

8. By mutually agreeing in 1947 to place the job here in dispute under the standard description and classification for the trade or craft job of Rigger, the parties acknowledged the existence of the craft job of Rigger in the Machine Shop. This the Board must accept as binding upon it. Otherwise, what were the parties describing and classifying? If the parties were not mutually recognizing the existence of such a craft job, their actions in applying the standard description and classification were meaningless.

9. The Board then is faced with the question of whether the duties of a recognized craft job properly may be dispersed among noncraft jobs. It is clear that the answer must be in the negative if due weight is to be given to the agreed system of using a standard job description and classification for acknowledged craft jobs irrespective of the scope of the actual duties performed. It must be inferred that any such dispersal of craft duties among noncraft jobs was not contemplated by the parties as being permissible. Of course, it should not be necessary to add that the scope of actual work performed by a craftsman may be changed within the context of the standard job description and classification.

10. Accordingly, the Board holds that the Company was not authorized to assign the duties of the Rigger in the Machine Shop to noncraft employees, so as to eliminate the Rigger position. In so doing, it laid off grievant from the position which he was entitled to hold on the basis of his seniority protected under Section 13.

AWARD

11. The grievance is sustained. Grievant shall be restored to the position of Rigger in the Machine Shop.

A—406. Worcester Works. May 21, 1953
Sylvester Garrett, *Chairman*

BACKGROUND

1. This grievance requests that the job of Conductor (Standard Gauge) at South Works Plant of Worcester Works be raised from Job Class 13 to Job Class 15 by application of the Group Leader Conventions.

2. Although prior to February, 1947, the Conductors were considered as Foremen, they were told at that time that they were thereafter to work as "Group Leaders" in the bargaining unit. The Company then proposed a new job description for the Conductors, dated February 19, 1947, and a classification at Job Class 13. This proposed classification was on the basis of the Group

Leader Conventions, relying on the fact that the Engineer (highest rated job in the group led) was classified at Class 11.

3. The local Union representatives did not sign the proposed classification for Conductor, but it was installed by local Management in March, 1947. As far as the local Union representatives were concerned, there was no dispute between the Union and the Company at this time, even though the classification was not signed by both parties. In fact, there was no indication of a difference of opinion locally as to classification of Conductors until December, 1948, when actions taken by the Company, described below, led to the present grievance.

4. The situation which arose in December, 1948 came after completion of a broad study undertaken by the Joint Wage Rate Inequity Committee covering transportation jobs throughout the bargaining unit. This over-all study resulted from numerous inquiries to the Joint Inequity Committee from various plants, as well as classification disputes in some, and continued through 1947 and into 1948, in an effort to develop a pattern for classification of transportation jobs in all plants covered by the Basic Agreement. Finally in May, 1948, the Joint Inequity Committee reached general agreement on a pattern of classification to be applied in the various Transportation Departments.

5. In the following months the Joint Inequity Committee reviewed the classifications of all Transportation Department jobs, including classifications previously agreed upon at the local level. Such classifications were adjusted where necessary to conform to the pattern agreed upon in May, 1948. As a result, some Engineer jobs were raised from Job Class 11 to Job Class 13.

6. In December, 1948, the job of Engineer (Standard Gauge) at Worcester was raised from Class 11 to Class 13; the Switchman was raised from Class 7 to Class 9; and the Fireman was lowered from Class 7 to Class 6.

7. At this time, however, the Conductors were not given an increase of two job classes under the Group Leader Conventions although there was no change in the duties required of them. This grievance in effect asks that the Company be directed to continue to treat the Conductors as Group Leaders, and give them two job classes above Engineers.

FINDINGS

8. The parties have agreed upon the description and classification of Conductor-Standard Gauge, at Worcester Works.

9. The Company holds that this amounts to an agreement that Conductors no longer should be regarded as Group Leaders, since the agreed codings under the various factors of the job negative any inference that the job was being classified as a Group Leader job.

10. The Union disclaims any knowledge, on the part of its Joint Inequity Committee representatives, that the Conductor job was treated as a Group Leader job. It insists therefore, that the Joint Inequity Committee could not be held to have decided that the job of Conductor no longer would be recognized as a Group Leader job.

11. It is unnecessary for the Board to resolve this difference of opinion. If local Management erred in treating the Conductor as a Group Leader in February, 1947, and Management at a higher level later discovered the error in the course of the Joint Inequity Committee proceedings, this would seem to provide a sufficient basis for the action taken in December, 1948. At that time, Management was entitled to conclude that the Conductors at Worcester were properly classified under the agreed description for Conductor-Standard Gauge, and that there was no basis for continuing to treat them as Group Leaders. No agreement by the Union was necessary for Management to discontinue an erroneous treatment of the Conductor job, instituted without Union signature of the classification in February, 1947, and corrected by application of the agreed description and classification of Conductor-Standard Gauge in December, 1948.

12. There is no showing that the Conductors at Worcester Works have any duties or responsibilities not covered by the agreed description of the job, hence the Board can find no basis to direct any increase in their job class.

AWARD

13. The grievance is denied.

A—677. Waukegan Works. June 30, 1954

Herbert L. Sherman, Jr., *Arbitrator*
Approved by Sylvester Garrett, *Chairman*

BACKGROUND

1. This grievance claims that an error was made in the initial classification of the job of Wire Drawer Machine (Wet) (Dry Reels), Plant Code 24-37, which handles certain continuous wire drawing machines in the Matt and Broom Department at the Waukegan Works. The job in dispute originally involved the wet drawing of fine wire on 4-cone Syncro machines with dry reels, and was classified by agreement in 1946, at 8.8 for Job Class 9. In July, 1947, during the so-called "second look" at the original agreed upon classifications in the plant, no action was taken concerning this job. In May, 1948, 2-cone Syncro Machines and a spooling attachment were added to the equipment operated by the job. A new description and classification were prepared, which merely resulted in a change in the title of the job and a change in the list of equipments of the job. It was again agreed at this time that the classification should remain at 8.8 for Job Class 9. The grievance was filed on August 25, 1953.

2. The Union contends that an error was made when the parties agreed at local level to assign Job Class 9 to the continuous machine wire drawer job in the Matt and Broom Department at Waukegan Works. Evidence was introduced to show that two Specimen Example Machine Wire Drawer jobs are classified at Job Class 10. The same is true of a job at South Works—Worcester, which was placed in Job Class 10 by the top Joint Wage Rate Inequities Committee, in the course of the disputes procedure. Reference is also made to Machine Wire Drawer jobs cited as Benchmarks under Factors 5 and 7 in the Classification Manual. Correction of the alleged mistake at Waukegan is sought under Section 9-I of the Agreement. The Union asserts that prior awards noted by the Company are distinguishable, and do not control this case.

3. According to Management, this grievance is barred by Sections 9-D and 9-H of the Agreement. In the alternative it denies that a mistake was made in the classification of the job in dispute.

DISCUSSION AND FINDINGS

4. The Union agrees that this grievance is not based upon a claim that there has been any significant change in job content of the job under consideration. Its sole contention is that a mistake was made when the locally agreed upon classification for the machine wire drawing job in this case did not follow precisely the codings of jobs which had been agreed upon at top level as Benchmarks and Specimen Examples.

5. This contention has, however, been fully considered in the Award in T-265, where the following language is found:

"The Board has often stated that, in the absence of a change in a job, it will not disturb a mutually agreed upon classification on the ground that a mistake of judgment was made in evaluating the content of the job . . ."

"To avoid any doubt it should be made clear that where the parties have described and classified a specific job at a given job class, and one party or the other *later* feels that an 'error' was made, no true error exists to be corrected by action unilaterally instituted under Section 9-I. As far as this Board is concerned the original agreed classification is correct . . ."

6. The two Awards cited by the Union to show that the Board has referred to Specimen Example jobs are not applicable to this case. In USC-371 there was a claim of a change in job content, while COL-69 dealt with a new job.

AWARD

7. The grievance is denied.

T—263. Fairfield Steel Works. July 24, 1953

Herbert L. Sherman, Jr., *Assistant to the Chairman*
Approved by Sylvester Garrett, *Chairman*

BACKGROUND

1. Grievants, Blacksmith Helpers in the Forge Shop at Fairfield Steel Works, request that the Board direct the Company to replace the present description for the job of Blacksmith Helper with the standard description, and to establish a description and classification for the job of Hammer Driver.

2. The Union refers to the April, 1951

Memorandum of Understanding, indicating that certain job descriptions and classifications should be reviewed. It contends that an oral understanding was reached during the course of the April, 1951 Review Program to replace descriptions in effect for all trade and craft and maintenance jobs and their helpers with standard descriptions if the jobs were not already so covered. Management denies the existence of any such all inclusive agreement, though it admits that it agreed in a number of instances to install standard descriptions where it was found that the incumbents were performing duties appropriately covered by the standard descriptions.

3. The Blacksmith crews consist of a Blacksmith and three Blacksmith Helpers. Six power hammers, ranging from 1500 pounds to 2500 pounds capacity, are located in the Blacksmith Department of the Forge Shop. Some of the Blacksmith Helpers are required to operate the hammer lever in hammer forging as directed by the Blacksmith. This duty was listed under Item 5 of the Working Procedure when the job description for Blacksmith Helper was originally approved. It reads as follows: "Manipulates hammer lever in hammer forging as directed." No change was made in this respect in the 1947 or 1951 Inequity Review Programs. Furthermore, there has been no change in the duties of the job since its description was initially agreed upon.

4. In 1946 the job in dispute, titled Blacksmith Helper "A", was classified at 5.6 points for Job Class 6. During the 1951 Review Program representatives of the parties visited the Blacksmith Department and observed the work performed by grievants. Minor revisions were then made in the job description, but the Primary Function and Working Procedure remained unchanged. Job Class 6 also continued in effect by agreement of the parties.

5. However, the total point value was raised at this time from 5.6 to 6.3 to give credit for the hammer driving duties in addition to the standard Blacksmith Helper duties. It was recognized that Specimen 910 for a Blacksmith Helper is classified with a total rating of 5.6 while Specimen 909 for a Hammer Driver operating controls of power hammers up to 3000 pounds capacity is classified with a total of 5.9 points for Job Class 6. Specimen 906 in Job Class 8 for a Hammer Driver operating controls of a 6000 pound steam hammer was also considered. It is clear that this Specimen Example would be inapplicable, however, even if a separate job of Hammer Driver did exist

at the Blacksmith Department in question because none of the hammers has a capacity in excess of 2500 pounds.

6. During the 1951 Review Program Blacksmith Helper jobs at the Fairfield Sheet Mill and the By-Product Coke Department of the Fairfield Steel Works, both classified at 6.3, were also agreed to by representatives of the parties, even though they are combination Blacksmith Helper and Hammer Driver jobs.

DISCUSSION AND FINDINGS

7. The April, 1951 Memorandum relied on by the Union does not disclose an agreement to replace descriptions for trade and craft and maintenance jobs and their helpers with standard descriptions. No reference is found in the Memorandum to any such understanding. Nor did the Union establish at the hearing a supplemental agreement to that effect. Although Union testimony clearly showed that standard descriptions were adopted for numerous jobs, the existence of a definite, comprehensive, and sweeping agreement to use standard descriptions in all cases of helpers to trade and craft employees, whether or not the duties currently performed were appropriately covered by a standard description, was not demonstrated.

8. The Union agrees that the job description and classification for Blacksmith Helper now in effect were signed by representatives of the parties, but asserts that an error was made. Its further contention, in line with its initial position that standard descriptions were to be used for all such Helper jobs, that approval of the descriptions in the 1951 Review Program was conditional and that it was agreed to substitute a standard description if it was later discovered that any of the descriptions were not standard was not supported by the testimony at the hearing. Undoubtedly, the misunderstandings brought to light in the present case arose out of the fact that standard descriptions were adopted for many other similar jobs. This fact cannot, however, be considered as establishing a general agreement to treat all jobs, no matter what the circumstances are, in like manner.

9. Nor is there any contractual basis, in the absence of an enforceable understanding, for the Board to require the Company to install a Hammer Driver description and classification in these circumstances. The grievance, therefore, cannot be sustained.

AWARD

10. The grievance is denied.

CI—217.   Ohio Works.   February 1, 1952
Sylvester Garrett, *Chairman*

BACKGROUND

1. This grievance arose in the Blast Furnace Department, Ohio Works, and involves a request that the job filled by the grievant, designated as Laborer, (Plant Code 2090-1359-1360) be described and classified. It is claimed that the job was not described and classified under the Wage Rate Inequities Agreements because of an oversight, and that the job description and classification of Laborer, to which the parties agreed, actually is not appropriate for the duties performed by the grievant as a Helper of the Moulder (Casting Maker) in the Blast Furnace. It is claimed that once the position is described and classified, the applicable standard hourly rate should be applied retroactive to January 4, 1944.

2. Immediately prior to June 13, 1946, the grievant was employed as Laborer, Gas Washer. On June 13, 1946 he was given a job in the Labor Gang on the day turn and assigned to work with the Moulder in the Cast House as a Helper.

3. For several years prior to the filing of the grievance on November 12, 1948, a Laborer from the Labor Gang had been regularly assigned to work with the Moulder. The job consisted in large part of digging sand holes for setting of patterns, wheeling and shoveling sand, moving patterns and cutters, cleaning up, etc., under the direction of the Moulder.

4. There are about eighty Laborers in all in the Blast Furnace Department. Some of the men in the day turn Labor Gang long have been given work assignments where the duties are deemed to fall within the broad category of labor, but the particular type of work performed varies somewhat from that performed by others in the labor category. At the time of the initial description of jobs under the Inequities Program these assignments included Ladle Loamer, Splasher Liner, Tractor Operator Helper and Pipe Threader, as well as the Moulder Helper. No doubt, in order in part to avoid a multiplicity of detailed job descriptions all falling within the same job class, Management and Union developed a single job description of Laborer 2123-37, the primary function of which includes "to work at various jobs in the Cast House as needed" and which the parties knew at the time would apply generally to Laborers in the Blast Furnace Department. Later, by mutual agreement, the parties separately described and classified the Threader Operator, and,

apparently, also the Tractor Operator Helper.

5. The Union points out that two other jobs in the Blast Furnace Department—Hot Metal Distributor and the Top Man—were overlooked in the original description and classification of jobs in the Department. As a result, job descriptions of the Hot Metal Distributor and Top Man jobs were prepared by the Company in September or October of 1948. The descriptions submitted to the Union at this time were investigated on the Union's behalf by Local President Camens, who visited the Blast Furnace Department for the purpose. At that time the grievant asked Camens why his job of "Moulder Helper" had not been separately described and classified. According to the Union, the Company acted under Section 17 of the current Collective Bargaining Agreement and under the provisions of the Wage Rate Inequities Agreements dated May 8, 1946 and January 13, 1947 in preparing job descriptions and classifications for Hot Metal Distributor and Top Man. It is asserted that the same obligation rests upon the Company in regard to the position of Moulder Helper.

FINDINGS

6. The Union's request is that the Board enforce an obligation said to be imposed upon the Company by the Wage Rate Inequities Agreements dated May 8, 1946 and January 13, 1947. There is no basis on which the Board can proceed with the merits of this case.

7. This appears to be the plain implication of the decision in Case A-372, dated May 5, 1951, where the Board left no doubt that it could not interpret or apply the Inequities Agreements between the parties except to the extent that they had been incorporated into the April 22, 1947 Basic Agreement under which the Board derives its authority.

8. There is nothing in the Basic Agreement which imposes on the Company an obligation to describe and classify positions which may have been overlooked in the course of the Inequities Program. It is true that part of Section 9-G declares as to unclassified jobs:

> "Rates now in effect plus the 12½¢ per hour shall remain in effect *until such jobs are described and classified* and such rates are adjusted *under procedures presently or hereafter agreed to* by the parties."

9. This language on its face imposes no obligation to describe and classify; it merely recognizes that at some future date the parties might describe and classify unclassified jobs under procedures designed for that purpose, and not included in the Basic Agreement. This conclusion is reenforced by the fact that Section 9-H declares that no basis shall exist for an employee to allege that a wage-rate inequity exists as to him.

AWARD

10. The grievance is dismissed for lack of jurisdiction.

USC—443. Ohio Works. December 17, 1954

Donald A. Crawford, *Arbitrator*

Approved by Sylvester Garrett, *Chairman*

FINDINGS

1. The request that a job of Moulder-Helper (Blast Furnace) be separately described and classified is denied. This work already has been covered by the description and classification of Laborer-General. The claim of oversight in failing to separately describe and classify the job of Moulder-Helper under the Inequities Program cannot be sustained. Nothing in the testimony of the man who did this work in the Blast Furnace in 1945 or the testimony of the man who performed it in 1948 indicates that the job differs essentially from Laborer-General.

2. The record of the action of the Plant Wage Rate Inequities Committee in describing Blast Furnace jobs does not permit a finding that the claimed Moulder-Helper job was overlooked. The Plant Committee, in fact, did describe and classify two of five specialized types of Labor jobs. There is no reason to suppose that Committee overlooked the facts as to this other job.

AWARD

3. The grievance is denied.

CHAPTER 2

CLAIMS CONCERNING TERMINATION OF JOBS

Claims concerning termination of jobs may arise in a number of different contexts. No attempt is made in this chapter to deal with the problem of crew reductions under the Local Working Conditions section of the Basic Agreements in the steel industry. Nor does this chapter concern itself with the termination of gangleader assignments, covered in Chapter 21 of this volume. Moreover, it should be noted that some of the cases in Chapter 4—Claim of Improper Assignment of Duties—present problems similar to those found in this chapter.

In the first section of this chapter the claim that a job continues to be performed and therefore has not actually been terminated is examined. The second section of this chapter presents cases involving a claim that Management had no right to terminate a job. Also included in the latter section are cases involving the related claims that an abandoned job must be re-established and that an existing job must be filled. The last two cases in this section—USC-615 and USC-782—deal with these two claims respectively.

Other relevant cases reported elsewhere in this volume are T-234 (p. 11), T-395 (p. 284) and A-799 (p. 85).

Section A. CLAIM THAT JOB NOT ACTUALLY TERMINATED

T—232. Fairfield Steel Works. April 24, 1953

Sylvester Garrett, *Chairman*

BACKGROUND

1. The issue in this grievance is whether the Company's action in terminating the jobs of Bottom Maker and Bottom Maker Helper in the Blooming and Billet Mills Department of the Fairfield Steel Works was authorized under the April 22, 1947, Agreement.

2. On October 1, 1951, the Company undertook to terminate the jobs of Bottom Maker (Job Class 10) and Bottom Maker Helper (Job Class 6) and assigned the grievants—incumbents of these positions—to the jobs of Soaking Pit Laborer and Stool Slurryman, both in Job Class 3. The Company asserts grievants no longer perform the work of Bottom Maker while the Union contends that their duties are still substantially the same. It is agreed that the Bottom Maker and the Bottom Maker Helpers did the same work prior to October 1, 1951, except that the Bottom Maker was the shift leader.

3. For years prior to 1951 both old type soaking pits and new type (Amsler-Morton) were used to service the Blooming Mill. Amsler-Morton pits were first introduced in 1938. The new pits have four holes each to be covered with saucer bricks in making

bottom instead of one hole per pit as in the old type. Two additional rows of Amsler-Morton pits were installed in 1951, and early in 1952 the Company began dismantling two rows of the old type pits and replacing them with three rows of new pits. At present there are 20 each of old type and new type pits.

4. The Company relies on an asserted change in the method of making bottoms on the Soaking Pits to justify its action. Prior to October, 1951, bottom making on the old pits involved the following duties. One of the bottom making crew went below the pit and notified the men working down there that a bottom was to be made. A bar was then inserted through a hole in a fender alongside the open pit and an attempt made to break the saucer brick with the bar. If the brick did not break, an occasional attempt was made to break it from below by use of a jack. Other methods were to have the Craneman punch it with a short ingot or to pull it out by tongs hooked on by the Bottom Making Crew. After the saucer brick was removed from the hole, the skull was broken with a heavy paddle by the Bottom Makers and pushed through the hole. Since the paddle would get hot in a few minutes, usually 15 or 20 would be available. The men

18

stood on a board, one end of which was on the pit cover and the other on the floor, to allow them to stand directly over the opening. After the skull was removed (which often required the assistance of the Craneman), the hole was sealed with new saucer bricks, positioned by use of a long-handled hook. The Craneman then dumped in coke breeze which the Bottom Makers at one time leveled with a long-handled rake. This function gradually was taken over by the Craneman who stirs and levels the coke with the tongs in a few minutes.

5. By October 1, 1951, the Company had decided that accumulated changes in the Soaking Pits, and their operation, justified a change in Soaking Pit manning. On this date it undertook to make still greater use of the Craneman in making bottoms on the old type pits and thus regularly assigned a fourth Craneman for the year around to absorb some of the added work of the Cranemen. Previously, the fourth Craneman had been used only in summer months. It was on this occasion that it terminated the jobs of the grievants.

6. The Cranemen always have made bottoms on the new type pits except for the placing of saucer bricks. Superintendent Glenn estimated that the bottom of an old pit is made about three times a week, and about every two weeks in new type pits. There are four crews, each of which handles five old pits and five new pits. He also testified that grievants formerly averaged about three hours a shift in breaking up and removing skull, which was hard manual work while exposed to a great deal of heat.

7. Estimates as to the amount of time consumed in positioning saucer bricks varied. One of the grievants claimed that the crew may handle two new pits and five old pits per shift, that a brick may fall out and have to be replaced, and that the holes may become enlarged, thus requiring the insertion of tin around the edges and the positioning of several saucer bricks. The Company brief asserts that not over 15 minutes' work on each turn is required of each grievant in placing saucer bricks. Superintendent Glenn testified that it might take about 30 minutes a day for a Bottom Maker to place saucer bricks in the old type pits, and about 30 minutes to place saucer bricks in the four holes of a new pit. An inspection of the operation at the plant, however, revealed that these estimates were too low.

8. In any event, it is clear that an appreciable amount of time is still spent by grievants in performing the duty of positioning saucer brick. It also is clear that the men are subjected to intense heat while this work is in progress. In addition, grievants are re-

quired at times to hook up tongs on ingots which have fallen over in the pits; to help get an ingot car, which has become derailed, back on the track; and to help in recovering an ingot which has fallen off the buggy. At irregular periods they must also clean the burners on the Amsler-Morton pits—an average of one burner a week. Though it ordinarily takes 15 or 20 minutes to clean a burner, it has occasionally taken several hours. These duties were performed by the grievants both before and after October, 1951.

9. Crew changes as of that date were also brought out at the hearing. On each shift, before the change there were three Charging Cranemen (a fourth was added to provide relief in summer), one Bottom Maker, two Bottom Maker Helpers, two Pit Laborers, two Stool Slurrymen. After the change there were four Charging Cranemen all year round, three Pit Laborers (with an extra Laborer on day turn to clean up), two Stool Slurrymen.

10. When grievants were demoted to Soaking Pit Laborers, the description for that job was revised by the Company to include the duties of positioning saucer bricks and of cleaning out slag and debris from around the burners of the new type pits. Management, nevertheless, believed that the Laborer classification should remain at Class 3.

FINDINGS

11. The changes made by the Company prior to October 1, 1951, were changes that —taken in the light most favorable to the Company—conceivably might be found to have affected the job content of the Bottom Makers and Bottom Maker Helpers to some extent, but certainly the changes relied upon are not enough to justify a claim that the jobs were terminated. Although use of the paddle by the Bottom Maker to break the skull was eliminated and the Soaking Pit Craneman was given greater responsibility for cleaning bottoms on all the pits, it is equally true that the Soaking Pit Craneman always did clean and make bottoms on all the new type pits and to a great extent on the old type. He assisted the Bottom Maker in breaking up the skull which was too hard to be broken up manually and removed large pieces of skull from the old type pits.

12. Section 9-D, insofar as relevant here, provides:

"The job description and classification for each job in effect as of the date of this Agreement shall continue in effect unless (1) Management changes the job content (requirements of the job as to the training, skill, responsibility, effort, and working conditions) to the extent of one full job class or more; (2) the job is terminated or not occupied during a period of one year; or (3) the description and classification are changed in accordance with mutual agreement of officially designated representatives of the Company and the Union."

13. From items (1) and (2) of the quoted language, it is clear that the parties carefully distinguished between the two situations of (a) when a job actually was terminated, and (b) when there was merely some change in job content. The purpose of the distinction is underlined throughout the elaborate and carefully drawn remaining provisions of Section 9-D, dealing with description and classification of *changed* jobs, as well as entirely new jobs. There is, of course, no provision in 9-D of the April 22, 1947, Agreement touching upon terminated jobs except as quoted above.

14. In their Inequities Agreement of May 8, 1946, to which reference is made in Section 9-D, the parties addressed themselves to the problem of classifying *changed* jobs in this wise:—

"In the subsequent reclassification of a job due to change in job content, consider only those factors affected by the change, move them into the next class only if the change in job content is at least one whole job class."

15. Manifestly, if one party or the other can effectively declare a job to be terminated, when there is a slight change in job content, the careful limitation which the parties set out in the above language will be rendered ineffective.

16. There thus was no proper occasion for declaring that the jobs of grievants were "terminated," and assigning them to the job title of Soaking Pit Laborer. It cannot be held that grievants, who continue at the same work station to perform substantially all of the tasks as before, are now incumbents of some other job within the meaning of Section 9-D of the Agreement. Rather, the jobs of Bottom Maker and Bottom Maker Helper, with their former incumbents, continue to exist, although they may now be changed jobs within the meaning of 9-D. The essence of the present holding is that the Company does not in truth "terminate" a job by merely assigning incumbents to a lower rate of pay under a different job title while they continue to perform the same duties with only relatively minor change. Accordingly, the Board will direct the Company to pay grievants at the established rates for Bottom Maker and Bottom Maker Helper.

17. This does not constitute a ruling that Management might not have been entitled on or after October 1, 1951, to establish new descriptions, and to review the classifications, for these jobs, on the basis that their content had been changed, in accordance with Section 9-D. The Board expresses no opinion at this time as to whether the Company might be so entitled. If Management now elects to proceed in this manner, however, such action will not be precluded by this Award. The Board does not speculate as to whether the Company will elect so to proceed, or as to what the eventual outcome might be in terms of rates of pay, following a proper application of Section 9-D.

AWARD

18. The grievance is sustained. The established rates for Bottom Maker and Bottom Maker Helper as they existed prior to October 1, 1951, shall continue to be paid, unless, and until, changes in the description and classification of these jobs are made in accordance with Section 9-D. Grievants are entitled to be made whole for loss of earnings resulting from discontinuance of payment of the rates for these two jobs.

G—56.   Geneva Works.   December 30, 1955
Sylvester Garrett, *Chairman*

FINDINGS

1. This grievance from the Plate Shipping Division, Rolling Mill Department, Geneva Works protests discontinuance on September 24, 1954, of a Plate Loader job (Class 9) at the Two Side Inspection Bed and the substitution therefor of a Slipmaker (Two Side) job, three job classes lower.

2. Plate Loader was described and classified September 15, 1947, when there were two work areas served by Plate Loaders. Normally one Plate Loader was assigned to the Shipping Dock and one or more to the nearby Two Side Inspection Beds.

3. The assignment of Plate Loaders to the two areas continued until the Company sought to improve its inventory control of finished plate by introducing a Plate Mill Product and Shippers list form for use at the Two Side Inspection Beds. It decided that the duty of filling out this form could be

combined with other duties performed by the Plate Loader at the Two Side Inspection Beds.

4. At the time of adding this duty, however, Management concluded that the Plate Loader job in effect was truly that of a Slipmaker, rather than Plate Loader. Accordingly it terminated the Class 9 job of Plate Unloader and installed instead a new job of Slipmaker in Class 6.

5. The Union contends that this action was in disregard of the job description and classification procedure under Section 9-D of the July 1, 1954, Agreement and the January 1, 1953, Job Description and Classification Manual. It stresses that Slipmaker is not really a new job, but merely a continuation of the Plate Unloader job under another name, with an added duty.

6. The Company points out that in October, 1952, a Plate Shipping incentive was installed omitting the Plate Loader at the Two Side Inspection Beds. When no Two Side Inspection work was required before this date the Two Side Plate Loader had moved to the Shipping Dock to work as member of the Shipping Crew.

7. As a result of the incentive there apparently was an informal realignment of actual duties performed by Two Side Plate Loader. The Company claims, for example, that the Two Side Plate Loader no longer directed any loading functions as did the Plate Loader on the Shipping Dock. There was, however, no change in either the description or classification of the Plate Loader job to reflect any change in duties at the Two Side Inspection Bed station.

8. The Company feels now that although the job of Plate Loader continued at the Two Side Inspection Bed for about two years after October, 1952, it really had ceased to be such in October, 1952. Hence it sees no impropriety in terminating the job in 1954 and installing in its place a new job of Slipmaker.

9. There is no doubt that a sufficient proportion of the duties of Plate Loader continued to be required at this work station to preclude a finding that the job in fact was terminated pursuant to Section 9-D of the Agreement.

10. The case here is essentially the same in basic facts as Case T-232. There the Board stated:

"Section 9-D, insofar as relevant here, provides:

'The job description and classification for each job in effect as of the date of this Agreement shall continue in effect unless (1) Management changes the job content (requirements of the job as to the training, skill, responsibility, effort, and working conditions) to the extent of one full job class or more; (2) the job is terminated or not occupied during a period of one year; or (3) the description and classification are changed in accordance with mutual agreement of officially designated representatives of the Company and the Union.'

"From items (1) and (2) of the quoted language, it is clear that the parties carefully distinguished between the two situations of (a) when a job actually was terminated, and (b) when there was merely some change in job content. The purpose of the distinction is underlined throughout the elaborate and carefully drawn remaining provisions of Section 9-D, dealing with description and classification of *changed* jobs, as well as entirely new jobs. There is, of course, no provision in 9-D of the April 22, 1947, Agreement touching upon terminated jobs except as quoted above.

"In their Inequities Agreement of May 8, 1946, to which reference is made in Section 9-D, the parties addressed themselves to the problem of classifying *changed* jobs in this wise:—

'In the subsequent reclassification of a job due to change in job content, consider only those factors affected by the change, move them into the next class only if the change in job content is at least one whole job class.'

"Manifestly, if one party or the other can effectively declare a job to be terminated, when there is a slight change in job content, the careful limitation which the parties set out in the above language will be rendered ineffective.

"There thus was no proper occasion for declaring that the jobs of grievants were 'terminated,' and assigning them to the job title of Soaking Pit Laborer. It cannot be held that grievants, who continue at the same work station to perform substantially all of the tasks as before, are now incumbents of some other job within the meaning of Section 9-D of the Agreement. Rather, the jobs of Bottom Maker and Bottom Maker Helper, with their former incumbents, continue to exist, although they may now be changed jobs within the meaning of 9-D. The essence of the present holding is that the Company does not in truth 'terminate' a job by merely assigning incumbents to a lower rate of pay under a different job title while they continue to perform the same duties with only relatively minor change. Accordingly, the

Board will direct the Company to pay grievants at the established rates for Bottom Maker and Bottom Maker Helper.

"This does not constitute a ruling that Management might not have been entitled on or after October 1, 1951, to establish new descriptions, and to review the classifications, for these jobs, on the basis that their content had been changed, in accordance with Section 9-D. The Board expresses no opinion at this time as to whether the Company might be so entitled. If Management now elects to proceed in this manner, however, such action will not be precluded by this Award. The Board does not speculate as to whether the Company will elect so to proceed, or as to what the eventual outcome might be in terms of rates of pay, following a proper application of Section 9-D."

11. The foregoing observations seem fully applicable here. The addition of duties to the Plate Loader job at the Two Side Bed in September, 1954, did not result in, or provide basis for, terminating the job.

12. Events occurring about two years earlier which were not significant enough to be reflected in a changed description or classification cannot support a claim now that the job in substance was nonexistent over such a long period.

AWARD

13. The grievance is sustained. The established rate for Plate Loader at the Two Side Inspection Bed under the September 15, 1947, Description and Classification shall continue to be paid unless, and until, changes in description and classification of the job are made in accordance with Section 9-D. Grievants who have suffered loss of earnings as a result of discontinuance of the Plate Loader rate at the Two Side Inspection Bed shall be made whole.

T—328. Ore Mines and Quarries. September 26, 1955
Sylvester Garrett, *Chairman*

BACKGROUND

1. This case is before the Board by stipulation, under the July 1, 1954 Agreement covering T.C.I. Mining and Quarry Operations.

2. The basic issue presented by the Union's objection to the descriptions of the two new jobs of Conditioning Operator (in Class 15) and Assistant Conditioning Operator (in Class 11) is whether the Company eliminated the three jobs of Crusher Laborer (Class 3), Scrap Picker and Feeder (Class 5), and Chute Attendant (Class 3) at the Ore Conditioning Plant in accordance with Section 9-C. The parties agree that the Board should pass only on this issue and that any issues of proper classification of new or changed jobs should be taken up only after the Board has decided this case.

3. At least two men—slotted as "Laborers" in Class 2—are now assigned each shift to work under the direction of an Assistant Conditioning Operator, who in turn assists a Conditioning Operator in regulating the flow of ore through the plant. The Union contends that all basic duties of the three eliminated jobs still must be performed, and are being performed, by the men assigned to work under the Assistant Conditioning Operator. Thus, the Union asserts that the Company is in violation of Sections 2-B and 9-C of the Agreement, and that the aggrieved employees should be compensated for such shifts as their occupations were required and were performed by Laborers in Job Class 2. Reliance is placed on two previous Awards of the Board—T-234 and T-232—where it was found that the Company had not in fact eliminated the jobs in dispute under Section 9-D of the Basic Agreement.

4. As noted particularly in Case T-232, it may be of considerable importance, in classifying a given job under the January 1, 1953 Manual, whether it is deemed to be "new" or merely a "changed" job, constituting a revision of an earlier job.

5. The Company holds that all essential duties of the three jobs have been eliminated, that such remaining duties as "cleans chutes and otherwise assists in getting ore through plant" and "cleans up spills" are covered by the existing description for Laborer in Class 2, and that rearranging certain job duties is discretionary with Management. Reference is made to the Awards of the Board in USC-417, USC-420, CI-257, and several others.

Effect of the Changes on the Crusher Laborer, Scrap Picker and Feeder, and Chute Attendant Jobs

6. During the summer of 1954 the Primary and Secondary Crusher sections of the Ore Conditioning Plant were remodeled. This was necessary due to increasingly greater use since 1948 of foreign ores, which are finer and of higher moisture content than the do-

mestic ores. Foreign ores caused a great number of choke-ups in the crushers, chutes and screens. Although close to a million dollars were expended in remodeling the plant and installation of numerous automatic devices, only those changes which have direct bearing on the three eliminated jobs in dispute will be noted in this analysis.

Crusher Laborer

7. Prior to the changes, it was necessary to station a Crusher Laborer throughout the shift at the discharge end of the Primary Crushers. His primary function was to keep the material flowing through the Primary Crusher. Since the discharge chute was not enclosed, he could observe the flow of ore in the chute while sitting in the chair provided for him. When a clog-up occurred, he could press a button to signal the Rotary Dump Operator to stop dumping. According to the Company clog-ups occurred several times a shift. The Union could not give an estimate, but noted that the number of clog-ups will depend on such factors as the weather and the condition of the ore being used. Together with Class 2 Laborers, when necessary, the Crusher Laborer would clean the chute by air pipe, shovel and bar, and then signal the Rotary Dump Operator by a buzzer to start dumping again. He was also required to assist in cleaning up around the Primary Crushers.

8. After the 1954 changes the necessity for constant observation of the discharge chutes, the signaling duties, and this location as a full-time work station were eliminated. It not only is unnecessary today to assign a man regularly to this location to observe the flow of ore, but it would be physically impossible for him to watch constantly the flow of ore in the discharge chute. As part of the improved dust collecting system, the chute has been enclosed. The only way to check the chute itself for a clog-up that may be building up is to open a door in the enclosure. But when the door is opened, the apron feeders for the Primary Crusher and the Crusher are automatically shut down.

9. If a clog-up does occur, an electrical device installed in the Crusher discharge chutes will automatically stop the apron feeders, and flash a light on the control panel at the Conditioning Operator's station in the Screening Building. The Conditioning Operator will then telephone the Assistant Conditioning Operator, who in turn will clean out the chutes or assign Laborers to do it. Although the conveyor belt below may still be running (the same as in the past), the apron feeders and crusher are shut down automatically while the door to the new enclosure is open. 48 new telephones—more than twice the old number—have been installed at the Ore Conditioning Plant, thus making it easier to locate the Assistant Conditioning Operator.

10. Clog-ups are removed with the same type of tools used by Laborers and the Crusher Laborer in past years. The new automatic devices, however, have eliminated the need for constant observation of the discharge chutes themselves by a Crusher Laborer. The buzzer used to signal the Rotary Dump Operator has been eliminated. Only occasional inspection of the chutes throughout the turn now is required to determine whether a gradual build up of fines is occurring, along with inspection of related equipment; and this inspection is supposed to be performed by the Assistant Conditioning Operator. Although the total amount of time spent inspecting these discharge chutes and cleaning them has been considerably reduced, the actual time depends on weather and ore conditions. A serious clog-up has taken up to 36 hours to remove.

11. Choke-ups in the Primary Crusher do not occur as often now, even though the same ores are going through the Primary Crusher. The former practice was for the Rotary Dump Operator to attempt to regulate the flow of ore to the Primary Crushers by dumping part of a railroad car at a time. When he was unsuccessful in regulating the flow and a choke-up occurred, the Crusher Laborer was already present, prepared to take action. With the installation of the new electrical equipment and devices, this rough method of regulation was abandoned. Now both the crushing operations carried on in the Primary and the Secondary Crusher buildings are remotely controlled by the Conditioning Operator stationed at his control board. By regulating the speed of the newly installed apron feeders ahead of the Primary Crushers (which replace the old straight chutes), he controls the flow of ore more effectively thereby reducing substantially the number of clog-ups. Only three or four really serious clog-ups have occurred at this point since September, 1954.

12. Another factor which has helped to reduce the number of choke-ups in the discharge chutes is the change in the size of the discharge chutes. They have been opened up and steepened to permit the ore to flow more freely.

13. One further elimination from the duties of the Crusher Laborer is the requirement that he assist the foreman in changing baffle plates for running foreign ore. This, however, is not a recent change, the elimination having been made three to four years ago.

14. The only difference in rating on the classification Factors for the Crusher Laborer and Laborer jobs are found on Factors 7, 9, and 11, where the Crusher Laborer job receives higher ratings. As a result of the changes installed by Management and their effect on the duties of the Crusher Laborer job, it is clear that Management has at least removed the original bases for the higher ratings on Factor 7—Responsibility for Operations and Factor 9—Mental Effort. Thus, if the Crusher Laborer job is viewed as a changed job and if only the duties of cleaning the chutes and the area around them remained, the proper rate of pay for such duties would be that assigned to Job Class 2 —the same as the job class for a Laborer. Certain other like duties, however, were substituted for the old Crusher Laborer duty of keeping a watchful eye on the discharge chutes, duties which the assigned Laborers thereafter were required to perform. As long as these duties (described under "Findings" below) are performed by the men now slotted as "Laborers," no justification exists for holding that the Crusher Laborer job was in fact eliminated rather than merely changed.

Scrap Picker and Feeder

15. Before the 1954 changes, a Scrap Picker and Feeder was stationed throughout the shift at each of the two ore conveyor belts leading from the discharge end of the Primary Crushers to the Secondary Crushers. An incumbent of this job sat in a protected chair beside the moving belt. When tramp iron was detected, he pressed a button to stop the belt until the foreign matter could be removed. At this time fine ore would drop through the old grizzlies for the Primary Crusher into the grizzly hopper. When the feed from the Primary Crusher diminished and the belt became empty, the Scrap Picker and Feeder operated the controls of the vibrating feeder to feed ore from the grizzly hopper onto the belt. When necessary, he also shoveled up spillage, cleaned the chutes, and helped to unchoke the Primary Crusher.

16. Today there is no need to station employees at these ore conveyor belts to watch for tramp iron. This location as a regular work station has been eliminated. Since an automatic metal detector has been installed, the belt is automatically stopped in three seconds after tramp iron passes under an inverted "U." This happens on an average of five times a turn for each of the two conveyor belts. The stopping of the belt also causes a signal to be flashed to the control board of the Conditioning Operator, who telephones the Assistant to remove the for-

eign matter from the belt and to push a button next to the belt to start it up again. The Assistant may direct one of his assigned Laborers to do this task. Duties involving the removal of foreign matter will consume an average of 35 to 40 minutes a turn. So far the automatic metal detector has not failed to detect tramp iron from the mines; the only difficulty is that it occasionally shuts the belt down when no foreign matter is passing through on the belt. During a plant visit the detector was tested a couple of times and it reacted properly.

17. The vibrating feeders, formerly operated by the Scrap Picker and Feeder, have also been removed along with the hoppers under the old grizzlies. Today the conveyor belts handle both the ore from the Crushers and the fines which drop through the new grizzlies. Although the Union argues that this elimination is immaterial because a Scrap Picker and Feeder was still assigned while the vibrating feeders were out of operation for a period during the Second World War, it is clear that these feeders were being operated from 1947 to 1954 and, from an examination of the reasons for the ratings on the Factors when the job was classified in 1950, that operation of the feeder controls provided a significant part in classifying it in Job Class 5. This conclusion is further supported by the fact that a job used up to 1952 and classified as Scrap Picker, which also removed foreign matter from the ore conveyor belts but which did not operate the controls of the vibrator feeder, was rated at Job Class 2. Hence, in view of the eliminations from the duties of the Scrap Picker and Feeder job, it must be concluded that this job no longer exists.

Chute Attendant

18. The job description for the Chute Attendant states that the primary function of this job is "to watch discharge from secondary crushers and prevent chokes in the discharge chutes." The working procedure reads as follows:

1. Observes material being discharged from crusher and screens, and dislodges any chokes which may occur.
2. Uses bar, hammer, etc., to dislodge pieces of ore or slate which wedge in chute and jamb flow of material.
3. Signals Rotary Dump Operator to slow down or stop, whichever is needed.
4. Stops crusher in emergency.
5. Cleans up ore which spills from conveyor belt.
6. Keeps working area clean.

19. It is not clear precisely what the in-

cumbent of the Chute Attendant job was doing immediately prior to September, 1954, since the parties do not even agree on which floor of the Secondary Crusher building he worked. In any event, at the time that the job was classified, his job was to watch for and prevent choke-ups in the Secondary Crusher discharge chutes and vibrating screens, where clog-ups occurred fairly frequently.

20. Normally, today, it is only necessary to clean these chutes on down days. Laborers are used to perform this task. The attention of a Chute Attendant to watch for clog-ups in these chutes is not needed. The number of clog-ups has been substantially reduced due to the regulation of the flow of the ore by the Conditioning Operator through his control board, and the newly installed apron feeders, the metal detectors on the belts conveying ore from the Primary to the Secondary Crushers, and the steepening and widening of the discharge chutes for the Secondary Crusher. Furthermore, it would be physically impossible for a Chute Attendant to watch the flow of ore in these chutes constantly because Management, as part of its improved dust collecting system, has enclosed these discharge chutes.

21. Thus, the following duties of the Chute Attendant job have been eliminated: regular observation of the material being discharged from the Secondary Crusher, signaling the Rotary Dump Operator to slow down or stop, and stopping the crusher in an emergency. The latter two duties have been eliminated by the replacement of the push buttons with newly installed electrical devices, which automatically flash signals on the control board of the Conditioning Operator when anything goes wrong.

22. The Union contends, however, that signaling the Rotary Dump Operator was the duty of the Screen Tender job despite the language in the Chute Attendant job description. In any event, the only duties which remain to be performed in connection with these discharge chutes involve cleaning the chutes and shoveling up spillage, and occasional inspection which is supposed to be made by the Assistant Conditioning Operator while he is making his rounds and examining all of the equipment.

23. The only differences between the classification ratings on the Factors for the Chute Attendant job (which is rated the same as the Crusher Laborer job) and the job of Laborer are found on Factors 7, 9, and 11, where the ratings for the Chute Attendant job are higher. As a result of the changes instituted by Management, it is apparent that the bases for the higher ratings on these Factors have been eliminated, and that the Laborer job description covers the remaining cleaning and shoveling duties around the Secondary Crusher discharge chutes.

24. Finally, although the Union believes that certain Laborers assigned for several months prior to July, 1955, to shovel spillage around the new screw conveyor and dribble chutes, at another work station near the fines discharge chutes, were performing the duties of the Chute Attendant, the Board cannot adopt this position. In the meantime, the screw conveyor has been removed. Whatever the proper classification of this job should have been, it must be found that the original Chute Attendant job was eliminated.

FINDINGS

25. The principal difficulty in this case is that while Management, as the result of the equipment end process changes enumerated, was entitled to eliminate all three of the disputed jobs and to establish the two new jobs to regulate the flow of the ore through the plant with the help of men who would do only Laborer work, in fact lower levels of Management (particularly the Turn Foreman) proceeded on a different basis by permitting a different practice to develop. And it is this clear practice which makes it impossible to find that the Crusher Laborer job in fact was eliminated in accordance with Section 9-C. The Crusher Laborer job, in practice, merely was changed by substituting similar inspection duties for the old inspection duties that justified the higher ratings on Factors 7 and 9.

26. As noted in Case T-234 the mere assertion that a job is "terminated," when in fact all of its substantial duties continue, cannot be held to terminate the job for purposes of Section 9-C if the integrity of the wage structure is to be preserved.

27. Although higher levels of Management may have expected the Assistant Conditioning Operator to make periodic rounds to examine the chutes and other equipment in both the Primary Crusher and Secondary Crusher buildings, and to direct his two assigned Laborers to perform only Laborer work as necessary, the Assistant actually used Laborers to "make the rounds" and inspect a substantial portion of the equipment, such as the discharge chutes and conveyor belts for the Primary Crushers, to determine whether fines were building up and whether the equipment was functioning properly. In the meantime, he inspected other equipment. In the words of the Superintendent of the Ore Conditioning Plant the Assistant "took advantage of his assigned Laborers." It is agreed, furthermore, that the Turn Foreman

must have known what was taking place, and must have approved of this procedure.

28. Shortly before a visit to the plant by a Board representative on July 18, 1955, the supervisors of the plant apparently decided that the Assistant Conditioning Operator was taking advantage of his assigned Laborers by having them perform part of his job, and that the Laborers were not cleaning up spillage and dirty areas to the extent expected. The supervisors agreed that the Turn Foreman should enforce the system which was expected to be followed when originally installed in September, 1954; on July 18, 1955, the Board representative witnessed the start of enforcement of the system contemplated by Management. It is not known what the practice has been since that date, nor is any issue as to this matter properly before the Board.

29. In September, 1954, therefore, the Crusher Laborer job was not eliminated but merely was changed, and the "Laborers" assigned by the Assistant Conditioning Operator to perform inspection duties (with at least the tacit approval of the Turn Foreman) were performing the revised duties of the Crusher Laborer job.

AWARD

30. The Scrap Picker and Feeder, and Chute Attendant jobs were eliminated at the Ore Conditioning Plant, in accordance with Section 9-C of the July 1, 1954 Agreement. After September, 1954 Laborers assigned to work under the Assistant Conditioning Operator actually performed inspection duties, in addition to unchoking chutes and shoveling spillage, and thus functioned as incumbents of a changed job of Crusher Laborer within the meaning of Section 9-C. Thus the job of Crusher Laborer was not eliminated, and the question remains under Section 9-C as to what changes, if any, were warranted in classification of the Crusher Laborer job. This decision does not consider whether the situation was changed by the direction in July, 1955, that the Assistant Conditioning Operator desist from using Laborers to perform certain duties under the job description of the Assistant Conditioning Operator.

USC—417, -420. Gary Sheet and Tin Mill. August 13, 1954

Sylvester Garrett, *Chairman*

BACKGROUND

1. These grievances result from conversion of the 42″ Hot Strip Mill Motor Room to an unattended Tin Mill Sub-station at Gary Sheet and Tin Mill. Case USC-417 protests, on behalf of employees in the Tin Mill Sub-station, Utilities Department, consolidation of the jobs of 42″ Motor House Operator (Class 14) and Tin Mill Sub-station Tender (Class 11) with subsequent payment of only Job Class 11 instead of Class 14. Case USC-420 presents a protest by two former 42″ Motor House Operators, against the transfer of the duties of the Operator job to Tin Mill Sub-station Tender at Class 11. These grievants, who were transferred to Sub-station Tender, seek to have the 42″ Motor House Operator job restored, as such, in Class 14.

2. The 42″ Hot Strip Mill Motor Room was built as part of the 42″ Hot Strip Mill in 1927. In addition to mill motor equipment, it also housed some items of equipment servicing the Tin Mill, including:

 2—15000 KVA 22000/2200 Volt Transformers and associated controls.
 2—1000 KVA 2200/250 Volt Transformers and associated controls.
 3—500 KW 250 Volt DC M-G sets and associated controls, control battery

and charger, sump pump, feeder circuit breakers, etc.

All 42″ Mill Motor Room equipment was tended by a Motor House Operator on each turn, and the job was classified under the Inequities Program in Class 14.

3. The 42″ Hot Strip Mill Room supplied power for the 42″ Hot Strip Mill, the Stainless Steel Department, the Tin Mill Cold Reduction, the Reversing Mills and Auxiliary Equipment. On October 29, 1948, operation of the 42″ Hot Strip Mill was discontinued, and all equipment in the Motor Room used directly to operate the 42″ Hot Strip Mill, was shut down. The 42″ Hot Strip Motor Room continued to be manned by the Operator in Class 14, and the seven items of equipment listed above, referred to by Management as "Sub-station" equipment of the Tin Mill, were kept in operation, except that one 15000 KVA Transformer and one 500 KW M-G set were taken off.

4. Although most of the equipment tended by the Motor House Operator did not operate after October 29, 1948, Management did not at this time either eliminate or change the job of Motor House Operator. This was for the reason that it had not been determined whether the 42″ Hot Strip Mill would be discontinued permanently. Indeed, at the time of the hearing, a decision to dis-

continue the 42″ Hot Strip Mill permanently still had not been reached.

5. The major portion of the 42″ Hot Strip Mill equipment is still there. In December, 1951, and January, 1952, the run-out tables were removed from their regular location and stored elsewhere in the Mill building, in order to make room for an increase in scarfing operations which were conducted in the 42″ Hot Strip Mill building for the 80″ Hot Strip Mill. The Coilers were removed in 1953, and one reduction unit was loaned to another plant.

6. Superintendent Ebert, who was in charge of the 42″ Hot Strip Mill in October, 1948, continues to hold the position of Superintendent of 42″ Hot Strip Mill. As late as August, 1952, Management considered using the 42″ Hot Strip Mill to roll skelp for the Tube Division, but found that the required skelp widths were too narrow for the 42″ Mill equipment.

7. Scarfing operations, servicing the 80″ Hot Strip, have been conducted in the 42″ Hot Strip Mill building since prior to October, 1948. Subsequent to that date, however, the extent of scarfing operations has increased substantially. To handle the increase in scarfing a new crane was put into scarfing service February 14, 1952. Prior thereto there had been 3 cranes available for scarfing operations.

8. In 1951, Management first gave consideration to converting the 42″ Hot Strip Mill Motor Room into an unattended Tin Mill Sub-station. There then existed a tie line between the No. 1 Sub-station of the Tin Mill and the 42″ Hot Strip Motor Room, and it appeared that by adding two feeder lines to supplement the tie lines, it would be possible to convert the 42″ Hot Strip Motor Room into an unattended Sub-station. By December, 1951, the new feeder lines were installed, and Management was ready to convert the 42″ Hot Strip Motor Room into a No. 2 Sub-station for the Tin Mill, but action was delayed for some months, in part upon request of the Grievance Committee.

9. In July, 1952, Management finally acted to terminate the Motor House Operator job, and assigned its duties to the job of Tin Mill Sub-station Tender, Class 11.

10. At this time several Motor House Operators were transferred to other jobs in Class 14, but two grievants in Case USC-420 were transferred to Sub-station Tender in Class 11. After combination of the two jobs into Sub-station Tender, this job serviced both the original Tin Mill Sub-station and the new No. 2 Tin Mill Sub-station, which formerly had been the 42″ Hot Strip Motor Room. Most of the time the men remained in the No. 1 Sub-station, but twice each shift they walked to the No. 2 Substation to check upon operation of the equipment, make necessary recordings, and any necessary adjustments and readings.

11. Management reviewed the revised job content of Sub-station Tender, but concluded that the added duties of inspecting and servicing the No. 2 Sub-station (42″ Hot Strip Mill Motor Room) did not change the classification of Sub-station Tender.

12. The Union supports the grievances both on Section 2-B-3 and Section 9-D. It believes that assignment of an Operator to the 42″ Hot Strip Motor Room gave rise to a local working condition protected under Section 2-B-3. Even if shutting down the 42″ Hot Strip Mill on October 29, 1948, might have justified a change in this arrangement under Section 2-B-4, the Company now is estopped to rely on this since it permitted three years and eight months to pass without any action in regard to the 42″ Motor House Operator job. Management's continuance of the Motor House Operator job for this period confirms that it deemed the job to be properly described and classified, according to the Union.

13. The Union stresses alternatively that Section 9-D provides that job descriptions and classifications in effect as of the date of the Agreement shall continue in effect unless:

"(1) Management changes the job content (requirements of the job as to the training, skill, responsibility, effort, and working conditions) to the extent of one full job class or more; (2) the job is terminated or not occupied during a period of one year; or (3) the description and classification are changed in accordance with mutual agreement of officially designated representatives of the Company and the Union."

14. The Union believes Case T-232 is similar to the present, and that the job of 42″ Motor Room Operator never *in fact* was terminated because the same duties are performed today as were performed prior to July, 1952. The only change is that Management now labels the work as that of a Sub-station Tender rather than continuing to treat it as the work of the Motor Room Operator. Hence the Union sees a violation of Section 9-B-3 as well as of 9-D.

15. The Company holds that nothing in the April 22, 1947, Agreement prohibited it from terminating the job of Motor House Operator and assigning its duties to Sub-station Tender. As to Section 2-B, the Company relies on a statement of the Board in CI-257 that,

"The mere fact that particular employees have performed certain duties could scarcely be said to give rise to a requirement that they will perform such duties continuously in the future without any change."

The Company also cites language from Case CI-257 dealing with Section 9-D, which the Company believes to constitute recognition that Management has absolute discretion in rearranging job duties.

16.   Finally, Management holds that the duties formerly performed by the 42″ Motor Room Operators, and now assigned to Sub-station Tenders, are of the same type as always performed by the Sub-station Tender job and thus already taken into account in its description and classification.

FINDINGS

17.   When the 42″ Hot Strip Mill was shut down on October 29, 1948, the direct result was to idle most of the equipment previously inspected and serviced by the Motor Room Operators. The extent of this impact is revealed in the following table covering all facilities in the 42″ Hot Strip Motor Room:

SURVEY OF OPERATIONS—42″ H. S. MOTOR ROOM AND SUB-STATION FACILITIES

42″ HOT STRIP MILL ELECTRICAL FACILITIES

#1—Wilson Snyder Descaling Pump	Shut down Oct. 29, 1948
#2—Wilson Snyder Descaling Pump	" " " " "
350 H. P. Vertical Edger Drives	" " " " "
#1—1800 H. P. Roughing Mill Drive	" " " " "
#2—1800 H. P. Roughing Mill Drive	" " " " "
#1—100 H. P. Ventilating Fan Motor	" " " " "
#2—100 H. P. Ventilating Fan Motor	" " " " "
#3—100 H. P. Ventilating Fan Motor	" " " " "
300 KW Exciter for Mill Drives	" " " " "
Switchgear for Mill Drives	" " " " "
Switchboard for Mill Drives	" " " " "
#1—3000 KW M-G Set for Mill Drives	" " " " "
#2—3000 KW M-G Set for Mill Drives	" " " " "
#3—3000 KW M-G Set for Mill Drives	" " " " "
1000 H. P. Cameron Descaling Pump	" " " " "
#1—200 H. P. Vertical Edger Motor	" " " " "
#2—200 H. P. Vertical Edger Motor	" " " " "
2500 H. P. Motor for #5 Pass	" " " " "
2500 H. P. Motor for #6 Pass	" " " " "
2500 H. P. Motor for #7 Pass	" " " " "
2500 H. P. Motor for #8 Pass	" " " " "
2500 H. P. Motor for #9 Pass	" " " " "
2500 H. P. Motor for #10 Pass	" " " " "
#1—Variable Frequency Set for Tables	" " " " "
#2—Variable Frequency Set for Tables	" " " " "

SUB-STATION FACILITIES

#83X—22 KV Incoming Line Oil Circuit Breaker
#85X—22 KV Incoming Line Oil Circuit Breaker
    (For Emergency Use Only)
#1   —15000 KVA 22000/2200 Volt Transformer
    (Removed from service Sept. 23, 1949)
#2   —15000 KVA 22000/2200 Volt Transformer
#1   —1000 KVA 2200/250 Volt Transformer
#2   —1000 KVA 2200/250 Volt Transformer
#1   —500 KW 250 Volt DC M-G Set
#2   —500 KW 250 Volt DC M-G Set
    (Load reduced by rearrangement of feeders 12-51)
#3   —500 KW 250 Volt DC M-G Set
    (Load reduced by 42″ H.S.M. Shut Down 10/29/48)

SURVEY OF OPERATIONS—42″ H. S. MOTOR ROOM AND
SUB-STATION FACILITIES

—200 KVA 2200/250 Volt Transformer (Removed from Service Nov., 1951)
Oil Circuit Breaker for 2200 Volt T.M.C.R. Feeder
Oil Circuit Breaker for 2200 Volt S.M.C.R. Feeder
Oil Circuit Breaker for 2200 Volt Pumphouse Feeder
Oil Circuit Breaker for 2200 Volt Slitter Feeder
Control Battery and Charger

MISCELLANEOUS FACILITIES

#1—Bury Air Compressor	Operation fully assumed by air
#2—Bury Air Compressor	Compressor Operators Aug., 1952

18. In view of the magnitude of these changes it is at first blush surprising that no action was taken to review the description and classification of the Motor Room Operator job at any time thereafter. After shutdown of the 42″ Hot Strip Mill, the only jobs which actually continued to operate were Motor Room Operator and jobs connected with scarfing to service the 80″ Hot Strip Mill. Nonetheless *no action was taken by 42″ Mill Hot Strip supervision to terminate any of the Operating jobs.* These no longer are carried on the pay scale, since they have not been occupied for a year or more. The reason for this seeming neglect lay in uncertainty whether the 42″ Hot Strip Mill might be put back into operation. Hence the Superintendent felt it unwise to change the description and classification of the Motor Room Operator job, or to terminate the other jobs. At least up until mid-1952 he believed that there was real possibility that 42″ Hot Strip Mill production would be resumed.

19. Moreover, it would not have been feasible to combine inspection and servicing of 42″ Hot Strip Motor Room facilities with Tin Mill Sub-station work, until the two additional feeder lines were installed in December, 1951. The feeder lines made it possible to eliminate use of 42″ Motor Room equipment and operate the facilities with power provided by the No. 1 Tin Mill Sub-station through the feeder lines, and vice versa. The essence of the arrangement was to achieve *flexibility* rather than to establish a different regular operating procedure. The fact that the feeder lines have been used only rarely since 1952, much emphasized by the Union, in all truth does not bear on the essential purpose of the feeder lines, and thus is irrelevant.

20. The substantial impact of shutting down the 42″ Hot Strip Mill on October 29, 1948, followed by installation of the new feeder lines, therefore provided a proper basis for Management to discontinue full-time use of the 42″ Motor Room Operator. Section 2-B-3 could not apply in these circumstances.

21. Nor does Section 9-D preclude action to combine the duties of the two jobs. In T-232 the Board held that discontinuance of the title and rate of "Bottom Makers" while the incumbents were required to perform the same duties substantially as before, but at a lower rate, constituted a violation of Section 9-D. This was for the reason that although Management had labeled the jobs of Bottom Maker and Bottom Maker Helper as "terminated," *in fact there had been no termination* for purposes of Section 9-D, since the *same duties* continued to be performed by the *same individuals* to the *same extent* in the *same work location.* The facts in the present case bear no reasonable similarity to those in T-232.

22. There remains a potential issue of proper classification of the job which resulted from combination of duties of Motor Room Operator and Sub-station Tender. Since this case was processed through the grievance procedure and before the Board on the basis of the Union's contentions that Management could not combine the duties of the two jobs because of restraints imposed by Section 2-B-3 and 9-D, the parties have not attempted to deal conclusively with description and classification of the new combined job. This matter remains open for the parties to consider and settle in the grievance procedure.

AWARD

23. The grievance is denied without prejudice to any issues which may arise as to proper description and classification of the job resulting from combination of duties of 42″ Hot Strip Mill Motor Room Operator and Tin Mill Sub-station Tender, in accordance with the procedures of Section 9-D.

USC—535. Youngstown District Works. November 23, 1955
Sylvester Garrett, *Chairman*

FINDINGS

1. This grievance from the Utilities Department, Maintenance and Utility Division, Ohio Works, Youngstown District Works, protests termination of the job of Substation Tender (O.W.) (Class 10), May, 1954, and assignment of remaining duties to Motor Inspectors.

2. When originally described and classified, the Substation Tender job was responsible for operation of two Rotary Converters. In 1948 responsibility for operation of a 1500 kilowatt electronic rectifier was added. This was located in the Open Hearth Shop, about 700 feet from the D.C. Substation where the Substation Tender normally worked. The rectifier (No. 1) was so installed as to permit remote operation from the D.C. Substation, using a supervisory cable. Besides remotely operating the No. 1 rectifier, the Substation Tender visited the Open Hearth Shop twice a turn to inspect the rectifier. These visits normally took a total of ½ hour per turn.

3. Early in 1952, the Company decided to replace the two rotary converters at the D.C. Substation with two new 1000 kilowatt rectifiers. Further, it was decided that the two new rectifiers, as well as the No. 1 rectifier, would be operated remotely from the D.C. Power House through supervisory cables. It was contemplated that these moves would permit conversion of the D.C. Substation to a remotely controlled unattended substation.

4. On December 19, 1953, one new rectifier (No. 3) was installed temporarily at the Substation to function along with No. 1 rectifier at the Open Hearth to carry the load until the rotary converters could be dismantled. The rotary converters (panels, switchboard, transformers and all other related equipment) then were dismantled and removed from the D.C. Substation.

5. On May 15, 1954, No. 2 rectifier was placed in operation. A supervisory control cable, which furnishes a battery impulse from the D.C. Power House to the Control Panel in the D.C. Substation, also went into operation. All three rectifiers could be remotely operated by the Switchboard Tender (Job Class 14) at the Power House as a result of these moves.

6. Thus the new equipment eliminated most duties of Substation Tender (O.W.). The Company therefore terminated the job and assigned some remaining duties to Mo-

tor Inspectors. These duties essentially were of an inspection, service and maintenance nature, such as long performed elsewhere in the plant by Motor Inspectors. Prior to May 15, 1954, moreover, Motor Inspectors were used to perform the more important repairs on No. 1 rectifier.

7. While the Motor Inspectors who now perform these duties make their headquarters at one or the other of the two rectifier stations, this does not establish that they are simply Substation Tenders (O.W.) performing the essential duties of that job rather than true Motor Inspector duties. Motor Inspectors often have such a station where they may be contacted easily when needed in any other portion of their assigned area. The Motor Inspectors in this case perform substantial duties in the Open Hearth, Bessemer and other parts of their assigned area, never performed by the eliminated job of Substation Tender (O.W.).

8. The Union in this case seems to suggest that as long as any duties of a job remain it cannot be terminated, with vestigeal duties assigned to another existing job. Thus, the Union feels that the Substation Tender (O.W.) job continues in existence under Section 9-D, even though perhaps a changed job. The situation here, however, is closely similar to that in USC-417 -420, where the Board stated:

"Nor does Section 9-D preclude action to combine the duties of the two jobs. In T-232 the Board held that discontinuance of the title and rate of 'Bottom Makers' while the incumbents were required to perform the same duties substantially as before, but at a lower rate, constituted a violation of Section 9-D. This was for the reason that although Management had labeled the jobs of Bottom Maker and Bottom Maker Helper as 'terminated,' *in fact there had been no termination* for purposes of Section 9-D, since the *same duties* continued to be performed by the *same individuals* to the *same extent* in the *same work location*. The facts in the present case bear no reasonable similarity to those in T-232."

For the same reasons as in USC-417 -420, this grievance cannot be sustained.

AWARD

9. The grievance is denied.

USC—631, -632. **Edgar Thomson Works.** February 28, 1958
Herbert L. Sherman, Jr., *Chairman*

BACKGROUND

1. The basic question presented by these two cases is whether Management of the Edgar Thomson Works obligated itself to continue an arrangement concerning the assignment of roll building duties, in the No. 2 Mill of the Rolling, Finishing and Fabrication Department, which was in effect from October 31, 1955 through 1956. According to the Union changes made in that arrangement constituted a violation of Sections 2-B and 9-D of the August 3, 1956 Agreement, and also of the Local Seniority Agreement. The Company denies that it had any obligation to continue beyond a reasonable period of time an arrangement requested by the Union and accepted by Management on the basis of a jointly held hope that the amount of business for the No. 2 Mill would be increased. There was no material change in business for the No. 2 Mill during 1956.

2. Prior to 1949 a crew of one Roll Builder and four Roll Builder Helpers provided roll building service on the day turn to No. 1 and No. 2 Mills, which rolled various rails and small slabs. At that time there were 30 operating turns per week. When required, the roll building crew also assisted on roll changes.

3. The roll building crew had originally been established to minimize interruption in continuous, around-the-clock rolling operations. This basis for the crew, however, gradually disappeared over the years. Starting in January 1949, the demand for product rolled on the No. 1 and No. 2 Mills began to decline steadily. There was a resultant decline in the number of operating turns. By October 1954, the No. 1 Mill had decreased successively from three rolling crews (15 turn operations) to two rolling crews (10 turn operations) to one rolling crew (5 turn operations), and finally on October 11, 1954 this Mill ceased operations. During this same period No. 2 Mill had reduced from three to two rolling crews with operations finally fluctuating between ten and five turns per week. By late 1954 the roll building crew had been reduced to three men.

4. Between October, 1954 and September, 1955 the number of operating turns fluctuated between 5, 8, 9 and 10 turns per week. Finally, on September 9, 1955, No. 2 Mill was shut down for extensive rehabilitation. When the necessary improvements were completed, it resumed operations on October 31, 1955. From that date through 1956 it operated mostly at a five turn a week level with some six turn weeks at the beginning of the period.

5. During October, 1955 several meetings were held by Management and Union representatives to discuss the necessary changes in the manning arrangements for No. 2 Mill to be installed upon resumption of operations. The Company took the position that the rolling crews should be reduced from two to one, and that roll changing duties, previously performed by the full operating crews assigned to operating turns, should be performed on non-operating turns by an eight-man crew which would also perform whatever roll building was necessary. For this crew Management contemplated establishment of two new jobs of Set-Up Man and Set-Up Man Helper. There were to be four incumbents of each job. Under this arrangement the incumbents of the Roll Builder and Roll Builder Helper jobs were to be demoted to the labor pool in accordance with the Local Seniority Agreement.

6. Among the objections raised by the Union at a meeting of October 21, 1955 was the fact that the incumbents of the Roll Builder and Roll Builder Helper jobs were not to be assigned to the proposed eight-man roll change crew. The Company agreed to consider the Union proposal that they be made part of that crew.

7. On October 27, 1955 another meeting was held. Management then agreed that members of the roll building crew would be included in the roll change crew if it could be shown that they had the necessary ability. The Company also proposed that if any of the regular Levermen were used on the roll change crew, they would be paid their regular rates rather than the proposed Set-Up Man and Set-Up Man Helper rates. At this point the Union noted that members of the roll building crew were not thoroughly familiar with roll change procedures. It withdrew its request that members of the roll building crew be included in the roll change crew. It contended that all members of the roll change crew should be regular Levermen, and that roll building should be performed by a separate crew.

8. Hope was expressed by both parties that business would improve and that No. 2 Mill would return to a higher level of operations. As stated by one of the Union witnesses in answer to a question as to whether the parties proceeded on the basis of a hope that there might be a return to 10 turns of operation a week, "They (the Company representatives) were as much hopeful as we were. They wanted qualified people at

their disposal when they wanted them. So they were as hopeful as the Union was in holding these people together." (Tr. p. 18.)

9. On this basis it was finally decided that there would be two full rolling crews with each crew being assigned to rolling on alternate weeks. During the off week of each crew, eight key Levermen were to be regularly scheduled as Laborers without regard to seniority in order that they would be available for roll changing as necessary on non-operating turns. Such roll building as still remained was to be performed on the daylight turn by a separate crew during this period.

10. By the end of 1956, since no improvement in the operating level of No. 2 Mill had materialized, Management concluded that continuation of such an arrangement was not justified. Moreover, there had been complaints about the fact that older employees were being required to participate in this working arrangement.

11. The Company then offered alternative proposals to the Union, but they were unacceptable. Finally, early in January, 1957, Management advised the Union that the two rolling crews would be merged into one with the excess employees displaced in accordance with the Local Seniority Agreement. Remaining roll building work was assigned to an eight-man crew which was scheduled on night turn for roll changing purposes. While this crew formerly consisted of qualified employees of the "off" rolling crew, the new roll change crew was selected from the employees displaced by the merger of the two rolling crews. These employees are scheduled as Laborers and are upgraded as the need arises to perform roll changing and roll building work.

12. The Roll Builder and Roll Builder Helper jobs were discontinued. By use of a Form G "Performs roll building functions as required" was added to the job descriptions for the following "higher rated" jobs on which the roll change crew members are carried:

No. of Men	Position	Job Class
1	Assistant Roller	17
1	Guide Setter	14
2	Leverman (First Rougher)	12
1	Leverman (Second Rougher) C.S.	13
1	Leverman (Second Rougher) R.S.	12
1	Leverman (First Finisher)	13
1	Leverman (Finisher)	13

13. On January 21, 1957 the present two grievances were filed. One grievance seeks restoration of the Roll Builder and Roll Builder Helper jobs, and asks that the former incumbents be reassigned to them from labor. The other grievance requests that roll building be deleted from the jobs constituting the new roll change crew.

14. Subsequent to the filing of the grievances No. 2 Mill went to four turn operations. At the time of the hearing the Mill was down.

CONTENTIONS OF THE PARTIES

15. The Union agrees that, due to the reduction in the level of operations over the years, the discontinuance of the No. 1 Mill and the rehabilitation of the No. 2 Mill, the situation in October, 1955 called for a rearrangement of the crews. It contends, however, that a memorandum prepared by Management in October, 1955, outlining the arrangement utilized from that time until January, 1957, reflected a local oral agreement under Section 2-B. The Union takes the position that this arrangement must be continued, under the alleged oral agreement which contained no time limit, until there is a sufficient change in underlying conditions under Section 2-B-4 of the Basic Agreement. Since there was no such change during the period in question, the Union argues that the practice followed from October 31, 1955 through 1956 is binding upon the Company under Section 2-B-3 of the Agreement.

16. Moreover, the Union contends that Section 9-D of the Agreement has been violated under the Board's reasoning in T-328 and T-234. And because the Union feels that the Roll Builder and Roll Builder Helper jobs have been improperly terminated, it also believes that the Local Seniority Agreement has been violated.

17. Management takes the position, disputed by the Union, that even if a local agreement were made in October, 1955, it would not be enforceable because it was not approved by the top representatives of the parties. The Company contends that without such approval no enforceable local working condition can arise under Section 2-B after April 22, 1947.

18. In any event, Management stresses its position that no such agreement as alleged by the Union was made in October, 1955. At the time there was considerable publicity concerning the rehabilitation of the No. 2 Mill. Witnesses for both parties indicated that they were hopeful that new business would be obtained so that No. 2 Mill would return to a higher level of operations. The Company points out that the

memorandum in dispute nowheres states that the parties agreed that roll building would be performed by a separate crew. In fact, the first time that the Union relied upon the alleged agreement was in the Fourth Step of the grievance procedure. Furthermore, Management claims that the changes over the years justified its action under Section 2-B-4.

19.   With respect to the Union argument based on Section 9-D of the Agreement, the Company asserts that prior Awards cited by the Union are clearly distinguishable. To support its position in this case, the Company cites the Board's Awards in CI-257, USC-417 and 420, USC-418, A-443, A-650, USC-526, T-316 and T-321.

DISCUSSION AND FINDINGS

20.   It is not necessary to decide in this case whether a binding local working condition may arise after April 22, 1947, without the approval of top representatives of the parties, under Section 2-B of the Agreement.

21.   Even if this Section were held to be applicable to these grievances, the parties recognized that such substantial changes in underlying conditions for the crews in dispute had taken place by October 31, 1955 that changes in the prior practices were warranted. And the Board cannot find that the parties locally agreed that the manning arrangement for No. 2 Mill which in fact prevailed during the following year must be continued in the absence of an improvement in operations. On the contrary, the testimony of witnesses for both parties convinces the Board that the Company was simply per-

suaded by the Union to adopt its manning proposals on the basis of a hope that No. 2 Mill would return to a higher level of operations. When that hope did not materialize after a reasonable period of time, Management was not obligated to continue the arrangement. Hence the Board cannot find that the Company violated a local agreement or practice under Section 2-B when it transferred the remaining roll building work to the new roll change crew on the night turn.

22.   Nor can it be found that there was any violation of Section 9-D of the Agreement. The Roll Builder and Roll Builder Helper jobs were in fact terminated when the remaining roll building work was transferred to the various position rated jobs in the new roll change crew. This is not a case where the same employees are performing essentially the same work on the same turn under a different job title. Neither is it a case involving dispersal of craft duties among noncraft jobs. Furthermore, there were substantial changes in underlying conditions, up to the time of the alleged local agreement, which greatly reduced the amount of roll building work required. Prior Awards of the Board cited by the Union deal with clearly distinguishable situations.

23.   Since the Union's contention that there was a violation of the Local Seniority Agreement is dependent upon a finding that the Roll Builder and Roll Builder Helper jobs should be restored, that contention must also fail.

AWARD

24.   The grievances are denied.

Section B.   CLAIM OF NO RIGHT TO TERMINATE A JOB

USC—520.   Gary Steel Works.   June 30, 1955

Sylvester Garrett, *Chairman*

BACKGROUND

1.   This grievance protests termination of the job of Test Report Clerk (Billet and 40″) in the Accounting Department of Gary Steel Works.

2.   Prior to the events giving rise to this grievance, there was duplication of forms, procedures, and effort in the determination of chemical and metallurgical test results at Gary Steel Works. Determination of test results was dispersed among employees in four different locations: (1) In the Billet and 40″ Mill, the chemical test check function was handled by Accounting Department Test Report Clerks (Class 7); (2) In the

36″ Slab Mill, the chemical test check function was handled by Special Products Inspectors who also performed substantial inspection duties; (3) In the 44″ Blooming and Rail Mill, the chemical test check function was handled by still other employees; (4) Metallurgical test analysis *for all products of the above operations* was handled by Physical Test Analysts (Macro) (Class 12) in the Metallurgical Department.

3.   Late in 1953 Assistant Chief Metallurgist Barnett was advised of customer complaints of delay in releasing shipments. Upon investigation Barnett learned of the dispersal of the chemical test check function among the above jobs and locations. Barnett

then undertook to simplify procedures for chemical and physical check analyses preliminary to release of semifinished steel to customers.

4. After discussion with the Accounting Department, Barnett decided to discontinue performance of the chemical test function by different employees in separate locations and to transfer the work to the physical Test Analysts (Macro) in his Department. At the same time various forms previously made out both by Test Report Clerks and Physical Test Analysts were eliminated entirely. Thereafter the results of chemical and physical tests for any given product were recorded on the back of production report forms which already were in use.

5. The working procedure of the Test Report Clerk job included eleven items as follows:

1. Lists in heat number sequence from Production Orders to check books— heat number, chemical analysis, specification number, and where rolled.
2. Prepares Spark Test Sheet showing heat number, analysis, number of tests, etc., from Production Orders and Specification File. Lists same information by heat number in Spark Book and gives test sheet to spark testers.
3. Prepares work sheet for each heat showing heat number, specification, chemistry range, date, customer, order number, etc., from information on Production Order, and test practice chart.
4. Consults specification file according to specification number on Production Orders.
5. Prepares drilling envelopes and order for chemical analysis form when drillings are required, copying drilling requirements as shown on specification card. Notes on back of Work Sheet the time and date drillings were sent to Chemical Laboratory.
6. Posts to Work Sheet by heat number and chemical analysis received from Chemical Laboratory noting time received and from whom.
7. Posts to Work Sheet by heat number the metallurgical test results received verbally from Metallurgical tester.
8. Compares chemical test results with specification requirements and if within specification tolerance prepares heat release forms. Mails copies to customers and other Departments and files one copy by heat number. Calls specification department when heats are outside specified ranges and gives

them all requested information, concerning heat from heat book, production order and spec. cards. Prepares order for extra test pieces as directed by Specification Department indicating heat number, ingot number, required tests, etc.
9. File all Work Sheets in Check File by heat number.
10. Posts to Check Analysis Book notice of heats held for extra checks by heat number.
11. Posts Spark Results to Check Book from Spark tester's results in Spark Book by heat number.

6. As a result of Barnett's analysis, items 1, 3, 4, 7, 9, 10 and 11, were eliminated in whole or in part. The remaining items— 2, 5, 6 and 8—which embraced a major portion of the Test Report Clerk job—were transferred to the Physical Test Analyst position.

7. When the Test Report Clerk job was discontinued and chemical test report duties of other jobs transferred to the Metallurgical Department, it became necessary to add four Physical Test Analysts. This was done by posting vacancies in the Metallurgical seniority unit. Three employees in the unit bid and were promoted. Consideration then was given employees outside the unit, and one Test Report Clerk was selected to fill the fourth vacancy as Physical Test Analyst. Remaining incumbents of the Test Report Clerk job are grievants in this case. At present they occupy various jobs in the Accounting Department, in most instances in a Job Class lower than Class 7.

8. Prior to termination of the Test Report Clerk job, and addition of four Physical Test Analysts, the situation was discussed with one of the Grievance Committeemen, and the Company's proposed course of action was outlined. It does not appear that the Company sought Union agreement to the proposed action, nor was any agreement reached as to how the matter might best be handled.

9. All grievants are female employees. They believe that they have been discriminated against because of their sex, and that the transfer of substantial Test Report Clerk duties to the Physical Test Analysts primarily was designed to eliminate female employees. The Union claims violation of Sections 2-B, 9-D and 13.

FINDINGS

10. The elimination of unnecessary functions, reports, and duplication of work, to provide better customer service in release

of semifinished steel products, provided proper basis to terminate the Test Report Clerk job and transfer functions of this and other jobs to Physical Test Analysts in the Metallurgical Department.

11. The basic problem here arises largely because the grievants were in an Accounting Department seniority unit while the remaining duties of their job were transferred to a job in a Metallurgical Department seniority unit. Thus grievants were not entitled to consideration for positions created in the Metallurgical seniority unit, ahead of employees bidding from within that unit.

12. The Union stresses that in the past incumbents have been transferred with their jobs when the duties were transferred from one seniority unit to another. It is conceded that whenever a job at Gary Steel Works is transferred *as such* to another seniority unit, the incumbents are transferred with the job and their continuous service is recognized in the new unit.

13. The Company did not apply this practice here because the Test Report Clerk job was not transferred intact, but was terminated, even though major duties of the job were transferred to employees in a job 5 classes higher. The Union believes it would have been possible first to transfer the Test Report Clerk job into the Metallurgical Department seniority unit, and then to terminate the Test Report Clerk job. This technique would have permitted the erstwhile Test Report Clerks to bid, as members of the Metallurgical seniority unit, for promotion to Physical Test Analyst.

14. It may be that grievants' seniority rights could have been given more substance by the technique suggested by the Union. If an agreement to this effect had been worked out locally, it might have provided a satisfactory means of precluding or settling the grievance. But the question before the Board is whether the Company's action violated some provision of the Agreement or of a local seniority rule.

15. Such a violation is not disclosed by the evidence. This is not a case of transferring a job intact from one seniority unit to another. Rather, duties performed by a number of different employees in different locations now are consolidated in a single higher rated job. Local modifications of rules for application of agreed seniority units are left to the parties under Section 13-B. Whatever may be the possible merit of the Union's suggestion for fuller protection of grievants' seniority rights, without undue prejudice to employees in the Metallurgical seniority unit, the Board cannot adopt it as a basis for deciding this case.

AWARD

16. The grievance is denied.

USC—521. Gary Steel Works. June 30, 1955

Sylvester Garrett, *Chairman*

BACKGROUND

1. This grievance protests termination of the Test Carrier job at the Nos. 1, 3 and 4 Open Hearths, Gary Steel Works.

2. Prior to this grievance one Test Carrier was assigned per turn in each shop, and worked with the Casting Crew.

3. The number of furnaces operating determines in large part the amount of Test Carrying required. Each incentive application in the three Open Hearths specified a maximum crew per turn of one Test Carrier at an 8 to 14 furnace level of operations, inclusive. Below the 8 furnace level no Test Carrier was assigned. At this level all Test Carrying was performed by Slaggers. The Test Carrying function was included in the Slagger job description as well as that for Test Carrier. The Slagger is in Class 4 and Test Carrier in Class 3.

4. Prior to April, 1954, there was a significant increase in the number of rim and mechanically capped heats. These type heats require more Casting Crew work than ordinary heats. Prior to April, 1954, the Casting Crews complained that they needed additional help because of the change in type of heats, and the Grievance Committeeman suggested addition of more Slaggers to the crews.

5. In the end, Management decided to add Slaggers to the Casting Crews but eliminated the Test Carrier job, as follows:

NO. 1 OPEN HEARTH SHOP CREW

JOB TITLE	MAXIMUM CREW PER TURN								
	Number of Furnaces Operating								
	14	13	12	11	10	9	8	7	6
(Crew Specifications Prior to 4/4/54)									
Slagger	4	4	4	2	2	2	2	2	2
Test Carrier	1	1	1	1	1	1	1	0	0
(Crew Specifications Effective 4/4/54)									
Slagger	5	5	5	5	3	3	3	2	2

NO. 3 OPEN HEARTH SHOP CREW—614 &
NO. 4 OPEN HEARTH SHOP CREW

(Crew Specifications Prior to 4/4/54)

Slagger	4*	4*	4*	4*	2	2	2	2	2
Test Carrier	1	1	1	1	1	1	1	0	0

(Crew Specifications Effective 4/4/54)

Slagger	5	5	5	5	3	3	3	2	2

* Size ranged from 2 to 4 and was based on percent of total heats produced per calendar day from ore charges.

6. As these figures reveal there was no decrease in number of employees as a result of this move. The crew sizes remained the same save that the No. 1 Open Hearth Crew was increased by two men per turn at the 11 furnace level of operation.

7. Elimination of Test Carriers and transfer of the work to Slaggers displaced 13 Test Carriers, while corresponding vacancies in the Slagger position were filled in accordance with Section 13. Several displaced Test Carriers were promoted to Slagger, but others—all of whom are women—were not able to promote because physically unable to handle the heavy work of Slagger. Several did promote to Slagger for awhile before concluding the work was too heavy.

8. Basically, the grievance claims violation of Section 2-B, in changing the Casting Crew, and also of Section 9-D, in terminating the Test Carrier job. Also, the Union suggests that those of the grievants who were women had been deprived of job security protected under Section 13, and were discriminated against because of sex.

FINDINGS

9. The change in nature of heats, as recognized in the request of the Casting Crew for additional Slaggers, provided basis for the Company's action here under both Sections 2-B and 9-D.

10. The Union claim that the additional Slaggers do not really work as such, but devote all their time to performance of the former Test Carrier duties, is not supported by the evidence.

11. While grievants believe themselves victims of arbitrary action, the record would not support a finding to this effect. Rather, there is no basis on which this grievance could be sustained. All grievants continue in the Company's employ in accordance with their seniority rights in the seniority unit.

AWARD

12. The grievance is denied.

USC—536. Ohio Works. February 23, 1956
Sylvester Garrett, *Chairman*

BACKGROUND

1. This grievance claims violation of Sections 2-B and 9-D of the July 1, 1954 Agreement by elimination of the Tallyman (43″ Scrap) job from the Mill Clerical Group, Accounting Division, Youngstown District Works.

2. Prior to the protested change the major function of Tallyman (43″ Scrap) in the 43″ Primary Rolling Mill was to report sulphur content (or alloy content, on occasion) of Bloom Butt Scrap in each individual box on each Narrow Gauge Buggy upon being cropped off the blooms. The butts dropped by conveyor into the boxes on the Narrow Gauge buggies. Each buggy held three boxes, and carried the scrap to the Open Hearth Department for charging.

3. In reporting sulphur content, the Tallyman posted to a form, showing average sulphur content of bloom butts in each individual box on each buggy, by box and buggy number. To ascertain the sulphur content of the butts, the Tallyman contacted the Shear Recorder by telephone.

4. After each turn the Tallyman's report was delivered to the Ingot Yard Stocker who

used it to prepare a Rolling Mill Scrap Report. Copies of this report then were sent to the Open Hearth Stock House Accounting Standard Cost and Primary Mills Inventory Clerk.

5. Under this system there were instances where high sulphur scrap was identified wrongly as low sulphur scrap and charged into low sulphur heats. In discussing this problem with Open Hearth Supervision, 43″ Primary Rolling Mill Superintendent Carr concluded that the existing scrap reporting system did not permit ready reference to source data in recording of sulphur content, so that it was not possible to check the recorded information for accuracy in case of doubt in any specific instance.

6. As a result, Carr decided to change the method of reporting sulphur and alloy content of bloom butt scrap so as to establish a buggy number on the source record.

7. Among changes effected at this time were: (1) elimination of the 43″ Mill Butt Scrap Report which had been filled out by the Tallyman, (2) introduction of a new Bloom Recorder's tally sheet with an added column to show percent sulphur content for each ingot rolled, (3) inclusion in the

new Bloom Recorder's tally sheet of a column for the numbers of boxes and buggies into which the bloom butts for each heat are dropped as they come off the Scrap Conveyor (with this actual recording of sulphur content by ingot, it is necessary for the Shear Recorder to indicate sulphur content only by buggies rather than by box), (4) installation of a new closed circuit telephone system between the Shear Recorder and Conveyor Man Scrap.

8.   To make it possible for the Shear Recorder to get the buggy numbers, the Conveyor Man Scrap now phones the Shear Recorder on the closed circuit telephone and gives him the number of each buggy as it moves into loading position beneath the conveyor. This then is recorded on the Bloom Recorder's tally sheet.

9.   Under the new method, a copy of the new Bloom Recorder's tally sheet is delivered to the Ingot Yard Stocker every two hours. The latter then calculates whether each buggy contains high or low sulphur bloom butts, and records this information on a new Rolling Mill Scrap Report. This last report represents a revision of the old Scrap Report form.

10.   Since the information formerly put into the 43″ Mill Scrap Report by the Tallyman now appears in more detailed and usable form in the new Bloom Recorder's tally sheet, and since the basic information for this purpose is provided by the Conveyor Man Scrap, it no longer is necessary for the Tallyman either to obtain this information or to transcribe it onto the old type report. Hence, the Company concluded that the job of Tallyman (43″ Scrap) should be terminated.

FINDINGS

11.   In view of elimination of the report compiled by Tallyman (43″ Scrap) and since the scrap content information is now provided by the Conveyor Man (Scrap) to the Shear Recorder over a closed circuit telephone, there was proper basis for Management's decision to terminate the Tallyman job. The record here discloses no violation either of Section 2-B or of Section 9-D.

AWARD

12.   The grievance is denied.

CWU—3.   Utah Plant.   November 14, 1957
Donald A. Crawford, *Arbitrator*
Approved by Herbert L. Sherman, Jr., *Chairman*

BACKGROUND

1.   The issue presented in this case is whether the Company has violated Section 9-D of the August 3, 1956 Agreement and the Local Seniority Agreement by requiring inspectors to perform duties included in the Conveyor Operator job.

2.   Beginning February 6, 1957, the Company moved conveyor controls so that the Final Inspectors could kick large diameter pipe onto and off the final inspection platform and rotate the pipe for inspection. Before this, the conveyormen performed these duties as well as conveying the pipe to and from the station and removing defective pipe from the area to a repair section. Since rotating the pipe for inspection required considerable time of the conveyormen, the change in set-up permitted reducing the number of conveyormen from two to one.

3.   The Union says that at the time the jobs were described and classified under the January 1, 1953 Inequities Agreement that all the conveyormen positions throughout the mill would be included in one job description—Conveyor Operators; that conveyor operation is not an inherent or specific requirement of the Inspector Final job. The

Union argues that Management has transferred the conveyorman duties to the Inspectors without eliminating any portion of the job. Accordingly, the Company has violated Section 9-D, which requires the continuation of existing job descriptions and classifications in effect unless terminated, changed one full job class, or changed by mutual agreement.

4.   In effect, the Union continues, the Company has terminated the conveyorman jobs at this location. To do so under these circumstances violates Section 9-D and the Board's rulings in cases T-232 and G-56.

5.   The Union notes that the two jobs are in separate seniority units, which further supports the position that operating conveyors is not an inherent function of the Final Inspector job. The Union concludes that the present arrangement creates a safety hazard. Formerly the conveyorman could see that both inspectors were out of the pipe, whereas now as either inspector comes out of the pipe, he can reach up to the horizontal pull rod and rotate the pipe while the other inspector is still inside.

6.   The Company position is that the Company's right to change job duties of position-rated jobs for legitimate needs has

been recognized by the Board in numerous cases (T-291, USC-418, USC-417, CI-257, COL-73); that Section 3-A of the Job Description and Classification Manual of January 1, 1953 (incorporated by Section 9-J-1 of the August 3, 1956 Agreement) specifically provides for Management changes in job content of less than a full job class, as in this instance; that Section 9-D-1 is not relevant because Management has not terminated the job in the plant or at this particular spot in the plant.

7. The Company says that the new set-up is less hazardous and more efficient. More efficient because the operation no longer requires the same coordination of inspector and conveyorman. Less hazardous because the inspectors who handle the pipe know better when to roll it than the more distant conveyorman.

8. The Company points out that only a function of the conveyorman job has been changed. The Company says that it is normal in this plant for the inspector to position pipe for his inspection by using turning rolls. The Company submits the job description for Preliminary Inspector (O.D. & I.D.—Large Diameter Mill), and notes that the first sentence of the "Working Procedure" reads: "Positions pipe section on conveyor or skid, using push-button controls or pipe rolling bar."

FINDINGS

9. *The Company has not violated Section 9-D nor created a safety hazard by assigning some conveyorman job duties to the Final Inspectors.*

10. The rule of T-232, decided under Section 9 of the Agreement, does not apply because the Company has not terminated the job of conveyorman—even at this particular work station. The job continues in effect at this area of the line with one incumbent instead of two because of the reduction in work load assigned to that job.

11. The assignment of the operation of the relocated conveyor controls to the Final Inspectors does yield more efficient operation and is consistent with the duties of other inspection jobs at different points along the line. The argument as to an increase in hazard is not persuasive. It seems obvious that the operation of controls by the men who may be injured by their own carelessness would result in greater safety than the operation of those controls by others who would not suffer the physical consequences of careless operation.

12. Thus, the re-assignment of job duties in this case cannot be held to violate Section 9-D or to create a hazard.

AWARD

13. The grievances are denied.

USC—615. South Works. June 18, 1957

Sylvester Garrett, *Chairman*

FINDINGS

1. This case involves composition of Narrow Gauge Engine Crews in the Yard and Transportation Department of South Works.

2. Some years ago the Board referred Case CI-194 back to the parties for settlement and they agreed on March 30, 1951, that Hostlers would be paid the Narrow Gauge Engineer rate when required to operate a narrow gauge engine.

3. On July 8, 1951, the parties also agreed upon an incentive application (No. 6340-901) with an understanding that Hostlers and Second men thereafter would be paid as Engineers or Switchmen. No men were assigned to either job thereafter, and former incumbents were slotted as extra Engineers or Switchmen.

4. In 1951 there were 4 or 5 steam locomotives, 1 in regular use. By 1954 the Company had discontinued steam locomotives entirely in favor of diesels, had installed a new intercommunication system and hold track, and had made other changes which eliminated most of the duties once performed by Hostlers and Second men. On March 9, 1956, the present grievance was entered in effect requesting re-establishment of the jobs of Hostler and Second man as additions to the Narrow Gauge Crews.

5. It is clear that no one has been slotted as Hostler or Second man since July 8, 1951, and that the jobs have not been occupied for years. Bearing in mind the terms of Section 9-D of the Agreement, there is no basis to direct the Company to re-establish these jobs in the Narrow Gauge Engine Crews.

AWARD

6. The grievance is denied.

USC—782.   Duquesne Works.   February 20, 1959
Sylvester Garrett, *Chairman*

BACKGROUND

1.   This grievance from the Accounting Department, Steel Producing Division, Duquesne Works, protests failure to assign a Floor Recorder (Class 7) (Plant Title— Test Carrier) in No. 2 Open Hearth when operations fall below the 8-furnace level. The Floor Recorder job is known locally as Test Carrier and also as Ingot Shipper Helper. It is not to be confused, however, with the Class 3 job of Test Carrier which formerly existed at No. 2 Open Hearth.

2.   The case arose during a period of curtailed operations commencing in the summer of 1957 when the number of operating furnaces was reduced below 8. Although the Union denies its existence, the Company's evidence is designed to confirm existence of an established local working condition protected under Section 2-B in No. 2 Open Hearth. This, according to the Company, contemplates that at 8-furnace, or higher, level of operation a Test Carrier will be assigned. Existence of the practice is reflected and elaborated in two grievance settlements —one in 1954, the other in 1955.

3.   In Grievance A-54-18 an issue was raised as to whether a Test Carrier should be assigned in No. 2 Open Hearth whenever operations were at a level of 6 or more furnaces. Following investigation, the Management representatives stated that in 1945, 1946, and 1949 when No. 2 Open Hearth operated at reduced levels, it appeared that a Test Carrier was assigned when operations were at the level of 9 or more furnaces, and removed when operations fell below 9 furnaces. The Third Step minutes dated April 2, 1954 include the following:

> "Although the records show that in the past the Test Carrier was not put on until a nine-furnace operation was reached, Management examined the work load of these men and found it had increased. They therefor concluded that the work load was such at present as to justify addition of the Test Carrier at an eight-furnace level of operations."

4.   Management thus decided in Third Step that (under existing conditions and barring change) the Test Carrier would be assigned at an 8-furnace or greater level of operation in No. 2 Open Hearth. This decision was not accepted by the Union, but there was no appeal from this settlement.

5.   In a related grievance (A-53-103), Management's Third Step decision was accepted January 26, 1955 to the effect that an assignment would be made to the position of Floor Recorder (Ingot Shipper Helper or Test Carrier, Class 7) whenever slab heats were made for shipment out of the plant on a hot run or for shipment out of the plant as cold steel to be converted at another plant. This settlement primarily related to whether an employee in the Floor Recorder job (known locally as Test Carrier or Ingot Shipper Helper) would be assigned rather than an employee in the Job Class 3 job of Test Carrier, which also then appeared in the rate structure for No. 2 Open Hearth.

6.   While the Company suggests that a question might be raised as to the status of the established practice in view of Section 2-B-5, it believes no real problem exists on this score since it does not deny the existence and applicability of the local working condition. Rather it is the Union which denies its existence.

7.   The Union stresses, moreover, that as a result of increased heat size, reduced overall heat time, and other technological changes, the number of tests which must be carried on any given turn has greatly increased since original establishment of the local working condition contemplating use of a Test Carrier at 8-furnace or higher level of operation. Accordingly, it believes that the Board should require assignment of a Test Carrier at some lower level of furnace operations. Its witness indicated a belief that years ago a Test Carrier had been regularly assigned at 6-furnace level of operations.

8.   In addition, the Union urged at the hearing that since the Ingot Shipper Helper job (Floor Recorder or Test Carrier) was separately described and classified, Management is obliged under Section 9-D to continue assigning an employee to this position at all levels of operation in No. 2 Open Hearth. Under this argument, the established local working condition would be of no significance.

FINDINGS

9.   Essentially the Union advances three alternative propositions in support of the grievance. *First,* it urges that the applicable local working condition requires assignment of a Test Carrier in No. 2 Open Hearth whenever operations are at a 6-furnace or higher level. *Second,* it holds that the gradually increased work load over the years (resulting from greater heat size, reduced tap-to-tap time, and like factors) requires adjustment of the established local working condition even if it has contemplated that a

Test Carrier will not be assigned until operations are at 8-furnace or higher level. *Third*, it believes that Section 9-D requires that the Test Carrier (Floor Recorder) job must be filled at all times since it represents an agreed job description and classification within the No. 2 Open Hearth.

10. The evidence is sufficiently clear that the applicable established local working condition at Duquesne Works contemplates assignment of a Floor Recorder (Test Carrier or Ingot Shipper Helper) at 8-furnace or higher levels of operation. The local working condition is not shown to require assignment of a man in this job at lower operating levels.

11. For reasons noted in Case A-461 and like decisions, the Board cannot undertake to equate the number of employees assigned to given jobs to any given level of work or performance where productivity or work load increases over the years. Accordingly, there is no basis in the evidence presented by the Union to disturb the established local working condition.

12. There likewise is no support for this grievance under Section 9-D, since the job has not been changed or eliminated. Section 9-D does not require that a job must be filled at all times, or at any given operating level.

AWARD

13. The grievance is denied.

CHAPTER 3

CLAIMS CONCERNING NEW JOBS

Two kinds of contentions are covered by the cases in this chapter: (1) a claim of failure to recognize that a new job has actually been established and (2) a claim that a new job has been improperly created. Comprehensive treatment of the coding of the classification factors for new jobs may be found in Part II of this volume.

Other relevant cases reported elsewhere in this volume are T-96 (p. 44), T-333 (p. 98) and T-494 (p. 262).

Section A. CLAIM OF FAILURE TO RECOGNIZE NEW JOB

N—197. Lorain Works. December 18, 1953

Herbert L. Sherman, Jr., *Assistant to the Chairman*

Approved by Sylvester Garrett, *Chairman*

BACKGROUND

1. This grievance requests a higher classification for the Repairman job performed by grievant at Lorain Works. The Union's claim that the job should be designated as Repairman Electronics in Class 18 is based primarily upon the detailed and specialized nature of the electronics work performed by grievant and upon his assumption of the duties of the Pyrometer and Meter Technician when that job was vacated in November, 1950. Seeking higher ratings on Factors 2, 3, 8 and 12, the Union asserts that the job can no longer be considered as falling in the craft of Instrument Repairman at Class 16. A detailed list of the new and modern electronic devices and communications equipment, which have been added to grievant's responsibilities since the job was classified, was presented to the Board along with supporting testimony.

2. The present ratings of the job in dispute (which is designated and classified as Instrument Repairman), and those proposed by the Union are as follows:

FACTORS	PRESENT RATINGS	PROPOSED BY UNION
1. Pre-employment Training.	C-1.0	C-1.0
*2. Employment Training and Experience.	H-3.2	J-4.0
*3. Mental Skill.	E-2.8	F-3.5
4. Manual Skill.	E-2.0	E-2.0
5. Responsibility for Materials.	E-1.6	E-1.6
6. Responsibility for Tools and Equipment.	C-.7 Med.	C-.7 Med.
7. Responsibility for Operations.	C-1.0	C-1.0
*8. Responsibility for Safety of Others.	A-Base	B-.4
9. Mental Effort.	E-2.5	E-2.5
10. Physical Effort.	B-.3	B-.3
11. Surroundings.	B-.4	B-.4
*12. Hazards.	B-.4	C-.8
Total	15.9	18.2

* Disputed Factors

3. Although Management admits that responsibility for maintenance of modern Audio and FM communication systems, newly installed in the No. 4 Seamless Mill, the No. 4 Blooming Mill and at the New Bessemer, has become a part of the job in dispute, it argues that the fundamental principles which govern maintenance of the communication systems have remained unchanged. Moreover, the Company asserts that grievant's claim, insofar as it is based on installation of the new Audio and FM systems, is untimely, because these changes were instituted prior to June, 1949, and the grievance was not filed until June, 1951. It appears, however, that there has been a con-

tinuous addition of new equipment and duties over the past few years.

4. To the Union's observation that the present job description contains no requirement of working with "electronics," the Company argues that all such work which grievant does is comprehended by the various items in the Working Procedure of the description. Management also refers to a reference to "electronics" in the Wireman's job description, but the Wireman's job, in Class 16, was distinguished by the Union on the basis of the limited type of maintenance work, in electronics (such as the removal of a tube), which is required of that job as contrasted with the complicated repair work on the latest devices assigned to grievant.

5. Great stress is placed by the Union on a comparison between the job in dispute and the job of Electronic Repairman in Class 18 at Gary Steel Works. This job is coded in Factor 2 at J-4.0 and in Factor 3 at F-3.5. Grievant performs almost all the duties listed in the Working Procedure of the job description for this job plus a few more. The Company admits that there are many striking similarities between the two jobs, but emphasizes language in the Gary job description which might indicate a few differences, such as building of electronic equipment, direction of a Repairman Carbometer, and research in the field of electronics.

DISCUSSION AND FINDINGS

6. The primary function of the job in dispute, as the result of the elimination of the Pyrometer and Meter Technician job, now involves responsibility for detailed and complicated work with numerous and different types of electronic devices, requiring a greater period of training and experience and a higher degree of mental skill than when it was agreed upon as an Instrument Repairman job. No longer does grievant have the benefit of close direction and instruction of the incumbent of the Technician job as he had prior to the elimination of that job by Management. Now he is required to work on his own to a much greater extent. Management explains the instruction given to grievant on the ground that he did not have apprentice training which was only recently installed. Nevertheless, grievant was considered a qualified Instrument Repairman, yet substantial instruction and training were given to him because of the specialized and complex equipment on which he was required to work. The changes in the duties take the job outside the scope of the craft job of Instrument Repairman for the purposes of rating Factors 2 and 3.

7. There is no specific Benchmark or Specimen for an Electronic Repairman job of the nature performed by grievant. Nor was there any pattern of non-Specimen Electronic Repairman jobs presented to the Board. On the other hand, it is not disputed that grievant, in addition to his past duties, has been required to perform most of the duties of the Pyrometer and Meter Technician since that job was vacated. The Union points out that the Technician job was a salaried job in Class 11 and that Class 22 under the Production and Maintenance Agreement is the closest equivalent to Class 11 under the Salaried Agreement.

8. It is agreed that only two duties of any significance appear in the job description for the Pyrometer and Meter Technician which grievant does not perform: direction of an Instrument Repairman and designing of electrical circuits by developing wiring diagrams or conduit layouts. Even so, grievant modifies schematic or wiring diagrams. Recognizing, however, that the Technician job and the job in dispute do differ in these respects, the Union emphasizes that it is seeking four job classes less than the equivalent job class of the Technician job.

9. The jobs most comparable to the job in dispute are the Pyrometer and Meter Technician job at Lorain and the Electronic Repairman job at Gary with respect to which there was testimony presented at the hearing. Two non-Specimen Youngstown Repairman jobs, introduced by the Company as exhibits, are difficult to evaluate in the absence of any testimony concerning the precise nature of the duties involved.

10. Although the Gary Electronic Repairman job is not considered as controlling the present grievance in view of the differences in some of the duties, it does provide some guidance, along with the Pyrometer and Meter Technician job, since most of the primary duties are also found in the job in dispute. Factor 2 is, therefore, coded appropriately at J-4.0 and Factor 3 at F-3.5.

11. Under the Board's findings with respect to Factors 2 and 3, there has been a change in classification. But since a new non-craft job is found by the Board, a new description must be prepared and all the other Factors must now be reviewed. The job cannot now be characterized as a craft job because the classifications for such jobs are standardized. Since all of the Factors were not considered by the parties either in the grievance procedure or at the hearing, the case is remanded to the parties for further consideration in the light of the findings in this Award.

AWARD

12.   Factors 2 and 3 are increased to J-4.0 and F-3.5 respectively. The balance of the case, involving the establishment of the description and the classification of the remaining ten Factors, is remanded to the parties for further consideration in the light of these findings.

USC—511.   Fairless Works.   September 26, 1955
Sylvester Garrett, *Chairman*

BACKGROUND

1.   This grievance from the Electrical Shop, Central Maintenance Shops, Fairless Works, asserts that grievant Electrician-Wireman is performing Cable Splicing work above and beyond the craft job of Electrician-Wireman, and that his work should be separately described and classified as a position rated job of Cable Splicer in Class 18.

2.   Before obtaining employment at Fairless Works, grievant had completed an apprentice training program as Cable Splicer for the Telephone Company and then had worked a number of years as Cable Splicer for the Telephone Company and several railroads. When he applied for employment at Fairless Works, he was told that there was no job of Cable Splicer, but that he could be hired as Electrician-Lineman. As Electrician-Lineman grievant worked up to 50% of his time cable splicing. After being carried as Electrician-Lineman for about 200 work hours, grievant was slotted as Electrician-Wireman because his work more properly fell under the scope of duties of Wireman.

3.   In view of the substantial time which grievant spends cable splicing, the Union believes that a job description and classification should be prepared covering his cable splicing duties, similar to a Class 18 job at Worcester Works (Wire Division) known as "Cable Splicer and Jointer." The Union believes that there is no essential difference between grievant's work at Fairless and the duties covered by the Class 18 position rated job at Worcester.

4.   The Company stresses that the Wireman-Electrician job description at Fairless is the same as the specimen job of Electrician-Wireman and refers to Cable under Materials Used. Item 6 of the Working Procedure also specifies "Makes all required splices and connector joints." In many other U. S. Steel plants cable splicing work is handled by Electricians-Wiremen in much the same manner as at Fairless.

FINDINGS

5.   The cable splicing work performed by grievant at Fairless falls within the scope of the trade and craft job of Electrician-Wireman at Fairless Works.

6.   The job description of a trade or craft job is required to reflect the scope of duties which a fully qualified journeyman may be called upon to perform in the plant. The parties also recognized under the Inequities Program that the varied qualifications and abilities of individual trade or craft employees had to be given recognition in describing and classifying trade or craft jobs.

7.   Since grievant apparently is the best qualified Electrician-Wireman at Fairless Works to handle cable splicing, it is not surprising that as much as 50% of his time has been devoted to performance of this type work. He is not the only Electrician-Wireman called upon to do such work, however, nor does he perform cable splicing to the exclusion of other Wireman duties. Since the work falls within the scope of duties of Electrician-Wireman and appears the same as performed by Wireman to a substantial extent in numerous other plants, there is no basis to sustain the grievance.

AWARD

8.   The grievance is denied.

USC—729.   Johnstown Works.   October 10, 1958
Sylvester Garrett, *Chairman*

FINDINGS

1.   This grievance from Johnstown Works broadly requests that Vicing Foreman jobs be described and classified under Section 9-D and filled in accordance with Section 13 of the August 3, 1956 Agreement.

2.   For many years Vicing Foremen have been used to fill temporary assignments where foremen are absent due to illness, vacation, or similar reason. In addition, there have been instances where men have served as Vicing Foremen for indefinite periods, running up to a year or more. The Company holds that the duties of all Vicing Foremen are supervisory in character and properly excluded from the bargaining unit.

3. One of the Union witnesses served as Vicing Foreman for 7 months some years ago, while the regular Foreman was attending a management school. The Union does not object to this type of arrangement, and recognizes that such an employee is a member of supervision, excluded from the bargaining unit.

4. The Union believes, however, that where an employee serves as a Vicing Foreman for an indefinite period, not merely to fill in during the absence of some identified regular member of supervision, the job must be regarded as within the bargaining unit, since Management continues to check off the employee's dues and does not authorize Vicing Foremen to handle grievances.

5. When the grievance initially was filed, it affected a substantial number of jobs. By hearing time a number of these jobs had been eliminated, other employees involved had been assigned as Foremen, and still others had ceased accepting Vicing Foreman assignments. The Union offered no detail at the hearing as to particular Vicing Foremen whom the Union believed should fall within the bargaining unit because of the duties which they performed. Although the Union referred to potential seniority problems which might arise concerning men serving as Vicing Foremen, no such issue is before the Board in a form which would warrant expression of opinion in this case.

6. The record provides no basis to hold that Vicing Foremen assignments in general constitute jobs within the bargaining unit which must be described and classified. If any of the employees involved in fact function as Gangleaders, which the Union suggested as a possibility, this could be demonstrated only on a case-by-case basis, with considerable attention to detail not present in this case. Thus, in the last analysis, the present grievance does not present any tangible issue calling for decision, and must be dismissed.

AWARD

7. The grievance is dismissed.

T—96. Ensley Works. January 25, 1949
Ralph T. Seward, *Chairman*

BACKGROUND

1. This dispute involves the following grievance, filed January 27, 1948, and signed by seventeen Gangleaders in the Rigger Shop, M. and E. Department, Ensley Works:

"We, the undersigned Riggers—(Gangleaders) request Management to establish the occupation of Working Foreman, Rigger."

2. The Union contends that these men perform work beyond that of Gangleaders, and cites three situations in support of the claim: *first,* when the Gangleader takes out his gang at the beginning of the shift, which consists of three or four to as high as twenty men, it might be necessary, because of the requirement of the work, to divide such gang into several groups and place them at different locations; thus, the Gangleader is required to supervise these several groups and by reason of that fact his status becomes higher than a Gangleader; *second* in some instances, after taking out his gang to perform a specific job, having received instructions from his foreman as to such job, the job originally scheduled to be done is changed. He must then perform the new job on his own, without benefit of the Foreman's instructions or advice thereon; *third,* that on the 3 to 11 shift there are two Gangleaders and that one of these is held responsible for and directs the other, thus assuming the status of a Foreman. The Union does not cite any section of the Agreement which has been violated or which supports the request in the grievance.

3. The Company contends that the Board does not have jurisdiction to direct the establishment of the occupation requested and that the employees in question are not being required to perform work over and above that of Gangleader-Rigger. The Company cites Sections 3, 7-B, and 9-D-4 of the Agreement as supporting its position.

FINDINGS

4. The job description and classification for Gangleader-Rigger were prepared in accordance with the standards of the Wage Inequity Program and signed by appropriate representatives of both parties in November, 1946. In the course of the application of the Inequity Program here, no provision was made for a classification of Working Foreman-Rigger. The men in question were classified as Gangleaders. There is no showing that the work of these employees has changed between the time of their classification or the agreed-upon job description, and the date of this grievance. No factual information has been presented to the Board to show that the job description does not cover the work of these men. While this

claim is presented presumably by the seventeen men who signed the grievance, it is also alleged that one of these men, on the 3 to 11 turn, is especially aggrieved. It is therefore uncertain whether this grievance is addressed to one man, seventeen men, or any other number. For example, if the seventeen were to be granted their request, one might reasonably wonder if the man on the 3 to 11 turn will not then ask for additional special treatment for himself. The Union does not show that the Company has violated any section of the Agreement. The Union has not cited any contract provision in support of its request. In view of these circumstances, it is unnecessary to engage in any further analysis of the case. The grievance should clearly be denied.

AWARD

5. The grievance is denied.

USC—276. Homestead District Works. September 14, 1953

J. O. Keller, *Arbitrator*

BACKGROUND

1. This grievance arose in the Blacksmith Shop of the Heat Treating and Forge Division, Homestead District Works, Carnegie-Illinois Steel Corporation, now United States Steel Company and is a request for job descriptions and classifications for the jobs of the crew of a 300-ton Hydro Press which replaced a 2,000 pound Steam Hammer.

2. By 1948, experience had proved to the Company that the 2,000 pound Steam Hammer was too antiquated to work 1,400 pound blooms in an efficient and safe manner. Accordingly the 300-ton press was purchased to produce such products as shafts, nuts, blocks, bars, hooks, washers, gear blanks and the like in sizes up to 8 inches square by 80 inches long and weighing up to 1,400 pounds. The 300-ton press was installed and in February, 1949, placed in regular operation.

UNION POSITION

3. The Union contends that the 300-ton press is a new installation in the Blacksmith Shop and that the operations of this equipment require that the positions involved are new jobs and that therefore in accordance with Section 9-D (Description and Classification of New or Changed Jobs) of the April 22, 1947 Agreement, the Union requests new job descriptions with appropriate classifications by the Company for these new jobs.

COMPANY POSITION

4. Management took the view that there was no appreciable change in the job content of the jobs of the crew operating the 300-ton press in place of the 2,000 pound hammer that was replaced by the press, that the job descriptions in use for the hammer operations adequately covered the operations of the 300-ton press, that the same product was produced on the press that had been produced on the hammer and that therefore there was no need for any new job descriptions and classifications.

DISCUSSION AND FINDINGS

5. In its brief, the Company stated that in the Blacksmith Shop of the Heat Treating and Forge Division, there are various types of blacksmithing craft activities to produce forgings of different sizes and shapes and the repairing of tools and equipment. The manipulation and shaping of iron and steel materials ranges from manual forging on anvils to the use of steam hammers and presses. All of the forging in the Blacksmith Shop is done by or under the control of employees occupying the trade or craft job of Blacksmith, a benchmark job established as Class 15 by the findings of the Inequities Program. When steam hammers are used, crews are made up to include Blacksmith Helpers and Hammer Drivers, as well as Blacksmiths.

6. The 300-ton press was purchased exclusively for the purpose of performing work previously done on the 2,000 pound hammer. The press is so constructed as to have two lengths of stroke, one being a short stroke for finish shaping, and the other is a full stroke for the rough shaping of forgings. Although used normally as a press, it can also be used as a hammer when required. The 300-ton press and a 50-ton press are the only presses used by the Blacksmith Shop, although there are three 1,500 pound Steam Hammers in operation in the Shop. The 300-ton Press is relatively small in comparison with the 2,000-ton to 12,000-ton presses used by the Press Shop of the Heat Treating and Forge Division, and it is comparable in size to the 2,000-pound Steam Hammer which it replaced. The operating crew on the 2,000-pound hammer consisted of one Blacksmith (Job Class 15), one Operator Hammer Driver (Job Class 6) and two Blacksmith Helpers (Job Class 6). The

same number of employees performing the same duties are required to operate the 300-ton press, as were required to operate the 2,000-pound Hammer.

7. Up to this point the Union substantially agreed with the statements made in the Company brief, except that the Union emphasized the fact that the new equipment is a press and not a hammer and implied at the second Third Step meeting that the operators of this press should be titled "Pressman," "Pressman Helpers," and "Press Driver." The Union also claimed that some of the work done on the 300-ton press was longer and heavier than had been done on the hammer. It was also explained by the Union that the small 50-ton press was not used as a forging press, but as a press for bending, straightening or stripping work. In this last statement the Company concurred.

8. It was at the third Third Step meeting that the Union presented a rack-up of the proposed job of "Pressman 300-tons" which contained specific recommendations to the effect that the job needed reclassification in so far as Factors 5, 6, 7 and 11 were concerned. No proposal was submitted for changes in factor valuations for reclassification of Pressman Helper or Press Driver by the Union up to the time of the hearings nor during the hearings.

9. The April 22, 1947 Agreement states in part under Sub-section 9-D (Description and Classification of New or Changed Jobs):

"The job description and classification for each job in effect as of the date of this Agreement shall continue in effect unless (1) Management changes the job content (requirements of the job as to the training, skill, responsibility, effort, and working conditions) to the extent of one full job class or more; * * *

"When and if from time to time the Company, at its discretion, establishes a new job or changes the job content (requirements of the job as to training, skill, responsibility, effort, and working conditions) of an existing job to the extent of one full job class or more, a new job description and classification for the new or changed job shall be established in accordance with the following procedure:

"1. Management will develop a description and classification of the job in accordance with provisions of the May 8, 1946 Agreement between the parties hereto.
"2. The proposed description and classification will be submitted to the grievance committee for approval, and the standard hourly wage scale rate for the job class to which the job is thus assigned shall apply in accordance with the provisions of Sub-section B of this Section.
"3. * * *
"4. In the event Management does not develop a new job description and classification, the employee or employees affected may, if filed promptly, process a grievance under the grievance and arbitration procedures of this Agreement requesting that a job description and classification be developed and installed in accordance with applicable provisions of the aforesaid May 8, 1946, Agreement."

10. The Union contention in essence is that this new equipment established new jobs and therefore Management is bound to develop new descriptions and classifications. The Company's contention is that the new installation did not establish a single new job, and that the old craft job of Blacksmith remained unchanged, except for a few slight changes of techniques, and that the job content (requirements of the job as to the training, skill, responsibility, effort and working conditions) were not changed at all.

11. One Union witness testified that while most of the work on the new press was the same as that done on the old hammer, some of the work was larger running up to 2,000 pounds in weight, eight inches square and as long as 120 inches. He also stated that the new press did work formerly done on the 2,000-ton press. He also stated, and another Union witness concurred, that the work on the press was more fatiguing than the work on the Hammer. However, Company witnesses stated that the same work was done on both machines and that no work had been taken off the 2,000-ton press and turned over to the 300-ton press. They testified that the maximum size of billet for the 300-ton press was 1,400 pounds, while the 2,000-ton press took ingots up to 48 tons. These witnesses also testified that the large presses were used for commercial work, where much of the craft skill was not needed to operate them. The elaborate sets of dies and the burning machines made it no longer necessary to use a blacksmith as press operator on the large presses doing commercial work and that a promotional sequence was used, starting with helpers, and running through Craneman, Manipulator man, Press Driver to Pressman. The Pressman did not need to be a craftsman but could come up from pressman helper. The 300-ton press was a maintenance machine and did not do commercial work. The operator has

to have craft skill since special dies are not used. There are only two sets of flat dies, one set to be used when the other set is being repaired. The 7,000-ton press is also used for commercial work and handles work up to 250 tons and down to as small as 65 tons or even 20 tons. The Company witnesses also said that while the 300-ton press could handle more product than the 2,000-pound hammer, the work took less effort. They stated that it takes ten blows of the old hammer to do what one squeeze of the press can do. These witnesses also said that the size of the work did not control whether craft skill was needed to operate a machine. The Company used to have a six ton hammer that was operated by a blacksmith which did work up to 18 inch by 18 inch blooms.

12.   One Union witness testified that he had prepared the rack-up for the new job of "Pressman 300-tons," and that in his opinion only the Factors 5, 6, 7, and 11 for the blacksmith job were out of line for the proposed Pressman job, and that the rest of the factors were all right. He explained that for the 2,000-pound hammer a chain block had been used to help hold the work, but that an air hoist was installed for the 300-ton press, which was more like the large cranes used to assist on the large presses.

13.   A Company witness testified as to why the craft jobs of Blacksmith, Blacksmith Helper, and Hammer Driver were considered adequate by the Company to fully cover the work of operating the 300-ton press as well as the 2,000-pound hammer, and why the Company believed that the job content had not changed enough to alter Factors 5, 6, 7, and 11 in so far as the craft job of blacksmith is concerned.

14.   His testimony as to each factor was substantially as follows:

Factor 5—Responsibility for Materials. Exactly the same material is handled by the 300-ton press as was handled by the 2,000-pound hammer. It could not be damaged more by the press than by the hammer. The classification for blacksmith was a benchmark job approved by both Union and Management when it was established, and therefore there should be no change in the factor valuation as originally set at D-1.1. While some material was worth more than $100, there would be a credit from the scrap value which would offset the loss. The witness testified that the loss through damage to materials should not run much more than $50.00.

Factor 6—Responsibility for Tools and Equipment. The 300-ton press would not lend itself any more to damage than the

2,000-pound hammer. The amount and grade given is that which was recognized for all such tools and on that basis it was felt no change should be made. The valuation was therefore retained at B-0.3.

Factor 7—Responsibility for Operations. For each tool, the same crew is used, the same complement of furnaces, and the same requirement for the delivery of product. Inasmuch as these items have remained constant there of course should be no change in the valuation of this factor. It was therefore left at C-1.0.

Factor 11—Surroundings. The surroundings improved with the installation of the press if anything. The furnaces were placed at a slight angle, which gave a little greater clearance and a lesser amount of heat. The substitution of the air hoist for the chain block permitted some part of the crew to be farther away from the hot material. It was therefore decided by the Company that the value of this factor should remain unchanged at B-0.4.

15.   This Company witness explained that even if the new description were adopted, which would remove the job from the craft of blacksmith the factors would have to receive the lower classification. He concluded that in his opinion the craft is clearly applicable to this job.

16.   Referring to the Inequities Program Manual containing the various Agreements, it is observed that Section 2 (Job Description) of the October 23, 1945 Agreement states in part:

"It is recognized that jobs of similar nature are referred to under various titles and that jobs of identical titles vary as to content (requirements of the job as to training, skill, responsibility, effort and working conditions) within plants of the Company. It is understood that accurate comparisons and correct groupings of jobs by title only are not possible, and that in the interest of proper job classification it is necessary to obtain full knowledge regarding the functions of a job and its requirements. Accordingly, the procedure set forth in the appendix attached hereto and identified as 'Instructions Regarding Review of Job Descriptions' is adopted by the parties and hereby made a part of this Agreement."

17.   Again referring to the Manual, Section 1 of the Agreement dated April 15, 1946, includes Blacksmith in the socalled "trade or craft jobs." Under paragraph (b) of Section 1 the Manual states:

"Such of the foregoing trade or craft jobs as are required in each plant shall be described and classified in accordance with procedures of the October 23, 1945, Intra-Plant Wage Rate Inequities Agreement. These descriptions shall reflect the scope of duties which a fully qualified journeyman may be called upon to perform in the plant, and the classifications shall reflect the job's requirements as to training, skill, responsibility, effort and working conditions."

18. From all the testimony presented the Board finds that the installation of the 300-ton press to replace the 2,000-pound hammer has not created any new jobs, that the job description for the craft job of blacksmith is applied correctly, and that the job content has not been changed to the extent of one full job class.

AWARD

19. The grievance is denied.

A—797. Worcester Works. November 26, 1958

Sylvester Garrett, *Chairman*

BACKGROUND

1. In this grievance from Worcester Works, a Tractor Operator (Class 8) who holds a Plumber's license from the State of Massachusetts, asserts that he should have been promoted to Pipefitter following posting of a Pipefitter vacancy in April, 1957.

2. The posting for Pipefitter at this time resulted from advice by the Inspector of Plumbing of the City of Worcester that certain plumbing work at the plant could be done only by a licensed plumber in view of a City ordinance and Massachusetts statute. After investigation, the Inspector advised that pipe equipment and fixtures which carried, or connected with, the City water supply and City sewer system should be serviced by employees licensed by the State of Massachusetts.

3. At this time, and for some years prior to description and classification of the Pipefitter trade and craft job under the Inequities Program, this work had been done by Pipefitters at Worcester Works. There is no substantial question as to qualifications of Pipefitters to perform the work, but most of them were not licensed by the State, and it became necessary in 1947 that licensed employees be obtained to do this phase of the pipefitting.

4. In discussions with the Mechanical Department Grievance Committeeman, he was concerned that, if some individual were assigned to perform all of the plumbing work for which a license was required, this might result in displacement of one of the Pipefitters then employed. This the Company agreed not to do. Accordingly, it posted a vacancy for Pipefitter under the caption "Pipefitter (Standard) (Journeyman Plumber's License Required)."

5. As a result of this posting, it was learned that Pipefitter Earl Dion in the Cable Works Division held a plumber's license from the State of Massachusetts. In addi-

tion, Grievant Louis Roy, a Tractor Operator in the Wire Mill Division, applied. Roy also held a plumber's license. The assignment was given to Dion rather than Roy because Dion already was a fully qualified Pipefitter who had been included in the Pipefitter Crew at the plant for a year and a half. Dion had substantially less continuous service than Roy.

6. In order to permit Dion to work throughout the plant handling plumbing duties, he was transferred from the Cable Works Division to Central Shops, and another Pipefitter was transferred from Central Shops to the Cable Works. This was done by agreement with the Union. Since this transfer, Dion has devoted the great majority of his time to plumbing work within the scope of the Pipefitter job at Worcester.

7. The Union claims that the seniority rights of Roy were violated in that he was not given an opportunity to promote pursuant to the Pipefitter posting. There is no promotional line between Production and Maintenance jobs in the plant and Trade and Craft jobs, but the Union believes that Roy should have been promoted since he had a license, and that the Company, in effect, created a new position rated job of Plumber, outside the scope of the Pipefitter job. Thus the Union denies that the situation was simply a matter of posting a job assignment within the Trade and Craft job of Pipefitter.

FINDINGS

8. Since the plumbing work in question fell within the scope of the Pipefitter Trade and Craft job at Worcester when it was described and classified under the Inequities Program, there is no basis on which the Union may insist that the Company is obliged now to establish a non-craft position rated job of Plumber at Worcester

Works. While the facts in this case differ somewhat from those in Cases USC-419 and T-234, the underlying basis for decision in those cases is applicable.

9. There is no indication here of fundamental change—as for technological reasons —in the conditions which existed when the Pipefitter job was described and classified at Worcester Works under the Inequities Program. Thus there is no basis upon which the Board could require breaking out of plumbing duties from the Pipefitter job, by establishment of a new position rated job.

10. The fact that Management unnecessarily posted what appeared to be a vacancy in the Pipefitter job does not establish either that a new job was created or that an additional man was to be added to the total number of Pipefitters. The evidence is clear that Management intended merely to as-

certain which of its Pipefitters at Worcester Works might hold a plumber's license from the State of Massachusetts which would provide a basis for his assignment to the plumbing duties in the course of his work as Pipefitter. If Management did not choose the least confusing method of ascertaining which Pipefitters thus might be assigned, this does not affect the substantive rights of either Grievant or Dion in the present case. Dion was a Pipefitter at the time of the posting, and properly was assigned to a new work station and given a predominant proportion of plumbing duties thereafter which fell within the scope of the activities for which he was licensed by the State of Massachusetts.

AWARD

11. The grievance is denied.

Section B. CLAIM OF IMPROPER ESTABLISHMENT OF NEW JOB

USC—419. Gary Sheet and Tin Mill. August 13, 1954
Sylvester Garrett, *Chairman*

BACKGROUND

1. This grievance, on behalf of Bricklayers in Central Maintenance Department of Gary Sheet and Tin Mill, protests establishment of a new position-rated job—Repairman, Floors (Class 5)—to perform duties covered by the Bricklayer job description at Gary Sheet and Tin.

2. The Bricklayer job at Gary Sheet and Tin was described June 28, 1946. The working procedure does not refer to installation or repair of wood block floors, but in listing materials used by the Bricklayer, the description includes: "Various types and sizes of brick, wood blocks, cement, sand, fireclay, plaster molding and casting cements, acid proof binding and insulating materials, quarry tile, etc." (Underscoring added.)

3. This inclusion of "wood blocks" in the Bricklayer's materials at Gary Sheet and Tin reflected that, at the time, all installation and repair of wood block floors there was done by Bricklayers assisted by Bricklayer Helpers. This had been true as far back as 1936 and continued up to February, 1953, when the grievance arose. In repairing floors not only are worn or broken blocks replaced, but also it may be necessary to break out and replace broken or cracked concrete subflooring. Prior to installation of the Repairman-Floors job, the Gary Sheet and Tin Bricklayers spent about 50% of their time working on installation and repair of wood block floors. Even today the Bricklayers spend about half their time working on the wood block floors.

4. This seeming anomaly results from a combination of three factors: (1) Management still uses Bricklayers for major wood block floor repairs; (2) the number of Bricklayers at Gary Sheet and Tin has been permitted to decrease over the years (From 1946 through 1949 there were 20 Bricklayers, but by 1953 this had dwindled to 16, of whom 2 were Gangleaders and the third had been out sick for some while); and (3) the area of wood block floors more than doubled from 1946 to early 1953.

5. Two men now fill the job of Repairman, Floors, and were promoted from Bricklayer Helper (Class 3) when the Repairman, Floors job was installed on February 1, 1953. No other Bricklayer Helpers were added to that classification. Thus, two Repairman, Floors have taken over work formerly performed by Bricklayers and Helpers.

6. The Union believes that this action violates the agreement of the parties establishing the trade and craft job of Bricklayer by taking a significant portion of the duties of Bricklayer out of the job and creating an entirely new noncraft job in repair and maintenance, at a substantially lower rate. It is a fundamental concept of trade and craft jobs, according to the Union, that such a job includes the entire scope of the craft duties performed by employees in that trade or craft job throughout the United States Steel operations covered by the agreement of the parties. This concept carries with it the corollary principle that an employee who is working on the trade or

craft job receives the craft rate classification even though at any given time he may be called upon to perform only a limited portion of the duties covered in the description of the craft job.

7. Hence the Union sees a violation not only of Section 9-B-4, but also of the requirement of Section 9-D that:

"The job description and classification for each job in effect as of the date of this Agreement shall continue in effect unless (1) Management changes the job content (requirements of the job as to the training, skill, responsibility, effort, and working conditions) to the extent of one full job class or more; (2) the job is terminated or not occupied during a period of one year or (3) the description and classification are changed in accordance with mutual agreement of officially designated representatives of the Company and the Union."

8. In addition the Union holds that Section 2-B-3 applies to protect the assignment of wood block floor installation and repair to Bricklayers at Gary Sheet and Tin. This is supported by the Decision of Acting Chairman Killingsworth in CI-238.

9. The Company holds that nothing in the August 15, 1952 Agreement prohibits it from establishing the job of Repairman, Floors, and asserts that all of the job descriptions and classifications involved in this case have continued in effect as required by Section 9-D. All that has been done has been to reassign certain duties from one job to a newly created position of Repairman, Floors. Section 9-D recognizes the right of Management to create new jobs. As to Section 2-B, the Company points to the statement in CI-257 that:—

"The mere fact that particular employees have performed certain duties could scarcely be said to give rise to a requirement that they will perform such duties continuously in the future without any change."

Management also urges that the Board in CI-257 recognized that Management has absolute discretion in establishing new jobs and changing existing jobs, and cites language in A-650 also supporting this view.

FINDINGS

10. While the parties have argued at length on the question of Management authority to make changes in assignment of duties among various jobs, the Board does not believe that this matter, in any sense,

controls decision in this case. The possible application of Section 9-D and 2-B to the assignment of duties among various jobs is more directly involved in USC-418, decided contemporaneously with the present case.

11. The true issue here is whether the agreed rate structure is properly observed when the Company breaks out a significant portion of the duties of a trade and craft job by establishing a so-called "position-rated" job, for maintenance and repair, at a lower rate of pay.

12. The status of trade and craft jobs under the Inequities Program is unique. In dealing with production jobs, the parties could describe and classify almost exclusively on the basis of specific duties constantly repeated at a given job location. Hence it was possible to describe the "job" as such, without particular note of peculiar skills which individuals filling the job might have as such. Not so, with trade and craft jobs, as to which the parties on April 15, 1946, took special note as follows:

"SECTION 1—REPAIR AND MAINTENANCE TRADE OR CRAFT JOBS

"It is recognized that due to the nature of the services to be performed in construction, rehabilitation of facilities, and in repair and maintenance work the requirements of the jobs as to training, skill, responsibility, effort and working conditions will vary from time to time. In addition to those considerations of job content, it is understood and recognized that the varying qualifications and abilities of the individual employees will be taken into account in the determination and elimination of intra-plant wage rate inequities and reduction of classifications to the smallest practical number. Therefore, it is agreed that:

"(a) . . . .

"(b) Such of the foregoing trade or craft jobs as are required in each plant shall be described and classified in accordance with procedures of the October 23, 1945 Intra-Plant Wage Rate Inequities Agreement. These descriptions shall reflect the scope of duties which a fully qualified journeyman may be called upon to perform in the plant, and the classification shall reflect the job's requirements as to training, skill, responsibility, effort and working conditions." (Underscoring added.)

13. The May 8, 1946 Inequities Agreement incorporated by reference all but Sec-

tion 3 of the April 15, 1946 Agreement. Later both the April 22, 1947 and August 15, 1952 Basic Agreements incorporated the applicable terms of the May 8, 1946 Agreement in Section 9-D for purposes of description and classification of new or changed jobs. In their January 1, 1953 Job Description and Classification Manual the parties again emphasized mutual recognition of the special nature of craft descriptions and classifications as follows:

"7. Due to the nature of the services to be performed in construction, rehabilitation of facilities, and in repair and maintenance work, the job content requirements of trade or craft jobs vary from time to time. Also, the varying qualifications and abilities of the individual trade or craft employees are involved. Therefore, the job description of a trade or craft job is required to reflect the scope of duties which a fully qualified journeyman may be called upon to perform in the plant, and the job classification is required to reflect the related job content requirements of the job . . ." (Underscoring added.)

14. Since Section 9-D declares that a job description and classification shall remain in effect, and Section 9-D-3 and -4 embrace the "job description and classification procedure of the May 8, 1946 Agreement" to implement the Basic Agreement, the special treatment of trade and craft jobs under the Inequity Program is fully protected and provides important guidance in the present case.

15. When the parties classified the Bricklayer job, installation and repair of wood block flooring was a significant part of the Bricklayer's work at Gary Sheet and Tin. That this work did not at all times require full utilization of Bricklayer skill is irrelevant. This is but the other side of the coin, since the steady assignment of Bricklayers to a particular kind of work—as furnace repair and rebuilds—conceivably would call for a higher classification than the Class 15 provided to the Standard Rate Bricklayer. At least the Board cannot assume otherwise, since the Bricklayer description must recognize that the requirements of the job as to skill, responsibility, effort, and working conditions will vary from time to time.

16. The dominant fact here is that the parties agreed that all duties of a given trade or craft job *in a given plant* would be lumped together in the single description. This was in marked contrast to the treatment of position-rated jobs. Hence the parties agreed at Gary Sheet and Tin that wood block floor installation and repair was part of the Bricklayer job there and provided no exception to this in the form of any limited purpose, assigned maintenance, or position-rated job.

17. The issue now is simply what job description and classification applied to the duty of installing and repairing wood block floors at Gary Sheet and Tin. The parties themselves provided the answer in 1946 and 1947 that this work called for payment of the Bricklayer rate. A unilateral attempt to substitute a new job description covering this work, so as to pay a lower rate, is inconsistent with the agreed rate structure, in the absence of any fundamental change in conditions on which the Bricklayer description was based. Since the Bricklayer rate is applicable, under 9-B-4, the Bricklayers are entitled to protest the work being assigned to men outside the Bricklayer craft, to the detriment of Bricklayer seniority rights protected under Section 13.

18. The present ruling passes no opinion on questions which may arise should fundamental changes occur—as for technological reasons—in the conditions which existed on January 13, 1947, when the trade and craft rate structure first was made effective. The increase in total volume of wood block floor repair work (assuming a constant level of operations and rate of repair) was not sufficient to change the nature of the duties required, or otherwise affect fundamental bases for the original description and classification.

AWARD

19. The grievance is sustained. Management shall discontinue use of the Repairman-Floors job to perform work covered by the description and classification of Bricklayer at Gary Sheet and Tin Plant.

T—436.   Ensley Works.   August 19, 1957
Sylvester Garrett, *Chairman*

BACKGROUND

1. This grievance from the Forge Shop, Blast Furnace Department, Ensley Works, initially protested that the job of Threading Machine Operator (B.F.) had not been properly classified.

2. After the grievance was carried to Fourth Step on issues as to coding various factors, the Union argued that Management

had violated Sections 9-D and 9-I of the July 1, 1954 Agreement by establishing a new job of Threading Machine Operator (B.F.) since operation of this type equipment fell under the Machinist classification at Ensley Works. Thus, the Union now holds that the work should have been assigned to Machinists and seeks a ruling to this effect, without prejudice to its arguments concerning proper coding should the Board's ruling be adverse.

3. The Union cites Cases USC-419 and T-234, where it was held that certain work fell within the scope of given craft jobs, and that incumbents of the respective craft jobs were entitled to perform such work at the applicable craft rate.

4. When the job was described and classified at Ensley Works, Machinists were employed in both a Central Machine Shop and the Blast Furnace Machine Shop. In the latter location were various machine tools operated by men classified as Machinists, with two Machinists Helpers. One piece of equipment was a Threading Machine, used for threading bolts. This was operated from time to time by various Machinists, as needed.

5. Late in 1955, the Company consolidated the Blast Furnace Machine Shop with the Central Machine Shop as part of a reorganization. Most of the equipment in the Blast Furnace Machine Shop was moved, and all of the Machinists transferred to the Central Machine Shop at this time. Since all bolts threaded on the Threading Machine first were processed in the Forge Shop adjacent to the old Blast Furnace Machine Shop, the Company decided to leave a Threading Machine at the old location together with a power Hacksaw. A partition between the old Blast Furnace Machine Shop and the Forge Shop then was removed and the area including the Threading Machine and the Hacksaw thus became physically part of Forge Shop and thereafter was operated as such.

6. All seniority problems concerning transfer of personnel to the Central Machine Shop were settled by mutual agreement.

7. For a number of turns following transfer, one Machinist was used to operate the Threading Machine and power Hacksaw at the old location, and to break in two other employees who now operate the equipment 6 days per week on day turn. A new Threading Machine to replace the old one was obtained about 10 days after the consolidation of the machine shops. The old machine in turn was converted later to a Horizontal Drill for drilling stopper rods. A new job description was prepared covering operation of the new Threading Machine and power hacksaw, together with a drill sharpener, drill press, and emery wheel. The new job was installed unilaterally in Class 8 on November 10, 1955. The description is dated September 15, 1955, and it does not appear whether the job was installed before or after the drilling of stopper rods was assigned to this position.

8. There is no essential difference in nature and function of the old and new Threading Machines. Since the old Threading Machine was operated exclusively by men in the Machinist classification in the Blast Furnace Machine Shop over the years, the Union holds that this work became recognized as part of the Machinist job at Ensley Works when trade and craft jobs were established at Ensley in 1946 and 1947.

9. The Company denies that operation of Threading Machines at Ensley was exclusively part of the Machinist job when the Standard Hourly Wage Rate structure was installed. At that time there also were such jobs at Ensley as Threading Machine Operator (FCE. REP.) (Plant Code E 45-230) operating a machine to cut and thread pipe for the Blast Furnaces. A Threading Machine Operator job, (Plant Code E 40-205), existed in the Pipefitters Shop at Ensley with primary function of setting up and operating pipe and bolt machines to cut and thread rods, bolts, and up to 16″ diameter pipe. One of these other jobs also operates a power hacksaw and emery wheel, while the other uses a drill press as needed. The Company stresses that neither the original Machinist description at Ensley (June 19, 1946), nor its September 1, 1951 revision, makes any reference to threading machines or threading bolts. It urges that Specimen Jobs 982 and 1069 reveal that the parties at top level recognized such position-rated jobs to exist.

10. It points also to a Threading Machine Operator job in the Forge Shop at Fairfield Steel (Plant Title—Bolt Cutter—Plant Code J 60-1015) with primary function to operate various sized Threading Machines in threading bolts and studs. There also is a Threading Machine Operator (Hand) job at Fairfield (Plant Title—Bolt Cutter—Plant Code J 40-310), with primary function of operating Bolt Cutting Machine to cut threads on various sized bolts, etc.

11. Concerning USC-419, the Company stresses that the Board there stated:

"The dominant fact here is that the parties agreed that all duties of a given trade or craft job in a given plant would be lumped together in the single description. This was in marked contrast to the treatment of position-rated jobs. Hence the parties agreed at Gary Sheet and Tin that wood block floor installation and repair was part of the Bricklayer job there and provided no exception to this in the form of any limited purpose, assigned maintenance or position-rated job." (Underscoring added).

12. The Company notes that in USC-419 the Board expressed no opinion concerning questions which might arise from changes in basic conditions which existed when a trade and craft job was described and classified initially. It urges that termination of the Blast Furnace Machine Shop with the removal of all machine tools (save the Threading Machine) constituted a fundamental change affecting operation of that machine, since the full skills of a Machinist no longer could be utilized at this location.

FINDINGS

13. In USC-419 the Board stressed that the scope of duties of a trade or craft job ordinarily must be determined on the basis of duties performed in the given plant when the job was described and classified under the Inequities Program.

14. The present case differs from USC-419. The evidence does not show that operation of threading machines for this type work at Ensley was recognized under the Inequities Program as exclusively within the scope of the Machinist job classification. The case differs also from USC-419 in that discontinuance of the Blast Furnace Machine Shop and transfer of all Machinists and machine tools (save the Threading Machine which became physically part of the Forge Shop) may have affected conditions which led to use of Machinists for this work in 1946 and 1947.

15. All questions concerning seniority of the Machinists have been settled by local agreement.

16. In these circumstances it appears that the only question which remains open for decision is the proper classification of the new job. Accordingly, the grievance will be returned to the parties for further consideration of this aspect in the grievance procedure.

AWARD

17. The grievance is returned to the parties for determination of any issues as to proper classification which may exist, in the light of the foregoing opinion.

A—650.   Worcester, South Works Plant.   October 19, 1953
Donald A. Crawford, *Arbitrator*
Approved by Sylvester Garrett, *Chairman*

BACKGROUND

1. This grievance arises under the terms of the April 22, 1947 Agreement. The major claim it presents is that a new job cannot be created which consists of some of the duties of an established higher rated job. The Union claims that the Company has split up an established job—not created a new job. Such management action, the Union says, makes Section 9 of the Agreement meaningless and destroys the job evaluation plan.

2. The Spring Mill Department, Rail Bond Division, manufactures Signal Bonds and Power Bonds. Before 1949, the finished products were visually inspected, counted, packed and bundled in the Shipping Unit by workers classified in Job Class 6 (Inspector and Shipper or Inspector-special). Around the middle of 1949, Management decided to change the method of inspection. Customers were complaining of broken Bonds caused by defects not discovered by final product visual inspection. The Company therefore decided to transfer inspection to the mill and to establish a job of Inspector to provide in-

process as well as finished product inspection. This job provided for spot check inspection of incoming material, material in process and finished product and was rated a Class 13 job.

3. The job was filled in the early part of 1950 and about the middle of 1950, inspection of finished Bonds was discontinued in the Shipping Unit. Visual inspection of the finished product was assigned to the Class 13 Inspector.

4. Production increased so that the Class 13 inspector could not perform both the in-process and final product inspection. Accordingly, the Company added a second inspector in early 1951. The new set-up provided that the Class 13 Inspector would continue to perform the in-process inspection, but would perform visual inspection of finished product only as he had time. The visual inspection of final product was assigned to a new job (Class 6), which was given to the second inspector.

5. The Union objects to the Class 6 rate not only on the major premise that the Class

13 job was split up in violation of Section 9 of the Agreement, but on other grounds as well. The Union contends that the second inspector is performing the Class 13 job; that an oral agreement has been broken; and that Section 2-B has been violated.

6. Mr. Savage, Union Grievanceman, said that when the Class 13 job was established, Mr. Connery, then Superintendent of the Finishing Department, said that if workload increased, "We would add an Inspector, the same way we do upstairs, when we need a man we will put him on." (Trs. pp. 14, 18, 19.)

7. Mr. Savage said this statement meant additional men would be paid the Class 13 rate, although he admitted that Mr. Connery did not specifically say that. (Trs. pp. 18, 19.)

8. The Union through another witness said that men assigned from the labor pool to higher rated jobs were paid the higher rate even though they did not perform all phases of the jobs. Similarly, another witness said that testers in the Wire Mill are paid the job rate even though they perform only one small portion of the testing job. The Union also said that the incumbent of the Class 13 Inspector job did not perform all of the job duties.

9. Other Union witnesses said that they knew of no other instance where the Company had taken part of a job and placed it in a separate, lower rated job. The Union, therefore, concludes that Section 2-B has been violated since the past practice has been to pay the job rate even though the employee is not required to do the whole job, and since past practice has been not to cut up higher rated jobs to create lower rated jobs.

10. The Company position can be summarized in this manner:

1. The need for additional inspection of finished Bonds has not been questioned.

2. The Company's right to establish the new job cannot be questioned. Board decisions in Cases A-463, A-464, and CI-257 affirm the principle that Section 9-D gives Management the right to introduce or change jobs, and that a job classification was not a contract protected by Section 2-B.

3. The Union does not claim that the new job is improperly classified. Moreover, the visual inspection performed on the new job is substantially the same as that formerly performed in the Shipping Unit at the same Job Class.

4. Board decisions in Cases CI-252 and A-557 recognize the principle that performance of one duty is not performance of the job.

5. The Union testimony concerning payment of the job rate to men for partial performance of a job is irrelevant. Those payments must be presumed to have been made in accordance with Section 9 and Board rulings as stated in cases A-228 and A-347. In any event, the alleged practice could have no bearing on the Class 13 Inspector job since it was not established until January, 1950. Section 2-B protects only practices in effect on April 22, 1947.

6. No oral agreement to pay the Class 13 rate to added inspectors was made. Mr. Anger, Superintendent of the Spring and Rail Bond Division, has testified that he knew of no such agreement and that his position requires that he know of such agreements. Mr. Magnusson, Rail and Bond Division Foreman, has said that he knew of no such agreement. Mr. Watson, then Assistant Labor Relations man, who attended a meeting to discuss the introduction of the Class 13 Inspector job, has said there was no agreement that any additional inspector would be paid the Class 13 rate. This testimony, the Company says, proves that there was no such agreement.

11. Moreover, Section 2-B-5 provides that a local agreement made after April 22, 1947, unless approved by top officials, is not enforceable if inconsistent with the Agreement. This alleged agreement was not so approved and would violate Section 9.

FINDINGS

12. *The grievance is denied. Section 9-D of the Agreement authorizes Management to create new jobs. The establishment of the new Class 6 Inspector job was a bona fide action to provide necessary final product inspection. The action as such was not rate cutting as the Union contends, but reasonable assignment of additional work. The Board has held (CI-257) that the assignment of particular duties to a job over the years does not create a local working condition under Section 2-B which prevents a legitimate re-assignment of duties. Therefore, the past practice argument (that Management has not previously cut up higher rated jobs) is not controlling.*

13. The facts show that the greater volume of work required more visual inspection of final product. The Class 13 Inspector could not handle this increased volume without sacrificing his spot check in-process inspection. To assign a second Inspector to perform this increased final product inspection is in the nature of adding a helper rather than the splitting up of an established job.

14. Obviously, a job which requires visual inspection of final product is not the same as a job which requires in-process inspection. The seven grades differential between the Class 6 job of visual inspection of final product (when it was done in the Shipping Unit) and the Class 13 job of in-process inspection in the mill recognizes this fact.

15. To pay these different jobs the same rate is unfair to the in-process Inspector. To say that Management cannot creat the second job when faced with a production need because the duties are part of the first job is a denial of Section 9-D. A carpenter may use a shovel but all who shovel are not carpenters.

16. In a real sense, the Class 6 Inspector job is a transferred job. For six months after the Class 13 job was established in the mill, visual inspection of final product, counting, bundling, and packing was continued in the Shipping Unit by the Class 6 Inspectors. Then the visual inspection of final product was assigned to the Class 13 Inspector in the mill. He could not keep up with this work, so the new Class 6 job was created in the mill. With this action, the transfer of the final product inspection task of the Class 6 Shipping Unit Inspector job was completed. These facts hardly show a rate cutting of a higher rated job.

17. The Union also cited instances of individuals who performed some part of a higher rated job and were paid the full job rate, as establishing past practice under Section 2-B. Some of these instances were temporary assignments under Section 9-B-3; others were examples of on-the-job learning required by men assigned from the labor pool; others were characteristic of testing work assignments.

18. This argument for paying the second inspector the grade 13 rate, however, is not in point. The assignment was to the grade 6, not the grade 13, Inspector job. Once the grade 6 job was properly established, the man was properly paid the grade 6 rate.

19. The Union argument that an oral agreement has been broken cannot be sustained. Committeeman Savage conceded that no mention of a grade 13 rate for added inspectors was made. Three Company witnesses (who said they would have known) denied knowledge of such a promise. One of them, Mr. Watson, who Mr. Savage said was present at some of the relevant discussions (trs. p. 18), testified that no agreement was made. On such evidence, the Arbitrator cannot find that an oral agreement was made. Moreover, an oral agreement, if made, must meet the requirements of Section 2-B-5.

AWARD

20. Since the grievant is not performing the Class 13 job but is performing inspection duties formerly performed by Class 6 Inspectors in Shipping, and since the job to which he assigned has been legitimately established, the grievance is denied.

USC—412. Irvin Works. March 31, 1954
Sylvester Garrett, *Chairman*

BACKGROUND FACTS

1. This grievance arose in the Magnetic Laboratory, Metallurgical Department, Vandergrift Plant of Irvin Works. It protests establishment of the new job of Control Technician (Torque Tester), Job Class 6, and claims that the duties of this new job should be performed by a Control Analyst (Special Testing), Job Class 13.

2. Prior to February 1, 1947, there was no torque testing in the Magnetic Laboratory at Vandergrift. On that date a Torque Magnetometer was installed in the Laboratory in connection with a grain oriented steel program which then was in the experimental stage at the Vandergrift Plant. The making of torque tests, with the Torque Magnetometer, was assigned to the Control Analyst (Special Testing). During the experimental stage of torque testing, the work required a high level of experience and ability. The practice in the Magnetic Laboratory was to assign operation of new and special equipment to the Control Analyst so that he might become familiar with it, detect irregularities, and make suitable adjustments.

3. 193 torque tests were performed by the Control Analyst from February 1, 1947, to April 22, 1947. During the remainder of 1947, as well as 1948 and 1949, the number of torque tests varied, but the total work amounted to approximately six hours per month. A single torque test takes about 12 minutes, and a total of about 300 tests was made in the entire year 1949. Thus, when the Control Analyst job was classified in March, 1949, the making of torque tests was a very small part of the duties of the job. During 1950, the volume increased, however, and in 1951 the Control Analyst performed approximately 4,624 torque tests.

4. By early 1952, Management concluded that the torque test had become routine and should be assigned to an employee under a job description and classification covering

torque testing only. Accordingly, a description of Control Technician (Torque Tester), in Job Class 6, was developed by Management. The Union objected to establishment of any such job, however, and did not agree to the description and classification. Management installed the job unilaterally on June 2, 1952. During 1953 there were 5,178 torque tests performed by men in the Control Technician job, but the job was not regularly manned during this interval. A few months prior to the hearing, Management assigned two employees to the Control Technician job on a regular basis.

5. The Control Analyst (Special Testing) job was not described and classified by the parties until March 15, 1949, since it was a "fringe" job. The description sets forth the primary function of the job as being "Prepare test samples and perform special and non-routine magnetic tests on steel samples obtained from various sources inside or outside of the plant." Under Tools and Equipment Used there are about 15 items listed. The Torque Magnetometer appears in this listing along with such items as punch press, scales, calipers, tongs, micrometer, strip tester, comptometer, core loss tester, permeameter, interlamination resistance tester, enamel tester, sample annealing equipment, high frequency and low induction tester.

6. Under Working Procedure for Control Analyst (Special Testing) there are 11 items set forth. Item 2 reads as follows:

"2. Performs special and non-routine magnetic testing for customer information, trade publications, development, research, etc., such as:

"a. Using core loss equipment to obtain separation, volt-amperes, core loss and AC permeability at normal inductions and commercial frequencies.

"b. Using permeameter to obtain DC incremental permeability.

"c. Using interlamination resistance tester to measure the effectiveness of special core plating materials and sheet oxides.

"d. Using high frequency and low induction tester to measure core loss and AC permeability at low inductions and high frequencies.

"e. Using torque magnetometer to determine degree of orientation of steels."

7. Some of the requirements of the job are well illustrated in the language used by the parties in assigning values to Factors 3, 4, 5 and 9 as follows:

"3. Mental Skill—Perform special and non-routine tests using a wide variety of physical testing equipment such as interlamination resistance tester, core loss tester, punch press, etc. Set up special apparatus; calibrates and wires for special testing.

"4. Manual Skill—Set up and operate a wide variety of physical testing equipment such as interlamination resistance tester, core loss tester, punch press, etc. Adjust and make minor repairs to equipment.

"5. Responsibility for Material—Use close attention for majority of turn to prepare and perform special and non-routine tests for customer's information, trade publications, development, research, etc. Error would result in inaccuracies in development and research projects.

"9. Mental Effort—High mental application required to prepare and perform special and non-routine tests using a wide variety of physical testing equipment such as interlamination resistance tester, core loss tester, punch press, etc.; set up special apparatus, calibrates and wires for special tests."

8. The new job of Control Technician (Torque Tester) has the following primary function, according to the description prepared by Management: "Prepare test specimens and perform torque measurements on steel specimens."

9. In the Union view, there was no material change in the nature or amount of torque testing in early 1952 which would justify the establishment of a new job. It believes that the performance of torque testing by the Control Analyst constituted a local working condition protected by Section 2-B-3. In addition the Union holds that by taking out from the duties of Control Analyst, the performance of torque tests, and setting up a separate job for that purpose, Management in effect deprived employees of the right to exercise their seniority under 13-B in seeking promotion to the position of Control Analyst. This is on the assumption that the volume of torque testing was such that by this time, another man would have to be assigned to the Control Analyst position in order to handle torque testing as well as the other requirements of the Control Analyst position.

10. As to the seniority argument, the Union cites the decision in Case T-233, where the Opinion observes that Section 13 imposes an obligation to refrain from juggling minor job duties where realignment of duties is not in fact necessary for efficient operations and where the known consequence is to defeat the right of a particular

individual employee to promote into a higher job.

11.   The Company denies any applicability of Section 2-B to this situation, and holds that it proceeded in conformity with Section 9-D in establishing the new job of Control Technician. In its view, the substance of the case is that when the performance of torque testing was sufficiently routinized and occurred in sufficient volume, it established a job to handle this duty so as to free the Control Analyst to handle other more important non-routine and special tests of the sort contemplated in the description and classification of that position. It asserts that the situation is no different from that in which a machine operator, in a relatively high job class, is called upon to perform sweeping duties from time to time. When the press of work is such that it is no longer practical to use the higher paid employee for such clean-up activities, Management is entitled to bring in a janitor to perform the clean-up duties. The Company can see no significant distinction between such a situation and the present case.

FINDINGS

12.   The issue in this case is essentially the same as that in Case A-650. There the Company had found it necessary, because of increased volume of work, to establish a Job Class 6 position of Inspector to perform only one portion of the duties previously performed by a Job Class 13 Inspector. In essence, the Job Class 13 Inspector was responsible for in-process inspection, while the Job Class 6 Inspector was responsible only for visual inspection of final product. In line with the Board's earlier decision in CI-257, the Opinion in A-650 states:

"To say that Management cannot create the second job when faced with a produc-

tion need because the duties are part of the first job is a denial of Section 9-D. A carpenter may use a shovel but all who shovel are not carpenters."

13.   The same thought applies here. It is manifest that the Control Technician performs only a minor portion of the duties originally assigned to the Control Analyst, and that the work has become routinized to the point where the full skill of the latter job does not seem to be required.

14.   The fact that the number of torque tests in 1952 was not much more than the number performed in 1951, does not bar Management from setting up the new job. Torque testing was started in 1947 and only relatively few torque tests were performed each year until 1951. When the Control Analyst position was described and classified on March 15, 1949, the relative volume of torque testing performed was small.

15.   There is no need to elaborate on possible applicability of Case T-233 to the present situation. Even though language may be found in T-233 which some may think relevant here, when taken out of context, the Decision in T-233 deals with an entirely different problem from that in this case.

16.   Finally, it should be plain that if there were merit to the contention that torque testing embraces the essence of the Control Analyst job, this would emerge in the proper description and classification of the Torque Tester job. The present decision passes only on whether Management is entitled to establish the new job. Nothing in this Opinion is intended to pass on the merits of any difference which may exist between the parties as to proper description and classification of the Torque Tester job.

AWARD

17.   The grievance is denied.

USC—563.   Ohio Works.   May 17, 1956
Sylvester Garrett, *Chairman*

BACKGROUND

1.   This grievance from Mechanical Maintenance Shops Department, Maintenance and Utilities Division, Ohio Works claims violation of Section 9-D of the July 1, 1954 Agreement, by establishment of an assigned maintenance crew, all of whom regularly are required to perform both Structural Painting and Sheeting work but under separate job descriptions and classifications.

2.   Early in 1955 Mechanical Maintenance Shops Superintendent Round posted a notice in all mechanical shops stating:

"A new organization is being established in the Boiler Shop to perform structural painting and sheeting. It shall be the function of this organization to perform both painting and sheeting work. Employees assigned to this organization will be paid Job Class 8 for structural painting work, and Job Class 10 for sheeting work.

"Employees of the Mechanical Shops Department who desire a transfer to the new organization may secure further details from their foreman."

Employees interested were interviewed by Superintendent Round and told that they would be trained both in painting and in sheeting work and required to do both types of work as need arose from time to time.

3. On March 14, 1955, the Company set up two separate job descriptions to cover the work of the new crew. One description was entitled Structural Painter and in part included the following:

"Primary Function:

To paint old and new metal structures as required.

"Working Procedure:

1. Sets ladders or scaffolding.
2. Stirs paint to mix ingredients.
3. Uses Safety devices to prevent falling.
4. Cleans surface, where necessary, using proper equipment; such as, scraper or pneumatic cleaning tool.
5. Sprays or brushes paint as required, painting structural work inside and outside.
6. Takes proper care of brushes and equipment.
7. Cleans up working area when job is finished.
8. Paints such places as roofs, stacks, structural work, sheathing, etc.
9. Cleans windows located in high places, where scaffold is necessary.
10. Patches roofs with canvas and roof cement, etc.
11. Carries paint and equipment to the job."

4. The other job description, designated Sheeter, included the following, in part:

"Primary Function:

To perform sheeting on all types of structural buildings.

"Working Procedure:

1. Inspects job to determine tools, equipment and materials necessary.
2. Orders materials for job.
3. Transfers tools and equipment to job.
4. Erects scaffolds, position ladders.
5. Secures safety devices.
6. Installs struts and purlin clips.
7. Hoists sheets and fastens in place by hand or hoist.
8. Cuts sheets for fitting with gas flame cutting torch or hand tools.
9. Cleans up working area upon completion of job, etc."

5. When Grievance Committeeman Kovacic was advised of this action, he protested to Rounds that there was no basis under Section 9-D, and the January 1, 1953

Manual to set up two separate descriptions and classifications for assigned maintenance duties to be performed from time to time by all members of the crew. Since all men in the crew would be trained for all of the duties in both descriptions and perform either type as need arose, Kovacic believed the duties properly to constitute a single assigned maintenance job.

6. Since March 1954, employees have been paid under the Sheeter job description about 48% of total time worked and paid under the Painter description 52% of the time. The Company has assigned a coding of 7.9 to the Structural Painter, and 9.8 to the Sheeter. The only differences in coding are under Factors 2, 3 and 4, where the Sheeting work receives higher ratings totalling 1.9.

7. Members of the crew (13 in all) share about evenly in performing work under the two descriptions. There has been no effort to apply Section 13 in distribution of the work, nor has Structural Painter or Sheeter as such ever been posted as a vacant job under Section 13. Apparently all men are paid Class 8, except when up-graded to Sheeter work in Class 10 for specific shifts.

8. When scaffolds are erected to perform sheeting, the same scaffolds are used by the same men in performing the necessary painting to complete the job. Foreman Owen estimated that this type of job (where painting is done from the same scaffolding as the sheeting) does not represent over 15% of the total work of the crew.

9. When members of the crew are sent out on an assignment, they do what is necessary in light of the condition of the building. If they find bad sheets in the course of painting, they contact the Foreman for authorization to replace the defective sheets, and complete the job with necessary painting. As need is apparent, the men apply roof cement in addition to painting.

10. In preparation for large sheeting jobs, the men may be required to handle, paint, and stack the sheets on the ground before actual sheeting commences. On one such occasion, their request for the Sheeting rate rather than the Painting rate (because of handling and piling the sheets) was denied.

11. The technique of paying separate rates for painting and sheeting at Ohio Works is not without a form of precedent. Under the Inequity Program a Sheeter job was described as such. Apparently the sheeting work was done by men who also performed duties in the Boilermaking trade and craft job when not sheeting. The structural painting was performed by men working under a description of Structural Painter (known colloquially as "Black Painters") who were absorbed into the trade and craft

job of Painter some time in 1948. The Structural Painter job thereupon was terminated.

12. Between 1948 and 1954 trade and craft Boilermakers and Painters, working separately, continued to perform some sheeting and painting work, although a large portion was sub-contracted. Since the Boilermakers and Painters were in different seniority units and worked separately, there was considerable inefficiency (as double erection of scaffolding) in using them to perform the functions now performed by the new crew.

13. The Union stresses that under Section B-7 of the January 1, 1953 Manual (page 6) the term "assigned maintenance job" refers to any job (other than trade or craft) on which the employees are assigned to operating and service units for the performance of field inspection, repair, replacement, installation, adjustment, and greasing and oiling of facilities and equipment within the assigned area. The Union also emphasizes that Section C-8 of the Manual states that the inherent nature of assigned maintenance work is such that the job content requirements of assigned maintenance jobs may vary from day to day within any given assigned area and as between areas.

14. The Company stresses that it retains exclusive discretion to establish new jobs. It finds nothing in Section 9-D which gives the Union basis to claim that the Company must create a "combination job" when in its discretion the Company has established two separate jobs. It points to the fact that separate rates (Blacksmith and Painter) have been paid in the past for the separate performance of sheeting and painting.

FINDINGS

15. This case does not present any challenge to Management authority to establish new jobs in conformity with the Agreement. Rather, the issue is whether there has been proper observance of the requirements of Section 9-D and the Manual. Since this is assigned maintenance work, the applicable portion of the Manual [p. 38, Paragraphs 8 and 8 (a)] states:

"8. The inherent nature of assigned maintenance work is such that the job content requirements of assigned maintenance jobs may vary from day to day within any given assigned area and as between areas; and, to achieve maximum productivity in any given area, employees engaged therein are called upon to perform varying duties in discharging the responsibilities of their assignments. Therefore:

"a. All assigned maintenance jobs are described on the basis of facts as they normally exist, classified in accordance with the foregoing Paragraphs of this manual, and identified by uniform titles which reflect the nature of the job."

16. This language requires that all assigned maintenance jobs be described *on the basis of facts as they normally exist.* It recognizes the inherent nature of assigned maintenance work to be such that job content may vary from day to day within any given assigned area, and that employees engaged in such work are called upon to perform varying duties from time to time in carrying out their assignments.

17. The present case thus turns on whether, in view of the manner in which the work has been organized by the Company and now is performed by the men at its direction, there truly may be said to be two jobs rather than one—within the contemplation of the above quoted language.

18. The evidence demonstrates beyond doubt that one assigned maintenance job in fact has been established. All men were recruited for, trained for, and must be able to perform, all duties assigned to the crew from time to time and place to place. Any crew member may be called upon at any time to perform any of the duties as required. There has been no application of Section 13, in filling a Sheeter job, in the manner contemplated when separate jobs actually exist. As performed, the work reflects interrelationship of relevant duties to a significant extent. The effort to describe in separate documents portions of the total duties regularly required of the men as needed, and to label them as separate "jobs," cannot override the requirements of the Manual defining assigned maintenance work and providing that assigned maintenance jobs must be described on the basis of the facts as they normally exist.

AWARD

19. The grievance is sustained. The assigned maintenance duties required of the men in this crew constitute a single assigned maintenance job, to be described and classified as such under Section 9-D and the Manual.

N—186. Lorain Works. August 13, 1954

Sylvester Garrett, *Chairman*

FINDINGS

1. This grievance was filed August 10, 1951, by two employees assigned to the job of Shipper Checker (Truck Shipments) in the Warehouse and Shipping Department at Lorain Works, and in effect contended that the job which grievants had bid for, and occupied, had been established in violation of the April 22, 1947 Agreement, particularly Section 2-B.

2. In light of various decisions of the Board subsequent to filing of this grievance, it is apparent that the grievance could not be sustained. This in effect was recognized by the Union in its presentation. A possible issue as to job classification was mentioned at the hearing, but is not involved in, or in any way affected by, the present decision.

AWARD

3. The grievance is denied.

A—812. Cuyahoga Works. July 25, 1958

Herbert L. Sherman, Jr., *Chairman*

BACKGROUND

1. In this grievance from the Wire Mill Division of the Cuyahoga Works employees in the Shipping Department claim that when the Company started to manufacture and ship welded wire fabric at the Cuyahoga Works, the additional shipping work should have been assigned to them under Section 2-B-3 of the August 3, 1956 Agreement.

2. Because of an anticipated substantial increase in the demand for welded wire fabric, the Company decided in 1956 to establish a new department for production of that product at Cuyahoga Works. That product had not previously been produced at this plant. For this department a new building was constructed next to the existing Wire Mill. This area, 120' x 400', was broken down into two parts—one half for production of the product on the new National Welded Wire Fabric Machines and one half for warehousing and shipping. In the latter area a truck dock, an internal railroad siding and two pulpit operated overhead traveling cranes were installed. Because the new product is subject to seasonal demand it is warehoused and shipped from stock.

3. Supervision was reorganized and new crews with new jobs were established for the warehousing and shipping in this area. The basic crew performs warehousing, but it is expanded as necessary to perform the shipping function. This crew stays in the new department; it is not dispatched to different areas like the old shipping crews. The new and different jobs were described and classified, and then posted. Since the Wire Mill Division is one seniority unit, employees on the existing shipping crews could have bid on these jobs. They did not do so because they claimed that this work should have been assigned to them anyhow.

4. The Union argues that the additional shipping work in the new area should have been assigned to the existing shipping crews because they had performed almost all of the shipping work in the past. It points out that the new product is a Wire Mill product and that the new facilities are in the Wire Mill Division. Because of a general reduction in business around the time that the new department went into operation in 1957, some of the men in the existing shipping crews were laid off. The Union contends that these men would have been retained if the disputed work had been assigned to the existing crews. (It should be noted that actually five of these men were assigned to the new jobs.)

5. Moreover, the Union does not believe that the differences in handling of the new product and the old product are significant, such as loading the new product on gondolas and flat cars with a pulpit operated crane as against loading the old product on boxcars with tractors and on trucks with electric hoists operated from the ground. Nor does it see any substantial difference in that the new crews perform warehousing functions and the old crews do not. Furthermore, although there is a separate Foreman for the new crew on the day turn, the Union notes that one Foreman supervises old and new crews on the afternoon turn.

6. Management argues that a local working condition is applicable and binding only within a given frame of reference, that it cannot be disassociated from its framework, and that it cannot exist outside its factual context. Illustrations are cited to show that the Board has identified practices with their areas of applicability under Sections 2-B, 9, 13 and 14 of the Agreement. Particular reliance is placed on the Board's Award in A-730, where two new Electric Welded

Fabric Machines were added to four old machines and it was found that no local working condition under 2-B-3 was applicable to the new condition. The Company therefore believes that there is no local working condition which restricts its right to assign the disputed work to the new crews.

DISCUSSION AND FINDINGS

7. At the outset it should be noted that grievants have not been deprived of any work on the old product which they have long loaded. Nor have any of the old crews been reduced by transferring any of their existing work to the new group.

8. When Management decided to purchase new equipment to produce a new product in a new building at Cuyahoga Works, it was not precluded from establishing a new department with the warehousing and shipping functions associated with this product as an integral part of the new department. Even though the old shipping crews had long loaded other products of the Wire Mill Division, Section 2-B-3 did not bar the Company from establishing new crews with new and different jobs in the new department to handle the new product. Under the evidence in this case there was no established local working condition applicable to the new situation.

AWARD

9. The grievance is denied.

A—870. Joliet Works. March 31, 1959
Sylvester Garrett, *Chairman*

BACKGROUND

1. This grievance from the Wire Mill Division of Joliet Works asserts that Management acted improperly in establishing a new job of Tractor Operator (Utilityman) (Class 8) in the Small Nail Packaging Department seniority unit. The grievance requests that tractor operator duties assigned to the new job be assigned to employees in the Transportation Department seniority unit.

2. Various types of small nails and fasteners are packaged by employees in the Small Nail Packaging Department seniority unit. Prior to the events causing this grievance, employees in three jobs normally were employed in the Small Nail Packaging Room to perform the necessary duties: Packers (Small Packages) (Class 3); Material Handlers (Class 6); and Packers (Assembler) (Class 4). The Packers (Small Packages), commonly called Hand Packers, weighed and packed nails and fasteners in small boxes (⅛ lb. to 25 lbs. per box) manually, then closed and labeled the boxes. The boxes then are placed in shipping cartons by the Packers (Assembler). The basic function of the Material Handler was to service employees on the two Packer jobs. He brought nails and fasteners (in cartons or kegs) from the nearby warehouse, dumped them on the Packers' workbenches, supplied the Packers with boxes and cartons, placed filled cartons on pallets, and removed loaded pallets of filled cartons to the warehouse. For this purpose he used a hand truck and a powered lift tractor (walking).

3. Up to around 1955, the items thus packaged were primarily small nails, tacks, and brads, but by 1955 an increasing demand began to develop for small packages of several larger types of nails for home use. Management, therefore, undertook to perfect a machine for automatically packaging such nails, and after considerable experimentation, a new set of equipment for mechanically packing such nails was installed near the other end of the main warehouse. Packing of nails, tacks, and brads continued as theretofore in the Small Nail Packaging Room. The new operation was installed as a part of the Small Nail Packaging Department, however, under the supervision of the same foreman.

4. Each of the two lines of the new packaging machine is manned by one Packer (Automatic Scales) plus one service employee in the Tractor Operator (Utilityman) job (Class 8). The Tractor Operator (Utilityman) performs about the same functions in relation to the Packer (Automatic Scales) as the Material Handler performs in respect to the Hand Packers. The one essential difference, which gives rise to this grievance, is that the Tractor Operator uses a powered lift tractor on which he rides, rather than a walking tractor such as used by the Material Handler. The new tractor is able to lift greater weights required in servicing the new packaging machine, is faster, and is better adapted to minimizing delays in operation. The Tractor Operator (Utilityman) also is responsible for packing filled boxes of nails in shipping cartons (done by the Packers (Assemblers) in the older operation) plus preparation of shipping cartons.

5. Despite the title of the job, the Tractor Operator (Utilityman) devotes most of his time to servicing the Packer (Automatic

Scales) and performing duties related to the packaging of the product. The time spent operating the tractor varies from about half an hour to an hour per turn, depending upon the type of product being packaged. The Tractor Operator (Utilityman) and Packers (Automatic Scales) are covered by a single incentive application.

6. The Tractor Operator (Utilityman) job was posted in the Small Nail Packaging Department seniority unit in February, 1958, and filled by promotion of a Material Handler. Grievants are Tractor Operators in the Transportation Department (a different seniority unit) who claim that operation of all powered mobile equipment servicing more than one department in the plant must be done by employees in the Transportation Department. They believe that since the Tractor Operator (Utilityman) must go from the Automatic Nail Packaging Machine into the warehouse to get items for packing, and also to store packaged product for ultimate shipment, this work must be assigned to employees in the Transportation Department.

7. The Union therefore asserts that by including operation of a tractor among duties of the Tractor Operator (Utilityman), the Company improperly combined two separate and distinct jobs in violation of Section 9-D of the Agreement. The Union broadly holds that whenever mobile power equipment is used at Joliet Works, it falls exclusively within the scope of the Transportation Department, and must be assigned to Tractor Operators in this department for operation. The Union feels that seniority units, as specified in the Local Seniority Agreement, cannot be modified or affected in any way save by mutual agreement.

FINDINGS

8. There is no evidence of a local agreement which would prevent Management from establishing a new job in the Small Nail Packaging Department which includes a small amount of tractor operation inci-

dental to performance of other major duties of the job. Since the amount of tractor operation is small, despite the title given the job, no issue of appropriate seniority unit for inclusion of the new job has been raised by the Union under Section 13-B. All that is sought is reassignment of the tractor duties, alone. The tractor work in question is substantially the same as long performed in this department by Material Handlers. The only difference is that the new tractor is of somewhat greater capacity and carries the operator as well as the load. Employees in departments and seniority units other than Transportation at Joliet operate various types of powered mobile equipment in transporting materials, supplies, and products.

9. The Union does not point to anything specific in the local Seniority Agreement (establishing the various seniority units) which might control disposition of this grievance, but cites a 1953 Third Step settlement in Grievance JOL-248, where Management agreed to restore a crew under an established incentive, protected under 9-F-2, where no changed condition within the meaning of Section 9-C-2 had occurred. This settlement involves an entirely different problem from that in the present case, and provides no guidance here.

10. Finally, the Union urges that decisions of Arbitrators Marwich (Procter & Schwartz, May 31, 1958), McCoy (American Bridge, October 18, 1958), and Seward (Bethlehem Steel, 25 L.A. 366) provide support for its position here, although in the latter case the grievances in fact were denied. But the essential facts in each of those cases differ from those here, and the Board ordinarily cannot give very much weight to general expressions of principle extracted from opinions of other Arbitrators dealing with different agreements, bargaining relationships, and fact situations. In these circumstances, the grievance must be denied.

AWARD

11. The grievance is denied.

N—283. National Works. September 23, 1959
Sylvester Garrett, *Chairman*

BACKGROUND

1. This grievance from the Inspection Department of National Works protests termination of the job of Conditioning Inspector (Class 9) and assignment of its inspection duties to a new job of Scarfer (Marker) (Class 8) when scarfing and inspection were mechanically changed and reorganized in July, 1958.

2. This occurred upon completion of changes in the #1 Peeler and related scarfing facilities which substantially affected the manner in which inspection, marking and scarfing of rounds was conducted.

3. Physical changes at this time involved relocation of scarfing operations, to place them adjacent to the #1 Peeler, plus installation of a mechanical conveyor be-

tween the #1 Peeler and a marking table. The new marking table was equipped with a mechanical rotating device to rotate peeled rounds while they were being inspected and marked for scarfing. Previously the Conditioning Inspector was required to use a pinch bar and wedge to rotate the rounds manually on the beds to inspect and mark them, prior to their being moved on down the beds for scarfing.

4. The new facilities also included mechanical conveying equipment to move the rounds from the new marking station to either of two new scarfing stations. Formerly there were 8 scarfing beds with a Conditioning Inspector, a Scarfer (Class 7), and a Scarfer Helper assigned to each when operating. Under the new arrangement, four employees are assigned to the new Scarfer (Marker) job in Class 8, and they rotate in filling assignments at the various work stations: one of the three marks at the marking table, while the other two scarf at the new scarfing stations. In addition, a new job of Quality Control Inspector has been created in Class 11, to selectively inspect the rounds after scarfing.

5. Prior to these changes in facilities and methods, the Peeler was located some distance from the scarfing area, and the peeled rounds were transferred to the 8 scarfing beds by crane. At the head of each bed the rounds were marked by a Conditioning Inspector, rotating them manually as required. The Conditioning Inspector also was responsible for O.D., size centering, squareness of ends, and stamping. He posted a blackboard report of the number of pieces inspected. When the Conditioning Inspector job was described and classified, moreover, it was required to inspect blooms primarily for shipment to Ellwood Works. With the passing of time, necessity for this work diminished, and was not often required prior to the events giving rise to this grievance.

6. After marking the rounds, the Inspectors rolled them down to the scarfing area on each bed. Here the Scarfers performed their work, with the aid of a Scarfer Helper in rotating the rounds during and after scarfing. Following the scarfing operation, a Conditioning Inspector made a spot check of scarfed rounds to ascertain whether scarfing had removed the defects as required or rounds were overscarfed.

7. The new Quality Control Inspector (Class 11) is within the same seniority unit as the former Class 9 Conditioning Inspector, and some of the former Conditioning Inspectors now work on the Quality Control Inspector job. None of the former Conditioning Inspectors have been assigned to the new Scarfer (Marker) job (Class 8), however, because in a different seniority unit. Thus some former Conditioning Inspectors have been demoted to Labor or assigned elsewhere in the plant in accordance with their seniority.

8. Although grievances currently are pending in respect to classification of the new jobs resulting from the methods and equipment changes, no classification issue is presented here. Rather the Union holds that Management has violated Section 9-D in that the primary function of the old Conditioning Inspector job has been combined with duties of the old Scarfer job. The Union feels that to combine the performance of primary functions of pre-existing jobs into a single job in itself violates Section 9-D. It seeks a ruling to this effect.

FINDINGS

9. The Union here seeks an interpretation of Section 9-D to solve the problem which arose as a result of mechanization and changed procedures displacing the Conditioning Inspectors. The equipment and methods changes which became effective about July 1, 1958 substantially affected the work of both Conditioning Inspectors and Scarfers, particularly in mechanizing the handling of rounds at both the marking work station and the scarfing work station.

10. Nothing in Section 9-D bars the Company in these circumstances from creating a new job to perform duties previously performed in part by two pre-existing jobs. Not only was performance of the marking duty by the Conditioning Inspectors affected by the mechanization, but also significant portions of the duties of the job were assigned to the newly created job of Quality Control Inspector in Class 11 as an incident to reorganization of the work.

11. In Case USC-418 the Board observed that, "Position-rated job descriptions provide only the basis for proper job classification. Responsible representatives of the parties long have understood that job descriptions did not constitute agreement that a job will continue to be performed in any particular way without change." In view of the equipment and methods changes here, this observation in USC-418 seems to apply with especial force. It might be noted also that the basic difficulty in this case seems to arise not as much from the combination of job duties, which the Union challenges under Section 9-D, as from local seniority arrangements covering the Inspectors which resulted in their demotion, in significant numbers, to substantially lower jobs.

AWARD

12. The grievance is denied.

CHAPTER 4

CLAIM OF IMPROPER ASSIGNMENT OF DUTIES

Under the broad heading of this chapter two groups of cases are considered. The first deals with claims that duties have been improperly distributed among jobs *within* the production and maintenance bargaining unit. The second group consists of claims of improper assignment of duties to jobs *outside* the production and maintenance bargaining unit—to supervisory personnel and to employees in other bargaining units.

For further claims of improper assignment of duties among trade or craft and assigned maintenance jobs, see Chapter 20 of this volume. The following cases reported elsewhere in this volume are also relevant to this chapter:

USC-412 (p. 55), USC-417, -420 (p. 26), USC-419 (p. 49), CWU-3 (p. 37), T-489, -490 (p. 120).

Section A.   AMONG JOBS WITHIN THE BARGAINING UNIT

CI—257.   Homestead District Works.   January 31, 1953
Sylvester Garrett, *Chairman*

BACKGROUND

1. These grievances present alleged violations of Sections 2-B, 9-D, 9-K-1, 13 and 14 of the April 22, 1947 Agreement. They grow out of a reorganization of clerical personnel instituted on June 25, 1950 in the 45″ Mill of Homestead Works.

2. Prior to June 25, 1950, the jobs here involved were manned on each turn as follows:

JOB TITLE	JOB CLASS	NUMBER OF EMPLOYEES
Clerk, Rolling Order	10	1
Clerk, Slab Yard	8	2
Incentive Recorder	6	2

The Rolling Order Clerk and Slab Yard Clerk positions existed without significant change at least from 1943 up to June 25, 1950. The Incentive Recorder position was created in December, 1947, as an incident of application by the Company of its management alignment program. Prior thereto incentive recording duties were performed by supervisory personnel.

3. During 1946 the Accounting Department of Homestead Works assumed responsibility for the Mill Clerical staff. At this time, the Accounting Department undertook to survey the clerical work being performed throughout the plant for the purpose of eliminating unnecessary reports and duplication of functions. Insofar as this study affected the jobs here involved, it appeared that both the Rolling Order Clerk and Slab Yard Clerk positions were performing useless functions. For example, Item 1 of the Rolling Order Clerk working procedure declared that the incumbent, "Verifies from knowledge of rolling order practices and mill limitations rolling order data and corrects where necessary by checking ingot specification, size, weight, type, code and pit. Checks slab length against ordered weight, checks stamping, production order letter, marking, painting and conditioning class." This function consumed about four hours time on each turn, but appeared to be merely a duplication of work already performed by Production Planning and properly the sole responsibility of Production Planning.

4. The study also revealed that the Slab Yard Clerk was required (Item 3 of working procedure) to perform the following: "From slab record cards, posts to slab conditioning schedule: P.O. numbers, serial number, heat number, turn rolled, date scarfed, date transferred, etc." This involved posting of various data on individual sheets in nine separate schedule books. It was discovered that the data thus posted in fact was not used by production personnel for whom it was prepared, and was of no practical value.

5. In view of these findings Management decided to discontinue the work covered by Item 1 of the Rolling Order Clerk's working procedure and Item 3 of the Slab Yard Clerk's working procedure. It also arranged to move the work location of the Slab Yard Clerk from the Slab Yard to a desk in the Mill Office opposite the desk of the Rolling Order Clerk. Incident to these changes Management realigned job duties and eliminated personnel so as to achieve greater efficiency—the crew was revised on each shift so that only one employee filled each of the three jobs here involved. This change in manning became effective June 25, 1950 simultaneously with an over-all realignment of job duties as follows:

Rolling Order Clerk: (a) Items 1 and 10 of the working procedure eliminated. (b) Item 3 of the Incentive Recorder's working procedure was transferred to the Slab Yard Clerk position with provision for the Rolling Order Clerk to assist the Slab Yard Clerk when needed. This item comprises, "Transcribes the following information from each Slab Yard Record card to Slab Yard Production Report and forwards to Time and Payroll Bureau: Section, date, turn, slab number, weight, gauge and classification. (c) The Rolling Order Clerk also was designated to assist the Slab Yard Clerk, when needed, in the performance of Item 4, preparing manifests for slabs transferred to shipped.

Slab Yard Clerk: (a) Item 3 of the working procedure eliminated. (b) Item 3 of the Incentive Recorder's working procedure was transferred to the Slab Yard Clerk with the assistance of the Rolling Order Clerk as described above. Prior to this reassignment of duties the Slab Yard Clerk, under Item 10 of the working procedure, was occupied to a small extent on this same duty. (c) Under Item 4 of the working procedure the Slab Yard Clerk was given the assistance of the Rolling Order Clerk as above indicated. (d) Item 9 of the working procedure, "Prepares rejection reports for slabs rejected in Conditioning Yards," was transferred from the Slab Yard Clerk position to the Incentive Recorder position.

Incentive Recorder: (a) Item 3 of the working procedure, "Transcribes the following information from each Slab Yard Record to Slab Yard Production Report and forwards to Time and Payroll Bureau: Section, date, turn, slab number, weight, gauge and classification," was transferred to the Slab Yard Clerk position to be assisted by the Rolling Order Clerk. (b) Item 9 of the Slab Yard Clerk's working procedure, "Prepares rejection reports for slabs rejected in Conditioning Yards," was transferred to the Incentive Recorder position.

6. During the period immediately following June 25, 1950, paper work piled up in the Mill Office to the extent that the Supervisor filled in as a Slab Yard Clerk on a number of shifts, and on June 28, an additional person was assigned to the Slab Yard Clerk position on the day turn. This assignment of an additional Clerk was continued indefinitely thereafter.

7. Subsequent to these changes additional duties were added to the position of Rolling Order Clerk; the major additional duty was added about 1951, and entails the making of periodic entries in connection with the Duquesne Hot Run. In addition to completing the Duquesne Hot Run report, the Rolling Order Clerk also has been given responsibility for seeing that the positions of Slab Yard Clerk, Incentive Recorder and Messenger are manned on each shift.

8. Sometime subsequent to June 25, 1950, there was assigned to the Incentive Recorder position the further responsibility of taking transfer slips from the Control Man when steel is transferred to the Slab Yard and delivering them to the 45" Mill Office. This additional responsibility consumes about five minutes per shift. The Incentive Recorder also has been given the responsibility of recording slab yard delays, but as yet this function has not been performed by the Incentive Recorders and supervision has not undertaken to require performance of this duty.

9. According to the Union, the foregoing realignment of duties and elimination of personnel imposed an unreasonable work load on employees filling the three positions. There was considerable evidence presented at the hearing to substantiate this claim. Rolling Order Clerk Reutzel testified that although Item 1 of the working procedure had been eliminated, this did not mean that no mistakes were being made in the rolling orders. Whenever mistakes occur and are detected in the mill, he is telephoned and asked to straighten out the difficulty. According to Reutzel, errors of this sort occur at least once a shift and sometimes from four to six times in the course of a single shift. Even though it may not be his assigned responsibility to correct such errors, the Production Foreman requests that he do so, and Reutzel spends from five to ten minutes helping to correct each such error by contacting Production Planning.

10. Reutzel also stated that considerable

work is entailed in assisting the Slab Yard Clerk in writing up incentive reports under the duties transferred from Item 3 of the old Incentive Recorder description. He spends from 1½ to 3 hours per shift working on this assignment, and sometimes has found it necessary to do the entire job because of the preoccupation of the Slab Yard Clerk with other more pressing duties. In addition, the Rolling Order Clerk spends a good deal of time working on the mill cards jointly with the Slab Yard Clerk. If the two employees are able to work together, this function takes about an hour of their time, but if the Rolling Order Clerk handles it alone, the assignment takes from 2 to 3 hours per shift. According to Reutzel, the Slab Yard Clerk ordinarily is so swamped with other duties that both employees cannot complete their assignments within the regular 8-hour shift.

11.   Slab Yard Clerk Piotrowski testified that although Item 3 had been modified in the Slab Yard Clerk's working procedure, the modification did not substantially affect the amount of time required to perform the work. She contended that the volume of work was so heavy that she no longer had adequate time to eat lunch, and sometimes was forced to eat with one hand while writing with the other.

12.   Incentive Recorder Gustashaw testified that he was unable to handle the Incentive Recorder position adequately because of conflicting demands on his time. There are three separate Slab Yards: A, B and No. 2. The A Yard in turn is divided into three separate scarfing pits. Since the Scarfers finish scarfing their slabs on one side in each of the pits at various times, it sometimes happens that two groups of Scarfers are ready to have their incentive recordings taken at the same time. On such occasions Gustashaw is unable to service both groups.

13.   Since the Scarfers are anxious to have their recordings taken promptly so that they can resume production, there is considerable pressure on Gustashaw to be in two places at once. According to Gustashaw and other witnesses, this results in the Production Foreman estimating the proper incentive recordings on the slabs scarfed and directing that the slabs be turned over so the scarfing may be resumed. The Foreman then turns over the information for the incentive records to Gustashaw later. On occasion Gustashaw has been contacted by his Supervisor with the complaint that such incentive recordings are too generous. Gustashaw stated that nearly every day two scarfing beds were ready for incentive recording at the same time.

14.   All three employees testified that the added pressure of work since June 25, 1950 had caused them considerable nervous tension. Gustashaw has lost about 15 pounds and is under a doctor's care for a nervous condition. He asserted that he had no time during which to eat lunch without interruption. Miss Piotrowski testified that the pressure of work made her nervous and gave her headaches, although she had experienced the same condition before June 25, 1950.

15.   The Union also sought to show that the realignment of duties has imposed such a burden on the employees that foremen frequently undertook to help out in the performance of their duties. There is no question that Supervisor Dorwart did perform clerical duties during the period immediately after June 25, 1950 until an additional Slab Yard Clerk was placed on the day shift. Beyond that, however, the Union asserts that foremen have continued to fill in for the Incentive Recorder by taking recordings when the Incentive Recorder is occupied elsewhere. According to Gustashaw, if foremen did not take incentive recordings, the time lost by the Scarfers would impair efficiency of the Mill. The volume of slabs scarfed has increased since June, 1950, and there is more recording work today for one Recorder than for both prior to the realignment of duties.

16.   The Chairman of the Grievance Committee works a day a month as Scarfer and testified that he had seen foremen continuously taking incentive recordings. Management denied that any substantial amount of incentive recording was being done by foremen in either the A or B Yard. Relief Foreman Kalupson testified that he had never taken incentive recordings except on one occasion when Gustashaw had not reported for work. Kalupson agreed, however, that Scarfers occasionally complained to him that there were not enough Incentive Recorders around, and on such occasions it was Kalupson's practice to go and find the Recorder. Kalupson agreed also that he had discussed the unavailability of the Incentive Recorder on one or two occasions with other foremen.

17.   He added that when he could not get the Incentive Recorder and the men wanted to go ahead, he did the following: "I say, wait until he comes over and takes the incentives. If they want to turn them over, tell the Cranemen to turn them over, give the incentives to the Recorder." Kalupson agreed that the Scarfers did direct the Cranemen to turn the slabs over in the absence of the Incentive Recorder, but declared that he actually never had seen it done himself.

18. One of the Union rebuttal witnesses, a Scarfer, claimed he had seen Kalupson himself take the incentive recordings on about 300 different occasions subsequent to June 25, 1950 *in the A Yard*. As to the B Yard, a Scarfer stated that when the Incentive Recorder is not available the Foreman takes the recordings himself and directs the Cranemen to turn the slabs over. This man estimated that he had seen this happen on five or six occasions subsequent to June of 1950. Kalupson is Foreman over the A Yard and it appears that the A Yard takes precedence over the B Yard where the Scarfers are ready for recording simultaneously in both yards.

19. The record supports the conclusion that a substantial amount of incentive recording has been done by supervisory personnel in A and B Yards, and that the Scarfers on occasion have been permitted to take their own recordings.

20. A large part of the Union's evidence with respect to the taking of incentive recordings by Foremen related to the situation in the #2 Conditioning Yard. This conditioning yard originally was established in connection with the 32″ Mill, and for a period it operated only on an emergency basis. In order to protect the seniority of employees assigned to the #2 Yard, the parties on July 22, 1949 reached a special agreement covering seniority of the 32″ Mill employees in the event that they should be displaced by discontinuance of operations of the 32″ Mill. The parties stipulated that "the 32″ Mill would be considered as a 'non-operative unit' as of June 30, 1949, for the purpose of placing 32″ Mill personnel in the 45″ Mill on the basis of job seniority." The Agreement went on to provide that "in the event the 32″ Mill should again operate, a crew would be picked from the 45″ Mill personnel for the emergency or temporary operation with no impairment to their seniority rating as established at the 45″ Mill after June 30, 1949."

21. Over a period of years the Company has had incentive recordings taken in the #2 Yard by Foremen. This long established practice was not changed in December of 1947 when, under the Management Alignment Program, incentive recording was removed from supervisory employees and included within the bargaining unit.

22. The Union interprets the above special seniority agreement as requiring the Company to discontinue the taking of incentive recordings by Foremen in the #2 Conditioning Yard. There is nothing in the special agreement, however, which touches upon the subject either directly or indirectly. It merely purports to set forth principles for protecting seniority rights of employees who work in the 32″ Mill and the 45″ Mill. The Board finds no obligation for Management to vary its established practice of having Foremen take incentive recordings in the #2 Conditioning Yard.

DISCUSSION AND FINDINGS

23. This case involves problems as to the meaning of Sections 3, 9-D and 2-B of the Agreement. In addition, a question is presented under Section 14. The Board finds nothing in Section 13 reasonably applicable to the situation in hand, nor does Section 9-K-1 have the significance attached to it by the Union.

24. It is notable that Section 9-K-1 is one of a number of provisions in Section 9-K covering developments to complete the program of the May 8, 1946 Agreement between the parties to eliminate inequities. Read in the context of Section 9-K it is apparent that the language of Section 9-K-1 was intended to convey the meaning that the Company would not establish performance standards for jobs except in connection with the establishment of incentives. If Section 9-K-1 were read to mean that management was not entitled to increase work loads because the mere fact of increasing a work load amounted to establishment of a "performance standard," then it would equally well follow that prior thereto there had already been established a performance standard, since there would be no generic difference between one level of effort and another. Since obviously the parties did not contemplate that there were already established performance standards in the sense that they were using the term for all non-incentive jobs, it would be fallacious to infer that they meant under Section 9-K-1 to provide that any increase in work load would constitute the establishment of a performance standard. This is especially true in view of the fact well known to both parties that the work load of jobs in large mills will vary greatly from one job to another, and also from time to time.

25. The major issue here lies in the Union contention that Section 9-D prohibits management from making any changes in job content or job duties, except where such changes affect the job to the extent of one full job class or more (unless there is mutual agreement as to the new description and classification). If this contention is sound, then all of the actions taken by management in this case were unauthorized. The significant language of Section 9-D provides:—

"The job description and classification for each job in effect as of the date of this Agreement shall continue in effect unless (1) Management changes the job content (requirements of the job as to the training, skill, responsibility, effort, and working conditions) to the extent of one full job class or more; (2) the job is terminated or not occupied during a period of one year; or (3) the description and classification are changed in accordance with mutual agreement of officially designated representatives of the Company and the Union.

"When and if from time to time the Company, at its discretion, establishes a new job or changes the job content (requirements of the job as to training, skill, responsibility, effort, and working conditions) of an existing job to the extent of one full job class or more, a new job description and classification for the new or changed job shall be established in accordance with the following procedure. . . ."

26. The primary purpose of this language is to establish the status of job descriptions and classifications. The description of a job, and its classification, are two separate matters. Preparation of a job description is a technical undertaking designed to provide as accurate a picture as possible of what duties and responsibilities are involved in the given job. It is only after all, or a representative group, of jobs in a given unit are described that the jobs may be classified intelligently *for rate purposes*. The classification proceeds on the basis of a comparison—direct or indirect—of all jobs in the given unit for the purpose of achieving equitable relationships in the rates of pay.

27. Thus, the end result in which the parties are interested is the *classification* of the job. The job description is a tool to achieve that result. Job descriptions are not and cannot be, perfect and complete representations of all of the nice details of each job. They merely represent the best effort that is possible to achieve an accurate representation. In recognition of this, the typical job description states that the working procedure outlined therein reflects the general detail considered necessary to describe the principal functions of the given job.

28. The task of describing and classifying many thousands of jobs in the steel industry is monumental. Once it has been accomplished, even though absolute perfection in a theoretical sense may not have been attained, it is nonetheless important in the interest of stability that the parties live with

the rate structure which has been developed unless it becomes necessary to recognize some *substantial* change which affects the *relative value* of a given job. In Section 9-D the parties were guided by this principle to the extent of providing that no job classification should be changed as a result of *changes in job content* unless such changes were sufficiently important to change the value or relative worth of the job for classification purposes by one full job class or more.

29. As to this much Section 9-D seems clear. The Union believes, however, that the Section goes further and requires that, because the *agreed job description* is not to be changed unless there is a total change of one full class or more in the job value, that the *job content* cannot be changed either. This argument rests on the assumption that the job description, instead of merely reflecting what duties and responsibilities management has assigned to a given job, is actually an *agreement* as to how the job will be performed over the future.

30. There are two reasons why the Board cannot accept this view. First, such an arrangement would be so contrary to normal experience in industry as to justify the belief that had the parties intended this far-reaching result they would have so indicated in clear and unequivocal language.

31. Second, Section 9-D includes language which confirms that Management has retained discretion to vary job assignments and duties as the legitimate needs of the business dictate, and except as other provisions of the Agreement in a given case may operate to limit such discretion. Section 9-D recites that management *"at its discretion"* may change job content to the extent of one full job class or more. In 9-D-4 it is provided that an employee may file a grievance where there has been a change in job content, *and the job has not been newly described and classified*. Plainly such grievance could have merit only if a change of one full job class or more is shown to have taken place. There is nothing in 9-D-4, however, to suggest that if the Board finds no such change in job *class,* it could direct the management to revert to the status quo. To read such an intention into 9-D-4 would be in effect to add language which would deprive management of all discretion to change job requirements in the absence of a change of one full job class.

32. Turning to the next phase of the case, it is urged that the assignment of two employees per shift in each of the positions of Shipping Clerk and Incentive Recorder, and the aggregate of job duties in these positions, as well as in the Rolling Order Clerk job,

constituted local working conditions within the protection of Section 2-B. Mr. Gall, representing the Union, elaborated this argument as follows:

"The assignment of the duties of Shipping Clerk and Rolling Order Clerk was a practice or custom, and this assignment of duties has the protection of 2-B. It definitely falls within the scope of other conditions of employment.

"Similar treatment should be accorded the assignment of the duties of the Incentive Recorder. Section 2-B-3 requires that the Company keep in effect those local working conditions which provide benefits in excess or in addition to benefits established by this Agreement. It certainly is a benefit to have two Shipping Clerks perform the duties as outlined in the job description for the Shipping Clerk. It is also a benefit to the Shipping Clerk not to have to perform the transcribing of incentives formerly done by the Incentive Recorder.

"Similarly, it is benefit to the Rolling Order Clerk not to assist in the performance of duties formerly done by the Shipping Clerk. The same consideration must be given to the Incentive Recorder.

"Freedom from the performance of time consuming tasks, and the freedom from mental effort is a benefit in excess of, or in addition to the benefits established elsewhere in the Agreement. Likewise the performance of a given amount of work by two people instead of one, is a benefit in excess of, or in addition to these benefits established elsewhere in the Agreement."

33. The argument that the bare assignment of particular duties to incumbents of a given job over the years gives rise to a local working condition, preventing the assignment of any other duties, seems unsupportable. The working conditions protected by Section 2-B are *customs or practices*. It must be recognized that these are not like physical objects. They are things which evolve out of human conduct, as the Board has had occasion to point out in Case N-146. Ordinarily, a custom does not arise unless a given type of recurring situation is handled in a given manner, or meets with a uniform response or reaction, where there is a reasonable choice of alternative courses of action available, but which are rejected in favor of the uniform response which ultimately achieves the status of a recognized custom. Some customs or practices may arise in a comparatively short space of time where the original decision to follow a given course of action in a given situation is of such importance that the initial conscious choice may be regarded as setting a pattern for the future.

34. The mere assignment of particular job duties to employees within a given job classification is a matter of almost casual importance in the over-all picture of plant operations. Some employees in a given job may be called upon continuously to perform all or most of the duties ascertained to be within the scope of the job when described, whereas other employees may not be called upon to perform as many of the duties involved. Changes in these assignments may occur from time to time, and doubtless have over the years. The mere fact that particular employees have performed certain duties could scarcely be said to give rise to a requirement that they will perform such duties continuously in the future without any change. The Board, therefore, could not hold that whether a given clerk did or did not fill out a particular report was a matter as to which a custom or practice could arise within the meaning of Section 2-B.

35. Another major question is presented by the Union argument as to crew size. The determination of how many employees will be used to man a given operation is a matter of substantial importance to Management and employees alike. As was held in Case N-146, a local working condition *may* arise as to the crew size. There the crews in question were established for Butt Mills and had been maintained thereafter over a period of years. It is certainly possible that a clear and definite practice may develop in regard to the number of employees manning a group of clerical jobs handling a given type of work. Admittedly, such a practice may not be as likely to arise, or as easy to define, in clerical jobs as in the case of production jobs tending machines which set the pace of operations. But this is a difference which goes only to the matter of proof of the practice.

36. The Union's presentation here was calculated to show that a local working condition had arisen in the form of an established clerical crew in the 45″ Mill. The Board believes it unnecessary to base any findings on such evidence, however, since it seems apparent that in any event Management was entitled to move under Section 2-B-4.

37. Section 2-B-4 recognizes that Management may change or eliminate any local working condition if, as a result of action taken under Section 3 "the basis for the existence of the local working condition is changed or eliminated, thereby making it unnecessary to continue such local working condition." In dealing with 2-B-4 there are two main questions: *First,* whether the basis for possible existence of any local working condition as to clerical crew of the 45″ Mill properly was changed by Management; *Sec-*

ond, if such a change in basis of the alleged working condition was affected, was there a proper causal relationship between the change in basis and the ultimate change in crew size.

38. In this case, the Board holds that Management was entitled to discontinue the performance of unnecessary clerical functions in the same manner that it is entitled to discontinue the performance of unnecessary machine operations in ordinary production processes. Thus the Company was entitled to eliminate the various items in the working procedures of the Rolling Order Clerk and Slab Yard Clerk which could be regarded as serving no useful function. In addition, it was entitled to move the work station of the Slab Yard Clerk so as to improve coordination of the activities of the clerical force.

39. There is not doubt also that the clerical jobs in the 45″ Mill could not reasonably be deemed to stand independent of each other. In many respects their work is similar, their duties have overlapped to some extent, and their work requires a certain amount of cooperation among them. Thus, if there were any established "crew" in this case, it presumably would have been a clerical crew consisting of employees in the jobs of Rolling Order Clerk, Slab Yard Clerk, and Incentive Recorder. As already noted, it is unnecessary for the Board to decide whether such a crew was established for purposes of Section 2-B.

40. Since the requirements of the Rolling Order Clerk and Slab Yard Clerk positions were affected substantially by the changes thus made, Management was not barred from acting under Section 2-B-4 to change any local working conditions as to crew size which might have been involved. As far as 2-B-4 itself is concerned, the actions of Management in this case appear to have been permissible, even were it conceded that a local working condition as to the crew had arisen.

41. Nevertheless, Management must comply with other applicable provisions of the Agreement in setting up new or revised jobs and in manning them. The Union has contended throughout that an undue burden has been imposed on incumbents of all three positions in violation of Section 14, and also that Foremen have performed work on a number of shifts, thereby depriving members of the bargaining unit of work to which they were entitled.

42. As to the health problem, the Union evidence tends to suggest possible overloading of the employees, at least of the Incentive Recorder. This matter was not sufficiently explored either in the grievance procedure or at the hearing, owing to preoccupation of the parties with the major issues of contract interpretation already discussed. It seems probable that the parties will be able to explore this matter to a satisfactory conclusion in further grievance proceedings now that the fundamental contract issues have been clarified.   ,

43. It is clear also that supervisors on a number of occasions performed work which properly should have been assigned to employees in the bargaining unit. This occurred when supervisors worked as Slab Yard Clerks for complete shifts on June 27 and 28, 1950, in the absence of any true emergency situation or other justifiable reason. Employees who thus were deprived improperly of the opportunity to fill these positions are entitled to be compensated for loss of earnings suffered as a result. The precise determination of which of the grievants thus suffered a loss is not possible on this record, however, and the matter can be cleaned up by the parties when they renew consideration of the grievances insofar as the issue of possible violation of Section 14 is explored.

44. The Board also leaves open for the parties the question of what action shall be taken to deal with the undoubted performance of incentive recording duties by foremen from time to time in the A and B Yards. In the present state of the case the dates and extent of such occurrences are not entirely clear, nor has the Board considered the problem of what remedial action might be proper in such situation.

45. The grievances will be referred back to the parties for further consideration in the grievance procedure.

AWARD

46. This case is returned to the parties for further consideration in the grievance procedure in light of the principles set forth in this opinion. In the event the parties do not reach final agreement within forty days from the date of this award, and have not agreed to extend the forty day period, the Union may return the case to the Board within ten days for further consideration.

USC—418. Gary Sheet and Tin Mill. August 13, 1954

Sylvester Garrett, *Chairman*

BACKGROUND

1. This grievance, on behalf of the Assigned Maintenance Crew of the Stainless Division, Gary Sheet and Tin Mill, protests that grievants are required to perform acid unloading duties which should be performed by Pipefitters and Pipefitter Helpers.

2. Unloading acid from tank cars requires connecting and disconnecting acid and air lines to the acid tank car and routing the acid line to a storage tank. This work includes removing and replacing eight bolts on the car and coupling the lines to the car connections. The operation involves two men and consumes about 20 minutes to make the connection and about 15 minutes to disconnect. One man stays at the tank car to watch the acid flow and level of acid in the storage tank, during the period between connecting and disconnecting the lines. This standby averages about 2¼ hours per car. Four types of acid are stored in Stainless Division storage tanks—nitric, muriatic, sulphuric, and hydrofluoric.

3. Years ago substantially all acid was delivered by railroad tank car, mostly from chemical plants in Louisiana and Texas. Receipt of acid by tank car has declined steadily since February 1952, however, due to the increased quantities received by tank truck from local suppliers. During 1951, one tank car a day of acid was received, on the average, although some days there were none, and other days 2 or 3. In the first 4 months of 1953 only 12 tank cars of acid were received in all, compared with 71 truckloads. (Operations were substantially reduced in these months, compared with 1951.) All acid received by truck is unloaded into the storage tanks by the truck driver. No Company employees are involved.

4. For years prior to July 1951, acid unloading at Stainless Division was done by Pipefitters and Pipefitter Helpers. This was unique, however, since assigned maintenance handled acid unloading at the five or six other locations where acid was received in tank cars.

5. When this grievance arose, local Management was seeking authority from Pittsburgh to obtain acid from suppliers in the Chicago area who would deliver by truck, with the truck driver taking care of the acid unloading. It was not until the Fall of 1951, however, that any substantial amount of acid was delivered by truck instead of by rail.

6. Use of Pipefitters at Stainless to unload tank cars involved some inefficiency since they were obtained from the Pipe Shop

upon request. The arrival time for acid tank cars at Stainless unloading dock never could be determined precisely in advance of actual arrival, since this was a matter controlled by the railroad. Hence, it was impossible to schedule Pipe Shop employees to be on hand with arrival of the acid. Because Pipefitters were assigned to various jobs throughout the plant, it generally was not possible to get a Pipefitter immediately. A call might be placed shortly before 7:00 a.m., but the necessary Pipefitter and Helper would not arrive for some time—occasionally not until the 3:00 p.m. to 11:00 p.m. shift.

7. It was to correct this situation that Management determined reassigned unloading acid tank cars to Stainless assigned maintenance, as in other departments. Thereafter men in a variety of jobs were assigned from time to time to the acid unloading, including Welder-Intermediate (Class 12), Repairman (Class 10), Greaser (Class 8), Electrician (Class 14), Millwright (Class 14), Gang Leader (Class 16), Tool Room Attendant (Class 7), and Motor Inspector (Class 14). Later Management concluded that this duty properly belonged to the Millwright and Repairman or Millwright Helper, since acid unloading is comparable to work normally performed by men in these jobs.

8. The Union contends unloading acid from tank cars is an inherent function of the Pipefitters trade and craft job and cannot be assigned to Millwrights, Repairmen, or other assigned maintenance jobs. It also believes that unloading acid tank cars in Stainless Division by Pipefitters constitutes a local working condition conferring a benefit on the assigned maintenance crew, within the meaning of Section 2-B-3, and thus protected against change by Management in the absence of circumstances calling 2-B-4 into play.

9. The Union case as to 2-B rests primarily on the Decision of Acting Chairman Killingsworth in Case CI-238. There the grievants were Millwrights at Ohio Works who protested the assignment of cleaning Open Hearth water strainers to them where this work had been done by Pipefitters for many years. The Acting Chairman sustained the grievance and directed the Company to cease assigning the cleaning of Open Hearth water strainers to Millwrights.

10. The Company believes that nothing in the Agreement prohibits assigning acid unloading to the assigned maintenance crew in Stainless Division. Management believes that CI-238 was improperly decided, and inconsistent with later decisions of the Board.

It cites Board Decisions in CI-257, A-650, and USC-412.

FINDINGS

11. There is no basis for the claim that unloading acid from tank cars is inherently a duty of the Pipefitter trade and craft job. When the Pipefitter job was described and classified at Gary Sheet, acid unloading was customarily assigned to jobs other than Pipefitter. Indeed, no Pipefitters have grieved over the assignment of this duty to Stainless assigned maintenance. The case thus differs from USC-419.

12. The remaining issue involves Section 2-B. In CI-238, Acting Chairman Killingsworth stated:

"We are left with two questions: (1) Did the assignment of the task of cleaning water strainers in the Open Hearth to Pipefitters (or, more accurately, to a group of employees other than Millwrights or Repairmen (Mechanical) (General) constitute a local working condition of the type protected by Section 2-B-3; and (2) if so, did the Company change or eliminate the basis for the existence of this local working condition and thereby justify the changing or elimination of the local working condition itself?

"The first question must be answered in the affirmative. The term, 'local working conditions,' is defined in Section 2-B as follows: 'Specific practices or customs which reflect detailed application of the subject matter within the scope of wages, hours of work, or other conditions of employment and includes local agreements, written or oral, on such matters.' The assignment of water strainer cleaning to Pipefitters was a specific practice or custom in the Open Hearth Department. This assignment had remained in effect for many years without change. There is no reason why the fact that different practices or customs prevailed in other departments and plants should remove this arrangement from the protection of Section 2-B. The question whether there could be a local practice or custom within the meaning of the Agreement in some unit other than a plant or department is not raised and not decided in this case.

"This practice or custom was clearly an instance of detailed application of subject matter within the scope of 'other conditions of employment,' both for the Pipefitters and the Millwrights. The work assignments involved in a particular job are usually as important a condition of employment as the wages paid. Conceivably a particular duty might be so trivial in nature that its assignment could not reasonably be considered a condition of employment within the meaning of the Agreement; but this is not true of a task that requires an average of at least 4 hours per week, and at times must be performed 24 hours per day. The assignment to perform such a substantial task must be regarded as a significant condition of employment.

"Section 2-B-3 requires that the Company keep in effect those local working conditions 'which provide benefits that are in excess of or in addition to the benefits established by this Agreement.' Did the local working condition provide such benefits (or advantages) to the Millwrights? Clearly it did. Especially since Millwrights in some other departments were required to clean water strainers, the long-standing practice under which this substantial task was assigned to a different occupational group in the Open Hearth Department provided a benefit or advantage to these Millwrights. Such benefit was in addition to those provided by the Agreement. Therefore, the practice falls under the protection of Section 2-B."

In seeming contrast to this langauge, the Board stated in CI-257:

"The argument that the bare assignment of particular duties to incumbents of a given job over the years gives rise to a local working condition, preventing the assignment of any other duties, seems unsupportable. The working conditions protected by Section 2-B are *customs or practices*. It must be recognized that these are not like physical objects. They are things which evolve out of human conduct, as the Board has had occasion to point out in Case N-146. Ordinarily, a custom does not arise unless a given type of recurring situation is handled in a given manner, or meets with a uniform response or reaction, where there is a reasonable choice of alternative courses of action available, but which are rejected in favor of the uniform response which ultimately achieves the status of a recognized custom. Some customs or practices may arise in a comparatively short space of time where the original decision to follow a given course of action in a given situation is of such importance that the initial conscious choice may be regarded as setting a pattern for the future.

"The mere assignment of particular job duties to employees within a given job classification is a matter of almost casual importance in the over-all picture of plant operations. Some employees in a given job may be called upon continuously to perform all or most of the duties ascertained to be within the scope of the job when described, whereas other employees may not be called upon to perform as many of the duties involved. Changes in these assignments may occur from time to time, and doubtless have over the years. The mere fact that particular employees have performed certain duties could scarcely be said to give rise to a requirement that they will perform such duties continuously in the future without any change. The Board, therefore, could not hold that whether a given clerk did or did not fill out a particular report was a matter as to which a custom or practice could arise within the meaning of Section 2-B."

13. From these quotations, there appears to be some conflict in the approaches of CI-238 and CI-257. No doubt in part this stems from lack of the detailed exploration of the problem which has occurred since decision of these two cases.

14. In retrospect, one major difference between CI-257 and CI-238 is apparent. The former dealt with position-rated jobs exclusively, and the latter touched upon the duties of a trade and craft job. While neither Opinion makes particular reference to this, it now is clear enough that opinions formed as to position-rated clerical jobs may not be valid when projected into the area of trade and craft jobs, or vice versa.

15. Such conclusion, at least, is indicated by the Inequities Program of the parties, insofar as its results are embodied in Section 9 of the Basic Agreements. Trade and craft jobs were described on the basis of "the scope of duties which a fully qualified Journeyman may be called upon to perform *in the plant*" at the time the various descriptions were written. This was by virtue of special agreement of the parties, first negotiated April 15, 1946, when it had become apparent that such jobs could not be handled on the same basis as "position-rated" jobs.

16. This basis for description and classification of trade and craft jobs has been preserved in subsequent agreements and is incorporated by reference in Section 9-D. While 9-D recognizes Management discretion to establish new jobs, or change job content, this is subject to the applicable provisions of the May 8, 1946 Agreement, which incorporates the April 15, 1946 Agreement. Thus,

for reasons detailed in USC-419, the facts which existed in each plant as a whole in 1946 and January, 1947, may determine whether particular work was recognized by the parties as covered by a given craft job for rate payment purposes *in the given plant*.

17. Position-rated jobs comprise the bulk of the jobs in the bargaining unit and the parties' treatment of them provides the key for determining the status of assignment of duties among various jobs for purposes of applying Section 2-B. Position-rated jobs were described on the basis of duties normally performed day in and day out at specific locations, where conditions affecting the job and its requirements remained relatively constant. Position-rated job descriptions provide only the basis for proper job classification. Responsible representatives of the parties long have understood that job descriptions did not constitute agreement that a job will continue to be performed in any particular way without change.

18. The status of these jobs under Section 9-D is clear: Management may change job duties or assignments, subject only to whatever limitations may arise directly or indirectly from other provisions of the Basic Agreement in a specific fact situation. As to this type job—distinct from trade or craft—the agreed procedure for classifying new or changed jobs ordinarily provides adequate protection against possible circumvention of the agreed rate structure by redistributing duties among "new" position-rated jobs.

19. These circumstances emphasize the unlikelihood that the parties could have believed that local working conditions covering assignment of duties among various jobs existed on any appreciable scale on April 22, 1947, when Section 2-B was written initially. It was primarily with this in mind that the Board observed in CI-257 that:

"The mere fact that particular employees have performed certain duties could scarcely be said to give rise to a requirement that they will perform such duties continuously in the future without any change. The Board, therefore, could not hold that whether a given clerk did or did not fill out a particular report was a matter as to which a custom or practice could arise within the meaning of Section 2-B."

20. While it is conceivable, in theory, that a written (or otherwise clearly demonstrated) agreement of this sort might have arisen under extraordinary circumstances, no opinion on the status of such an arrangement, in view of Section 9-D and the May 8, 1946 Agreement need be expressed here. There is no evidence of any agreement as to

assignment of acid unloading to others than assigned maintenance, or anything to suggest an established custom or practice other than a bare showing that Pipefitters were utilized in the past.

21. In truth, the present grievance comes down to a claim that *no other duties* can be assigned to grievants save those they have performed over the years, unless they consent, or 2-B-4 applies. Section 2-B was not intended to introduce such a rigidity into direction of the work force. The parties left no doubt that Section 2-B should receive a practical construction, since they state that its provisions "provide general principles" and furnish "guideposts" both to the parties and the Board. In view of this the Board must, as it did in CI-257, recognize the practical difference between determination of crew size and spell-time arrangements, on the one hand, and the assignment of particular duties among employees in various jobs. Determination of crew size directly affects work load, rest and relief, labor cost, and ofttimes safety conditions. Men and Management alike are keenly interested in such questions the moment a new crew is organized. The assignment of job duties—apart from its direct and recognized effect on job classification—is simply not the sort of thing that both men and Management reasonably could regard as setting a pattern for the future within the protection of Section 2-B. There is no suggestion here, moreover, that the particular reassignment of duties was a mere subterfuge to effect a reduction in established crew.

22. Another issue was suggested at the hearing by evidence as to adverse effect on Surroundings, Hazards, and other Factors, of the assigned maintenance jobs, as a consequence of this new assignment. It appeared also that various jobs had been given acid unloading duties before it was concluded this work should be assigned to Millwright and Repairman, or Millwright Helper. No opinion is expressed on any of these implied issues as to proper job classification, or rate payment, since they were not fairly considered either in the grievance procedure or the hearing. If there is any substance to these matters, presumably they can be cleaned up by the parties without serious difficulty.

AWARD

23. The grievance is denied. No opinion is expressed as to issues which may exist as to proper classification, or rate payment, as a result of the requirement that men in various assigned maintenance positions handle unloading of acid.

CI—238. Ohio Works. April 14, 1952
Charles C. Killingsworth, *Acting Chairman*

BACKGROUND FACTS

1. The grievants in this case are employed as Repairmen (Mechanical) General, more commonly known as Millwrights, in the Open Hearth Mechanical Unit at the Ohio Works. They protest the action of Management in assigning to them in June 1949 the task of cleaning certain water strainers in the Open Hearth Department.

2. For a number of years prior to the assignment of this task to the Millwrights it was performed by Pipefitters in the Open Hearth Department. In this grievance the Millwrights seek to have the duty returned to the Pipefitters. There are four strainers involved, three in the north end of the Open Hearth and one in the No. 1 Boilerhouse. They range from 10 inches to 24 inches in size. The Company estimates that the task requires about four hours per week, averaged over a period of a year. The Union's estimate is higher, but both sides agree that during certain periods of the year, when the plant gets "bad water" because of floods or heavy rains, the task must be performed 24 hours a day. Two strainers in the Open Hearth are still cleaned by Pipefitters, but the Company points out that in the Blast Furnace Department, Millwrights do part of this work and Tuyeremen do part of it; while in the Pumphouse, a fuel oil strainer is cleaned by Fuel Unloaders. The Millwright job is one job class higher than that of Pipefitter.

3. The Union contends that certain functions are inherent in a craft job such as Pipefitter, and that the Wage Inequity agreements forbid the Company to "dissect" these inherent functions from craft jobs and assign them to maintenance jobs. The cleaning of water strainers is an inherent function of the Pipefitter's craft, the Union argues. The Union further contends that the Company has no right under the Agreement to make unilateral changes in job content. The Union also argues that the cleaning of water strainers by Pipefitters constituted a local working condition within the meaning of Section 2-B, and that the Company's change in this local working condition is in violation of the Agreement. Finally, the Union contends that the safety provisions of the Agreement were

violated by the assignment of this unfamiliar task to the Millwrights.

4. The Company contends that the Agreement grants it the right to make changes in job content by reassigning duties from one job to another. The Company also argues that there cannot be a local working condition within the meaning of Section 2-B in an area such as this one, in which the parties have specifically reserved to Management the freedom to act. The Company explains the shift under consideration on the ground that, as a result of its Management Alignment Program, supervision of the Pipefitters was transferred from the Open Hearth Department to the Pipe Shop in the Maintenance Division. This division made a survey of the duties performed by its shop employees and concluded that certain of these duties, including the cleaning of water strainers, was of a routine nature that should properly be performed by Millwrights of the Open Hearth Department. The latter department supported this conclusion of the Maintenance Division because it had experienced difficulty in getting proper attention for the water strainers from the Pipefitters following the shift of supervisory authority. This, the Company says, was the basis for the decision to reassign this task to the Millwrights: first, because it is work that properly falls within their jurisdiction, and second, because this arrangement results in more efficient performance of the task.

FINDINGS

5. Certain of the Union's arguments can be disposed of readily. The testimony does not support the claim that the cleaning of water strainers by Millwrights creates a safety hazard. The testimony also fails to show that the performance of this task is an inherent part of the craft job of Pipefitter; this same task has long been performed by employees other than Pipefitters in other parts of this plant, apparently without protest by the Union. Therefore, it is not necessary for this Board to rule on the Union's contention that an inherent function of a craft job may not be assigned to non-craft employees.

6. This Board must also disagree with the contention that the 1947 Labor Agreement and its supplements forbid the Company to make any changes in job content. There are certain provisions that, taken alone, might conceivably be interpreted as the Union argues. However, such an interpretation is made impossible by the presence of certain other provisions which are clearly based upon the proposition that the Company does have the right to make changes

in job content. These provisions are found in the Wage Inequities Agreements, which are incorporated in the 1947 Labor Agreement by reference. The following are examples:

"It is further understood that new job descriptions shall be prepared from time to time when and if a new job is established or the content of any given job is changed by management." (Agreement of October 23, 1945, Sec. 2.)

"It is further understood that when and if from time to time management establishes a new job or changes the content of a job to the extent of one full job class or more a new classification for the new or changed job shall be established." (The same, Sec. 3.)

"The job description and classification for each job, established by agreement of the parties under provisions of the May 8, 1946 Agreement and in effect as of January 13, 1947, shall continue in effect unless: (1) management changes the job content. . . ." (Agreement of January 13, 1947, Sec. III.)

This Board would have to ignore the obvious intent of the foregoing provisions in order to rule that the Company has no right to make changes in job content.

7. This right is not unqualified, however. Among other things, this right is subject to the so-called "local working conditions" clause when it can be shown that a particular assignment constitutes a local working condition within the meaning of Section 2-B of the 1947 Labor Agreement. This section provides in relevant part as follows:

LOCAL WORKING CONDITIONS

The term 'local working conditions' as used herein means specific practices or customs which reflect detailed application of the subject matter within the scope of wages, hours of work, or other conditions of employment and includes local agreements, written or oral, on such matters. It is recognized that it is impracticable to set forth in this Agreement all of these working conditions, which are of a local nature only, or to state specifically in this Agreement which of these matters should be changed or eliminated. The following provisions provide general principles and procedures which explain the status of these matters and furnish necessary guideposts for the parties hereto and the Board.

* * *

3. Should there be any local working conditions in effect which provide benefits

that are in excess of or in addition to the benefits established by this Agreement, they shall remain in effect for the term of this Agreement, except as they are changed or eliminated by mutual agreement or in accordance with Paragraph 4 below.

4. The Company shall have the right to change or eliminate any local working condition if, as the result of action taken by Management under Section 3—Management, the basis for the existence of the local working condition is changed or eliminated, thereby making it unnecessary to continue such local working condition; provided, however, that when such a change or elimination is made by the Company any affected employee shall have recourse to the grievance procedure and arbitration, if necessary, to have the Company justify its action.

8. We are unable to agree with the Company that the foregoing is over-ridden by the management clause of the Agreement. The clause in question, which is Section 3, reads as follows:

SECTION 3—MANAGEMENT

The Company retains the exclusive rights to manage the business and plants and to direct the working forces. The Company, in the exercise of its rights, shall observe the provisions of this Agreement.

The rights to manage the business and plants and to direct the working forces include the right to hire, suspend or discharge for proper cause, or transfer, and the right to relieve employees from duty because of lack of work or for other legitimate reasons.

It is axiomatic that every provision of an agreement is subject to every other provision, and that each provision should be interpreted in such a manner as to allow the fullest possible scope to other provisions. These general principles are reinforced in this instance by the fact that Section 3 specifically provides that: "The Company, in the exercise of its rights, shall observe the provisions of this agreement." Thus we are forced to conclude that Section 2-B limits and qualifies Section 3. To rule otherwise would render Section 2-B meaningless; if Section 3 were given primacy, the Company could change or eliminate any conceivable local working condition without regard for the limitations of Section 2-B. To give the latter section primacy does not make Section 3 meaningless, because under it the Company still retains the right (subject to whatever limitations

there may be elsewhere in the Agreement) to change or eliminate the basis for the existence of any local working condition, and then to change or eliminate the local working condition. Thus the two sections taken together limit and qualify, but do not destroy, the Company's right to make changes in job content when such job content constitutes a local working condition.

9. We are left with two questions: (1) Did the assignment of the task of cleaning water strainers in the Open Hearth to Pipefitters (or, more accurately, to a group of employees other than Millwrights or Repairmen (Mechanical) General) constitute a local working condition of the type protected by Section 2-B-3; and (2) if so, did the Company change or eliminate the basis for the existence of this local working condition and thereby justify the changing or elimination of the local working condition itself?

10. The first question must be answered in the affirmative. The term, "local working conditions," is defined in Section 2-B as follows: "Specific practices or customs which reflect detailed application of the subject matter within the scope of wages, hours of work, or other conditions of employment and includes local agreements, written or oral, on such matters." The assignment of water strainer cleaning to Pipefitters was a specific practice or custom in the Open Hearth Department. This assignment had remained in effect for many years without change. There is no reason why the fact that different practices or customs prevailed in other departments and plants should remove this arrangement from the protection of Section 2-B. The question whether there could be a local practice or custom within the meaning of the Agreement in some unit other than a plant or department is not raised and not decided in this case.

11. This practice or custom was clearly an instance of detailed application of subject matter within the scope of "other conditions of employment," both for the Pipefitters and the Millwrights. The work assignments involved in a particular job are usually as important a condition of employment as the wages paid. Conceivably a particular duty might be so trivial in nature that its assignment could not reasonably be considered a condition of employment within the meaning of the Agreement; but this is not true of a task that requires an average of at least 4 hours per week, and at times must be performed 24 hours per day. The assignment to perform such a substantial task must be regarded as a significant condition of employment.

12. Section 2-B-3 requires that the Company keep in effect those local working

conditions "which provide benefits that are in excess of or in addition to the benefits established by this Agreement." Did the local working condition provide such benefits (or advantages) to the Millwrights? Clearly it did. Especially since Millwrights in some other departments were required to clean water strainers, the long-standing practice under which this substantial task was assigned to a different occupational group in the Open Hearth Department provided a benefit or advantage to these Millwrights. Such benefit was in addition to those provided by the Agreement. Therefore, the practice falls under the protection of Section 2-B.

13. As already stated, the Agreement does not forbid management to make unilateral changes in those local working conditions that are protected by Section 2-B; it provides only that, in order to justify a change in or elimination of such a local working condition, the Company must show that the basis for its existence has been changed or eliminated, thereby making it unnecessary to continue the local working condition. Therefore, we must now consider whether the Company has made such a showing in the present case. As was stated above, the Company concluded from a survey that strainer cleaning was properly Millwright work rather than Pipefitter work. This conclusion represented merely a change in management's opinion concerning the proper assignment of the work in question. It is the objective facts on which the original opinion was based, and not the opinion itself, that constituted the basis for the existence of the local working condition. If a mere change in management's opinion were held to satisfy the requirement of 2-B-4, there would be no real difference between Section 2-B and Section 3 (Management); under either, management would be free to change or eliminate any local working condition, provided only that it decided to do so. To avoid nullification of Section 2-B, we must consider the

objective facts, and not merely the opinion formed from them. Section 2-B-4 requires a change in those objective facts, and further requires the Company to show a reasonable relationship between a given change in a local working condition and the change in its basis which is cited as justification.

14. The only change in the objective facts that the Company has shown is a reorganization which transferred supervisory authority over the Pipefitters from the Open Hearth Department to the Pipe Shop. The Pipefitters remained in the Open Hearth physically, and they continued to clean some of the water strainers there. The Company contends that the change in supervisory authority made the old arrangement inefficient for the cleaning of certain of the water strainers. We need not decide whether this reorganization of management is the kind of change contemplated in Section 2-B-4. The Company failed to show that the alleged inefficiency was a necessary result of the change in supervisory authority. Neither did it show that reassignment of the task was the sole or best method of remedying the alleged inefficiency. Thus the record does not establish a reasonable relationship between the elimination of the local practice and the other change which is relied upon for justification. For the lack of such a relationship the Company's case must fall, without consideration of other questions that might be raised if the relationship had been established.

AWARD

15. The grievance is granted. The Company is hereby directed to cease assigning the cleaning of water strainers in the Open Hearth Department to the employees known as Millwrights or Repairmen (Mechanical) General, unless and until it eliminates or changes the basis for the departmental practice of assigning this task to Pipefitters, and thereby justifies the elimination of the practice.

COL—73. Pittsburg Works. December 30, 1955
Sylvester Garrett, *Chairman*

FINDINGS

1. This grievance protests addition of bundling duties to the Tractor Operator job in the Wire & Wire Products Department of Pittsburg Works on June 11, 1954.

2. The Tractor Operator job description dated September 14, 1945, stated, under "Working Procedure":

"Driving is performed in semi-crowded

areas adjacent to Bundlers and Inspectors.

Drives tractor to storage and picks up skip of wire by manually operating controls on electrically driven lift.

Transports wire to scale and backs tractor away from skip while wire is weighed by weigher, picks up skip and deposits in proper place for bundling and inspection, picks up bundled wire and delivers to scale for weighing and then to storage.

Delivers wire to Nail Mill, Wire Galvanizer, Fence Dept. or S & C. Machines, and returns rejects to Wire Drawing and delivers scrap to scrap bundler.

Delivers and picks up wire for paper wrapping machine.

Receives orders from Turn Foreman or General Foreman.

Changes batteries, except in case of female operators who must have a helper to change battery per instructions of the Safety Department."

3. Over ensuing years significant changes occurred in the method of handling and tying wire. *First,* the old bundling conveyors, on which bundles had been tied by hand, were replaced by Signode Strapping Machines. As noted, the primary function of the Tractor Operator job was to transport wire from storage to the bundling benches and then to pick it up after bundling and inspection for delivery to storage. Most wire now is tied automatically by Signode Strapping Machines, with only a very small portion still tied by hand. *Second,* introduction of Signode Strapping Machines made it practicable to use a ram type tractor rather than the platform tractor operated by job here in dispute, to convey the bundles either to storage or shipping areas. A new ram tractor

was acquired and put into operation moving the bundles away after processing through the Signode Strapping Machines.

4. There is no protest here against removal of this work from the Tractor Operator job here involved. This change in working procedure drastically reduced the amount of platform tractor work required on certain shifts; perhaps by as much as 50%.

5. Under the notice of job change (dated January 29, 1954, but issued June 11, 1954) the additional work of bundling coarse wire on the bundling benches was included in duties of the platform Tractor Operator position. This produced a change in classification of .5 but not in job class. In making this move the Company was influenced by the fact the Tractor Operators were experienced in bundling, since the normal progression was from Bundling to Tractor Operator.

6. The only issue raised in the grievance is whether Management is precluded under Section 9-D from adding these new duties to the Tractor Operator job. There is no claim under Section 2-B.

7. In view of earlier decisions of the Board, as in Case CI-257, USC-418, and T-291, it is clear that the present grievance cannot be sustained.

AWARD

8. The grievance is denied.

T—261. Ensley Works. March 31, 1954

Herbert L. Sherman, Jr., *Arbitrator*

Approved by Sylvester Garrett, *Chairman*

BACKGROUND

1. The Union contends in this grievance that the Company has improperly combined the jobs of Greaser and Car Repairman at the Ensley Works. The basis for this complaint rests in Management's proposed action of requiring both jobs to oil and grease both narrow gauge and standard gauge rolling stock if necessary. Prior to August, 1952, the Greaser job, in job class 4, was only required to oil, grease and inspect narrow gauge rolling stock, while the Car Repairman job, in job class 5, was required to oil, grease and inspect standard gauge rolling stock. The reason for the higher job class for the Car Repairman job is found in the additional duty of replacing bearings and springs on charging pan cars and ladle trucks.

2. In August of 1952, grievants understood Superintendent Stone of the Open Hearth to tell them that the Greasers would be subject to call to perform the duties of the Car Repairman and that the Car Repair-

man would be subject to the requirement of performing the Greaser's duties. The Company asserts, however, that it never contemplated that the Greasers would be required to replace bearings and springs on charging pan cars and ladle trucks, but that it only intended to extend the duty of oiling and greasing narrow gauge rolling stock to standard gauge rolling stock and vice versa. Grievants admitted in their testimony that Superintendent Stone did not state expressly that the Greasers were to replace bearings and springs. The proposed revisions of the job descriptions did not indicate that the Greasers are to be required to perform this duty. And, according to the Union testimony, no Greaser has yet been required to perform this duty. In fact, it is agreed that there are no appreciable changes in the duties which would warrant a change in classification.

3. The Union relies on the fact that Management has not changed the job content

one full job class or more, the jobs have not been unoccupied for one year, and the classifications have not been changed by mutual agreement. Since, the Union says, there has been no change to warrant the Company action, Managemnt has violated Section 9-D of the Agreement by combining these two jobs. The Union also argues that the continued existence of these two jobs at separate rates of pay is assured as a local working condition protected by Section 2-B of the Agreement.

4. On the other hand, the Company denies a combination of the two jobs as alleged by the Union. It asserts further that its realignment of some of the duties was due to the cumulative effect of certain improvements, such as installation of roller bearings to replace brass bearings and the relocation of bearings and journals from positions adjacent to the inner side of the wheels to the outer side of the wheels. The Company estimates that oil or grease is applied to brass bearings once or twice a week while it is applied to roller bearings once or twice every sixty days. According to Management the net effect of the various changes resulted in a considerable reduction of the time required for oiling and greasing. The interchange of the oiling and greasing duties was therefore proposed, including the assignment of the Car Repairman for part of his turn to the Mold Yard where he receives his regular rate for cleaning up and tightening bolts. Even under the original job description the Car Repairman is required to tighten draw head bolts.

FINDINGS

5. The Board finds that the job of Greaser and the job of Car Repairman still exist as two separate jobs with different rates of pay. The duty of replacing springs and bearings was the most distinguishing feature between the two jobs when they were classified. It continues to distinguish the two jobs under the Company's proposed extension of the oiling and greasing duties. Incidentally, no Greaser has yet been assigned in fact to oil or grease standard gauge rolling stock and no Car Repairman has been assigned to oil or grease narrow gauge rolling stock.

6. There has been no reduction in either the number of Greasers or the number of Car Repairmen, but at most only a realignment of some of the duties which require the same skills and responsibilities. In accordance with the previous holdings of the Board, it cannot be found that the Company's action in this case constitutes a violation of Section 9-D or Section 2-B of the Agreement. Since the grievance as originally filed requested a new job description and classification, it appears that a misunderstanding had arisen as to the true extent of the changes proposed by the Company.

AWARD

7. The grievance is denied.

T—291. Fairfield Tin Mill. December 23, 1954
Sylvester Garrett, *Chairman*

BACKGROUND

1. In this grievance men in the job of Production Checker "A" (present title "Loading Checker") in Fairfield Tin Mill protest change in their job duties.

2. In December, 1950, the primary function of Production Checker "A" was "to check each bundle of tin, terne, ferrostan, and black plate packed." At the same time the primary function of the job of Car Rechecker (Warehouse and Shipping Dock) was "to be personally responsible for correctness of all tin plate and by-products loaded, and exercise authority in releasing cars for shipment, or replacing packages in cars, that are incorrect." The Car Rechecker job was in Class 9, whereas Production Checker "A" was in Class 11.

3. Both jobs are in the Comptroller's Department under the immediate direction of Head Stock and Production Clerk Fleet. When they originally were described and classified in 1946, shipments of tin plate and related products were made by rail and the primary function of the Car Rechecker job was performed in connection with such rail shipments. By 1950, however, shipments by motor truck were not unusual, and in June, 1950 the Company revised the Car Rechecker description to include specific references to truck shipments. At that time and over the ensuing six months substantially all releasing of trucks for shipment was handled by men in the Car Rechecker job.

4. In December of 1950 a railroad strike of six days duration resulted in great expansion of the number of shipments by truck. As a result, men in the Production Checker job, particularly on the 3 p.m. to 11 shift, were directed by the Company to check truck shipments. On December 21, 1950, a grievance was filed by the Production Checkers protesting "the responsibility being placed on us by Management of checking plate be-

ing shipped by trucks." This grievance (No. 155-858) was processed through the 4th Step but not appealed to arbitration.

5.   Since the present grievance on behalf of the Production Checkers not only is signed by three of the original grievants in 155-858 but also presents the same substantive issue, the Company believes that its consideration is barred by failure to appeal in Case 155-858. The Union stresses, however, that in January, 1951, all trucks were barred from entering the plant after 2 p.m. with the result that there was no occasion to utilize the services of Production Checkers on the 3 p.m. to 11 turn for checking plate shipments by truck. Since Car Recheckers are scheduled on the 7 to 3 turn there was no necessity for utilizing Production Checkers for truck shipments during such turn.

6.   The prohibition of trucks entering the plant was continued until October, 1952. Thereafter truck shipments apparently were resumed to a small extent on the 3 p.m. to 11 turn and Production Checkers were directed to handle the checking of plates for truck shipments occasionally.

7.   In June, 1953, the Company presented to the Union an exhibit "G" including changes in the description for Production Checker "A" and specifying as item 10 of the revised working procedure, "Checks plate loaded on trucks for shipment and prepares proper reports as required." This form "G" precipitated the present grievance which in effect asserts that no such duty can be added to the Production Checker job description since the duty falls within the statement of the primary function of the Car Rechecker position. Apparently the Union believes that if any checking of plate shipments by truck is to be carried on during the 3 p.m. to 11 turn a man in the Car Rechecker job (Class 9) must be called out for the purpose instead of having it done by a man in a Class 11 job.

FINDINGS

8.   For various reasons which need not be detailed here, it is doubtful whether the failure to appeal from the 4th Step in grievance 155-858 would bar consideration of the merits of the issue presented in the present case.

9.   But the present grievance must be denied on the merits. It presents a broad claim that no duty involving checking of plate shipments by truck can be included in the description of the Production Checker position. This apparently is on the basis that no duty encompassed in the principal function of one job description ever can be assigned to employees in another job.

10.   There is nothing in the Agreement which supports this argument, nor can it be reconciled with the fact that many jobs covered in the Inequity Program have overlapping duties. It would be extremely difficult —if not impossible—to run the business efficiently if this were not recognized. Management authority to change job requirements in order to meet legitimate needs of the business, moreover, is recognized in Cases CI-257, USC-481, and USC-417-420, among others.

11.   There appears to be no legitimate basis for a claim that the volume of checking of plate shipments by truck on the 3 p.m. turn is such to warrant assignment of a Car Rechecker in Job Class 9. From January 1, 1954, to October 1, 1954, only 7 trucks were loaded after 4 p.m. During the same period shipments of plate by truck checked by Production Checkers on the day turn, rather than Car Recheckers, totaled 11. The total number of truck shipments over the same period was 1,386. Head Production Clerk Fleet agreed that if a substantial volume of truck shipments developed on the 3 p.m. to 11 turn a Car Rechecker should be assigned to handle such work.

12.   Hence no reason appears why the Company is not entitled to change the description of Production Checker "A" in such manner as to reflect *actual requirements* of the job as to checking plate shipped by truck. The Board has no occasion to pass on whether the revision embodied in exhibit "G" *accurately reflects the nature and extent of the duty* which Management has assigned to the Production Checkers in this regard. This is a matter for the parties. All that is decided here is that Management is not barred from assigning such duty to Production Checkers.

AWARD

13.   The grievance is denied.

T—375. Fairfield Steel Works. May 17, 1956
Herbert L. Sherman, Jr., *Arbitrator*
Approved by Sylvester Garrett, *Chairman*

FINDINGS

1. In this grievance, the Union protests, under Sections 2-B and 9-D of the July 1, 1954 Agreement, the requirement that the incumbent of the Tire Repairman job, in the Motor Transportation Department of Fairfield Steel Works, perform work on Saturdays not listed in his job description. No change in classification of the job is sought.

2. For many years prior to July 9, 1954, an Automotive Serviceman was scheduled on the day shift Monday through Friday and a Tire Repairman was scheduled Tuesday through Saturday. On Monday a Relief Man was scheduled as a Tire Repairman and on Saturday as an Automotive Serviceman. Both jobs are in Job Class 5. On July 9, 1954, the Relief Man was removed, an Automotive Serviceman having previously been added Monday through Friday on the 3-11 turn. The removal of the Relief Man was protested by grievant in a prior grievance. It was settled in the Third Step by an agreement that the Tire Repairman would be given help whenever needed while working with large tires.

3. Originally, the present grievance, filed on March 11, 1955, sought relief for three men on the ground that they were being required to work outside their job descriptions. In the Fourth Step, the Union amended the grievance to eliminate Automotive Servicemen Larkin and Harris because their job description specifically listed "Changes and repairs tires." But grievant Davis, Tire Repairman, continued to protest the assignment of certain duties on Saturdays, such as greasing and changing oil (listed in the Automotive Serviceman job description), since these duties are not also listed in his job description.

4. Whether the Tire Repairman was always required to perform occasional greasing work is disputed. In any event, neither Section 2-B or Section 9-D precludes assignment of additional duties to a job. Previous Awards of the Board cited by the Union are not on point. And finally, any issue as to the necessity for Management to schedule an Automotive Serviceman on Saturdays must be considered as having been settled in the prior grievance.

AWARD

5. The grievance is denied.

A—658, -659. Worcester Works. March 31, 1954
Donald A. Crawford, *Special Assistant to the Chairman*
Approved by Sylvester Garrett, *Chairman*

BACKGROUND

1. These grievances are combined because they present aspects of one action. The Company reassigned the rereeling and inspection of a product from a class 11 job to a class 9 job. The Union questions the Company's right to make the transfer and the rate of pay applied to the transferred work.

2. RR (rubber over rubber) cable of certain sizes had been processed for many years by James Moen, one grievant and the regular inspector in the rubber braiding department. Rejections on inspection of this single conductor cable had been running as high as 30%. Product improvements had failed to solve the problem, and so the product was transferred to the repairman, class 9, in the rubber insulating department. The thinking was that the coiled cable, after vulcanizing, stood too long while hot before rereeling. This delay caused cross-overs and other defects. To prevent this delay and incidentally to lower transportation costs, Management in January, 1953, rerouted the product to the coilers downstairs and adjacent to the vulcanizer, which were operated by the repairmen.

3. In the unit downstairs, there were three coiling machines operated on a two or three turn basis, making available six or nine turns per day. Upstairs, a very large part of the time, there was the one coiling machine being operated by Moen on the day turn. Therefore, less turns per day were available upstairs and a delay (often several days) occurred between vulcanizing and rereeling. As a result of the elimination of the delay and better quality control, because the Foreman of the rubber insulating department could know the condition of the product before it left his department, rejections dropped to 5% (trs. pp. 22-24).

4. Before the rerouting of the work flow, Moen had spent about 70% of his time processing RR cable. There were three ma-

chines in the rubber braiding department, but for many years Moen had been the only one regularly performing the inspector job. Moen said that for a period prior to the change, there were two men, including himself, working on RR cable, and one man on navy cable. Since the change, Moen has been the only inspector and at times he has had to bid for work in the labor pool, sometimes being off altogether and sometimes doing lower paid work (trs. pp. 2-7).

5. Repairman Walsh, another grievant, said that repairmen were not required to run RR cable before the change, although they did run other single conductor cable; that now he was spending two-thirds of his time working RR cable; that a third shift has been added; that the task is performed in the same manner as it was performed by Moen; that it requires slower operation, fussier work, hand inspection without gloves, completing a preliminary inspection tag, and involves the only hot cable run (trs. pp. 9-15).

6. The Union contends that the Company, in transferring the assignment of RR cable from the inspector job to the repairman job, violated Sections 2-B and 9-D. The managerial function specified in Section 3 is limited by Section 2-B. The assignment required 70% of the inspector's time, existed for many years, was a specific practice in the rubber braiding department, was a detailed application of subject matter within the scope of "other conditions of employment" (work assignments are usually as important as wages paid), and provided benefits to both the inspector and repairman.

7. The Union distinguishes the general practice in the cable works of assignment and reassignment of products to machines and jobs and departments from this specific departmental practice. Here, the Union cites Case G-8 where Chairman Seward sustained a 2-B-3 practice of a paid lunch period for a few employees in spite of a general plant practice of unpaid lunch periods. The Union argues that 2-B-4 is not applicable since there was no change in equipment or process. Reasons of economy and efficiency are not sufficient. As the Board said in USC-278, "Section 2-B-4 does not authorize a change in established local working conditions solely on the basis of considerations of relative cost."

8. Case CI-238, the Union says, is the only decision dealing with the application of Section 2-B to changes in job content and work assignment made by Management, and sustains the Union position. All but three of the Company citations are decisions of ad hoc arbitrators and made prior to CI-238. CI-257, A-461, and A-464, decided later, are not in point. But the dicta of CI-257 (a 2-B-4 case) does say, "Section 9-D includes language which confirms that Management has retained discretion to vary job assignments and duties as the legitimate needs of the business dictate, and except as other provisions of Agreement in a given case may operate to limit such discretion." Clearly, the Board recognizes that the right to change assignments may be limited by Section 2-B.

9. As regards Section 9-D, the Union contends that the assignment of RR cable belonged to the inspector job alone at the time the job descriptions and classifications were made, and the parties recognized this fact. Section 9-D established a classified rate structure and did not intend a subsequent dissecting of higher class jobs by transfer of substantial tasks to lower class jobs. This rule is especially pertinent in this case, because the repairman job was created by an agreement deskilling the patcher job (class 13) to make the cold patcher or repairman job (trs. pp. 45, 46).

10. The Board held in TCI-232 that Section 9-D does not permit the Company to terminate a job by merely assigning incumbents to a lower rate of pay under a different job title while they continue to perform the same duties with only minor changes. The Union adds, that the inspector job is now performed only by Moen, and he has been forced to take lower rated work because 70% of his job is gone.

11. The Union concedes that the Company has the right to change job content. But in this case, where only efficiency and cost are involved, the delay which caused the rejections could have been solved by applying inspectors on a three shift basis on the two machines in the rubber braiding department that can process RR cable.

12. The Union concludes that if the Company wants repairmen to perform 70% of the inspector's job, the Company is required to pay them the higher rate.

13. The Company position may be summarized as follows:

14. (1.) Regardless of the effect, if any, on the job content of the repairman job, nothing in Section 9-D prohibited the Company from assigning to repairmen the task of rereeling and inspecting RR cable; and, in any event, the Company's determination that this task was covered by the repairman job description was neither challenged in the grievance procedure nor shown to be incorrect at the hearing.

Section 9-D of the Agreement and Section B-5 of the January 1, 1953, Manual recognize Management's right to change job content at its discretion. This principle has been determined by the Board in CI-257, USC-327, 329, N-187 and A-453, 4.

Since the Company has the right to add duties not presently in the job description, it has the lesser included right of requiring performance of duties within the job description, but not previously performed. This principle has been sustained in such awards as A-369 and A-322 and applies directly to this case.

The record demonstrates that there was no change in job content of the repairman job. The claim was not made in grievance meetings, and both step 3 and 4 minutes contain Union admissions that the task is part of the repairman job as described. The Union claim of change in job content made at the hearing was unsupported and came too late. The Board cannot now determine the question of change in job content (T-3).

The Union suggestion that repairmen be paid class 11 when processing RR cable overlooks the fact that processing RR cable is a task of both jobs. Even if it were not, performance of one task does not constitute performance of the job (G-22, CI-252).

15.   (2.) No limiting practices with respect to the assignment of products to particular jobs or equipments or departments has been established as a fact.

The record shows, through the testimony of Mr. Nicholson, division superintendent of the cable works, that the assignment or reassignment of products in the cable works is customary (trs. pp. 25-45). This general practice with respect to transfer of products to machines, jobs, and departments embraces the assignment of RR cable.

16.   (3.) The alleged practice, even if established as a fact, could not constitute a local working condition under Section 2-B.

Section 3 as well as Section 2-B must be given reasonable effect. The Union theory would eliminate Management authority to direct the working forces in the important area of assignment of job duties. Neither Section 9-D nor Section 2-B provide for the freezing of job assignments (CI-22, A-322, A-369, A-443, A-480, CI-257, A-461, A-464).

CI-238, relied upon by the Union, is inconsistent with the general rule, was decided by an ad hoc chairman before CI-257, and involved a craft job. T-232 found simply that the job had not been terminated in spite of the Company's claim. The ruling is irrelevant to this case which involves the right to change job content.

Moreover, the exercise by Management of its discretion in a consistent way over a period of time does not result in a binding practice under Section 2-B-3. The Company

may exercise its discretion in a different way thereafter (COL-11, 19).

FINDINGS

17.   (1.) *The basic problem in this case arises from the fact that both job descriptions appear to cover substantially the same duties, but are classified at different rates of pay. The primary function of each job as stated in the description is almost identical.*

The inspector job description says the primary function is: "To operate equipment for measuring, sparking and inspecting insulated wire." The repairman description reads: "To measure, inspect, spark and repair (unvulcanized patch) single conductors without braided, wound or knitted coverings, sizes 2 and smaller, also to braze solid or wire strand ranging in sizes 10 and smaller." (Co. Ex. A and B)

The apparent difference in the two jobs on the face of the description is that the repairman job requires some brazing and patching not required on the inspector job. The patching consists of cutting out the bad section, and wrapping self-vulcanizing tape around the bared wire level with the insulated wire.

The equipment and tools used, as listed, are essentially the same, as are the materials. The working procedure is substantially the same, except for the repair and brazing task.

The Company says that, "Even a casual examination of the respective job descriptions will disclose a marked similarity between the two jobs. Both require essentially that electrical conductor cable should be rereeled, inspected and spark tested, measured and cut. Both jobs encompassed the performance of substantially similar tasks on substantially similar products. The reasons for the difference in job classes does not appear from the record and is, in any event, immaterial since these respective job descriptions and classifications have been agreed upon by the parties. (Co. Post-Hearing Brief, p. 3.)

The Company did point out that on each job various products are run, and that identical functions are not always performed with respect to each product. The repairman sometimes cold patches and brazes the products. The inspector performs a very minute visual inspection when lacquer finished wire is run (trs. pp. 20, 21).

It is true, as the Company says, that the inspector processes other wire, but the function and duties in this connection are not essentially different from the inspection of RR cable. The Company's reference to minute visual inspection of lacquer finished cable is not significant. The task hardly could be considered as a duty distinct from the hand and visual inspection performed on RR cable. The use of microscopes or glasses is not involved. In short, the differences in product do not create significant differences in duty on the inspector job.

On the other hand, judging from the testimony of Walsh, the inspection of RR cable entails different work elements (or degrees thereof) than required for the work normally done by repairmen over the years.

18. (2.) *The processing of RR cable requires payment of the inspector rate.*

The Company contends that processing RR cable is merely one of the tasks of both jobs; that even if the task were not part of the repairman job, its performance would not entitle repairman to the inspector rate. Performance of one task of a job does not constitute performance of that job. To be entitled to the rate of a job, an employee must show that he is required to "regularly perform the substance of the duties" of that job (G-22).

The rule is sound. As applied to this case, however, it supports the Union case, since the repairmen working RR cables in fact are required to "regularly perform the substance of the duties" of the inspector job. The duties involved in rereeling, measuring, sparking and inspecting RR cable are the *substance of the inspector job quantitatively and qualitatively*. The measuring, sparking and inspection of other insulated wire by an inspector does not involve duties significantly different (when they differ at all). The bare transfer of the product from one machine to another cannot transform duties of an inspector job into duties of a repairman job. Historically, the parties have treated the job as two separate jobs, and the measuring, sparking and inspecting of RR cable as part of the inspector job. The presumption is for maintenance of the status quo, particularly where the evidence confirms, in the testimony of Walsh, that a sufficient difference exists between RR cable inspection and repairman work to warrant the original separate description and classification.

19. As Chairman Garrett said in Case T-230 in denying a Union demand that the grievant be relieved of duties going beyond the precise language of the job description:

20. "He has performed substantially these duties during most of his 12 years of service in his present job . . ."

21. "It is not uncommon, of course, that the parties fail to achieve perfection in describing the duties of a job. While this may give rise to troublesome problems for the parties, the Board is not authorized under the Basic Agreement to disturb the situation when it is clear that *the job actually is being performed in the same manner as it was when described and classified. The Board has no standing to attempt to improve upon the results achieved* by the parties under their Inequities Program."

22. Even though the jobs appear to be essentially the same, the separate treatment afforded them by the parties under the Inequities Program must be preserved. In Case G-22 the Board held that it was without authority to revise vague and overlapping job descriptions. Nor can the Company in effect disregard an agreed description and classification. In many cases the vague or overlapping nature of descriptions can be clarified only by reference to the actual operating conditions when the job was described and classified. The Company cannot now treat the inspector job as a repairman job by a mere transfer of the great bulk of the inspector work to men in another job class.

23. In view of the finding, the Union's argument over the application of Section 2-B as a limitation on the Company's right to change job content and work assignments is irrelevant. Even though Management may change job assignments, the specific work is still considered to constitute the essence of the inspector job no matter where it is performed. There is no change in job content or job classification.

24. Obviously, the repairmen concerned in grievance #1168 are entitled to the retroactive pay they claim for performing the inspector job. The claim of inspector Moen in grievance #1167 has been satisfied in the sense that the finding determines that the work performed is work which was rated by the parties as the essence of the inspector job. If Moen has suffered loss of pay because of the performance of the inspector job in the rubber insulating department, in violation of any applicable seniority rights, he is entitled to compensation for such loss. No ruling is made on this point since the seniority phase was not explored at the hearing.

AWARD

25. Grievance #1168 is sustained. The Company shall pay the inspector rate retroactively to repairman for time spent in performing the inspector job.

26. Grievance #1167 is sustained in the sense that the decision holds that the disputed work scheduled for job class 9 in the rubber insulating department is, in fact, work which calls for the rate of the class 11, inspector, job. If the grievant has sustained loss because of the performance of this work by other men, and the assignment of other men to the inspector work violated his sen-

iority rights, the Company shall pay him for such loss. This is a matter to be determined by the parties in light of this Award and any seniority rules which may be applicable.

A—799. Cyclone Waukegan Works. June 26, 1958
Sylvester Garrett, *Arbitrator*

BACKGROUND

1. This grievance from the Assembly Department of Cyclone Waukegan Works asserts that Management violated Section 9-D of the August 3, 1956 Agreement when it reassigned work previously performed by a Threading Machine Operator.

2. The dispute involves threading of rods, which has been done at various times over the years by three jobs: (1) Factory Gate Assembler (Web Tier), Class 6; (2) Factory Gate Fabricator, Class 6; and (3) Threading Machine Operator, Class 5. For convenience the three jobs, respectively, are referred to as Fabricator, Assembler, and Operator.

3. The Fabricator and Assembler jobs long have existed at Cyclone Waukegan Works, and were placed in Class 6 under the Inequities Program. The Fabricator primarily assembles framework for gates, using pipe and fittings, and the Assembler essentially fastens the mesh or web to the assembled frame. About 90% of the gates produced are in standard sizes, and the rest are made to customer specifications.

4. A part of the gate assembly consists of truss rods to add rigidity to the frame. The truss rods are threaded at one or both ends.

5. Until 1947, all truss rods were purchased in random lengths, with necessary cutting and threading done, for the most part, by Assemblers. In 1947 the Company started to buy rods precut to standard lengths, so that truss rods for standard size gates thereafter required only threading. A new job of Threading Machine Operator was established in Class 5 on February 28, 1947 as a single-purpose job to thread most standard size truss rods, leaving the Fabricators and Assemblers more time for assembly work.

6. In 1950, equipment and method changes affected the Fabricator and Assembler jobs. These included installation of new equipment to cut and thread truss rods at the Fabricators' work station. The placing of truss rods in gate frames thereafter was assigned to Fabricators rather than Assemblers, and cutting and threading of non-standard truss rods was taken over by the Fabricators.

7. In November, 1950, a new incentive was installed for Assemblers. A new incentive for Fabricators was installed November, 1956, including standards for cutting and threading non-standard truss rods, performed by Fabricators since 1950.

8. Between 1947 and November, 1956, the Threading Machine Operator job was filled on day shift, while Fabricators and Assemblers worked two or three shifts per day as needed. Even on day turn the Operator job was not always filled on a full-time basis. For ten consecutive months in 1954-1955, no one was assigned as Operator. In many pay periods between 1955 and early 1957 the Operator worked less than 40 hours per week. Because of this situation an understanding was reached by the Grievance Committeeman and Foreman that when the Operator job was filled as much as 20 hours per week, it would be posted and filled under the seniority provisions of the Agreement. For some time prior to November, 1956, and into early 1957, the Operator job was filled in accordance with this understanding.

9. Early in 1957, the number of hours worked by the Operator dropped substantially. For example, in the pay period ending January 26, 1957 the job was filled 5 hours; in the period ending February 9, 5 hours; in the period ending February 23, 8 hours; and in the period ending March 23, 3 hours. By April, 1957, the Company had concluded that it would be more efficient for the Fabricators to thread all rods, both standard and non-standard lengths. A Form G, spelling out operation of the threading machine in the duties of Fabricators, was presented to the Grievance Committee on April 15. The latter, however, protested because there had been layoffs and he did not believe that the Union should give up any jobs. In view of this protest, and since threading had been done by Fabricators since 1950, the Form G was withdrawn the next day. The Fabricator incentive was modified about this time so as to include standards for threading rods, only, since the existing standards covered both cutting and threading by Fabricators and would be too loose for application to any substantial amount of standard rod threading.

10. While the Operator job has not been terminated, it has been filled for only a few hours since April 15, 1957, in threading a special lot of bolts for another department.

11. The Union asserts that the Company,

in substance if not in form, has terminated the Threading Machine Operator job. Under the decisions in Cases G-56 and T-232, it urges that the Company has violated Section 9-D, and holds that the Company should be directed to reassign threading of standard length rods to the Operator job. Alternatively, the Union suggests that principles outlined in Cases A-658 and -659 are applicable if the job is not deemed terminated for purposes of Section 9-D.

12. The Company feels that the case turns on interpretation and application of Section 9-D, citing decisions in Cases CI-257, N-187, A-463-464, USC-418 and N-210.

A—686. Joliet Works. December 23, 1954

Sylvester Garrett, *Chairman*

BACKGROUND

1. This grievance, on behalf of Crane Hookers, protests that no Crane Hooker was called out to work on each of four special turns in the Roll Shop of Joliet Works on October 24 and 31, 1953, where only extra roll necking work was done.

2. At this time the Roll Shop was operating 15 turns per week, manned as follows:

Job Assignment	TURN ASSIGNMENT		
	7-3	3-11	11-7
Operators [1]	13	12	3
Template Maker	1	–	–
Bearing Repairman	1	–	–
Roll Builder Helper (Bearings)	2	–	–
Roll Builder	1	1	1
Roll Builder Helpers	3	3	3
Craneman	1	1	1
Crane Hooker	1	1	–
Total	23	18	8

[1] Operators include Roll Turners, Roll Turner Apprentices, and Roll Turner Trainees.

3. The following equipment operated on these turns normally:

Equipment	TURN ASSIGNMENT		
	7-3	3-11	11-7
Conventional Lathes	5	5	–
Profile Lathes	1	1	1
Engine Lathes	2	2	2
Merchant Mill Lathe	1	1	–
Belt Driven Lathes	2	1	–
Grinders	2	2	–
Total	13	12	3

FINDINGS

13. While threading standard size rods now is done by Fabricators in Class 6, the Union believes this work should be done by Operators in Class 5, so as to protect the integrity of the rate structure.

14. Since Fabricators have threaded rods commencing as far back as 1950, and in light of earlier decisions of the Board dealing with like problems, there is no basis to sustain this grievance.

AWARD

15. The grievance is denied.

4. On the four extra turns (2 each on October 24 and 31) only a Profile Lathe and 2 Engine Lathes were operated. On the 7-3 turn on each of these days 5 men were called out, including 3 Operators, a Template Maker and a Craneman. On the 3-11 turn 4 employees were called out, including 3 Operators and a Craneman.

5. Since no Crane Hooker was present on the four extra roll necking turns, the Operators performed whatever hooking was required in connection with their work. No other crane hooking was performed.

6. The Union sees violation of Section 2-B-3 in the failure to use a Crane Hooker on each of the four extra roll necking turns. It believes that a Crane Hooker should have been called out to perform crane hooking on these turns because the primary function of the Crane Hooker job in the Roll Shop provides "To follow the crane and render all necessary service from the floor (Assists over entire department)." The Union believes that this language (and particularly the "all necessary service") establishes that no crane hooking shall be performed in the Roll Shop save by Crane Hookers.

FINDINGS

7. Section 2-B-3 does not apply here since the four turns in question were special roll necking turns. Any local working condition as to crew size for regular turns would not apply for reasons spelled out in Cases USC-327, USC-329, A-653 and A-654.

8. Nor does the stated primary function of the Crane Hooker require that all crane hooking in the Roll Shop be performed only by Crane Hookers. Job descriptions, standing alone, do not constitute agreements that certain types of work will be performed only by men assigned to given jobs. Actu-

ally, the job description of Roll Turner here, in four places, refers to occasional crane hooking by the Roll Turner. The job description for Roll Necker also includes clear reference to crane hooking by Roll Neckers. Under the regular manning arrangement during normal 15 turn operations, no Crane Hooker was scheduled on the 11 p.m. to 7 a.m. turn. Hence it is clear that some crane hooking has been per-formed by Operators in the Roll Shop over the years. Under the evidence presented, moreover, the nature and amount of crane hooking on the four disputed turns did not differ materially from that normally involved on the 11 p.m. to 7 a.m. turn.

AWARD

9.   The grievance is denied.

USC—873.   Fairless Works.   September 30, 1959
Sylvester Garrett, *Chairman*

BACKGROUND

1.   This grievance on behalf of Stockers (Hot Strip Finishing) (Class 10) in the Hot Strip Finishing unit, Cold Reduction and Sheet Finishing Department, Fairless Works, asserts that Management cannot, under the Agreement, assign the duty of inspecting hot rolled ship coils to Stockers.

2.   From 1952 until July, 1957, the responsibility for making sure that hot rolled ship coils were of proper gauge, and for marking individual coils as to whether conditioning was required to meet customer specifications, was assigned at various times to different groups of employees (both supervisory and non-supervisory) in the Operating and Metallurgical Departments. Also, the method of inspecting hot rolled ship coils by Metallurgical Inspectors from time to time had varied (and still does) from an individual coil basis to a spot-check basis.

3.   Beginning about April, 1957, customer complaints, particularly as to off-gauge coils, became frequent enough to require reconsideration of the inspection process. By July, 1957, Management concluded that having the Stockers make an individual coil for coil inspection, supplemented with spot checks by Metallurgical Inspectors and Supervision of both the Operating and Metallurgical Departments, would best insure the desired results. On July 19, 1957, a Form G was prepared for the Stocker job, reflecting a net change of .7 of a job class, due to the additional inspection duties. The Form G was submitted to the Union, which then filed Grievance A-57-198, contending that the classification of Stocker should have been increased from Class 10 to Class 13. On November 25, 1957, Grievance A-57-198 was remanded from Third Step to Second, where it was withdrawn.

4.   The present grievance was filed June 30, 1958 and reflects a contention that Sections 1 and 9 of the August 3, 1956 Agreement prevent Management from adding an inspection function to the Stocker job, because this type of work previously was performed by Metallurgical Inspection personnel. Although Metallurgical Inspectors continue to perform the same type of inspection—sometimes a spot check and sometimes coil by coil—the Union seems to believe *all* inspection should be done by Metallurgical Inspectors.

FINDINGS

5.   There have been many cases (such as CI-257 and USC-418) where the Board has observed that nothing in the Agreement precludes Management from changing the assignment of duties among position-rated jobs. This case involves only a protest that Management is not entitled to take such action. The classification problem has been dealt with in the earlier grievance and is not before the Board. There is nothing in the facts to support the view that Management was not entitled to add the inspection duty to the Stocker job.

AWARD

6.   The grievance is denied.

T—362.   Ensley Steel Works.   December 23, 1955
Sylvester Garrett, *Chairman*

BACKGROUND

1.   In this grievance Ingot Tracers in the Open Hearth Department of Ensley Steel Works protest being required to perform the duties of Test Carrier.

2.   The Open Hearth at Ensley includes a No. 1 Shop with 5 furnaces and a No. 2 Shop with 4 furnaces. The two Shops are separated by the Converting Department.

3.   Between 1940 and 1954 one Ingot Tracer has been scheduled per turn with one

Test Carrier, servicing both Shops. On September 26, 1954, No. 2 Open Hearth Shop was shut down temporarily and No. 1 continued to operate with 4 furnaces. Three days later a fifth furnace was put in operation in No. 1.

4. With the Ingot Tracer's duties thus confined to No. 1 Shop, the Company discontinued scheduling a Test Carrier and assigned test carrying to the Ingot Tracer. The arrangement was continued thereafter at 5 furnace level of operations.

5. The primary function of Ingot Tracer is "to keep various records on heats, ladles, slag pots, skull and rubbish, etc., and to check test reports and forward to laboratory." The primary function of Test Carrier is "to carry tests to laboratory." The coding of the two jobs is as follows:

Factor	Ingot Tracer	Test Carrier
1. Pre-employment Training	B-0.3	A-Base
2. Employment Training and Experience	C-0.8	A-Base
3. Mental Skill	C-1.6	A-Base
4. Manual Skill	A-Base	A-Base
5. Responsibility for Material	D-1.6	A-Base
6. Responsibility for Tools and Equipment	A-Base	A-Base
7. Responsibility for Operation	D-2.0	A-Base
8. Responsibility for Safety of Others	A-Base	B-0.4
9. Mental Effort	D-1.5	A-Base
10. Physical Effort	B-0.3	C-0.8
11. Surroundings	C-0.8	B-0.4
12. Hazard	C-0.8	B-0.4
Totals:	9.7	2.0

6. The above codings differ under all Factors save two, and Test Carrier is coded higher than Ingot Tracer in Factors 8 and 10.

7. The Company contends that test carrying always has been an inherent part of the Ingot Tracer job. Superintendent Stone testified that he carried tests when he served as Ingot Tracer in 1932 and 1933 during three-furnace operation. When operations were reduced from March 4, 1940 to June 24, 1940, the Ingot Tracers also carried tests. Between June 25, 1940 and May 14, 1954 more than 5 furnaces operated continuously, except during strike periods.

8. When the job was described and classified in 1946, operations were, and long had been, above the 5 furnace level. The

Ingot Tracer Plant Title states "Ingot Tracer (4 or more furnaces)." This the Company explains on the ground that there was an incentive plan in effect at the time (terminated in 1950) providing a lower base rate for Ingot Tracer when 3 or less furnaces were operating. The Company at this time maintained a separate job description for Ingot Tracer at the lower level of operations, rating it seven cents per hour lower than Ingot Tracer at 4 or more furnace operations.

9. This separate description specifically included the test carrying duty. The parties never described or classified a lower rated job of Ingot Tracer at 3 furnace or less level of operations. In the Review Program of 1951 there was no change in title or description of Ingot Tracer, although apparently the classification was raised.

10. During a period from May 16, 1954 through June 5, 1954 when 5 furnaces only were operated (in the No. 1 Shop) a grievance was filed on behalf of Test Carriers protesting the failure to schedule them. The grievance was dropped because of a seniority issue.

11. During Third Step here the Grievance Committee asserted that the Company had failed to comply with Section F of the January 1, 1953 Job Description and Classification Manual. In response, the Company held that carrying tests was an inherent part of the job of Ingot Tracer.

FINDINGS

12. Test carrying is not an inherent function of Ingot Tracer. When the job was described and classified Ingot Tracers had not carried tests for more than six years. The language of Item 8 of Working Procedure of Ingot Tracer precludes a finding that test carrying is part of the job of Ingot Tracer. The brief period of reduced operations in 1940, when tests were carried, is too remote and inconclusive to establish a practice significant enough to show that the parties understood that carrying to be an inherent part of the Ingot Tracer job.

13. Evidence that the Company maintained a separate job description and rate for Ingot Tracer at 3 furnace or less level of operations seems to confirm this conclusion. The Union was not party to this description and classification, which was not adopted under the Inequity Program.

14. There was no proper occasion for the Company to assign test carrying to the Ingot Tracers, yet hold that this constituted no change in job content of Ingot Tracer. This is not to say that there may not be proper occasion for the Company to assign

test carrying to Ingot Tracers in order to meet changed conditions which arise in the future. There is no occasion for the Board to express an opinion on any such issue here.

AWARD

15. The grievance is sustained to the following extent: (1) test carrying duties were added to the job of Ingot Tracer on September 26, 1954; (2) test carrying is not an inherent part of the job of Ingot Tracer, nor is now included in any part of the Test Carrier description; (3) the provisions of Section 9-D of the July 1, 1954 Agreement and Section F of the January 1, 1953 Job Description and Classification Manual are applicable; (4) failing compliance with the requirements of these Sections, the Company was not, and is not, authorized to add test carrying duties to the job of Ingot Tracer.

T—563. Ensley Steel Works. July 30, 1959
Donald A. Crawford, *Arbitrator*
Approved by Sylvester Garrett, *Chairman*

BACKGROUND

1. The Ingot Tracers in the Open Hearth Department of the Ensley Steel Works protest the combining of the Test Carrier duties with their job and the Test Carriers protest the elimination of their job.

2. The Open Hearth includes a No. 1 Shop with five furnaces and a No. 2 Shop with four furnaces, the Shops being separated by a Bessemer Converter. During periods when six furnaces or more are scheduled, the Test Carrier, Job Class 2, carries the Open Hearth samples in a bucket or wheelbarrow to the Chemical Laboratory about six to nine blocks away. One Test Carrier is scheduled per turn. The task of carrying tests when two furnaces are being tapped simultaneously, or one immediately after the other, has also been included in the job of Pit Laborer, Job Class 3.

3. There is also one Ingot Tracer assigned per turn. His job is to keep records on heats, ladles, slag pots, skull and rubbish, etc., and to check test reports and forward them to the laboratory. The Ingot Tracer job, Job Class 10, is rated as high as the Test Carrier, or higher, on all factors except as to Factor 8, Responsibility for the Safety of Others, and Factor 10, Physical Effort.

4. From January 1, 1958 to March 7, 1959 the Open Hearth Department was either shut down or operated on a five furnace and less basis. During this period the Company did not schedule a Test Carrier (Tr. 39 and seq.) and the Ingot Tracer was assigned the duty of carrying the tests. On March 3, 1958 the Company issued a Form G adding the duty "carries test pieces with report to laboratory as directed" to the Ingot Tracer job description. No change was made in classification.

5. Open Hearth Superintendent Stone testified that past periods of low operations have occurred in 1932 and 1933 and March 4, 1940 to June 24, 1940. During these periods of five furnace or less open hearth operation, he said, the Ingot Tracers carried the tests and the Test Carrier job was discontinued. From June 25, 1940 to May 14, 1954, more than five furnaces operated continuously, he said, except during strikes.

6. From May 16, 1954 to June 5, 1954, the Open Hearth again underwent a period of low operations. Again the Ingot Tracer was required to carry the tests. A grievance was filed concerning this action, and in Case T-362 the Board of Arbitration sustained the grievance, to a limited extent as will appear more fully below. Since this award, there have been high level operations until January, 1958, which brings us to the present dispute.

7. As additional background the Company submitted its unilateral job descriptions from past days. The first of these three job descriptions for Ingot Tracer is dated April 10, 1937, and states that he carries ladle tests to main laboratory. The second, dated September 21, 1929, says: "Carries test pieces to the laboratory when less than five or six furnaces are operating." The third, dated December 15, 1943, again provides: "Carries test pieces to the laboratory when less than five or six furnaces are operating."

8. When the job of Ingot Tracer was described and classified in 1946, under the mutual administration of the Inequity Program, operations were, and long had been, above the five furnace level. The Ingot Tracer plant title states: "Ingot tracer four or more furnaces." This the Company explains on the ground that there was an incentive plan in effect at the time (terminated in 1950) providing a lower base rate for Ingot Tracer when three or less furnaces were operating. The Company at this time maintained a separate job description for Ingot Tracer at the lower level of operations, rating it 7 cents per hour lower than Ingot Tracer at four or more furnace operations. This separate description specifically

included the test carrying duty. The parties, however, never described or classified a lower rated job of Ingot Tracer at three furnace or less level of operations. In the Review Program of 1951 there was no change in title or description of Ingot Tracer, although apparently the classification was raised. (See Paragraphs 8 and 9 of T-362.)

9. The Union takes the position that this grievance has been tried once before in the period of low operations just preceding that involved in this grievance, and that the Board sustained the Union in its position. The Union says that the only difference since then is that the Open Hearth is busier so that the Ingot Tracer and Test Carrier have more work to do. In addition the Company has issued a Form G. The Union says that it does not understand how the Company can hope to reverse a previous award by such a transparent maneuver as issuing a Form G. The Union cites the language of Section F of the January 1, 1953, Job Description and Classification Manual, which is incorporated by reference through Section 9-J-1 of the August 3, 1956 Basic Agreement:

"It is equally as important to maintain the job descriptions and classifications in constant adjustment to fit new or changed conditions as it is to make accurate determinations in the first instance."

10. In short, says the Union, "new or changed conditions" are the basis for an Exhibit G. Since nothing has changed since 1954, there is in fact no basis for the issuance of an Exhibit G. It adds that any change that has occurred since the parties agreed upon the classification of the Test Carrier and Ingot Tracer jobs in 1946 have increased the productivity of the furnaces so that more test carrying per furnace is now necessary.

11. The Union argues that Section 2-B, Section 9-D, and Section 13 are involved. In putting the Test Carrier's duties on the Ingot Tracer, the Union claims the Company crossed seniority lines. On this score, the Union cites decisions of Arbitrators Kendall D'Andrade (Lukens Steel Company) and Whitley P. McCoy (American Bridge Company, Roanoke, Virginia).

12. The Union emphasizes the point that the Company's unilateral job descriptions included the duty "carries test pieces to the laboratory when less than five or six furnaces are operating"; that, however, the joint job description of 1946 for Ingot Tracer does not contain the duty of carrying test pieces. Hence, reasons the Union, the Company is actually taking its own unilateral job description and putting it into effect unilaterally through an Exhibit G.

13. The Union invites the Arbitrator to find one case where an Arbitrator has allowed the Company, after failing to get an agreement from the Union, to accomplish the same end unilaterally. The Company cannot agree to a joint job description with the Union, then go back to its office and nullify the description agreed to by sitting down with a pencil and writing out unilaterally a Form G. If it can, then the Union does not have a contract with the Company.

14. As to Superintendent Stone's testimony concerning past practice, the Union points out that he gave the same testimony in the prior case, and the Board held that no significant practice existed.

15. Moreover, the Union points out through the testimony of Ingot Tracer Herman Shoppe that the job of Ingot Tracer is itself a full eight-hour job and that the addition of carrying tests has made the job literally impossible for one man to do; that as a result he has had to secure the help of his buddies or let the work be done improperly.

16. In its brief the Union cited a Board decision (USC-852) based on Section 2-B, which it said was a parallel case and decisive of the present case. As to Section 13, Seniority, the Union in response to a question from Company counsel said, "I don't intend to make much out of it, to be honest with you."

17. The Company summarizes its position as follows: that none of the grievants in this case are Test Carriers according to the Company's records; that the award in Case T-362 was based on the Company's failure to comply with Section 9-D of the Agreement and Section F of the Job Description and Classification Manual; that in this case, however, Management has, in strict compliance with Section F-3-a(1), issued an Exhibit G showing the addition of test carrying to the Ingot Tracer job; that the Company's right to add duties to a job without Union concurrence has been ruled on by the Board so many time (as evidenced by the decisions in CI-257 and T-291) that there can no longer be any question concerning it; that the Union's reliance in its brief on USC-852 cannot be supported by the facts in the instant case; that if seniority should be considered a factor in this case, the only relevant Board decision is that in Case A-443 where Acting Chairman Forrester said:

"Section 13-B and the local Agreement, dated January 19, 1948, contain no language which can be fairly said to limit the rights of the Company to reassign work. The 'existing seniority units' referred to in Section 13-B are still in existence and have been allowed to 'remain in effect.' The departments set up in the Agreement of January 19, 1948, have not been changed. It is true that the Company, by reassigning work, has diminished the amount of work available in one of the departments in some degree, but the existing seniority units and departments still remain in effect as required by Section 13-B and the Agreement of January 19, 1948."

18. In conclusion the Company points out that the Job Description and Classification Manual, Section B-5, reads, "The job description of a job shall serve only as the basis from which to classify the job . . ."; that there have been many Board rulings that the job description does not constitute an agreement that the job shall be performed in the same way in the future; that in any event there has been no change because whenever there has been a five furnace level of operation or less, no Test Carrier has been scheduled; that the Company has complied completely with the award in Case T-362, and so this grievance should be dismissed.

FINDINGS

19. *There is no contractual violation in the Company's assignment of test carrying to the Ingot Tracer job and the discontinuance of the Test Carrier job.* In Case T-362 the Board awarded as follows:

"The grievance is sustained to the following extent: (1) test carrying duties were added to the job of Ingot Tracer on September 26, 1954; (2) test carrying is not an inherent part of the job of Ingot Tracer, nor is now included in any part of the Test Carrier description; (3) the provisions of Section 9-D of the July 1, 1954 Agreement and Section F of the January 1, 1953 Job Description and Classification Manual are applicable; (4) failing compliance with the requirements of these Sections, the Company was not, and is not, authorized to add test carrying duties to the job of Ingot Tracer."

20. In this award the Board rejected the Company's major premise that test carrying was a part of the Ingot Tracer job and accepted the Union's contention that test carrying duties had in fact been added to the Ingot Tracer job (items 1 and 2 of the award). The transfer of the primary function of one job to another established a prima facie case for the conclusion that the Company had changed the job content of the Ingot Tracer job. As Chairman Garrett wrote in arriving at this award (Paragraph

14): "There was no proper occasion for the Company to assign test carrying to the Ingot Tracer, yet hold that this constituted no change in job content of Ingot Tracer." Accordingly the Board ruled that Section 9-D and Section F, which require the Company to follow prescribed procedures when it changes the job content of a job, were applicable and sustained the Union on the basis that the Company did not follow these procedures (items 3 and 4 of the award).

21. Nothing in the award and opinion in T-362, however, supported the Union argument, advanced in the instant case, that Section 9 and Section F, or a jointly approved job description, precludes the Company from changing job requirements unless there has been a new or changed condition. As the Company points out, the Board has already decided this question adversely to the Union's position in earlier decisions. In CI-257 (Paragraph 31) Chairman Garrett said:

"Second, Section 9-D includes language which confirms that Management has retained discretion to vary job assignments and duties as the legitimate needs of business dictate, and except as other provisions of the Agreement in a given case may operate to limit such discretion."

And in T-291 (Paragraphs 9 and 10) he stated:

"But the present grievance must be denied on the merits. It presents a broad claim that no duty involving checking of plate shipments by truck can be included in the description of the Production Checker position. This apparently is on the basis that no duty encompassed in the principal function of one job description ever can be assigned to employees in another job.

"There is nothing in the Agreement which supports this argument, nor can it be reconciled with the fact that many jobs covered in the Inequity Program have overlapping duties. It would be extremely difficult—if not impossible—to run the business efficiently if this were not recognized. Management authority to change job requirements in order to meet legitimate needs of the business, moreover, is recognized in Cases CI-257, USC-461, and USC-417-420, among others."

22. And in accordance with these earlier decisions, the Board in T-362 did not preclude the combining of test carrying work with Ingot Tracer. In the same paragraph (14) referred to earlier (in which the Board held that the Company could not

assign test carrying to Ingot Tracer while maintaining that the content of that job had not been changed) added:

"This is not to say that there may not be proper occasion for the Company to assign test carrying to Ingot Tracers in order to meet changed conditions which arise in the future. *There is no occasion for the Board to express an opinion on any such issue here.*" (Emphasis supplied.)

23. Thus with respect to the instant case, when it is considered that the job of Test Carrier even under the conditions of full scale Open Hearth operations, includes work as a Cinder Pit Laborer as required, the transfer of test carrying to Ingot Tracer under the impact of a 40 per cent (or greater) reduction in Open Hearth operations in 1958 would appear to be a legitimate response to changed business conditions. Insofar as this issue in T-362 is concerned, the Board did not find it necessary to express an opinion, having resolved the case on the basis of the threshold issue raised by the Company's action in not following the procedures prescribed in the Agreement.

24. When, four years later, low level Open Hearth operations caused the Company to assign test carrying to the Ingot Tracer job, the Company proceeded in accordance with Section F-3-a(1) of the January 1, 1953 Job Description and Classification Manual:

"a. When Management changes a job, but the job content is changed less than one full job class, a supplementary record shall be established to maintain the job description and classification on a current basis and to enable subsequent adjustment of the job description and classification for an accumulation of small job content changes as follows:

(1) Management shall prepare, on the form set forth as Exhibit G of this manual, a record of the change involved, such record to become a supplement to the job description and classification and be transmitted to the appropriate Union representative through the procedure of Section D of this manual. This record shall contain statement of the additions to or deletions from the job description, the factor classifications in effect before the job was changed, the proposed new factor classifications, and the net total change."

25. In accepting the Company's issuance of a Form G as complying with the sense of the decision in T-362, the Board is not necessarily agreeing with the Company that the Ingot Tracer job has not been changed as to factor ratings. But on the basis of the foregoing discussion, the Board finds that there was no contractual violation in the assignment of test carrying work to the Ingot Tracer job.

26. With respect to the discontinuance of the Test Carrier job, the Union also argues that this Company action violated Section 2-B-3. Case USC-852, on which the Union relies, does not support the Union's contention. In that case the Board wrote:

"For 30-odd years the Mixer Operator and Weigher jobs have been filled whenever the Open Hearth Department has operated at Clairton, except for one instance when operations were reduced to one or two furnaces. At this time no Mixer Operator was assigned because the Mixer was not in operation and cold iron was being charged into the furnaces. The evidence warrants finding an established working condition contemplating assignment of employees to both the Weigher and Mixer Operator jobs when the Open Hearth is in operation under present conditions, at the 4-furnace level, and using hot metal from the Mixer . . ."

27. In the instant case, however, in the few periods five and less furnaces were operated—1932, 1933 and March 9 to June 24, 1940—the Test Carrier job had been discontinued and the Ingot Tracer assigned to the task of carrying tests. Therefore there is no confirmation of the existence of a practice in this case protected by Section 2-B-3.

28. Furthermore, since the Test Carrier may be required (even under high level Open Hearth operation) to work as a Cinder Pit Laborer, there appears to be no legitimate basis for a claim that the volume of test carrying during a period of drastically reduced operations was such as to warrant the assignment of a Test Carrier.

AWARD

29. The grievance is denied.

USC—327, -329.   Homestead Works.   January 31, 1953
Sylvester Garrett, *Chairman*

BACKGROUND

1. These cases include six grievances which arose in the 48″ Universal Plate Mill, Slabbing and Plate Division of Homestead Works. In three of the grievances, members of the Shearing Crew who were not scheduled for work on a non-operating shearing turn, claim that they should be compensated for the turn lost, on the ground that their duties were performed by other crew members who worked on the special non-operating shearing turn. In the other three grievances, members of the Shearing Crew who were called out on the non-operating shearing turn protest against having been required to perform duties of crew members who were not called out for work.

2. On rare occasions in the 48″ Mill, special non-operating shearing turns become necessary when there is an accumulation of product to be salvaged or of a special nature which must be sheared from stock which cannot be sheared efficiently on an operating turn. Such an occasion arose in January, 1951, and resulted in the calling out of an extra shearing group on a non-operating daylight turn on January 17, 1951. Since the regular shearing crew already had worked 5 operating turns in that workweek, the special shearing group was paid for the sixth day at overtime rates. The special crew called out was composed of a Layerout Marker, a Layerout, a Stamper, a Shearman, three Shearman Helpers, and one Weigher. This crew differed from the regular operating crew in that a Layerout Helper, a Slip Recorder, a Piler, and 5 Piler Helpers were omitted. Thus on the special turn an 8-man crew was used in contrast to the regular shearing crew of 16 men.

3. The reasons underlying Management's decision not to call out men in the four positions of Layerout Helper, Slip Recorder, Piler, and Piler Helpers are as follows:

1. Layerout Helpers. Under normal operating conditions, where speed is of paramount importance, a Layerout Helper is scheduled to assist the Layerout. On the special shift the Company did not believe that speed was required owing to the nature of the product being sheared, and concluded that the Layerout needed no Helper. Superintendent King of the 48″ Mill testified that operating speed on the special shearing shift was controlled not by any delay in the laying out and marking of the plates for cutting, but rather by time required in the preliminary phase of sorting plates, removing dust therefrom, and identifying them by stamped symbols. On the special shift only 324 plates were sheared in contrast to a shearing of 2000 or more plates on a normal operating turn.

2. Recorder. Superintendent King did not contemplate that any recording functions would be performed on the special shearing shift, but that the Recorder on the next regular rolling shift would perform the recording functions. As it happened, the Weigher had substantial free time on the special shearing turn and undertook on his own initiative to do functions which the Recorder normally performed.

3. Piler and Piler Helpers. The Company did not believe that a piling crew was necessary since the plates were all of one size and for one customer. The principal duty of the Piler on a normal operating turn is to check the rolling order, and to direct the Piler Helpers in piling plates according to customer. Since the plates were all for one customer, the short plates were pulled out by the Shear Crew and dropped off the casters to the piling bed immediately behind the shears. This practice is usual on the regular production shift, and is included in the job description of the Shear Crew.

4. The Union contended that elimination of the Layerout Helper in setting up the crew for the special shearing shift in fact resulted in slowing down shearing. According to the Union, the bottle-neck in the operation consisted of sorting out and identifying the plates to be sheared. Since the special shift was characterized by considerable confusion in sorting out and identifying the plates, it is the Union's belief that an additional man would have speeded the whole operation. The Union also stresses that part of the special shearing job for this particular customer was completed on the next operating shift and that 106 plates were sheared by the regular crew within about one hour.

5. The Layerout Marker, who worked on the special shift, testified that the duties of Layerout Helper were performed during the special shift by himself (the Marker), by the Stamper, or by the "Sketcher." He testified that all of the four items under the working procedure of the Layerout Helper job description were performed by one or the other of these men.

6. In regard to the Piler Crew, the Union agrees that there was no necessity on the special shift to sort and direct the piling of

plates according to customer. It asserts, however, that for this particular customer there were a number of orders and different gauges of steel which required some segregation. Management agrees that this was the case, but points out that all of the production sheared could have been delivered to the shipping room for sorting there, since that is the ultimate responsibility of the Shipper.

7. The Union contends that under Section 2-B, Management was precluded from taking the action in question since there was a local agreement on May 24, 1950, to the effect that in the 48″ Mill regular employees would be given all of the available work. The Union also asserts that a local working condition arose as to crew size under Section 2-B, and that since operations were performed under conditions requiring the performance of most of the duties of all members of the regular crew, that such working condition required use of the full crew on the special shearing shift.

8. In addition, the Union stresses Section 9-D of the Agreement, and particularly the provision that a job description and classification for each job shall remain in effect unless certain specified conditions arise, none of which have occurred in this case. In effect the Union looks upon the job description as an agreement that there will be no change in the duties of the job, and that as long as any duties of the job are performed at any given time, an incumbent of such job will be assigned to do such work.

9. The Union also relies on a local practice or understanding that job seniority shall determine assignment to given positions in a period when less than a full crew is required. Moreover, it asserts that under such practice as to job seniority, overtime should be distributed in accordance with job seniority.

10. The Company holds Section 2-B to be entirely inapplicable on the ground that there was no local agreement covering the situation and that no local working condition could have arisen as to the manning of a special non-operating shift since such situation had arisen only once previously as far as anybody could recollect, and at that time less than a full crew was used. No grievance was filed on this occasion.

FINDINGS

11. The evidence does not sustain the Union's view as to the scope of the local agreement of May 24, 1950. There is no reasonable basis on which this agreement could be held applicable to the present case. Nor does it appear that any local working condition as to crew size on the regular operating shifts could be held to apply to the special type of situation which arose on January 17, 1951. The only comparable situation occurred in 1950, and was handled in the same manner by the Company.

12. It seems reasonably clear that the shearing performed on January 17, 1951, could not have been handled conveniently on a normal operating turn. Management thus was required to decide in what manner it could best get the work done. It is not for the Board to decide what was the most efficient manner in which this objective could have been accomplished. Decisions of this sort have been reserved to Management as recognized in Section 3, subject only to the limitation of other provisions of the Agreement. The question, therefore, is whether anything in the Agreement prohibits the action taken. Section 2-B does not, nor does Section 13, even as supplemented by the local agreement as to job seniority relied upon by the Union.

13. It is only in connection with Section 9-D and 9-B-2-a that some question arises as to the propriety of Management's action in this case. It appears that substantially all of the duties of the jobs included in the normal rolling crew were performed by the men assigned to the special turn. This sort of scrambling of job duties, on which the agreed rate structure is based, poses some threat to the stability of the rate structure which the parties have gone to great pains to develop. If Management were to undertake such action on a regular production shift, in a situation where Section 2-B might not be applicable, it is obvious that the provisions of Section 9-D as to description and classification of the jobs would come into play. On the other hand the Board finds no merit in the Union contention that Section 9-D-4 freezes the job descriptions and prohibits any reassignment of various job duties as necessity dictates during the course of operations.

14. In the present case it appears that all of the miscellaneous functions performed by members of the crew on the special shift were functions which properly could be regarded as less important functions of the jobs not used on the shift, and in each instance, with one possible exception, were part of a job in the same or a lower job class than that of the man who actually did the work during the special shearing shift. The one possible exception arises from the

fact that duties of the Piler to some extent were performed by the Shearman Helper. But even here the Piler's primary function of responsibility for directing separation of the plates according to customers is not in-volved. Accordingly, the evidence would not justify any remedial action by the Board.

AWARD

15.   The grievances are denied.

Section B.   TO JOBS OUTSIDE THE BARGAINING UNIT.

USC—783.   Fairless Works.   February 16, 1959
Sylvester Garrett, *Chairman*

BACKGROUND

1.   This grievance by three Riggers from Central Shops at Fairless Works claims that they should be paid four hours' reporting allowance under Section 10-E of the August 3, 1956 Agreement because two Foremen performed Riggers' work on the 7-3 turn, November 23, 1957.

2.   Prior to the turn in question, a crated wood lathe apparently weighing several tons had been placed in the Sintering Plant, in a passageway at the end of two filter drums. The lathe was over 16 feet long and had been brought there in order to true-up several wooden filter drums, which were about 16 feet in length and 12 feet in diameter. The lathe was to be moved from its crate in the passageway to a position on a special platform parallel with one of the filter drums, so that it then could be operated to true-up the drum.

3.   Carpenter Foreman Kelly anticipated that it would be necessary to hoist the lathe out of the crate and over the top of one of the filter drums in order to swing it ninety degrees and lower it into position parallel to the drum. Accordingly, Kelly (several days earlier) had requested the Rigger Shop to send Riggers to the Sintering Plant to remove the lathe from its crate and position it for operation on the morning of November 23. Meanwhile, in preparation of the drums for turning on the lathe, two Carpenters were at work removing slats, screws and nails from the drums. About 11:30 A.M. on November 23, Foreman Kelly, together with a Turn Foreman, went to the Sintering Plant to check the job and found that the Carpenters had completed their preliminary work and were waiting for the Riggers to move the lathe out of the crate and into position.

4.   Noting that there was a chain fall on a monorail directly above the lathe, Kelly then checked to see whether it was possible to attach a sling to the lathe so as to raise it from the crate for inspection prior to actual movement by the Riggers to the operating position. While one of the Carpenters went to fetch a sling, Kelly ascertained that a sling could be passed through a hole in the middle of the lathe in such position that it would not slip. Kelly and the others proceeded to prepare to lift the lathe with the chain hoist, and raised it from the crate. On inspection it appeared that the lathe was complete and in proper operating condition. According to Kelly, more or less by accident, it appeared as the lathe was raised that it could be cleared easily past the drum next to which it would have to be positioned. Rather than wait longer for the Riggers to arrive to handle the operation, Kelly directed the men to proceed to "horse" the lathe into operating position, using the monorail and chain fall.

5.   Kelly testified that in guiding the lathe in the course of this move, he actually placed his hand on it for not more than 5 minutes in order to assure that it did not smash into a nearby control panel. In any event, the move was completed by the Carpenters and the two Foremen, who thereupon left around noon.

6.   Shortly thereafter the three Riggers arrived, found the lathe already in position, and were told by the Carpenters how it had been moved with the help of the Foremen. The present grievance resulted.

7.   In seeking 4 hours' reporting allowance for each of the grievants, the Union holds that this is required under an oral agreement reached with the then Assistant Vice President, Labor Relations, Shaver in a meeting at the plant on November 19, 1957, attended by District Director Carcella and others.

8.   This meeting had been preceded by numerous instances in which grievances had been filed protesting performance of bargaining unit work by Foremen, with the Union asserting that no effective action had been taken by Management to terminate such activity. After discussion, Assistant Vice President Shaver advised the Union that in future instances of this sort, grievances should be filed requesting 4 hours' reporting allowance. The Union believes this suggestion to imply a commitment that in all future instances of Foremen performing bargaining unit work, the affected employees would receive 4 hours' reporting

allowance as a penalty upon Management.

9. The Company stresses that in the November 19, 1957 meeting the Union referred to performance of bargaining unit work by Foremen in the context of stressing that many employees were laid off, or working short time.

10. The Company policy long has been that supervisors will not perform bargaining unit work except in cases of emergency, training, or experimental work. In advising the Union as to the means whereby it could obtain effectuation of this policy at Fairless, according to the Company, Assistant Vice President Shaver in effect merely was stating what already was obvious—that where a grievant not at work was able to prove that a foreman had done his work, he could file a grievance requesting 4 hours' reporting allowance since he would have been entitled to a minimum of 4 hours' pay (Reporting Allowance) if he had been called in to do the work performed by the foreman.

11. At the hearing the parties widely disagreed as to what actually was said in the meeting of November 19, 1957. No minutes of the meeting were kept, nor was any memorandum of understanding signed.

12. In addition to scouting the claim of agreement contemplating 4 hours' pay as a penalty in all such situations, the Company stresses an argument that the amount of work here performed by Kelly and the Turn Foreman was so small as to fall within the de minimis doctrine.

13. Even if the de minimis doctrine is not applicable, moreover, the Company believes the appropriate relief to grievants necessarily would depend upon the amount of time actually lost from work by them, as in Case T-520.

FINDINGS

14. For many years it has been the Company's policy, under the successive Basic Agreements, that supervisory employees not perform work of production and maintenance employees within the bargaining unit, save in situations involving emergencies, training, or experimental work. It is against this background that the decision in Case N-252, dealing with this problem in terms of Section 2-A of the August 3, 1956 Basic Agreement, is best understood. In N-252, the Board directed that a foreman discontinue performing work of employees in the bargaining unit. In the more recent case of T-520, the Board directed that a maintenance employee be made whole for time he lost when a foreman performed his work. The question here is whether the same

type remedy is appropriate, or the more stringent penalty urged by the Union.

15. In the absence of any minutes of the November 19, 1957 meeting, or any memorandum of agreement, it is understandable that the parties should have substantially different recollections of what happened. Considering all the evidence, however, the Board is satisfied that Assistant Vice President Shaver did not commit the Company to a flat policy that thereafter any instance of foremen performing any amount of bargaining unit work would be dealt with by applying a penalty in the form of 4 hours' reporting pay to any adversely affected employee.

16. The Union recognizes that Mr. Shaver's remarks did not clearly spell out the commitment here suggested, or imply such a commitment, but believes that for some months thereafter the Fairless Management recognized the existence of the commitment, by granting 4 hours' pay in all cases like the present. In fact, however, the present case arose only 4 days after the November 19, 1957 meeting. Moreover, several grievance settlements since November 19, 1957, have provided for payment of one-half hour of pay to employees adversely affected by foremen performing bargaining unit work. Still another grievance resulted in payment of 4 hours' reporting pay to an employee who was not at work on the shift in question when a foreman performed bargaining unit work, but who would have been called in to perform the work had not the foreman done so. There apparently also have been numerous instances where employees have received 4 hours' pay in grievances protesting performance of bargaining unit work by foremen subsequent to November 19, 1957, but these cases are not reflected in any written records since settled prior to filing of a written grievance.

17. In balance, it appears that the then Assistant Vice President-Labor Relations in all likelihood intended to go no further than to indicate that Management meant to enforce its policy that foremen should not perform bargaining unit work (except in cases of emergency, training, or experimentation), and that employees affected by failure of foremen to observe this policy could file grievances requesting payment for time lost. In the circumstances which existed, it was understandable that he should speak in terms of employees not at work when such an incident occurred, and who might therefore have a valid claim for a minimum of 4 hours' pay (Reporting Allowance) on the assumption that they would have been called out to do the work had it not been done by a foreman.

18. The Board thus proceeds to dispose of the present case on the basis that where an employee is adversely affected by performance of bargaining unit work by a foreman, he is entitled to be made whole in the same manner as in Case T-520 for the amount of work presumably lost.

19. There is, of course, always the question of whether the total amount of work is so trifling that no remedial action is in order. Here the grievance arose against a background of numerous similar instances over prior months, and specifically four days after the meeting where the Company policy against performance of such work by foremen was reiterated by Assistant Vice President Shaver. It would be manifestly inappropriate in this context to apply the de minimis doctrine to any but the most trifling instance of performance of bargaining unit work by members of supervision.

20. While Foreman Kelly seemed to believe that the physical work which he did in connection with the disputed Riggers' work consumed no more than 5 minutes, it is clear that the entire transaction consumed up to 30 minutes of Kelly's time together with that of another foreman and the two Carpenters. Since the Board cannot measure such a matter with absolute precision, it would appear sound to hold that grievants are entitled to compensation for one-half hour additional pay on the day in question, based on the presumption that they would have worked a total of 30 minutes longer on November 23, 1957 had they performed this work.

AWARD

21. The grievance is sustained to the extent that grievants shall be compensated for an additional half hour of work on November 23, 1957.

N—252. Christy Park Works. December 19, 1957

Herbert L. Sherman, Jr., *Chairman*

BACKGROUND

1. In this case the Union claims that Foreman Mihalek at the Christy Park Works is performing work that should be performed by a job in the bargaining unit. Violation of the clause recognizing the Union as exclusive bargaining representative and Sections 1, 2-A, 9-B and 9-D of the August 3, 1956, Agreement is alleged.

2. On May 26, 1948, a job of Toolman (Job Class 11) was established for the High Pressure Cylinder Department. The primary function for this job read: "Directs grinding operations on tools and maintains supply of tools such as ring dies, hammer dies, punches, etc., used on various operations in the mill." This job was filled by a man in the bargaining unit from June 1, 1948, through July 31, 1951. It was occupied periodically by another employee in the bargaining unit from January 28, 1952, to December 11, 1953, when the High Pressure Cylinder Department was discontinued. Although the job was not formally terminated until much later, no one was thereafter assigned to that job to direct the work of die grinders. It is true, however, that the job was filled for about five pay periods in 1954 and for five pay periods in 1955 for the purpose of taking inventory only. Since the job was not occupied during 1956, it was formally abandoned on February 4, 1957.

3. It was shortly after issuance of the formal notice of abandonment of the Toolman job that the Union claims that Foreman Mihalek assumed duties listed in the job description for that job. The Union asserts that the use of a foreman for most of these duties should be discontinued. It questions the right of the Company to assume the directional duties of the Toolman job, which is conceded to be comparable to a Group Leader job, by way of abandonment of the job instead of issuance of a notice of change in the job description and classification. Although the Union agrees that Management may assume the directional duties of the old Toolman job, it believes that the Company should re-establish the old job and reclassify the remaining duties as a job to be posted for employees in the bargaining unit, or at least assign the remaining duties to such employees.

4. In support of its position, the Union quotes from a Bethlehem Steel Award. Although the Union recognizes that the issue in that case was different, it feels that some of the language used is applicable to this case.

5. Management contends that Mihalek is not performing any duties inappropriate for a foreman. It reviews his background during the last couple of years when there was decreasing activity at the Christy Park Works, and his present responsibilities. One large government order was completed on December 31, 1955, another on March 31, 1957. On January 1, 1956, Mihalek was transferred from General Foreman, Tool

Room—Shell Finish to Turn Foreman, Tool Room—Shell Finish. He became foreman of fourteen employees assigned to the job of Tool Sharpener. Starting April 1, 1957, the number of Tool Sharpeners was gradually reduced to two. During the reorganization that took place in the following period three Die Grinders, one Saw Operator, three Lathe Operators and one Tow Motor Operator were added to Mihalek's supervision. Except for the Die Grinders these jobs work in the Machine Shop of the Special Job Works Department. During the intevening months the number of employees on these jobs has sometimes been less.

6. Prior to April, 1957, the Die Grinders were under the supervision of other Turn Foremen. During the course of a turn Mihalek now spends about two hours in his direction of the Die Grinders, checking stock and expediting the preparation of die rings and punches. He works 8-5, while the Die Grinders work 7-3 and 3-11. Mihalek also performs other duties clearly appropriate for Management personnel.

7. The Company contends that it may fill the Toolman job or not, according to its judgment of the need for assigning someone to the job, and it asserts that no one is now needed on the Toolman job. Since the Toolman job is comparable to a Group Leader job, Management relies on the following quotation from the Board's Award in USC-616:

"Cases T-140 and USC-413 recognize that direction of the working force is a Management function, and that it rests in Management discretion whether—at any given time—it desires to utilize the services of employees in Gangleader capacity. On February 17, 1953, Management made plain that it would not thereafter utilize the services of a Machinist—Groupleader in connection with auto repair work. The Board cannot reverse this determination, which is a proper exercise of Management discretion in direction of the working force."

DISCUSSION AND FINDINGS

8. At the outset it should be noted that the Toolman job has not been occupied at all since 1955, and that it had only been used occasionally for inventory taking purposes for a substantial period prior to 1955. During the intervening years Turn Foremen have directed the Die Grinders and performed the related work of checking stock and maintaining a supply of tools for them by writing requisitions, placing orders, keeping records, etc. These are duties which have long been performed by Management personnel and which cannot be deemed inappropriate for Foreman Mihalek to perform. It lies in the Company's discretion as to whether it wants to assign a man to the Toolman job to assist in the performance of these duties.

9. On the other hand, there is evidence that Mihalek has on occasion gone beyond the scope of these proper assignments to him. He has performed a certain amount of manual work inappropriate for a foreman and not justified as a safety measure in an emergency. For example, he has been observed performing certain maintenance work, such as oiling punches and other equipment, and cleaning threads on punches and dies. Performance of such manual work by Mihalek must be discontinued. Such work properly belongs to employees in the bargaining unit, and should be assigned to them. Mihalek obviously does not fall within the definition of an employee in Section 2-A of the Agreement. To allow him to perform such work undermines the status of the Union which, in the opening section of the Agreement, is recognized as the exclusive representative of the employees in the bargaining unit.

AWARD

10. The grievance is sustained to the extent that Foreman Mihalek is directed to discontinue his performance of maintenance repair work. In other respects the grievance is denied.

T—333.   Fairfield Sheet Mill.   September 26, 1955
Sylvester Garrett, *Chairman*

BACKGROUND

1. This grievance contends (1) that supervisors in the Salvage Department of Fairfield Sheet Mill are performing duties which (under Section 2-A of the July 1, 1954 Agreement) should be performed by employees in the bargaining unit, and (2) that these duties should be described and classi-

fied as an Assemblyman job under Section 9-D of the Agreement.

2. To the Company argument that the grievance is untimely under Section 6, the Union replies that this defense was waived by the Company's failure to raise it prior to submission of its brief. Secondly, the Union urges that failure of the employees to file this grievance between establishment of

the Salvage Department in 1950 and August 19, 1954 was because the tonnage originally did not warrant services of a full-time Stocker or Assemblyman. It feels that today there is ample tonnage to justify assignment of a full-time Assemblyman.

3. Management asserts that it retains exclusive right to manage the plants and direct the work force. It denies that an Assemblyman job is necessary in the Salvage Department; in the Warehouse and Shipping Department four Assemblymen are assigned each turn only because of the much greater tonnage handled per month. It further denies that it has in substance established a new job of Assemblyman in the Salvage Department. On the contrary, the Company argues that the Turn Foreman-Salvage and other supervisors in this Department are performing only duties appropriate for supervisory employees.

FINDINGS

4. Since it is clear that the grievance must be denied on its merits, no useful purpose is served by passing on the question of timeliness.

5. The supervisory force in the Salvage Department consists primarily of the Superintendent and four Foremen—two on the day shift and one on each of the other two shifts. The Union is objecting to the performance of certain duties by all of these supervisors, but particularly to the performance of certain duties by Foreman Freeman on the day shift.

6. Although some of these disputed duties reflect surface similarity to duties of an Assemblyman, they appear upon analysis to involve either directional work appropriate for a Foreman, or to involve more discretion than that exercised by the Assemblyman job in the Warehouse and Shipping Department of the Fairfield Sheet Mill.

7. It is the latter job, among several submitted to the Board, which the Union relies on most heavily to support its contention that Foreman Freeman is performing an Assemblyman's job.

8. Each day Freeman checks customer orders on file in order that he may determine, when rejected product is shipped into the Salvage Department from four different lines, whether such product will meet the requirements of those customers who will take less than prime. When the product arrives in his department, Freeman *in his discretion* determines what disposition shall be made of it. Inspectors note the grade or quality of the material, but make no disposition of it.

9. Freeman, for example, decides whether to apply it to an existing order or whether to send it to stock. He may send material to the shears to have the rough edges cut down. If so, he makes up the shear tickets and determines how much the material is to be cut. If he sends material to the oiling machines, he determines how it is to be stacked as it comes off the machines. If he applies material directly to a customer order, he decides whether to send it to the warehouse or to the wrapping rows.

10. Or, Freeman may decide to send material to one of several departments for further processing. He determines what processing is necessary to make a saleable product. Such further treatment may involve sending the material to the temper pass (to get the "kinks" out of it by rerolling it), to pickling and oiling, to box annealing, or to scrub and dry (a light cleaning action). Sometimes a combination of these processes is required. This sort of discretion must be exercised both for disposition of material coming into the Department, and for material in stock.

11. Freeman picks up the reject lift ticket, and directs the Hookers to take the material to the location which he has decided upon. If, among the numerous possibilities, he directs the Hookers to place material coming into the Department in storage, he specifies the particular location. Then, when a customer order comes in, Freeman or the Schedule Clerk will go through the extra flaps torn off the identification tickets to determine whether satisfactory material is in stock. In such a case Freeman's duty to dispose of material in this Department also includes the requirement that he locate stock and determine what further processing, if any, is needed. If he decides that no further treatment is necessary, he sends the material to the scale for weighing. Finally, although a Union witness stated that he had heard that Freeman took inventory on weekends, this testimony was not substantiated and Freeman flatly denied it.

12. Most of the duties which Freeman performs—which bear surface similarity to duties of an Assemblyman in the Warehouse and Shipping Department—actually are but a phase of his truly important duties requiring exercise of discretion, and the giving of directions, as a member of the Management group. Viewing his duties as a whole, therefore, and noting their obvious interrelationship the Board finds that they are appropriate for a Foreman to perform *under the conditions which prevail in the Salvage Department.*

AWARD

13. The grievance is denied.

T—260. Fairfield Steel Works.   December 31, 1953
Sylvester Garrett, *Chairman*

BACKGROUND

1. In substance this grievance protests against the assignment of certain weighing functions to employees outside the Production and Maintenance Bargaining Unit.

2. While very little evidence was presented at the hearing, the Board has been able to piece together a reasonably adequate picture of the facts from the briefs and exhibits.

3. When the Blast Furnaces at Fairfield Steel Works were placed in operation in 1928, a railroad track scale known as the Hot Metal Scale was installed at the north end of the Open Hearth Scrap Storage area. Since that time hot metal from the Blast Furnaces has been weighed on the Hot Metal Scale. This weighing at all times was the responsibility of employees in the Rail Transportation Department and was done by them except for a very few instances mentioned below. Employees of the Rail Transportation Department are included in a separate bargaining unit and covered by a separate agreement. No representative of Local 3662, (Transportation Department) has participated in any stage of the processing of this case. Apparently both Yardmasters and Conductors in Rail Transportation handle the weighing. Yardmasters occupy a supervisory position.

4. Prior to April 1949, carloads of scrap were weighed on the Ingot Scale between the Open Hearth and Soaking Pits. In April 1949, however, the weighing of cars of scrap was transferred to the Hot Metal Scale. When this was done, Management directed incumbents of the Stock-Weighman job at the Open Hearth to go to the Hot Metal Scale as required to weigh cars of scrap. This action resulted in a grievance by the Stock-Weighman complaining about having to go to the Hot Metal Scale while still being held responsible for weighing done on a Stock Yard Scale by Open Hearth operating personnel. This grievance was settled on July 6, 1949, with the understanding that Stock-Weighmen no longer would be sent to the Hot Metal Scale to weigh scrap.

5. Following this settlement the Company added another Ingot Weighman and assigned him to weigh scrap at the Hot Metal Scale on the day turn only. The services of a Time and Production Clerk from the salaried Bargaining Unit were utilized from 6:00 p.m. to 9:00 p.m. to weigh scrap during these hours at the Hot Metal Scale. The Time and Production Clerk is included in the salaried bargaining unit at T.C.I., covered by a separate rate agreement. Local No. 2210 (salaried unit) has not participated in any of the steps in which this grievance has been considered.

6. For the remainder of the 24-hour period, Rail Transportation Department personnel weighed any scrap which came across the Hot Metal Scale. This was from 9:00 p.m. to 7:00 a.m. and apparently left three hours without anybody specifically assigned to the weighing of scrap at the Hot Metal Scale, between 3:00 p.m. and 6:00 p.m.

7. Thereafter, the amount of scrap weighed increased to the point that on January 12, 1951, the Company established a new wage rate job under the title of "Hot Metal Weigher," the primary function of which was recited in the description to be "to weigh and record weights of ladles of hot metal, cars of scrap, scale, miscellaneous materials and empty railroad cars."

8. The new job of Hot Metal Weigher was manned 7 days a week, *but only on the 7:00 a.m. to 3:00 p.m. turns.* During this turn, most of the scrap passing over the Hot Metal Scale was weighed. Scrap weighed during other hours was weighed by a Time and Production Clerk (salaried unit) and by Rail Transportation Department employees as had previously been done. Substantially all weighing of hot metal at the Hot Metal Scale still was done by Rail Transportation Department employees despite inclusion of such duty in the description of the Hot Metal Weigher job. In short, although the description appeared to contemplate the performance of this function, the Hot Metal Weigher worked only on day turn and in fact was confined to weighing scrap. The rare instances in which the man filling the Hot Metal Weighman job did weigh hot metal occurred when the Rail Transportation Department Yardmaster or Conductor was unable to come to the scale.

9. Incident to expanding Open Hearth capacity at Fairfield it later was decided to transfer scrap weighing to an entirely new location. A new scrap scale was built on the west side of the Open Hearth building. This location was selected in the belief that it provided a more direct line for the flow of scrap from the mills to the Open Hearth. This new scrap scale was placed in operation in August, 1952, and a new job of Scrap Weigher was established.

10. The Scrap Weigher is in Job Class 7, as was the Hot Metal Weigher. The description and classification of the new job were agreed to by the parties and the job put into effect January 18, 1953. At this time the incumbents of the Hot Metal Weigher job

were transferred to the new job of Scrap Weigher to perform the function of weighing scrap which they previously had performed at the Hot Metal Scale. Rail Transportation Department employees continued to weigh hot metal on the Hot Metal Scale.

11. At the same time, the Time and Production Clerk who had been assigned to weigh scrap at the Hot Metal Scale from 6:00 p.m. to 9:00 p.m. daily also was transferred to the new Scrap Scale to perform the same work at the new location. Similarly any scrap weighed at the new Scrap Scale from 9:00 p.m. to 7:00 a.m., was weighed by Rail Transportation Department employees.

12. With the installation of the new job of Scrap Weigher on January 18, 1953, the Company terminated the old job of Hot Metal Weigher on the basis that all of the functions actually performed by such job had been transferred along with the incumbents to the new job at the new Scrap Scale. The weighing of hot metal at the Hot Metal Scale involves approximately 40 to 50 minutes during an entire 8-hour turn. Six casts must be weighed during each 8-hour turn normally. This work always has been performed by Rail Transportation Department employees with unimportant exceptions.

13. The Union contends that the job of Hot Metal Weigher has not in fact been abolished since the scrap weighing work covered by the job *in practice* still is being performed, although at a different location. From this the Union infers that the work covered by the Hot Metal Weigher job description belongs to the employees in the bargaining unit, and should not be performed by employees in the Rail Transportation Department, or in the salaried group.

14. Also the Union asserts that to the extent that "supervisors perform work on the 3:00 to 11:00 turn at the new scale" the contract is being violated. This is on the ground that application of the contract and seniority of the men entitled to the weighing work does not depend upon the turn when weighing services are being performed. In no event, says the Union, may such weighing work be assigned to supervisors (apparently referring to the Yardmaster in Rail Transportation) in the absence of some emergency or like special circumstance.

15. Irrespective of the broad language of the description of the Hot Metal Weigher job, the Company maintains that the weighing of hot metal always has been performed by employees in the Rail Transportation Department. The weighing of scrap, which constituted the true reason for establishing the job under the title of Hot Metal Weigher, in

fact has been fully transferred to the new Scrap Scale. Hence the Company holds that its action terminating the Hot Metal Weigher job is authorized by Sections 3 and 9-D of the Agreement.

16. While hot metal functions continue to be performed, the Management holds that they never in fact were performed by the incumbent of the Hot Metal Weigher job. Hence there is no application of Section 13-A to the performance of hot metal weighing by employees in the Rail Transportation Department, rather than in the Production and Maintenance unit.

FINDINGS

17. While the original grievance in this case specified four sources of difficulty which the Union wished to have corrected, only two of these were still present in the case when heard by the Board and call for any consideration by the Board. These involve: (1) a claim that the Hot Metal Weigher job has not been abolished and that *hot metal weighing* functions must be assigned to Production and Maintenance employees, and (2) a claim that Management is not entitled to assign *scrap weighing* functions to employees outside the P & M bargaining unit.

18. On point (1), since all of the duties *actually performed* by the Hot Metal Weigher job were transferred to the new job of Scrap Weigher at the new Scrap Scale, there is no basis on which the Board could hold that Management was not authorized to discontinue the Hot Metal Weigher job. Management was fully entitled to put the new Scrap Scale into operation and transfer the performance of duties from the Hot Metal Scale to the Scrap Scale.

19. All hot metal weighing now is performed by employees in the Rail Transportation Department as was true (with unimportant exceptions) prior to the creation of the Hot Metal Weigher job in the first place. There is no basis to hold that Management cannot assign hot metal weighing functions to employees in the Rail Transportation Department (represented by Local 3662) rather than production and maintenance employees represented by Local 1013. Local 3662 has not appeared in any stage of this case, and the Board will not speculate as to the position of Local 3662 in this matter. It would be improper for the Board in this case to pass on matters involving the assignment of work *within* the Rail Transportation Department without participation by Local 3662 in the proceedings.

20. On point (2), a somewhat different situation appears, when this grievance was being processed through the first four steps

apparently a substantial amount of scrap weighing was performed by employees outside the P & M bargaining unit. Most of this weighing was done either by Rail Transportation Department, or salaried employees, both represented by Locals not involved in this case. It is unclear whether some of this weighing may not have been done by production supervision also. Management since has moved to adjust this situation by adding two Scrap Weighers on February 27, 1953. A Scrap Weigher is present from 8:00 a.m. to 4:00 p.m. and from 8:00 p.m. to 4:00 a.m. each day, apparently. Most scrap weighing can be concentrated into these shifts. At the present time, the Board cannot determine from the record whether any scrap weighing is performed, in the absence of Scrap Weighers, by supervisory personnel from production and maintenance.

21. The Board cannot find any violation of the Agreement in assigning some scrap weighing to Rail Transportation and salaried employees. The Board would not make such a finding in any event in the absence of participation in these proceedings of the Local Unions directly concerned. Thus, there has been a failure to establish by reliable evidence that any actual violation of the Agreement has taken place. The grievance thus cannot be sustained.

AWARD

22. The grievance is denied.

USC—654. Fairless Works. May 9, 1958
Herbert L. Sherman, Jr., *Chairman*

BACKGROUND

1. This grievance from the Paint Shop of the Maintenance and Utilities Division at Fairless Works constitutes a claim by trade and craft Painters that certain painting assignments always performed by Fire Inspectors should be taken away from the latter job and given to the Painters. In dispute is such painting work as the painting of targets areas behind fire extinguishers so that the extinguishers can be recognized from a distance.

2. The principal argument of the Union is that the painting work involved is obviously covered by the Painter job description, and that such work cannot be assigned, under Section 2-A of the 1956 Agreement, to employees outside the Production and Maintenance bargaining unit. The Fire Inspectors are presently represented by a union other than the Steelworkers.

3. Management replies that the painting work involved in this case has never been performed by the Painters, and that the Painter job description, read in the light of the existing facts, never contemplated that Painters would perform this work. The Company points out that when Fire Inspectors were first hired at Fairless Works, a standard job description was installed. This job description was identical to that used in other plants and agreed to by the Steelworkers. The Fire Inspector job description refers to "brushes," "paint," and "Paints and polishes fire fighting equipment for ready recognition."

4. The Union notes that it was not a party to the Fire Inspector job description at Fairless Works. Furthermore, the Union states that past practice is irrelevant because the Union was unaware of it and because it denies grievants benefits in violation of Section 2-B-2 of the Agreement.

FINDINGS

5. Whether the disputed painting work is an inherent part of the trade and craft job of Painter at Fairless Works must be determined by reference to the treatment accorded such work by the parties.

6. The Fire Inspectors have always examined the target areas behind the fire extinguishers and repainted them as necessary —both before and after certification of the Steelworkers at Fairless Works. The same is true of the guards around the fire hydrants and equipment in the foamite building. Since there are 1500 fire extinguishers at Fairless Works and 177 fire hydrants, the Union claim that it was unaware of the practice cannot be accepted. Moreover, the Board cannot find that grievants are being deprived of some benefit under the Agreement in violation of Section 2-B-2. They have never performed the work in dispute. It has always been performed by employees excluded from the bargaining unit under Section 2-A of the Agreement. In view of these facts, the grievance must be denied.

7. Other awards cited by the parties, though providing some guidance, are distinguishable.

AWARD

8. The grievance is denied.

CHAPTER 5

CLAIM FOR HIGHER RATE OF PAY WHILE PERFORMING CERTAIN ASSIGNMENTS

Included in this chapter are cases where the claim is made that an employee is entitled to a higher rate of pay during the period of time in which he is required to perform certain specifically assigned duties. This type of claim is to be contrasted with the claim that an employee's job should be assigned a higher job class because of significant changes in job content. The first and last cases in this chapter shed some light on the question of which approach should be pursued in a given set of circumstances.

G—105.   Geneva Works.   May 26, 1959
Sylvester Garrett, *Chairman*

BACKGROUND

1. This grievance from the Structural Mill Department, Rolling Mills Division, Geneva Works, claims violation of Sections 9-B-3 and 9-J-3 of the August 3, 1956 Agreement, and requests correction of an error in application of rates of pay, as contemplated in Section 9-H. The Union asserts that Management, in view of these provisions, cannot require an employee to spell another on a higher job for any period of time (including brief periods for lunch or personal relief) without paying him the higher rate of the job on which he spells.

2. The Structural Mill at Geneva began operating early in 1944, and on March 21, 1947 the first Steelworkers Agreement covering P. and M. employees at Geneva Works became effective. It adopted for the Geneva employees the original Inequities Program developed by the parties, and made it retroactive to March 9, 1947. Description and classification of Geneva jobs under the Inequities Program was completed later, and all standard hourly wage rates became effective April 18, 1948.

3. The original descriptions and classifications at Geneva included the jobs particularly involved in the present grievance: Breakdown Operator (Class 18) ("Screwman"); Breakdown Manipulator Operator (Class 16) ("Manipulator"); Roll Motor Operator (Class 8); Structural Mill Crane Operator (Class 8). The grievance arose when Screwman Dockery was sent to the dispensary for a physical examination, one day late in 1957. During Dockery's absence of several hours, Manipulator Warren moved up

to fill the Class 18 job, and Roll Motor Operator Jensen moved up into Warren's Class 16 job. In turn, the Craneman filled the Roll Motor Operator job which is in a lower job class but enjoys a higher out-of-line differential. It was not apparent who moved into the Craneman job. None of the men was paid the higher rates of the job which they filled during Dockery's absence, which apparently ran over a substantial portion of the turn. In Second Step, Management agreed that it had erred, and later paid each of the men for the time spelling on a higher job because of Dockery's absence. This did not settle the grievance, however, since by this time the parties had become involved in serious differences concerning proper interpretation of the Agreement. The present grievance, therefore, seeks authoritative determination of these issues.

4. Since 1944 Management has required the Breakdown Manipulator Operator to relieve the Breakdown Operator, the Roll Motor Operator to relieve the Breakdown Manipulator Operator, and Structural Mill Crane Operator to relieve the Roll Motor Operator, and so on, while the respective higher rated employees were eating or on personal relief. All of these moves are made in accordance with an agreed promotional sequence. While there was much haggling in the grievance procedure, as to whether such spelling was *"required"* by Management, this was largely a matter of juggling words, and not persuasive as far as the Board is concerned. It is clear that Management has failed to make any other arrangement for relief spelling, and it obviously finds the

arrangement advantageous and expects the men to spell in this manner.

5. From 1944 until 1951, the employees involved were paid the higher rate for the job on which they spelled for these purposes. In 1951 the Company, however, developed an incentive based on the assumption that the spelling practice would continue, but that the employees no longer would be paid the higher job rate for time spelling higher rated employees. There is no provision for a spell job in the incentive, which states that the performance standards will be applied to production each turn, providing the standard crew is used.

6. When the incentive was installed, the old practice of paying the higher rate for spelling thus was discontinued. There was no protest at the time, but the present grievance now seeks a return to the pre-incentive practice on the basis that this reflects the proper application of Sections 9-B-3 and 9-J-3 at Geneva Works, and so is necessary in order to comply with the controlling provisions of the August 3, 1956 Agreement.

7. The Company's primary position is that the grievance is untimely under Section 6-D-1-a of the August 3, 1956 Agreement, which requires that a grievance be filed promptly in writing. Since the old practice of paying employees the higher rate for time actually spent spelling on higher rated jobs was discontinued in 1951, the Company holds that if grievants had a claim under Section 2-B-3, it should have been filed in 1951.

8. The Union replies that this is a rate of pay question, not a problem under 2-B-3, and that under Section 9-H of the Agreement, grievants are entitled at any time to require correction of an error in application of the rates of pay. The Union deems the application of Section 9 at Geneva Works to be clear in this case, and so asserts that the timeliness defense cannot bar determination of the merits of the grievance, even though it might preclude retroactivity for the period prior to actual filing of the grievance.

9. As an alternative to its untimeliness defense, the Company insists that the grievance lacks substantive merit. The basic question, it holds, is the meaning of Section 9-B-3: "The established rate of pay for each production or maintenance job . . . shall apply to any employee during such time as the employee is required to perform such job." It is the Company's position that the type of relief involved here is not encompassed by the Section 9-B-3 provision: Throughout the industry employees relieve each other for brief periods; higher rated employees frequently relieve lower rated employees and lower rated employees relieve

higher rated employees on an informal basis that cancels out on a total-time-worked basis.

10. Such relief is deemed by the Company to be primarily for the benefit of the employees because it enables incentive covered operations to proceed without interruption and with maximum time worked. If the Roll Motor Operator is deemed to become a Manipulator for 20 minutes of relief, says the Company, then two men are filling one position simultaneously. Likewise, there is a vacancy in another position. This amounts to a non-standard crew situation, and for these 20 minutes the entire crew would be on unmeasured work. It reasons, therefore, that the production during that time could not be used in the calculation of incentive performance and the crew would be paid the standard hourly wage rate for that period.

11. The time involved in spelling is not recorded on a minute-by-minute basis, but according to the Company the practice is recognized indirectly through incentive plan allowances. Such a practical flexibility of work arrangements, says the Company, was recognized in USC-392 when the Board stated:

"Although grievants do perform a certain amount of guide setting work, it appears that they have long performed these duties, as part of their contribution to the traditional teamwork which is found in this type of operation under an incentive plan, in order to cut down on the time required to change rolls and guides."

12. The Union, on this score, stresses that the men spell each other as a matter of convenience and necessity both from their own viewpoint and that of Management. Operations frequently could not continue unless employees moved up for temporary relief on the crucial jobs at certain periods.

13. The Union holds that there is nothing in the incentive plan which could change any of the operating procedures relative to personal relief or for a lunch period. In fact, the Roll Builder (Class 11) is required, as a regular diet, to relieve the Traveling Table Operator (Class 13) and *is paid the Traveling Table Operator's rate while acting as relief* to the 4 Table Operators each turn, totalling 80 minutes.

14. The jobs of Traveling Table Operator and Roll Builder are covered in the *same incentive* brochure as the jobs particularly involved in the present grievance. Had it been intended that the incentive cover lunch and relief spell time, says the Union, it would not then be necessary to pay the Roll Builder the Table Operator rate while relieving.

15. Section 9-B-3 establishes the rate of pay for each job in effect and requires that an employee be paid on the basis of such rate. The Union sees only one alternative to this requirement which might be relevant here: Management might establish spell-hand jobs, to provide relief periods for the occupants of other jobs in the regular operating crew. Since this has not been done, the Union believes Section 9-J-3 plainly controlling.

FINDINGS

16. Errors in application of rates of pay may be corrected at any time, under Section 9-H, notwithstanding any other provisions of Section 9. Since the Union asserts that the Company since 1951 has erred in not applying Sections 9-B-3 and 9-J-3 as written, the substantive merits of this question now must be determined by the Board. If the Union is correct in asserting that Management has erred in application of Sections 9-B-3 and 9-J-3, then the time limitations of Sections 9-D and 6-D-1-a would apply only to cut off retroactivity in remedying the violation of Section 9.

17. Section 9-B-3 states that the standard hourly wage rate for a given job "shall apply to any employee *during such time as the employee is required to perform such job.*" Section 9-J-3 contemplates that in the event an employee *"is assigned temporarily at* the request or direction of Management from his regular job *to another job"* the employee *"shall receive the established rate of pay for the job performed"* in accordance with Section 9 (among other requirements of Section 9-J-3).

18. Although neither party has mentioned Section 9-D, it seems to the Board that this provision is of critical importance in determining proper application both of Section 9-B-3 and 9-J-3. Only by reference to 9-D can it be ascertained what are the various "jobs" for purposes of the other two provisions. A "job," for this purpose at least, may be thought of, as a given bundle of duties to which the parties have assigned a specific job classification which is protected against change, save as contemplated under Section 9-D itself. Obviously, spelling briefly on other jobs may or may not be included in a given job, depending upon the relevant facts in each case.

19. The practice of spelling higher rated employees on lunch or personal relief, where employees work as a crew under a single incentive, long has been common in basic steel operations. It has by no means been a uniform, or universal, practice, however, as far as the Board is aware. Where such a practice existed when given jobs were de-

scribed and classified, the spelling sometimes was mentioned in the descriptions, but in other instances was not mentioned. While the parties' January 1, 1953 Job Description and Classification Manual provides special techniques for handling two types of "spell hand" jobs, these provisions (Section C-11-a, -b, and -c, pp. 41-43) by their terms do not apply to "relief resulting from the practice of permitting the occupant of one job in a crew to move up for short periods and perform the work of a higher job, thus to acquire training on such job . . ."

20. As far as the Board is concerned, it is immaterial for purposes of Section 9-D whether the practice of spelling employees for brief periods on higher rated jobs without payment of the higher rate (where it existed) was mentioned *specifically,* or not, in the original description. In neither instance could the practice be relied upon later to claim an increase in job class (or payment of a higher rate for such spelling under 9-J-3), when it had been in effect from the time of original classification without payment of the higher rate.

21. When the jobs involved in this grievance were described and classified at Geneva, in 1948, however, it was customary for employees who moved up to higher rated jobs, in spelling other employees for their lunch period or personal relief, to be paid the higher rate applicable to the job on which they spelled. This continued for about three years thereafter. Thus, it might reasonably be urged that the original job classifications did *not* contemplate spelling without payment of the higher rate, so that for purposes of Section 9-D (and so, of 9-B-3 and 9-J-3) the jobs did *not* include any such spelling requirement.

22. Basis for this view may be found in earlier Board decisions, in rate of pay cases, to the effect that the description and classification of jobs must be interpreted and applied in light of the actual facts as they prevailed when the job was described and classified. Thus, even though some duties were not mentioned specifically in the working procedure of a job, this fact—standing alone—has provided no basis for the Board later to direct redescription and classification of the job in absence of actual change in the duties performed, whether or not such duties were spelled out in the description. This is but one aspect of the broad policy that the Board must refrain from "correcting" what amount to *claimed* "errors" in job descriptions and classifications as they were mutually agreed upon. This policy has been developed and applied in numerous cases, such as CI-217; T-202; T-230; T-232; T-234; USC-293; and A-406. Adoption of a con-

trary view would invite a flood of efforts to change or "correct" job descriptions and classifications where no real change in actual job duties has taken place, and so tend to undermine the parties' policy of maintaining stability in the agreed rate structure.

23. In USC-392, Hot Bed Operators in Class 6 requested that they be paid a Guide Setter rate (Class 13) under Section 9-B-3 for brief periods when they performed certain minor guide setting duties. The grievants always had performed the duties in question, and their job description stated that the Hot Bed Operators were required "to assist" in roll and guide changes. The Union argued that the word "assist" in the job descriptions plainly indicated that the Hot Bed Operators were not to be required to perform guide setting duties alone, but it was clear that the Hot Bed Operators long had performed the minor guide setting duties, and specifically had done so when their job was described and classified. In denying the grievance, the Board noted also that the performance of these duties by the Hot Bed Operators was part of the traditional teamwork in such an operation under incentives, in order to cut down on time required to change rolls and guides.

24. Earlier an apparently different result was reached in Case A-347 (Acting Chairman Harbison), but this case was decided March 9, 1951, before the Board had adequate opportunity to study the full scope and ramifications of the entire problem. The later decisions in USC-392 and related cases above mentioned reflect the firmly established principle that the Board will not require any change in job classification or method of payment on the basis of spelling arrangements which existed when a job was described and classified, unless there has been a relevant change since the original description and classification.

25. Here the practice of paying employees for all time spent spelling was in effect when the jobs were described and classified, so that it cannot be inferred that such spelling, without payment of the applicable higher rate, was covered in the original description and classification. In fact, the contrary appears and—had there been no change in relevant facts since 1948—the Board would be required to apply Sections 9-D, 9-B-3 and 9-J-3 in light of the facts which prevailed when the jobs were described and classified in 1948, thereby sustaining this grievance in full.

26. Thus the critical question here is whether the situation which developed at the time of installation of the incentive in 1951, entailing discontinuance of the higher rate for brief periods of spelling, effectively changed the scope of the jobs in dispute for purposes of 9-D, 9-B-3, and 9-J-3.

27. It is well known that, among the many factors tending to enhance earnings under a well constructed incentive covering a crew of substantial size under common standards, good teamwork is essential. Reduction in total lunch and personal relief, as well as other lost time, may be significant where employees spell each other freely and do not hesitate to help out as needed on other jobs in order to keep production flowing smoothly.

28. If discontinuance of payment for spelling on some jobs in 1951 had the effect of adding to the jobs a requirement for purposes of Section 9-D, which might materially have affected job content in light of relevant Specimen Jobs, this would have been such an obvious consequence that any complaint for purposes of job classification should have been presented in 1951. Section 9-D-4 provides that a grievance may be processed "if filed promptly," where Management has failed to develop a new description or classification as required in Section 9-D. Since all relevant facts were well known to the interested parties in 1951 when the new incentive was installed under Section 9-C, the policy thus set forth in 9-D-4 would seem to foreclose the present argument of the Union.

29. In closing, it should be emphasized that the original problem which precipitated this grievance properly called for application of Section 9-B-3 and 9-J-3. When employee Dockery went to the infirmary for a physical examination involving several hours away from his work station, his absence clearly was not akin to the usual taking of lunch or personal relief. There is no suggestion of any relevant understanding or practice contemplating spelling or relieving other employees for prolonged periods without payment of the higher rate. The foregoing discussion thus is limited entirely to brief periods of spelling, such as for lunch and personal relief, where such spelling is required by the nature of the operation. Accordingly, the grievance here has merit to the extent already conceded by Management. It is denied insofar as it seeks to apply 9-B-3 and 9-J-3 to brief periods of spelling of higher rated employees (for lunch and personal relief) where such spelling has been a normal and usual incident of the operations under an established incentive since 1951.

AWARD

30. The grievance is denied to the extent that it seeks relief beyond that already granted by Management.

USC—392. Gary Steel Works. March 31, 1954

Herbert L. Sherman, Jr., *Arbitrator*

Approved by Sylvester Garrett, *Chairman*

BACKGROUND FACTS

1. This grievance arose in the 20″ No. 1 Merchant Mill at Gary Steel Works. The Hot Bed Operators in Job Class 6 request, under Section 9-B-3 of the Agreement, that they be paid the rate for the Guide Setter job, in Job Class 13, when they perform certain guide setting duties. The Company claims, however, that grievants have always performed these duties, that no change has taken place since the job was classified, and that consequently, the grievance must be denied. Grievants concede that they have always performed guide setting duties at their end of the Mill, but assert that prior to March 1, 1952, such work was performed through the joint efforts of the Hot Bed Operator, the Assistant Roller, and the Guide Setter.

2. Around March 1, 1952, the Union contends, the responsibilities of grievants were changed by direction of Management, so that grievants now have responsibility for the following duties:

1. The adjustment of delivery guides on stands 4, 5, 6 and 9 as necessary during rolling operations.
2. The setting of delivery guides on stands 4, 5, 6 and 9 when the mill is down for the purpose of changing passes and rolls to process a different section.
3. The setting of delivery guides for spare stands 4, 6 and 9.
4. Occasional adjustments to roll settings both for the spare stands and the aforementioned stands on the roll line.

3. Management flatly denies any change of responsibility or that any instructions were ever issued to that effect. It asserts that for decades grievants have worked alone when performing the duties listed in Items 2 and 3 above. With respect to duties listed in Items 1 and 4, the Company also denies any change and holds that any work which has been done by grievants concerning the adjusting of guides and rolls during rolling operations is limited to trial runs or an emergency. To that extent, such work, Management contends, has always been performed by incumbents of the Hot Bed Operator job as part of the traditional teamwork in this type of operation.

4. The Union disclaims any argument that a mistake was made when the job was classified, and notes that the job description for the Hot Bed Operator reads under Factors 9, 10 and 12 that incumbents "assist" with roll and guide changes. It argues that a comparison with the Guide Setter job description shows that the Hot Bed Operator job was not given credit for the setting of guides without assistance. Nor does the word "assist," as shown by job descriptions for other jobs in the 20″ Mill, embrace grievants' duty of setting guides alone. To this the Company replies that the word "assists" is found in various job descriptions and that it means different things. It must be interpreted to mean whatever the incumbents of the particular job were doing at the time that the job was classified. Management also points to the Working Procedure of the job description which reads "performs assigned tasks on Roll, Section and Pass changes."

DISCUSSION AND FINDINGS

5. This grievance is based in large part upon a claim that Management directed a change in the responsibilities of the Hot Bed Operators in March of 1952. In order for grievants to prevail in this case, the Board must find that the evidence in favor of finding a change in responsibility outweighs the evidence which indicates that no change has taken place.

6. Of the two Hot Bed Operators who testified in support of the alleged changes, Whitaker stated that, among other verbal reprimands, he was reprimanded by his Turn Foreman in March, 1952, for not having certain guide setting work completed on the stands at his end of the mill while the mill was shut down, that he was told he should not wait for help from the Guide Setter who works on the stands at the other end of the mill, and that previously he performed these duties by helping the Guide Setter only when he had time. The other Hot Bed Operator denied that Management had instructed him as to any change in his responsibilities. The Guide Setter who testified also denied that he was ever informed that his duties or responsibilities were changed. He did say, however, that at one time he went from the east end of the Mill (where stands 1, 2, 3, 7 and 8 are located) to the west end of the Mill (where stands 4, 5, 6 and 9 are located) to work on guides for *special* sections, but that his work today keeps him busy at his end of the Mill. He also agreed that he would go to the other end of the Mill today if necessary for a special section since the crew is under an incentive plan. He empha-

sized that such teamwork is the practice under any incentive plan. Finally, he testified that he suffered a lost time accident in 1948 while working between No. 4 and 5 stands, but he admitted on cross-examination that this occurred during the regular rolling operation.

7. The second Hot Bed Operator testified that prior to March, 1952, he set the guides on stands 4, 5, 6 and 9 but did not feel that he had the responsibility, and that the Hot Bed Operators know their jobs so well today it is not necessary for the Assistant Roller or Guide Setter to assist them in setting the guides.

8. Management witnesses who testified included all three Turn Foremen, the General Foreman, and the Assistant to the Division Superintendent who was Superintendent of the 20″ Mill prior to July, 1953. Each of these witnesses categorically denied any change in responsibility or duties of the Hot Bed Operators had taken place, or that instructions to that effect had ever been issued by Management. It was also testified that the Assistant Roller continues to set guides on the entry side of the No. 9 stand, and that the Table Operator continues to set the guides on the entry side of stands 4, 5 and 6. It was further testified that the Hot Bed Operators have always been responsible for setting delivery guides alone on stands 4, 5, 6 and 9, that they still receive occasional assistance from the Assistant Roller as in the past, but that it has never been a practice for the Guide Setter to work on guide changes in the west end of the Mill.

9. Management also relies on an exhibit which shows that a higher job class for the Hot Bed Operator job was considered during the 1947 Review Program. Higher ratings were recommended by the local Union and Management Classification Committees for Factors 5, 7, 9 and 10. Although the top Committee did not approve the increased classification, the Company notes that the proposed higher rating for Factor 9 at that time was partly based on the duty of the Hot Bed Operators to "make pass and guide changes, and assist on roll changes."

10. In the light of the testimony and evidence presented to the Board, it cannot be found that any significant change took place in March of 1952 in the duties and responsibilities of the Hot Bed Operator job. The evidence which tends to show that a change has occurred is certainly not stronger than the evidence which indicates that no change has taken place. The Board finds that Management did not issue any instructions to change the responsibilities of grievants. Although grievants do perform a certain amount of guide setting work, it appears that they have long performed these duties, as part of their contribution to the traditional teamwork which is found in this type of operation under an incentive plan, in order to cut down on the time required to change rolls and guides. Accordingly, the grievance must be denied.

AWARD

11. The grievance is denied.

T—602. Ensley Steel Works. August 6, 1959
Donald A. Crawford, *Arbitrator*
Approved by Sylvester Garrett, *Chairman*

BACKGROUND

1. The issue here is whether the grievants, who worked on repair of No. 5 Blast Furnace at Ensley Steel Works on various of 20-odd turns in July, 1958, should have been paid as Laborers (Class 2) or as Bricklayer Helpers (Class 3), under Section 9-B-3 of the August 3, 1956 Agreement.

2. On these turns pallets of brick were unloaded from freight cars by fork lift trucks and placed in the yard. Subsequently the bricks were placed alongside the beginning of a conveyor system erected at the site for repair of No. 5 Furnace.

3. On the turns in dispute (while the repair was in progress), three or four of the grievants were required to select bricks from the pallets outside the cast house and load them on the conveyor. The conveyor carried the brick from the ground to the cast house

floor some 12 to 15 feet above. One grievant was stationed at a turning point in the conveyor system at the cast house floor level. His job was to deal with any congestion of brick and to relay orders originating with the Brickmasons as to what type of bricks to put on the conveyor.

4. Three or four more grievants, on the cast house floor, removed the brick from the conveyor and stacked it opposite the tuyere openings into the shell of the Blast Furnace. Bricklayer Helpers placed the brick onto other conveyors which carried the brick inside the furnace, where still other Bricklayer Helpers put it in tubs. The tubs were hoisted by an engine to the scaffolding on which some 9 Bricklayers worked. Here another group of Bricklayer Helpers removed the brick from the tubs and placed it in reach of the Bricklayers.

5. In addition, the grievants supplied the Bricklayers with insulation packing, black patch, water-cooled blocks, and bond clay, and furnished Carpenters with lumber to build scaffolds. Grievants also cleaned up broken brick and debris made by the Bricklayers.

6. Some 12 kinds of brick were required for the relining. Four types constituted about 90% of the total. The Brickmasons specified the type of brick by instructions relayed to Brickmason Helpers and to the grievants.

7. The Union says in addition that one of the two clay mixers on each turn was classified as a Laborer. The Company replies that this was not brought out in the grievance procedure and thus should not be considered here.

8. The Union points out that all the grievants were Brickmason Helpers who had been bumped to Labor. The Union's position is that there is no justification for the cutoff line between Bricklayer Helper's and Laborer's work; that the supplying of brick to the Bricklayers from the end of the conveyor system to the top of the conveyor system was one continuous process; that there was no substantial difference in the work performed; that the job descriptions have no reference to any tuyere holes as some kind of magic dividing line for purposes of pay.

9. The Union emphasizes the fact that the Company concedes that there is no difference in skill required between the Helper's and the Laborer's work. The Union argues that the work performed by the grievants was that stated as the primary function of the job of Bricklayer Helper:

"Supplies bricklayers with brick, mortar, and miscellaneous materials."

And the working procedure:

"Wheels materials from storage to working area. Mixes mortar as required. Passes brick to bricklayers either manually or by roller conveyor. Cleans up old brick and debris torn out by bricklayers. Upon completion of job, removes planks and unused materials and returns to storage."

10. The Union says that the grievants supplied the Bricklayers with some 12 varieties of bricks, selecting the bricks as required by the orders; that the grievance involves a substantial amount of work; that the job performed was not that of Laborer. The Laborer stores bricks, but does not feed bricks to the Bricklayer when he is depending on them to get the work done.

11. The Union refers to a previous settlement of the same issue, albeit without prejudice, on the same basis as requested here. The Union concludes that it is not claiming an inequity but requesting the proper rate of pay for an established job, a demand not precluded by past success of the Company in paying the wrong rate.

12. The Company replies that what the Union has established is that some of the Bricklayer Helpers were overpaid. For certainly the Helpers passing brick into the furnace shell were not performing the full scope of the Bricklayer Helper job.

13. The Company emphasizes the fact that in such low rated jobs as these—Job Class 2 and Job Class 3—the duties are simple and often overlap, and the skill requirements do not differ much. Handling brick is such a duty. Thus the job description for Laborer makes clear that handling material is a part of that job. Item 4 of the Working Procedure specifies, ". . . loading, unloading and handling materials . . ." And "roller conveyor" is one of the listed equipment.

14. The Company points out that brick was just one of many items of material that were unloaded and brought to the casting house floor in the same manner by the Laborers for use by the various crafts. Hence brick was just another item of material, and handling materials has always been part of the Laborer job.

15. The Company agrees with the Union that picking up bricks and putting them through the tuyere openings is not higher level work than the Laborers were doing. But historically the Company has always used Bricklayer Helpers to do this task. And historically the Company has always used Laborers to unload brick and place it outside the blast furnace shell for the Bricklayer Helpers, who supply the Bricklayers inside the furnace as needed. The only difference from the prior Blast Furnace reline jobs at Ensley is that an elevator and wheelbarrows were used before to bring the brick to the casting house floor instead of pallets of bricks and conveyors. In 1946 when the jobs of Bricklayer Helper and Laborer were classified, this historical cutoff line was in effect.

16. Accordingly, "the Board is not authorized under the Basic Agreement to disturb the situation (since) it is clear that the job is being performed in the same manner as it was when described and classified. The Board has no standing to improve upon the results achieved by the parties under their Inequities Program." (T-230, Paragraph 8).

17. The Company also refers the Board to Case CI-231. The Company concludes that the Union's case stripped to its essentials is a claim of an inequity. A grievance therefor is expressly barred from the grievance

procedure by Section 9-G of the August 3, 1956 Agreement.

FINDINGS

18. *The job performed by the grievants on the relining of No. 5 Blast Furnace was that of Laborer.*

19. Section 9-B-3 of the August 3, 1956 Agreement provides that: "The established rate of pay for each production or maintenance job . . . shall apply to any employee during such time as the employee is required to perform such job."

20. Most recently, in Case G-105 the Board reiterated the rule in rate of pay cases. The Board said:

"Basis for this view may be found in earlier Board decisions, in rate of pay cases, to the effect that the description and classification of jobs must be interpreted and applied in light of the actual facts as they prevailed when the job was described and classified. Thus, even though some duties were not mentioned specifically in the working procedure of a job, this fact —standing alone—has provided no basis for the Board later to direct redescription and classification of the job in absence of actual change in the duties performed, whether or not such duties were spelled out in the description. This is but one aspect of the broad policy that the Board must refrain from 'correcting' what amount to *claimed* 'errors' in job descriptions and classifications as they were mutually agreed upon. This policy has been developed and applied in numerous cases, such as CI-217; T-202; T-230; T-232; T-234; USC-293; and A-406. Adoption of a contrary view would invite a flood of efforts to change or 'correct' job descriptions and classifications where no real change in actual job duties has taken place, and so tend to undermine the parties' policy of maintaining stability in the agreed rate structure."

21. The record in this case is that the simple function of bringing brick to a point outside the tuyere openings has always been considered as Labor work. Thus when the jobs were classified and described under the Inequities Program, the understanding and application of the relevant job descriptions was that men who brought brick to the point outside the tuyere opening, were performing the Labor job. The change from wheelbarrows and elevators to conveyors does not change the duties in any significant way. No matter how arbitrary this line between the 16 Bricklayer Helpers and 13 Laborers supplying the 9 Bricklayers may be thought to appear, a practical line must be drawn somewhere, and by practice this is the line drawn by the parties. As such it is not a case of "past success of the Company in paying the wrong rate" but rather of past definition and application of relevant job descriptions and job rates for performance of the job in dispute.

22. The foregoing applies, of course, only to the actual handling of brick in various stages between the freight car and the Bricklayers. The existence of a "cut-off" point, recognized in practice, is irrelevant to such work as mixing mortar to proper consistency for prompt use by the Bricklayers. This undeniably is the work of Bricklayer Helpers.

23. If in this instance, as the Union says, some of the grievants actually mixed mortar on various turns, the Company must consider such claims (which are included within this grievance) and, where meritorious, pay the Bricklayer Helper rate in accordance with Section 9-B-3.

AWARD

24. The grievance is denied, except that any grievant who can show that he mixed mortar shall be paid the Bricklayer Helper rate for the turn involved.

T—427.   Fairfield Coke & Chemical Works.   March 27, 1957

Sylvester Garrett, *Chairman*

FINDINGS

1. In this grievance the Bricklayer Helpers in the Bricklayer Shop at Fairfield Coke Works request that they be paid at the rate of Mortar Mixer for all time spent mixing mortar for Bricklayers.

2. The Bricklayer Helpers have mixed mortar for the Bricklayers for many years, both by hand and using a concrete mixer.

The concrete mixer normally has been used when the work in progress requires a substantial amount of mortar at one location. Until Steptember 28, 1955, there was no separate job description and classification at Fairfield Coke Works for the job of Mortar Mixer. During 1955, the Union called attention to the fact that elsewhere in the Corporation a Mortar Mixer job was described and classified separately where a concrete mixer was used. A new description and classification of Mortar Mixer was installed at Fairfield Coke Works by mutual agreement effective October 2, 1955.

3. The present grievance was filed about eleven months later, seeking reimbursement of the difference between the Job Class 3 (Bricklayer Helper) and Job Class 5 (Mortar Mixer) for all hours worked mixing mortar by hand since August 4, 1955.

4. The Union holds that all time spent mixing mortar, either by hand or using of the concrete mixer, should be paid at the Mortar Mixer rate rather than the Bricklayer Helper rate. The Company holds that the Mortar Mixer job was established solely to cover mixing of mortar with the concrete mixer. There is no question that it has been applied to all mortar mixing, using the concrete mixer.

5. The Union case rests largely on the proposition that the coding of various factors in the Mortar Mixer job, makes no reference to operation of a concrete mixer. To illustrate, under Factor 3, the Mortar Mixer is coded B-1.0 (with no reference to the concrete mixer) whereas the Bricklayer Helper is coded A Base. In reply the Company points out that the working procedure of the Mortar Mixer refers clearly to "using concrete mixer." There is no contradiction of Company evidence that, when the Mortar Mixer job was established, both parties knew that it would be applied only to operation of the concrete mixer in producing mortar.

6. Under the evidence there is no basis to sustain this grievance.

AWARD

7. The grievance is denied.

G—22. Geneva Plant. February 19, 1953

Sylvester Garrett, *Chairman*

BACKGROUND

1. In this grievance the Bearing Repairmen of the Roll Shop at the Geneva Plant request that they be paid the Bearing Maintenance Man rate when working on a turn to which no Bearing Maintenance Man is assigned. The Union relies on Section 9-B-3 of the May 7, 1947, Agreement, which provides that the established rate of pay for each job shall be paid to any employee during the time that he is required to perform such production or maintenance job.

2. When the job titles of Repairman-Bearing and Bearing Maintenance Man were established in 1948, the Roll Shop operated only during the day turn. From March to June, 1949, however, operation was on a three-turn basis with both Bearing Repair-Men and Bearing Maintenance Men assigned to all three turns, because of an increase in the number of roll changes. In June, 1949, the Company again revised the assignments of incumbents of the two jobs to various turns because of a belief that there was not sufficient work for the Bearing Maintenance Men on all three shifts. All Bearing Maintenance Men, therefore, were assigned to the day turn, with the Bearing Repairmen assigned over the three turns. In December, 1949, the Company split the Bearing Maintenance Men between the day and evening shifts because Mesta Oil Bearings and Hydraulic Jacks needed more frequent repairs. Since filing of the grievance early in 1950, there has been no change in the distribution of the Bearing Repairmen over the turns, but the Bearing Maintenance Men sometimes have worked only the day shifts. At other times they have been split between the 8-4 and the 4-12 shifts, depending on the state of repairs needed and equipment available. They have not worked on the 12-8 shift since filing of the grievance.

3. The description of the Repairman-Bearing job was completed in January, 1948. Under "Source of Supervision" it states that the Repairman works under direction of the Bearing Maintenance Man. In March, 1949, additional foremen were assigned to the Roll Shop, however, and turn foremen began to assume directional duties formerly exercised by Bearing Maintenance Men, along with supervising the enlarged crews.

4. Also relevant to the change in assignments was completion of a new Roll Storage building in February of 1950. Thereafter, the Bearing Repairmen worked almost entirely in the new building, while the Bearing Maintenance Men remained in the Roll Shop proper. As a result, the differences in the nature of the duties of the two jobs became more apparent.

5. The work of Repairman-Bearing now consists mainly of removing and replacing roller bearing assemblies on the roll neck journals. The Bearing Maintenance Men are concerned with more intricate work, including inspection, tearing down, overhauling, and building up bearing assemblies and the hydraulic jack.

6. In August, 1950, the Company unilaterally revised the job descriptions of Repairman-Bearing and Bearing Maintenance

Man, deleting any reference to direction of the Repairman by the Bearing Maintenance Man.

7. This revision, of course, has no bearing on the merits of the present grievance. The fact that Management took such action, however, seems to be symptomatic of the underlying difficulty which has plagued the parties, and now the Board, in the handling of this grievance. This underlying difficulty lies in the fact that the difference between the two jobs is not clear and apparent on the face of the descriptions. Actually, significant elements of the working procedure of the two jobs are identical.

8. In an effort to minimize difficulty since filing of the grievance, Management has striven to limit actual work done by the Repairmen to functions which clearly are not those of Maintenance Men. Again, however, this action is irrelevant to the Board's determination of this case, since the Board must look primarily to the existing agreed job descriptions in determining job content. The Board has no authority in this type of situation to revise a job description or to disregard its essential provisions. If the existing fuzziness of the descriptions as written is to be eliminated, this is a matter for the parties, not for the Board.

9. Prior to filing of the grievance Management paid Bearing Repairmen the higher rate of Bearing Maintenance Man whenever it felt that a Repairman was performing the substance of the Maintenance Man job. Between June and December, 1949, this occurred 25 times.

FINDINGS

10. The question here is whether the Repairmen-Bearing in practice have been performing the duties of a Bearing Maintenance Man, on shifts where no Maintenance Man is assigned, to such an extent that the Company should be required regularly to assign a Maintenance Man to each shift. The same result would be accomplished in substance, if the Board were to direct the Company to pay the rate for the Maintenance Man job to at least one Repairman on each shift, on the basis that he presumably was performing the duties of the Maintenance job.

11. Since the descriptions of the two jobs are agreed upon and the Board cannot revise them, we proceed on the basis of the descriptions actually in effect in deciding this case. The question then is a factual one— that is, whether the Union has established that Repairmen-Bearing regularly perform the substance of the duties of a Bearing Maintenance Man on shifts where no one in the latter job is assigned. The evidence submitted does not support the Union's claim in this regard. The grievance, therefore, must be denied.

12. This does not affect in any way the right to file a grievance whenever it is felt that on a given shift a Bearing Repairman has been required to perform the substance of the Bearing Maintenance Man job without being paid the higher rate.

AWARD

13. The grievance is denied.

CI—240. Johnstown Works. January 31, 1953
Sylvester Garrett, *Chairman*

FACTS

1. This grievance seeks, under Section 2-B-3 of the April 22, 1947 Agreement, to require the Company to maintain an established practice of using two Topmen at the Cupola of the Iron Foundry at Johnstown Works.

2. For 30 years prior to this grievance two men were assigned as Topmen to charge the Cupola. On February 21, 1950, one of the incumbent Topmen was discharged for cause. Thereafter, Grievant Albert Schein was assigned to perform the duties previously performed by the discharged Topman, but was classified as a Topman Helper (Job Class 4) rather than as Topman (Job Class 7).

3. In thus eliminating one of the two Topmen jobs, Management acted in accordance with its understanding of discussions between the parties in late 1945 when the Joint Inequity Committee described and classified the jobs of Topman and Topman Helper. Management seemingly was under the impression that agreement had been reached at that time that when a vacancy occurred in one of the two Topman jobs, it would be filled by a Topman Helper and the practice of using two Topmen thus discontinued.

4. When the Standard Hourly Wage Scale was put into effect in 1947, however, no action was taken to designate the job of one of the two incumbent Topmen as properly that of Topman Helper. Thus, the out-of-line differentials of both incumbents were calculated on the basis that the Standard Hourly Rate for the Topman job was properly applicable to each. This was explained

by the Company at the hearing as a technical error which Management was entitled to correct under Section 9-I.

5. On these facts it is apparent that the case turns upon the question of whether an agreement such as Management alleges actually arose between the parties when the jobs were described and classified.

6. The evidence is clear that no such agreement arose between the parties, nor were the circumstances of their discussions such that the Union should reasonably have inferred that Management intended ultimately to eliminate one of the two Topmen.

7. At the time of original description and classification of these positions, charging of the Cupola was manned not only by the two Topmen but also—from time to time as tonnage required—by one or more laborers who were assigned to help out. Grievance-man Rugh at the time requested that a description and classification be developed to cover the work of laborers thus assigned on an as needed basis. It was the understanding both of Rugh and of Grievance Committee Chairman Zwiener, who served on the Joint Inequities Committee, that the description of Topman Helper, developed following Rugh's request, was specifically for the purpose of covering work done by the laborers previously assigned and who had been paid only

the labor rate up to that time. Zwiener denied that Management representatives at any time had indicated that the Helper description should cover the work of one of the two men then filling the Topman job.

8. It is clear also that both of the incumbent Topmen, DeBeck and Gembinski, performed the full duties of the Topman position as described, and continued to do so until the time of Gembinski's discharge on February 21, 1950. Thereafter, grievant continued to perform the same duties that had been performed by Gembinski.

9. The failure to pay grievant the Topman rate was in violation of Section 9-B-2-a, since the job description and classification of the position continued in effect and there is no doubt that grievant performed the duties of the position. It is thus unnecessary to pass upon the question of possible application of Section 2-B in this situation.

AWARD

10. The grievance is sustained. Grievant Schein is entitled to reimbursement for all wages lost as the result of being compensated at the Helper rate rather than the higher rate of Topman while occupying the position previously filled by Gembinski.

T—274.I. Farifield Steel Works. September 13, 1954

Herbert L. Sherman, Jr., *Arbitrator*

Approved by Sylvester Garrett, *Chairman*

DISCUSSION AND FINDINGS

1. This grievance seeks to implement the award in Case T-234, which was previously heard by the Board. The Crane Hookers in the Machine Shop at Fairfield Steel Works, request that they be paid the difference between a Crane Hooker's rate and a Rigger's rate for the period during which a Rigger by the name of Salter was improperly removed from the Machine Shop. The Rigger job was eliminated on November 14, 1951; it was restored pursuant to the Award in Case T-234, on May 10, 1953.

2. The Company contends in this case that the Award in T-234 is wrong. Most of the Company's testimony bears on the amount and type of work performed by Salter, and is repetitive of the testimony offered in the previous case. In addition, a Management witness testified that while Salter was absent, one of his duties—the requisitioning of slings to replace those which are worn out—was assigned to the Tool Foreman. The Company argues, in effect, that the Crane Hookers did not perform any of Salter's

duties which are not proper for a Crane Hooker. It is clear, however, that the only regularly performed duty of the Rigger which was not performed by some Crane Hookers during his absence involves the requisitioning of slings. Although Management contends that the Crane Hookers were not "required" to perform a Rigger's duties, it is also clear that the Crane Hookers as a group, at least on the day shift, were expected to do the work previously done by Salter, with the exception of the one minor duty already noted. During the period in question there was no change in the type of work coming into the Machine Shop, and on no more than two occasions were Riggers brought in from the Rigger Shop to relieve the Hookers from the obligation of handling extra large and hazardous jobs on which Salter would have exercised supervision and rendered assistance. While the Company relies in part on the deletion of the words "Rigger directs closely" from the job description of the Crane Hooker during the 1951 Review Program, this was a natural revision to reflect the fact that the Rigger directs less than half the Hookers in the Machine Shop—those on the day shift only.

3. The Union urges that all the grievants should receive the same rate of pay which Salter received (Job Class 14). It must be acknowledged that the decision in USC-419 lends support to the view that non-craftsmen who *are required* to do recognized craft work should receive the established craft rate. But this principle would not fit the facts in this case, since no individual grievant has been identified as having performed *all* of Salter's duties as Rigger for any given period of time. Rather it appears that the removal of Salter from the Machine Shop affected in some degree the duties of all Hookers who otherwise would have worked with him, but no one of whom was required to take over all his duties. Thus, it is not surprising that no provision of the Agreement was cited at all by the Union except Section 9-D in the grievance as it was originally filed. In any event the extent to which the classification of the Crane Hooker job may have been affected during the period in question was not adequately explored by the parties at the hearing by appropriate references to the classification program.

4. Another question before the Board is whether the principal duties performed by Salter devolved upon all Crane Hookers, or merely those on the day shift. The Rigger job in the Machine Shop only works on the day shift. Six Crane Hookers are assigned to the day shift, five to the afternoon shift, and three to the night shift. There is no clear evidence to show that the Hookers on the afternoon or night shifts performed any specific work which would otherwise have been performed by Salter, despite a general assertion by the Union that they too were required to perform part of his work. Thus, for aught that appears in the present record, it seems that Hookers on the afternoon and

night shifts were not required to perform Salter's duties. They were not deprived of Salter's direction and assistance, since they never did have the benefit of such help.

5. One further question remains. The Company argues that the grievance is untimely because it was filed on October 23, 1952—more than eleven months after the date on which the Company eliminated the Rigger job. Although a Union witness stated that the reasons for the lapse of time were its reliance on a Company promise to assign Riggers to the Machine Shop from the Rigger Shop when Management thought it necessary and its hope that the grievance in T-234 would be settled at an early date, these explanations are not sufficient to justify a gap of eleven months. But the payment of an improper rate under Section 9 constitutes a continuing violation of the Agreement, hence the lapse of time before the filing of the grievance cannot bar any remedy even though it will affect the retroactivity of any rate adjustment, should such later appear to be required.

6. In summation, the Board reaffirms its rulings in Case T-234, that it was improper to eliminate the Rigger position in the Machine Shop, and that Salter was removed from that position in violation of his seniority rights under Section 13. However, in the light of the contractual arguments presented to the Board in this case and the findings made in this Award, the case is remanded for further consideration of all the circumstances under Section 9-D of the Agreement.

AWARD

7. The grievance is remanded for further consideration under Section 9-D as to the extent to which the classification of the Crane Hooker job may have been affected between October 23, 1952, to May 10, 1953.

T—274.II.   Fairfield Steel Works.   December 17, 1954
Herbert L. Sherman, Jr., *Arbitrator*
Approved by Sylvester Garrett, *Chairman*

DISCUSSION AND FINDINGS

1. In this case the Crane Hookers in the Machine Shop at Fairfield Steel Works seek a Rigger's rate of pay during the period that the Rigger job was improperly eliminated. The Rigger job was restored pursuant to the Award in T-234 on May 10, 1953.

2. The parties had acknowledged the existence of duties calling for the use of a Rigger, in the Machine Shop at Fairfield Steel Works, for many years. When the Rigger was removed, his duties and responsibili-

ties, except for the requisitioning of slings, devolved upon the Crane Hooker job. The reason for the need of a Rigger in the Machine Shop for so many years was undoubtedly because bulky, heavy, and hazardous lifts had to be handled carefully in order for them to be positioned properly for the Machinists. Yet neither at the time the Company removed the Rigger from the Machine Shop and required grievants to perform his duties, nor during his absence, was there any change in the volume or type of work coming into the Machine Shop.

3. Included among the normal duties of the Rigger in this Machine Shop is the direction of Crane Hookers on the day shift while moving particularly large pieces of equipment around the shop. Equipment must often be precisely positioned for the Machinists to work on it. Such large and heavy items as the housing of a shear mill, the bell and hopper of a blast furnace, certain "foreign orders," a blooming mill crankshaft, a blooming mill roll or a plate mill roll are moved about in this shop. The weights of the equipment must be estimated so that the details of moving the equipment may be properly planned. The cables on unbalanced pieces of equipment must be carefully choked and adjusted in order that the piece may be positioned exactly as the Machinist needs it. Sometimes a piece is so heavy, such as a plate mill roll or a blooming mill sideguard, that its weight is approximately that of the capacity of the crane. In these situations extra care and skill are, of course, required because of the hazards involved to both material and other employees. There is also occasional lashing of equipment to railroad cars. At times pieces must be assembled in housings, such as the shear mill housing.

4. It is clear that the Rigger in the Machine Shop has substantial responsibilities and must exercise a considerable amount of skill in connection with the movement of these types of heavy equipment and structures. An examination of the Rigger job description shows its applicability to the functions described above.

5. Some pertinent parts of the Rigger job description read:

"Estimates weight of load to be handled. "Loads and unloads heavy or bulky machinery, equipment, fabricated structural members, spare parts, castings, etc.

"Moves, sets in place, erects, assembles, or dismantles machinery and equipment. . . ."

The illustrations given include "mill housings" and "blast furnace bells."

6. The Board finds no indication in the job description for the Crane Hooker in the Machine Shop at Fairfield Steel Works or in the job description of Specimen Example 986 for a Hooker that the incumbents have a Rigger's responsibility for handling such equipment. The language is very general. The more detailed language in the Rigger job description provides concrete illustrations covering bulky equipment handled by grievants.

7. If no other considerations were involved, it would seem that under Section 9-D of the Agreement the codings for the Rigger job might well be the proper codings for the duties performed by grievants during the period while the Rigger was absent from the Machine Shop. But the difficulty with this position is that the Rigger job is a craft job and craft jobs are rated in part on the basis of skills which incumbents may be called upon to utilize but which may not actually be required in their daily duties. Also, there are three levels of rates recognized for the Rigger—starting, intermediate and standard (Job Classes 10, 12 and 14, respectively), and the Rigger's duties here primarily were performed by 6 Crane Hookers on the day shift.

8. An awkward remedial problem has been created by the unauthorized removal of the Rigger from the Machine Shop, a problem which the parties were unable to resolve by themselves after full opportunity to do so under the prior remanding of this case. If the changes in grievants' jobs, considered as a whole, are evaluated in the light of the job descriptions and classifications for the Crane Hooker and Rigger jobs, with due allowance for the special features of the trade and craft classification program and the fact that not all individual grievants were affected in like degree, this results in changes in codings of the various factors of the job except Factors 8, 9, 10 and 11.

9. The changed Factors are as follows:

FACTOR	RATING
1. Pre-Employment Training	B .3
2. Employment Training and Experience	D1.2
3. Mental Skill	C1.6
4. Manual Skill	B .5
5. Responsibility for Materials	C1.8
6. Responsibility for Tools and Equipment	B .2
7. Responsibility for Operation	C1.0
12. Hazards	C .8

All codings here found appropriate are the same as those for Specimen 1021—Repair (Mech.), Plant Title "Rigger," save Factors 5 and 11 where the present facts warrant a higher rating in one instance, and a lower in the other.

10. The added duties have devolved only on Crane Hookers on the day shift, and the remedial revised classification is limited to men whose work was thus affected.

11. The Union, however, now urges that Section 9-B-4 is fully applicable here, with each grievant affected therefore receiving the Rigger rate since called upon to handle some portion of the Rigger duties.

12. It may be that both parties believe that whichever technique—Section 9-D, or 9-B-4—is applied to remedy the original violation here, it will constitute a long-range precedent for all cases where men in position rated jobs are directed to perform substantial duties of craft jobs. If such fears exist, however, it should be borne in mind that the facts in the present case are of such unique nature that it would be difficult to duplicate them in any subsequent case. Here the Board's only concern is to find a permissible and proper remedy under the Agreement for a violation involving unique facts, and which long since has been discontinued. The result in this case, therefore, in no sense is conceived as a precedent for future action by the Board.

13. Actually, there seems to be no immediate need to deal with the case under Section 9-B-4 other than to observe that—if applied here—the Board would not be inclined to hold that this group of grievants would be entitled to any rate higher than the Learner rate for Rigger. As it happens, this is at the Class 10 rate already found appropriate under the analysis contemplated in Section 9-D.

14. One final observation. As indicated in the previous Award, grievants are not entitled to relief in the period prior to the filing of the grievance.

AWARD

15. Grievants, whose work as Crane Hookers on the day shift was affected by addition of the Riggers duties from October 23, 1952, to May 10, 1953, were entitled to payment at the Job Class 10 rate during this period.

T—313. Fairfield Steel Works. March 31, 1955
Sylvester Garrett, *Chairman*

FINDINGS

1. Grievants protest that they were paid as Measurer (Class 8) instead of Second Layerout (Class 10) for laying out plates for shearing in the Fabricating Shop, Fairfield Steel Works, between November 1953 and March 1954.

2. The plates in question were diverted to the Fabricating Shop from the Plate Mill for lay out and shearing. They would have been sheared in the Plate Mill had not the work on hand exceeded the shearing capacity there. The shearing schedule in the Fabricating Shop was increased from 10 to 20 turns per week during this interval to handle the diverted plates.

3. Grievants' work as Measurer in the Fabricating Shop entails marking plates with templates. There are only rare occasions on which templates are not used. In marking the plates diverted from the Plate Mill, grievants were unable to use templates. Instead they were required to use a large square, a straight-edge, a tape and other tools to lay out and square the plates for proper shearing. In so doing, grievants were instructed by the Foreman to maintain an adequate supply of marked plates for shearing so that the shear did not fall idle.

4. The evidence leaves no doubt that, in marking the plates diverted from the Plate Mill, the Measurers in the Fabricating Shop were called upon to perform the principal function and virtually the entire substance of the job of Second Layerout. Grievants were entitled to receive the Class 10 rate for those periods of time during which they were required to perform this work.

AWARD

5. The grievance is sustained.

A—750. Joliet Works. June 28, 1957
Sylvester Garrett, *Chairman*

FINDINGS

1. This grievance protests the rate paid to Hookers for assisting in taking inventory in the Rod Mill Billet Yard at Joliet Works on September 30, 1956.

2. For some years prior to the 1956 inventory, both Stockers (Class 12) and Hookers (Class 6) were utilized to take inventory because of their knowledge of the product. Substantial elements of the Stocker job were involved in this work, and the Company paid the Stocker Standard Hourly Wage Rate to all men utilized in taking inventory.

3. During the interval between the 1955 and 1956 inventories incentives were applied to both the Stocker and Hooker jobs. When it became necessary to take inventory in 1956, operations in the Billet Yard were scheduled for 6 days per week, Monday through Saturday and Illinois law prohibits 7 days of work by any employee. Thus it

was necessary that Stockers or Hookers who worked taking inventory on Sunday, September 30, 1956, should not be scheduled for work on one of the operating days during the rest of the week. Thus Stockers utilized to take inventory at Standard Hourly Wage Rate on Sunday, September 30, would thereby lose opportunity for incentive earnings on a production turn later in the week. To offset this potential loss of earnings for the Stockers, the Company decided to pay them their respective average incentive earnings (based on pay periods in June) for time worked taking inventory on September 30, 1956. A similar decision was reached with respect to Hookers, but based on each individual Hooker's earnings under the Hooker incentive. Where the individual Hooker's average earnings were less than the Stocker Standard Hourly Rate, the latter rate was paid.

4. Three Stockers and 10 Hookers participated in the inventory of September 30, 1956. The Hookers protest that they should have received pay based on average hourly earnings of the Stockers rather than the higher of their own individual average incentive earnings, or the Stocker Standard Hourly Rate. The Union feels it is discriminatory for Stockers and Hookers to be paid different individual rates for the same hours taking inventory. The Union urges that taking inventory is not truly part of the Stocker job, and that the Company in effect has established a rate for a new job of inventory taking, based on the average hourly earnings

of the Stockers. Moreover, it suggests that over the years the practice has been for all Hookers and Stockers to get the same rate while taking inventory, and that this is a local working condition protected under Section 2-B-3.

5. This case turns on application of Section 9-J-3. The earnings' protection there specified is a personal protection, so that an employee assigned to some job other than his regular job receives either the established rate for the job performed, or that rate plus "such special allowance as may be required to equal the earnings that otherwise would have been realized by the employee." Applied to the present case this requires that Hookers who took inventory receive either the Stocker Standard Hourly Rate, or that rate plus an allowance sufficient to equal earnings which each Hooker otherwise would have realized. It seems clear that the Company has complied with this requirement, even though the result is that Hookers might receive differing compensation both as among themselves and as compared with Stockers.

6. It is urged that some of the Hookers, had they not participated in taking inventory, would have worked as Stockers later in the week for at least one turn. The evidence does not establish, however, that any Hooker actually missed a turn as Stocker because he took inventory.

AWARD

7. The grievance is denied.

CI—252. Homestead District Works. March 7, 1952
Donald A. Crawford, *Acting Chairman*

BACKGROUND

1. These two grievances present the claim of 4 hookers (*Job Class 5*) that they should be paid the higher press helper rate (*Job Class 8*), pursuant to Section 9-B-3 for time they spent cleaning scale out of the press pit.

2. Scale is usually removed by the 7,000 ton press crew from the press pit during inactive periods, normally twice in 24 hours. This task requires about thirty minutes for each of the seven press crewmen.

3. On *very rare occasions* when the press crew works on forge operation until the end of the turn, and when a press crew is not scheduled for the next turn, hookers are used to clean the pit. When using 4 hookers, it takes approximately 4–4½ hours to remove the scale. Since 1943, when the 7,000 ton press was installed, there have been very few occasions when the hookers

have done this task. The Union claims the two occasions creating the present grievances are the first occurrences.

4. The hookers are carried in a separate seniority unit from the press crew, and the hooker job description contains no reference to this work. The press helper job description provides, as one of its duties, cleaning scrap, scale, and refuse out of the press pit.

5. The Union contends that the time the hookers spent removing scale from the press pit should be compensated at the press helper rate, since this work is part of the press helper job. Management denies this primarily on the ground that the performance of the simple clean-up duty itself does not entitle the grievants to the job rate. Conversely, it is agreed that when a hooker performs the press helper's job during forging operations, he receives the press helper rate.

FINDINGS

6. The Board denies the grievance, since it finds that the hookers did not actually perform the press helper job. They simply did one task of the job (cleaning out scrap, scale and refuse—labor work) and this when the normal tasks of the job could not be done. Under the *facts of this case* the performance of *this* one duty is not enough to constitute the performance of the job.

7. The press was not operating, the press crew was not working, the press helper's job was not being performed. True, the hookers did one duty normally performed by press helpers, but *this* one duty *performed* under these circumstances, although under others it might, does not constitute performing the job. Since the press was not operating, only this one task would be performed, and it was work less skilled than regular hooker work.

8. The Union has stressed Case No. A-347, in which the Board held that yard cranemen were performing the mill craneman's job whenever they operate the mill cranes. But in that case the Board found that the Company paid, or did not pay, the higher rate solely on the basis of the length of time the yard craneman worked on the mill craneman's job, where in this case, the distinction is not length of time, but rather that the hooker was not doing the press helper job because the press helper job was not operating. True, the Board in Case A-347 did not require that the yard craneman, to secure the mill craneman's rate, do all the tasks performed by the mill craneman. But the Board did find that there were no limitations on the tasks which may be performed by the yard craneman in supplementing the mill cranemen, whereas in the present case, the press was not in operation and the press crew was not working. There existed the actual limitation that only a single duty—removing scale from the pit, a less skilled work than normally performed by hookers—could be done. Therefore, the two cases are differentiated on the basis of difference in fact. Thus, where a press helper is relieved by a hooker when the crew is working, and it happens that the hooker only relieves long enough to remove scale, the hooker nonetheless would be entitled to the press helper rate.

9. Section 13, Seniority, has not been discussed since it does not affect these grievants.

10. This award is limited to the precise facts presented in this case, and is not to be construed as sanction for Management to regularly schedule workers to additional duties in disregard of the duties embraced in the agreed upon job descriptions.

AWARD

11. The grievance is denied.

USC—294. Edgar Thomson Works. March 16, 1953

Frederick Harbison, *Arbitrator*

BACKGROUND FACTS

1. Among the employees in the Open Hearth Department are the laborers in the Labor Gang whose primary function is stated to be "To operate a compressed air gun to remove slag from open hearth slag pockets." This job, classified as Job Class 5, is not occupied by regularly assigned incumbents but by members of the Labor Gang who are paid the Class 5 rate when they operate the pneumatic hammer. Prior to the rate classifications which became effective on February 9th, 1947, the members of the Labor Gang, while performing any kind of so-called "hot work" on the furnaces, were paid at the rate of *Pneumatic Hammer Operator* irrespective of whether or not they actually operated the gun.

2. The Union contends that the operation of the hammer is only one function of the several involved in hot furnace work. It points out that, in addition to operating the hammer for part of a turn, the grievants while engaged on hot work are required to perform semiskilled tasks such as setting checkers, hooking cables around large pieces of slag to be pulled out by crane, and using several types of hand tools for tearing out furnace checker and cinder pocket bulkheads. Such tasks, it points out, are not included in the job of general laborers. To support its case, the Union claims that the work actually performed is better described by a Homestead Works job description entitled *Laborer, O.H.—Assignment 2.* (Job Class 5.) The primary function of this latter job is described as follows: "Tears out Open Hearth furnace checker and cinder pocket bulkheads, cleans or tears out and replaces checkers or uses pneumatic hammer for breaking and removing cinder from Open Hearth cinder pockets." Indeed, the witnesses for the Union testified that they actually performed the type of work set forth in this latter description, and their testimony was not questioned by the Company. The Union contends, therefore, that the grievants should

be paid the job class 5 rate for all hot work on slag pockets irrespective of whether or not the hammer is used.

3. The Company bases its case on the contention that the primary function of the *Pneumatic Hammer Operator* Job is the operation of the air gun. It argues that the difference between this job and the general labor job (Class 3) is dependent upon the requirement of operating the hammer, this difference being reflected in Factor Values 4—Manual Skill, 6—Responsibility for Tools and Equipment, 9—Mental Effort, and 11—Surroundings, in the descriptions of the two jobs in question. The Company contends that, since the classifications became effective in 1947, it has paid the Class 5 rate for "hot work" only when the hammer is used. The Company admits, however, that it has been liberal in applying this rate, since it has given the members of the labor gang the higher rate even if they were required to operate the hammer for very short periods of time on a turn. Indeed, a witness for the Company admitted that this rate would apply even if a laborer was required to use the hammer for only one hour or even less during an 8-hour turn. According to the testimony of the principal Company witness, "If he (the laborer) uses the gun he maybe uses it two or three times on a turn, maybe an hour and a half at a clip. So we pay him the eight hours on the gun."

4. The Union attempted to show that there was an established practice for paying the higher rate even when the hammer was not used, and the Company attempted to show that there was no such practice. In the opinion of the Arbitrator, these contentions are irrelevant for the proper disposition of this grievance, as is also the contention of the Company that the Union is alleging a wage-rate inequity.

5. The sole issue to be resolved is whether or not the grievants are in effect performing the job entitled *Pneumatic Hammer Operator* (Class 5) or the job entitled *Laborer #1* (Class 3) when they are engaged on "hot work" on the furnace.

FINDINGS

6. The Arbitrator finds that the differences between the two jobs in question are not dependent solely upon the requirement of operating the air gun.

7. In the *Hammer Operator* Job, a rating of D 1.6 on Factor 11—*Surroundings*— is given because of "heat, dirt, dust (work with hot slag)" as compared with a rating on the *laborer* job of C.8 for "inside—outside, continually dirty, dusty, work. Heat in

summer." The difference of .8 in the two ratings appears to be dependent solely on the nature of "hot work" required on the furnaces and has no connection at all with the use of the air gun.

8. With respect to Factor 9—*Mental Effort,* the *Hammer* job is rated B.5 for use of "simple tools for rough work of a repetitive nature, whereas the *Laborer* job is rated A—Base for performance of rough tasks closely directed." The witnesses for the Union contended that the setting of checkers and other tasks as required in the *Hammer Job* were more complicated than the mere replacement of checker-work and related tasks, as called for in the lower rated job. The Company did not question the testimony of the witnesses on this score. It must be assumed, therefore, that the difference in rating of .5 with respect to this factor is not *solely* attributable to use of the air gun.

9. With respect to Factor 6—*Responsibility for Tools and Equipment,* the difference of .2 on the two jobs is specifically dependent only upon use of the hammer.

10. With respect to Factor 4—Manual Skill, there is a difference of .5 between the two jobs. This is accounted for in the *Hammer* job description by the words: "operate power tool" *and also* by the words: "use chain on cable slings." This means that the difference may not be solely dependent on the use of the air gun.

11. The work on the hot furnaces described by the witnesses in the case bears little resemblance to the work described in the *Laborer #1* job, and the Company made no attempt to demonstrate how the "hot work" could be considered to fall within this latter job description. The Arbitrator is forced to conclude, therefore, that when engaged on the "hot work" job, the members of the labor gang *are not performing* the *Laborer #1* job.

12. It is true, however, that they are not performing *all* the functions of the *Hammer Job* when they are not required to operate the air gun. Yet, in the opinion of the Arbitrator, the work performed even without operating the air gun appears to be closer to that envisaged in the *Hammer Job* than in the *Laborer #1 job.* This opinion is fortified by the practice of the Company in paying the higher rate for a full eight hour turn even if the grievants are required to operate the hammer only for a part of that turn.

AWARD

13. The grievance is granted.

T—489, -490.   Ensley Steel Works.   March 21, 1958
Clare B. McDermott, *Assistant to the Chairman*
Approved by Herbert L. Sherman, Jr., *Chairman*

BACKGROUND

1. In these two cases from the Iron Foundry of the Ensley Steel Works, the Union claims that Management has improperly treated the job of Moulding Craneman (No. 6) (Job Class 9) under Sections 9-D and 9-J-3 of the August 3, 1956 Agreement.

2. **T-489** In January, 1957 there was a reduction in operations in the Iron Foundry. Thereafter no hot metal was poured on the C turns (2-10 p.m.) on Friday, Saturday and Sunday, thereby reducing the number of pouring turns from 14 to 11. Hence the job of Hot Metal Craneman (Nos. 4 & 5) was not scheduled on the week-end C turns. However, when ingot mold castings were poured near the end of the B turns on the week-end, the molds had to be partially lifted off the stools and blocked up on the C turns to prevent further shrinking of the casting to the point where it sticks to the central core. The Moulding Craneman was directed, starting January, 1957, to lift the molds on these turns. On other turns this function is performed with the No. 4 or No. 5 crane by the Hot Metal Craneman (Job Class 11) or the Shake-Out Craneman (Job Class 10). Prior to January 27, 1957 this function was performed by the Hot Metal Craneman on the week-end C turns.

3. Two grievances were then filed in February, 1957, by the Moulding Craneman, requesting payment at the Hot Metal Craneman rate for the 2-10 p.m. shifts on the week-ends. These grievances were not settled in the grievance procedure and were eventually docketed as T-488. While these two grievances have been pending, the Company has paid Hot Metal Craneman rates to the Moulding Craneman for some of the work performed by him on week-end C turns. How much is not clear.

4. Management issued an Exhibit G on May 20, 1957, adding the following items to the working procedure of the Moulding Craneman job:

"16. Pulls up moulds, for shake-out crew, that are to be partially stripped at required time.

"17. Strips chills from moulds and sets aside.

"Note: Cranes Nos. 4, 5, or 6 may be used in performing the above duties."

5. This Exhibit G, issued to the Union in May, 1957, was made effective January 27, 1957. Nevertheless, the Company continued to pay grievants at the Hot Metal Craneman rates for some of the work performed on the week-end C turns until shortly before the hearing in the present cases in January, 1958.

6. This is the background of the case docketed as T-489. This grievance was filed in May, 1957.

7. **T-490** In April, 1957, the Company decided that ingot mold stools could be cast at the Ensley Steel Works Iron Foundry by utilizing re-usable metal molds or chills rather than the conventional flasks and sand molds. After sufficient cooling the stools are removed from the chills by lifting them out with a magnet.

8. Sometime thereafter the Moulding Cranemen were required to remove the stools from the chills. The Company claims that this work is almost identical to lifting stools with a magnet to load them on railroad cars, and that such work has always been performed by Moulding Cranemen. The Union, on the other hand, believes that lifting the stools from the chills is part of the Shake-Out Craneman's job (Job Class 10), which operates on the A turn the same crane operated on B and C turns by the Hot Metal Craneman.

9. On January 16, 1958 Management issued another Exhibit G to the Union, adding Item 18 to the working procedure of the Moulding Craneman's job. It reads: "Uses magnet to lift stools from permanent molds (chills)." This Exhibit G was made effective April 11, 1957. Since this Exhibit G was issued shortly before the hearing in these cases, the Union states that it should not be considered.

10. This is the background of the case docketed as T-490. This grievance was filed in July, 1957.

CONTENTIONS OF THE PARTIES

11. The Union contends that it was improper for the Company to assign the duties in dispute to the Moulding Craneman job. According to the Union the Exhibit G of May, 1957 was issued with retroactive effect to force a settlement of the two earlier grievances in which the parties had been unable to agree on the amount of time on week-end C turns for which the Hot Metal Craneman rate should be paid to grievants. The Company recognized, says the Union, the applicability of Section 9-J-3 when it paid the Hot Metal Craneman rate for some

of the work performed by grievants on the week-end C turns. The Union asserts that Management has abused the letter and spirit of the Classification Manual.

12. The Union points out that the Hot Metal Craneman continues to perform his job with all its old duties four days a week. Similarly, the Moulding Craneman's duties are unchanged on those four days. It is only on the week-end C turns, when the Hot Metal Craneman is not scheduled, that the Moulding Craneman is required to lift molds for blocking. The Union believes that this is a temporary situation, and that the present problem will no longer exist when pouring on 14 turns is resumed. For these additional reasons the Union believes that issuance of an Exhibit G was improper.

13. In the Union's view there has been no change in the Hot Metal Craneman job or in the Shake-Out Craneman job. Since Management has not changed the job content of these jobs within the meaning of Section 9-D of the Agreement or within Section F-3-a of the Classification Manual, the Union believes that the work of these jobs has been improperly "stretched out" into the Moulding Craneman job.

14. Management takes the position that these cases simply present the question of its right to make changes in the duties of position rated jobs; that this right has been upheld by the Board in numerous prior cases; that its right to change the duties of a job is not affected by the time in which the duties are to be performed; that an Exhibit G is merely a recording device; that there are many jobs that have duties that are performed only occasionally; and that duties overlapping two jobs of different job classes are common, examples in this very Foundry being certain of the duties of the Hot Metal and Shake-Out Craneman jobs.

DISCUSSION AND FINDINGS

15. Because of a reduction in the number of pouring turns in January, 1957, a Hot Metal Craneman was not scheduled for the week-end C turns. Nothing in Section 9-D or the Classification Manual required assignment of a Hot Metal Craneman to these turns. Nor did Section 9-D preclude assignment of the duties in dispute to the Moulding Craneman job. To rule otherwise would be to depart from principles previously established in numerous other cases by the Board.

16. Management has not, however, pro-

ceeded properly in these two cases. When the Company assigned additional duties in both of these cases on a regular basis to the Moulding Cranemen, it was obligated to proceed under Section 9-D of the Agreement and the Classification Manual.

17. The Company is not free to proceed under Section 9-J-3 when duties have been assigned as a regular part of a job, even when the duties are to be performed only on certain turns. And this is true whether the classification of the job remains unchanged or whether the classification, obviously applicable to all turns, is increased. To rule otherwise would sometimes mean that the Company could avoid paying a higher classified rate.

18. In these two cases the Company violated the Agreement of the parties. It should have promptly considered the effect on the classification of the Moulding Craneman job when it added to that job types of duties previously performed by the job of Shake-Out Craneman (Job Class 10) and by the job of Hot Metal Craneman (Job Class 11). In this connection it should be noted that Management has copied duties from the working procedures of these two jobs and added them to the working procedure of the Moulding Craneman job (Job Class 9).

19. Whether the added responsibility of the Moulding Craneman job warrants a higher job class should be determined by the parties. Both parties indicated at the hearing that they did not wish the Board to make any ruling on this question in the present Award.

AWARD

20. (1.) Section 9-D of the Agreement did not require assignment of a Hot Metal Craneman in the Iron Foundry on the week-end C turns starting January 27, 1957.

21. (2.) Section 9-D of the Agreement did not preclude assignment of the disputed duties to the Moulding Craneman job.

22. (3.) Management was obligated, under Section 9-D of the Agreement, to proceed promptly in determining the effect on the classification of the Moulding Craneman job when it added to that job types of duties previously performed by the Shake-Out Craneman and Hot Metal Craneman jobs.

23. (4.) The parties should determine whether the additional duties require a higher job class for the Moulding Craneman job. The Board makes no ruling on this question.

CHAPTER 6

CLAIM OF NO SIGNIFICANT CHANGE IN JOB CONTENT

Many cases involve the claim that there has been no significant change in the job content of a disputed job and therefore that there should be no change in the classification of that job. In this chapter cases raising that issue are set forth chronologically in each of three groups. The first group consists of awards by Sylvester Garrett; the second group consists of awards by the editor of this book; and the third group consists of awards by Ray Forrester, Frederick Harbison, Donald Crawford, Jacob Blair and John Coleman.

See also Chapter 14 "More of the Same" Principle.

Other relevant cases reported elsewhere in this volume are: T-239 (page 344), T-265 (page 7), A-754 (page 296), A-755 (page 259), USC-293 (page 232), USC-367 (page 172), USC-371 (page 273), USC-383 (page 277).

CI—224.   Edgar Thomson Works.   October 2, 1951
Sylvester Garrett, *Chairman*

BACKGROUND

1.   This grievance involves the job of Rail Driller in the Finishing Department of the Rail Mill. The Union contends that the relative worth of Factors 5, 9 and 11 of the subject job have been changed by installation of a hand-operated wedge on the end stop of the rail drilling machine. Before reaching the drill presses which are operated by the Rail Mill Drillers, all rails are inspected on beds and easily distinguishable marks are placed on the rail to show if either or both ends of the particular rail are not square. The mark indicates that the end must be squared on a milling machine.

2.   Prior to adoption of the hand-operated wedge, rails with properly squared ends were moved onto the drill presses by the operators and drilled to meet specifications. When the mark on the end of a rail indicated that it was not square, however, the rail was not drilled but instead was channeled to a milling machine where the end was squared properly. Thereafter, the rail was drilled by other operators at another location.

3.   In an effort to improve operations, management instituted use of a hand-operated wedge or plate 3/16 of an inch thick, which was inserted on the shaft of the end stop block and left in position for all rails with properly squared ends. When a rail marked as having a bad end came along, it was no longer necessary to divert it for mill-

ing elsewhere, since the wedge then could be pulled out to permit the end stop to be pushed 3/16 of an inch back. Then the holes could be drilled in the off-square rail that much further from the end. Off-square rails thus drilled could be properly squared later, leaving the drilled holes in proper position to meet customer specifications. Use of the wedge was started in March, 1949, and on the average, about 10 to 12 off-square rails are drilled each turn through use of the device.

4.   The subject job, known as Driller, Plant Code No. 4311-051 was described and classified by representatives of the parties under the Wage Inequities Program prior to installation of the standard hourly wage rates on February 9, 1947. The question here presented, therefore, is whether the change in method incident to adoption of the wedge in May, 1949 has so changed the nature of the job that it now should be classified at a higher level.

5.   As to Factor 5—Responsibility for Materials, the Union contends that the job now requires frequent checking and adjusting of the wedge to insure proper drilling. This alleged increased attention is the result of the changed set-up.

6.   As to Factor 9—Mental Effort, it is contended that the job now requires moderate mental or visual application required to check markings and adjust wedge for proper variance. The Union believes that the visual concentration required by the

122

job has increased to a measurable extent application of the change.

7. As to Factor 11—Surroundings, it is the Union's position that introduction of the wedge, which was accompanied by an enlargement of the end stop, has resulted in blocking the flow of water used to cool the drills. This prevents the water from flowing off the rails as freely as had been normal prior to introduction of the change. With the enlarged end stop and inserted wedge, water normally now runs down over the rails to an extent which was not previously true. Thus when the rails are manipulated by the Drillers, they become wet to an appreciably greater degree than previously.

8. It is the Company's position that there has been no change in the job content. As the Company visualizes the situation, there merely has been a slight increase in the number of rails drilled per turn, which of itself does not change the job content, and therefore the existing job description and classification is proper and must remain in effect under the provisions of Section 9-D of the April 22, 1947 Agreement.

DISCUSSION AND FINDINGS

9. The Union's position in the present case was carefully presented by three witnesses, all of whom at one time or another had served as Rail Drillers on this particular job. It thus was possible, together with the other evidence, for the Board to obtain a satisfactory picture of the job as it was performed prior to installation of the new device, and as it has been performed subsequent thereto.

10. After a careful review of the evidence presented by the Union witnesses, it appears to the Board that the introduction of the gadget did not materially change the requirements of the job under either Factor 5 or 9. With respect to Factor 11, there definitely was an increase in the amount of wetness to which the Rail Drillers were subjected. In recognition of this fact, however, management made adjustments to the end screw which had the effect of facilitating the flow of water off the rails as they were being drilled, and substantially restored the situation to what it had been prior to introduction of the new device.

11. The Board was impressed with the fact that the subject job was initially described and classified in accordance with the Wage Inequity Program, and that at that time the plant representatives of the parties were unable to agree on the classification of the subject job. This dispute was thereupon referred to the Cooper-Maloy Committee which resolved the question, agreeing upon and signing the description and classification form. This had the effect of classifying the subject job at the same level as a similar job at Gary Works. Thereafter, plant Union representatives endeavored to have the matter of the subject job's classification re-examined once more during the "review period." Plant management declined to join the Union in this request for a review, and as a result the job remained in the classification assigned to it by the Cooper-Maloy Committee. From the testimony of the Union witnesses at the hearing, it appeared that dissatisfaction with the initial classification has persisted to some extent, and was largely responsible for presentation of the instant grievance.

12. Under all of the evidence it is clear that the introduction of the new device in May of 1949 did not produce a sufficient change in the requirements of the Rail Driller job to warrant a higher job classification, within the meaning of Section 9-D of the Agreement.

AWARD

13. The grievance is denied.

A—697. Joliet Works. May 27, 1955
Sylvester Garrett, *Chairman*

FINDINGS

1. The Union seeks Job Class 17 for the job of Boiler House Operator, now in Job Class 12, at Joliet Works. Higher ratings are sought on Factors 1, 2, 3, 4, 5, 6, 7, 10 and 12. Installation of new water treating equipment at the Boiler House in February, 1952, gave rise to the present grievance. The new equipment replaced the former equipment for treating the water, and caused some deletions and additions in the duties of the Boiler House Operator.

2. Instead of changing four water strainers per turn as was previously required, the Operator now only changes one strainer. He no longer operates valves at the old feed regulator tank to regulate the flow of a chemical solution from a chemical mixing tank. Nor does he add a caustic solution to the old feed regulator tank. On the other hand, he must now check the new pumps

and the new sediment tank every two hours and draw off the sediment as necessary, which requires about five minutes every two hours when the Water Treater is not present.

3. Actual mixing of the chemicals and charging them into the water are the duties of the newly created job of Water Treater, whose primary function is the operation of the new water treating equipment. This job operates only on the day turn. Several times each turn when the Water Treater is not scheduled, the Operator must check the water level in the new soda ash, lime and adjunct tanks and he must operate a valve to increase or decrease the water level if necessary. Occasionally, he may shut off the flow of the solution from these tanks.

4. No new duties have been added to the job of Boiler House Operator, which require higher skills or a higher degree of responsibility or effort than have already been credited by the existing classification. Nor have the hazards of the job been increased. In view of Specimens 550, 552, 554, 555 and 556 for a Boiler House Operator (all of which are in Job Class 11 or 12) and the previous Awards of the Board, it must be found that the job in dispute is appropriately classified.

5. Further contentions of the Union are based upon duties and conditions which, though they may not have been detailed in the original job description, do not represent actual changes in job content from the time that the job was originally described and classified. The grievance cannot be sustained on the basis that certain duties, always performed, are now found listed on the written job description. Such duties and conditions involve directing minor maintenance work (for example, removing and replacing broken grate bars and shear pins), packing pumps and valves, and the absence of a foreman on the afternoon and night turns.

6. Nor can the Board increase the classification of the present job merely because a Boiler House Operator—Leader at the Worcester Plant has been assigned a higher job class. The Board is obliged to confine its decision to the applicable Specimen Examples and cannot classify the present job on the basis of an isolated job at the Worcester Plant. And finally, although the Union urges application of the Group Leader Convention to this case, it must be noted that the job with the highest job class in the group led by the Boiler House Operator is in Class 8. The new job of Water Treater, which also falls under the Operator's direction, is in Class 7. Application of the Convention, therefore, would not sustain the Union's position that a higher job class than Class 12 is warranted for the job in dispute.

AWARD

7. The grievance is denied.

T—350. Fairfield Tin Mill. March 30, 1956
Sylvester Garrett, *Chairman*

FINDINGS

1. This grievance from the Assorting Warehouse and Shipping Department of Fairfield Tin Mill asserts that the job of Supplyman (Class 5) is coded improperly in view of changes in job requirements.

2. The Supplyman job initially was in Class 4, but was raised to Class 5 during the 1951 Review Program at T.C.I. The Working Procedure, as of May 29, 1951, declares:

"1. Sizes up product to be reckoned and/or wired to determine amount and sizes of platforms and all other supplies needed in order that Reckoners and Wiremen, Package will have proper supplies to complete their turn's work.

2. Plans necessary routine for the delivery of supplies in the most convenient routing in assigned section.

3. Obtains hand truck and goes to Box House for supplies and loads same on hand truck as required.

4. Pulls hand truck to various working positions and places supplies in most convenient manner.

5. Cuts and folds wrapping paper as required.

6. Carries excess supplies back to Box House.

7. Makes out a written report of all shortages of supplies in Box House and turns same over to immediate Foreman.

8. Relocates supplies in Assorting Room to meet changing conditions.

9. Reports any needed repairs to hand truck.

10. Returns hand truck to proper place at end of turn.

11. Maintains a neat and properly sup-

plied location for the different sizes, grades, and other types of supplies in Assorting Room and Box House.

12. Helps unload or stack supplies from store house.

14. Stamps code on lacquered or black plate tickets and labels or code labels as required."

3. Effective December 17, 1953, a Form G was issued changing Item 14 of the Working Procedure to Item 13, and adding two items as follows:

"14. Opens up bundles returned from warehouse as required.

15. Assembles, weighs, and records weight of extra supplies, required by special orders, to be loaded in boxcars or trucks."

4. As a result of adding a scale to be used in weighing extra supplies, the Company revised the coding of Factor 6 from A-Base to BL-.2. The Union holds that this action does not suffice to reflect changes in job duties which justify increased codings, and Factors 1, 3, 5, 6 and 10 now are in dispute.

5. The differences between the parties on the Factors are as follows:

FACTOR	PRESENT CLASSIFICATION	UNION'S PROPOSAL
* 1	A-Base	B 0.3
2	B 0.4	B 0.4
* 3	B 1.0	C 1.6
4	A-Base	A-Base
* 5	A-Base	B 0.8
* 6	BL 0.2	CL 0.4
7	C 1.0	C 1.0
8	B 0.4	B 0.4
9	B 0.5	B 0.5
*10	C 0.8	D 1.5
11	A-Base	A-Base
12	B 0.4	B 0.4
	4.7	7.3

6. Much of the Union evidence concerns duties and conditions affecting the job which existed well before the Review Program in 1951. Much stressed as to Physical Effort, for example, is the fact that a new storage room, accessible by ramp, was put in use in 1950. This reflected the need for greater variety and larger sizes of packaging supplies, which had developed over the years. Also in this vein, the Union emphasizes the Mental Skill involved in determining and selecting proper packaging materials to supply the Reckoners and Wiremen.

7. There is no doubt, however, that the added duties reflected in the December 17, 1953 Form G are not of great significance in the disputed Factors. They are performed only on very few occasions through the year, and appear to have been dealt with adequately by the adjustment in Factor 6 already made.

8. The Board cannot go behind the 1951 Review Program to re-evaluate Factors which have not been affected materially by the added duties set forth in the Form G, or otherwise arising since 1951.

AWARD

9. The grievance is denied.

T—361. Ensley Steel Works.   April 24, 1956
Sylvester Garrett, *Chairman*

BACKGROUND

1. This grievance involves the effect of additional duties on the classification of the job of Hammer Driver in the Forge Shop at Ensley Steel Works. The job in dispute has always operated the controls for an 1100 lb., 1500 lb., 2000 lb., or 3000 lb., hammer. Effective January 3, 1955, by use of a Form G, "electrically operated jib crane" was added to the Tools and Equipment of the job, and "Operates jib crane to handle material to and from furnace and hammer" was added to its Working Procedure. Operation of the new jib crane and hammer by one man at a single physical location is practically identical with the part-time operation of an electrical jib crane and hammer by a Blacksmith Helper job at Fairfield Steel Works. The new crane at Ensley replaced an old jib crane, of a different type, which was usually handled by a Blacksmith Helper.

2. Management took the position that these changes did not have any effect on the classification of the Hammer Driver job. Consequently, the present grievance was filed on January 6, 1955, requesting a new description and classification. While the grievance was being processed, the Company also changed the location of the controls for the furnace doors, so that grievants must also operate these controls to charge the materials into the furnaces. Previously, the

controls for the furnace doors were located beside the furnace, and were operated by the Blacksmith crew.

3. During the 1951 Review Program the description and classification for this job were replaced. From 1946 to 1951 the job was known as Blacksmith Handyman "A" in Job Class 9. The new job description was copied, almost word for word, from Specimen Example 909 for a Hammer Driver, and the new codings were identical with those for Specimen 909, resulting in a total of 5.9 points.

4. Although the Union argues that operation of an E.O.T. crane in the Blacksmith Shop storage yard has also been added to the Hammer Driver Job since 1951, there has been no significant change in the assignment of such duties since 1949 when the Stockyard Crane was installed. At that time a separate job description and classification, in Job Class 6, were installed for a Stocking Craneman. Since 1949 both Hammer Drivers (called Blacksmith Handymen prior to 1951) and Blacksmith Helpers have been assigned to the operation of this crane as required—usually no more than one hour a day. These duties were not added to the old job description for a Blacksmith Handyman "A." Nor were they incorporated in the new Hammer Driver job description in the 1951 Review Program. Even though an incumbent of the Hammer Driver job on the afternoon shift is assigned fairly regularly, for a short period of time, to the job of operating the Stockyard Crane, it is clear that some of the Hammer Drivers are not assigned to this task. In fact, it appears that some are not able to operate the E.O.T. crane. In the absence of some agreement of the parties, or change in the assignment of such duties, operation of the Stockyard Crane cannot be considered as having been transferred from a Stocking Craneman job to the Hammer Driver job.

5. The following table shows the present classification codings of the Hammer Driver job and the codings proposed by the Union:

FACTOR	PRESENT CLASSIFICATION		UNION POSITION	
* 1. Pre-Employment Training	A	Base	B	.3
* 2. Employment Training and Experience	B	.4	C	.8
3. Mental Skill	C	1.6	C	1.6
4. Manual Skill	B	.5	B	.5
5. Responsibility for Materials	C	.5	C	.5
* 6. Responsibility for Tools and Equipment	B	.3	C	.4
* 7. Responsibility for Operation	B	.5	C	1.0
* 8. Responsibility for Safety of Others	B	.4	C	.8
9. Mental Effort	C	1.0	C	1.0
*10. Physical Effort	B	.3	C	.8
*11. Surroundings	B	.4	C	.8
*12. Hazards	A	Base	B	.4
Total		5.9		8.9

*Factors in dispute

DISCUSSION AND FINDINGS

6. The most appropriate guides to evaluate the effect of the changes in the job in dispute are the Specimen Examples for Blacksmith Shop jobs; Specimen 703 for a Jib Crane Operator; and the Blacksmith Helper job at Fairfield Steel Works which operates, on a part-time basis, both an electrical jib crane and a 2,500 lb. hammer. The duties of the latter job have remained unchanged since sometime prior to 1951. When it was reviewed by the parties in the 1951 Review Program, the total point value was raised from 5.6 to 6.3.

7. Other jobs presented to the Board are distinguishable. The Forge Driver (Axles) job in the Forge Shop at Fairfield Steel Works, relied upon by the Union, is not comparable. That job operates a five-ton hammer and a jib crane in roughing and finishing axles. It was obviously classified by reference to Specimen 906 for a Hammer Driver Job which operates a 6,000 lb. hammer.

8. On Factor 1, like the job in dispute, both Specimen 909 for a Hammer Driver who operates a 3,000 lb. hammer, and Specimen 703 for a Jib Crane Operator, are coded at A Base. The same is true of the Blacksmith Helper job in the Forge Shop at Fairfield Steel Works, which requires the same skills as grievants in the operation of the hammer and the jib crane. On the "skill" Factors this job provides a very appropriate guide. For Factor 2 Specimen 909 receives a rating of B .4, while Specimen 703 is coded at A Base. The Blacksmith Helper job at Fairfield Steel Works is assigned B .4 on Factor 2, the same as the job under consideration. Since the present ratings on Factors 1 and 2 for the Hammer Driver job at Ensley Works are as high as those found on the most closely related job, they must be considered appropriate.

9. With respect to the "responsibility"

Factors, however, the Blacksmith Helper job at Fairfield Steel Works is distinguishable, both because it operates the hammer and the jib crane for a limited amount of time, and because it is physically impossible for that job to operate the furnace doors from the hammer driver location. As in the prior situation at the Ensley Forge Shop, the furnace doors are operated at the furnace by various members of the Blacksmith Crew. No such responsibility is placed on one job by the use of electric controls at the back of the hammer.

10.   Grievants now must exercise a higher degree of care and attention under Factor 6—Responsibility for Tools and Equipment. Because of the possibility of harm to the furnaces from improper operation of the new equipment by control buttons located behind a hammer which partially obstructs grievants' view, the Board concludes that, in the light of Specimen Example jobs for a Blacksmith Shop, the Union request for C .4 must be granted.

11.   For Factor 7 Specimen 909 is coded at B .5 and Specimen 703 at C 1.0. With the added duties there is no reason why the job in dispute should not also be coded at C 1.0 in this Factor. Grievants have greater responsibility for operations than they had when they merely operated the hammer controls to control the rapidity and the force of the hammer blows. By operation of controls for handling material to and from the furnace and hammer, and by operating the furnace doors to charge material into the furnace, they also have greater responsibility for operations than incumbents of Specimen 909. Considering the combination of the old and new duties in the light of the applicable Specimen Examples, the Board finds that C 1.0 is the appropriate rating for Factor 7.

12.   The additional duties have likewise increased grievants' Responsibility for Safety of Others under Factor 8. While the Blacksmith Helpers are positioning a piece on the die, the Hammer Driver not only controls the hammer lever, which keeps the piece on the die, with his left hand, but he also operates the jib crane controls with his right hand at the same time. Negligence on his part could seriously injure the Blacksmith or Helpers. Moreover, because the position of the air valves, which control the opening and lowering of the furnace doors when the furnace is being charged, is behind the hammer, he must lean over in order to see the furnace, and must exercise considerable care and attention to prevent injury to the Blacksmith and his Helpers.

13.   The resultant combination of duties gives him a degree of Responsibility for Safety of Others more like that of Specimen 906, and therefore requires a higher degree of care and attention than either Specimen 909 for a Hammer Driver or Specimen 703 for a Jib Crane Operator, both of which receive B .4 on this Factor. Under all the evidence the Board concludes that the Hammer Driver job should be coded at C .8 for this Factor.

14.   There has been no significant change to affect the ratings on Factors 10, 11 and 12. The average degree of physical effort is substantially the same. The surroundings are the same. The work station is the same, and is out of reach of the new jib crane.

AWARD

15.   The grievance is sustained to the extent that the rating on Factor 6—Responsibility for Tools and Equipment is raised from B .3 to C .4, the rating on Factor 7—Responsibility for Operations is raised from B .5 to C 1.0, and the rating on Factor 8—Responsibility for Safety of Others from B .4 to C .8. Since the new ratings result in an increase of one full job class, grievants are entitled to retroactive compensation from January 3, 1955.

USC—589.   South Works.   November 9, 1956
Sylvester Garrett, *Chairman*

FINDINGS

1.   This grievance from the Chemical Laboratory, Metallurgical Division, South Works, claims changes in job content requiring redescription and reclassification of 12 jobs:

1.   Laboratory Laborer
2.   Chemical Technician (#2 Elect. Fce.)
3.   Chemical Technician (#2 O.H. Ladles)
4.   Chemical Technician (#3 O.H. & Bess. Ladles)
5.   Samplers
6.   Supply Man
7.   Test Preparer (Drillings)
8.   Test Preparer Helper (Drillings)
9.   Spectrographic Technician (Preparation)
10.   File Clerk—Lab. Office
11.   Test Clerk Report
12.   Chemical Technician—#2 O.H. Floor (Pre.)

2. The bulk of the evidence in support of this grievance constitutes a restatement and reanalysis of the original job elements which were present when the job was described and classified under the Inequities Program. There is no persuasive showing of changed job content in these jobs for purposes of Section 9-D.

AWARD

3. The grievance is denied.

USC—586. Fairless Works. December 21, 1956
Sylvester Garrett, *Chairman*

FINDINGS

1. This grievance claims a change in the job of Tractor Operator (Hooker) in the Sheet Annealing Department, Sheet and Tin Division, Fairless Works, to the extent of one full job class or more since original description and classification of the job. It requests that the job be reclassified in accordance with Section 9-D of the July 1, 1954 Agreement.
2. The Union believes that the duty of placing thermocouples in the outer wraps of top coils in the annealing furnace was imposed on the Tractor Operator (Hooker) after the job was classified by agreement on February 25, 1954. The Company holds that the function was performed by the Tractor Operator (Hooker) prior to February 25, 1954, and was too insignificant in any event to warrant inclusion in the job description at that time. Moreover, it stresses that even if such a duty had been added, it would not warrant increase in the agreed job class under Section 9-D.
3. The evidence reveals that the disputed duty was performed by the Tractor Operator (Hooker) to a significant extent prior to February 25, 1954, even though also performed occasionally by Assistant Annealers as a matter of teamwork among the crew. The situation in this respect does not appear to differ materially today, and there has been no change in job content for purposes of Section 9-D.

AWARD

4. The grievance is denied.

G—87. Geneva Works. June 25, 1957
Sylvester Garrett, *Chairman*

FINDINGS

1. In this grievance the Pig Machine Operators, Blast Furnace Department, Geneva Works, protest against being required to perform minor maintenance repairs to the Pig Machine at the Pig Machine Operator rate of Class 10, rather than at the rate for Millwright, Class 14.
2. The job description of Pig Machine Operator includes "directs and assists in making minor repairs and lubricating equipment." The tools and equipment mentioned in the description include sledge, chokers, and bars—all used in making repairs to the Pig Machine chain as needed. There is no question that when the job description was written Pig Machine Operators were performing, and had performed, this type of maintenance work. On the other hand, it is clear that Millwrights are used for major repairs to the Pig Machine of a sort not involved in this case. Under the evidence the grievance lacks merit.

AWARD

3. The grievance is denied.

USC—605. Youngstown District Works. June 25, 1957
Sylvester Garrett, *Chairman*

BACKGROUND

1. This grievance from the Operating Maintenance Department, Blast Furnace Division, Ohio Works, requests that the Electric Crane Repairman (Central Maintenance) (Class 11), be redescribed and classified because of claimed gradual changes in the job commencing about 1950.
2. The job description, dated August 23, 1946, provides:

PRIMARY FUNCTION:
To make general repairs to electrical and mechanical equipment in the field.

CLAIM OF NO SIGNIFICANT CHANGE IN JOB CONTENT 129

TOOLS AND EQUIPMENT:
Wrenches, sledges, jacks, bars, block and tackle, chain blocks, slings, power grinder, drills, burning equipment, etc.

MATERIAL:
Cables, armatures, gears, bearings, cable, drums, motors, driveshafts, brake wheels, shoes, brakes, etc.

SOURCE OF SUPERVISION:
Electrical Turn Foreman (B.F.). Receives work instructions from Motor Inspector when assisting them on repair jobs.

DIRECTION EXERCISED:
None.

WORKING PROCEDURE:
Repairs all types of electrical and mechanical equipment as changing cables, armatures, gears, bearings, cable drums, motors, drive shafts, brake wheels, shoes, brakes, etc.

Makes hitches to handle material by crane block and tackle, chain blocks, etc.

Uses burning outfit for rough work.

Selects tools from repairs.

Assists the Motor Inspector on major repair jobs handling heavy equipment, etc.

3. The Electric Crane Repairmen in the Blast Furnace work in a Bull Gang, day shift only and perform major repairs. Because there is some new equipment and replacements of old equipment and some change in the direction of the Repairman by Motor Inspectors, the Union believes there has been a substantial increase in the responsibilities of the job.

4. On this basis the Union feels that the job now is comparable to Crane Repairman (Class 14) at the Homestead Works, where the job description, dated July 1, 1946, states:

PRIMARY FUNCTION:
To repair and maintain all electric and mechanical equipment on cranes, charging machines and transfer buggies throughout the plant.

TOOLS AND EQUIPMENT:
200-Ton press, hoisting pulley burning torch, air drill and grinder, sledge chisels, block and tackle, jack, miscellaneous wrenches, etc.

MATERIAL:
All types and sizes of electrical equipment, grease, oil, wire, cleaning fluid, etc.

SOURCE OF SUPERVISION:
Gang Leader.

DIRECTION EXERCISED:
Helpers.

WORKING PROCEDURE:
Reads blueprints and lays out repair work.

Operates 200-ton press in fitting up and assembling shafts, gears, pinions, track wheels and armature shafts on various kinds of equipment.

Operates hoisting pulley and air hoist.

Assembles brakes gearing and main contact poles on crane installed by American Bridge Company or cranes in service.

Inspects main hoist cables on hot metal cranes.

Inspects and makes final adjustments and newly installed equipment.

Directs and Assists in:
Changing bridge drivers and followers, trolley drives and track wheel bridge line shafts and hoisting trolley shafting and gearing, main hoist, drums, lifting beams, hoisting cables, and various motors from 5 H.P. to 9000 H.P.

Making minor repairs to electrical equipment, cleaning insulators with wireman, etc.

Installing panels and control boards, main feeder and contact rails.

Dismantling shafting, motors, controllers, limit switches, contact rail and salvages same on equipment taken out of service.

Moving or handling any equipment in plant as required.

Assists wireman in installing large overhead feeders or in performing any major jobs that require help.

Directs and assists salvage and disposition of steel and copper scrap.

Directs and assists cleaning of working area.

In addition the Union cites Crane Repairmen jobs at Fairless Works, Irvin Works and Youngstown Sheet and Tube, all in Class 14.

5. The Company agrees that there have been equipment changes since original description and classification of the job, but the evidence reveals no essential change in the actual work done.

6. There has been some change in the manner in which the Crane Repairmen work with Motor Inspectors. In 1946 it was customary for the Crane Repairmen frequently to work directly with the Motor Inspector in whose area a major repair was necessary. In 1948 the Crane Repairmen were moved to

Central Maintenance for payroll and supervision purposes, and a Gang Leader position was established to direct the work of the Crane Repairmen. Because of this more regular source of on-the-job direction, the proportion of their time spent working directly with Motor Inspectors gradually diminished. In 1954 the Crane Repairmen were returned to the Blast Furnace for supervisory and payroll purposes, but continued to work less frequently with the Motor Inspectors. This has been feasible in part because a Turn Foreman now is directly in charge of the Crane Repairmen and keeps in touch with their work at the various locations. Where substantially all of the Gang is working on a major repair job, the Turn Foreman is present through most of the job. But if several small groups of Repairmen are at work simultaneously in various parts of the Division, the Turn Foreman must divide his time among the various locations. Thus, to some extent, not precisely measurable, the Crane Repairmen may receive less on-the-spot direction from the Turn Foreman than they once received from Motor Inspectors in 1946, or from the Gang Leader in 1951.

7. As to this the Company cites numerous specimen and comparable other jobs indicating that even if some measurable change had occurred in the disputed job in this respect, there still is no basis for change of one job class in accordance with Section 9-D.

FINDINGS

8. This case has been presented with considerable care by both parties, and is of more than passing interest in view of inevitable changes over the years in equipment serviced by assigned maintenance jobs throughout the Corporation.

9. Modernization of equipment serviced, alone, does not necessarily indicate change in duties and responsibilities of the assigned maintenance jobs concerned with repair and maintenance of such equipment. On the other hand, logic dictates that some such changes may arise which will affect the job content. The Union believes that this has happened in the present case, and also that there has been significant change in direction of the disputed job.

10. Even assuming change in this regard, however, the evidence does not show it to be of such magnitude as to require new description and classification within the meaning of Section 9-D. Under Specimens 1020, 1022 and 1027, and various other jobs cited by the Company, there is no basis to require a change of one full job class. The Homestead, Gary, Fairless and Irvin Works jobs cited by the Union, are largely distinguishable because of extensive inspection responsibility (as overhead, or Hot Metal Cranes), use of blueprints for laying out work, making final adjustments in new equipment, or the like.

11. Finally, it appears that the present grievance to a large extent involves a claim of inequity, and extends an effort launched by the Union in 1950 to correct what then was felt to be an error in the original description and classification of the job.

AWARD

12. The grievance is denied.

USC—351. Edgar Thomson Works. October 6, 1953
Herbert L. Sherman, Jr., *Assistant to the Chairman*
Approved by Sylvester Garrett, *Chairman*

BACKGROUND

1. This grievance requests that the classification of the job of Spectrographic Technician at Edgar Thomson Works be increased from Class 13 to Class 17. There is no dispute that two duties have been added to the job: analysis of silica brick and analysis of soluble aluminum. At the Union's request the job description was revised to make it clear that these duties were part of the job in dispute.

2. Also relied upon by the Union in arguing that determinations of high alloy content must be made is an incident which occurred on May 17, 1951. Grievants were required to analyze samples of three heats for copper content by the wet chemistry method. Although the job description provided for wet chemical analysis, this duty was confined to the same class of materials on which spectrographic determinations were made. The spectrographic method could not be used at this time, however, because the existing conversion scale was too low to reflect the quantitative copper content indicated. The copper content found in these tests, though very high, was not present for the purpose of obtaining an alloying effect. Edgar Thomson does not make alloy steels as such. It was a freak occurrence.

3. The difference between analysis of soluble aluminum and an ordinary steel sample is that a solution is used to make the test for soluble aluminum rather than a flat piece. There does not appear to be any other

significant difference in the procedure followed except that a different type of electrode is used and the arc spark stand must be cleaned with acid after each run. The use of acids in wet chemical analysis is not new. In the case of silica brick the polarity of the Spectrograph must be reversed, the grating doors opened, and the proper filter selected after some trial runs. No appreciable change has been made in the equipment.

4. Ratings sought by the Union for the job in dispute and the present factor values relied upon by Management are shown in the following tabulation:

FACTOR	COMPANY CLASSI-FICATION	UNION CLASSI-FICATION
1. Pre-Employment Training.	C-1.0	C-1.0
*2. Employment Training and Experience.	F-2.0	G-2.4
3. Mental Skill.	E-2.8	E-2.8
4. Manual Skill.	C-1.0	C-1.0
*5. Responsibility for Materials.	D-1.6	D-2.4
*6. Responsibility for Tools and Equipment.	C-.7 Med.	D-1.5 Med.
*7. Responsibility for Operations.	C-1.0	D-2.0
8. Responsibility for Safety of Others.	C-.8	C-.8
*9. Mental Effort.	D-1.5	E-2.5
10. Physical Effort.	A-Base	A-Base
11. Surroundings.	B-.4	B-.4
12. Hazards.	B-.4	B-.4
Total	13.2	17.2

* Disputed Factors.

DISCUSSION AND FINDINGS

5. Late in 1950 the Spectrographic Technician job at Edgar Thomson was reviewed by the Joint Wage Rate Inequity Committee as part of the disputes procedure. The Union was seeking Job Class 15 while the Company asserted that Class 12 was proper. The factors in dispute were 2, 3, 5 and 9. It was decided to adopt the Union's position on Factors 2 and 3, thus placing the job in Class 13.

6. Also reviewed in the disputes procedure by the Joint Wage Rate Inequity Committee and coded identically with grievants' job was a Youngstown Spectrographic Technician job whose primary function is: "Responsible on one turn (3-turn position) for spectrographic determination of manganese, silicon, copper, chromium, nickel, molybdenum, tin, vanadium, titanium and zirconium in Blast Furnace iron, Bessemer steel and Open Hearth steel, blooms, slabs, billets produced at the Ohio Works; shapes and bars produced at McDonald and Union Works, as well as samples furnished by Metallurgical Department and customers, and for spectrographic determinations of manganese, copper, magnesium and silicon in aluminum, or performs the same analysis by wet chemical methods when required."

7. Likewise, another Spectrographic Technician job was classified by the parties at Youngstown precisely the same as the job in dispute and in accordance with the ratings found to be proper for the Youngstown job reviewed by the top Committee. Its primary function requires "analysis of all ferro-alloys, brass, bronze, babbitts, silica brick, water analysis, aluminum." (Underscoring added.) Among other items in the working procedure, the following are found: "Makes spectrographic analysis of shot aluminum and aluminum alloys," and "Makes spectrographic analysis of silica brick."

8. Specimen Example 4826 for a Spectrographer is in Class 11. Deviation from this Specimen in the case of the two Youngstown and the Edgar Thomson jobs was based upon the requirement of performing wet chemical analysis. Specimen 4823 for a Spectrograph Operator is in Class 7. Non-Specimen Spectrographic Technician and Analyst jobs presented to the Board range from Class 7 to 13. None are higher, although some non-Specimen Chemical Technician jobs with different basic functions are as high as Class 17. The present classification of the job in dispute adequately reflects the training, responsibility, and effort required by the added duties.

AWARD

9. The grievance is denied.

N—206. Ellwood Works.   October 6, 1953

Herbert L. Sherman, Jr., *Assistant to the Chairman*

Approved by Sylvester Garrett, *Chairman*

BACKGROUND

1. The Car Blockers at Ellwood Works request in this grievance that their job classification be increased from Class 6 to Class 8. The Union contends that Factors 1, 5, 7, 8, and 10 have been affected by the addition of truck blocking to the duties involved in blocking railroad cars.

2. The present Chairman of the Grievance Committee, who was Committeeman for the Car Blockers at the time that the job was classified, asserts that he was told by a Management representative during the Inequity Program that the Car Blocker job would receive Class 7. It is not disputed, however, that the Chairmen of the local Inequity Committees, both Company and Union, agreed upon Job Class 6 as the proper classification. A review of the classification was requested in June, 1947, but no change was made. Continual protest has been made over the failure to assign Class 7 to the Car Blockers.

3. According to Company testimony the Car Blockers have blocked trucks at least since 1943, but it is conceded that the number of trucks to be blocked has increased over the years. Carpenters have been called upon to assist in the rough carpentry work of blocking when the Car Blockers fall behind in their work. Although the original job description does not refer specifically to blocking trucks, a change in the job content record in October 1952 incorporates this duty along with blocking of railroad cars. Management explains that this action was taken to preclude any refusal of the Car Blockers to block trucks on the ground that no specific reference to trucks was made in the job description.

4. Ratings sought by the Union for the job in dispute and the present factor values relied upon by Management are shown in the following tabulation:

FACTOR	PRESENT CLASSI- FICATION	UNION CLASSI- FICATION
*1. Pre-employment Training.	A-Base	B-.3
2. Employment Training and Experience.	B-.4	B-.4
3. Mental Skill.	B-1.0	B-1.0
4. Manual Skill.	C-1.0	C-1.0
*5. Responsibility for Material.	B-.3	B-.8
6. Responsibility for Tools & Equip.	B-.2 Low	B-.2 Low
*7. Responsibility for Operations.	B-.5	C-1.0
*8. Responsibility for Safety of Others.	B-.4	C-.8
9. Mental Effort.	B-.5	B-.5
*10. Physical Effort.	C-.8	D-1.5
11. Surroundings.	B-.4	B-.4
12. Hazards.	B-.4	B-.4
Total	5.9	8.3

* Disputed Factors.

DISCUSSION AND FINDINGS

5. Although truck blocking is not precisely mentioned in the original job description of the Car Blockers, it appears that the incumbents have blocked trucks at least as far back as the time that the job was described and classified. This is so even if the Union's assertion is adopted that Car Blockers as such were established during the Inequity Program and that certain former Carpenters of various classes who had previously blocked cars and trucks became the incumbents of the Car Blocker job. Under Section 9-D of the Agreement, therefore, the present classification, established by the local Inequity Committees, must remain in effect.

6. Furthermore, if it is taken as established that truck blocking was not performed at the time that the job was classified but was subsequently required of grievants, the Board must find that such a duty has not affected the classification ratings. The evidence does not show any substantial difference between car blocking and truck blocking insofar as the factors in dispute are concerned.

AWARD

7. The grievance is denied.

A—663. Joliet Works.   March 31, 1954
Herbert L. Sherman, Jr., *Arbitrator*
Approved by Sylvester Garrett, *Chairman*

BACKGROUND

1. This grievance requests that the job of Scale Inspector at the Joliet Works be placed in Job Class 16. The job in dispute was originally described and classified in 1946 as a Scale Repairman in Job Class 11. It involved the primary functions of inspection, maintenance, repair and installation of the various weighing devices in use throughout the plant. Part of the job required that test weights be transported by a hand buggy to the various locations of the scales.

2. In July, 1951, a small three wheeled tractor was assigned to the only incumbent of the job so that he could pull a buggy containing the necessary tools and test weights to the various scale locations. At approximately the same time the Company decided that it would no longer call in outside servicemen about once a year to "seal out" the scales.

3. A new description was then prepared for the changed job of Scale Repairman. Management classified it identically with Specimen 1090 for a Scale Inspector except that Factor 6 was rated, because of the duty of occasionally operating the tractor, at C-.7 rather than B-.2. This increased the total classification of the original job from 10.5 to 12.1. Specimen Example 1090 has a total point value of 11.6.

4. Although the new job description is not disputed, the Union seeks higher ratings on Factors 3, 4, 7 and 9. At the second Fourth Step Meeting the Union also requested that the rating on Factor 8—Responsibility for the Safety of Others be increased from B-.4 to C-.8 because of the necessity for operating the tractor. This factor, however, is no longer in dispute, since Management announced at the beginning of the hearing that the Union had been notified that its proposed rating on Factor 8 was acceptable to the Company. This brought the total classification to 12.5 for Job Class 13.

5. The Company and Union positions on the factors remaining in dispute are shown by the following table:

FACTOR	COMPANY	UNION
3. Mental Skill	D 2.2	E 2.8
4. Manual Skill	C 1.0	E 2.0
7. Responsibility for Operation	C 1.0	D 2.0
9. Mental Effort	C 1.0	D 1.5

DISCUSSION AND FINDINGS

6. Many of the duties upon which the Union relies were already performed by grievant when the Scale Repairman job was classified. These include the planning of the details of his work, the making of replacement parts and sketches, the inspection and repair of complicated scales, and the direction of machinists and millwrights on major installations or repairs. Although there is disagreement as to whether automatic printing scales or merely hand operated printing scales were in operation at the time that the job was originally classified, the Scale Repairman job description clearly covers "automatic recording" scales. The Union adds, however, that grievant has been required to adjust the printomatic attachment to the Fairbanks Scale so that it will stamp with sufficient force to print one more copy of the correct weight than it was originally set up to print. The Union also asserts that grievant must now requisition parts for his repair work, such as bearings. Nevertheless, these duties cannot justify higher ratings than those presently assigned to the factors in dispute.

7. To the Union argument that grievant's source of supervision is the Machine Shop Foreman while the incumbent of Specimen 1090 derives his supervision from a Scale Foreman, the Company notes that this does not represent a change in his job. The only incumbent of grievant's job has always been directed by the Machine Shop Foreman. The Union's further reliance on the removal of grievant's helper when the tractor was provided cannot serve to increase grievant's responsibility for operations. Nor can the duty of working from manufacturers' data sheets increase the classification since this duty was performed at the time the job was originally classified and is covered by both the job descriptions for the Scale Repairman and for Specimen 1090.

8. Lastly, the new duty of "sealing out" must be considered as being encompassed by the job description and classification for Specimen 1090. It is true, as the Union contends, that the words themselves are not found in the job description. But "sealing out" merely means that precise adjustments must be made at various points around the dial of the scale. The scale could be adjusted properly for weights at 250 pounds, yet it might be inaccurate for weights at 500 pounds. "Sealing out" is the final adjustment

to assure the accuracy of the scale. Specimen 1090 and the job in dispute not only have the same materials and equipment, including various precision instruments, but Specimen 1090 also requires that the incumbent "adjust to weigh correctly in all weight ranges . . . , repair or rebuild scales as required . . . , determine length and lever multiple of each lever . . . , install lever system, (and) check lever system for plumb, level, and square."

9. The changes which have taken place cannot serve to increase the classification of the job of Scale Inspector beyond the Job Class 13 proposed by the Company. The ratings on Factors 3, 4, 7 and 9 for Specimen 1090 adequately reflect the necessary mental skill, manual skill, responsibility for operations and mental effort required in grievant's job.

AWARD

10. The grievance is denied.

N—211. Ellwood Works. September 29, 1954

Herbert L. Sherman, Jr., *Arbitrator*
Approved by Sylvester Garrett, *Chairman*

DISCUSSION AND FINDINGS

1. This grievance requests that the total point value of the job of Charger (Hot Mills Nos. 5, 7 and 8) at Ellwood Works be changed from 8.4 to 10.9. Increases are sought on the ratings of Factors 2, 3, 7 and 9. At the time of the initial classification program, the Grievance Committeeman in this case asked that this Charger job be reviewed, but the Chairman of the Local Union Inequity Committee signed despite his request.

2. Approximately ten duties of the job in dispute are stressed by the Union. Some of them, however, are expressly covered by the job description, and most of the others, though not specifically listed in the job description, were performed at the time that the Charger job was described and classified. Although the Union testimony shows several changes which took place prior to this crucial period, the only changes in the duties of the job established by the Union, which took place after the job was described and classified, involve preparation of a heat slip, visual inspection of alloy rounds to determine if they have been machine centered with a different size hole, checking for center holes in test pieces for stainless steel, and possibly locating steel and throw-outs in a different area from the Steel Yard.

3. The working procedure of the original job description sets forth the following:

"Compiles 'Report of Steel Charged to Hot Mills' setting down work order, size and weight of steel, pieces, cradle numbers, heat numbers, grade, etc., and how steel was charged in furnace."

4. Starting in 1951, Chargers were required to prepare a heat slip by transcribing the work order number and the heat numbers from the "Report of Steel Charged" to a small slip of paper. Copies of the heat slips are then furnished to three different departments.

5. At the time the job in dispute was originally described and classified, Chargers visually examined rounds which had been centered by torch-cutting or drilling a small hole into one end of the rounds. It was their responsibility to make sure that the rounds had been centered. Adding the duty of visually checking machine-centered holes and of checking centers in test pieces in 1953 could not affect the classification of the job. No instruments are used in making this examination since the checking involved is not so precise as to require them. It has not been shown how the additional duties with respect to inspecting center holes have affected the Factors in dispute.

6. The added duties are not significant changes in the duties of the job as it was actually performed at the time it was described and classified. Although the Union presented to the Board several non-specimen job descriptions and classifications for other jobs with higher classifications, which it feels are comparable to the job in dispute, the Company pointed out certain distinguishing features. In any event, in the absence of any appreciable change in job content of the Charger job, the Board is not authorized to disturb the original classification.

AWARD

7. The grievance is denied.

A—775.　Donora Steel and Wire Works.　February 21, 1958
Herbert L. Sherman, Jr., *Chairman*

FINDINGS

1. In this case the Union claims that changes installed by the Company have affected the classification of the job of Rod Mill Weigher, P.C. 41-06, at Donora Steel Works. Higher ratings are sought, under Section 9-D of the August 3, 1956 Agreement, on Factors 2, 5, 6, 7, 10, 11 and 12.

2. The job in dispute was originally Specimen Example 4539. Numerous changes are claimed by the Union. Some of the alleged changes, however, involve duties that have always been performed, changes in workload, or minor changes that obviously would not affect job content for classification purposes.

3. Among the changes which might be considered as affecting job content are the following:

4. (1.) With the construction of a new cleaning house, the work station of the Rod Mill Weigher was moved to a relocated scalehouse. No substantial difference in conditions was effected by this change.

5. (2.) Counting has largely replaced weighing. Instead of weighing the bulk of the rods produced for Wire Mill use, the Rod Mill Weigher now multiplies the bundle count for all Wire Mill rods, obtained from mechanical and IBM counters, by a pre-determined average bundle weight. This function involves only simple arithmetic. No greater skills are required than formerly when the weights were added.

6. (3.) Previously the Rod Mill Weigher recorded by weight, rolling time, order number, customer billet length, etc. Now he must record Rod Mill production by count—hardly a significant addition.

7. (4.) The Rod Mill Weigher has always weighed Normalizing production. Now, in addition, he must weigh Radiant Tube production a couple of times a turn at the Radiant Tube scales. This duty was previously performed by another job coded on all Factors the same as the job in dispute.

8. (5.) Grievants are now required to verify the end of each order or heat by physically checking against the rolling schedule the first and last bundle on the conveyor. To perform this duty grievants walk from the scalehouse to the conveyor to pick up heat tags and make the proper check. Although the Union claims that surroundings and hazards are affected by this duty, the changes in average surroundings and hazards are not sufficient to require higher ratings on Factors 11 and 12.

9. (6.) The Rod Mill Weigher has been assigned the duty of checking production indicated on the new IBM counters against the "line up sheets" of the Production Planning Department. If there is a discrepancy, it may indicate that the counters are not counting properly. The Weigher's duty is simply to advise the Foreman.

10. (7.) If the regular counter becomes inoperative, grievants must also push a button at that time and after it is fixed in order to record the elapsed time of the breakdown. During the breakdown of mechanical and IBM counters, the Weigher must count the bundles of rods. The Weigher has no responsibility for repair of the new counters and recorders. The possibility of grievants' causing damage to the new equipment is remote.

11. (8.) Although the Union claimed that grievants had been assigned primary responsibility for taking inventory, Management stated that no change was intended. It was agreed to insert the words *"Assists in taking physical inventories. . . ."* in the job description so as to be consistent with the previously performed duties.

12. The positions of the parties with re-

	1	2	3	4	5	6	7	8	9	10	11	12	TOTAL	JOB CLASS
						FACTORS								
Company position	.3	.8	1.6	–	C 1.2	B .2	1.0	–	1.5	–	–	–	6.6	7
Union position	.3	1.2	1.6	–	D 1.6	B .5	2.0	–	1.5	.3	.4	.4	9.8	10
Specimen 4539	.3	.8	1.6	–	C 1.2	B .2	1.0	–	1.5	–	–	–	6.6	7
Specimen 4551	.3	.8	1.6	–	C 1.2	B .2	1.0	–	1.5	–	–	–	6.6	7
Specimen 4550	.3	.8	1.6	–	C 1.2	B .2	1.0	–	1.5	–	–	–	6.6	7
Specimen 4538	.3	.8	1.6	–	C 1.2	B .2	1.0	–	1.5	–	–	–	6.6	7
Specimen 4544	.3	.8	1.6	–	C 1.2	B .2	1.0	–	1.5	–	–	–	6.6	7
Specimen 4545	.3	.8	1.6	–	C 1.2	B .2	1.0	–	1.5	–	–	–	6.6	7

spect to appropriate ratings on the Factors for the job in dispute are shown by the following table. Also included in the table are the ratings on Specimen Examples 4539, 4551, 4550, 4538, 4544 and 4545, all of which were Donora Weigher jobs. The incumbent of Specimen 4550 previously weighed the Radiant Tube production now weighed by grievants. The Rod Mill Weigher is also now performing some of the duties previously performed by the incumbent of Specimen 4551.

13.   After examination of all the changes claimed by the Union, the Board concludes that job content of the job in dispute has not been affected to the extent of requiring higher ratings on the Factors.

AWARD

14.   The grievance is denied.

A—776.   New Haven Works.   February 21, 1958
Herbert L. Sherman, Jr., *Chairman*

BACKGROUND

1.   This case involves two grievances, arising under Section 9-D of the August 3, 1956 Agreement, from the New Haven Works. One claims that changes in the job of Wire Rope and Rope Products Inspector, P.C. 28-25 (Job Class 9), require increases in the ratings on Factors 2, 3, 6, 7, 8 and 11; the other claims that changes in the job of Wire Rope Inspector (Process), P.C. 28-23 (Job Class 11), require increases in the ratings on Factors 4, 5, 6, 7, 8, 10 and 12. The fact that the incumbents of these jobs are employees with many years of service is stressed by the Union.

2.   The present classification of each of these jobs and the ratings sought by the Union are shown by the following table:

3.   No specific rating on Factor 12 for the Process Inspector job was suggested by the Union.

PRODUCTS INSPECTOR

4.   Dissatisfaction over the classification of this job has been expressed by Grievance Committeeman Grottele, one of the present grievants, for many years. In 1953 a grievance, making many of the same claims as presented in this case, was filed. This earlier grievance was withdrawn in 1954 without prejudice to the Union claim.

5.   Again, in the Spring of 1956, the Union claimed that a series of changes had affected the classification of this job, requiring revision of the job description. In June

FACTOR	PRODUCTS INSPECTOR		PROCESS INSPECTOR	
	PRESENT	UNION	PRESENT	UNION
1. Pre-employment training	B .3	B .3	C1.0	C1.0
2. Employment training and experience	C .8	D1.2	F2.0	F2.0
3. Mental skill	C1.6	D2.2	D2.2	D2.2
4. Manual skill	B .5	B .5	B .5	C1.0
5. Responsibility for materials	D2.4	D2.4	D1.6	D2.4
6. Responsibility for tools and equipment	B .2	B .5	B .2	C .7
7. Responsibility for operations	B .5	C1.0	B .5	C1.0
8. Responsibility for safety of others	A Base	B .4	A Base	B .4
9. Mental effort	C1.0	C1.0	D1.5	D1.5
10. Physical effort	C .8	C .8	B .3	C .8
11. Surroundings	A Base	B .4	B .4	B .4
12. Hazards	B .4	B .4	B .4	?
	8.5	11.1	10.6	?

of 1956 Management prepared a draft of a new job description for this job, which the parties agreed reflected the job content of this job as of that date. An analysis of this draft, however, discloses that for the most part it is simply an elaboration or paraphrase of the original description.

6.   The inspection function of the job in dispute has two aspects: (1) comparing papers connected with the prospective shipment with the papers connected with the customer's order and specifications, and (2) comparing the product to be shipped with the customer's order and specifications. The comparison of shipping papers with the customer's order and specifications is done by

one of the incumbents in the mill office. The other function is performed in the mill by other incumbents. For the past few years five men have rotated on a weekly basis in the performance of paper work in the office.

7. The Company claims that comparison of shipping papers was assigned to the job in 1944. According to the Union the task was assigned in the latter part of 1945 after the original job description was signed. In any event, the Board concludes that no higher skills are required in this part of the inspection function than in the other.

8. At one time the Products Inspector sent the shipping papers, after making the proper comparisons, to the Head Shipping Clerk before they were transmitted to the Billing Office. This procedure was changed in 1948 so that the shipping papers are sent directly to the Billing Office. This change, however, did not affect grievants' responsibility. Since 1944 the Head Shipping Clerk had performed no function in connection with these papers except for routine transmittal.

9. Although the Union contends that customer specifications have become more rigid over the years, it is not clear whether they are any tighter than the Company's own specifications. As to the latter, grievants have always had to check for conformity. And it is obviously expected of an Inspector that he will keep up with changing specifications for new product.

10. Additional gauges, similar to those always used, are now used by the job in dispute. Such an addition does not affect the classification ratings.

11. The Union contends that there has been an increase in congestion in the warehouse area over the years, and that it is difficult to move large objects. According to the Company there has been an increase in the volume of some products warehoused, but a corresponding decrease in others. It appears that the area in question has always been congested, and that no significant change in job content has been effected in this respect.

PROCESS INSPECTOR

12. The Primary Function of this job has always been, since the job was originally described, "To inspect, test and approve material for customer's inspectors or for stock . . ." These duties are performed at various locations in the plant. The number of incumbents has varied from four to seven.

13. To perform the testing functions, grievants have always used certain testing machines. Under Tools and Equipment in the original job description "Olson testing machine, Warner Life testing machine, [and] Baldwin—Southwich testing machine" are mentioned. The tests are frequently made in the presence of the customer's inspector. Grievants must ascertain that the product is in conformity with the Company's standard practices and with the customer's specifications. Inspection and testing records are also maintained.

14. In the early part of 1954 a Riehle testing machine was added to the equipment of the job. It is used by grievants to test the tension of wire rope slings. Management's conclusion that this addition did not affect the classification of the job, as set forth on the Form G issued at that time, was not challenged by the Union in 1954. The function performed by this machine was previously performed by a hydraulic jack. According to the Union prestressing of rope products is performed on this machine and this is a production function. The Company denies that prestressing is ever done; it claims that only prooftesting is performed. In any event, it does not appear that higher degrees of skill or responsibility are required than already reflected in the present ratings on the Factors for operation of other testing machines. The fact that servicemen are also used by grievants to help in putting the slings on this machine does not alter this conclusion.

15. Additional gauges for the job in dispute, similar to those always used, do not affect its classification.

16. Since 1953 grievants have prepared a Cummar solution. They mix the solution, after weighing out the parts, for use by strand inspectors on the brass plating of cord. The degree of danger from this solution is disputed. Safety devices reduce the hazards involved, and moderate accident hazards for this job are already recognized by the rating of B.4 on Factor 12. This particular duty was apparently raised for the first time at the hearing. On the basis of the evidence presented on this point, no higher rating on Factor 12 can be justified.

SUMMARY OF FINDINGS

17. Most of the principal changes alleged by the Union for the two jobs in dispute have been set forth above. Many other items cited by the Union are not new duties, are similar to duties always performed, or are too minor in nature to affect job content for classification purposes. Such items, therefore, cannot affect the present classification of the jobs in dispute. Other jobs cited by the Union are not in point. None of the changes in duties set forth

above affect job content to the extent of requiring higher ratings on the Factors.

18. However, a couple of other changes also require analysis. Starting in 1956, incumbents of the Products Inspector job were required to go to the Smedley warehouse (a commercial warehouse) to inspect and tag rope before shipment. This assignment required work under outside conditions, since inspection was performed on an open platform. Although the Company states that this was a "nonrepetitive" situation and was due to congestion at the plant at the time of a public "Open House," the Union points out that it continued for eight to ten months. The frequency of inspection at this location is disputed.

19. In any event, further outside work has been added to this job. On June 1, 1957, "Tags material stored in yard, occasionally, as required" was added, by use of a Form G, to the Products Inspector job. Although this change took place after the grievance was filed, the Company is willing that it be considered by the Board. A Product Inspector has been sent outside to inspect product for about a half hour every other day. It appears to the Board that the tendency of the Company in recent years to assign work involving outside conditions to incumbents of this job justifies an increase in rating from A Base to B.4 on Factor 11 for this job.

20. Also on June 1, 1957, "Cut samples from material stored in yard, occasionally, as required" was added, by use of a Form G, to the Process Inspector job. Factor 11 —Surroundings for this job is not in dispute. It is already rated at B.4 anyhow.

AWARD

21. The grievances are denied except that the rating on Factor 11—Surroundings for the Products Inspector job should be increased from A Base to B.4.

CI—195. South Works. October 5, 1951

Ray Forrester, *Acting Chairman*

BACKGROUND FACTS

1. On November 12, 1948, sixteen employees in the Centerless Grinding Shop of the Stainless Steel Warehouse, Alloy Bar Department, South Works, Carnegie-Illinois Steel Corporation (now United States Steel Company), filed the following grievance in the Second Step of the grievance procedure:

"We ask supervision of the Alloy Finishing End to comply and follow Section 2, paragraph B-2, page 7; Section 9, paragraph D, page 35; and Section 14, paragraph A, page 62 of the April 22, 1947 Agreement, and refrain from operating the Centerless grinding machines without the assistance of Helpers."

2. The Union alleges that a Centerless Grinder Operator Helper had been assigned to each Centerless Grinding Machine at all times, regardless of the size of the product, until shortly before this grievance was filed. The Union alleges that the elimination of the Helper on certain small sizes violated Sections 2-B and 14. In addition, the Union alleges that there have been certain changes in material, tolerances, and methods of processing which require a new job description and classification under Section 9-D.

3. The Company denies the existence of any practice of always assigning a Helper to each of these machines. The Company contends that it has added a foot control to the machine which makes its operation even safer than theretofore. The Company denies any changes sufficiently significant to require a new description and classification under Section 9-D.

FINDINGS

4. The evidence does not support the Union's allegation of a past practice of always assigning a Helper to each machine regardless of the size of the product involved. The Union's own witness testified that while Helpers might report on each of the machines, they were periodically transferred from such machines whenever smaller sizes were run and were assigned to other work, such as boxing and packaging material; and the Operator ran the machine without a Helper. This evidence affirms the Company's position.

5. Similarly, there is no evidence to establish a violation of Section 14. The Union witness testified that an Operator could operate this machine without a Helper on the smaller sizes, and had, in fact, done so in the past. The only change in method of operation resulted from the new foot control which was installed for the purpose of making the operation safer than it had been prior to the time of this grievance.

6. In connection with the request for reclassification under 9-D, it is unnecessary to consider the individual elements which the Union alleges have been changed. Nor

is it necessary to engage in any lengthy analysis of the testimony of the witnesses presented by the parties, except to quote some of the statements of the Union's witness. For example, there is the following statement:

"It is the same operation, has been all the way through. The only thing, some jobs require a little closer application. Maybe the customer is a little more particular on the product that he gets, requires a smoother surface or finer finish."

7. On another occasion the Union witness stated:

"The only difference would be, naturally as business goes along, maybe a customer will want a smoother bar, better ground bar. That would be the only difference."

8. Then still further, he stated:

"As far as types of steel goes, I don't think there would be too much difference."

9. In view of these and other similar admissions by the Union's witness, the Board finds that there is no basis for a change in the job description and classification under Section 9-D, and therefore the grievance must be denied.

AWARD

10. The grievance is denied.

CI—225. Homestead Works.—December 19, 1951
Frederick H. Harbison, *Acting Chairman*

FACTUAL BACKGROUND

1. In June 1949 a new 20-ton Porter Diesel Electric locomotive was put into operation in the #2 Structural Yard (of the Company's Homestead Works) for shifting and transferring products to and from various locations in that area. The new locomotive replaced a power unit known as the 10-ton Brookville Transfer Car. Because of this change in power units, the Union contends that there has been a change in job content of more than one full job class within the meaning of Section 9-D of the Agreement.

2. The grievance reads:

"Employees request new job description and classification on new diesel electric locomotive at #2 Structural Yard."

3. The Company contends that the mere changing of the type of power unit for transfer operations does not change in any respect the job classification of the Transfer Car Operator. The Union contends that changes are warranted in Factors 1, 2, 3, 5, 6, 9 and 12. The details of the Union's contentions are included in the Fourth Step minutes.

FINDINGS

4. A careful examination of the evidence presented by the parties, an examination of the job in question, and a discussion with one of the operators involved leads the Board to make these findings with respect to the changes which have been made in the job of Transfer Car Operator.

5. (1.) The new diesel power unit, though somewhat different from the old Transfer Car, does not require greater training, skill or mental effort to operate. Indeed, the controls on the new diesel locomotive are, if anything, easier to operate. There is less jerking and skidding because of the greater capacity of the new unit to handle heavy loads. The new unit pulls heavy loads more easily than the old unit (in its last years of operation) pulled lighter loads. The operators did not contend that the new power unit is more complicated or difficult to maintain. It was shown that a man could learn to operate the new unit in a week's time, provided that he had the necessary experience in performing the job with the old equipment. Though the direct visibility from the cab of the new unit is limited to one side, the operator can indirectly view objects from the other side of the cab through a safety mirror.

6. (2.) The new power unit did not result in any major changes in operating procedures in the job. The track layout and number of bays served are identical. The product hauled on the cars is the same. The same number of cars are customarily handled by the new power unit, namely four in front and one in back. As was the case when the old power unit was used, the operator is required to do switching, and to couple and uncouple cars. Although he may sometimes get assistance in such tasks from other men in the mill, the evidence indicates that such help was "voluntary" when the old unit was used and is still "voluntary" under present conditions. This matter has been a source of controversy between the parties for some time. The Union, in fact, filed a separate grievance on this score, requesting the Company to put in a switchman on this job.

7. (3.) There is evidence that the new power unit can push more *loaded* cars than the old power unit. It is also certain that the new unit can push and haul cars at greater speed than the old unit. No evidence was introduced, however, to show that the allowed or required speed of operation of the new unit was greater than the old. The evidence further indicates that the old power unit, when new, could and did haul practically the same number of loaded cars as the new unit currently handles under normal operating conditions.

8. (4.) It would appear that the new power unit can transfer the same amount of material with less switching and coupling than would have been the case with the old unit, at least in its latter years in use. The operators testified that more product was being handled with the new unit than with the old, but this is probably attributable to the higher level of activity in the Structural Mill as a whole.

9. On the basis of the findings above, the Board can find no significant changes in the job of Transfer Car Operator occasioned by the introduction of the new diesel power unit. The introduction of the new unit does not seem to change in any way what appears to be the major complaint of the operators, namely that the Company should add a switchman to perform the switching and coupling operations. The net result of the introduction of the diesel is to provide a more efficient, better operating, and easy to maintain power unit to push and haul cars loaded with the same products which have customarily been handled by a less efficient power unit with the same operators. For these reasons the Board sees no justification for any of the Union's contentions with respect to changes in the job due to training, experience, skill, responsibility, effort, and hazards.

AWARD

10. The grievance is denied.

CI—226. Homestead Works. December 19, 1951

Frederick H. Harbison, *Acting Chairman*

FACTUAL BACKGROUND

1. On December 6, 1948, the Union filed a grievance requesting that the job of Pump Station Operator, #1 Pump House, in the Company's Homestead Works, be redescribed and reclassified because of alleged changes involved as a consequence of introduction of new equipment. The grievance reads as follows:

"Request change in classification due to change in content of Pump Station Operator's job at #1 Pump House."

2. The Union alleges that Management has violated Section 9, Subsection D of the current Agreement because the installation of new chlorinating equipment has changed the job duties and requirements more than one job class.

3. The parties are agreed that the only relevant changes involve the introduction of the chlorinating unit. This equipment was installed in a building approximately 6' x 6' attached to the #1 Pump House, and consists of a mechanical pump, cylinders of chlorinated gas, and other minor collateral mechanism.

4. The Union contends that the total factor values in the job should be increased from 9.6 to 12.6 points. The Company contends that no increases are warranted in any factor values. The Union proposes increases in values in Factors 2, 4, 5, 8, 11 and 12.

FINDINGS

5. In the Fourth Step minutes, it is noted that the parties ascertained that the Pump Station Operator on two of the three turns per day is required to operate the chlorinating equipment for a period of one and one-half hours per turn. This operation consists of starting the equipment, observing that it is in proper working order, periodically during the one and one-half hour operation visiting the area for the purpose of checking, and finally, shutting the equipment down. The building is well ventilated with windows and a fan, and the door of the building is about six strides from the Pump House.

6. After an examination of the job, the Board has reached the following conclusions:

7. (1.) With respect to Factor 2—Employment Training and Experience, the Union proposes a change from D-1.2 to E-1.6, presumably because the new equipment is more complicated to operate than other equipment in the Pump House. This contention was denied by the Company and also by one of the Operators interviewed. The Union introduced no supporting evidence to justify its position.

8. (2.) With respect to Factor 4—Manual Skill, the Union proposes an increase from B-.5 to C-1.0 on grounds that the Operator works with the maintenance crew on major repair jobs involving the chlorinating unit. The Union introduced no evidence to

support this contention. It is difficult to see why the chlorinating equipment requires more manual skill than other machinery in the Pump House. The position of management as set forth in the Fourth Step minutes is therefore unchallenged.

9. (3.) With respect to Factor 5—Responsibility for Material, the Union proposes an increase from B-.3 to C-.8 because of close attention for part of the turn for frequent inspection of conditions of boiler, feed water, waste fuel, steam and chlorine gas. The Board fails to see how inspections of condition of boiler, feed water, waste fuel, etc., are influenced by the addition of the chlorinating unit. The operation of this unit requires relatively little time on the part of the Operator. The position of the Board in this respect was confirmed by conversations with one of the Operators.

10. (4.) With respect to Factor 8—Responsibility for Safety of Others, the Union proposes an increase from A-Base to B-.4 on grounds that the Operator operates equipment where others are occasionally exposed. It was ascertained that only the helper is in the area of the chlorinating unit except when a laborer carries chlorine tanks to the door of the building approximately once every two weeks.

11. (5.) With respect to Factor 11—Surroundings, the Union proposes an increase from A-Base to C-.8 on grounds that the Operator is exposed to all weather conditions and exposed to wetness, acid and fumes. The Board finds that the Operator works inside except for a few trips each turn to the chlorinating unit, the door of which is only six strides from the Pump House. The addition of the chlorinating equipment cannot significantly change the job with respect to exposure to acid, wetness, steam or smoke. The exposure to fumes from the chlorine gas is not deemed sufficient to warrant an increase in this factor of the magnitude proposed by the Union. Substantial exposure to the chlorine gas would occur only in event of an emergency such as breakdown in the equipment, faulty gas lines, etc.

12. (6.) With respect to Factor 12—Hazards, the Union proposes an increase from B-.4 to C-.8 on grounds that the Operator handles or controls caustic, inflammable or volatile liquids. The handling of the chlorine gas, however, is within closed vessels and pipes. Such operations specifically call for a B-.4 rating according to the Manual.

13. In the light of the conclusions set forth above, the Board finds that the addition of the chlorinating equipment does not change the job of Pump Station Operator (Plant code 7410-237) one job class or more.

AWARD

14. The grievance is denied.

USC—296.   South Works.   August 6, 1952

Donald A. Crawford, *Arbitrator*

BACKGROUND

1. This grievance requests the advancement of the job of loader from class 8 to 9, effective February 13, 1951, (date grievance filed) because of an alleged change in job content in May 1950, of one full job class. During May 1950, conditioning of slab was discontinued, and the job of inspector stopped. The loaders were then told to visually inspect the edges of piled slabs for tears, sponges, scabs, overfill and the like, and set aside defective unconditioned slab. Additionally, the loaders were instructed to prepare part of a Conditioning Report (rejection card) for rejected slabs.

2. Concerning this change the Union, through the testimony of a loader, stressed that the loader, after May 1950, was required to make the same inspection that was formerly made by the inspector and perform some foreman duties as well. In grievance proceedings, the Union specified that the loader was required after the change to inspect surface and edges for sponge, tears, flatness, pipe and off-section, and gauge all slabs not within flatness tolerances. If the slab was unsatisfactory, the loader had to make out a rejection card, and if salvageable, cut it back to maximum length.

3. Management replied that the loader's inspection of unconditioned slab consists of casual observation for obvious defects on slab edges by walking around piled slabs, whereas inspection for conditioning by scarfing involved careful examination of both surfaces and all edges of each slab for minute defects that were difficult to distinguish. Concerning the specific duties itemized by the Union in grievance proceedings, the Company answered that sponge and tears were easily seen, that flatness was determined by observation without gauges, that pipe was not observed unless noted by the painter, and that observing for section was a normal part of the loader's occupation. If the slab was unsuitable because of flatness, the loader directed the slab to an area for straightening. If the slab was salvageable, the

loader determines the salvage possibility by checking orders and marking the product for burning. These changes, the Company said, were very minor.

4. The Union claimed, also, that the conditioning foreman had been removed and the loader given some of his duties. Namely, the loader must see that a full crew is on the job. If not, he must go to the pit foreman or labor foreman and get a man. In the event of crane trouble, the loader must get a repairman. Finally the loader fills out switch orders and scrap reports formerly done by the foreman.

5. The Company pointed out the messenger nature of these assignments concerning crew and repairman, and that, of the reports listed by the Union (Union Exhibits #5-#10), only #5, Conditioning Report, was used by the loader prior to the grievance date.

6. On this score, the arbitrator has restricted his findings to changes in job content prior to February 13, 1951, the grievance date. Hence the reports identified as Union Exhibits #6 to #10 and changes in the loader's occupation resulting from the establishment of a salvage unit in this department have not been considered.

7. The Union in presenting the case did not specify which factors were undervalued. Accordingly, there was little discussion of factor ratings.

FINDINGS

8. The grievance is granted. The change in job content which occurred in May 1950, has increased the Responsibility for Material factor requirement 1.1, from C.7 to C1.8. Since this change totals more than one full job class, Section 9-D of the 1947 Labor Agreement requires that the Union demand for raising the loader job by one job class (8 to 9), effective February 13, 1951, be granted.

RESPONSIBILITY FOR MATERIALS
Present C-.7   Award C-1.8

9. Before the change, the loader job required close attention for part of the turn in directing the handling and loading of semi-finished material. The loader could mix or load improperly. The consequence was expense in ascertaining identification and freight, switching, sorting and handling cost.

10. Now the loader job additionally requires visual inspection of the edges of piled slabs for tears, sponges, and the like, and the separation of defective unconditioned slab from acceptable unconditioned slab. The loader can err by accepting defective slab. The consequence is expense of shipping costs, other adjustment and customer complaint. The probability is indicated by the fact that normally 2% of the slabs are rejected by the loader, and that customer complaints have occurred.

11. Additionally, responsibility for material has been increased by an actual lessening of supervision. Formerly the Department was supervised by a Conditioning Foreman. With the change in product, the Conditioning Foreman was eliminated and the Department placed under the foreman of the 54" mill. The result is that less supervision is given to the department so that the loader has less review or observation of his decisions.

12. The loader is now responsible, with less constant supervision, for the handling and loading of the product and the separation of defective unconditioned slabs. Accordingly, the cost of error has increased from C.7 under $50.00 to C1.8 under $500.00.

AWARD

13. Since the change in job content in May 1950, was one full job class, the grievance is granted. The job of Loader, Code #4350-151, shall be raised one full job class effective February 13, 1951.

CI—231.   Clairton Works.   June 8, 1953
Jacob Blair, *Arbitrator*

THE ISSUE

1. Under the Statement of the Grievance and its subsequent development in the grievance procedure, two issues developed. The first issue is whether the grievance is timely with respect to the April 22, 1947, Agreement. The second issue involves the merits of the allegations made by the Union that the assignment of additional duties to the job of cinder pitman or third helper in the

Open Hearth has changed this job to the extent of more than one full job class.

BACKGROUND

2. This case appears to have arisen out of a meeting held between Management and the Union sometime in 1947. At this meeting the evidence seems to be clear that the duties of the Third Helper were clarified. What is not clear and is a matter of con-

troversy is whether this clarification involved the assignment of additional duties, as the Union has contended, or whether the purpose of the meeting was simply to advise the Third Helpers of what their duties were with respect to the Job Description. The latter position is taken by the Company.

3. The facts of the case are clear in showing that for a considerable period of time prior to April 22, 1947, the Third Helpers did assist the First and Second Helpers in the performance of various duties. Then later, following April 22, 1947, the effective date of the contract of that year, the Third Helpers did complain that the work they had previously assisted on had been given to them as assignments. This work, according to the Union, was accumulative so that discussions of the alleged assignments began in the latter part of 1947, carried through to the submission of the grievance on September 13, 1948, and then to the Fourth Step meeting held April 14, 1950.

CONTRACTUAL PROVISIONS INVOLVED

4. Section 9-D of the April 22, 1947, Agreement reads:

"The job description and classification for each job in effect as of the date of this Agreement shall continue in effect unless (1) Management changes the job content (requirements of the job as to the training, skill, responsibility, effort and working conditions) to the extent of one full job class or more; . . ."

CONTENTIONS OF THE PARTIES

5. On the merits, the Union contends, that Factors 3, 6, 10 and 11 should be increased by a total of 3 points, raising the job from Class 6 to Class 9. More specifically, the Union contends that Factor 3—Mental Skill—should be increased from A-Base to Code B at a value of 1.0; Factor 6—Responsibility for Tools and Equipment—increased from Base to Low B with a point value of .2; Factor 10—Physical Effort—to be increased from D with a value of 1.5 to E, with a value of 2.5, and Factor 11—Surroundings—to be increased from C with a value of .8 to D with a value of 1.6. This request, according to the Union, is based primarily upon the claim that after April 22, 1947, the Third Helpers were assigned the following work:

1—Operation of the dolomite machine;
2—Filling and leveling floors;
3—Mixing materials such as cold patch and chrome ore;

4—Making the cinder line over the heat;
5—Adding ferro-manganese for reboils;
6—Removing and replacing of paddle blades on the rabbling machine.

6. These duties, in the opinion of the Union, deserve the increases in the factor values, as previously outlined.

7. The Union also maintains that the Third Helper at another plant is in a higher classification because of the operation of the dolomite machine, a condition not credited to the Third Helpers in the instant plant.

8. The Union further contends that the grievance is timely. In this respect the Union points to the meeting held sometime in 1947, at which the Third Helpers were specifically assigned the six previously enumerated duties. At this time the Third Helpers expressed dissatisfaction with their classification. Oral discussions continued in the hopes, according to the Union, of securing some kind of an amicable settlement. Failing to reach such a settlement, the Union then filed its grievance on September 13, 1948. Under these circumstances, the Union claims that the grievance is timely.

9. The Company denies the claims made by the Union and contends that the job should be held in Job Class 6. It points out that the work of the Third Helpers has always been that of assisting the First and Second Helpers. The work described under the Union contention was performed in exactly this manner and so continues. Regular assignment of such work is therefore today no different than what practice has been prior to April 22, 1947.

10. On the point of the evaluation of the Third Helper job at another plant, the Company points out that here the work of operating the dolomite machine is specifically assigned, together with the full responsibility of the maintenance and care of the equipment. At the instant plant this does not prevail since all employees on the Open Hearth use the machine, as needed, in order to reduce the arduous physical toil in the job.

11. On the question of timeliness, the Company maintains that the Union must establish that the changes claimed were made after April 22, 1947. Claiming that the Union has failed to do this, it asks that the grievance be denied.

FINDINGS

12. This grievance must be decided on the facts of the job content of the Third Helper after April 22, 1947, as compared with the work performed by this occupation prior to this date. Careful examination of the

evidence shows that the Union contention cannot be sustained under the facts of the case. The grievance is therefore denied.

13. In the preliminary consideration of the issues involved, the Company raised the question of "a consideration of the questions of timeliness and the factual question of when these changes were made." It then followed by the statement that "We would like to get to the merits of the case as well." (Record page 24)

14. From the manner in which the case was presented, it is desirable to decide the issue based upon the merits of the Union claim that the changes alleged were the result of the assignments made after April 22, 1947. Accordingly, the facts will be considered as against the date when the job was allegedly changed, together with the nature and extent of the change. In order to develop this fully, the evidence in regard to each of the disputed factors will be considered separately.

15. *Factor 3—Mental Skill.* The Union is asking that this factor be advanced from Base to Code B with a value of 1.0. This requires that the conditions of the job be such as to, "make minor changes in routine or sequence on repetitive jobs involving selection, positioning and recognition of obvious defects or adjustments where tolerances are liberal."

16. This claim of the Union is based primarily upon the use of the dolomite machine by the Third Helper. One argument is with reference to the evaluation of the job in another plant of the Company. Examination has therefore been made of the evaluation sheets of this occupation, as submitted by the Company in their Exhibit 5. This examination shows that the dolomite machine is used in three other plants of the Company. In only one is Code B given. In that plant one of the primary functions of the Third Helper is designated as operating the dolomite machine. In the other two plants its use is mentioned in Working Procedure. But in neither is Factor 3 evaluated differently than in the plant in which the grievance arose.

17. The basic distinction therefore between the instant plant and that used by the Union for comparison is that in the latter the dolomite machine is regarded as a primary function and is credited accordingly. In the instant plant, the evidence is clear that the operation of this machine is not assigned to anyone but that, instead, all use it as a means of making their work easier. No grounds are found therefore for sustaining the Union contention based on the use of the dolomite machine.

18. There is also a considerable amount of evidence to show that the dolomite machine was put into operation sometime in September, 1945 (Company Exhibit 6). From this point on there is no question but what the Third Helpers, as well as others, used the dolomite machine (record page 66). Thus, it is clear that the use of the machine was a condition prior to April 22, 1947, and during the period that the job of Third Helper was being described.

19. *Factor 6—Responsibility for Tools and Equipment.* The Union claim is again based upon the use of the dolomite machine. It is claimed that this operation satisfies Code Low B providing, "recognize obvious trouble and shut down routine machines and power hand-tools to prevent or minimize damage."

20. Since the use of the dolomite machine, together with its maintenance, is not assigned to the Third Helper and moreover, since it is not a primary function, no grounds are found for sustaining the Union contention in regard to this factor.

21. As pointed out under Factor 3, the evidence is clear that the dolomite machine was used during the period that the job of Third Helper was being described and evaluated, or prior to 1947. Thus it was a condition that existed at the time the job was described and consequently must be considered as having been included in the initial evaluation of the job.

22. *Factor 10—Physical Effort.* The Union claims that the Third Helper should be evaluated in Code E, with a value of 2.5 on the condition of the "extreme physical effort. Extremely heavy lifting, pushing or pulling" as allegedly required on the job.

23. In making this contention the Union rests its case, to a large extent, upon the work involved in the removal and replacing of paddle blades on the rabbling machine; the mixing of cold patch; the requirement that Third Helpers assist on any one of the six furnaces as contrasted with the assignment of the Second Helper to just one furnace and finally the addition of ferromanganese to reboils. These contentions, the Union claims, were made following the meeting sometime late in 1947.

24. Basic to the consideration of this claim is whether the duties were assigned or continued on the same basis as before April 22, 1947, when the Third Helpers gave such assistance to the First and Second Helpers as was required. Controlling in this determination is the question of whether such work was specifically assigned. On this point the testimony of Management is clear. Concerning the meeting in the latter part of 1947, the superintendent stated that this was held for the purpose of clarifying the duties of the Third Helper. This clarification was based upon the job description. Management at

this time took the position that the Third Helpers should continue their duties as assisting the other members of the Open Hearth crew. Most of this controversy appears to center on making the cinder line and repairing the bottoms of the furnace. Reference to Item 3 under "Working Procedure" shows that such a duty was described in the initial classification of the job (Record Pages 127 to 131). Moreover there is evidence that making cinder line and repairing bottoms was a part of the Third Helper's job prior to April 22, 1947. (Record Pages 79, 80). From the evidence, therefore, it is clear that after April 22, 1947, the Third Helpers continued to perform the same duties with respect to making bottoms and cinder line as they performed prior to this date. (Record Pages 79, 80).

25. The same conclusion must be reached concerning the removal and replacing of blades on the rabbling machine, the mixing of cold patch and the handling of ferro-manganese.

26. Concerning the removal and replacing of blades on the rabbling machine, a Union witness testified:

"Q. When did you begin to burn off these paddles?
A. Oh, we didn't get the paddles until, I don't know, around 44 or 45, something like that. Maybe it might have been before that, I don't know.
Q. When did you start burning them off? When did you have to make the changes of paddles?
A. Well, always did, ever since we got the paddles. . . ." (Record Page 45)

27. Concerning the work of mixing the cold patch, the evidence also indicates that this was assigned to the Third Helpers, "back in 1946 and 47" (Record Page 81).

28. On the work of adding ferro-manga-nese it appears that this varies with the sulphur content of the steel and then only at infrequent intervals (Record Page 154 to 155), but here again the Third Helpers, acting under the instruction of the First or Second Helpers, assisted in this work on the occurrence of an emergency (Record Page 64).

29. Thus, the evidence shows that the duties in question continued on a basis of assisting the First and Second Helpers, in the same manner as prevailed prior to April 22, 1947. No change in the job content is therefore noted and, as a consequence, this contention of the Union must be denied.

30. *Factor 11—Surroundings.* The Union contends that this factor should be advanced from Code D to Code E with a value of 3.0 based upon the extreme heat both in front of as well as in back of the the open hearth furnaces attended by the Third Helpers. More specifically, this contention rests upon the assignment of Third Helpers to assist on banks of six furnaces where they perform work both in the front and in the back of a furnace. In addition, the Union contends that the surroundings are made more difficult because of the task of making cinder line above the heat.

31. As reviewed under Factor 10, the evidence shows that the Third Helper has always assisted, as a member of the Open Hearth crew, in the making of the cinder line above the heat. Similarly, there is no evidence to show that the number of furnaces over which the work of the Third Helper is distributed has been changed in any way since April 22, 1947. In view of this evidence, the Union contention on Factor 11 must be denied.

AWARD

32. The grievance is denied.

USC—914, -915.   Ohio Works.   September 15, 1959
John R. Coleman, *Assistant to the Chairman*
Approved by Sylvester Garrett, *Chairman*

BACKGROUND

1. In the summer of 1957, the Company purchased a Northwest 2½ cubic yard diesel powered shovel to replace an old Lorain two cubic yard shovel at the Youngstown Ohio Works. This new shovel, like its predecessor, is used primarily for loading such materials as limestone, flue dust, coke, and refuse slag in the plant area. Both shovels carried a crew of two men: a Shovel Craneman (or Operator) and a Shovel Craneman Helper (or Oiler). The incumbents on the Lorain shovel jobs took over the duties on the new Northwest shovel.

2. The job incumbents, through the Union, are contending that their work is so changed by the new shovel that a higher classification for both jobs is justified. By the time of the hearing before the Board of Arbitration, the disputes had been narrowed down to four factors (Factors 5, 8, 10, 12) on the Operator's job and three factors (Factors 6, 8, 10) on the Helper's job. Subsequent

to the original filing of the grievances, the Company had agreed to an increase in Factor 6 (Responsibility for Tools and Equipment) on the Operator's job from Med.—D 1.5 to High—D 2.0, but this resulted in a change of less than one full job class and hence left the Job Class unchanged at 11. No changes have been agreed to in the Helper's job which the Company has left at Job Class 3.

3. The Union and Company proposals for the two jobs may be summarized as follows:

SHOVEL OPERATOR:

FACTORS	UNION POSITION	COMPANY POSITION
5. Responsibility for Materials.	C .7	C .5
8. Responsibility for Safety of Others.	D 1.2	C. 8
10. Physical Effort.	D 1.5	C .8
12. Hazards.	C .8	B .4
Total Classificaton	13.3	11.6
Job Class	13	11

SHOVEL OPERATOR'S HELPER

FACTORS	UNION POSITION	COMPANY POSITION
6. Responsibility for Tools and Equipment.	Med. C .7	A Base
8. Responsibility for Safety of Others.	B .4	A Base
10. Physical Effort.	C .8	B .3
Total Classification	4.9	3.3
Job Class	5	3

FINDINGS

Shovel Operator (Case No. USC-915)

4. *Factor 5 (Responsibility for Materials).* The Union's request for a C .7 rating here in place of the present C .5 rests primarily upon the handling by the Operator of a new type of lumite slag. The Operator was under instructions to be particularly careful not to get dirt into the slag when shoveling it out of the pit for shipment. But there has only been one instance of the production and handling of this slag, and there is no reason to believe that it will become a permanent part of the Ohio Works operations. The Union's request thus cannot be supported. Basically the responsibility for materials handled is the same today as with the old shovel.

5. *Factor 8 (Responsibility for Safety of Others).* The Operator contends that the mechanical set-up of the Northwest shovel presents him with new risks of hurting others when the shovel is travelling through the yard. While the shovel is moving forward, the boom cannot be swung from one side to the other to avoid hazards which suddenly appear. But most of the time there are no men other than the Helper near the shovel while it is operating. When the shovel moves through the yard, the Operator is customarily accompanied by the Helper who offers the same measure of protection against hazards along the way as was true with the old shovel. It appears that the standard rating of C .8, which is to be found on a wide variety of shovel operating jobs throughout the Company's plants, is fully applicable here as elsewhere.

6. *Factor 10 (Physical Effort).* The Union's primary case for an increase in Factor 10 is based on the added effort in replacing worn cables on the new shovel. It is clear that the effort involved here is greater in each individual instance of changing cables, but these instances occur so rarely that no justification exists for an increase in the factor rating. The average physical effort is not greatly changed by an event which at a maximum has occupied one half of a day during each six-month period since the shovel was purchased.

7. *Factor 12 (Hazards).* The Union suggests that the positioning and swivel arrangement of the cab seat presents hazards to the Operator if he should ever be forced to get out of the cab in a hurry. But this arrangement is very similar to the one which prevailed for seven or eight years with the old shovel; there is no reason to believe the hazards are greater now than they were then. Such Operator jobs as are rated in the Company's plants at the C .8 requested by the Union invariably have some special hazard to them that is absent on the Ohio Works job. The present rating of B .4 adequately covers the hazards on the new shovel.

Shovel Operator's Helper
(Case No. USC-914)

8. *Factor 6 (Responsibility for Tools and Equipment).* The present shovel is more expensive and complicated than the old one; this has led the parties to agree on a higher rating for Factor 6 for the Operator on the new shovel. But there does not appear to be any case for a similar increase in the Helper's rating. Essentially his job is no more complicated than it was on the Lorain shovel. There are more fittings which need attention, but this is a change in quantity of work, not in quality. The consequences of leaving some fitting unoiled or ungreased are seemingly no more serious here than with the

previous equipment. In all respects, the Factor 6 responsibility seems just about the same now as it was before.

9. *Factor 8 (Responsibility for Safety of Others)*. No convincing case for any change on Factor 8 was offered. The parties agreed on a rating of A-Base on the Lorain shovel, and nothing has changed sufficiently with the Northwest shovel to call for a new rating on the responsibility for other men's safety.

10. *Factor 10 (Physical Effort)*. The same findings on the matter of changing cables apply here as were set out for the Operator above. The only remaining basis for a higher rating on physical effort is the extra climbing called for to get at certain of the boom fittings for greasing. This does not appear to be enough to warrant the higher rating requested by the Union. The present B .3 rating is correct for the job.

AWARD

11. The grievances are denied.

CHAPTER 7

CLAIM OF SPECIAL RULES FOR CHANGED JOBS

Special rules have been developed for the classification of changed jobs as distinguished from new jobs. The parties have agreed that "In the subsequent reclassification of a job due to change in job content, consider only the factors affected by the change. Move the job into the next job class only if the change in job content is at least one whole job class." The first three awards in this chapter illustrate application of the first sentence in this quotation, while the last three awards show the significance of the second sentence in the quotation.

Other relevant cases reported elsewhere in this volume are N-148 (p. 314), T-489, -490 (p. 120) and USC-532 (p. 325).

T—179, -180. Ensley Works. April 24, 1953
Sylvester Garrett, *Chairman*

BACKGROUND

1. The grievances seek retroactive pay to June, 1949, due to changes in the jobs of Blowing Engineer and Gangleader (Blowing Engineer) in the Blast Furnace Department at Ensley Works. The decision in T-179, covering the Blowing Engineer, will determine the result in T-180, covering Gangleader (Blowing Engineer), in light of the groupleader conventions agreed upon by the parties on February 14, 1947.

2. In May, 1949, two blowers were added to the Turbo Blower Building, and the Company revised the job class of Blowing Engineer from 9 to 10 to reflect the change in job content. This job was called Turbo Blower Operator Second Class in the initial job description and classification program, and it was placed in Job Class 9. Likewise, in May, 1949, the job previously known as First Blowing Engineer-Turbo was given the title of Gangleader (Blowing Engineer), although the job class remained unchanged at Grade 12. A grievance protesting the Blowing Engineer classification was filed on June 1, 1949. The Gangleaders' grievance, filed June 3, 1949, requested a revised job description and classification.

3. Shortly thereafter a revised job description for the Gangleaders was developed and jointly approved, though the parties continued to disagree as to proper classification. As a result of further study, the job class for the Blowing Engineers was changed from 10 to 11 later in 1949, effective to the date of filing of the grievance. Similar treatment was

accorded the Gangleaders, the Company installing Job Class 13 retroactive to the date of their grievance.

4. The Union did not agree with the classification for either of these jobs, and the grievances were processed through the grievance procedure and docketed by the Board on April 24, 1950. While these cases were pending before the Board, the parties launched a joint review program in 1951. This was conducted for the purpose of eliminating wage rate inequities, which both parties felt existed in spite of the original description and classification of jobs by mutual agreement under the Inequities Program. After considering the entire rate structure the Union submitted about 1,200 jobs for review at this time, and the Company about 65. Approximately 750 jobs were revised rate-wise, following this comprehensive review.

5. Despite the fact that cases T-179 and 180 were pending before the Board, the two jobs here involved were included in the broad review, and adjustments were made in the classifications of both jobs. Blowing Engineer was increased from Class 11 to 13, and the Gangleader job from 13 to 15. These changes became effective September 23, 1951.

6. The Union now seeks retroactive application of the adjustments thus made in 1951 to the dates of the original grievances. It asserts that Management in effect has admitted a mistake in applying the May 8, 1946, Inequities Agreement by agreeing in

1951, that the job class for the Blowing Engineer should be 13 instead of 11 as installed by the Company in 1949. The contractual provision on which the Union's claim for retroactivity is based is Section 9-D-3 of the April 22, 1947, Agreement providing:—

"If Management and the grievance committee are unable to agree upon the description and classification, Management shall install the proposed classification, and the standard hourly wage scale rate for the job class to which the job is thus assigned shall apply in accordance with the provisions of Subsection B of this Section. The employee or employees affected may at any time within 30 days file a grievance alleging that the job is improperly classified under the job description and classification procedure of May 8, 1946, Agreement between the parties hereto. Such grievance shall be processed under the grievance and arbitration procedures of this Agreement and settled in accordance with the job description and classification provisions of the aforesaid May 8, 1946, Agreement. If the grievance is submitted to the arbitration procedure, the decision shall be effective as of the date when the disputed job description and classification were put into effect." (Underscoring added.)

7. It is argued by the Union that the two jobs involved are *new jobs* within the meaning of Section 9-D, and that the final determination of the disputed classification should be based upon a comparison with benchmark and specimen jobs retroactive to June, 1949. In the alternative, it is argued that if the Blowing Engineer is merely a *changed* job, then the Board should consider all of the classification factors in the light of benchmark and specimen jobs, which would result in finding that Job Class 13 was proper at that time. Such finding, the Union holds, must be given retroactive effect to the date of initial installation of the disputed description and classification.

8. The Company contends that the jobs were originally classified by mutual agreement, and were correctly described and classified under the Inequities Manual in 1949, to reflect the changes made at that time. It asserts that the increase in classification under the 1951 Review Program to eliminate wage rate inequities has nothing to do with changes in job content made in 1949. Stress is placed on the argument that even if there was no change in job content, the Blowing Engineer would have ended up in Class 13 under the Review Program just as a similar job did at Fairfield Blast Furnaces.

It points to Paragraph 5 of the April, 1951, Memorandum of Understanding, covering the joint review, and declaring that the ". . . change shall become effective as of the first day of the first pay period after transmittal of the approved description and classification as specified below."

FINDINGS

9. Here the Board must decide what was the proper classification of the disputed jobs during the period from June, 1949 to September 23, 1951. The decision must be based on the Agreement of the parties, as applied to the facts of the situation presented. In view of the provisions of the Agreement, the Board must take up first the question of whether the job of Blowing Engineer was a *new* job which came into existence when the two new blowers were installed in May, 1949, or was a *changed* job. If it is merely a changed job, then the Board must proceed under that part of the Manual (Instructions) for Job Classification of the May 8, 1946, Inequities Agreement which reads as follows:

"In the subsequent reclassification of a job due to change in job content, consider only those factors affected by the change. Move them into the next class only if the change in job content is at least one whole job class." (Underscoring added.)

10. The addition of two Turbo Blowers, with resulting changes in duties and responsibilities, was not sufficient to characterize the job of Blowing Engineer as an entirely new job. In Case T-232, the present parties were in roughly reverse positions as to what constitutes a "new" job. There the Company declared that changes in job duties had resulted in complete elimination of a Bottom Maker position, and the Union declared the job was continued even though the duties may have been changed somewhat. The Board ruled that the job was not eliminated but merely changed. The same appears to be true here. The added duties did not eliminate the old job and create a new one. Rather, it was a changed job which might have required reclassification to a higher level.

11. Therefore, under the Manual, the Board properly can concern itself only with the factors affected by the change in job duties.

In short, the Union contention that the Board now should determine retroactivity on the basis of the parties' ultimate agreement as to proper classification of the jobs, runs afoul of the provision of the May 8, 1946, Agreement quoted above, and cannot be sustained by the Board, even though the parties could have agreed, in the review program, to treat these jobs in a different manner. They did not choose to do so. The Board therefore, must determine, in light of the evidence, which of the 12 factors of the job reasonably could be regarded as having been affected by the change in job content. In this way, the Board properly separates the consequences of the review program, as to these jobs, from the consequences which flow from the required application of the Inequities Agreement during the period from June 1, 1949, to September 23, 1951.

12. The following table shows the status of the various factors of the Blowing Engineer job at relevant times:

From this table, it appears the parties have not, at any time here relevant, been in disagreement as to the classification under Factors 1, 3, 4, 6, 7, 8, and 10. As to the remaining Factors—2, 5, 9, 11, and 12—the Board must ascertain which of them were *affected by the change in job content* reflected in the revised description effective June 1, 1949.

13. It is immediately apparent from consideration of the nature of the changes in job duties that Factors 2, 5, and 9 reasonably could be deemed to have been affected by the addition of responsibilities in the operation of more equipment.* In the case of Factor 11—Surroundings, and Factor 12—Hazards, no evidence has been presented

	ORIGINAL CLASSIFICATION*	CLASSIFICATION INSTALLED RETRO. TO 6/1/49	ORIGINAL UNION REQUEST**	PRESENT AGREEMENT
1. Preemployment Training	B-0.3	B-0.3	B-0.3	B-0.3
2. Employment Training and Experience	C-0.8	D-1.2	E-1.6	E-1.6
3. Mental Skill	C-1.6	D-2.2	D-2.2	D-2.2
4. Manual Skill	B-0.5	B-0.5	B-0.5	B-0.5
5. Responsibility for Material	C-0.5	C-0.5	C-0.7	B-0.3
6. Responsibility for Tools and Equipment	CH-1.0	DH-2.0	DH-2.0	DH-2.0
7. Responsibility for Operations	E-3.0	E-3.0	E-3.0	E-3.0
8. Responsibility for Safety of Others	A-Base	B-0.4	B-0.4	B-0.4
9. Mental Effort	C-1.0	C-1.0	D-1.5	D-1.5
10. Physical Effort	B-0.3	B-0.3	B-0.3	B-0.3
11. Surroundings	A-Base	A-Base	B-0.4	B-0.4
12. Hazards	A-Base	A-Base	B-0.4	B-0.4
	9.0	11.4	13.3	12.9

* The original classification under the Inequities Program was completed for the job as then designated "Turbo Blower Operator 2nd Class." See Step 4 Meeting No. 2, Minutes, March 28, 1950.

** As revealed in Step 3, Meeting No. 4, minutes, November 28, 1949.

which reasonably could be held to support a finding that these were affected. The Company consistently has asserted the contrary, emphasizing that conditions in the Turbo Blower Building actually were improved by installation of air conditioning, and hazards were not increased by mere installation of additional equipment of the sort already in operation. On this record, the Board agrees as to these two factors.

14. In determining the proper values to be assigned Factors 2, 5, and 9, the Board is required to apply all relevant benchmark and specimen jobs. While these were not discussed at the hearing, they have remained the same at all times relevant to a determination of this case, and the parties' own agreement during the review program is the

best available evidence as to how they must be applied in this case. Nothing was presented at the hearing to demonstrate any impropriety in this approach. Looking at these factors, then, it is apparent that had the Manual for Job Classification been applied, in the manner specifically required, to those

* The Company recognized change in Factor 2, when it revised the value from C-0.8, to D-1.2. As noted in this opinion, the proper value should have been E-1.6. On this basis alone the job class as of June 1, 1949, should have been 11.8 (Job Class 12) and the grievance sustained to that extent. Thus, consideration of Factors 5 and 9 does not affect the result in this case.

factors actually affected by the change in job content on or about June 1, 1949, the job value would have been 12.1, or Job Class 12. The coding on Factor 2 should have been E-1.6, instead of D-1.2; on Factor 5, it should have been B-0.3, instead of C-0.5; and on Factor 9, it should have been D-1.5, instead of C-1.0.

15. To this extent, only, the grievance will be sustained. To make retroactive any higher classification would be in effect to apply the parties' later review program to a period earlier than the parties expressly stipulated. This would entail giving incum-bents of the jobs affected a windfall retroactive payment, not received by numerous other employees in positions originally classified too low, and raised under the review program.

AWARD

16. The grievances are sustained in part. Retroactive adjustments for Blowing Engineer (Plant Code 901-485) and Gangleader (Blowing Engineer) (Plant Code 901-480) at Job Class 12 and Job Class 14, respectively, shall be made from the date of initial installation of the disputed classifications up to September 23, 1951.

A—716, -717. Trenton Works. March 26, 1956
Sylvester Garrett, *Chairman*

FINDINGS

1. These grievances protest classification of Factors 2, 5, 11 and 12 of two Tractor Operator jobs at Trenton Works: Tractor Operator (Wire Mill), Plant Code 06-09, and Tractor Operator (Finishing), Plant Code 22-11.

2. The grievances followed addition to the job in February, 1955, of the duty of weighing, using Print-O-Matic scales. As a result of this addition, the Company increased coding of Factor 5 from C.3 to C.5 for each job.

3. Table A includes present and requested codings of the disputed jobs and Specimens 1527, 1528, 1594, 1681, 2119, 2352 and 2386. (Table A below.) All of the cited Specimens include tractor operation and weighing.

4. Factors 2 and 5 of the disputed jobs appear to be in line with the Specimens, and no basis has been presented to indicate that the Specimens are not fully applicable.

5. Concerning Factors 11 and 12, the Union stresses (1) exposure to all types of weather conditions and (2) traffic hazards, both inherent in crossing a main thorofare of the city of Trenton which bisects the plant. Both conditions existed at the time of original description and classification of the jobs.

6. While the Tractor Operators believe the original classification, in line with the Specimens, to have been erroneous, this is not a matter which could be corrected by the Board, even if there were some basis for such a belief. As such, it would amount to a claim of error in original description or classification, which is barred by Section 9-H. In reclassification of a changed job, the Manual permits consideration only of the Factors affected by the change. Absent material change affecting these Factors, there is no basis for the requested higher codings.

AWARD

7. The grievances are denied.

TABLE A

FACTORS

JOB	1	2	3	4	5	6	7	8	9	10	11	12	Total
Disputed Jobs	.3	.4	1.6	.5	C.5	C.7	1.0	1.2	1.0	3	.4	.4	8.3
Codings Requested													
by Union:	.3	.8	1.6	.5	C.7	C.7	1.0	1.2	1.0	.3	.8	.8	9.7
Specimen 1527	.3	.4	1.6	.5	.3	.7	1.0	1.2	1.0	.3	.4	.4	8.1
Specimen 1528	.3	.4	1.6	.5	.3	.7	1.0	1.2	1.0	.3	.4	.4	8.1
Specimen 1594	.3	.4	1.6	.5	.3	.7	1.0	1.2	1.0	.3	–	.4	7.7
Specimen 1681	.3	.4	1.6	.5	.3	.7	1.0	1.2	1.0	.3	.4	.4	8.1
Specimen 2119	.3	.4	1.0	.5	.3	.7	–	1.2	1.0	.3	.4	.4	6.5
Specimen 2352	.3	.4	1.6	.5	.5	.7	1.0	1.2	1.0	.8	–	.4	8.4
Specimen 2386	.3	.4	1.6	.5	.5	.7	1.0	1.2	1.0	.3	–	.4	7.9

TABLE A

FACTORS

JOB	1	2	3	4	5	6	7	8	9	10	11	12	Total
Tractor Operator (W.M.) (54-2— Worcester)	.3	.4	1.6	.5	C.5	C.7	1.0	1.2	1.0	.3	.4	.4	8.3
Tractor Operator (SPM) (72-10— Worcester)	.3	.4	1.6	.5	C.5	C.7	1.0	1.2	1.0	.8	Base	.4	8.4
Tractor Operator (44-33—Joliet)	.3	.4	1.6	.5	B.3	C.7	1.0	1.2	1.0	.3	Base	.4	7.7

T—569. Fairfield Tin Mill. July 14, 1959

Donald A. Crawford, *Arbitrator*

Approved by Sylvester Garrett, *Chairman*

BACKGROUND

1. The Union contends in this case from the Fairfield Tin Mill that the Coil Trimmer (or Coil Dresser) job (Temper Mills), re-evaluated by the Company to reflect a change in job content, should be in Class 4 instead of 3.

2. The change in job content was from use of a hammer and chisel to use of a pneumatic chisel, in cutting out damaged coil edges. The Company increased the ratings on Factors 4 and 6 (Manual Skill and Responsibility for Equipment, respectively), changing the total point rating for the job from 2.9 to 3.6, a net change of 0.7 point. There is no dispute as to these codings. The job continued in Class 3, however, since the change in job content did not amount to one whole job class.

3. Among other changes shown in the Exhibit "G" (Notice of Job Description and Classification change) submitted to the Union was a change in the factoring language under Factor 2, Employment Training and Experience, from "3 to 6 months inclusive" to "0 to 2 months of continuous progress." The original job classification sheet read: "3 to 6 months inclusive. Code A-base."

4. Specifically the Union (1) objects to this reduction in training time specified for learning the Coil Trimmer job, and (2) argues that rating of the disputed job in Factor 2 should be increased from A-base to B-.4, thereby increasing the total number of points for the job to 4.0—or Job Class 4.

5. It says that the disputed job was originally (June 20, 1946) incorrectly rated A-base in Factor 2 instead of B-.4, which is the coding specified in the Manual for a 3 to 6 month period of employment training and experience necessary to become proficient in a job. The Union stresses that it was not permitted to correct this error in

coding, and that if it took 3 to 6 months to become proficient in the original Coil Trimmer job, it still requires that period of time and more to achieve proficiency in the job and learn the use of the new power-driven chisel. Since the parties originally agreed that it took 3 to 6 months to learn the disputed job, the Union reasons that the Company cannot now seek to reduce this time to a period of 0 to 2 months on the basis of correcting an alleged mistake in the original language used in coding this Factor.

6. The Union further cites Specimen 689 (Chipper), which is rated B-.4 in Factor 2, and contends that the chipping hammer is not as large nor as difficult to operate as the pneumatic chisel. It argues further that by improperly using the pneumatic chisel the Coil Trimmer can cut through thousands of wraps of coil, thus causing greater damage than could be done by the improper use of a hammer and chisel; that in the specimen jobs on which the Company relies the power-driven hand tools are used to break bulk concrete, grind rough burrs off steel rail ends and ingot molds, and similar rough work; that therefore these specimen jobs are not comparable with the disputed job. Finally, the Union refers to the testimony of the Committeeman in the Cold Reduction Department, who has seen this equipment in operation, that it requires 3 to 6 months to become proficient in the use of the pneumatic chisel.

7. The Company's position in brief is that the parties usually agree on the coding before writing the factoring language and that therefore the error was made in writing the factoring language under the disputed factor; that the change from hammer and chisel to the pneumatic chisel had not added any significant training time to the Coil Trimmer job.

FINDINGS

8. A determination of whether error arose in the language used in coding Factor 2 originally is not necessary. The job was rated A-base in the disputed Factor and has been so classified since 1946. And, as provided in Section C-5-g of the January 1, 1953 Job Description and Classification Manual, in a subsequent re-classification of a job due to a change in job content, only the factors affected by the change can be considered.

9. Accordingly, the change in job content of the disputed job cannot be used by the Union as the occasion for the correction of an alleged error. (The Board notes incidentally that the Union accepts the coding of the Coil Trimmer job in A-base in Factor 1, although the factoring language ("Perform work of semi-repetitive nature where judgment is required to gain results") is the Manual code B language, and if applied, would place the job in Class 5.) Hence the question here is whether Factor 2 actually has been affected significantly by the change in job content.

10. The primary function of the Coil Trimmer job is to prepare coils for Temper Mill rolling. In the transport of the coils from Annealed Cold Storage to the Temper Mill by crane the coils are often bent over several wraps either on the inside or outside of the coil by the hooking or clamping devices. In order to prevent the succeeding wraps from sticking when the coils are unwound, the Coil Trimmer as part of his work of dressing the coils for the Temper Mill cuts out the bent coil edges. The cutting out of the damaged coil edges is now being done by a pneumatic chisel instead of by hammer and chisel.

11. The Board finds that learning how to connect the pneumatic chisel to a source of power, insert the chisel and manipulate it (gauge the cutting effect) does not add significantly to the training time required in the disputed job. This conclusion is supported by fact that the twelve specimen jobs cited by the Company (3 Chipper jobs, 2 Pneumatic Hammerman jobs, and 7 Grinder jobs), all of which involve the use of power-driven hand tools in the performance of the duties of the job, are rated A-base in Factor 2—0 to 2 months training time.

12. The Union objection to these specimen jobs for comparison purposes on the basis they are less skilled jobs than the disputed job is not persuasive. The specimen jobs classified in Job Classes 3, 4 and 5 are rated B-.5 in Manual Skill (with one exception which is rated A-base) the same as the Coil Trimmer job. And with respect to Mental Skill requirements, 5 specimen jobs are rated A-base as is the disputed job, and 7 are rated higher, at B-1.0. Obviously the skills to be learned in the disputed job are no higher than in the 12 specimen jobs in which no more than 2 months training time is necessary for attainment of proficiency.

13. Specimen No. 689, which the Union cites in support of its position, is the job of Final Inspection Chipper in the Finishing and Shipping Department in the Bar and Strip Mills and is classified in Job Class 7. The incumbent is required to "exercise judgment in positioning product and removing defects from finished product." This job is rated C-1.6 in Mental Skill as compared with the A-base rating for the disputed job; and both jobs are rated B-.5 in the Manual Skill Factor. It is apparent that Specimen No. 689 (which involves recognizing and removing various types of defects in final products) and the Coil Trimmer job are not comparable with respect to skills to be learned, and therefore the B-.4 rating of the specimen job in Factor 2 cannot be used to justify the same rating for the disputed job.

14. In these circumstances the Union request for the rating of the Coil Trimmer job at B-.4 in Factor 2 must be denied.

15. The Company concedes, on the other hand, that it cannot make the change in factoring language in Factor 2 to which the Union objects. Therefore it will be directed to restore the original factoring language in Factor 2—and also in Factor 1 which it also changed in the form G it submitted to the Union in connection with the change in job content in the Coil Trimmer job.

AWARD

16. The grievance is denied to the extent that it seeks an increase in coding of Factor 2. The Company shall delete the changes in factoring language as to Factors 1 and 2 made on the Exhibit "G" for the Coil Trimmer (Temper Mills) job.

USC—319. Wood Works. April 30, 1953
Herbert L. Sherman, Jr., *Assistant to the Chairman*
Approved by Sylvester Garrett, *Chairman*

BACKGROUND

1. This grievance, which arose out of the continuous use of a standby Normalizing Furnace at the Wood Works, requests a higher job classification for the Furnace Operators.

2. Prior to the installation of the new "B" Normalizing Furnace in 1948, there were four furnaces in the Annealing Unit— "A" Normalizing Furnace, two Muffle Furnaces and one Box Annealing Furnace. The crew consisted of an Operator, three to four Feeder-Catchers on "A" Normalizing Furnace, two Helpers on the Muffle Furnaces, and two Loaders on the Box Annealing Furnace when necessary. In 1948 the crew assigned to the "A" Furnace was transferred to the new "B" Furnace, the "A" Furnace being used only as standby equipment during emergencies. About the middle of 1950, however, "A" Furnace was put into continuous operation. At that time three additional Feeder-Catchers per turn were assigned to "A" Furnace. In the meantime, automatic temperature controls had been installed on the "A" Furnace similar to those with which the "B" Furnace had been equipped from its initial construction.

3. During the processing of the present grievance in February, 1951, plant representatives of the parties agreed upon a new job description for the Furnace Operators which incorporated the changes occasioned by the operation of two Normalizing Furnaces. According to the Company, agreement was also reached on the classification ratings for all Factors but Number 6—Responsibility for Tools and Equipment, the Company asserting that C-Hi-1.0 is the proper coding for that Factor and the Union contending that E-Hi-3.0 is warranted. As a result of these meetings, the Company did agree to raise Factor 5—Responsibility for Materials from C-1.2 to C-1.8 to reflect the additional production. Management takes the position, however, that no change in job class has been effected because the provisions of Section 9-D of the April 22, 1947 Agreement require a change of one full job class or more.

4. At the hearing the Union initially argued that the Fourth Step Minutes were misleading or erroneous in stating that the plant representatives had previously agreed on the values of all the classification factors except Number 6. Alternatively, it holds that the Board should examine all the factors anyhow since the job class itself is still in dispute. Specifically, the Union seeks changes in the original ratings on Factors 5, 6, 7, 8, 9, and 10. It is further contended by the Union that, in any event, the provisions of the Agreement requiring a change of one full job class or more to warrant a higher job class do not apply to the situation presented by this grievance. Since it is agreed that there was a change in job content as is evidenced by the Company's willingness to increase the rating of Factor 5, the Union feels that the job of Furnace Operator should be reclassified to a higher level.

DISCUSSION AND FINDINGS

5. A review of the record, supplemented by a visit to the plant, leads the Board to the conclusion that Factor 5—Responsibility for Materials is the only Factor that may be properly increased under all the evidence. The increased production resulting from the continuous use of the standby Normalizing Furnace justifies the change in rating on this Factor from C-1.2 to C-1.8. However, the other Factors have not been sufficiently affected to warrant a change in the coding.

6. Both before and after the institution of the practice of using two Normalizing Furnaces continuously, the Operator was required, among other things, to adjust the gas to maintain temperatures in the Box Annealing Furnace, to direct the laborers in loading this furnace, to regulate the speed of the Normalizing Furnaces, to regulate the timers on the Muffle Furnaces, to make out production and other reports, and to locate material. Of course, there are five furnaces (counting the Box Annealing and the Muffle type) for which the Operator is now responsible instead of the previous four, but the manner of operation has not changed appreciably. Although the location of the office was changed, there has been no marked change in the nature of the duties performed.

7. Furthermore, installation of automatic temperature controls for the two Normalizing Furnaces, which the Operator checks periodically, has eased his workload to some extent. When the job of Operator was originally classified by mutual agreement, the temperatures on the "A" Furnace were manually controlled. Now there is less danger of damage to the furnaces by reason of improper heating since the automatic instruments will turn the gas off, and thus less attention is required. A visual inspection of

the operation revealed that the Operator can see the controls and recorders of the "B" Furnace and Muffle Furnaces in his office where he makes out his reports, and the controls for the "A" Furnace are located on a couple of posts about fifty feet away. Also, both the Normalizing Furnaces and the Muffle Furnaces are located quite close together.

8. The Union argues nevertheless that a sustained high degree of care and attention must be exercised in the operation of this equipment because of its variety. However, "B" Normalizing Furnace with automatic controls was already in continuous operation when "A" Normalizing Furnace was put into continuous use with similar controls. And the other furnaces remained unchanged except that a temperature recorder was added for the Box Annealing Furnace which made for more accurate readings. This automatic recorder is also located in the Operator's office and helps the Operator to determine when a trip to the Box Annealing Furnace is necessary. Moreover, there have been periods over weekends when temperatures on the furnaces have been controlled without the presence of an Operator. Since the degree of attention required to prevent damage to the furnaces and conveyors has not increased to such an extent as to justify a higher coding under Factor 6—Responsibility for Tools and Equipment, the Board must find that C-1.0 is still the proper rating.

9. It should also be noted that "probable damage" to equipment was already rated as "High" and that this is the highest level for this aspect of the classification. Thus, the fact that damage from improper heating may be quite extensive, as was true in one instance when the temperature "got away," cannot increase the rating of probable damage. Nor can the operation of an additional furnace.

10. One further question remains. As a result of the increase of .6 (C-1.2 to C-1.8) in the coding of Factor 5, the total value of the job of Furnace Operator is raised from 11.9 to 12.5. If this were a new job, it would be classified as Job Class 13 under the Manual. But a changed job is treated differently. Section 9-D of the April 22, 1947 Agreement speaks of a new job classification when the Company "changes the job content (requirements of the job as to training, skill, responsibility, effort, and working conditions) of an existing job to the extent of one full job class or more." (Underscoring added.)

11. The Manual makes specific reference to the procedure for handling changes in job content. It reads:

"In the subsequent reclassification of a job due to change in job content, consider only those factors affected by the change. Move them into the next class only if the change in job content is at least one whole job class." (Underscoring added.)

12. The parties have therefore agreed that the impact of changes made by the Company on job content must be ten tenths or more in order to change the job class of an existing job. This interpretation has been embraced by special arbitrators in previous awards. The reasons for the differentiation between new jobs and changed jobs by the parties are apparent. Once an equitable rate structure has been mutually agreed upon for existing jobs, it is desirable that some measure of stability be assured. The parties did not intend fluctuation of the rate structure up and down to reflect relatively minor changes in job content. Only where the impact of the changes on job content are so substantial as to amount to a job class or more is it intended that a lower or a higher rate should be assigned to the job.

13. For these reasons the request for a higher job class for the Furnace Operators must be denied.

AWARD

14. The grievance is denied.

A—621. Worcester, South Works Plant. November 6, 1953

Donald A. Crawford, *Special Assistant to the Chairman*
Approved by Sylvester Garrett, *Chairman*

BACKGROUND

1. This grievance involves a question of proper pay for a changed job.—Press and Bench Operators, Job Class 3. In 1950, the Company installed an abrasive cut-off wheel to cut springs to length, because press-cutting left a burr.

2. The major issues presented at the Hearing, however, were the Union's contention that Section 9-D requires the Company to prepare a new job description and classification before joint evaluation in grievance meetings, and the Company's procedural objection that the Union could not introduce the issue of job evaluation and description because its grievance procedure claim had

been that the grievants were performing another, higher rated job.

3. Thus, at the Hearing, International Representative, Joseph J. Kelleher, said that the issue is simply whether or not Management must prepare a new job description and classification. Kelleher claimed that it is impossible to evaluate the changed job without a new job description, and that Section 9-D requires that when jobs are changed, and the job class is in dispute, new job descriptions and classifications should be prepared. He added that if a future evaluation of the changed job should result in a higher evaluation, the new rate should be effective as of the grievance date, September 27, 1950.

4. The Union believes, Kelleher said, that the addition of the abrasive cut-off wheel has changed the job value as regards Factor 11, Surroundings, and Factor 12, Hazards, to the extent of more than one job class. Management's refusal to prepare a new job description means in effect that Management considers itself the sole judge as to whether a job is changed one full job class.

5. The Company position at the Hearing consisted of the procedural argument that the Union cannot change the nature of the demand at the Hearing, and expect the Board to act on its new claim. The Company contended that throughout the grievance procedure, the Union's claim has been that the grievants are doing the Hand Grinder job —a position entirely different from the relief now requested.

6. The Company cited an award by Ralph Seward, then Board Chairman (Case A-195) in which he said that, "Where the Union is making a claim of contract violations, the burden is on the Union to make a case and should make that case clear long before it gets to this Board. It ought to know the facts, and management should be informed of the facts which it has."

7. The Company pointed out that other Board decisions adopt the same rule. Similarly the Company cited a Seward decision at Bethlehem Steel (Lebanon Plant, Grievance #2353, Decision No. 19, March 11, 1953). There Seward refused to hear the claim of improper job evaluation because the grievance procedure argument had been a claim for payment of the applicable job rate.

8. The Company further emphasized that this grievance was filed in September, 1950; that the fourth-step final meeting was on March 6, 1951; that the case was appealed to the Board on April 23, 1951, but was not docketed with the Board until March 6, 1953—two years after the final fourth-step meeting. The Company asked that this procedural matter be considered in deciding this case.

FINDING

9. *The grievance is remanded to the parties to evaluate the effects of the changes in the job of Press and Bench Operator (Plant Code 56-54) pursuant to Section 9-D. The Union's demand that the Company first prepare a job description and classification is denied. The Board holds that it has no power under the 1947 Agreement to direct the Company to prepare a new job description unless it first is found that there has been a change of one full job class.*

10. The Board does not find the Company's procedural argument (that the Union changed its demand) persuasive. The history of the grievance does not support the Company conclusion. True, the principal Union claim was that the employees have been performing the hand grinder job and should be paid the rate. But throughout the grievance procedure the Union also argued the issue of proper evaluation of the Press and Bench Operator job.

11. In third step, the Union claimed that: "The Operators in cutting to length the brake cable are required to use care in seeing that the ends are square, which is precision work." (Third Step Minutes). And that: ". . . the use of an abrasive cut-off wheel . . . changes the job description and classification . . . The Union believes that the job should be classified at the same level as that of Hand Grinder, Job Class 6."

12. The Company said, in grievance meetings, that: ". . . the use of the small cutting wheel . . . has tended to simplify the work and is not sufficient to change the classification of the job." (Fourth Step Minutes).

13. The Union filed the grievance as a violation of the Section 9-D (classification of new or changed jobs) as well as Section 9-B (application of wage scale).

14. Therefore, the issue of proper evaluation of the job constituted an important element of grievance meeting discussions. Accordingly, the Union demand at the Hearing for a new job description and classification for purposes of evaluation has not introduced a new theory of the grievance nor a new claim for relief.

15. The Union's request that the Company prepare a job description and classification as a prerequisite to evaluation cannot be supported under the 1947 Agreement. Under that Agreement, Section 9-D requires a change in job content of one full job class as a condition precedent to the Company's preparation of a new job description

and classification. The Board, therefore, is in agreement that it has no power to direct the Company to prepare a new job description unless it *first* is found that there has been a change of one full job class. (This issue, of course, has since been clarified by Section F-3 of the January 1, 1953 Job Description and Classification Manual).

16. Since the issue of job evaluation remains, the Board refers the grievance back to the parties to determine whether in fact there has been a change in job content of one full job class as provided in Section 9-D of the 1947 Agreement.

17. The issue of timeliness is not compelling in the decision on this issue. The Union did appeal the case to the Board within the specified time limits. The obvious inference from the delay—that the grievants did not strenuously press their claim on the merits—does not effect the issue here decided.

AWARD

18. The grievance is remanded to the parties to determine whether in fact there has been a change in job content of one full job class in the Press and Bench Operator job (Plant Code 56-54) pursuant to Section 9-D. If the parties are unable to agree on this matter, the case may be referred back to the Board for decision as to whether there has been a change of one full job class.

19. The Union's demand that the Company first prepare a job description and classification is denied. The Board holds that it has no power under the 1947 Agreement to direct the Company to prepare a new job description unless it first is found that there has been a change of one full job class.

20. The Company's procedural objection to the Board's consideration of the grievance is over-ruled.

CI—247, -248.   South Works.   June 12, 1952
Donald A. Crawford, *Arbitrator*

BACKGROUND

1. Between August 1948 and July 1949, the Company enlarged the No. 5 Power Station and installed new equipment: Two 12,500 H.P. Turbo Blowers, two 75 MM Gal. Per Day Turbo Driven Service Water Pumps, one 1000 GPM Turbo Driven Boiler Feed Pump (and a Drip Tank), four Motor Driven Circulating Water Pumps for condensers, and a Boiler.* The Union contends that these additions caused changes in job content requiring an upward evaluation of two grades in the jobs of Pump Tender, 1st, Grade 10 to 12 (Case CI-248), and Engine Turbine Attendant, Grade 12 to 14 (Case CI-247). The Company contends that its review of the revised and agreed upon job descriptions shows that no upward adjustment is proper.

2. The Union, however, has agreed with the Company that the present factor ratings for the Pump Tender job on nine out of twelve factors are correct, and that for the Engine Turbine Attendant job eight out of the twelve are correct. Thus the arbitrator has been limited by the parties to a finding on three and four factors respectively.

FINDINGS

PUMP TENDER, 1ST.

3. The arbitrator finds that the content of Pump Tender, 1st, has not been changed

* Additional equipment has since been added which by agreement is not to be considered in these grievances.

to the extent of one full job class, and so the grievance must be denied. Responsibility for Tools and Equipment, however, has increased in value from 1.0 to 1.5 and the total point value from 10. to 10.5.

4. *Mental Skill—Present C-1.6 Union Claim D-2.2:* The Union believes that the new requirement of training and directing an Oiler-Wiper, the removal of the 2nd Engineer as supervisor, the requirement of a Stationary Engineer's license, and the operation of expensive new equipment, has increased the mental skill needed on the job. The Union agrees, however, that the training duties are evaluated under Factor 1 and its value is not contested (Trans. p. 23) and, also, agrees that an Engineer's license was a requirement of the job before the changes, but not enforced because of wartime conditions.

5. The removal of the 2nd Engineer is not relevant because this supervisory change occurred after (1951) the series of changes involved in this grievance.

6. The Arbitrator finds that the addition of new pumps has not increased the know-how, judgment or ingenuity required to inspect, operate, or repair pumps. Each of the new pumps has its counterpart in one or more similar older pumps, and if the attendant knows how to operate one, he knows how to operate the other. Since stand-by pumps are always available, no increase in judgment or ingenuity is needed.

7. *Responsibility for Tools and Equipment—Present High C-1.0 Union Claim*

Medium D-1.5. The Company claims that there is no increase in this responsibility because the new equipment is similar to the old, and because the nature of the job does not warrant a higher classification. That the present valuation of "Moderate attention and care required to prevent damage to dies, power driven cutting tools . . ." is proper. That close attention is not required nor given as the attendant walks around a big station and the consequences are no more than burning out a bearing or causing a leak in the pumps or possibly a ruined shaft or broken housing. That no different kind of accident could occur now than before, and the responsibility at any one time is the same.

8. The parties evaluated the job previously as requiring moderate attention and care, *high.* Now there are five circulating pumps running continuously instead of three, and five Turbo-driven pumps instead of two. The value of equipment in operation has been significantly increased. The Turbo-driven pumps are susceptible to more costly damage than the motor driven because, if a bearing drops, a rub on the turbine blade may develop, and a turbine blade be ripped up. These changes increase both the probability and the cost of damage which may occur at any one time. With more pumps operating more damage may occur at any one time.

9. If, therefore, this factor was properly rated before as requiring a high level of moderate care and attention, it follows that the change in equipment with its resultant effect upon the probability and cost of damage now requires a higher degree of responsibility. Accordingly the 1.5 rating is indicated.

10. *Responsibility for Operations—Present D-2.0 Union Claim E-3.0.* The Union contends that the responsibility for operations has been increased because the Pump Tender, 1st, now pumps and maintains water for the entire plant system. Actually, these pumps supply some, but not all, of the water for the entire plant. The station formerly supplied about one-third whereas it now supplies about one-half of the water for the plant—and can supply in emergency about 75%.

11. The increase in amount of water supplied, however, has not added to the responsibility for operations. The added equipment furnishes the Pump Tender, 1st, with stand-by pumps, which pick up load as needed. He always has time to shut down a pump, repair it, or get it repaired, and go back into operation. Thus the obligation for maintaining pace has not increased.

12. For these reasons, the grievance is

granted to the extent of raising the evaluation of the Pump Tender, 1st, job by .5 to 10.5.

ENGINE TURBINE ATTENDANT

13. The Arbitrator finds that the content of Engine Turbine Attendant has not been changed to the extent of one full job class, and so the grievance must be denied. Responsibility for materials, however, has increased in value from .3 to .5.

14. *Employment Training and Experience—Present E1.6 Union Claim F-2.0.* The Union contends that additional training time is required to learn to operate the new equipment. The two new Turbo-blowers are very similar to the three older models. The starting, stopping and control apparatus and the make-up of the control panels are the same. Accordingly there is no significant additional training time required to learn to run five rather than three.

15. *Mental Skill—Present D-2.2 Union Claim E-2.8.* The Union argues that the Engine Turbine Attendant now directs an Oiler-Wiper-Checker; receives no supervision from the 2nd Engineer who has been removed; is required to hold a Stationary Engineer's license; and must have the mental skill to operate the new equipment.

16. The Union admits, however, that the direction of the Oiler-Wiper-Checker is valued under another factor, the rating of which is not contested (Trans. p. 18). The Union, also, agrees that the Stationary Engineer's license was required before the changes, but not enforced because of manpower shortages during and immediately after the war.

17. The removal of the 2nd Engineer, since it did not occur until 1951, is not relevant to this grievance.

18. The Arbitrator finds that the mental ability, job knowledge and judgment to reason through and plan the job have not changed since the two new Turbo-blowers are started, stopped, observed and controlled in the same way as the older three.

19. *Responsibility for Materials—Present B-.3 Union Claim C-.5.* The Company argues that this factor has not changed because the material for which the Engine Turbine Attendant is responsible is air supplied by blowers, whether three or five blowers, and the attention required is relatively constant and not for part of the turn, that it is the same type of attention required to prevent wasting of air by unnecessary blowing.

20. The five Turbo-blowers service five blast furnaces whereas the three served three blast furnaces. The blowers must be

operated manually four times a day when the furnaces hang. The furnaces hang spasmodically—there may be no hanging for a week or two and then they may hang during two weeks. The increase in the amount of manual operation is in direct line or proportion to the increase in Turbo-blowers. The Turbo attendant was not out of control with three Turbo-blowers proportionally more than with five.

21. The Arbitrator finds that this additional manual operation has increased the difficulties of supplying the material (air) in adequate and varying amounts. The care or attention required by the direct ratio increase in manual operation has changed the responsibility for materials from ordinary care or avoiding negligence in operation to close attention for part of turn. Accordingly, the .5 instead of .3 rating is indicated.

22. *Surroundings—Present A-Base Union Claim B-4.* The Union argues that since Pump Tender, 1st, is rated .4 on surroundings, this job should also be .4. The Union additionally claims that the heat has increased. The Pump Tender's job, however, is rated .4 because of dirt and grease which are not present near the Engine Turbine Attendant's station. Also, the heat is less near the Turbine Attendant's position than in the area nearer the boilers where the Pump Attendant works. The Arbitrator finds that the changes in the Power Plant have not altered these conditions for the Turbine Attendant.

23. For the foregoing reasons, the grievance is granted to the extent of raising the Engine Turbine Attendant job by .2 to 12.6.

24. Both grievances must be denied because the changes in job content did not increase the value of the factors submitted to arbitration to the extent of one full job class. The grievances, however, are partially granted in that higher point values have been established. These new ratings naturally will be considered in evaluating any changes in job content resulting from added equipment or other causes subsequent to those herein evaluated.

CHAPTER 8

CLAIM THAT GRIEVANCE NOT TIMELY

Most of the preceding cases contain substantive rulings which bear upon the stability of the rate structure. In this chapter the cases show that the status quo may be mainained, with no decision reached on the merits of a dispute, either because no grievance was filed promptly or because no proper appeal was made within the grievance procedure.

The award in G-105, set forth on p. 103 is also relevant to a claim that a grievance is untimely.

N—254. Lorain Works. February 21, 1958
Clare B. McDermott, *Assistant to the Chairman*
Approved by Herbert L. Sherman, Jr., *Chairman*

BACKGROUND

1. The issue in this case from the Maintenance Department of the Lorain Works is whether this grievance, protesting the Job Class 9 assigned to the new job of Grader Operator, was filed in a timely fashion under Section 9-D-3 of the August 3, 1956, Agreement. This was the only question explored by the parties in the grievance procedure, and the hearing before the Board was likewise limited, as will be this Award.

2. On August 14, 1956, Management put a road grader into service in the Yard Labor Division of the Maintenance Department. On August 23, 1956, employees in the Crane Service Division of the same department filed a grievance asking that the job of Grader Operator be put in their seniority unit. On September 11, 1956, after discussion of the description and classification of the job with the grievance committeeman of the zone involved, which was customary in the plant, the classification was installed.

3. The grievance seeking placement of the job in the Crane Service Division was processed through to the Fourth Step, when on March 14, 1957, it was sustained, and Management agreed to man the grader with Crane Service personnel. The minutes of that Fourth Step meeting were presented to the Union representative for signature on April 10, 1957, and they were signed by him on April 18.

4. Finally, on May 20, 1957, the grievance now in arbitration was filed, requesting that the job of Grader Operator be put in Job Class 12.

5. The classification of the job was installed and presented to the grievance committeeman on September 11, 1956, and the classification grievance was not filed until May 20, 1957. In view of the more than eight months' time lapse, the Company argues that the grievance is untimely because not filed within the 30-day limit of Section 9-D-3. The Union would agree with this position but for the fact of the favorable settlement of the earlier grievance, which transferred the job to the Crane Service Division. The Union argues that the 30-day period for filing the classification grievance should not begin to run until settlement of the earlier grievance because not until that date was the job put within the area of the Crane Service grievance committeeman who was more familiar with the equipment and the proper classification of the job.

6. There is no complaint that the Union was unaware of the fact that the classification for the Grader Operator job had been installed. When the classification was installed on September 11, 1956, Management told Committeeman Davis, whose zone included the Yard Labor Division, that the job would be put in Job Class 9, that that was the comparable classification for the same job at other of the Company's plants including the Fairless, Duquesne and Gary Works, and that the Union had thirty days from that date to file a grievance relating to classification. In fact, Committeeman Roberts, whose zone included the Crane Service Division, testified that Davis had told him that the job had been put in Job Class 9. Therefore, it is very clear that, during the processing of the seniority-unit

grievance, Roberts was aware of the classification of the job. During the six months following installation of the classification, the seniority-unit grievance was being processed through the various steps and was finally sustained in mid-March of 1957. Surely the classification grievance should have been filed before this, particularly in view of the fact that the committeemen from both zones were aware that the job was classified in Job Class 9.

7. Section 9-D-3 reads in part as follows:

". . . The employee or employees affected or the grievance committee may at any time within 30 days file a grievance alleging that the job is improperly classified under the job description and classification provisions of the Manual. . . ."

8. It is true, as Committeeman Roberts stated, that the classification was never formally presented to him, but that was unnecessary since it had been properly presented to Committeeman Davis back in September of 1956. Moreover, in spite of all this, the Union did not see fit to have Davis file a classification grievance with the latter's foreman.

9. Even assuming, however, that there is merit in the Union's argument that the Board may look beyond the date of installation of the classification and that it may look to the date of settlement of the seniority-unit grievance, still the present grievance must be denied because even on that basis it is untimely since it was not filed within thirty days of that date.

AWARD

10. The grievance is denied.

CI—220. South Works. June 29, 1951
Sidney L. Cahn, *Acting Chairman*

BACKGROUND

1. The grievant, a Motor Inspector, requests that Management be required to abide by the job description for Motor Inspector or create a new job description which will cover his specific duties. He also requests a retroactive pay adjustment.

2. The job of Motor Inspector is a "Bench Mark" job, indicating that the duties of the job holder are encompassed by the actual job content of a Motor Inspector.

3. The grievant claims that despite the fact that he holds a Bench Mark job, he has been required, in addition, to perform some of the work of a Millwright, which work is not covered by the job description for Motor Inspector.

4. The Union contends that under such circumstances, Management should be required either to limit the duties of the grievant to that of Motor Inspector, or create a new job description and rate adequate to cover and compensate the work actually performed.

5. Management argues: (1) that the instant grievance is identical with a prior grievance from which no appeal was taken after the 4th Step grievance decision of Management to deny the grievance, and thus the instant grievance must likewise be denied. (2) that the Union, in the instant grievance, failed to allege a violation of the 1947 Labor Agreement, which, under Section 6-C, precludes the Union from processing the grievance. (3) that the grievance was untimely filed and is thus violative of Section 6-D-1-a.

(4) that if the Board assumed jurisdiction of this grievance it would violate the provisions of Section 7-B of the 1947 Agreement.

6. The prior grievance (A-48-8) was denied by Management in the 4th Step upon two grounds. (1) "That the request was not proper subject matter for the grievance machinery inasmuch as there is no claim of violation of the April 22, 1947 Labor Agreement on the part of the Company as provided by Section 6-C, Definition of Grievance." (2) That the job in question had been properly described and classified by agreement of the parties, and therefore there was no basis for creating a new description and/or classification.

7. Section 6-D (Paragraph 61) provides that if the 4th Step grievance decision is not duly appealed to arbitration, the grievance shall be considered settled on the basis of such decision, and precludes further appeal.

8. It is the opinion of the Board that Section 6-D-2 (paragraph 61) is conclusive of the rights of the parties. A determination having been made in the 4th Step of the old grievance, which determination has not been duly appealed from, is contractually final and binding.

9. This determination makes it unnecessary to discuss other points raised by Management and the Union.

AWARD

10. The grievance is denied.

CI—210. Youngstown District Works. November 4, 1953

J. Orvis Keller, *Arbitrator*

BACKGROUND

1. This grievance arose in the Number 18—43 inch strip mill of the McDonald Mills, Youngstown (Ohio) District, Carnegie—Illinois Steel Corporation, now United States Steel Corporation, and is a request that the Coiler Operator Job be given a higher job classification than was originally mutually agreed upon by the Company and the Union as the result of the addition of certain new coiling equipment to the original installation and the consequent additional controls to be operated by the Coiler Operator.

2. The grievance was originally filed in the Second Step on December 24, 1948 by Ralph Hughes, one of the coiler operators.

3. This Number 18—43 inch Hot Strip Mill was built and commenced operations about the year 1935. The position of Coiler Operator was described and the description agreed upon by the Company and the Union pursuant to the Wage Rate Inequities Program on June 6, 1945. Later the job was classified in Job Class 11 with the mutual agreement of both parties and this classification was installed on February 9, 1947.

4. The final step in rolling an order on a strip mill is the disposition of the hot rolled product. The product may be cut into shorter lengths and piled, or handled by the hot coiling method. The essential requirements of the coiler equipment are to receive the material at mill speeds and coil it tightly without excessive tension, telescoping, scratching or marking and, finally to discharge the finished coil quickly without damage.

5. The delivery end of the Number 18—43 inch Strip Mill is served by two Coiler Operators, who when the strip is being coiled, alternate in regulating and disposing of the coils by electrical push button and air valve controls from a pulpit. There are two pulpits, one for each coiler operator.

6. Prior to July 24, 1948, Management decided to make certain changes in this mill coiling equipment in an attempt to improve the entry of strip into the coilers and to reduce the number of cobbles. The Grievance Committeeman, who was also the Chairman of the Grievance Committee, was notified by the Company. Since it was impossible for either the Union or Management to predetermine what job changes if any would be caused by the new equipment, the Union representative did not wish to take any action until after the new equipment was placed in operation.

7. The new equipment, consisting of a larger and relocated pinch roll and a coiler aligning device, known as an escuer, both operated by electrical controls, was installed on July 24, 1948. The old pinch rolls were dead rolls, while the movement of the new ones were subject to control. Shortly thereafter, the Union, upon being notified of the installation, made a request that a study be made by Management of the changed operations and asked that the coiler operation job classification be revised upward. From this point there is disagreement as to what transpired between the Management representative and the Union grievanceman. The matter is dealt with further during the early portion of the "Discussion and Findings."

8. Prior to the installation of the new pinch rolls, the Mill experienced numerous cobbles in the coilers and pile-ups on the tables, since occasional strips with bad front ends, usually cambered strips, would not enter the coiler, while others would enter part way and stall and/or stick in the coiler. On such occasions the Operators were required to manipulate the coiler controls continuously or coordinate their efforts with other members of the crew when the Burner burned off the end of the coil before coiling. After the installation of the new pinch rolls and the escuer, the coiler troubles from cobbles were greatly reduced.

9. Management made a restudy of the coiler operator job after the request from the Union, but found no change in the job content of the job. Consequently no new job description nor new job classification was necessary in the opinion of Management representatives. The matter was discussed according to the Union grievanceman until Management gave its final decision in December, 1948 stating that there would be no new job classification. The Union then entered the instant grievance on December 24, 1948 in the Second Step. At the Third Step Meeting of February 16, 1949, the Union submitted a suggested job description and classification. It contained no change in the job description, but showed an increase in the valuation Factors 3, 5, 6 and 7 over the former mutually agreed-upon classification. The proposed classification totaled 13.8 points which would place the job in Job Class 14 instead of Job Class 11, the former classification.

POSITION OF THE UNION

10. The Union in its brief contends that the Coiler Operators now manipulate, operate and observe eleven more levers, controls, buttons and gauges than they had prior to the installation of the new equipment in July, 1948. Their duties have been increased greatly and their responsibilities are far greater now. Previously they had no control whatsoever over production. If a strip of steel entered the Coiler properly and no difficulties developed, a good coil possibly resulted and production was maintained. If the strip cobbled as it hit the pinch roll or Coiler, the Coiler Operator was powerless in preventing the strip from becoming so entangled at the Coiler that it had to be scrapped and more than likely several other strips following the cobble had to be scrapped. If a strip of steel came off the mill cambered, the Coiler Operator was powerless in preventing its telescoping while it was being coiled.

11. These difficulties have almost all been entirely eliminated at the present time. If a cobble develops, the Coiler Operator can in most instances, by manipulating his controls, levers and buttons, extract the cobble from the Coiler very quickly, correct the situation, coil the strip with the least possible delay and thus prevent the scrapping of that strip and other strips following it. If a strip comes off the mill cambered, the Coiler Operator can manipulate the escuer in such a fashion as to prevent the telescoping of the coil and thus produce a resultantly good coil.

12. The Union brief also states that prior to the introduction of the new equipment the percentage of scrap loss on the #18—43 inch Mill was exceedingly high, some estimates placing it as high as 50% of production. In addition to the scrap loss, the lost time involved in the burning of cobbles, and in the extraction of cobbles from the Coiler was very great. These and other factors resulted in a great loss of production on the mill.

13. The Union brief asserts that an analysis of the duties and responsibilities entailed in the performance of the job of Coiler Operator prior to the installation of the new pinch roll and escuer with the collateral installation of 11 new levers, controls, buttons and gauges compared with an analysis of the duties and responsibilities in connection with the Coiler Operator job as it is being performed today, will lead to but one conclusion, and that is, the job merits an increase of 3 Job Classes or from Job Class 11 to Job Class 14.

14. According to the Union the value of four factors in the classification has been enhanced as the following table of Factor comparisons shows:

	CODE	CLASS
Factor 3—Mental Skill		
Present—Judgment required to keep pace with mill and to control any variation from routine. Operate tension on coilers for coiling product uniformly.	C	1.6
Union Proposal—Uses considerable judgment to keep pace with mill and to control any variation from routine. Operate tension on coilers for coiling product uniformly.	D	2.2
Factor 5—Responsibility for Materials		
Present—May wrap coils too tight causing reel digs. On cut material overlapping or jamming ends may cause scrapping of product. 4 slabs x 3 tons @ $21/ton $250. ($36—$15)	C	1.2
Union Proposal—May wrap coils too tight causing reel digs. On cut material overlapping or jamming ends would cause scrapping of product. Jamming of lapped coil in mechanical rollers could cause damage to same. 4 slabs x 3 tons @ $21/ton—$250. ($36—$15)	D	1.6
Factor 6—Responsibility for Tools and Equipment		
Present—Ordinary care and attention required to prevent coil from dropping off coiler onto motors.	Med C	.7
Union Proposal—Close attention required to prevent coil from dropping off coiler onto motors. Jamming of lapped coil in rollers as coil enters coiler.	Med D	1.5
Factor 7—Responsibility for Operations		
Present—Operates an important section of major producing unit. (Coiler and Piler)	D	2.0
Union Proposal—Operates an important section of a major producing unit. (Coiler and Piler)	E	3.0

15. On the question of timeliness of the grievance, the Union submits that the matter of an appropriate job description and classification was taken up by the Union immediately upon the installation of the new equipment in July, 1948. The Grievance Committee pursued the matter with local plant management and refrained from filing a grievance prior to December 24, 1948, because Management indicated from time to time that a settlement might be reached. The Union did not sleep on its rights, as Management contends, neither did it fail to pursue its rights as provided in the collective agreement. The Union view as stated in its brief is that if matters can be settled without resorting to grievance machinery, both Management and the Union are happier to exhaust all efforts in that respect, before implementing the grievance procedure. The Union asserts that its request for a higher classification was then in the discussion stage from the time of the introduction of the new equipment until the month of December, 1948. When the Company finally declined to talk about the matter further, the Union had no recourse but to file a grievance and obtain the Company's answer in writing as the first step in pursuing its rights through the grievance machinery and arbitration.

16. The Union sincerely submits that the Company erred in declining to re-evaluate Factors 3, 5, 6 and 7 in the classification of the position of Coiler Operator and should be directed to re-evaluate those factors as requested by the Union, such classification to result in a total point value of 13.8 for the job, and place it in Job Class 14. It is further claimed that the Company did not reclassify the Coiler Operator position pursuant to the provisions of Section 9-D of the collective agreement. Consequently the Union contends that the Company must be found in violation of the collective agreement, and be directed to reclassify the instant position in Job Class 14, effective the date the new equipment was placed in operation; and further be directed to reimburse the Coiler Operators at the rate of Job Class 14 back to such date.

POSITION OF THE COMPANY

17. The Company requests the Board to dismiss this grievance for the reason that it was not filed promptly in writing in accordance with the provisions of Section 6-D-1-a (Paragraph 40) of the 1947 Labor Agreement.

18. Without waiving its position as to timeliness in filing this grievance, the Company further presents its position on the merits of the claim.

19. As the result of the addition of the new pinch roll and a coiler alignment device to the No. 18—43 inch Strip Mill, the operation of certain electrical controls to regulate this equipment was added to the Coiler Operator job. To the claim of the Union that the responsibility for operating these additional controls increases the classification values of certain basic factors of the total job classification, the Company replies that such additional requirements are not such as would increase the separate valuations for any of the factors, and that under no circumstances would the job content be increased to the extent of one full job class or more as provided under Section 9-D of the 1947 Labor Agreement. In fact the improvements in operation resulting from the addition of the new equipment have, if anything, simplified the work of the Coiler Operators.

20. The Company, therefore, submits that the addition of the new coiling devices did not cause a change in the job content (requirements of the job as to the training, skill, responsibility, effort, and working conditions) of the Coiler Operator job to the extent of one full job class or more, and accordingly the claim of the Union, based upon the provisions of Section 9-D of the 1947 Labor Agreement, has no standing.

21. Management, therefore, requests the Board to dismiss this grievance.

DISCUSSION AND FINDINGS

22. There is considerable disagreement as to how expeditiously the Union prosecuted its claim prior to entering a written grievance. Mr. Paul M. Jones, as the Union Grievance Committeeman testified that he was in fairly constant touch with the representative from Management, Mr. J. E. Foldessy, who was Assistant Superintendent of the Number 18—43 inch Hot Strip Mill at the time the new equipment was installed until the grievance was entered in written form. Mr. Foldessy's superior was the Superintendent, Mr. A. H. Werner. The Company claimed that right after the study was made of the Coiler Operator job by Management at the request of the Union, it was determined by Management that no change in Job Class was warranted. This information was at once passed on to the Union representative according to Management testimony. However, Mr. Jones implied that this was not the case and that discussions with Mr. Foldessy were carried on for a couple of months. As proof of this assertion the Union introduced as an exhibit a photo-

static copy of the original grievance form dated December 24, 1948 containing a decision of the date of December 30, 1948, and signed by A. H. Werner with initials J.E.F. under the signature. The decision reads: "Job description and classification will be revised and negotiated with Union." The Company in its brief stated, "Although the Union representative discussed the classification on several occasions with a Management representative, no attempt was made to file a grievance before December 24, 1948, five months after the new equipment was placed in operation. There was no good reason for not filing the grievance promptly and then, if further discussion was in order, the grievance could have been held pending."

23. Management asks that the grievance first be dismissed on account of the matter of timeliness and cites the Agreement of April 22, 1947. Paragraph 125 of Subsection 9-D reads in part:

"The job description and classification for each job in effect as of the date of this Agreement shall continue in effect unless (1) Management changes the job content (requirements of the job as to the training, skill, responsibility, effort and working conditions) to the extent of one full job class. . . ."

24. Paragraph 130 states in part:

"In the event Management does not develop a new job description and classification, the employee or employees affected may, if filed promptly, process a grievance under the grievance and arbitration procedures. . . ."

25. Management also refers to Subsection 6-D-1-a of the Agreement which reads:

"A grievance which has not been settled within two days as a result of the discussion required by Subsection B to be considered further, must be filed promptly in writing."

26. Management called the attention of the Board to three former cases in which the Grievance was dismissed because the grievance was not filed promptly. These cases were T-71, T-97 and CI-256. In giving careful study to these cases, it would appear that the grievants in each case were utterly neglectful in the prosecution of the respective grievances. In this instant grievance such would not appear to be the case. *The Board, therefore, finds that the grievance is not untimely and the matter must rest on its merits.*

27. Since the proposed Union classifica-

tion contains the same description as the original agreed-upon description and classification with the exception of an addition dated September 13, 1948, on the original description, and since there is mutual agreement between the Company and the Union on all of the classification Factors except 3, 5, 6 and 7, the attention of the Board will be given to these four Factors in dispute. (As an aside the added notation on the description dated September 13, 1948 reads: "Operates electrical push buttons to control coiler pinch rolls and hold down.")

28. The method employed for making a job classification was outlined clearly by the Assistant Plant Industrial Engineer, a Company witness. In essence he stated that certain regulations are followed in making a job classification; an attempt is first made to compare the job under consideration to a "bench mark" job in each of the Twelve Factors that go to make up a total classification. If there are no "bench mark" jobs that can be used for a comparison, an applicable "specimen job" is sought and if possible several such specimen jobs. But if there can be found neither a "bench mark" job nor a "specimen" job that applies to the Factor being considered, then the Manual must be used to help select a value for rating any particular Factor. This witness further testified that there are no Coiler Operator Jobs in the United States Steel Corporation which are classified higher than the one at McDonald, in other words higher than Job Class 11.

29. The Company also introduced as an exhibit a Job Classification Analysis which compared the Youngstown Coiler Operator Job with four specimen Coiler Operator Jobs for one 38 inch, one 42 inch, and two 80 inch Hot Strip Mills and one sample job of the Coiler Operator Job for an 80 inch Hot Strip Mill at the Irvin Works. All of these Coiler Operator jobs are classified as Job Class 11 and from the job descriptions of these jobs furnished also in exhibit by the Company, it can be seen that the controls on many of these jobs are as complex as on the 42 inch Hot Strip Mill Coiler Operator job at Youngstown.

30. The Board gave careful consideration to the four factors in dispute and gives its comments concerning these Factors in numerical order.

Factor 3—Mental Skill. All of the four specimen and the one sample job on the Job Classification Analysis value this Factor at C-1.6. Insofar as mental skill is concerned, the job requires semi-routine performance of duties involving some variety of detail and requiring judgment. The new control equipment would not appear to alter the mental skill required, which essentially is to maintain the tightness of the coil. The Board finds that the new equipment did not add anything to the mental skill necessary for the operation of the Coiler, and that the value of C-1.6 is equitable for Factor 3.

Factor 5—Responsibility for Materials. Prior to the installation of the new control equipment, both parties mutually agreed that the responsibility of the Coiler Operator for materials on this job was in the amount of $250.00. The new equipment does not change the value of the materials at all. The amount of attention required by the Operator has, therefore, a large bearing upon the amount of waste material or scrap resulting from the operation. The original classification mutually agreed to by the Union and the Company was the description given in Code C for this Factor and reads "Use close attention for part of turn." The numerical classification in the manual for $250.00 is given as 1.2 points. To increase this to Code D for $250.00, the job requirements would read "Use close attention for majority of turn." From the evidence submitted the Board is of the opinion that the new control equipment does not increase the time for which the operator is required to give close attention to the operation, certainly not for a majority of the turn. The Board finds that the original valuation of C-1.2 appears to be equitable.

In referring to the Job Classification Analysis, only the 38 inch Hot Strip Mill coiler operator job is given the C-1.2 classification rating. The 42 inch specimen job and the three 80 inch jobs are rated at D-1.6. From the description of duties given on the Job Classification Analysis there is no question insofar as the Board is concerned that the operation of the 80 inch Hot Strip Mills require more attention from the Coiler Operator than does the 42 inch Hot Strip Mill at Youngstown. However, there is some slight doubt about the 42 inch Hot Strip Mill Specimen Job (Number 2018). Since this latter is a specimen job, both Management and the Union agreed on the D-1.6 rating and on the description which reads in part "Use close attention for majority of turn...."

The Board recognizes that for the job on the 42 inch Hot Strip Mill at Youngstown, the Management and the Union also mutually agreed on the C-1.2 rating before the new control equipment was installed. The Board is clearly of the opinion that the installation of the new control equipment has not increased the amount of attention required by the operator, and in fact may have actually reduced the time for which the operator is required to give close attention.

Factor 6—Responsibility for Tools and Equipment. In this case all of the specimen jobs and the sample job have a value for Factor 6 of C-0.7. It would appear that the new equipment does not add any additional equipment to which more than ordinary care is required to prevent damage. The highest valued items are the Coiler Motors and these are the same as when the operation did not have the new equipment, at which time Factor 6 was mutually agreed upon at a value of C-0.7. The Board finds that for Factor 6 the value of C-0.7 is equitable.

Factor 7—Responsibility for Operations. Again the value given for Factor 7 on all the jobs listed in the Job Classification Analysis is D-2.0. The new equipment did not change the job content in this Factor. The Coiler Operator originally received the strip as it came from the mill and had to maintain the same pace as the mill maintained; but with the new control equipment, there is no obligation for the Operator to maintain a pace which is determined by someone else.

The Union contended that the language used in describing this Factor 7 on the back of the job classification sheet was most similar to the language that is used in the Manual for the numerical classification of E-3.0. The Company representative testified that the language chosen for this factor was selected for the 42 inch Hot Strip Mill specimen job as well as for the 42 inch Hot Strip Mill Youngstown job and at the time of classification the value of D-2.0 was mutually agreed upon by the Company and the Union not only for the Youngstown Coiler Operator job, but elsewhere at the time the specimen jobs of Coiler Operator were classified. Since all of the specimen jobs as well as the sample job on the Job Classification Analysis give the same rating of D-2.0 to this Factor, the Board holds that this rating of D-2.0 is equitable for the Youngstown job.

31. In conclusion the Board finds that the present classification of the Coiler Operator job at the McDonald Mills is an equitable classification at Job Class 11.

AWARD

32. The grievance is dismissed.

PART II

CODING THE CLASSIFICATION FACTORS

CHAPTER 9

LIMITATION ON ARBITRATOR'S AUTHORITY

For this brief introductory chapter to Part II of this volume two paragraphs have been excerpted from an award in a case between United States Steel Products Division of United States Steel Corporation and the United Steelworkers of America. These paragraphs, in a case decided by the editor of this book on December 12, 1955, contain some important observations on the purpose of a job classification program and on the arbitrator's authority in job classification disputes. They read as follows:

"From the number of Factors in dispute, the wide disparity of codings thought appropriate by the parties, and the various contentions made at the hearing, it is obvious that the parties hold widely divergent views as to the nature of their agreed upon classification program. Hence, a few preliminary observations on the over-all program are in order.

"To adopt all the codings sought by the Union would create serious wage rate inequities within the scope of the present wage structure. The object of the classification program was to create and preserve an equitable wage rate structure. To the extent that any inequities may have crept into the classification of jobs in the original program or that inconsistencies may exist, they can be corrected only by a joint review by the parties. The Arbitrator is not empowered to make any such corrections in the present case. He is bound by the existing agreements of the parties, and must decide the grievances before him by using as guides the jobs agreed upon by the parties as Benchmarks."

CHAPTER 10

IMPORTANCE OF SPECIMEN EXAMPLES

As noted in the Historical Sketch of the Wage Rate Inequity Program, set forth at the outset of this volume, the parties at top level described and classified about 2,500 Benchmark and Specimen Example jobs. The present chapter shows the significance to be attributed to these job descriptions and classifications.

Other relevant cases reported elsewhere in this volume are: USC-293 (page 232), USC-342 (page 290), A-865 (page 264), COL-69 (page 301).

A—681. Worcester Works. September 29, 1954

Herbert L. Sherman, Jr., *Arbitrator*
Approved by Sylvester Garrett, *Chairman*

1. This grievance requests a higher classification for the job of Bench Operator-Springs in the Spring Mill of the Worcester Works on the ground that incumbents were required to perform certain duties in connection with the inspection of a rejected lot of brake cable assemblies during August and September, 1953. Although at an early stage of the processing of the grievance, it was thought that grievants were paid as Assemblers (Brake Cable), it was finally established that they were paid as Bench Operators. The confusion arose because the Assembler job performs similar duties on original shipments of brake cable assemblies (such as gauging the brake cable assembly for length) and because of the fact that both the Bench Operator job and the Assembler job are in Job Class 3.

2. In August, 1953, two truckloads of brake cable assemblies were returned to the Spring Mill from a customer since some of the assemblies were defective in either cable length or fittings. The Union believes the shipping of defective product was due to the relaxation of the amount of inspection in the preceding months. Because the entire shipment was rejected, a check of all the assemblies was required to salvage the good product. Prior to this incident there had been no rejection of brake cable assemblies in such a large lot. In those instances in the past when small amounts of faulty brake cable assemblies were returned by a customer, each cable was tagged as to the exact nature of the defect. Management or the Inspection Department handled the matter in a few minutes by visual examination.

3. Because the returned lot in August, 1953, was so large Management decided that the checking, sorting and counting should be done in the Spring Mill Division. According to the Working Procedure of a job description prepared by the Union, the following duties were involved:

Measure brake cable in go or no-go gauge.

Correct cables placed in box for shipment.

Short cables placed in one pile and long cables placed in another pile.

Inspect each cable to see that proper number of fixtures are attached.

Record results of inspection on forms.

4. Management assigned these tasks to the Bench Operator job because that job, according to unrefuted testimony, has for many years been used to recheck and sort other rejected materials in order to salvage the good product. For example, incumbents of that job have rechecked and sorted Contact Fingers by checking the height of the arc to see if it was too high or too low. The pieces were pushed under a red and green light gauge. The Bench Operators watched to see which light lit up, and then sorted the pieces accordingly. Flat Springs, Clock Springs and Fulcrum Rings have also been rechecked and sorted by Bench Operators by using different gauges and by visual examination for obvious defects.

CONTENTIONS OF THE PARTIES

5. The Union contends that there was sufficient change in the job content of the Bench Operator job to warrant a new description and classification at Job Class 5. The Union's proposed classification assigns higher ratings on Factors 3, 4, 5, 7 and 11 than the present ratings found for those Factors for the Bench Operator job.

6. On Factor 3—Mental Skill a rating of C 1.6 is sought because the language under Code C in the Manual reads, "Sort material according to size, weight or appearance." C 1.0 is assigned by the Union under Factor 4—Manual Skill. Reference is made to language in the Manual under Code C which calls for "dexterity of a high degree." It is the Union's position that the special Convention for Inspectors should apply under Factor 5—Responsibility for Material. Attention is also called to the language in the Manual under Code D: "Inspect and classify finished product." For Factor 7—Responsibility for Operations, the Union assigns a rating of B .5 because two men coordinated their efforts in checking the rejected product. And finally, B .4 is sought for Factor 11 —Surroundings since the Spring Mill is housed in an old building with a low ceiling which makes for disagreeable conditions.

7. While Management concedes that checking and sorting rejected material are not specifically mentioned in the job description for the Bench Operator job, it points out that such tasks were part of the actual job content of the job as it was being performed at the time it was described and classified. It contends that under Section 9-D of the Agreement no change in classification is in order. The Company points to two items in the Working Procedure of the job description:

"Inspects springs for height and O.D. (outside diameter) using set gauge or special equipment.

"Inspects springs **intermittently.**"

8. Attention is called also to the notation under Factor 3 for the Bench Operator job: "Recognize obvious defects." Moreover, the Assembler job, which is given credit in the applicable incentive brochure for checking brake cable assemblies in their original fabrication (though not listed expressly in the job description), is in Job Class 3.

9. By way of summation, the Company takes the position that whether the duties involved in rechecking the brake cable assemblies be considered as assigned to the Bench Operator job, the Assembler job, or as giving rise to a new job of "Rejection Sorter," the resulting classification is still no higher than Job Class 3.

DISCUSSION AND FINDINGS

10. In checking and sorting the returned brake cable assemblies, incumbents of the Bench Operator job were required to make a visual examination of each cable to determine if the fixtures were in their proper places. The length was checked in a "go-no-go" gauge. Good product was set aside while faulty product was put in various piles depending on the defect involved. Finally, the number of assemblies in each pile was counted and noted on a form.

11. Although the Union argues that grievants had responsibility for final inspection of brake cables during August and September, 1953, the testimony shows that an Inspector Special or Factory Inspector in Job Class 13 regularly spot-checked all good product segregated from the rejected product before any of it was returned to the customer. Likewise, the same Inspector job, prior to the return of the two truckloads involved in this case, spot-checked brake cable assemblies made by the Assembler job for original shipments.

12. The Board agrees with the Union that the literal language of the job description for the Bench Operator job does not cover the inspection and sorting of returned brake cable assemblies during the two-month period in 1953. On the other hand, it cannot be found that there has been a change in actual job content to the extent of one job class or more. Gauges similar to the "go-no-go" gauge have long been used by the Bench Operator job. The other duties with respect to sorting and counting returned brake cable assemblies likewise do not affect the classification to the extent of one job class or more.

13. The Union stresses certain language under the codings in the Classification Manual. These words, however, must be interpreted in the light of the meaning attributed to them by the parties. On Page 37 of the Classification Manual, the following agreed upon provision is found:

"The description and classification of each job shall be consistent with and properly related within the framework of the descriptions and classifications of the appropriate 'Benchmark' and 'Specimen Example' jobs listed in Exhibit A of this manual which, by reference, are hereby made a part of the manual."

14. Thus, the broad, abstract language found under the Factors in the Manual must be given only such meaning by the Board, in

evaluating the effect of changes (if any) in the duties of a job on the classification of the job, as was attributed to it by the parties in applying it to concrete cases in the course of reaching agreement upon the "Benchmark" and "Specimen Example" jobs. And finally, as a check to determine the proper interpretation and application of "Benchmark" and "Specimen Example" job descriptions and classifications, the Board must consider any relevant evidence before it which provides proper guidance in that respect. For example, it is relevant for the Board to consider how the parties have applied "Benchmark" and "Specimen" job descriptions and classifications to other jobs similar to the one in dispute.

15. Specimen Example 1756 covers a job of Packer in a Spring Mill. Included in the duties are the following: "May count number of springs for each container," and "Inspects springs as packed." In the Spring Mill at Worcester Works there are similar jobs to the one dispute. A Sorter (Steel Terminals), with a plant title of Bench Operator-Gauge Steel Terminals, gauges steel terminals in a "go" and "no-go" gauge. He also "inspects terminals for length and obvious defects visually," and sorts them accordingly. An Inspector and Packer job "inspects rail head bonds for all possible defects such as angle of crimp in stands, diameter of terminals, welds at terminal, broken stands, improper plating." The job also counts and packs the bonds. A Packer (Lightweight) job is required to "weigh, sort, count and pack lightweight springs or other Spring Mill products," and to make out shipping tags. In the Spring Mill at Waukegan Works, a job of Bench-Operator Springs must "inspect and perform necessary hand finishing operation to springs." Also, "grain tubes are inspected and laid on bench between two predetermined marks."

16. None of these jobs are classified higher than Job Class 3. Specimen 1756 is in Job Class 2. None of the Factors on any of these jobs are rated higher than the ratings of the Factors for the job in dispute, except for Factor 5 for the Sorter (Steel Terminals) job which is rated at C .5. Nor does the subsequent installation of an electrically operated detector table to check original shipments of brake cable assemblies for some of the same items involved in grievants' inspection of rejected product indicate that the job in dispute should receive a higher classification. The placing of the Operator job for this machine in Job Class 4 was obviously based on the duties involved in operating that type of equipment. Thus, on the basis of the evidence presented to the Board, it cannot be found that the job content of the job in dispute has been changed to the extent of one full job class or more.

AWARD

17. The grievance is denied.

A—738. Duluth Works. February 4, 1957
John R. Coleman, *Assistant to the Chairman*
Approved by Sylvester Garrett, *Chairman*

BACKGROUND

1. This grievance arose out of the establishment of new jobs at Duluth Works on a fence post galvanizing unit installed in the spring of 1954. One of the jobs, that of Galvanized Post Bander, PC 22-65, was originally assigned a Job Class 4 rating by the Company. Subsequently the Company reclassified the job and gave it a Job Class 5 rating with a point score of 5.4. The Union has accepted the original Company description of the job and also the revised description offered by the Company at the Third Step in the grievance procedure. But the Union disputes the Company's codings under Factors 1, 2, 3, 5, and 7, and seeks a Job Class 7 rating.

DISCUSSION AND FINDINGS

2. The Union's case rests primarily upon references to the language of the Job Classification Manual. No benchmark or specimen jobs are referred to in the brief or testimony. For its part, the Company makes brief reference to three specimen jobs, Specimens 777 (Bander), 716 (Bundler), and 1680 (Piler), in its brief, but depends principally upon comparison with the nonspecimen job of Fence Post Handler (Unracker), Plant Code 22-13, for its argument that the present job is properly classified.

3. The Union asserts that the Unracker's job is not a close fit with that of the Bander, and that comparison with specimens and other jobs is irrelevant. It believes rather that the language of the Manual under each factor should be controlling. This view is erroneous, since the parties fully agree that specific job comparisons, making the fullest possible use of the specimens, is the only practical way to give adequate meaning to the Manual in specific cases.

4. Summaries of the Union and Company positions on the Bander's job, together with the classification of the Unracker's job, follow:

5. Each of the five factors in dispute will be considered in turn.

6. *Factor 1. Pre-Employment Training.* The Bander job requires relatively simple in-

PLANT CODE	PLANT JOB TITLE	FACTORS												TOTAL CLASSI- FICATION	JOB CLASS
		1	2	3	4	5	6	7	8	9	10	11	12		
22-65	Galvanized Post Bander														
	Company Proposal	—	.4	1.0	.5	B.3	B.2	.5	.8	.5	.8	—	.4	5.4	5
	Union Demand	.3	.8	1.6	.5	C.5	B.2	1.0	.8	.5	.8	—	.4	7.4	7
22-13	Fence Post Handler (Unracker)	—	—	1.0	.5	B.3	B.2	.5	—	.5	1.5	—	—	4.5	5

spection, recording, and sorting. Most of the work is repetitive. These considerations make A-Base the appropriate rating on this factor whether one looks to the manual for guidance or to the job of Unracker which is similar in this respect.

7. *Factor 2. Employment Training and Experience.* The job descriptions and the testimony in the case suggest that the Bander's job should receive a higher rating here than the Unracker's job, because of the fact that the Bander does in fact need to know more in order to perform his job proficiently. The Company has already recognized this in its new classification of the Bander's job where a B-.4 rating has been assigned, in contrast to the A-Base for the Unracker. This classification seems to make adequate allowance for the extra training time involved, and no case has been established for pushing this rating still higher.

8. *Factor 3. Mental Skill.* Of the different tasks involved in the Bander's job, the inspection function appears to require the greatest degree of mental skill. The revised description of the job, as agreed to in the Third Step of the grievance procedure, states that inspection here is confined to checking for "obviously faulty surface coating or excessive camber." The flaws for which the Bander looks meet the naked eye. This inspection is thus not up to the level of the inspecting done in such specimen jobs as Specimens 4000-4021 and 4032-4034, all of which carry a rating of C-1.6 or better on Factor 3.

9. It is probably true, as the Union claims, that the Bander's job requires more mental skill than does the Unracker's job. But the difference here is not so great as to justify putting the Bander's job in a higher classification. The Unracker's job too con-

tains some rough inspection work ("Inspects posts for quality when placing on bundling tables"). Moreover, the Bander's mental skill required to prepare bundle sizes to customer requirements is not justly comparable to the mental skills which are called for in any of the benchmark jobs classified at C-1.6 in the Job Classification Manual. Bander and Unracker are close enough to one another in the degree of skill involved to make the B-1.0 rating for both an equitable one.

10. *Factor 5. Responsibility for Material.* The primary argument advanced by the Company for a B-.3 rating on Factor 5 is that there is little likelihood of any damage being done. Yet the Specimen inspector jobs typically reveal that, while there is little chance of damage in the direct sense, the job nonetheless receives a C rating because of the amount of attention required during the turn to avoid passing products not up to specifications. The Bander can do little damage to the posts. But he can do a poor job of inspecting and let unsatisfactory posts pass on to the customer. Such cases have occurred and the Bander has been criticized for poor inspection. Similarly he has also been instructed upon occasion to be particularly careful in the inspection of certain shipments.

11. The fact that the Fence Post Galvanizing Operator usually is not in a position to observe the posts carefully as they pass out of the spelter furnace and through the air and water rings means that an appreciable amount of inspection of the total product is left solely to the Bander.

12. From the evidence, it appears that this is an assigned responsibility which entails exercise of care in recognizing faulty galvanizing, rough surface coating, and excessive camber. For example, a nine-foot post with more than ½" bend must be re-

jected by the Bander. To meet this assigned responsibility, therefore, requires close attention for part of the turn, of the sort illustrated in Specimens 1627 and 1628, rather than Specimens 1680, 777, and 716. The inspection on the Bander's job may also be distinguished from the Unracker's job by the fact that the latter inspection is shared by at least three other men whereas no one else sees posts passed by the Bander. Company and Union agree that the relevant dollar amount for possible damage is less than $50.00. Thus a coding of C-.5 is appropriate for this Factor.

13. *Factor 7. Responsibility for Operations.* There is little in the Bander's job to support the Union's request for a rating higher than the B-.5 assigned here by the Company. The Bander has none of the responsibility for operations which falls on the Operator. He has adequate time to get one storage rack cleared of posts while the second one is filling up. Only rare and unusual circumstances could produce a jamming at his position. The job is correctly classified at B-.5.

AWARD

14. The grievance is sustained only to the extent of raising Factor 5 from B-.3 to C-.5. This raises the total point score to 5.6 and the Job Class to 6.

USC—367. Duquesne Works. October 6, 1953

Herbert L. Sherman, Jr., *Assistant to the Chairman*
Approved by Sylvester Garrett, *Chairman*

BACKGROUND

1. This case involves two grievances. Both request a higher classification for the Weighers at #1 and #2 Open Hearths at Duquesne Works. Job Class 7 is presently assigned to the job. The Union seeks Job Class 10.

2. In dispute are the following Factors:

FACTOR	PRES-ENT CLASSI-FICA-TION	UNION CLASSI-FICA-TION
1. Pre-Employment Training	B-.3	C-1.0
2. Employment Training and Experience	C-.8	E-1.6
3. Mental Skill	C-1.6	D-2.2
7. Responsibility for Operations	C-1.0	D-2.0
9. Mental Effort	C-1.0	D-1.5

3. During 1948 and 1949, the job of Weigher at #1 and #2 Open Hearths at Duquesne was studied on plant visits, along with other Weigher jobs at Donora and National Works, by members of the Joint Wage Rate Inequity Committee. In April, 1949, the classification for the job of Open Hearth Weigher at Duquesne was agreed to in Job Class 7, established as a Benchmark, and issued as Specimen Example 4522. On August 20, 1950, the standard hourly wage scale was made effective for all "fringe jobs." In less than three months the first grievance was filed, claiming that numerous "extra duties" had been assigned to the Weighers and that the job should be redescribed and reclassi-

fied. Management replied that there had been no change in the assigned duties of the job. The Company contends that the first grievance amounts to a claim of a wage rate inequity which is barred by Section 9-H of the Agreement.

4. The "extra duties" listed by the Union are as follows:

"Primary Functions:
Determines the quantity of hot metal, ore and scrap to be charged to secure the proper melt carbon for the scheduled heat. No. of furnaces—#1 O.H. 106 to 120 inc.—#2 O.H. 121 to 132 inc.

"Tools & Equipment:
#2 O.H.—Public address system, teletype machine.

"Working Procedure:
Posts and totals accumulative tonnage report daily, weekly and monthly.

Hot metal report ascertaining the amount of hot metal in mixer and also in furnaces twice weekly and monthly.

Places orders for hot metal to be charged in each furnace.

Determines by arithmetical calculations and deviates from standard charge the quantity of hot metal, ore and scrap to be charged due to:

(1) condition of scrap
(2) silicon in iron
(3) amount of cast iron charged
(4) charging alloy heats
(5) scrap charges (due to lack of ore, shortage of hot metal or furnace conditions)

Contacts production planning at the start of each turn for schedule of alloy heats and informs the stock foreman of the type of alloy scrap to be charged.

Weighs and records all scrap from other departments and other sources:

(1) Skull Crackers (for the payment of tonnage)
(2) Scrap from rolling mill
(3) Boiler Shop
(4) Blacksmith Shop
(5) Pipe Shop

Contacts Laboratory by telephone for analysis in an emergency. Relays information received normally on teletype to proper persons.

After each drag is weighed and divided, informs operating personnel as to amount and type of material each furnace being charged still requires.

Calls in expected tap times to Production Planning to determine new change for co-ordination between the Open Hearth and Production Planning to maintain operating schedule for rolling mills.

Calls Production Planning for order at melt and issues order slip to operating personnel.

Issues order changes for reasons listed below:

(1) Production Planning convenience
(2) O.H. Furnace conditions
(3) High alloys
(4) Low melts

Makes out order slips on General Store-room for safety clothing, tools and equipment.

In case of accident issue hospital cards for authority on Hospital.

Takes all furnace fuel changes from Curry Hollow and informs all First Helpers of said change and makes record as to time change received and completed and notifies Curry Hollow at time of completion.

Posts on delay sheet the number of buggies of scrap used per heat.

Posts on delay sheet number of heats per furnace of roof life."

5. The second grievance was filed in October, 1951. It arose out of the new requirement that grievants calculate theoretical ingot weights. Except for periodic test weighing by the Ingot Weigher position, scale weighing of ingots was eliminated. Manage-

ment also admits that two other duties have been added. The Weigher is required to check the "Ingot Production Report" for each heat made in #2 Open Hearth, and to contact the Open Hearth Ingot Shipper or Metallurgical Supervisor in the event of omissions or errors. At #1 Open Hearth the Weigher now receives the bi-weekly pay checks from Accounting supervision and distributes them to each Foreman.

6. Attached to the Fourth Step minutes are six exhibits listed by the Union. They consist of new instructions by Management to #1 and #2 Open Hearth Weighers. Two other similar instructions were introduced as exhibits at the hearing. According to the Company these instructions are related to duties performed at the time the job was classified or to the new duties which are admitted, and do not affect the classification.

DISCUSSION AND FINDINGS

7. *First Grievance.* The Union's contentions are based primarily on a favorable comparison between the "extra duties" in the job in dispute and the duties of Specimen 4526 (a Benchmark) for an Open Hearth Charging Scale Weigher in Job Class 11, and to some extent with a Homestead Weigher job. The difficulty with these contentions, however, is the lack of change in job content between the time that the job in dispute was classified and the filing of the first grievance. From the testimony of one of the grievants and the testimony of the Assistant Works Auditor, it is clear that no duty of any consequence was added in this period to the job as it was previously performed. The requirement that the number of buggies of scrap used per heat be posted to the Delay Sheets merely involves transcription of a number from the work sheet. Although Superintendent Fox stated that certain minor tasks such as issuing hospital cards in case of accident were not necessarily "required" duties of grievants at the time that the job was classified, they were nevertheless performed by grievants at that time and are continued on the same basis today.

8. Management also disputes the assertion that the job "determines the quantity of hot metal, ore and scrap to be charged to secure the proper melt carbon for the scheduled heat." It states that this has always been the responsibility of higher supervision in the Open Hearth Department and notes that this language was copied from the primary function of Specimen 4526. There is considerable testimony on this point. It appears that grievants do make some determinations such as determining the amount of hot metal to be charged by reference to a standard chart,

They make arithmetical calculations, but do not determine the total charge. In any event, one of the grievants referred to this function and stated that he had always performed it, or at least for five or six years, even though it is not expressly listed in the job description. There are, moreover, some differences between the more comprehensive determinations made by the incumbent of Specimen 4526 and those made by grievants.

9.   It was this function of determining and adjusting quantities of materials for charging Open Hearth Furnaces which was emphasized by the parties in classifying Specimen 4526. Reference is made to it not only in the primary function but also in the classification of Factors 1, 3, 5, 7 and 9. The Board cannot question at this time the weight which has been given to these differences by the parties.

10.   Since there was no change in the job content of any consequence from the time of classification of the job in dispute to the filing of the first grievance (whether or not the duties performed were precisely itemized in the job description), the Board has no authority to sustain the grievance.

11.   *Second Grievance.* As to the second grievance, it is obvious that the only added duty which might appear on the surface to affect the ratings on the Factors in dispute is the calculation of theoretical ingot weights. The other new duties are not complicated

and clearly do not require a higher degree of mental skill or effort or more employment training than that already recognized in the present classification. The instructions from Management to grievants, contained in the Union Exhibits, refer to such matters as recording additional data in the possession of the Weighers on certain reports, relaying information by a telephone call, addition of figures, checking a report for an omission, and calculation of theoretical ingot weights.

12.   To perform the last mentioned duty, the Weigher obtains the theoretical weights by referring to a Weight Manual and by making relatively simple computations based on the type of top, the cross section size of the mold, and the block or height of pour. The basic information is furnished to grievants. At the time that the job was classified, incumbents were also required to compute theoretical weights of slab heats. This, however, does not involve use of a Weight Manual nor was it specifically listed in the job description. On the other hand, the job description clearly contemplates basic arithmetical calculations. No change has been made in the job content of the Weigher job as performed at the time it was classified which is sufficiently substantial to justify higher ratings on the Factors in dispute.

AWARD

13.   The grievances are denied.

USC—289.   Duquesne Works.   October 6, 1953

Herbert L. Sherman, Jr., *Assistant to the Chairman*
Approved by Sylvester Garrett, *Chairman*

BACKGROUND

1.   This grievance involves classification of the new job of Loader Helper (Hot Beds) 40″ (Trade) at the Duquesne Works. Management classified it at 5.2 for Class 5 which was made effective June 2, 1950, the date the grievance was filed. The Union argues for Job Class 7. Since use of the 40″ Hot Beds was discontinued on April 25, 1952, the present grievance concerns retroactive compensation.

2.   In April, 1950, a new loading procedure was introduced for the 40″ Hot Bed product going to the trade in order to eliminate extra handling at the Section 30 Conditioning Yard. A locomotive crane, equipped with a magnet, began loading the steel from the 40″ Hot Beds into railroad cars after grievants had performed the necessary switching duties in guiding the crane while the cars were positioned for loading from the spurs or main track. Blocking was placed in the cars, and, as the steel was loaded,

grievants were required to nail and complete the blocking. Also assigned as a new duty to grievants was direction of the crane in the positioning of lifts evenly so that the car was properly balanced. The Loader Helper then directed the Craneman in moving the loaded cars to make room for the empties.

3.   Previously, grievants as Loader Helpers in Class 4, though they drifted cars down the spur to the Hot Beds for loading and stopped them with a brake, were not required to perform switching duties. Blocking was simpler. And grievants merely assisted in the mechanical pushing of the steel into the cars. The old job of Loader Helper 40″ Hot Beds remained on the wage scale because only 85% of the product was shipped directly to customers. The new loading procedure was more like the practice followed by the Loader Helper (Hot Beds) 38″ (Trade) job which has a total point value of 5.2. However, the incumbent of that job need not know how to perform

switching duties in the manner required of grievants. He merely "spots" the cars for loading.

4. The job description for the new job is agreed upon, but the Union asserts that the switching duties warrant the same factor values as those received by a Broad Gauge Switchman. The Board is also referred to the job of Locomotive Crane Helper. Following is a tabulation which shows the respective positions of the parties.

FACTOR	COMPANY CLASSI-FICATION	UNION CLASSI-FICATION
1. Pre-Employment Training	A-Base	A-Base
* 2. Employment Training and Experience	A-Base	B- .4
* 3. Mental Skill	B-1.0	C-1.6
4. Manual Skill	B- .5	B- .5
* 5. Responsibility for Materials	B- .3	C- .7
6. Responsibility for Tools and Equipment	A-Base	A-Base
7. Responsibility for Operations	B- .5	B- .5
* 8. Responsibility for Safety of Others	B- .4	C- .8
9. Mental Effort	B- .5	B- .5
10. Physical Effort	C- .8	C- .8
11. Surroundings	C- .8	C- .8
*12. Hazards	B- .4	C- .8
Total	5.2	7.4

* Disputed Factors.

DISCUSSION AND FINDINGS

5. At the outset it must be noted that the Union's position that the job in dispute should be given the identical factor values as a Switchman cannot be adopted by the Board. Railroad switching is the reason for the existence of the Switchman job; it is the primary function involving pulling, coupling, and switching cars for the Engineer. The Loader Helper's switching duties are more of an incidental part of the job and are performed in an area where danger of injury to others is not very great. Likewise, the job of Locomotive Crane Helper, though more comparable to the Loader Helper job than a Switchman, cannot be considered as controlling the factor values since the Crane Helper follows the crane into various areas of the plant for any purpose.

6. On the other hand, there is no reason why the rating on a particular factor for the job in dispute cannot be the same as that found for the Switchman or Locomotive Crane Helper. Factor 2—Employment Training and Experience is coded at B-.4 for Specimen 706, a Loader Helper job. Non-Specimen Loader Helper jobs presented to the Board range from Job Class 3 to Job Class 6. Factor 2 for these jobs is coded at A-Base or B-.4.

7. The Working Procedure for Specimen 706 reads in its entirety as follows: "Assists Loader in: measurement of car, calculation of skid lumber needed, ordering of lumber and moving of lumber of yard to car, placing of lumber and lifts in car, locating material in finishing end and transporting by crane to car." By way of comparison the new job of Loader Helper at Duquesne was required to check with the Gang Leader as to which cars were to be loaded; to gather the proper skids and blocks; to switch cars to position for loading which involved coupling and uncoupling cars, throwing switches for the Craneman, and signaling the Craneman; to place and nail initial blocking in cars; to complete the blocking as the steel was loaded; and to direct the crane in positioning of lifts evenly so that the car was properly balanced. At times loaded cars had to be switched back and forth by grievants on the spurs for purposes of straightening the loads or clearing the way for other cars. Using Specimen 706 as a guide, the Board finds, by comparing and balancing the duties of the two jobs, that B-.4 for Factor 2 is justified for the job in dispute.

8. Under Factor 3—Mental Skill, not only is Specimen 706 rated at B-1.0, but Specimen 837 for a Locomotive Crane Helper which switches for locomotive cranes is also coded at B-1.0. The duties of the job in dispute certainly do not require any higher degree of mental ability. No non-Specimen Loader Helper job presented to the Board receives a higher coding than B-1.0 in Factor 3.

9. Factor 5 concerns Responsibility for Materials. Nothing in the Loader Helper job in dispute warrants a higher rating than B-.3, which is the rating on this Factor for Specimen 706—a Loader Helper, Specimen 837—a Locomotive Crane Helper, and for every non-Specimen Loader Helper job presented for the Board's consideration.

10. With respect to Factor 8—Responsibility for the Safety of Others, Specimen 706 is coded at B-.4. Although Specimen 837 receives a C-.8, that job involves the guiding of the Craneman "to various plant locations." Grievants' regular switching was confined to limited car movements in one area about 100 yards long and 30 yards

wide. There is a difference of opinion as to whether grievants or Locomotive Crane Helpers on occasion guided the locomotive crane to the shop for repairs. The requirement that the Loader Helper set out safety signs, flags and lanterns to protect automobiles while loading was taking place is found in the Section 30 Loader Helper job at Duquesne. It is coded at B-.4 for this Factor. No safety signs were placed at the switches by the Loader Helper. It is true that the functions of throwing switches and giving standard signals by the Loader Helper job in dispute are the same as those for the Locomotive Crane Helper. Nevertheless, the Crane Helper receives a higher rating because of his greater responsibility for the safety of others based upon the area he covers, sometimes congested, the numerous crossings which he must consider, and his primary function. On the whole, B-.4 must be considered as appropriate for the Loader Helper on this Factor.

11. In the grievance procedure the reason advanced by the Union for a higher rating than B-.4 under Factor 12—Hazards was that grievants were required to climb on moving stock. It seems clear, however, that such was not a requirement of the job, and was, if true, a violation of instructions from Management. All of the Loader Helper and Locomotive Crane Helper jobs presented to the Board—both Specimen and non-Specimen, receive B-.4 for this Factor. Nothing in this case warrants a higher rating for the job in dispute.

12. Since the rating on Factor 2 is increased to B-.4, the new job of Loader Helper is classified at 5.6 for Job Class 6. When Management classified the job at Class 5, it made retroactive adjustments to grievants, who had been paid at Class 4, on the basis of 85% which represented the amount of steel shipped to trade from the 40″ Mill Hot Beds during the period involved. This was done because no accurate record was available for the actual hours worked on the new job and the hours worked on the old job at Class 4. This solution seems to have been agreeable to the parties concerned. It is assumed that retroactive compensation under this Award will be made in like manner for the period between June 2, 1950 and April 25, 1952, the date when utilization of the 40″ Hot Beds was discontinued.

AWARD

13. The grievance is sustained to the extent that the new job of Loader Helper (Hot Beds) 40″ (Trade) is placed in Job Class 6.

T—286.   Fairfield Sheet Mill.   June 2, 1955
Sylvester Garrett, *Chairman*

BACKGROUND

1. This grievance involves classification of a new job, established unilaterally by the Company in Job Class 4 effective March 28, 1953, in the Shearing and Finishing Department at Fairfield Sheet Mill. The new job, titled Hooker (Heavy Duty Shear), performs most of the functions performed by the Class 6 job of Stocking Crane Hooker (Cut Bar) prior to March 1953. Grievant, the only present incumbent of the new job, was also an incumbent of the Stocking Crane Hooker job. The physical area of the Mill where grievant now works is the same as that in which he worked as a Stocking Crane Hooker.

2. This job, as well as the Stocking Craneman job in the Rolling and Annealing Department, was discontinued when two Jobbing Mills and the Bar Shears at the Sheet Mill were removed. The Coil Storage area for the Heavy Duty Shear Line then became a part of the Shearing and Finishing Department. Since the two old jobs had been discontinued, the Company established two new jobs to provide crane service for the storage of coils and for the entry end of the Heavy Duty Shear Line in the Shearing and Finishing Department: Heavy Duty Shear Craneman and Hooker (Heavy Duty Shear). At a meeting with the grievance committee on March 28, 1953, there was agreement on the proposed description and classification of the Heavy Duty Shear Craneman and also on the description of the duties of the occupation Hooker (Heavy Duty Shear). There was no agreement on the classification of this job.

3. In the grievance procedure the Union contended that the proposed job of Hooker (Heavy Duty Shear) was not in fact a new job but was merely a changed job derived from the old position of Stocking Crane Hooker. At the hearing, however, the parties agreed that the job was a new position and should be classified as such.

4. At the hearing it also developed that the parties hold widely different views as to the essential nature of the work of this new job. In the Company view it is merely a

Crane Hooker position. In the Union view the new job is essentially a Stocking job which should be classified by reference to Specimens covering Stocking jobs.

5. The Union stresses that the job of Hooker (Heavy Duty Shear) in substance involves the same working procedure as did the job of Stocking Crane Hooker. According to the Union a comparison of the new job description with that for the discontinued job shows that the removal of the two Jobbing Mill furnaces did not eliminate the stocking functions in this area of the Sheet Mill. In addition it can find no essential difference between the actual duties of the Hooker (Heavy Duty Shear) job and those set forth in the working procedure of Specimen 2153, Standard Title—Stocker, which is classified at 6.2.

6. The agreed working procedure of the Hooker (Heavy Duty Shear) is as follows:

"1. Receives instructions as to material to be handled and material identification tickets from Turn Foreman—Shearing, or Tallyman (Processor).

"2. Hooks and unhooks for crane in servicing heavy duty shear line entry conveyor and related storage areas.

"3. Hooks and unhooks lifts to load or unload railroad cars and coil conveyors.

"4. When unloading coils, paints coil number, width, gauge and other special markings on inside wrap of coil, as shown in chalk on coil.

"5. Marks, on back of coil ticket, location in which coils are stored, and takes coil ticket to office for further handling.

"6. Places skids in desired locations to receive or block coils.

"7. Performs necessary crane hooking to repair and maintain equipment in assigned area.

"8. Keeps working area clean."

7. This compares with the working procedure of the former job of Stocking Crane Hooker as follows:

"1. Receives instructions and material identification tickets from Jobbing Mill Turn Foreman, Turn Foreman—Shearing, or Schedule Clerk—Jobbing Mill & Bar Yard as to material to be handled.

"2. Performs necessary crane hooking to service entry conveyors for jobbing mill furnaces and heavy duty shear line, and related storage areas.

"3. Hooks and unhooks lifts to load or unload railroad cars and coil conveyors.

"4. When unloading coils, paints coil number, width, gauge and other special

markings on inside wrap of coil as shown in chalk on coil.

"5. Marks, on back of coil ticket, location in which coils are stored, and takes coil ticket to office for further handling.

"6. Performs necessary crane hooking to repair and maintain equipment in assigned area.

"7. Keeps working area clean."

8. The working procedure of Specimen 2153 is as follows:

"1. Checks shearing schedule to determine work sequence.

"2. Locates coils in storage area or gondola railroad cars and positions necessary identification marks on coils.

"3. Hooks for and signals Craneman in removing coils from gondola cars to storage or doubling lines, or from storage to doubling lines.

"4. Hooks for crane in removing scrap from doubler lines to scrap compressor or in loading scrap into cars.

"5. Records coil and heat numbers on shearing orders, reports cars unloaded and records location of coils placed in storage."

9. The Company distinguishes this Specimen job in that the incumbent must check the shearing schedule to determine the sequence of the coils to be stocked at the doubling lines, and he records more information than grievant. To this the Union points out that grievant must check a bundle of tickets to determine the sequence of the coils to be stocked at the entry to the Shear Line, and he performs the recording function of reporting the exact bay and the exact row where he has decided to store a given coil. The Union does not believe that it takes any more skill or responsibility to work from a prepared schedule than it does to follow a prepared bundle of tickets, which could even become mixed up during the course of stocking the coils.

10. The Union further notes that coils of a very substantial number of different gauges are handled and stocked by the disputed job. In this respect it contends that the new job differs materially from the Class 4 job of Crane Follower (Processor), which is cited by the Company as closely similar to the disputed job. The working procedure of the Crane Follower (Processor) is as follows:

"1. Receives loading tally, coil tickets, or verbal instructions as to material to be moved.

"2. When unloading coils, notes width, gauge, etc., written on coils, to determine proper storage location.

"3. Secures skids and positions them for the placing of material.

"4. Hooks and unhooks lifts for servicing Processing Lines, Heavy Duty Shear Line, and related equipment.

"5. Hooks and unhooks for loading or unloading railroad cars, trucks, and coil conveyors.

"6. Paints coil number, width, gauge, and other special markings on inside wrap when unloading coils, as shown in chalk on coils.

"7. Marks on back of coil ticket location in which coils are stored, and forwards coil ticket to office for proper filing.

"8. Hooks and unhooks other lifts, as required.

"9. Cleans up working area, as required.

"10. Performs other related work, as required."

11. Other local Sheet Mill Hooker jobs are also relied upon by Management. Although the Union believes that they are distinguishable from the job in dispute on the ground that they receive direction from a Stocker (while grievant does not have the benefit of this assistance), the Crane Hooker (Cold Reduced Shear) is not supervised by a Stocker. This Hooker receives his directions from his Foreman or through a Tractor Operator.

12. In addition, the Company cites Specimen 2472, Standard Title—Hooker, which is classified at 4.4. The working procedure for this job, which is coded precisely the same on all Factors as the job in dispute, is as follows:

"1. Hooks for crane in transporting material to and from Finishing Department processing units, scales, warehouse storage areas, package floors, loading conveyors, railway cars and motor trucks.

"2. Follows crane to destination, places proper skids and unhooks lift.

"3. Selects proper carrier equipment and hooks to crane to accommodate various products."

FINDINGS

13. There is no doubt that the disputed job performs functions going beyond those covered in the working procedure of Specimen 2472 for a Hooker. On the other hand, no substantial difference from a classification standpoint has been shown to exist between the new job and Specimen 2153 for a Stocker, which also performs a considerable amount of hooking work. It is, therefore, not necessary for the Board to consider the various plant jobs, with the various similarities and distinctions relied upon by the parties.

14. When coils are brought to the Coil Storage area by gondola cars for stocking, grievant is handed a ticket for each coil, giving the coil number, weight, decimal thickness, heat number and coil width. After checking the information shown on the outside of the coil in chalk against the material identification ticket, he then paints these special markings on the inside wrap of the coil. Grievant must then determine the most appropriate row of the 62 rows in the 15 bays, to stock the coil. He hooks and unhooks the lifts, and tries to stock coils of the same width in the same row. Not too much attention is paid to the gauge at this point. Coils usually are piled two high in the respective rows and bays and occasionally three high. As a safety precaution, it is necessary to place the wide coils on the bottom. After the coil has been properly stored, grievant marks the row number and bay number on the ticket, and returns it to the office.

15. To service the Heavy Duty Shear Line entry conveyor, grievant is able to determine the sequence of the coils needed by checking a bundle of tickets transmitted to him. From the tickets, which are arranged in sequence, he can locate the bay and row number of a given coil. He then checks the coil numbers of the particular coils in that row against the tickets to make sure that he is hooking up the proper coils to be placed on the entry conveyor.

16. Another function of this job is to hook and unhook lifts of coils returned on a conveyor from the Heavy Duty Shear Line. This involves re-storage of coils which have been partly sheared. The bay and row numbers for these coils are marked for grievant by the Foreman or Shipper.

17. The following duties of grievant's job may be compared with the numbered duties in the Working Procedure of Specimen 2153 for a Stocker, as set forth above:

1. Checks material identification tickets to determine the sequence of the coils to be placed on the entry conveyor for the Heavy Duty Shear Line.

2. Locates coils in storage area. Paints necessary identification marks on coils.

3. Hooks for and signals Craneman in removing coils from gondola cars to storage, or from storage to the Heavy Duty Shear Line.

4. Hooks for crane in removing partly used coils on return conveyor from Heavy Duty Shear Line.

5. Determines appropriate location for coils unloaded from gondola cars and records location of coils placed in storage.

18. The added duties of the incumbent of the Specimen job to copy the coil and

heat numbers on the shearing schedule and to report the number of cars unloaded cannot justify different codings for the job in dispute. The Board finds, therefore, that all Classification Factors of this job should be coded in accord with Specimen 2153.

AWARD

19. The grievance is sustained. The new job of "Hooker (Heavy Duty Shear)" should be coded for each Factor with the same codings as Specimen 2153—Stocker, for a total coding of 6.2 (Class 6).

USC—318. Edgar Thomson Works. December 30, 1953
Sylvester Garrett, *Chairman*

AWARD ON REQUEST FOR REVIEW

BACKGROUND

1. On March 16, 1953, Special Arbitrator Harbison issued his Award under Section 7-J of the August 15, 1952, Agreement. Pursuant to Section 7-J, the Company on March 26, 1953, requested a review of the Special Arbitrator's Award. On November 10, 1953, a hearing was held by the Board, at which both parties presented argument on the question of whether the Special Arbitrator's Award should be modified.

2. Under Section 7-J, the Board's review is limited to an analysis of matters already in the record of the case at the time of the Special Arbitrator's Decision, including the agreements of the parties. This policy first was announced by the Board in Case COL-34. The review in COL-34, as here, was governed by the principle that the Special Arbitrator's findings of fact should be regarded as final and binding if supported by the evidence.

3. As far as evaluating the evidence is concerned, the purpose of the review under Section 7-J is limited to determination of whether (a) there is credible evidence to support the Special Arbitrator's findings, or (b) relevant findings required by the evidence were not made where essential to proper determination of the case. Where there is room for judgment in determining the credibility of witnesses or as to which of various possible inferences may be drawn from evidence, the Board will not disturb the findings of the Special Arbitrator. Apart from this limited evaluation of the evidence, there is a second phase of review under Section 7-J; namely, the determination of whether the Agreements of the parties have been applied correctly.

4. This case involves a grievance which arose in the Plant Protection Department of Edgar Thomson Works. Basically, the grievance alleged that there had been sufficient changes in duties of the Plant Guard job to require development of a new job description and an increase in classification from Job Class 8 to Job Class 13. Among other things, the Union stressed three asserted changes in job duties after the original description and classification of the Plant Guard position as follows: (a) a requirement to carry firearms at all times while on duty, (b) handling an inventory of dynamite and dynamite caps, (c) handling of equipment and responsibility incident to taking of gas tests in the Plant on an increasing basis, and (d) other additional duties such as ordering Dri-Ox. The difference between the parties as to classification under various factors in dispute is indicated in the following table:

FACTOR	PRESENT CLASSI-FICATION	UNION PROPOSAL (IN FOURTH STEP)
4—Manual Skill	B-0.5	C-1.0
5—Responsibility for Materials	C-1.8	C-3.7
6—Responsibility for Tools and Equipment	B-M-0.3	C-H-1.0
7—Responsibility for Operations	A-Base	B-0.5
8—Responsibility for Saftey of Others	B-0.4	C-0.8
10—Physical Effort	B-0.3	C-0.8
12—Hazard	B-0.4	C-0.8

5. Some of the essential findings of Special Arbitrator Harbison on the record before him are as follows:

"An analysis of the briefs, the minutes of the third and fourth Step grievance meetings, and the hearing, reveals the following facts:

"a. Starting in April, 1951, the Plant Guards were required to carry revolvers at all times when on duty, in order that they would be better equipped to safeguard plant facilities in view of the state of emergency arising from the Korean conflict. Prior to this time, it was customary for the guards to be armed only when transporting or guarding the payroll. The job description specifically refers to 'firearms' under *Tools and Equipment* and under Factor 4—*Manual Skill,* so that the occasional use of revolvers was recognized as part of the job when it was classified. Formerly, however, only a few of the guards were required to have revolvers and then only while guarding the payroll. After April, 1951, all guards were required to carry revolvers at all times.

"b. The guards at Edgar Thomson have been given increasing responsibility for making gas tests in various parts of the plant. This requires use of a simply operated portable instrument which shows the concentration of CO (Carbon monoxide). The planning of gas tests is done by a supervisory employee—the gas coordinator—but most of the actual tests are made by the guards, and the equipment is maintained by them. In the working procedure of the job description, specific mention of this task is referred to as follows, 'May use CO indicator or any other safety device as required.' Many of the guards now spend a substantial portion of their time making gas tests, while others never perform this function. Of 68 men in the Plant Guard Force, 39 are trained to make gas tests, and normally 18 are used regularly on this assignment. No claim was made that this task involves greater skill, mental effort, or responsibility than other tasks included in the guard's job.

"c. Only a small number of guards have any tasks connected with dynamite or dynamite caps. Management claims that the procedure, with respect to dynamite and caps, is for the guards to count and tally them on the sheet, and not to handle the dynamite or caps. Witnesses for the Union were unable to show that they were *required to handle* dynamite or caps themselves. The counting and tallying of dynamite, however, was a new task for the guards starting in 1950. This particular task is not specifically mentioned in the job description.

"d. Very few guards have anything to do with ordering Dri-Ox. When performed, this task is limited to responsibility for handling and recording telephone calls between the Oxygen Storage and the Linde Air Company for the purpose of ordering Dri-Ox. This function is not specifically mentioned in the job description, but it could be subsumed under the following task, 'Uses telephone in making reports and answering requests for information. Operates Switchboard at plant entrances when assigned,' which is found under *Working Procedure* in the job description. Tasks related to Dri-Ox require only a fractional part of a few guards' time.

"e. The methods of checking, inspection and record keeping at the plant gates appear to have been changed in some respects, perhaps requiring greater care on the part of the guards. This function, however, is rather completely set forth in the working procedure of the job description as follows, 'Guards plant entrances. . . . controlling admission or exit of employees, visitors, vehicular traffic and materials after establishing their identity . . .' and 'Prepares records and reports as required by established procedures.' "

6. On the basis of findings which were amply supported by the evidence, the Special Arbitrator concluded that there was no basis for any increase in the codings under Factors 4, 6, 7, 8 and 10. The Special Arbitrator properly applied the Agreement in ruling that the present codings for the Plant Guard job under these factors were correct.

7. The substantial questions now before the Board involve the correctness of the Special Arbitrator's conclusions with respect to Factors 5 and 12. The reasons for the conclusions of the Special Arbitrator as to Factor 5 appear as follows:

"With respect to the final Factor 5—*Responsibility for Material*—there is reason to believe that arming of the guards is a recognition of the necessity for closer attention to prevent loss of Company property under conditions of the Korean emergency. The Union proposes an increase in the factor from C-1.8 to C-3.7, but fails to give much concrete evidence to justify this increase. It is certainly reasonable to think, however, that the possible loss of Company property, as evidenced in the decision of the Company to arm the guards, has been increased from $500 to at least $1,000.

"This conclusion is fortified by the testimony of the Superintendent of Plant Protection who said, 'In 1950 there was in the country an emergency, and *we felt there could be a very large effort at sabotage.* So in 1950, we started to prepare against that by increasing our force to 23 more people and *having them commissioned and armed in 1951.'* (Italics inserted) It is true that the guards were similarly armed during World War II, but there is conflicting evidence regarding pay practices on this score throughout the Corporation. The experience of World War II, however, is irrelevant because the present job Classification system was introduced several years afterwards. The Plant Guard Job Description, as we have pointed out, did not contemplate that all guards would ever be armed at all times. The Arbitrator thus finds that the value rating of this factor should be increased from C-1.8 to C-2.5."

8. Particularly with regard to Factor 12 the Special Arbitrator declared:

"With respect to Factor 12—Hazard—the Union proposes an increase in value from B-.4 to C-.8 on the basis that the likelihood and nature of injury to the guards is greater by reason of carrying firearms at all times. The principal argument of the Union is that, when the guards are carrying guns, they would probably be attacked by persons intending to damage plant facilities who were also armed with guns rather than with less deadly weapons. The Company contends that the guards would be exposed to at least as much hazard of injury if they were unarmed. However, the very fact that the Company now requires the guards to be armed is in itself a clear recognition that there is more hazard of attack in the job as a consequence of the Korean emergency. The Arbitrator thus finds that the hazard of the job has been increased and agrees with the Union's proposal to increase the factor value by 0.4 points."

9. The Company asserts that in directing increases in the codings under Factors 5 and 12, the Special Arbitrator has gone well beyond the Agreement of the parties in rendering a decision *which has the effect of changing the description and classification of a Specimen-Example job when there in fact has been no change in job content under undisputed evidence.* It stresses that the carrying of firearms was specifically mentioned under "Tools and Equipment" in the Specimen Job Description, and that the duty of carrying firearms was given full consideration in all 12 factors involved in classification. This, it asserts, was not, and cannot be, controverted in view of the fact that the use of firearms was specifically mentioned in the coding under Factors 4 and 6.

10. The Company also asserts that Specimen Example No. 1284 covering the Plant Guard job was negotiated at Job Class 7.8 by officially designated representatives of the parties as the Standard Job Description and Classification for Plant Guard in all plants of the Company.

11. As to probable monetary loss under Factor 5, the Company asserts that the loss figure for which the Plant Guard was deemed responsible was reached by agreement of the parties at C-1.8 ($500.00) whether or not Plant Guards were required to carry firearms. The Company points out that at Edgar Thomson the Guards occasionally carried guns at the time the description and classification was negotiated and that responsibility for damage remains the same at Edgar Thomson—as in all other plants—whether or not all Guards carried guns. In the other plants, where the Specimen-Example is equally applicable, the Company stresses that some Plant Guards may have carried guns regularly, and others not, and that the responsibility for the damage to plant material or property was set at the same level for all Plant Guards. Such variations in actual detailed duties were contemplated by the parties when the Standard Job Description and Classification was developed, negotiated and issued as the Specimen-Example.

12. As to Factor 12, the Company position is that if the Special Arbitrator's reasoning is sound:

". . . the hazards of all employees in a plant should now be increased as a result of the Korean emergency because of the possibility of sabotage being greater now than it was in 1946. Furthermore, if the Korean emergency has caused an increase in the hazard of the guards, such increase in their hazards would be present whether or not they carried arms.

"Of primary importance, however, is the fact that the 'carrying of firearms' was given classification credit in all Factors, including Factor 12—Hazards, and consequently, since there is no change in job content, any decision increasing this Factor level is unwarranted."

FINDINGS

13. The issues raised by the Company's request for review are of first-rank importance since they involve the integrity of the job classification program developed by the parties. *All of the material contentions of the Company are supported either by undisputed evidence or by the terms of the agreements of the parties.*

14. When the job description of Plant Guard throughout the operations of United States Steel was developed under the Inequity Program, it was known by both parties that the actual duties performed by various men in the Plant Guard job were variable both from plant to plant and within specific plants. The situation at Edgar Thomson Works today is merely an illustration of this fact—some men handle the making of gas tests and others do not; some have handled the issuance of dynamite and dynamite caps but others have not.

15. After ascertaining that the actual duties of various men in the Plant Guard job varied somewhat, the Joint Wage Rate Inequity Committee concluded that it would be best to develop a Standard Job Description for the Plant Guard job in line with what had been done in regard to such jobs as Millwright or Motor Inspector. Thus, a standardized job description was developed

by mutual agreement as representative of all important functions of the job, even though they varied somewhat from plant to plant and within given plants.

16. In short, the record leaves no room for doubt that the parties strived to establish a broad job description, somewhat general in nature which would cover the range of functions that a Plant Protection Guard would be expected to perform.

17. The parties understood that the standardized job description would be adopted at all plants of the Company. All Plant Guard jobs in the Central Operations Division are coded at 7.8, and the job descriptions are identical.

18. It thus is apparent that no proper basis exists for the Special Arbitrator's conclusion that the codings under Factors 5 and 12 should be increased because of claimed special circumstances at Edgar Thomson Works. Such an Award would defeat the joint effort of the parties to achieve simplification of description and classification of the Plant Guard job.

19. The petition for review must be granted, the Special Arbitrator's Award set aside, and the grievance denied.

AWARD

20. The petition for review is granted and the grievance is denied.

USC—344. Gary Steel Works. July 24, 1953

Sylvester Garrett, *Chairman*

1. This grievance involves classification of the new job of Fireman (Oil or Gas) in the new Turbo Blower Boiler House at Gary Steel Works. The job description has been mutually agreed upon. Failing to reach agreement on the classification, Management on February 5, 1950, unilaterally installed Job Class 9 effective August 9, 1949. The Union, seeking Job Class 11, disputes the ratings on Factors 2, 3, 7, and 11.

2. The following is a tabulation showing the factor evaluations as developed by Management and the values sought by the Union:

FACTOR	COMPANY CLASSIFICATION	UNION CLASSIFICATION
1. Pre-employment Training	B-.3	B-.3
*2. Employment Training and Experience	D-1.2	E-1.6
*3. Mental Skill	C-1.6	D-2.2
4. Manual Skill	B-.5	B-.5
5. Responsibility for Materials	C-.5	C-.5
6. Responsibility for Tools and Equipment	C-1.0 Hi	C-1.0 Hi
*7. Responsibility for Operations	C-1.0	D-2.0
8. Responsibility for Safety of Others	C-.8	C-.8
9. Mental Effort	C-1.0	C-1.0
10. Physical Effort	B-.3	B-.3
*11. Surroundings	B-.4	C-.8
12. Hazards	B-.4	B-.4
TOTAL	9.0	11.4

* Disputed Factors

DISCUSSION AND FINDINGS

3. In two of nine Boiler Houses at Gary Steel Works, the jobs of Fireman (Oil or Gas) were classified and issued as Specimen Examples. Specimen 579 (Fireman for #2 Blast Furnace Boiler House) was placed in Job Class 7; Specimen 564 (Fireman for #4 Boiler House) was placed in Job Class 9. The new job in dispute has been coded on all the factors by the Company with the same ratings as found in the higher of these two Specimens.

4. To support its positions on Factors 2 and 3, the Union's testimony stressed the differences in equipment and duties between the #2 Boiler House and the Turbo Blower Boiler House. The evidence clearly indicates that higher ratings on these two factors for the job in dispute are called for than those given the Fireman job at the #2 Boiler House (Specimen 579). However, credit for the longer training period and the greater skill required has already been given by the Company's assigning D-1.2 instead of B-.4 on Factor 2 and C-1.6 on Factor 3 instead of B-1.0. The Fireman job in question is presently classified two job classes higher than the Fireman job at #2 Boiler House.

5. On the other hand, the evidence does not justify higher codings on these factors than those assigned to the Fireman job at #4 Boiler House. It is true that the Fireman at the new Turbo Blower Boiler House has a couple of duties not required of the #4 Fireman. He must run certain standard chemical tests on the water for hardness, alkalinity, and chlorides, and he assists the Operator in blowing down the boilers. These duties, nonetheless, are not uncommon for Firemen who assist Operators and have not been considered as providing a basis for

higher ratings on Factors 2 and 3 than those presently assigned. It should be noted that to give the Fireman D-2.2 on Factor 3 would be to rate this job on this Factor as high as the Operator whom he assists.

6. As to Factor 7—Responsibility for Operations, the number of pieces of equipment which must be checked by the Fireman was emphasized by grievant. A Company witness stated that, if anything, the Fireman at #4 Boiler House is normally more "on his own" because of the greater length of the House. At the Turbo Blower Boiler House the Fireman is in at least as favorable a position to get directions from the Operator. Also, the Foreman of the latter has an area of responsibility which is confined to the Turbo Blower Boiler House and, therefore, is normally immediately available for advice,

whereas the responsibility of the Foreman for #4 Boiler House extends to other areas and he is not so readily available. Neither Fireman job requires direction of the work of others. A rating of C-1.0 for this Factor is therefore an adequate reflection of the job's responsibility for operations.

7. With respect to Factor 11—Surroundings, an examination of the ratings of other jobs in this area reveals that B-.4 has been considered appropriate and therefore B-.4 must be deemed to be proper for this job also. No higher rating on this Factor can be granted to the Fireman job than that received by the Boiler House Operator under the facts of this case.

AWARD

8. The grievance is denied.

USC—345. Gary Steel Works. July 24, 1953
Sylvester Garrett, *Chairman*

BACKGROUND

1. This grievance involves a request for Job Class 16 for the new job of Engineer (1st) Turbo Blower in the Turbo Blower Station at Gary Steel Works rather than the Job Class 13 installed by the Company. The job description is agreed, but the values for Factors 1, 2, 5, 6, 8 and 11 are in dispute.

2. The following tabulation shows the codings of Management and those sought by the Union:

FACTOR	COMPANY CLASSI-FICATION	UNION CLASSI-FICATION
*1. Pre-employment Training	B-.3	C-1.0
*2. Employment Training and Experience	F-2.0	G-2.4
3. Mental Skill	D-2.2	D-2.2
4. Manual Skill	B-.5	B-.5
*5. Responsibility for Materials	B-.3	C-.5
*6. Responsibility for Tools and Equipment	D-2.0 Hi	E-3.0 Hi
7. Responsibility for Operation	E-3.0	E-3.0
*8. Responsibility for Safety of Others	B-.4	D-1.2
9. Mental Effort	C-1.0	C-1.0
10. Physical Effort	B-.3	B-.3
*11. Surroundings	B-.4	C-.8
12. Hazard	B-.4	B-.4
TOTAL	12.8	16.3

* Disputed Factors

DISCUSSION AND FINDINGS

3. The job in dispute is responsible for operation of three Turbo Blowers. It has received the identical ratings on all factors as those given to the Engineer (1st) Blowing at Homestead and to the Engineer (1st) Blowing at #2 Power House at Edgar Thomson. The Homestead job operates six Turbo Blowers and the Edgar Thomson job three Turbo Blowers. These two jobs have not been issued as Specimen Examples although they were original benchmarks.

4. Specimen 546-Engineer (1st) Blowing (Turbo Blower Engineer), responsible for the operation of one Ingersoll-Rand Turbo Blower and one Todd Steam Blower, is also coded by the Company the same as the job in dispute except for Factors 2 and 9. Factor 9 is not in dispute and Factor 2 received a lower rating for Specimen 546 than the new job in the Turbo Blower House. The result in both instances is Job Class 13.

5. Under Factor 1—Pre-Employment Training and Factor 2—Employment Training and Experience, Union testimony stresses that the new Turbo Blower Station is blowing the three largest furnaces on the line, that it is delivering wind at the average rate of 250,000 cubic feet per minute, and that it would take three gas engines to blow any one of the three furnaces served. Specimen 542—Engineer (1st) for #5 Power Station at Gary—is urged upon the Board as providing a proper guide for granting C-1.0 for Factor 1 and G-2.4 for Factor 2. This job is responsible for three Turbo Generators which produce electricity that ties in with other plant generating facilities, and is also

responsible for numerous facilities for the pumping of water to other operations. Grievants, however, point out that they must be familiar with certain auxiliary equipment not found at #5 Power Station, such as air filters on the roof, and steam extraction lines which take part of the steam to preheat the condensate water. They must also watch for high and low pressures and may be required to change from a blower to a gas engine without dropping the pressure.

6. As further support for its proposals, the Company points to the following jobs: Specimen 544—Engineer (1st Blowing for #2 Gas Engine House at Gary; Specimen 545—Engineer (1st) Turbine for #1 Power Station at Gary; Specimen 547—Engineer (1st) Blowing for #1, #2, and #3 Blowing Engine Houses at Gary; and Specimen 548 —Engineer (1st) for #1, #2, #3 and #4 Power Houses at Gary. Specimens 544, 545, 546, 547 and 548 all rate Factor 1 at B-.3. Specimens 544, 545 and 546 rate Factor 2 at E-1.6; Specimens 547 and 548 at F-2.0.

7. The incumbents of these five Specimens are, however, under the direction of Blowing Engine House Operators or Power Station Operators, while grievants only receive direction from the Turn Foreman. On the other hand, the Homestead and Edgar Thomson benchmark jobs referred to above receive directions from the Turn Foreman. And there are automatic controls at the new Turbo Blower House to control the speed, barometric pressure and temperature of incoming air. Thus, the presently assigned ratings of B-.3 and F-2.0 for Factors 1 and 2 respectively may be deemed to be proper.

8. Materials under Factor 5 are steam, compressed air, oil and water. The parties agree that probable monetary loss is under $50, only the level of attention remaining in dispute. Grievants testified that after a unit is placed in operation, they must keep a constant check on blast pressure to maintain the allowable pressure of 28 lbs. maximum and 5 lbs. minimum. Steam, air, and oil leaks are watched for.

9. Grievants are charged with the responsibility of hourly readings of all charts, gauges, oil temperatures, atmospheric temperature, and barometric pressure. Turbos must be greased, cleaned, thrust bearings checked and vibration readings taken. Checking and cleaning of air filters, oil filters, filter bags and filter cartridges, packing of pumps, and greasing of pumps are their responsibility, though grievants concede that the latter is a small part of the job. Management does not disagree that these duties are performed but asserts that rules and procedures emphasized by Union testimony are normal and usual for such Engineers.

10. According to the Company, deviations from proper operations are discovered by routine inspections and interpretation of data reflected on instrument panels.

11. All of the Specimen Examples urged upon the Board except 542 grant B-.3 for this Factor. Specimen 542 for #5 Power Station receives C-.5. But that Engineer (1st), in addition to maintaining his load and inspecting for lubrication and vacuum, must also care for different types of water. There are seven boiler feed pumps (4 steam driven, 3 motor driven) for #4 Boiler House, two transfer pumps to supply condensate water for #5 Open Hearth, three transfer pumps which transfer condensate water to the Turbo Blower Station, and another pump for the treated water. The Engineer (1st) must see that the water is properly heated and that it goes to the right place. He is responsible for maintaining a nice balance to see that none of the pumps run out of water. This apparently is the main justification for the higher rating for Factor 5 in Specimen 542. This being so, B-.3 must be considered proper for the job in dispute in the light of the other applicable Specimens.

12. With Respect to Factor 6—Responsibility for Tools and Equipment, grievants note that failure to detect poor lubrication may result in major repairs. They assert that they are responsible for as many bearings as the Engineer (1st) at #5 Power Station, whose classification at 3.0 under Factor 6 follows the statement "Failure to detect poor lubrication—burn out bearing—may result in major repairs." Also, grievants must watch for fires or an explosion in the blast main though the #5 Power Station Engineer (1st) does not have this problem. In 1944 the pressure dropped too low at the Ingersoll-Rand Turbine at #3 Blowing Room and there was an explosion. Excessive vibrations around the turbines must be watched for. According to grievants the worst thing that can happen at #5 Power Station is to burn up a generator. Thus, E-3.0 is claimed to be the proper rating for Factor 6. Management notes that improper maintenance of the pumps at #5 Power Station could cause the water to shut off, resulting in a boiler explosion and that this has actually happened.

13. Equipment falling under control of the job in dispute is as follows: 3 De Laval Turbo Blowers, one auxiliary oil pump per unit, two condensate preheaters per unit, one lube oil cooler per unit, one condenser per unit, one steam air ejector per unit, two condensate pumps per unit, one circulating water pump per unit, and one oil filter and one air filter per unit.

14. Company testimony emphasized the

similarity between the Ingersoll-Rand Turbo Blower and the Turbo Blowers in the new Station. Specimen 546—Engineer (1st) for the Ingersoll-Rand Turbo Blower—is coded at D-2.0 for this Factor. A Management witness stated there is no material difference in the operation of Ingersoll-Rand and De Laval Turbo Blowers except that there are two more controls on the De Laval: a hydraulic check control which is a quick means of reducing speed, and a density corrector control. One of the grievants agreed that although he has more controls, they are about the same. He also pointed out that the Ingersoll-Rand is smaller and that the Engineer (1st) there works under the direction of a Blowing Engine House Operator. In the new Turbo Blower Station there are correction motors that are designed to correct automatically the temperature and the pressure but they do not always work properly. Also there are automatic steam purges on two furnaces which would tend to prevent an explosion.

15. In addition to the Homestead and Edgar Thomson benchmark jobs, which do not have the benefit of direction from Operators, Specimens 546, 545, 544, 547 and 548 all receive D-2.0 for Factor 6. It cannot properly be held that the evidence in this case warrants a higher coding than that established by this pattern.

16. As to Factor 8—Responsibility for the Safety of Others, not only do Specimens 544, 545, 546, 547, 548 and the Homestead and Edgar Thomson jobs receive B-.4 —the same as the job in dispute, but also

the Engineer (1st) at #5 Power Station. In the light of this pattern, testimony that there is danger of explosion if the blast pressure gets too high or too low, and that the breaking open of steam lines could injure other persons is not sufficient to justify a higher coding. Such dangers do not go beyond the established Specimen Examples.

17. Factor 11 concerns Surroundings. Grievants are subjected to disagreeable noises from the Pressure Reducing Valves in the Boiler House as well as the Turbo Blowers. The Union asserts that although the Engineer (1st) at #5 Power Station receives A Base for this Factor, the instant job is not comparable for this purpose. It is hot and grievants do not believe that the fans have helped much. Furthermore, they are exposed to blast furnace gas and must occasionally wear oxygen apparatus when the precipitator chambers are inspected. The schedule of inspection is one precipitator chamber every eight months. There are four chambers in that location.

18. All of the applicable Specimens rate this Factor at B-.4 which likewise has been considered appropriate for related jobs in this same vicinity. The heat and noise are not any greater than are found in the new Boiler House. Nor is the noise any greater than the noise which prevails in the working area of the Homestead benchmark job. B-.4 is therefore determined to be the proper rating on this Factor for the job in dispute.

AWARD

19. The grievance is denied.

USC—389. South Works. December 30, 1953

Herbert L. Sherman, Jr., *Assistant to the Chairman*
Approved by Sylvester Garrett, *Chairman*

BACKGROUND

1. In this grievance the Gas Washer Pump Tenders in the Blast Furnace Division of South Works request that their job be reclassified from Class 8 to Class 11 with the same ratings on the Factors as those assigned to the Gas Washer Operator job at South Works. The Company admits that new duties have been added to the job in dispute. Since the filing of the grievance, Management has unilaterally raised the initial Class 8 to Class 9 by increasing the ratings on Factors 9 and 10.

2. When the job was classified, grievants were required to attend and service four Gas Booster Fans in the Gas Booster Station which maintains fuel pressure for the North End Mills. At that time servicing of the 5-10 Blast Furnace Gas Washer Pumps, which

consumed about forty-five minutes a turn, was part of the duties of the Gas Washer Operator for the 5-8 Theisen Gas Washers. Two developments have taken place in the meantime: the 5-8 Theisen Gas Washers have been discontinued and Nos. 11 and 12 Blast Furnaces have been erected. Grievants have been assigned the added duty of checking for proper operation, and lubricating the 5-12 furnace group pump houses. These include several water pumps, gas washer pumps and precipitator pumps. In addition, incumbents may be required to change over to stand-by pumps when repairs are being made. Water strainers must be changed when the screens become clogged and the pressure is low. A round of the three pump houses every eight hours, including the work at the No. 11 and 12 Pump House, takes about one hour and fifteen minutes.

3. Starting in April, 1950, grievants were assigned the task of flushing once on the day turn the three precipitators on Nos. 11 and 12 Blast Furnaces, and once every four hours the duty of flushing the sprays on top of the furnace precipitators. Also, checking of the rectifiers was assigned to grievants.

DISCUSSION AND FINDINGS

4. During the Inequity Program the parties agreed upon the Gas Washer Operator and the Gas Washer Pump Tender jobs as two separate jobs. The primary duties of the Gas Washer Operators at South Works are to operate gas washer equipment, such as Theisen Gas Washers, and to regulate the pressure in gas holders that supply fuel for the Power Station and Blowing Engine Rooms. Grievants are not responsible for Theisen Gas Washers nor for the careful regulation of pressure on gas holders which requires that somebody be at the controls all the time. If a gas holder collapses, it would result in the loss of a furnace or electrical generators. Although there was no gas holder under the supervision of the Gas Washer Operator job for the 5-8 Theisen Gas Washers at the time that the Gas Washers were eliminated, this job was responsible for a gas holder at one time, which supplied gas for three different locations.

5. Grievants' new duties involving the servicing of pumps cannot justify higher ratings than those presently assigned to their job. Specimen Examples 97, 572, 30, 31, 580, 577, 63, 3385 and 583 for Pump Tender jobs, ranging from Class 5 to Class 8, indicate that the present ratings for the job in dispute more than reflect the credit which pump tending functions alone would warrant.

6. With respect to flushing of the pre-cipitators once on the day turn, this involves the opening of several 3-inch valves, allowing them to remain open about five minutes, and then closing them. Actual flushing of the precipitators is not observed by grievants nor do they control the flow of gas through the precipitators. Flushing the sprays on top of the furnaces requires the opening of two stop cocks on each for five minutes and then closing them. To ascertain whether the rectifier is functioning properly, grievants merely check the electric arc or check the voltmeter and ammeter readings. If the rectifier is not functioning properly, that condition is reported to the Foreman. Grievants are not allowed to do anything else to the rectifiers or the precipitators.

7. For the above reasons it cannot be found that the job in dispute has been transformed into a Gas Washer Operator job of the nature agreed upon by the parties. Furthermore, even though grievants' duties do involve work on some gas washing equipment (the precipitators), Specimen Examples 91, 549 and 570 for Gas Washers indicate that the present ratings are appropriate. Specimen 91, which operates (like grievants) under the supervision of a Foreman, is coded at Class 9, all of the Factors being rated identically with the job in dispute except that Factor 6 for the latter is coded C-1.0 rather than C-.7 and Factor 11 is coded B-.4 instead of C-.8. Although Specimen 549 is coded in Class 12, it directs Specimen 570 for a Gas Washer in Class 8. Specimens 130 and 594 for Gas Washer Helpers are in Class 3 and Class 4 respectively. Thus, the Board finds that the grievance must be denied.

AWARD

8. The grievance is denied.

USC—467. South Works. January 31, 1955

Herbert L. Sherman, Jr., *Arbitrator*
Approved by Sylvester Garrett, *Chairman*

BACKGROUND

1. This grievance requests a new description and classification for the drivers of two "Auto Car" trucks, #120 and #121, at South Works. The operation of these trucks is presently covered by the existing job description and classification for Truck Driver (Heavy) at Job Class 9. The Union believes, however, that these trucks should be characterized as "Extra Heavy" with a higher job class assigned to the drivers.

2. The two trucks in question were put into service in the Yard and Transportation Department about February 15, 1953. They have three ranges of gear shifts, and are larger, heavier, and cost more than the trucks which the Company had at the time of the original classification program. The rated capacities of the new trucks are 15 tons and 18 tons respectively, though the actual capacity, according to the Union, is higher. Some of the heavy loads which they now haul were formerly handled by outside trucks or railroad cars. Comparison of the new trucks with the old heavy trucks shows that the new trucks handle heavier loads. There is no difference, however, in the units at which materials are loaded or in the units to which materials are taken.

3. Prior to the classification program at South Works, three different rates were paid Truck Drivers depending upon the rated capacity of the trucks. Because of this background the parties at South Works agreed to establish two truck driver job classifications: Truck Driver (Light) at Job Class 8 and Truck Driver (Heavy) at Job Class 9. The former applied to trucks of less than 5 ton rated capacity, the latter to trucks of 5 tons or more rated capacity. At that time 10 tons was the highest rated capacity of the trucks on hand. Because of the higher rate senior employees are assigned to the heavy trucks.

4. Although the Union suggests that the Board might raise the ratings on other Factors, specific higher ratings are proposed only on Factors 2, 3, 4, 6 and 7. Following is a tabulation showing the present classification for the job of Truck Driver (Heavy) at South Works, and the proposed ratings of the Union to cover operation of trucks #120 and #121:

FACTOR	PRESENT CLASSIFICATION		UNION PROPOSAL	
1. Pre-Employment Training	B	.3	B	.3
2.* Employment Training and Experience	B	.4	D	1.2
3.* Mental Skill	C	1.6	D	2.2
4.* Manual Skill	B	.5	C	1.0
5. Responsibility for Materials	C	.7	C	.7
6.* Responsibility for Tools and Equipment	D	1.5	F	3.0
7.* Responsibility for Operation	A	Base	C	1.0
8. Responsibility for Safety of Others	D	1.2	D	1.2
9. Mental Effort	C	1.0	C	1.0
10. Physical Effort	C	.8	C	.8
11. Surroundings	B	.4	B	.4
12. Hazards	B	.4	B	.4
Total		8.8		13.2

* Factors specifically disputed.

DISCUSSION AND FINDINGS

5. The extent to which the operation of the new trucks differs from the operation of the older trucks must be measured, in determining its impact on the classification of the truck driver jobs, by consulting the appropriate Specimen Example jobs and the patterns which have emerged at South Works and other plants of the Company. These patterns provide guides which aid in the interpretation of the Specimen Examples. Specimens 841 and 851 for Truck Drivers, both in Job Class 8, are most closely related to the jobs in dispute. Specimen 1200 for a Crane Truck Driver (Job Class 8) and Specimen 1282 for a Fire Truck Driver (Job Class 9), though similar, are distinguishable.

6. Specimens 841 and 851 are rated the same as Truck Driver (Heavy) on Factors 2, 3, 4 and 7. Factor 6 for these Specimen Examples is rated C .7. On the South Works Truck Driver (Heavy) job, Factor 6 is given D 1.5. Specimens 841 and 851 also show that incumbents are expected to operate different types of trucks with varying gear shifts and transmissions; yet the classification is not affected by these differences.

7. Of the thirty some job descriptions and classifications for non-Specimen truck driver jobs presented to the Board, only one has a higher job class than Class 9. That is the Tank Trailer Driver job at Fairless Works in Class 10, which not only drives a tractor trailer but also repairs tank pumps, gas line drips, steam traps and couplings on gas collection lines. The only ratings of that job which are higher than those assigned to the Truck Driver (Heavy) job at South Works are the ratings on Factors 4 and 7. The reasons given for the classification of these Factors easily explain the differences in the ratings: Factor 4 "Use hand tools in making repairs to drips, traps, and other related condensate collection equipment"; Factor 7 "Remove coke oven gas condensate and maintain plant condensate collection lines in proper operating condition." Six other Fairless Works truck driver jobs are assigned the same or lower ratings than those assigned to the jobs in dispute.

8. Other non-Specimen jobs presented to the Board cover the operation of numerous trucks of widely different types, sizes, and capacities, yet no distinction in classification has been made on that basis in rating Factors 2, 3 and 4. All of these jobs are rated the same as the Specimen Examples on Factors 2, 3 and 4, except for one Duquesne job which operates a construction truck with pole derricks and double drum winches, and works as a member of the electrical crew when the truck is not being driven. This job has a higher rating on Factor 2.

9. No job was presented to the Board with a higher numerical rating on Factor 6 than the D 1.5 already assigned to the disputed jobs in accordance with the pattern established at South Works for heavy trucks. With respect to Factor 7, a few of the thirty some jobs submitted to the Board are given credit for responsibility for operations where

truck driving is an integral part of the operating process. No evidence was presented, however, to show that the operation of trucks #120 and #121 involves any more responsibility for operations than is involved in the duties of the drivers of the older heavy trucks. The fact that heavier loads are hauled on the new trucks cannot affect the rating on this Factor.

T—425.   Fairfield Steel Works.   April 16, 1957

Herbert L. Sherman, Jr., *Arbitrator*

Approved by Sylvester Garrett, *Chairman*

BACKGROUND

1.   Upon the purchase of a new 2½-ton Mack tractor and a 45-ton low-boy trailer, Management issued an Exhibit 3, dated November 22, 1954, to bring the existing job description for Trailer Truck Drivers in the Motor Transportation Department at Fairfield Steel Works up to date. No change was made in the classification ratings.

2.   The Union claims that by introducing a massive new tractor-trailer, the Company has created a new job. The new tractor-trailer differs from the old equipment covered by the existing job description in that it is longer and wider. It also transports much heavier and more expensive loads, which were previously handled by outside firms. A special permit is required to operate the new tractor-trailer on State highways, and it is not allowed on such highways after dark.

3.   Grievants are responsible for determining that material is properly loaded. While the tractor-trailer is being loaded, grievants must operate a winch on the back. At times they have used cables, chains and heavy timbers in loading. The new tractor has two driving ranges, each having five forward speeds. Emphasized is the fact that grievants must operate in congested areas and on narrow roads. They must determine what routes they will take, some roads being unsafe and not providing enough clearance for big loads. Thus, the Union argues that the incumbents of the job must do more than merely drive a truck.

4.   Management disagrees with the argument that any significantly new type of duty is required of grievants. After making comparisons with the operation of other tractor-trailers covered by existing job descriptions, the Company contends that operation of the new equipment, though it is larger and capable of carrying greater loads, is not basically different. The low-boy trailer is used less than one half of the time.

5.   Following is a table which shows the

10.   Since it has not been shown how the existing job description and classification are inadequate to cover the operation of trucks #120 and #121, the grievance must be denied.

AWARD

11.   The grievance is denied.

present classification ratings for Trailer Truck Drivers at the Fairfield Steel Works and the ratings sought by the Union to cover the operation of the new equipment and related duties:

		EXISTING CLASSI-FICATION		UNION POSITION	
1. Pre-Employment Training		B	.3	B	.3
*2. Employment Training and Experience		B	.4	C	.8
*3. Mental Skill		C	1.6	D	2.2
*4. Manual Skill		B	.5	C	1.0
*5. Responsibility for Material		C	.7	C	1.8
*6. Responsibility for Tools and Equipment		CM	.7	DH	2.0
*7. Responsibility for Operations		A Base		B	.5
8. Responsibility for Safety of Others		D	1.2	D	1.2
*9. Mental Effort		C	1.0	D	1.5
*10. Physical Effort		C	.8	D	1.5
11. Surroundings		B	.4	B	.4
*12. Hazard		B	.4	C	.8
Total			8.0		14.0

* Factors in dispute.

6.   According to the Union, Specimen Examples 841, 851 and 1200 for Truck Drivers and the twenty-two descriptions and classifications for Truck Drivers at the T.C. & I. Division of the Company, relied upon by Management, are not adequate to resolve this grievance. Resort must be had to the Classification Manual.

7.   The Board is urged by the Union to adopt the distinctions made in the description and classification of truck driver jobs by the Oliver Iron Mining Company, where

operation of small trucks is Job Class 8, operation of large trucks with low-boys is in Job Class 10, and operation of Euclid trucks is in Job Class 11. Moreover, the Union cites a Truck Driver job at Fairless Works in Job Class 10 and a Truck Driver (Heavy) job at South Works in Job Class 9.

8. With respect to the Company's reliance on the twenty-two job descriptions and classifications for Truck Driver jobs at T.C. & I., the Union notes that only 17 are in Job Class 8, the other 5 having been classified at Job Class 7. Arguing that the Class 7 jobs have departed from Specimen Examples 841 and 851, the Union contends that a higher classification than Job Class 8 may properly be assigned to the job in dispute. The Company points out, however, that no distinction has been made in the pattern of classifying truck driver jobs at T.C. & I. in terms of size of load or capacity of the trucks and tractor-trailers. Though Job Class 7 was assigned to some jobs, Factor 3—Mental Skill and Factor 8—Responsibility for Safety of Others, were coded lower than the ratings on Specimen Examples 841 and 851 on the ground that incumbents operated trucks primarily inside the plant. But truck driver jobs which must operate outside the plant, like the job in dispute, are in Job Class 8, the same as Specimen Examples 841 and 851.

FINDINGS

9. In resolving this grievance, the Board is bound by the Classification Manual as interpreted by the parties in the coding of Specimen Examples applicable to the "Steel Producing Operations" of the Company. Since different Benchmark jobs are used under the Oliver Iron Mining Company Classification Manual, the Oliver job descriptions and classifications cannot control the present grievance.

10. Nor is the Fairless Works job cited by the Union of much help in this case, since that job, in addition to driving a tank trailer, repairs tank pumps, gas line drips, steam traps and couplings on gas collection lines, and maintains them in proper operating condition. But it cannot be found that grievants' duties are of a different type from those outlined in the job descriptions for Truck Driver jobs.

11. No distinction has been made in the coding of Specimen Examples 841 and 851 for Truck Drivers—the most closely related Specimen Examples, or in the coding of numerous T.C. & I. Truck Driver jobs, on the basis of different types, sizes or capacities of trucks. With respect to the South Works Truck Driver job cited by the Union, the Board's Award in USC-467 noted the unusual distinction developed at that plant. In the light of Specimen Examples 841, 851 and 1200 (all in Job Class 8), the Board must find that no higher ratings on the Factors can be granted in this case.

AWARD

12. The grievance is denied.

T—349. Fairfield Tin Mill. March 30, 1956
Sylvester Garrett, *Chairman*

BACKGROUND

1. This grievance from the Fairfield Tin Mill seeks a new description and classification of Electrolytic Tinning Line Operator.

2. The job presently is classified at 15.5 (Class 16), in line with Specimen 2340, and all other Electrolytic Tinning Line Operator jobs in the Corporation. The most recently classified Electrolytic Tinning Line Operator job in the Corporation is at Fairless Works, dated July 31, 1953. The Fairless job, like the disputed job, is coded the same under each Factor as Specimen 2340.

3. The Union stresses that since original description of the disputed job in 1946, line speeds have been increased, with about an 18% increase in tonnage per turn. New equipment has been added to the No. 1 Electrolytic Tinning Line, as follows: (a) new Beta-ray gauge for thickness determination, (b) new type guides and pin hole detectors, (c) additional piler, (d) electrostatic oiler with auxiliary drive bridle, (e) additional pickler tank, rinse tank, and scrubber system, (f) 4 new plating tanks, (g) larger panel board, (h) 6 additional generators, (i) additional motor driven brush rolls, and (j) additional circulating pumps.

4. While most of these equipment changes appear to have been made in 1951 and 1952, the Union stresses them particularly as part of a cumulative process which it believes has affected the substance of the job in three Factors: 5—Responsibility for Materials; 10—Physical Effort; and 12—Hazards.

5. The positions of the parties as to the disputed Factors may be summarized as follows:

6. *Factor 5*—The Union urges that a formula exists for determining Estimated Cost of loss under this Factor. While there is no formula under Specimen 2340, the

Union stresses that the Fairfield job in dispute recites as part of the reason for classification under Factor 5 "Estimate 2 hours production before detection." Since average production per turn on the No. 1 and No. 3 Lines at Fairfield has increased about 18%, or 350 base boxes, since 1946, the Union calculates this to mean that around 88 more defective base boxes could be produced before detection now than in 1946. With this figure, the Union proceeds to Specimen 2343 (Hot Dip Tinning Foreman) where (under Factor 5) the parties in 1946 referred to the value of a base box as $3.35. The Union believes the conclusion inescapable that the cost of material under Factor 5 has increased at least $300.00 above the "up to $500.00" figure which the parties used at that time. Thus the Union believes Factor 5 now must be coded at D-3.5 rather than D-2.4.

7. The Company points out that Specimen 2340 includes no formula under Factor 5. If the formula now urged by the Union actually had been applied to the 1946 production, a fantastic situation would have resulted:—the true loss (as now calculated by the Union) would have been about $1600.00 for two hours production, whereas Factor 5 recites only "up to $500.00." Thus the Company denies that any formula properly may be applied under this Factor. It stresses that all Electrolytic Tinning Line Operator jobs in the Corporation are fundamentally the same, but that necessarily there are differences in line speeds and tonnages from Line to Line. Just before this grievance was filed, for example, average tons per line turn varied between 115 on the No. 3 Line at Irvin Works and 171 on the No. 1 Line at Gary Sheet and Tin. During this same month (February 1954) tonnage per turn at Fairfield was 132 on the No. 1 Line and 138 on the No. 3 Line. At Fairless, the No. 1 Line averaged 155 tons per turn.

8. *Factor 10*—The Union seeks B-.3, whereas this Factor is A-Base at present. The major item stressed here by the Union is that about 30 rolls have been added to the number which the Operator must keep in proper condition. This requires polishing, using sandpaper on an 8 to 10 foot two by four. Added physical effort also is entailed in handling a greater number of anodes (particularly on the No. 1 line) than in 1946. This results from the addition of plating tanks, and the introduction of differential plating as well as heavier plating than in 1946. The Union also cites added physical effort related to servicing the new Oiler, as well as other new equipment, and increased use of acids, etc.

9. The Company agrees that there has been some increase in physical effort, but only to an unimportant degree. Thus the total time spent exerting appreciable physical effort is not substantial enough to affect the average degree of muscular exertion in its judgment. Before addition of 30 odd rolls, the Operator spent about 3.7% of his time polishing rolls. The Company estimates that this figure has been increased 30 to 35% by the new rolls. On increased handling of anodes, tin consumption per line turn averaged 1290 pounds, compared with 1305 in 1955. Thus, while plating capacity on the No. 1 Line has doubled since 1946, actual use of tin has not increased to this extent because higher coating rates are not run constantly. Since anodes are positioned by air hoist, with the aid of a Laborer, the Operator's main effort in the handling of anodes involves pushing the anodes into proper alignment on the dovetail. This positioning of the anodes apparently consumes not more than 4%, on an average, of the Operators' time. The figure is higher (up to 6%) on the No. 1 Line, where the higher coatings are run.

10. *Factor 12*—Now coded at A-Base; the Union seeks B-.4. It stresses increased acid exposure, based primarily on the new Pickler and greater acid use, plus increased hazard of falls from ladders used in filling the Oiler tank and acid tanks. Use of stairs to a basement, carrying chromic acid chips, is noted. Polishing of additional rolls, characterized as moving equipment, also is emphasized.

11. The Company denies that acid exposure is measurably greater today than in 1946. It stresses that the new Pickler Unit, on one Line only, replaced a hot alkaline cleaner which itself presented greater hazard than a Pickler Unit. The plating unit solution is irritating to the skin, and will deteriorate nonwoolen clothing, but is not as dangerous as the sulphuric acid in the picklers. The requirement of adding oil to the Oiler tank averages only 2 or 3 times a week.

FINDINGS

12. A job coded identically with the relevant Specimen may be changed to such an extent that new codings are required under some, or all, Factors. The question in each case is whether significant changes in job requirements are shown to have taken place.

13. The reliance of the Union upon a formula derived from language in the disputed job classification of Factor 5, and language from Specimen 2343, seems misplaced. Such a formula could not be reconciled with the actual coding of Factor 5 in

Specimen 2340. The latter Specimen is controlling here.

14. In view of recent application of Specimen 2340 in coding the relevant job at Fairless Works, with considerably greater line tonnage per turn than here, the Board finds no merit in the Union's position in this case concerning Factor 5.

15. The Union evidence as to Factors 10 and 12, likewise does not establish a sufficiently material change in conditions to affect coding. Specimen 2340 continues to provide the appropriate reference for coding each Factor.

AWARD

16. The grievance is denied.

T—538. Fairfield Steel Works. January 9, 1958
Sylvester Garrett, *Chairman*

BACKGROUND

1. This grievance protests that the job of Tractor Craneman (Class 8) (Plant Code J60-375) at Fairfield Steel Works is improperly classified because of change in the equipment operated, and addition of new duties. On June 10, 1957 the Company replaced the old 5-ton Tractor Crane with an 8-ton Tractor Crane, both operating primarily in the Machine Shop area.

2. The Union contends that the old 8.1 Classification no longer reflects correct evaluation of job content and urges that the job now must be coded the same as Truck Crane Operator, Construction Department (Plant Code J50-55), in Class 12. It emphasizes that the new 8-ton vehicle has greater capacity, a longer boom, and greater versatility than the old, and is utilized to perform a variety of tasks beyond the capabilities of the discarded unit. The plant area in which the equipment operates has been greatly expanded.

3. The Company holds that no factual basis exists for increasing the present job classification under the applicable Specimens since the sole effect of the change in equipment is to increase the pay load. It holds the construction department job of Truck Crane Operator (J50-55) not comparable because it requires use of a bucket in excavating for foundations, sewers, pipelines, loading and unloading materials, and backfilling.

4. With the Union proceeding on the basis of Plant Code J50-55, the following table shows the positions of the parties on the Factor Ratings of the disputed job:

FACTORS	PRESENT CLASSIFICATION	UNION PROPOSAL
1. Pre-employment Training	B .3	B .3
*2. Employment Training and Experience	B .4	D1.2
*3. Mental Skill	C1.6	D2.2
*4. Manual Skill	B .5	C1.0
5. Responsibility for Materials	C .7	C .7
*6. Responsibility for Equipment	CM .7	DM1.5
7. Responsibility for Operations	C1.0	C1.0
*8. Responsibility for Saftey of Others	C .8	D1.2
9. Effort-Mental	C1.0	C1.0
*10. Effort-Physical	B .3	C .8
11. Surroundings	B .4	B .4
12. Hazards	B .4	B .4
Total	8.1	11.7

* Factors in dispute

FINDINGS

5. The old 5-ton tractor was used primarily as a towing device to transport materials from the Forge Shop, Foundry and Fab Shop to the Machine Shop. Two or three buggies were hooked to the rear of the tractor and these were usually loaded by means of the crane, located on front of the tractor. The boom measured 9' 6" and the Operator manipulated 10 control mechanisms.

6. The new 8-ton equipment, like its predecessor, is gasoline operated. It has outrigging fore and aft which acts as stabilizer to support the machine and its load when actually lifting. It has a 21' 9" boom which can turn 360°, power brakes, and 7 controls. It is equipped with a hook by which its pay loads are raised, lowered, and transported. It has been assigned to work a small percentage of the time in the Blast Furnace, Open Hearth, and Blooming Mill, in addition to working in the Storage Yard at the Machine Shop. Among other items handled are hot tops, flasks, patterns, etc.

7. The Union particularly emphasizes two situations believed to have substantial bearing on proper coding.

8. The first relates to trips made to the Storage Yard. The route followed requires the tractor to pass under two trolley lines suspended from poles. These lines are approximately 18 to 20 feet above the ground and carry 220 volts. On one occasion a foreman was operating the tractor and the boom knocked down the wires, with resultant fireworks. A similar accident took place on another occasion while a salesman was demonstrating the machine. In neither case was anyone hurt. The Union contends that, since the boom is capable of being raised approximately 28 feet above ground, there is danger that the boom will contact the trolley lines while passing under them in frequent trips to and from the Storage Yard. The Company holds that with reasonable caution such an accident will not happen, and none has occurred under actual working conditions over more than a year.

9. The Union's second major point relates to work done by the Tractor Crane at the Open Hearth. There has been an appreciable amount of work at one end of the Open Hearth Floor, which the Union believes to expose the Operator and other workers to danger. In addition, the Tractor Craneman now works with Riggers in removing frames of damper doors, as they require replacement at the Open Hearth. To do this the Operator must position the boom at ceiling level, within less than 1 foot of a hot tar line passing almost directly over the opening—at floor level—through which the damper door frame must be lifted by the Crane. Previously this work was performed entirely by Riggers, with whom the Tractor Craneman now works.

10. Should the boom contact and rupture the hot tar line, it would be likely to burn the employees in the immediate vicinity, as well as cause property damage. Although only three or four such jobs have been performed by the Tractor Craneman since purchase of the new 8-ton Tractor, these are the only instances when flue-stack damper door frames have been replaced in that time.

11. When the Tractor Craneman goes on the floor of the Open Hearth, it is in locations that cannot be reached by other pieces of equipment to perform lifts. This work is minimal in nature, and on occasion has entailed removal and replacement of water and slag troughs, working with Ironworkers. When the lumber yard crane was out of service because of a tornado on one occasion, he did some crane work at that site.

12. The Company notes that the Tractor Craneman never has removed furnace doors in the Open Hearth, but has worked only on flue-stack dampers in the basement. Company evidence indicates that the 8-ton tractor has been used in and about the Blast Furnace and Open Hearth about 2% to 3% of the Tractor Craneman's total work time. It is clear that when a gantry crane blew down, the new equipment temporarily spent considerable time loading and unloading trucks at the lumber yard.

13. The Company stresses that while the Union seeks Class 12 for this job, it actually cites no applicable Specimens and relies only on Plant Code J50-55. The Company points to Specimens 980, 1105, 1200 and 1201 as comparable. None is classified higher than Class 8. As to Specimens 830, 831, 832, 842 and 1221, which fall in Job Class 12, the Company emphasizes that these entail higher classification only because the equipment includes a bucket or shovel attachment, operated in construction work. They call attention to the fact that the truck crane in question operates only with a hook and cable.

14. The fact that this equipment ranges over a wide area is not of itself sufficient to warrant higher codings, for example, of Factors 6 or 8. Inspection of typical areas serviced does not support higher codings than under Specimens 980, 1105, 1200, and 1201 cited by the Company.

15. It is conceivable that coding of some of the Factors in this job may be affected by future developments, such as an expansion of the type of activity involved in working with the Riggers in the Open Hearth. Manifestly, addition of a bucket or shovel will warrant review in light of the Specimens. As the job now operates, however, the appropriate references are the Specimens cited by the Comany. Thus, there is no basis for the Board to find an increase of one job class or more.

AWARD

16. The grievance is denied.

CHAPTER 11

RELEVANCE OF NON-SPECIMEN JOBS

Although the Benchmark and Specimen Example jobs constitute the proper frame of reference for consideration of disputed job classifications, the parties often rely additionally upon numerous non-Specimen job descriptions and classifications to support their positions. And, of course, when there are no relevant Specimen Example jobs available for comparison with the disputed job, the parties must rely upon whatever relevant non-Specimen job descriptions and classifications that may be found. The cases contained in this chapter illustrate the use that has been made of non-Specimen Example job descriptions and classifications.

Other relevant cases reported elsewhere in this volume are: A-681 (page 168), T-425 (page 188), A-715 (page 223), USC-342 (page 290), A-865 (page 264).

USC—559. Gary Steel Works. June 13, 1956
Sylvester Garrett, *Chairman*

BACKGROUND

1. This grievance, from the Coke Production Department at Gary Steel Works, protests the Job Class 8 assigned to the job of Screenman (Coke) at the new No.3-6 Station. After the Company described and classified the job in September, 1954, the parties reached agreement upon the job description. The grievance, objecting to the classification, was filed in the Second Step on February 22, 1955. In the Third Step the Union reduced its request for Job Class 10 to Job Class 9. Ratings on Factor 2—Employment Training and Experience, Factor 6—Responsibility for Tools and Equipment, and Factor 7—Responsibility for Operations are protested.

2. Following is a table which shows the positions of the parties with respect to the coding of the Factors:

FACTOR	COMPANY	UNION
1. Pre-employment Training	B .3	B .3
*2. Employment Training & Experience	B .4	C .8
3. Mental Skill	C1.6	C1.6
4. Manual Skill	B .5	B .5
5. Responsibility for Materials	B .3	B .3
*6. Responsibility for Tools & Equipment	C .7	C1.0
*7. Responsibility for Operations	C1.0	D2.0
8. Responsibility for Safety of Others	B .4	B .4
9. Mental Effort	C1.0	C1.0
10. Physical Effort	B .3	B .3
11. Surroundings	C .8	C .8
12. Hazards	B .4	B .4
	7.7	9.4

* Factors in dispute

3. In arriving at its proposed classification for the job in dispute, Management recognized that the alternate methods of processing the product at the new screening station, resulting from the installation of interchangeable facilities, required higher ratings on Factor 3—Mental Skill and Factor 9—Mental Effort than those assigned to Specimen Example 37 for a Screenman (Coke) job. The higher ratings on these two Factors are the same as those assigned to the Screenman job at Fairless Works. The Union stresses the fact that loading is controlled at two tracks by grievants through the use of more equipment, while at the old screening stations the Screenmen normally control loading at a single track. In addition, the Union notes that grievants service four coke oven batteries at their new station. Screenmen at the old screening stations at Gary, operating under Specimen 37, service only two batteries apiece.

4. The Company argues that no higher classification ratings are warranted on Fac-

tors 2, 6 and 7 in the light of Specimen 37. It notes that only probable damage is disputed under Factor 6, and not the level of care and attention for tools and equipment. If the Screenman exercises the same degree of care and attention as under the Specimen, the probability and extent of damage to the new equipment, according to Management, will be less than that at the old screening stations. Facilities for recognizing trouble and shutting down the new equipment are emphasized.

5. With respect to Factor 7, the Company contends that the Screenman job in dispute has the same relationship to the batteries, in terms of maintaining a coke processing operation, as the Screenmen at the old screening stations. Storage and standby facilities, along with the possibility of diverting coke to other stations, are also cited. Various types of distinctions are offered to explain the coding of D 2.0 on Factor 7 on several similar jobs at other plants.

DISCUSSION AND FINDINGS

6. Specimen 37 is the only Specimen Example under the Classification Manual for a Screenman job. There are, however, over a dozen Screenman or Coke Loader jobs throughout the Corporation, which disclose the manner in which Specimen 37 has been applied in practice.

7. All of these jobs, except a Coke Loader job at Cleveland Coke Works with more extensive duties than grievants, are coded at B.4 in Factor 2. The classification pattern shows that even those jobs required to service four batteries and load on two tracks are rated at B.4 on this Factor. No higher rating is warranted for the job in dispute.

8. Likewise, the present coding of C.7 on Factor 6 is proper. Of the various jobs presented to the Board, only the Clairton Coke Loader jobs are coded higher than C.7 on this Factor. A rating of C1.0 is granted to those jobs in Factor 6 because of possible damage to the loading boom. The evidence in the present case does not justify a higher rating than C.7 on Factor 6 for the job in dispute.

9. Factor 7—Responsibility for Operations, now coded at C1.0, presents the most difficult question. Of the six Screenman or Coke Loader jobs in the Corporation which have similar responsibility for servicing four or more coke oven batteries, four of them (2 at Clairton, 1 at Joliet, and 1 at T.C.I.) are coded at D 2.0 on this Factor. Though Management attempts to explain the higher coding in each of these cases by individual distinctions, none of these distinctions can be accepted as valid. Each distinction is undermined when considered in the light of analysis of the whole pattern.

10. The Board must examine the appropriate Specimen Example and determine how the parties have interpreted it in practice. Such an analysis discloses that in most cases where four or more batteries are serviced by a Screenman or Coke Loader, the parties have assigned a rating of D2.0 on Factor 7. At Fairless Works, where the parties most recently applied the classification procedures, Factor 7 for the Screenman job is coded at C1.0. But it is to be noted that the Fairless job services only two batteries.

11. The Board must conclude, in the light of the particular classification pattern established by the parties under Specimen 37, that the job in dispute, which services four batteries, should be coded at D 2.0 on Factor 7. Since this rating results in one higher job class, grievants are entitled to retroactive compensation under Section 9-D-(3) of the July 1, 1954 Agreement.

AWARD

12. The grievance is sustained to the extent that the coding on Factor 7—Responsibility for Operations, for the Screenman job at the No. 3-6 Station in the Coke Production Department, is raised from C1.0 to D 2.0.

T—275.   Fairfield Steel Works.   March 31, 1954
Herbert L. Sherman, Jr., *Arbitrator*
Approved by Sylvester Garrett, *Chairman*

BACKGROUND

1. This grievance seeks a higher classification for the new job of Tractor Shovel Operator in the Open Hearth Department at Fairfield Steel Works than the Job Class 8 installed by the Company on March 22, 1953. Although the job description was jointly approved by representatives of the parties, the ratings on all of the factors except Factors 1 and 9 remain in dispute.

2. The ratings proposed by the parties on all twelve factors are as follows:

FACTOR	COMPANY'S CLASSIFI-CATION	UNION'S CLASSIFI-CATION
1. Pre-employment Training	B- .3	B- .3
* 2. Employment Training and Experience	C- .8	D-1.2
* 3. Mental Skill	C-1.6	D-2.2
* 4. Manual Skill	B- .5	C-1.0
* 5. Responsibility for Materials	A-Base	B-1.8
* 6. Responsibility for Tools and Equipment	CM- .7	DM-1.5
* 7. Responsibility for Operation	A-Base	C-1.0
* 8. Responsibility for Safety of Others	B- .4	D-1.2
9. Mental Effort	C-1.0	C-1.0
*10. Physical Effort	C- .8	D-1.5
*11. Surroundings	C- .8	D-1.6
*12. Hazards	C- .8	D-1.2
Total	7.7	15.5

* Disputed Factors

3. The job in dispute, which works twenty-one turns a week, is primarily responsible for operating an Emco Rocker-Shovel Tractor in handling and loading slag and debris around the furnaces and the ladle stands. It is assigned exclusively to the Open Hearth Department and works in the pit most of the time. The machine is mounted on caterpillar tracks. Attached to two arms is a bucket which goes over the cab to dump the load in rubbish cars. There are seven levers to control the operation of the machine.

4. Priority is given to the cleaning out of slag pockets which takes an average of two to three shifts each week. The balance of the time is devoted to a general cleaning up of the rest of the pit. To clean out a slag pocket, the machine must go down an incline and then back out with the load in the bucket and deposit the load in a rubbish car. When a furnace is taken down for a rebuild, the ladle crane tries to break the slag first. Then one of the grievants starts to clean the slag out so that the brick masons can rebuild the wall.

5. Job descriptions and classifications for the following jobs were introduced by the Company for the Board's consideration: Specimen 95 for a Bulldozer Operator in the Blast Furnace Department; a Bulldozer Operator in the Construction Department at Fairfield Steel Works; a Tractor Shovel Operator in the Yard Department at Fairfield Steel Works; a Tractor Shovel Operator in the Open Hearth Department at the Ensley Plant (over which a grievance was once filed but withdrawn); a Traxcavator Operator in the Maintenance Shops at Geneva Works; a Bulldozer Operator in the #4 Open Hearth Shop at Homestead; a Tractor Operator in the Open Hearth Department at Edgar Thomson Works; a Bulldozer Operator in the #5 Open Hearth Shop at Homestead; and a Tractor Operator in the Open Hearth Department at Clairton Works. The Union submitted for the Board's guidance a description and classification for an Overhead Shovel Operator job in the Open Hearth Department at Lorain Works.

DISCUSSION AND FINDINGS

6. To support its proposed rating on Factor 2, the Union alleges that the Loader Operator job at the Company's Ore Mines receives a rating of D-1.2 on this Factor. To this the Company replies that the Ore Mines job was coded under a different agreement with a different classification manual and different benchmark jobs. With respect to Factors 3 and 4, the Union urges the Board to consider the job of Charging Machine Operator as an appropriate guide.

7. One of the grievants who testified, however, stated that he had previously operated a bulldozer and that the controls on a bulldozer and those on his Tractor Shovel are the same except for the difference between a blade and the bucket attachment. Of all the jobs for which descriptions and classifications were submitted, none receives a higher rating on Factors 2, 3 and 4 than the ratings now assigned to these factors for the job in dispute. The Board finds that the present ratings on these factors, involving employment training and experience, mental skill, and manual skill, are appropriate.

8. Materials for the Tractor Shovel Operator job are slag, used brick, steel skulls, debris, spittings, oil and grease. Every job presented to the Board receives a rating of A-Base for Factor 5—Responsibility for Materials. The Board finds, therefore, that A-Base is the proper rating for grievants' job under Factor 5.

9. For purposes of coding Factor 6—Responsibility for Equipment, grievants' main piece of equipment is obviously the Tractor Shovel. The Union is not disputing the probable damage to the equipment, but only the amount of care and attention required. There is testimony that such Loaders become damaged quite a bit from the rough handling to which they are subjected.

Nevertheless, no reference was made to any other job with this type of equipment which is rated higher than the C level in Factor 6. All job classifications introduced as exhibits, including the Lorain job, are assigned the C level in Factor 6. The Board finds that a higher level for the job in dispute is not warranted.

10. Under Factors 7 and 8 the ratings on the jobs presented to the Board vary. It is clear from the pattern, however, that a distinction is made between jobs assigned solely to Open Hearth Departments, particularly when they work in the pits, and those jobs which are assigned to other Departments. The jobs in the latter category may work in a variety of areas involving the leveling of debris at dumps, the grading of ground, the excavation and backfilling of trenches, etc. Of the jobs assigned exclusively to Open Hearth Departments for removing slag and debris, the Ensley job receives lower codings than the prevailing pattern on Factors 7 and 8, while the Lorain job receives higher coding on these two factors. The Ensley job, however, does not work in the pit, while the Lorain job not only spends most of the time cleaning out slag pockets but it also has some responsibilty for direction of a Flagman. The codings on these two factors for the four other jobs assigned to Open Hearth Shops (two at Homestead, one at Edgar Thomson and one at Clairton) fall in between the ratings on the Ensley and the Lorain jobs with the exception of Factor 7 for the Homestead job at #4 Open Hearth which is coded at A-Base. The other three jobs are given a rating of B-.5 for Factor 7, and all four of these jobs are coded at C-.8 in Factor 8. In view of the purpose of bringing such a Tractor into the Open Hearth pit to expedite the rebuilding of the furnaces and in view of the necessity for avoiding injury to other workers in the area (about twenty employees are regularly assigned to the pit at Fairfield Steel Works), it appears that Factor 7—Responsibility for Operation should be coded at B-.5 and Factor 8—Responsibility for Safety of Others should be coded at C-.8 in line with the prevailing pattern.

11. Factor 10 involves Physical Effort. None of the jobs presented to the Board receives a higher rating than C-.8 on this factor. It cannot be found that the physical effort required in the job in dispute to operate the controls of the Tractor Shovel warrants a higher rating than C-.8.

12. With respect to Factor 11—Surroundings, the dirty, dusty and hot conditions were emphasized by the Union. Sometimes the slag which must be removed is red hot. Under Factor 12—Hazards, the Union points to testimony that grievants have sometimes received slight burns, that occasionally the machine tips up on end, that at times part of the contents of the overhead bucket spills out on top of the cab, and that there is a possibility that a brick might fall from the arches of the slag pockets when grievants are working in that area. The only job classification submitted to the Board with a higher rating than C-.8 on Factor 11 is the Lorain job. Four of the other five jobs assigned solely to Open Hearth Departments receive C-.8 on this factor; the fifth one is coded even lower at B-.4. A plant visit did not disclose average surroundings for the job in dispute which would justify departure from the prevailing pattern of C-.8 for Factor 11 for similar type Open Hearth jobs which are also obviously exposed to extreme heat at certain times. All of these jobs, including the Overhead Shovel Operator job at Lorain relied on by the Union, are coded at C-.8 under Factor 12. It must be concluded that C-.8 is the appropriate coding for Factors 11 and 12 respectively for the Fairfield Shovel Operator job in dispute.

13. Since Factor 7 is coded at B-.5 instead of A-Base and Factor 8 at C-.8 rather than B-.4, the new job of Tractor Shovel Operator in the Open Hearth Department receives a total of 8.6 points. Grievants are, therefore, entitled to retroactive compensation to March 22, 1953, the date that the job was installed.

AWARD

14. The grievance is sustained to the extent that Factor 7 is coded at B-.5 and Factor 8 at C-.8 for the new job of Tractor Shovel Operator in the Open Hearth Department. Since the ratings on the factors total 8.6 for Job Class 9, grievants are entitled to retroactive compensation to the date that the job was installed.

N—223. **Lorain Works. March 8, 1955**
Sylvester Garrett, *Chairman*

BACKGROUND

1. This grievance protests classification of the job of "Lubrication Man," Auto and Truck Repair Division, Central Maintenance Department, Lorain Works. Grievant operates a mobile lubrication unit, which consists of a Mack truck with lubricating equipment mounted on the rear. He drives to various plant areas and lubricates mobile gas powered and diesel powered equipment. He also assists in the repair of such equipment.

2. On January 8, 1954, the description and classification for this job were installed without Union agreement, as provided in Section 9-D-3 of the Agreement. Prior thereto, grievant lubricated two types of equipment (total of 8 pieces) at the slag yard. Although some lubrication work was performed by other incumbents of the Automotive Repairman Helper job at the diesel garage, most of it was done by the operators of the various types of tractors in the field. In his new job grievant must lubricate a total of 54 pieces of equipment which fall into 23 different types.

3. The truck which grievant operates weighs about 8 tons. The exact amount of driving required is not clear, but the lubrication truck consumes about 7 gallons of gasoline per turn. Some of this is consumed in operation of a "Blue Brute" air compressor mounted on the truck. The plant areas serviced by the truck are about the same as serviced by the Fuel Truck at Lorain Works. Both trucks service the same equipment, except that the Fuel Truck also fuels the Narrow Gauge diesel locomotives.

4. Both trucks carry "Danger" signs on their sides with warnings of flammable products. Management asserts, however, that the lubrication truck signs are merely extra precautionary measures, and that the oil and grease transported by the lubrication truck should not be regarded as flammable. Gasoline in containers is transported in this truck to equipment in the field or to other areas only in emergencies, such as on occasion when a mechanic is driven to equipment in need of repair.

5. The current coding of the job is 8.5 or Class 9. The four disputed Factors are:

Factors	2	6	8	12
Company				
Classification	B.4	C.7	C.8	B.4
Union Claim	C.8	D1.5	D1.2	C.8

6. The other Factors are rated as follows:

Factor 1—B .3		Factor 7 —B .5
Factor 3—C1.6		Factor 9 —C1.0
Factor 4—B .5		Factor 10—C .8
Factor 5—C .7		Factor 11—C .8

The Contentions

7. *Factor 2.* Although the Union seeks C .8 here, it recognizes that separate credit is not given for each separate type function of a combined job with the separate credits then being added to provide the appropriate rating under this Factor. The Union nonetheless feels that the new greasing functions, with vastly more types of equipment involved than under the old Automotive Repairman Helper job, plus the truck driving requirement together warrant a higher rating than B .4.

8. The Company notes that truck driving uniformly calls for a rating of B .4 on this Factor, and holds that in classifying Factor 2 for a job which embodies the functions of two jobs, the appropriate technique is to consider only the duty which requires the greatest skill. It cites Specimen Examples 250 (Roll Greaser), 591 (Oiler), 592 (Oiler and Wiper), 836 (Hostler), 1034 (Millwright Helper), 1036 (Oiler and Greaser), 1038 (Oiler and Greaser), 1041 (Oiler and Greaser), as Specimens involving lubricating and mechanical work. All are coded at B .4 under Factor 2.

9. The Company also cites Specimen 851 (Truck Driver) and Specimen 1200 (Truck Driver—Crane) as well as 12 Tractor Operator jobs coded at B .4 under Factor 2. Finally, it calls attention to Specimen 2192 as an example of a job requiring performance of unrelated functions (operation of tractor and assisting in welding or burning operations). This job is coded at B .4 under Factor 2, even though a Tractor Operator as such receives the same coding as a Burner.

10. *Factor 6.* For this Factor the Union seeks D 1.5 by reference to the Truck Driver (Fuel) job at Lorain Works. The Company attempts to distinguish this job on the ground that it transports fuel, but the Union stresses that the reason for classification of the Fuel Truck job at D 1.5 in Factor 6 is: "Close attention in driving through congested areas to prevent damage to truck." There is no appreciable difference between the areas serviced by the lubrication truck and the fuel truck. The Union believes, therefore, that there is no escape from the conclusion the

lubrication truck operates in congested areas as the parties themselves have defined the term. The Union asserts also that the fuel truck is no larger, no more complicated, and no more expensive than the lubrication truck, which carries $3,000 worth of special equipment.

11. The Company refers to the same Specimens cited under Factor 2, all of which are coded at C .7 or lower for this Factor. It feels that the fuel truck driver job is essentially different because gasoline is included among the fuels transported, and suggests that a mistake was made by the parties in stating the reason for classification of Factor 6. It also argues that this job may have been erroneously classified too high on this Factor, and that the Board should look to the Specimen Examples rather than to what actually has been done by the parties at Lorain Works, in classifying a comparable job.

12. *Factor 8.* For this Factor the Union claims a rating of D 1.2. The Company refers to the descriptive language in the Manual under Code C: "Operate power driven mobile equipment where others are exposed, but probability of accident is low." It cites 14 Specimen Examples for Truck Driver and Tractor Operator jobs, 9 of which are coded at D 1.2, the others at C .8. Although the Manual calls for a rating of D 1.2 where a job is required to "operate power-driven mobile equipment in congested areas," the Company feels that grievant does not operate in congested areas.

13. The Union holds that the appropriate comparison is to Truck Driver jobs, and not to Tractor Operators. Specimen 851 for a Truck Driver is coded at D 1.2; Specimen 1200 for a Crane Truck Driver at C .8. Of the truck driver jobs at Lorain Works, some receive D 1.2 on this Factor, others C .8—depending on the areas in which they operate. Again the Union relies on the Truck Driver (Fuel) job, coded at D 1.2, which covers about the same "congested" areas as grievant.

14. *Factor 12.* A higher rating is sought here because grievant must stand on straddle trucks (Ross Carriers) about seven feet off the ground, without scaffolding, to lubricate. It is particularly hazardous in the winter, asserts the Union, when ice may have accumulated on the equipment.

15. Management cites numerous Specimens and plant jobs involving lubrication work to support its rating of B .4. It stresses that the Straddle Truck Operator was coded at B .4 under Factor 12 originally, even though required to lubricate his equipment

prior to the assignment of this function to the Lubrication Man. It also notes the descriptive language in the Manual under Code B ("exposed to falls such as may occur when walking or climbing over bins, stock buggies, and low scaffolds"), as contrasted with the language under Code C ("exposed to falls such as might occur when working on high scaffolds, structures and roofs" and "perform heavy maintenance work involving climbing and rigging to repair, set up or tear down equipment and mills").

FINDINGS

16. *Factor 2* is properly rated at B .4. The parties agree as a general proposition that credit is not assigned to each of the various separate functions of a "combined" job and then added to reach a grand total. Under the Specimen Examples and other jobs presented here, there is no basis to find that either the lubrication work of grievant or his operation of the truck warrants a higher rating.

17. Under *Factor 6* the extent of probable damage at "medium" is not in dispute. The only difference is as to level of responsibility. No directly comparable job has been found in other plants in the Company. It must be recognized that a very difficult issue is presented, with practical considerations at play. In the last analysis, there is no escape from the conclusion that the only fairly comparable truck operation as far as this type responsibility is concerned, is the Fuel Truck at Lorain Works.

18. Since both jobs are responsible for the operation of special service trucks, of about the same size and value, for the purpose of servicing mobile powered equipment in the same areas, the Board must hold that a rating of D 1.5 is proper on this Factor.

19. The classification of *Factor 8* must be considered on the same basis. Not only are the Fuel Truck Driver job and certain other Lorain truck driver jobs coded at D 1.2 on this Factor, but further support for this coding is derived from Specimens 841 and 851 for Truck Drivers. It must be concluded that D 1.2 is the appropriate coding for the job in dispute.

20. Finally, the evidence does not justify a higher rating than B .4 for *Factor 12*. The hazards involved in greasing the Straddle Trucks are not such as to warrant the "C" level under the Classification Manual.

21. Since Factor 6 is raised from C .7 to D 1.5 and Factor 8 from C .8 to D 1.2, the total point value of the job in dispute is raised from 8.5 to 9.7 or Job Class 10,

AWARD

22. The grievance is sustained to the extent that Factor 6 of the job in dispute is coded at D 1.5 and Factor 8 is coded at D 1.2. The total point value is 9.7 or Job Class 10.

USC—653. Fairless Works. July 14, 1958

Donald A. Crawford, *Arbitrator*

Approved by Sylvester Garrett, *Chairman*

THE BACKGROUND

1. The Union protests the classification of the Stocker (Temper Mill) job in Job Class 9 instead of 12.

2. One of the original group of some 600 jobs established at Fairless Works, the Temper Mill Stocker job was deferred until a later date for description and classification. The primary function of this job, located in the Sheet and Tin Division, is to direct the flow of coils to the Sheet Temper Mill. The values assigned to the classification factors for the job in question by the Union and Company are presented below:

FACTOR	COMPANY		UNION	
1. Pre-Employment Training	B	.3	B	.3
* 2. Employment Training and Experience	C	.8*	E	1.6*
* 3. Mental Skill	C	1.6*	D	2.2*
4. Manual Skill	A	Base	A	Base
* 5. Responsibility for Materials	C	.7*	D	1.6*
6. Responsibility for Tools and Equipment	B	.2	B	.2
* 7. Responsibility for Operations	D	2.0*	E	3.0*
8. Responsibility for Safety of Others	B	.4	B	.4
9. Mental Effort	D	1.5	D	1.5
10. Physical Effort	B	.3	B	.3
11. Surroundings	B	.4	B	.4
*12. Hazards	B	.4*	C	.8*
Total		8.6		12.3
Job Class		9		12

* Disputed Factors

At the Hearing the Union withdrew its objections to the value assigned by the Company to Factor 12—Hazards.

3. The Union argues that the Temper Mill Stocker job is closely related to the Stocker (Pickling) job, classified in Job Class 10, and the Stocker (Cold Strip Finishing), Job Class 12, since the incumbents in the three jobs perform identically the same work in the same general area; that the subject Stocker job requires at least 24 months of training and experience to become proficient as does the Cold Strip Finishing Stocker job; that conditions of changing schedules and rush orders, plus the necessity to consider widths of the Temper Mill, require considerable judgment in feeding the Temper Mill and the Shears and Recoil Lines—indicating mental skill requirements equal to that of the Cold Strip Finishing Stocker; that the subject Stocker job should be rated as high as the two related Stocker jobs on Factor 5, Responsibility for Materials, since the former job also requires close attention to the work throughout the turn; that inasmuch as the continuous operation of the Cold Strip Finishing Lines is directly dependent upon the flow of materials from the Temper Mill and since the Temper Mill Stocker is charged with maintaining continuity of operation of the Tempering line, the job in question should be rated E-3 on the Responsibility for Operations factor as are the two comparable Stocker jobs.

4. The Union also contends that the pattern of specimen jobs to which the Company attempts to relate the instant job are in essence nothing more than Hooker jobs in that their primary function is to locate material only; that the specimen jobs (evaluated in Job Classes 6, 7 and 8) are not responsible for the flow of product to producing units as is the Temper Mill Stocker; that the duties of the specimen jobs are repetitious in nature, not subject to change and do not require decisions to be made in the absence of the turn foreman; that on the other hand Item No. 9 in the description of the working procedures of the Temper Mill Stocker specifies that he "makes temporary or emergency changes in operating schedules when necessary to minimize production losses based on information obtained from the operations."

5. The Company argues that the Temper Mill Stocker job was classified within the agreed Corporation-wide framework of classification for similar specimen Stocker jobs and the pattern of classification for comparable Stocker jobs at Fairless Works; that the pattern of classification for Stocker jobs recognizes a Job Class 8 pattern and a Job Class 10 pattern of Stockers with a few odd jobs falling within Job Classes 9, 11 and

12 because of differences in factors such as Manual Skill, Physical Effort, Surroundings, etc.; that the Job Class 8 Stockers cannot deviate from the schedule prepared by Production Planning; that the Job Class 10 Stockers are required to depart from the sequence specified in the schedules to minimize production delays; that the disputed job falls within the Job Class 8 pattern since the Stocker cannot deviate from the schedules except to the extent he can skip to the next coil in the sequence when a coil is missing or overheated; that the instant job is classified in Job Class 9 because of external factors such as Surroundings, Safety for Others, etc.; that the language of the job description for the Fairless Cold Reduction Mill Stocker (which also falls with the Job Class 8 pattern) has an item in its working procedures that is identically the same as Item No. 9 in the working procedures of the subject Stocker job; that the coils which the Temper Mill Stocker loads on flat cars for the Recoil and Shear lines are moved well in advance of the needs of those operating units and the direct stocking for those lines is performed by another Stocker.

THE FINDINGS

6. *The Stocker (Temper Mill) is properly rated C-.8 on Factor 2, C-1.6 on Factor 3, C-.7 on Factor 5 and D-2 on Factor 7.*

7. The Temper Mill Stocker works from a schedule which lists the coils in sequence by number that he is to locate in the storage area for removal by the Craneman to the entrance of the conveyor to the Sheet Tempering Mill. So that he can readily locate the coils specified on his schedules the subject Stocker maintains two binders in which he keeps a running inventory of the coils arranged in 75 rows in the storage area. He lists the coils by number and row in his binders, and as coils are removed, changed in position from one row to another, or new ones brought in to the storage area, he notes the changes in his binders.

8. If a change in operating schedule is necessary, the instant Stocker is notified of the new sequence of number coils he is to locate to maintain continuity of operations of the Sheet Temper Mill. After so doing he reverts to the original schedule. At no time can he deviate from an original or revised schedule except in the very limited sense of skipping to the next numbered coil in sequence under these two conditions; when the specified coil is not available for processing, or when the prescribed coil is above temperature, which fact he determines by feeling the coil. When the foreman is avail-

able, however, the Stocker gets him to check his action.

9. The Pickling Stocker works from a schedule prepared by Production Planning, but he can deviate from the schedule within prescribed limits as illustrated by the following examples. When notified of operating problems in the Pickling line, such as roll changes, shear knife changes, etc., which require it to function differently than originally scheduled, he will make adjustments in the sequence specified in the schedule. If specified coils are not immediately available because of storage problems, he substitutes other coils of the same width and general characteristics as the coils listed on the schedule. He substitutes other coils of the same type for coils that show obvious defects. He uses judgment, including deviations from the scheduled sequence of coils, in order to accomplish the best flow of production through the Pickling line by feeding coils in terms of width and shear limitations and schedule changes.

10. The specified coils on the schedule given the Cold Strip Finishing Stocker are listed by widths and lengths and delivery dates. Within these limits he selects the material to feed the Finishing lines to gain the maximum utilization of the operating units. He tries to run the same widths and lengths and to gradually reduce or increase widths and lengths, while at the same time meeting priorities in delivery dates.

11. It is clear from the above discussion that the disputed Stocker job requires less know-how and responsibility than the grade 10 and 12 jobs cited by the Union, and fits the Corporation-wide mutually agreed upon Job Class 8 pattern. The Union is therefore not persuasive when it argues that the grievant Stocker exercises the same degree of responsibility for operations as do the Pickling and Cold Strip Finishing Stockers by reason of the following language of Item No. 9 of the working procedures of the Temper Mill Stocker job: "Makes temporary or emergency changes to operating schedule when necessary to minimize production losses based on information obtained from operations." In fact, an incumbent of the job in question testified that he does not deviate from the sequence of coils specified in the schedule. Additionally, the Fairless Cold Reduction Mill Stocker job, which is classified according to the Job Class 8 pattern, has the same language as part of its working procedures.

12. The time to learn and the mental skills (Factors 2 and 3) of the Pickling and Cold Strip Finishing Stockers are higher because greater knowledge of product and

processes is necessary as a basis for the judgment required to deviate from the schedules. This is especially so with respect to the Finishing Stocker, who serves 7 operating units —2 Shear lines, the Recoil operating line and 4 finishing processes. Additionally, the Pickling Stocker must be able to operate a Downtilter and Power Conveyor and the Cold Strip Finishing Stocker a Ram or Tow Tractor, inasmuch as they themselves feed the coils directly to the lines instead of through a Craneman as does the Temper Mill Stocker. The perpetual inventory that the disputed Stocker maintains is of the simplest kind, one in which he records the product by number and row. In finding the row in which the specified coil is located and marking it for the Craneman, he also performs essentially a semi-routine task.

13. The attention required (Factor 5) is less for the job at issue because of the extensive record keeping time involved and the fact that the job is not tied in with line operations as closely and continuously as the Stocker jobs cited by the Union. Close attention is required only when the Stocker is locating the numbered coils to meet his schedule and checking on the movement of the coils by the Craneman from storage. On the other hand, the location of coils specified in the schedules, the reasoning out of the changes that may be required in the schedules, and the operation of the conveying or towing equipment to feed directly the processing lines involve a variety of detail and frequent checking that require close attention for most of the turn on the part of the Pickling and Finishing Stockers. Insofar as Factor 7 is concerned, it is abundantly clear from the discussion of the three Stocker jobs that the responsibility for operations imposed on the subject Stocker in following a sequence of number coils without variations to perform his primary function is less than in the case of the two Job Class 10 pattern Stocker jobs.

THE AWARD

14. Grievance No. A-57-12 is denied.

USC—595.   Gary Sheet and Tin Mill.   May 14, 1957

Herbert L. Sherman, Jr., *Arbitrator*

Approved by Sylvester Garrett, *Chairman*

BACKGROUND

1. This grievance arose in the Tractor Repair Shop of the Central Maintenance Division at the Gary Sheet and Tin Mill. It claims that changes recorded on a Form G dated May 18, 1955, along with other changes, have affected the classification ratings, particularly on Factors 5, 6 and 8, for the job of Tractor Repairman.

2. Added to Tools and Equipment on the Form G are: "pneumatic wrenches, acetylene burning equipment, floor-controlled overhead traveling crane, towing equipment, electrical tractor testing and charging equipment." To Materials propane gas and acetylene and oxygen tanks have been added. And the Form G notes that grievants must procure material and supplies from Stores. A Union witness testified that the skills, responsibilities and working conditions of the job have been affected in particular by the following: use of charging equipment with higher voltage, and occasional hooking of two panel boards to one generator in the charging set when the other fails, repair of propane powered tractors, use of a floor operated crane and acetylene burning equip-

ment, repair and testing of larger, more complicated and more expensive tractors in a new location with a smaller working area, towing more disabled tractors longer distances to the Repair Shops in all kinds of weather, sketching and altering electrical circuits to slow down the speed of Ross Carriers, and the occasional repair of a diesel locomotive on the night shift.

3. Management contends that some of the duties relied upon by the Union have always been performed by the incumbents of the job in dispute, that others are specifically covered by the language in the original job description, and that none of the duties warrant an increase in the classification ratings. With respect to those duties particularly stressed by the Union in connection with Factors 5, 6 and 8, the Company argues that they do not affect the classification ratings on these Factors because of the relative infrequency with which they are performed and because they are an incidental part of the job.

4. Following is a table which shows the present classification ratings for the Tractor Repairman job and the ratings sought by the Union:

FACTOR	PRESENT		UNION	
1. Pre-employment training.	C	1.0	C	1.0
*2. Employment training and experience.	G	2.4	H	3.2
*3. Mental skill.	E	2.8	F	3.5
4. Manual skill.	D	1.5	D	1.5
*5. Responsibility for materials.	D	1.1	D	2.4
*6. Responsibility for tools and equipment.	C	.4	D	1.5
7. Responsibility for operations.	C	1.0	C	1.0
*8. Responsibility for safety of others.	B	.4	D	1.2
9. Mental effort.	D	1.5	D	1.5
10. Physical effort.	C	.8	C	.8
*11. Surroundings.	B	.4	C	.8
*12. Hazards.	B	.4	C	.8
Total	13.7		19.2	

* Factors in dispute.

FINDINGS

5. A review of the evidence in the light of the original job description, Specimen Example 945 for an Automotive Repairman, and the job descriptions and classifications for eighteen jobs which perform similar duties leads to the conclusion that no higher classification ratings are appropriate for the job in dispute. Some of the duties relied upon by the Union have always been performed by the incumbents of the job and do not represent a change in job content. And an analysis of the numerous job descriptions and classifications submitted to the Board shows that the new duties added to the job in dispute do not affect the ratings on the Factors. The classification pattern of the most closely related jobs, as distinguished from the jobs cited by the Union, is identical with the codings presently assigned to the Factors for the job in dispute.

AWARD

6. The grievance is denied.

USC—462.   South Works.   January 31, 1955
Herbert L. Sherman, Jr., *Arbitrator*
Approved by Sylvester Garrett, *Chairman*

BACKGROUND

1. This grievance, signed by 87 employees, stems from the installation of two way radios on Narrow Gauge Railroad locomotives at South Works. The Union is seeking a higher classification than Class 11 for the Narrow Gauge Engineer, and a higher classification than Class 7 for the Switchman. Though the Union believes that other Factors might be affected, its case is built primarily on its claims that the Engineer has greater responsibility for the safety of others and that the Switchman is exposed to greater hazards.

2. Two way radios were installed on the locomotives at South Works in September, 1952. The equipment in the cab consists of a loud speaker and an instrument which is much like a telephone. Both of these instruments may be turned on and off by the Engineer. He may also control the volume of the loud speaker in the cab as well as the volume of the loud speakers located on the footboards of some of the engines.

3. The purpose of the new equipment is to permit two way communication between supervision and engine crews, and between the engine crews. The Yardmaster transmits radio messages from his shanty to the Engineer in his cab,

DISCUSSION AND FINDINGS

4. Grievance Committeeman Fahey testified that his duties as a Narrow Gauge Engineer required him to operate his new equipment in the same manner as he would operate a telephone except that he presses a button to speak and releases the button to hear. The Engineer, it is argued, has greater responsibility for the safety of others because of the requirement that he answer the telephone, sometimes when the engine is moving. There is conflict in the testimony as to whether the Engineer on occasion must use two hands to operate the radio equipment. According to Union testimony, the Engineer at times must hold the telephone receiver with one hand and adjust the button for the transmission of messages by loud speaker with the other. On the other hand, a Company witness testified that it was only necessary to use one hand to operate the new equipment, thus leaving the other hand free to operate the engine controls. Nor is there agreement as to whether the Engineer must ever take his eyes off the track, when backing up, in order to use the radio equipment.

5. Messages are transmitted to Switchmen by the loud speakers located on the footboards of the engine. Sometimes messages are relayed by the Engineers. Prior to

installation of the new equipment Switchmen often had to walk to the nearest telephones to receive their instructions. The Union claims that the blaring of the radio is startling to the Switchman, thereby increasing the hazards of the job while coupling and uncoupling. Although it is recognized that there are P. A. systems in effect in areas where the jobs in dispute work, with greater volume than is found on the radio loud speakers on the engines, grievants point out that they do not work so close to the P. A. loud speakers as to be startled by them.

6. Management takes the position that the hazards of the Engineer and Switchman jobs have, if anything, been reduced. The basis for this assertion is that the Engineers may be warned more quickly of track conditions by radio, and the fact that all engines receive every radio transmitted message.

7. Although Management refers to numerous non-railroad jobs which use radio sending and receiving equipment, the Board agrees with the Union that the jobs in dispute should be compared with other Locomotive Engineer and Switchman jobs. Specimens 833 and 848 for Locomotive Engineers show that a distinction is made between limited area switching and general or interchange switching. Locomotive Engineers who perform limited area switching are in Class 11, the general switching Engineers in Class 13. This distinction explains the Class 13 assigned to the Fairless Works Locomotive Engineer job upon which the Union relies in part. Although all engines at Fairless Works have been radio equipped since the plant went into operation, no additional credit is found on any of the Factors for the Locomotive Engineer job because of the use of the two way radio. Nor has the addition of such radio equipment to numerous Locomotive Engineer jobs in other plants of the Company affected the established classification ratings.

8. Specimens 835 and 849 for Switchman jobs likewise show a distinction between limited area switching and general switching involving the use of interchange tracks and the exchange of traffic with common carriers. The Switchman (Limited Area) is in Class 7, while the Switchman (General) is in Class 9. But again, the installation of two way radios on the locomotives at Fairless Works, and elsewhere, did not provide a basis for higher classification ratings on the Switchman job.

9. And finally, despite an assertion by the Union that the installation of the radios caused two engines and several gangleaders to be displaced, thereby increasing the responsibilities of grievants, the supporting testimony does not clearly establish this claim. The engines were retired in April, 1952, while the radios were installed in September, 1952. Although several gangleaders were laid off in some period, the particular date is not clear. Management states that there was a reduction in force due to curtailed operations. In any event, it is not shown how any such displacement has affected the classification ratings of the jobs in dispute. In view of the classification pattern established by other locomotive engineer and switchman jobs, where two way radios have been added, the present ratings on the jobs in dispute must be considered appropriate.

AWARD

10. The grievance is denied.

USC—444.   McDonald Mills, Youngstown District.   June 30, 1955
Donald A. Crawford, *Arbitrator*
Approved by Sylvester Garrett, *Chairman*

FINDINGS

1. Grievance No. 53-3, which requests that the new job of Bulldozer Operator, McDonald Works, Youngstown District, be rated at Job Class 9 instead of Job Class 8, is denied. The Union believes that Factors 4, 7, and 8 are underrated by the Company. The major bases of the Union position are that the Ohio Works Bulldozer job is classified higher in these three factors and that the Specimen Bulldozer Job (Class 8) differs in that it is used for work outside the mills. The Union points out that the disputed Bulldozer job requires work *inside* (and outside) the mills, particularly on furnace rebuild jobs.

2. The Board in reviewing the factors ratings has been governed by the parties' application of the factors, as required by the relevant Agreements, and finds no basis for increasing them.

3. *Factor 4,* Manual Skill, Company: B .5 Union: C 1. Award: B .5

Some 31 Bulldozer job descriptions and classifications in effect in Central Operations (Co. Ex. 9) show that no one, except for the Ohio Works job, is rated higher than B. 5. Since several of these Bulldozer jobs involve operating the Bulldozer in congested and close areas (blast and open hearth furnaces, foundries) like the furnace areas concerned in this job, the Board must follow the B .5 ratings of the Specimen job rather than the exception expressed in the Ohio Works job.

4. *Factor 7,* Responsibility for Operations, Company: A .0 Union: C1.0 Award: A. 0

Some 13 of the 31 bulldozer jobs receive higher than the A Base rating on this factor. These job descriptions indicate that the Bulldozer operation is coordinated with processing units, shipping or construction so that there is a responsibility for maintaining other operations. If the disputed Bulldozer job were used a substantial amount of the time in connection with furnace rebuild or other mill operations, its rating would be increased. The evidence is, however, that the amount of time spent on this type of work is slight.

5. *Factor 8,* Responsibility for Safety of Others, Company: B. 4 Union: C .8 Award: B. 4

Some 14 of the 31 Bulldozer jobs receive higher than the B .4 rating. The job descriptions indicate that the Bulldozer is moving material with crews and/or in congested areas, such as blast furnace, open hearth or foundry. Again if the disputed Bulldozer job worked a substantial amount of the time in the furnace or mill areas, a higher rating would be required. But it does not.

For these reasons, the grievance cannot be sustained.

AWARD

6. The grievance is denied.

T—363. Fairfield Coke and Coal Chemical Works. April 24, 1956

Sylvester Garrett, *Chairman*

BACKGROUND

1. This case involves two grievances, both of which were filed on April 15, 1954 in the By-Product Coke Department of Fairfield Coke and Chemical Works. The first grievance protests the classification of the Tar Stillman job, in Job Class 18, in the new Tar Distillation and Naphthalene Refining Plant; the second grievance protests the Job Class 10 assigned to the Tar Stillman Helper job. The disputed classifications were installed unilaterally, effective March 22, 1954.

2. Both job descriptions were approved by representatives of the parties. The Working Procedure of the Tar Stillman job is worded almost identically with that for the Tar Stillman job, in Job Class 19, in the Coke Plant of Clairton Works, and the Tar Stillman Helper job description is quite similar to that for the Tar Acids Stillman Helper, in Job Class 9, at Clairton Works.

3. Only Factors 6 and 8 are in dispute for the Tar Stillman job, the other Factors having been coded the same as the Tar Stillman job at Clairton Works. The Union urges that Factors 6 and 8 also be coded the same as the Clairton job, which would require that Factor 6 be raised from D 2.0 to E 3.0 and Factor 8 from C .8 to D 1.2. The Union further contends that the Helper job should be coded the same as the Tar Acids Stillman job at Clairton.

4. Management refers, for purposes of coding Factors 6 and 8 on the Tar Stillman job, to two Specimen Examples for Benzol Stillmen, to a Job Class 15 Benzol Stillman at Fairfield, and to other Stillman jobs. It points out that the Clairton Tar Plant is larger and argues that certain safety features in the Fairfield operation decrease the degree of attention required of the Tar Stillman, to prevent damage to his equipment and to prevent injury to others, to such an extent that the Clairton Tar Stillman job is not comparable.

5. Operation of the Fairfield Tar Plant consists primarily of pumping crude tar through tar heaters where it is heated to optional temperature and passed through chain recovery equipment consisting of flash tanks, fractionating columns and condensers to separate the tar into its component parts —solvents, naphthalene, anthrocene, creosote and pitch. Finished products are then pumped directly into tank cars or storage tanks from which they are loaded and shipped out according to customer requirements.

6. For 10 of the 15 storage tanks at Fairfield, there are high level indicators to warn the Stillman that the tanks will overflow if he does not take action to reduce the flow. The high level alarm system consists of lights over the panel board in the control room. When the danger point is reached in the 10 smaller storage tanks, the lights will brighten and a siren at the corner of the control room will be set off. This alarm system, however, does not prevent the storage tanks from overflowing, which could burn anybody coming into contact with the material. Nor is the alarm system connected to the direct loading of tank cars. The smaller tanks are diked, the five larger tanks are not. At Clairton the 6 larger tanks are not diked; the 9 smaller tanks are set in a deep pit. The only signal light consists of a red light on the No. 4 Still, which warns the Tar Pump Tender or the Tar Stillman that the hot pitch tank may overflow.

7. At Fairfield there are also other automatic safeguards, such as safety valves to cut off fuel gas flow and relief valves to protect against excessive pressures. An electric "fire eye" looks at the flame in the burners and shuts off the gas if the flame goes out. Although the high pressure shutoff valve is supposed to cut off the gas automatically when a tube is coking up and the pressure is increasing, due to the failure of a Flowrator the safety valve did not operate the only time that a tube did coke up. Hence, the amber light over the panel board did not warn the Stillman, nor did the siren go off. As at Clairton, the valves had to be turned off by hand.

8. Numerous dials in the control rooms at both Fairfield and Clairton must be checked by the Tar Stillman to determine whether adjustments need to be made in temperatures and pressures. Temperature controls for the fire box are adjusted manually. The various dials, among other things, record temperatures and pressures. If the pressure is too low, it may indicate a vapor leak from a break in the tubes. If the pressure is too high, it may indicate that a tube is becoming plugged. This in turn can cause vapor leaks. Where there are vapor leaks, there is danger of fire and explosion from ignition of vapors by the gas burners. When tubes coke up, great expense is involved in cleaning them out or replacing them.

9. At Clairton a Creosote Stillman, under the direction of the Tar Stillman, is stationed in a control room adjacent to the stills where the gas burner valves are located. Dials in his control room, like the dials in the control room of the Tar Stillman, indicate increases and decreases in pressure, and also record temperatures. Even when the Tar Stillman leaves his control room to inspect the equipment and check his various gauges, the Creosote Stillman is in a position to note from his dials whether he should turn off the nearby gas valves to prevent fires or plugging of tubes. The Creosote Stillman also shares responsibility with the Tar Stillman for maintaining a proper balance in the production of pitch-tar mixture in blending tanks. Likewise, the Tar Stillman relies on the Tar Pump Tender to check the pressure gauges of the coal tar pumps, and to count periodically the strokes of the feed pumps. Although the Tar Pump Tender stays at these pumps most of the time, he also occasionally checks the Hot Tar Pumps, the Transfer Pumps, and other pumps. On the other hand, storage tank pumps and their pressure gauges are checked by a Tank Yard Pump Tender, also under the direction of the Tar Stillman. And finally, a Tar Plant Utilityman, in Job Class

10, is available, as required, to assist in the performance of any of these operating positions in the Tar Plant.

10. At Fairfield the Tar Stillman, who has the primary responsibility for operation of the coal tar distillation unit, is assisted generally by the Tar Stillman Helper. The latter job periodically inspects the equipment to assure its proper operation. A Dockman, under the direction of the Tar Stillman, is responsible for the loading operation.

DISCUSSION AND FINDINGS

11. There is no Specimen Example which is exactly comparable with the two jobs in dispute. Management itself has recognized, at both Fairfield and Clairton, that codings on a number of Factors for a Tar Stillman, who has the primary responsibility for operation of a Tar Plant, should differ from the codings assigned to certain other types of Stillman jobs. Of the various other types of Stillman jobs examined by the Board at Fairfield and Clairton, which are required to exercise a lesser degree of care and attention, some are responsible only for a batch process, and not a continuous process; some are responsible for units which are steam heated rather than by gas burners; and some of these Stillman jobs do not have the top responsibility for their equipment. At both Fairfield and Clairton the Tar Stillmen have top responsibility for *continuous* operation of a coal tar distillation unit where there is danger of igniting vapors from the gas burners.

12. The Board finds that the Tar Stillman job in dispute should be coded the same on Factors 6 and 8 as the Tar Stillman job at Clairton, the most closely related job. With respect to the coding of Factor 6, the parties are in disagreement only as to the requisite degree of attention and care. Both parties agree that probable damage should be rated "High."

13. Although the Tar Stillman job at Fairfield has the benefit of a number of automatic safety features, it is clear that a considerable amount of responsibility is placed on the operator to prevent damage to equipment and injury to others. Obviously, responsibility is not placed entirely on automatic devices. Even though, as Management contends, there are differences between the Clairton and Fairfield Tar Plants, the Board finds that the degree of care and attention required under Factors 6 and 8 for the two Tar Stillman jobs is not so dissimilar that different ratings on these Factors are justified. It must be remembered that although the Tar Stillman at Clairton does not have the benefit of the safety devices

installed at Fairfield, he does have the benefit of assistance, in checking the equipment for proper operation, of two Pump Tenders, a Creosote Stillman, and a Utilityman.

14. With respect to the Tar Stillman Helper job in dispute, no directly comparable job was presented to the Board. In any event, the Tar Acids Stillman job at Clairton, relied upon by the Union, is not an appropriate guide. That job is not a "Helper" or an "Assistant" job. It is not under the direction of the Tar Stillman. It is an entirely separate job, at a different physical location, with primary responsibility for the equipment which produces refined tar acid products.

15. The Helper job in dispute is already coded one job class higher than the Tar Acids Stillman Helper. And it is in the same job class as the Utilityman at Clairton. Upon analysis of all the evidence the Board concludes that Job Class 10 is appropriate for the Tar Stillman Helper at Fairfield.

AWARD

16. Factor 6—Responsibility for Tools and Equipment should be coded at E 3.0 for the Tar Stillman job, and Factor 8—Responsibility for Safety of Others at D 1.2. The Tar Stillman Helper job is properly classified at Job Class 10.

USC—277. Clairton Works. September 17, 1953

J. O. Keller, *Arbitrator*

BACKGROUND

1. This grievance concerns the job classification of a newly created job of Tournapull Operator in the Labor and Transportation Department of the Clairton Works. The equipment concerned is known as a Le Tourneau Diesel Tournapull machine complete with carryall, identified as a Model C Roadster Tournapull with Model E-16 Scraper Carryall, and manufactured by R. G. Le Tourneau, Inc.

2. The Carryall has a maximum capacity of approximately 16 cubic yards and is used to move earth, coal and similar materials by scooping up, transporting, and spreading or dumping. The Tournapull is operated along the same general principles as bulldozers, road-graders, tractors and the like, and has finger tip electric controls for steering and operating.

3. Between April 20, 1949, and February, 1951, Clairton Works rented Tournapull machines from time to time and on February 1, 1951, it purchased three of them. The rented and purchased equipment were not identical, but were basically alike, the differences being improvements of the new machines over the rented machines, including an enclosed operator's cab, equipped with heater and cooling fan.

4. The Tournapulls at the Clairton Works are primarily utilized in the coal storage areas, four in number, to move coal from place to place as desired. When material is being stocked they pick up coal at the initial point of delivery and spread it at the desired location. During the de-stocking periods, they scoop the coal from the piles and haul it to and dump it at points where

it can be reached for loading into other means of transportation.

5. When the first Tournapull machine was rented on April 20, 1949, a description of the job of Tournapull Operator was prepared by Management pursuant to the terms of Section 9-D of the April 22, 1947 Labor Agreement, and was later accepted by the Union representatives. The original classification from this description made by Management was a proposal of Job Class 9 (total point value 9.1). The Union disagreed with this proposal and further review of the values resulted in an increase in Factor 8 (Responsibility for Safety of Others), from B-0.4 to C-0.8. This raised the total points to 9.5 and the Company assigned Job Class 10 to this position. The Union declined to accept Job Class 10, contending that the job properly belonged in Job Class 13.

6. On June 6, 1949, the Company proceeded to install the proposed classification in accordance with the directive of Section 9-D-3 (paragraph 129), of the April 22, 1947 Labor Agreement and the Union filed the instant grievance in the Second Step on June 24, 1949. This grievance was appealed to the Fourth Step initially on August 1, 1949.

7. Subsequently, the operation of the Tournapulls was suspended and on March 3, 1950, the grievance was withdrawn from consideration in the Fourth Step with the understanding that the matter could be reinstated by the Union without prejudice to the rights of either party should the Tournapull operation again become operative.

8. A short time later Tournapull operations recommenced and, failing to secure agreement on the Job Classification at the

Plant level, the grievance was reappealed on May 1, 1950, for fourth step consideration. From there it found its way to Arbitration and hearings were held Tuesday afternoon, December 2, 1952.

UNION POSITION

9. In their brief the Union sets forth the Factor values continuing in dispute as follows:

	UNION	COMPANY
Factor 3 (Mental Skill)	D-2.2 Use considerable judgment in operating heavy duty mobile equipment.	C-1.6 Performs semi-routine job involving some variety of detail and judgement.
Factor 4 (Manual Skill)	C-1.0 Manipulate controls at a rapid pace of heavy duty equipment.	B-0.5 Operate variable controls in operation of high speed heavy duty equipment.
Factor 5 (Responsibility for material)	C-1.8 Estimated cost of $500.00. Use close attention part of time to prevent combustion.	B-0.4 Estimated cost of $100.00. Use ordinary care to prevent damage. Can cause spontaneous combustion in coal pile by improper spreading and compaction.
Factor 6 (Responsibility for tools and equipment)	D-1.5 Close attention and care required to prevent damage to high speed mobile equipment.	C-0.7 Moderate attention and care required to prevent damage to mobile equipment.
	UNION'S PROPOSAL	COMPANY'S PROPOSAL
Total	12.8 points	9.5 points

10. The Union requests that the Board find in accordance with applicable provisions of the May 8, 1946 Agreement and pursuant to Section 9-D of the April 22, 1947 Agreement that the aggrieved employees be classified in Job Class 13, effective on the date that the operation of Tournapull was initially installed.

COMPANY POSITION

11. The Company contends that the Tournapull Operator job was classified in accordance with the provisions of Section 9-D of the 1947 Labor Agreement and was properly evaluated in Job Class 10. In view of this, the Company requests the Board to dismiss this grievance in toto.

DISCUSSION AND FINDING

12. From the testimony and evidence submitted at the hearings the Board finds that the job description of the Tournapull Operator #6150-3666 as prepared by the Company was accepted and agreed to by the Union. In the classification installed by Management from this description there is mutual agreement on all Factors except 3, 4, 5 and 6. On these four factors, however,

the Union disagrees with the valuation assigned by Management.

13. Factor 3 has to do with Mental Skill. Here is to be considered the mental ability needed to perform a job, the judgment required to do the work, the ingenuity involved. This factor has nothing to do of itself with size or weight of machine or of materials, unless they require a great deal of thought to operate. In other words a very large machine might require less thought to operate than a tiny machine. On the Job Classification Analysis entered as an exhibit by the Company, the two specimen jobs of Bulldozer Operator and Truck Driver, and the six similar jobs of Youngstown Tournapull Operator, Clairton Truck Driver, Clairton Truck Craneman, Clairton Craneman (Machine Shop), Clairton Bulldozer Operator, and Gary Steel Works Bulldozer Operator all are evaluated for Job Class 3 at C-1.6 the same as is given by the Company for the job under consideration, namely the Clairton Tournapull Operator #6150-3666. The Union contention for a higher value rests on the fact that the operator performs a complete operation, he loads, conveys and discharges the material. However, the factor asks how much thought and ingenuity does

this require. The Union compares this Tournapull to heavy duty cranes at the Gary plant. But again the size has nothing to do with this factor, but rather how much mental effort. The Board finds that the Company evaluation is equitable for Factor 3.

14. Factor 4 has to do with Manual Skill. Here muscular effort and dexterity as well as other physical ability are to be considered. Here the Company selected the Manual description which states, "Operate variable controls, such as rheostats, and levers, to control movement of machines or passage of material through equipment where jogging, frequent regulation and precision of adjustment is required." The Union has selected the higher value for which the Manual states, "Manipulate controls of complex machines at a rapid pace involving a high degree of coordination." All eight jobs on the Job Classification Analysis assign the Company value to this Factor 4 of B-0.5. From the evidence submitted by both parties, the Board would not consider the Tournapull as operating at a rapid pace. The Board finds that the Company evaluation is equitable for Factor 4.

15. Factor 5 considers the responsibility of the operator for Materials. Here we must consider the obligation of the worker imposed upon him either by his supervisors or by the essential character of the job. This responsibility exists only to the extent that it is controllable by the workman, that is, the damage is a direct result of an act by him or negligence on his part. The Company selected this requirement from the Manual, "Mechanically handle or transport material not easily damaged," while the Union feels that the higher Manual requirement more accurately applies which reads, "Mechanically handle and transport material subject to damage from handling devices." In the Job Classification Analysis, the specimen job of Bulldozer Operator, and the sample jobs of Youngstown Tournapull Operator and Gary Bulldozer each receive a lower value for Factor 5 than the value the Company gives the Clairton Tournapull Operator. The Clairton Bulldozer Operator gets the same value for Factor 5 namely B-0.4. The specimen job Truck Driver, and the three sample jobs of Clairton Truck Driver, the Clairton Truck Craneman, and the Clairton Craneman (Machine Shop) all receive higher ratings; in the case of the first three C-0.7 and for the last mentioned job C-1.2. The Company explains that the higher ratings are given because the material handled is subject to damage from handling devices. Such material consists of high priced equipment such as generators, motors, expensive machine parts and the like. The Union con-

tended that damage to the coal results from fires caused by spontaneous combustion when the coal is not properly compacted. The Management stated that the Company has not had any fires caused by spontaneous combustion on any coal stocked by Tournapulls. The Company admitted that prior to the use of Tournapulls there were a number of such fires, and stated that since rating the Tournapull job at Clairton, the Tournapull experience relative to fires caused by spontaneous combusion, would incline the Management to rate this Factor 5 at the base or lower rate. The Board again finds that the present Company rating is equitable for Factor 5.

16. Factor 6 has to do with the responsibility of the worker for tools and equipment. Here must be considered the obligation on the workman for attention and care to prevent damage to tools and equipment with which he is actually working or which come under his control. The degree of responsibility is determined by the probability and cost of damage which might occur at any one time. The Company selected this statement from the Manual, "Moderate attention and care required to prevent damage to light mobile equipment such as tractor, trucks and light cranes." The Union selected the following from the Manual as being more nearly correct, "Close attention and care required to prevent damage to heavy duty mobile equipment such as locomotive cranes and heavy duty cranes." The Union made much of the fact that in the Job Description for the Clairton Tournapull Operator the Company uses the phrase "heavy duty equipment" in several of the factors, but in Factor 6 just the phrase "mobile equipment." The Company explained that the phrases used are relative. Locomotive cranes and heavy duty mobile cranes generally weigh in the neighborhood of 100 tons, while the Tournapull weighs empty in the neighborhood of 17 tons. The Job Classification Analysis gives the same value to Factor 6 for all the specimen and sample jobs as is given to this Factor 6 for the Clairton Tournapull Operator, with the exception of the Clairton Bulldozer Operator. This Bulldozer job is rated slightly lower than the Tournapull job. The Board agrees that the Company evaluation of the Tournapull job for Factor 6 is equitable.

AWARD

17. The grievance is denied.

Note: On a petition for review this award was affirmed by Chairman Garrett on December 31, 1953.

A—748. Joliet Works. May 14, 1957

Herbert L. Sherman, Jr., *Arbitrator*

Approved by Sylvester Garrett, *Chairman*

BACKGROUND

1. This grievance, filed on December 12, 1955, involves a dispute over the proper classification of the new job of Packer (Automatic Scales) (PC 44-06) at the Joliet Works. The job description is mutually approved.

2. Following is a table which shows the classification ratings installed by Management and the ratings sought by the Union:

FACTORS	COMPANY		UNION	
* 1. Pre-employment training	A	Base	B	.3
* 2. Employment training and experience	A	Base	B	.4
3. Mental skill	B	1.0	B	1.0
4. Manual skill	C	1.0	C	1.0
* 5. Responsibility for materials	B	.4	D	.8
* 6. Responsibility for tools and equipment	B	.3	C	.7
7. Responsibility for operations	A	Base	A	Base
8. Responsibility for safety of others	A	Base	A	Base
* 9. Mental effort	B	.5	C	1.0
*10. Physical effort	B	.3	C	.8
*11. Surroundings	A	Base	B	.4
*12. Hazards	A	Base	B	.4
Total	3.5		6.8	

* Factors in dispute.

3. Grievants start up, operate, and make adjustments to an automatic packing and weighing machine in the Small Nail Packaging Department and perform related duties. A Material Handler fills a hopper with nails which run through a chute on a magnetic conveyor. By observing the amount of nails on the magnetic conveyor, grievants determine whether the proper amount is coming through the chute. When necessary, they adjust the flow of nails at this point by moving the chute gate up or down. Two controls for the hopper vibrators and three controls for the chute vibrators may also be adjusted. The parties do not agree as to who adjusts these controls, but it appears that in practice they have not been adjusted very often. Nevertheless, such duties are part of grievants' job.

4. The nails on the magnetic conveyor are dumped into a split hopper, one half to go to one automatic scale and the other half to go to another automatic scale. From the split hopper the nails fall on vibrators which feed the nails into unscramblers. The purpose of the unscramblers, which must be adjusted by grievants, is to straighten out the nails. From the unscramblers the nails vibrate out two chutes for each scale and fall into the packages placed on the automatic scales by grievants. Grievants must adjust four rheostat controls at the front of the machine—two for each scale. One control is for the volume of the flow and one is for dribble. The proper flow and the proper dribble must be synchronized in order to control the feed of the nails into the packages.

5. A mirror attached to the split hopper must be observed by grievants to determine whether too many nails are coming through, which would block the unscramblers. If the unscramblers became blocked, and the conveyors were not shut off by grievants by their foot pedal, the split hopper could fill up and overflow, thus causing the nails to become bent. When necessary, grievants use a hand rake to release nails jammed in the hopper.

6. The Packer folds packages and places them alternately on the two automatic scales. When the packages are full, the machine cuts off automatically. If the feeders are not adjusted properly, either too many or not enough nails may go into the box. When the scale shows that the weight in the package is not correct, the Packer must remove or add the proper number of nails, and make any necessary adjustments. Grievants must also use test weights to make sure that the scales are balanced, and they must lubricate the motors about every two hours.

7. According to the Company the initial adjustments take about 15 or 20 minutes, and different adjustments are normally required only when there is a change in the size or type of nail being run—about once every two or three days. The Union disputes these estimates as to the frequency with which the machine has to be set up and adjusted for different sizes or types of nails. The nails, usually one of three types, are packed in 1, 2 or 5 pound packages.

8. When the package on the scale is full, the Packer folds the top and places it on a belt conveyor. At the other end of the conveyor the Packer places the packages in a

50 pound carton which he has folded and stitched together, seals the carton, stencils it, and slides it to a pallet on the floor.

CONTENTIONS OF THE PARTIES

9. For purposes of comparison the Union relies principally on a description and classification, proposed by local Management in 1950, for a job of Machine Packer —Set Up (Job Class 10). The Company claims, however, that no one was ever paid on the basis of this description and classification. There was experimentation with a machine that was installed, but it was finally discarded as unworkable. Moreover, although the scale weighing mechanism of that machine was similar to grievants', the equipment as designed also included a multigraph machine which had to be set up and adjusted, and various heads and plungers on automatic package folding equipment had to be removed, replaced and aligned on size changes. Moreover, a package closing unit had to be removed, replaced and set up for each box size change. Grievants are not responsible for such complex machinery.

10. According to the Company adjustments required of grievants are less complicated. It believes that more appropriate references may be found in Specimen Example 1756 for a Packer (Job Class 2) and in a job of Packer—Small Packages (Job Class 3) in the Small Nail Packaging Department at Joliet Works. The latter job performs essentially the following: folds small cardboard packages, manually weighs the required amount of nails on a balance scale and fills the packages, closes and labels the packages, places the packages in shipping cartons, and closes and labels the cartons.

11. Management contends that Factors 1 and 2 for the job in dispute should be rated no higher than the Packer—Small Packages job. With respect to Factor 5, the Company notes that the Packer—Small Packages job handles the same material and it is coded in the "B" level. Furthermore, it characterizes the Union position on this Factor as an afterthought. Only after the Company referred in the Fourth Step of the grievance procedure to a Rankin Works job of Packer (Automatic Scale) (Job Class 3), coded at D.8 in Factor 5, did the Union request a higher rating on this Factor. For Factor 6 the rating, according to Management, should not be as high as that for a truck driver—in the "C" level.

12. The Company believes that Factors 9 and 10 should be coded the same as for the Packer—Small Packages. The greatest physical effort of the job in dispute is found in the handling of 50 pound cartons. Incumbents of the job of Packer—Small Nail Orders at Joliet Works handle more 50 pound cartons and heavier orders, yet even that job is coded at B.3 in Factor 10. On heavy orders, however, the Union claims that two girls in the latter job work together. With respect to Factor 11, Management notes that all other jobs in the Small Nail Packaging Room are coded at A Base. And the noise of the vibrators on the new machine, cited by the Union, is not appreciably greater than the noise to which the Packers—Small Packages have always been subjected since their job was described and classified. For Factor 12, the Company claims, the rating should be the same as for Packer—Small Packages, because the latter handles nails manually all the time. No greater danger of nail punctures or scratches exists in the job in dispute.

13. The Union stresses that the incumbent of Specimen Example 1756 and the Packer—Small Packages at Joliet Works simply perform hand packing operations and related duties. The same is true of a Rankin Works job of Packer (Nail Packaging, Small Packages), relied upon by the Company. Moreover, the Union notes that the coding of a Rankin Works job of Packer (Automatic Scale), stressed by Management in its brief, was not followed in the Company coding of the job in dispute. And finally, the status of the classification of this Rankin Works job was further clouded by conflicting testimony of witnesses from Rankin Works as to whether a timely grievance, protesting the classification, is pending.

FINDINGS

14. It is clear that no useful purpose would be served in this case by a prolonged and extensive analysis. The new machinery operated by grievants is unique. All jobs cited for the Board's consideration are obviously distinguishable from the job in dispute with the possible exception of the Rankin Works job of Packer (Automatic Scale). The classification of that job, however, cannot be given any controlling significance. Not only did the Company depart from the ratings of that job in the coding of several Factors for the job in dispute, but a grievance protesting the classification of that job may also be pending.

15. On the other hand, although no job called to the Board's attention is identical with the job in dispute, there are some similarities between grievants' job and the jobs relied upon by the parties. Using descriptions and classifications for all of these jobs as

guides, the Board concludes that the following ratings are appropriate for the job in dispute.

FACTORS	PROPER CODING	
1. Pre-employment training.	B	.3
2. Employment training and experience.	B	.4
3. Mental skill.	B	1.0
4. Manual skill.	C	1.0
5. Responsibility for materials.	D	.8
6. Responsibility for tools and equipment.	B	.3
7. Responsibility for operations.	A	Base
8. Responsibility for safety of others.	A	Base
9. Mental effort.	B	.5
10. Physical effort.	B	.3
11. Surroundings.	A	Base
12. Hazards.	A	Base
Total		4.6

AWARD

16. The grievance is sustained to the extent that the job of Packer (Automatic Scales) is placed in Job Class 5.

T—288. Fairfield Tin Mill. March 31, 1955
Herbert L. Sherman, Jr., *Arbitrator*
Approved by Sylvester Garrett, *Chairman*

BACKGROUND

1. In this grievance the Union seeks a higher job class than Class 4 installed by the Company for the new job of Floor Sweeper Operator at the Fairfield Tin Mill. This job, whose primary function is to operate a gasoline powered sweeper with a vacuum cleaner attachment to suck up the dust and dirt in the aisles and other nearby areas, was installed unilaterally by the Company in March, 1952, after the parties had failed to reach agreement on the description and classification.

2. To support its proposed ratings, Management relies on the Floor Sweeper Operator job at the Fairfield Sheet Mill, coded identically with the job in dispute, and nine Floor Sweeper Operator jobs, also in Job Class 4, in Central Operations. The Fairfield Sheet Mill job was originally installed in Job Class 3. During the 1951 Review Program, however, this job was reviewed and placed in Job Class 4 by agreement of top level representatives of the parties. The nine Job Class 4 Floor Sweeper Operator jobs in Central Operations consist of one at Duquesne Works, two at Fairless Works, four at the Gary Sheet and Tin Mill, and two at Gary Steel Works.

3. The Union emphasizes that there is no Specimen Example for a Floor Sweeper Operator, and asks the Board to take a "fresh look" at the job in dispute. It argues that the classification pattern established in Central Operations is not controlling. The Union further asserts that the Sheet Mill Floor Sweeper Operator job is distinguishable because the Sheet Mill is not as large as the Tin Mill, and does not have as much active floor space. It feels that since there

may be more equipment and employees in the path of grievant, his job should receive higher ratings on Factors 1 and 2, and particularly on Factors 6 and 8. Also stressed by the Union was the fact that grievant goes outside several times each day to empty his machine and to shovel his dirt into Dempster Dumpster containers. In addition, grievant sweeps an outside area immediately adjoining the M. and E. building. The Union, therefore, seeks a higher rating on Factor 11 —Surroundings.

4. With respect to Factor 7—Responsibility for Operations, the Union calls attention to the fact that grievant follows a printed, definite schedule, and that operating personnel look for him at stated times during the day.

5. Finally, the Union notes that the Floor Sweeper Operator job at New Haven Works, which was considered by the Board in A-557, is in Job Class 5. That job has higher ratings on Factors 6, 8 and 11 than the job in dispute. Management notes, however, that the Board was not classifying the New Haven job in that case, and that, in denying the grievance, the Board only considered the four Factors in dispute. Those Factors—1, 2, 3 and 9—are coded the same as the present job in dispute.

DISCUSSION AND FINDINGS

6. On a plant visit the Board devoted over two hours to an examination of the Floor Sweeper Operator jobs at the Fairfield Tin Mill and the Fairfield Sheet Mill. The entire routes followed by incumbents were covered. The equipment used and the surrounding circumstances were observed.

7. The Board finds no significant differ-

ence between these two jobs. The working procedures of these jobs are identical. Both jobs operate Tennant floor sweepers. Both jobs follow definite, printed schedules. Incumbents of both jobs go outside several times each day to dump their loads and to shovel dirt into Dempster Dumpster containers. Both jobs do a relatively small amount of sweeping in outside areas immediately adjoining the buildings. Although the Tin Mill may have more active floor space than the Sheet Mill, the Board finds no significant difference in this respect in the Floor Sweeper Operator jobs servicing these Mills. Both jobs operate in many open areas, and in many areas which may be characterized as congested. Both jobs go off the aisles and sweep as close to equipment and materials as the practicalities of the situation allow. There are areas in both Mills which the Sweepers cannot clean because of congestion of equipment and materials.

8. On the basis of the Board's observations, it must be concluded that the job in dispute is properly classified at Job Class 4.

AWARD

9. The grievance is denied.

A—309. Worcester Works. January 25, 1949

Ralph T. Seward, *Chairman*

BACKGROUND

1. The dispute in this case involves the following grievance filed on April 4, 1947:

"This grievance is entered against the classification on the Lewis Travel Cut Str. & Cut Machine. We believe that there has not been enough consideration given to some of the factors. (Factors 3-5-6-7-9-10.) Entered under the 1-13-47 Agreement. We ask that this job be reviewed and corrected."

2. Under the Wage Inequity Program, the Union and the Company established job descriptions and job classifications for occupations throughout the entire Company, including jobs on various Straighten and Cut machines. This was done at the Worcester Plant for the Operator of the Straighten and Cut Machine in the Rail Bond Division of the Spring Mill, and the Operator of the Large Lewis Travel Cut Machine in the Straighten and Cut Division of the Wire Mill.

3. Subsequently, the Company installed the Lewis Travel Cut 10-F Machine and prepared a proposed job description and classification for the Operator on this machine. The parties agreed on the description, but were unable to agree upon the classification. Therefore, on or about March 5, 1947, the Company installed its description and classification despite the lack of agreement. The above mentioned grievance was then filed.

4. The parties are in agreement on the following factors for purposes of classification:

FACTOR	CODE	CLASSI-FICATION
1—Pre-employment Training	B	.3
2—Employment Training and Experience	C	.8
4—Manual Skill	B	.5
8—Responsibility for Safety of Others	B	.4
	Total	2.0

5. The parties are in disagreement concerning the following factors:

FACTOR	COMPANY CLASSIFICATION CODE	COMPANY CLASSIFICATION	UNION CLASSIFICATION CODE	UNION CLASSIFICATION
3—Mental Skill	C	1.6	D	2.2
5—Responsibility for Material	C	.7	C	1.2
6—Responsibility for Tools and Equipment	C low	.4	C	.7
7—Responsibility for Operations	C	1.0	D	2.0
9—Mental Effort	C	1.0	D	1.5
10—Physical Effort	C	.8	D	1.5
	Total	5.5	Total	9.1

6. The Company's evaluation at 7.5 places the job in Labor Grade 8. The Union's evaluation at 11.1 would place the job in Labor Grade 11.

7. In support of its position, the Company points out that throughout all the other plants the Union and the Company have uniformly evaluated Straighten and Cut Operators at 6.6, or Labor Grade 7, and that the point value assigned by the parties to each of the elements in dispute in this case is identical with that assigned by the Company.

(Special allowances on Factor 8, "Responsibility for Safety of Others," and Factor 9, "Mental Effort," were made on this machine because it is located in unusually crowded quarters and because it is used occasionally to handle strand wire. These two special elements account for the Company's placing the job in Labor Grade 8, rather than 7 as elsewhere, but they are not material for the purposes of this dispute. According to the Company, there is no consequential difference otherwise between this machine and the various other machines throughout the Company.)

8. The Union contends that these elements should be adjusted upward in order to give proper weight to them in view of the work of the Operators, and that it is inequitable to give the same evaluation on the disputed elements as was given on the other Straighten and Cut machines in Worcester, since the requirements on the Lewis Travel Cut 10-F Machine are much more difficult.

FINDINGS

9. In the briefs and during the hearing, the parties proceeded at length to support their respective positions and went into great detail as to the operation of the Lewis Travel Cut 10-F Machine and the work of the Operator. The Board feels that it is unnecessary to reproduce the evidence, factor by factor, or to engage in a detailed analysis of the various arguments.

10. It appears to the Board that the sources of the Union's desire for a higher classification are the nature of the material processed and the role this machine plays in the plant, rather than any differences in the machine itself. According to the Union, the other machines generally have long runs of the same material, with a relatively narrower range of sizes, and with fewer die changes, etc. This machine, however, is, in effect, a jobbing machine. It is used to process many types of miscellaneous material. There are, according to the Union, very short runs with frequent change-overs to other sizes. These conditions necessitate frequent die changes; and, according to the Union, the Operator is required to be more adept at such things.

According to the Union, an inept Operator on this machine can be a bottleneck for a number of other operations which depend on the output of this machine for raw material.

11. It will be noted from this summary that the Union's case rests primarily upon the difficulty of operating the machine itself under these circumstances, as contrasted with other Straighten and Cut machines at Worcester in certain respects. Very little, if any, comparison was made with the bench mark jobs set forth in the official Wage Inequity Manual of the parties. No comparison or contrast was made with regard to Straighten and Cut machines in other plants of the Company. In a nutshell, the Union says this Operator has some problems.

12. The Company not only disagrees with the stress placed by the Union on the responsibilities of the Operator of this machine, but also points out that no other Straighten and Cut Operator in the entire Company received the evaluations requested by the Union for the elements in dispute here. The Company claims that the problems alleged by the Union are also common to machines in the other plants. There is no evidence from the Union to refute this information. It might be added that the Board has knowledge of at least one other substantially similar, if not identical, Straighten and Cut Machine in another plant which is operated on a jobbing basis, processing a great variety of material for relatively short runs. This machine occupies the same role in that plant as the machine in dispute occupies in Worcester. The classification of that Operator by the parties there is identical with the proposal of the Company here.

13. Considering all the arguments of the parties and particularly the classifications which the Company and the Union have established throughout the entire Company, the Board concludes that the evidence in this case does not warrant granting the Union's request.

AWARD

14. The grievance is denied.

A—327. Worcester South Works.   January 25, 1949
Ralph T. Seward, *Chairman*

BACKGROUND

1. The dispute in this case involves the following grievance, filed on April 5, 1947:

"This grievance is entered against the classification of the job of Str. and Cut

Helper Lewis Travel Cut. We feel that it takes as much, or more, mental effort to be a helper here as on some of the other helpers jobs. We ask that this job be reviewed and corrected. Filed under the January 13, 1947 Agreement."

2. The background and history applicable to this particular grievance have already been discussed by the Board in Case A-309, which involved the Operator on the same machine, and the Board feels it unnecessary to repeat the discussion in A-309.

3. The parties are in agrement on the following factors for purposes of classifications in this case:

FACTOR	CODE	CLASSI- FICATION
1—Pre-employment Training	A	Base
2—Employment Training and Experience	A	Base
3—Mental Skill	B	1.0
4—Manual Skill	B	.5
5—Responsibility for Material	B	.3
6—Responsibility for Tools and Equipment	A	Base
7—Responsibility for Operations	B	.5
8—Responsibility for Safety of Others	A	Base
Total		2.3

4. The parties are in disagreement concerning the following factors:

FACTOR	COMPANY CODE	CLASSIFI- CATION	UNION CODE	CLASSIFI- CATION
9—Mental Effort	B	.5	C	1.0
10—Physical Effort	C	.8	D	1.5
Total		1.3		2.5

5. The Company's evaluation at 3.6 places the job in Labor Grade 4. The Union's evaluation of 4.8 would place the job in Labor Grade 5.

6. The Union contends that the disputed factors should be re-evaluated in accordance with the Union's request in order to give what the Union considers to be proper weight to these elements on the job in question. It will be noted that the grievance makes reference to an allegation that this

job is as difficult as some other Helpers' jobs in the mill. The Union did not name any such job during the discussion of this case in the Third or Fourth Step, according to the minutes thereof. Towards the end of the hearing the Union finally made an offhand reference to one or two Helpers' jobs, but did not proceed to make any detailed comparison.

7. The Company contends that proper weight has been given to the elements in dispute. The Company claims that this job is similar to that of the Straighten and Cut Helper on the large Lewis Machine in the Wire Mill, where the allowances made by the parties jointly on these factors are identical with those made by the Company here. It further points out that in the instance of Straighten and Cut Helpers throughout the Company, the parties jointly gave the same point evaluations to these factors as those given by the Company here, and that the other jobs are substantially similar or identical to the job in question. All the Straighten and Cut Helpers are placed in Labor Grade 4 with the exception of one situation where the Helper was placed in Labor Grade 3. Nowhere was the Helper placed in Labor Grade 5.

FINDINGS

8. The source of the Union's complaint and the procedure followed by the Union in advancing its claim are substantially similar in nature to the situation in Case A-309. The elements in dispute here were also in dispute in Case A-309.

9. The position taken by the Company is likewise substantially similar to the position it took in A-309.

10. Here, as in A-309, the factor comparison made by the Company between this job and the same job on similar or identical machines throughout the Company, has not been refuted by the Union.

11. In view of the foregoing facts as applied in A-309, since the reasoning and the conclusions are equally applicable to the job involved in this case, the Board does not feel that the evidence would justify the granting of the Union's request.

AWARD

12. The grievance is denied.

T—69. Ensley Works.   September 15, 1948
Ralph T. Seward, *Chairman*

BACKGROUND FACTS

1. The dispute in this case involves the following grievance filed in the Blowing Engine House, Bessemer Converters, Open

Hearth Department, Ensley Works, on July 21, 1947:

"Management has combined the occupations of Blowing Engineers, Plant Code

911-385 and Second Blowing Engineer, Plant Code 911-390 and has submitted a new job description and classification, Plant Code 911-390, 1st Blowing Engineer. We allege that the new job is improperly classified under the job description and classification procedure of the May 8, 1946 Agreement. We request that this job be reclassified and consideration given to the added duties and responsibilities.

Signed: J. G. Carter 1757
G. H. Morris 1756
W. R. Kaler 1745"

2. These employees operate one 4,000 HP G. E. electric blower, one 2,800 HP Ingersoll-Rand steam turbo-blower, and one cross-compound Allis-Chalmers blowing engine, as required, to supply air blasts for making steel in the Bessemer converters. The Allis-Chalmers blowing engine, however, is used only when one of the other blowers is down for repairs or inspection, and is considered principally a stand-by unit.

3. For several years prior to December, 1946, the Blowing Engineer operated the electric blower, and the Second Blowing Engineer operated the steam turbo-blower. When the parties classified the various jobs in accordance with the May 8, 1946 Agreement, the Blowing Engineer was placed in Job Class 13 and the Second Blowing Engineer was placed in Job Class 9.

4. In December, 1946, the control panel of the electric blower was moved to a position adjacent to the steam turbo-blower. One man is now able to operate both units at the same time. This resulted in the elimination of the position of Second Blowing Engineer except on those occasions when it is necessary to use the Allis-Chalmers blowing engine.

5. On July 10, 1947, the Company presented a new description and classification to cover the above changes. The occupational title was changed from Blowing Engineer to that of First Blowing Engineer, but the job classification remained Job Class 13.

6. The parties agreed to the new job description, but were unable to agree upon the appropriate job class. Thereupon, the Company installed the classification effective July 13, 1947, and the employees filed the grievance previously quoted, asking for Job Class 15.

7. The parties have agreed upon the following factors and points assigned to them on the First Blowing Engineer occupation:

JOB CLASSIFICATION FACTOR	POINTS
2. Employment Training and Experience	F-2.0

3. Mental Skill	D-2.2
4. Manual Skill	B-0.5
7. Responsibility for Operations	E-3.0
9. Mental Effort	C-1.0
10. Physical Effort	B-0.3
12. Hazards	B-0.4
Total	9.4

8. The parties are in disagreement regarding the following factors and points:

		POINTS	
JOB CLASS FACTOR		COMPANY	UNION
1. Pre-Employment Training		B-0.3	C-1.0
5. Responsibility for Materials		B-0.3	C-0.5
6. Responsibility for Tools and Equipment		DH-2.0	EH-3.0
8. Responsibility for Safety of Others		B-0.4	C-0.8
11. Surroundings		B-0.4	C-0.8
	Totals	3.4	6.1

9. According to the Company's calculations, the job has a point value of 12.8 and therefore belongs in Job Class 13. According to the Union's calculations, the job has a point value of 15.5, which would place it in Job Class 16; but the Union is asking for only Job Class 15.

10. It would appear from the Fourth Step Minutes in this case that the principal item of the disagreement, according to the Union, is Factor 6, Responsibility for Tools and Equipment.

FINDINGS

10. With regard to its contention concerning Factor 1, Pre-Employment Training, the Union bases its claim on ". . . the requisites of familiarity with numerous signals, ability to read temperature charts, gauges, etc., and proper application of water." No additional evidence is offered. However, it is interesting to note that all those things were required, and are still required, of the Second Blowing Engineer; and yet the parties agreed that 0.3 was correct. Accordingly, the Board is unable to see why a point value of 1.0 should be granted for those duties alone in view of the other agreement.

11. With regard to Factor 5, Responsibility for Materials, the Union simply calls attention to the fact that this is the point value given to Turbine Engineer and the Pressure Pump Engineer on this Factor. Be-

yond calling the Board's attention to that fact, the Union offers nothing to support its claim. There is no evidence to show any similarity between the Turbine or Pressure Pump Engineer and the First Blowing Engineer on this score. Nor is any reason shown why the value of 0.3 which the parties previously established for both the old Blowing Engineer and Second Blowing Engineer should not be continued. Consequently, there is no basis for accepting the Union's argument on this point.

12. According to the Fourth Step Minutes, the principal source of dissatisfaction seems to stem from the Company's evaluation of Factor 6, Responsibility for Tools and Equipment. The Union claims that the situation here is comparable to that of the Turbine Engineer, who received 3.0, on the grounds that the same high degree of sustained care and attention is required. However, the Board has been given this contention with virtually no factual evidence to support the claim of similarity.

13. The Company denies the similarity alleged by the Union, pointing out first that a turbo-generator costs about five times as much as a turbo-blower. (The Union argues that the relative expensiveness of the equipment is immaterial.) The Company claims the conditions on these two operations named by the Union are wholly different. According to the Company, the new job is more nearly comparable to that of the Blast Furnace Blowing Engineer, who received 1.0 by agreement of the parties, or the First Steam Engineer, who operates four steam engines blowing air for the Bessemer converters, and who was assigned 2.0.

14. It is difficult for the Board to see why the relative value of the equipment is not a relevant factor in determining the responsibility for tools and equipment and the probable damage which might be caused by the employee.

15. As to the degree of care and attention, since the Union supplied no factual data, the Board has compared the job de-

scriptions of First Blowing Engineer and the Turbine Engineer and has been unable to find any such evidence as would establish the alleged similarity. If anything, the various job descriptions show at least as much, if not more, similarity between the First Blowing Engineer and the occupations named by the Company.

16. Therefore, the evidence before the Board is not such as would justify the Board's establishing a point value of 3.0 for this element.

17. As to Factor 8, Responsibility for the Safety of Others, the Union argues that the change ". . . involves more people working around the Bessemer Converter." Except for the fact that the First Blowing Engineer controls both blowers, there has been no change in operations, certainly not at the site of the vessels. The First Blowing Engineer is still at the same distance from the converter and is still directed by signals from the Bessemer Blower as in the past. There has been no increase in the number of vessels. The Board is unable to see how this change alone at the Blowing Engine House should suddenly result in an increase in the number of people present in the vicinity of the Bessemer converter. The parties previously agreed on 0.4 for both the Blowing Engineer and the Second Blowing Engineer on this Factor, and the Board believes that allowance is equally applicable here.

18. The last point of disagreement is Factor 11, Surroundings. An analysis of the facts indicates that, if anything, the Union's argument is based upon a feeling that the original allowance of 0.4 for the Blowing Engineer and the Second Blowing Engineer is inadequate. The First Blowing Engineer is still working in the same vicinity, and the mere movement of a panel could not have increased the previous dirt, grease, or noise.

19. For these reasons, the grievance is denied.

AWARD

20. The grievance is denied.

USC—764. Homestead District Works. May 15, 1959

John R. Coleman, *Assistant to the Chairman*

Approved by Sylvester Garrett, *Chairman*

BACKGROUND

1. The installation of a 160″ Plate Treating Line at the Homestead District Works, Central Operations, United States Steel Corporation, in 1956, gave rise to a dispute as to

the proper classification of the job of Plate Leveler Operator (4456-4988). On February 21, 1957, this grievance was entered.

2. The Union's requests compared with present classification are as follows:

FACTOR	COMPANY'S PRESENT CLASSI-FICATION	UNION'S PROPOSED CLASSI-FICATION
2—Employment Train-ing & Experience	B- .4	C- .8
3—Mental Skill	C-1.6	D-2.2
5—Responsibility for Materials	C- .5	C-1.2
7—Responsibility for Operations	C-1.0	D-2.0

3. The job in question was viewed by the Arbitrator, as were two other jobs on which Company or Union placed heavy reliance for comparative purposes. The Company's choice of a comparable job was the Leveler Operator in the 100″ Normalizing Mill; the Union chose the job of Roller Leveler Operator (0632-0662) in the Heat Treating and Forge Department, known as the Harvey Shop. Both the 100″ Normalizing and the Harvey jobs were seen in operation, but the subject job was not in normal operation at the time of the Arbitrator's visit. However, the operator on the job made several passes of plates through the leveler to demonstrate its functioning.

4. The Plate Leveler Operator works in a pulpit above the 160″ Plate Treating Line. Here he operates controls to move plates back and forth through a McKay Leveler on which he has made settings in accordance with his information as to the size of the plate and his manual on the machine. His normal inspection of plates to see if they are satisfactorily flattened by the Leveler is visual from the booth; occasionally, however, he makes a visual inspection from the floor level beside the line. But he does not use instruments for any precise determination of relative flatness.

5. There has been variety in the types of plates processed through the Leveler, but the major emphasis is upon stainless steel plates which are treated cold. When the quench in the Plate Treating Line works well, the hot plates passing through the line do not require leveling.

DISCUSSION AND FINDINGS

Factor 2—*Employment Training and Experience*

Union position	—	C- .8
Company position	—	B- .4

6. There are a number of jobs of Leveler Operator (Specimen 369 and the First Leveler Operator on the 100″ Plate Mill at Homestead are examples) rated as the Union urges here. But there are also jobs with similar titles (Specimen 2233 and the Leveler Operator on the 100″ Normalizing Mill) rated at the Company's lower figure of B-.4. An on-the-spot study of the subject job suggests that it has more in common with what appears to be the content of the lower-rated jobs than with the content of the higher ones. The training time for this job must be less than for the C-.8 examples since the latter call for building up a body of skills and a sense of judgment, in set-ups and operations alike, greater than is expected of the 160″ Operator. A training period from three to six months adequately reflects the requirements of this latter job. Hence the rating of B-.4, proposed by the Company, is a better fit than the Union's suggested seven to twelve months and .8 points.

Factor 3—*Mental Skill*

Union position	—	D-2.2
Company position	—	C-1.6

7. A rating of D-2.2 as requested by the Union cannot be sustained either by comparison to other jobs observed or to specimen jobs in the Manual or by reference to the language of the Manual. The Plate Leveler Operator's work is semi-routine in nature, encompassing the degree of variety and judgment incorporated in a rating of C-1.6. Certainly the mental skill called for in the Harvey Shop job, rated at D-2.2, is considerably higher than in the subject job. The Harvey Shop operator is called upon to make judgments on such matters as whether or not a particular plate should go through the leveler, and whether or not dummy plates need to be run through with it to produce the desired straightness. The mental skill required in knowing how and where to use dummy plates for the optimum results is by itself more than is called for from the job in dispute here.

Factor 5—*Responsibility for Materials*

Union position	—	C-1.2
Company position	—	C- .5

8. The dispute here concerns only the dollar value to be attached to the degree of responsibility. Kinking of the plate or a nicked or battered plate end is the most likely form of damage which the operator of the leveler might cause. From the evidence presented, it seems clear that a rating of C-.5, representing up to $50 damage, adequately considers the cost involved in salvaging any plate so harmed.

Factor 7—*Responsibility for Operations*

Union position	—	D-2.0
Company position	—	C-1.0

9. The core of the Union's case for a higher rating here is comparison with the Harvey Shop job and with such other leveler jobs as Specimens 369, 2233, and Leveler Operator (4640-4648) on the 100″ Plate Mill at Homestead. The comparison with the Harvey Shop job is not a good one, however, since the incumbent there directs the work of a crew of at least six men. Moreover, all of the specimen leveler jobs rated at 2.0 appear from their descriptions to be jobs more intimately tied in to a whole production line or else to involve more operations pressure through working with a larger fraction of hot plates than the Leveler Operator on the 160″ line normally encounters. There is no subsequent operation at Homestead dependent on the work of the Leveler Operator. It is true that this operator may upon occasion have to call the Plate Treating Furnace Operator to ask him to hold up on sending further plates through to the Leveler, but this is infrequent enough and involves little enough interference with production to make a rating of C-1.0 right for the job. This is essentially an individual processing unit where continuity of production is expected; the Company's proposed rating of C-1.0 correctly reflects this.

AWARD

10. The grievance is denied. The Company has properly classified the job of Plate Leveler Operator in the 160″ Plate Treating line at 7.0 for Job Class 7.

USC—765. Homestead District Works. May 15, 1959
John R. Coleman, *Assistant to the Chairman*
Approved by Sylvester Garrett, *Chairman*

BACKGROUND

1. This grievance arose out of installation of a 160″ Plate Treating Line at the Homestead District Works, Central Operations, United States Steel Corporation. The Union claimed on February 21, 1957, that the Company had improperly classified the job of Plate Treating Furnace Operator (4456-4981) on this new installation.

2. Specifically, the Union requests the following ratings on seven disputed factors:

FACTOR	COMPANY'S PRESENT CLASSI- FICATION	UNION'S PROPOSED CLASSI- FICATION
1—Pre-employment Training	B- .3	C- 1.0
2—Employment Training & Experience	D-1.2	F-2.0
3—Mental Skill	D-2.2	E-2.8
5—Responsibility for Materials	D-1.6	D-3.5
6—Responsibility for Tools & Equipment	Med. D-1.5	High E-3.0
7—Responsibility for Operations	D-2.0	E-3.0
9—Mental Effort	C-1.0	D-1.5

3. The Union's case rests primarily upon comparison between the job of Plate Treating Furnace Operator and another Homestead job, Forging Heater (0631-0601), which is classified at 18.2 for Job Class 18.

The Arbitrator observed those two jobs and one other furnace job, Normalizing Furnace Operator (4657-4774), at the Homestead Works.

4. For its part, the Company relies on a broad range of jobs of furnace operators in the industry, such as Specimens 618, 2225, 2226, and 3350, and jobs numbered 0240-0283 and 5762-6452, to name only six of the total of sixteen cited as examples. All of these other jobs are in Job Class 12 or less with the exception of two, Specimen 618 and Job 5540-4510, which are in Job Class 13 principally because of Factor 9.

5. The job in question is a control job. The operator, working in a booth above the plating line, controls furnace and quench roller tables, plus transfer cars and by-pass tables, enabling him to move steel plates through his hardening furnace, into a water quench, into a tempering furnace or into a stainless steel heat-treating furnace. Engineered capacity is 6000 tons of plate a month. Television viewers, colored lights, and sound systems supplement visual controls over the process.

6. The operator gets the number of each plate going through his line from the craneman who delivered it to the furnace. An order sheet then tells him the proper temperature and time for the hardening of that plate in the furnace. The water quench is a matter of judgment for the operator. On the average, plates go through the line about once every 20 minutes; but it is possible for the operator to have several plates in his line at once, each in a different furnace.

DISCUSSION AND FINDINGS

Factor 1—*Pre-Employment Training*

Union position	—	C-1.0
Company position	—	B- .3

7. A rating here of B-.3 appears to be well substantiated by comparison with the many specimens cited by the Company (for example, Specimens 255, 618, 2226) and by reference to the language of the Manual ("Perform work of a nonrepetitive or semi-repetitive nature where judgment is required to obtain results . . . Set up and operate machines or processes requiring a variety of adjustments.") Certainly the mentality required to learn the job of Forgings Heater, rated at C-1.0, is greater than for the present job. The complexity of the details associated with the Forgings Heater's job cannot be found in sufficient degree in this new job to justify any rating above B-.3.

Factor 2—*Employment Training and Experience*

Union position	—	F- 2.0
Company position	—	D-1.2

8. Again the specimens cited by the Company, all rated at D-1.2 or lower, are more comparable to this Furnace Operator's job than is the Forgings Heater's job. There is considerable learning required, but this is adequately compensated for in a rating of D-1.2, representing 13 to 18 months' training time.

Factor 3—*Mental Skill*

Union position	—	E-2.8
Company position	—	D-2.2

9. There is complexity to the total unit under the Furnace Operator's responsibility, and this complexity is not removed by the presence of various automatic controls and guiding devices. But parallels to this job are found in many specimens in the Manual rated at D-2.2. This would appear to be just the kind of job that the Manual refers to in its language for D-2.2 ratings: "Use considerable judgment in operating equipment." This rating is a much closer fit than would be obtained through applying the E-2.8 classification of the Forging Heater. The Heater normally is engaged in considerably more planning in the placing of forgings in his furnaces and in the strict maintenance of temperatures than is expected of the Furnace Operator. The D-2.2 rating proposed by the Company is correct for the Furnace Operator.

Factor 5—*Responsibility for Materials*

Union position	—	D-1.6
Company position	—	D-3.5

10. The only difference between the parties on this factor concerns the dollar value of any plates damaged passing through the treating line. It seems evident from all the testimony that it is normally possible to re-treat any plates which may not meet standards after their initial heat treatment. Only where a plate buckles so badly that it has to be burned out is there likely to be sufficient damage to warrant the rating sought by the Union, and this situation occurs so seldom that the rating sought by the Union is unsupportable.

Factor 6—*Responsibility for Tools and Equipment*

Union position	— High —	E-3.0
Company position	— Med. —	D-1.5

11. The possibility of damage to equipment on this job is certainly sufficient to call for reasonably close attention from the operator throughout the turn. However, his speeds are not so high nor are his ways of damaging equipment so numerous that he needs to give his work the sustained high degree of care characteristic of jobs rated at E-3.0 in the steel industry. The Company's specimen comparisons here are apparently valid. A rating of Med.—D-1.5 correctly describes the factor of responsibility for equipment.

Factor 7—*Responsibility for Operations*

Union position	—	E-3.0
Company position	—	D-2.0

12. The Furnace Operator's work is not closely tied in with other operations at Homestead. The 160″ Heat Treating Line is a physically large unit, as the Union has pointed out, but this by itself does not make it the "major producing unit" spoken of in the Manual's job requirements for a Factor 7 rating of 3.0. In the absence of any relevant specimen jobs to support the Union's claims for a higher rating, the rating of 2.0 proposed by the Company must stand as correct.

Factor 9—*Mental Effort*

Union position	—	D-1.5
Company position	—	C- 1.0

13. Once again, when the Furnace Operator is compared with the Forgings Heater, it is evident that the former's job is the less demanding of the two. The Furnace Oper-

ator does not have as narrow tolerances to work with, does not make the same level of decisions in building and maintaining heats on his job, and is generally not required to make the same fine adjustments as is the Forgings Heater. His job obviously requires alertness throughout the turn, especially since the various control and detection devices are not yet functioning at a high level of efficiency. But the absence of high speeds, close coordination, and close tolerances makes it a C-1.0 job rather than a D-1.5 job such as the Forgings Heater.

AWARD

14. The grievance is denied. The Company has properly classified the job of Furnace Operator on the 160″ Plate Treating Line at 11.8 for Job Class 12.

CHAPTER 12

FACTOR BY FACTOR APPROACH

The first two cases in this chapter, decided by Sylvester Garrett, contain passages relevant to the point suggested by the title of the chapter. The next two cases, decided by the editor of this book, should be read together as an illustration of the factor by factor approach. And the last two cases, decided by Jacob Blair, are related to each other and should be read together. The award in USC-532, which may be found at p. 325, is also relevant to this chapter.

USC—741. Fairless Works. December 22, 1958
Sylvester Garrett, *Chairman*

BACKGROUND

1. This grievance protests classification of a new job (6520-6216), Tractor Operator, in the Fairless Works. The job was established specifically to operate a flat body Clark Truck-Tractor to service plant track labor gangs in the Transportation and General Services Department.

2. The Tractor Operator hauls tools, materials and equipment to the track gangs when they work in areas not easily serviced by a Rail Car Operator whose operations transporting tools and material are limited to the intra-plant rail system, and subordinate to other uses of the railroad. When not transporting materials, the Tractor Operator works as a member of the track gang, about 60% of his time.

3. The job has been classified by the Company at 7.0 for Job Class 7. The Union contends that the codings of Factors 3, 7 and 8 are inappropriate and the job belongs in Class 9. During Fourth Step, however, the Union indicated that Class 8 would be acceptable.

4. The Company maintains the job is coded properly on the basis of similar jobs at the Fairless Works, and stresses that the Tractor Operator performs exactly the same function as the Rail Car Operator job (6520-6219), also in Class 7 and in the same department. It believes a higher coding for the Tractor Operator in this circumstance would be manifestly unsound.

5. The Union stresses that a similar one-ton Clark Truck-Tractor in the Masonry Department at Fairless Works is operated by an employee in Job Class 8. Thus it seems grossly inequitable to the Union for the Operator of similar equipment in Transportation to receive a lesser rate. The Union also notes that, exclusive of the disputed job, 27 of 30 Tractor-Operator jobs in the Fairless Works are above Job Class 7.

6. The parties' positions as to Factor ratings are as follows:

FACTOR	COMPANY	UNION
1. Pre-Employment Training.	.3	.3
2. Employment Training and Experience.	.4	.4
*3. Mental Skill.	1.0	1.6
4. Manual Skill.	.5	.5
5. Responsibility for Materials.	B .3	B .3
6. Responsibility for Tools and Equipment.	C .7	C .7
*7. Responsibility for Operations.	Base	.5
*8. Responsibility for Safety of Others.	.8	1.2
9. Mental Effort.	1.0	1.0
10. Physical Effort.	.8	.8
11. Surroundings.	.8	.8
12. Hazards.	.4	.4
Total	7.0	8.5

* Factors in dispute.

7. The Company cites Specimens 317 and 980 as proper references for the instant job, and points also to numerous Class 6 and Class 7 Tractor-Operator jobs in Gary Sheet and Tin, Irvin Works, Gary Steel,

Johnstown Works, Duquesne Works and Fairless Works.

8. In reference to the Union's allegation that a Tractor-Operator job (8722-7450) in the Masonry Department is in Class 8 for operating identical equipment, the Company points out that actually there is no job separately described and classified for this purpose. Job 8722-7450 operates a fork lift tractor in coordination with Masonry crews and is in Class 8. There is also a Class 8 Truck Driver job filled from time to time in the Masonry Department. The fork lift tractor, the truck, and the Clark Truck-Tractor all are operated by employees scheduled out on the Tractor-Operator job (8722-7450) who are assigned as Truck Drivers to operate the truck as needed. Only rarely are such employees assigned to operate the Clark Truck-Tractor, since this equipment is used but rarely in the Masonry Department. To this the Union replies that, if a job operating the Clark Truck-Tractor were separately described and classified in the Masonry Department it probably would be in Class 8, because the Fork Lift Tractor Operator and Truck Driver already are in Class 8.

CONTENTIONS

9. *Factor 3:* The Union stresses that 28 of 30 Tractor-Operator jobs at Fairless are coded at 1.6 in this Factor. The Company cites Specimen 317 as operating the same type of equipment, hauling test pieces from the Billet and 40″ Blooming Mills to the laboratory, coded 1.0. The Company also stresses the Rail Car Operator job in this department with identical coding, doing the same work with the same labor gangs as the job in question. While the Company agrees that many Tractor-Operator jobs at Fairless are coded at 1.6, it notes that the specific job responsibilities of each job must be the basis for such a coding. As to Plant Code 8722-7450, coded 1.6, the Company notes that this results from operating a fork lift, which must be raised and lowered by variable controls in handling pallets and other materials. Job 8722-7452 at Fairless, Truck Driver, rates 1.6 under this Factor according to the Company because he operates a more complicated vehicle, is required to park in close quarters, and must have a thorough knowledge of the extensive plant roadway system.

10. *Factor 7:* This Factor is now at A-Base, while the Union seeks B .5. The Union feels that B .5 is amply justified in that 24 of 30 Tractor-Operator jobs at Fairless are coded 1.0. The Company argues that Base is proper because the Tractor Operator ob-

viously has exactly the same responsibility for operations as does the Rail Car Operator which is coded A-Base.

11. *Factor 8:* This now is rated .8 and the Union seeks 1.2 noting that 18 of 30 Tractor-Operator jobs in Fairless are coded 1.2, as are 2 of 3 jobs the Company cites to justify its Class 7 coding. The Company avers that since the incumbent spends 60% of his time working along with the Labor Gang the .8 is justified. It notes that Job 6520-6210 (Track Repairman) receives only .4 for this Factor and thus the Tractor Operator here is really in a .4 category 60% of his time. Specimen 317 gives .8 also, and the Operator there spends his time hauling material in and about the plant the same as occurs in the disputed job. Again, it calls attention to the Rail Car Operator receiving .8 even though he works less time with the Labor Gang. The Company admits Job 6174 gets D-1.2, but attributes this to the fact that the Operator is consistently working under congested conditions in the Roll Shop.

FINDINGS

12. *Factor 3* is properly rated at 1.0 on the basis of Specimens 317 and 980. Nor is there basis here to find substantial difference between this job and the Rail Car Operator for purposes of this Factor. Plant Code 8720 also seems fairly comparable. The Union's reliance on the fact that a preponderance of Tractor-Operator jobs at Fairless are coded 1.6 is not convincing since the coding of each job must be on the basis of a factor-by-factor analysis considering the specific requirements and circumstances relevant to each such factor.

13. *Factor 7* also is properly rated at Base in light of Specimens 317 and 980 and the Rail Car Operator job.

14. *Factor 8* is properly rated at .8. Specimen 317 is similarly coded and encompasses the operation of similar equipment in comparable type areas. The Rail Car Operator job, also coded at .8, operates in the same general areas, although on rails. Even assuming the areas here were sufficiently congested to warrant a D-1.2 coding for full time operation of the Tractor, moreover, about 60% of the Tractor Operators' work time consists of working along with the track labor gang, with employees coded at .4 in this Factor.

AWARD

15. The grievance is denied.

A—715. Joliet Works. July 25, 1956

Sylvester Garrett, *Chairman*

BACKGROUND

1. This grievance arises out of transfer from the Chicago Warehouse, into Joliet Works, of a job of Splicer (Wire Rope), PC 46-01. The job description was written March 25, 1953, preparatory to moving the work into the Joliet bargaining unit, and accepted by the Union. The Union contends that the description justifies Job Class 15 for the job, while the Company has instituted a rating of Class 11. The present grievance seeks to resolve this difference.

2. The major arguments of the Company and Union involve comparisons of the Joliet job with Specimen 1079 (Splicer); two comparable jobs at other works (24-33, Expert Splicer, at New Haven, and 20-21, Expert Splicer, at Trenton); a job of Welder (Rope Products), 26-13, which was broken out of the Splicer's job at New Haven in March, 1952, and the trade and craft Welder job.

DISCUSSION AND FINDINGS

3. The Splicer jobs at Joliet, New Haven, and Trenton are roughly comparable but involve important differences in amount and type of welding. Welding and burning at New Haven and Trenton take only a relatively small amount of the total time of men in the wire rope warehouses. Such work is performed either by special Welders at New Haven, or by a Gangleader at Trenton (assisted to a minor extent by two Splicers who have learned to burn and weld to the limited extent necessary). Welding at Joliet is more varied and an integral part of the work of all Splicers, who spend about half their time using welder's tools. In particular, Joliet Splicers are required to weld becket loops into rope ends, rather than simply to weld rope ends to prevent fraying, or to burn off strand ends after splicing. The nature and extent of this additional welding activity has led the Union to place considerable emphasis here on comparison with the trade and craft Welder Specimen, 1095.

4. The differing views of the parties as to Factor coding, as well as codings for other jobs thought relevant in the course of the proceedings, appear below:

	FACTOR	1	2	3	4	5	6	7	8	9	10	11	12	JOB CLASS
46.01	Splicer (Wire Rope)													
	Company Position	1.0	1.6	2.2	1.0	C .7		B .2		1.0	.4	1.0	.8 .4 .4	11
	Union Position	1.0	2.0	2.2	1.5	D 1.6		C .7		1.0	.8	1.5	1.5 .8 .8	15
Spec. 1079	Splicer (Rope & Cable)	.3	1.6	2.2	1.0	C .7		A Base		1.0	.4	1.0	.8 .4 .4	10
24-33	Expert Splicer (New Haven)	1.0	1.6	2.2	1.0	C .7		B .2		1.0	.4	1.0	.8 .4 .4	11
20-21	Expert Splicer (Trenton)	1.0	1.6	2.2	1.0	C .7		B .2		1.0	.4	1.0	.8 .4 .4	11
26-13	Welder (Rope Products) (New Haven)	.3	1.2	1.6	1.0	D 1.1		B .2		.5	.4	1.0	.3 .8 .4	9
Spec. 1106	Welder, Arc	1.0	1.2	2.2	1.5	D 1.1		B .2		1.0	.4	1.5	.8 .8 .4	12
Spec. 1095	Welder (Trade and Craft)	1.0	2.4	2.2	1.5	E 1.6		B .2		1.0	.4	1.5	.8 .8 .4	14

5. The following discussion concerns the nine factors in dispute.

6. *Factor 2. Employment Training and Experience.* Specimen 1079 (Splicer), and the Splicer jobs at New Haven and Trenton carry ratings of E-1.6 for this factor. The fact that the Joliet Splicers do considerably more, and different, welding than contem-

plated in the New Haven and Trenton jobs does not seem to warrant a higher coding for this Factor. Both Specimen 1106 (Arc Welder) and Welder (Rope Products), 26-13, at New Haven are rated at D-1.2. The plain difference between this job and the trade and craft Welder Specimen, calling for a higher coding, needs no elaboration under this Factor. Thus, the rating of E-1.6 adequately reflects the employment training and experience required here.

7. *Factor 4. Manual Skill.* The Joliet job involves both substantially more, and different type, welding than either the New Haven or Trenton Cable Splicer jobs. At Joliet, about half the Splicer's total work time involves use of the welding equipment. No Splicers now are required to weld at New Haven since all this type work was concentrated in the special purpose Welder job in 1952. Before 1952 the burning of rope and cable ends probably did not exceed 15% of the total time worked. At Trenton, welding has been done principally by a Gangleader for the Splicers (Job Class 13). Only a very small amount of welding is done by two others of the six Splicers in the department, so as to release the Gangleader for other duties. The Joliet situation is explained both by differences in work coming into the three mills, and by absence of a swaging machine for use in attaching becket loops. While Trenton also has no swaging machine, the orders coming into that mill made it possible to get along with only tapering and zincing of ends until three years ago, when regular welding was introduced. It is clear, therefore, that work of the Joliet Splicer cannot be compared only with other Splicers, but also must be considered in the light of Welder job codings. The Welder (Rope Products) at New Haven is rated at C-1.0, while both the trade and craft Welder Specimen (1095) and Specimen 1106 (Arc Welder) are coded D-1.5. There is no doubt that the welding of Splicers at Joliet is more complex than that performed at New Haven since it entails considerable work welding becket loops into rope ends. On the other hand, the language used in coding Factor 4 of both Specimen 1095 and Specimen 1106, as well as the detailed working procedures, show reliance on considerably more variety and difficulty of welding than that done by the Splicers at Joliet. In balance, it appears that the latter welding is akin to that specifically contemplated in the Manual at C-1.0, even though somewhat more complex than at New Haven.

8. *Factor 5. Responsibility for Materials.* The New Haven Welder (Rope Products) and Specimen 1106 (Arc Welder) are coded at D-1.1. This same coding seems appropriate at Joliet where the Cable Splicers weld

about half their total working time, and in effect are welders as much as they are splicers. This far exceeds the small amount of burning and welding done by New Haven or Trenton Splicers, and differs qualitatively as well. Thus a coding of D-1.1 is required here.

9. *Factor 6. Responsibility for Tools and Equipment.* The tools used here lend themselves more easily to damage than do those in Specimen 1079, which carries a rating of A-Base. On the other hand, the likelihood of damage actually occurring is not as great as the Union suggests. The proper rating for the Joliet Splicer is B-.2, the same rating as the New Haven and Trenton Splicers and the New Haven Welder (Rope Products).

10. *Factor 8. Responsibility for Safety of Others.* The Splicer must exercise ordinary care and attention to prevent injury to others. In the normal course of his job, few others come close enough to him to expose themselves to any personal danger. The rating is therefore properly B-.4, the rating carried by all of the other jobs mentioned.

11. *Factor 9. Mental Effort.* Such differences as exist in mental effort in the Splicer jobs at the three mills are small. Splicers from each are occasionally required to go to the site of customer's operations to undertake a splicing job. The blueprints which are used are relatively simple ones and tolerances expected are seldom finer than ± ¼". The correct Factor 9 rating is C-1.0.

12. *Factor 10. Physical Effort.* There are no clearly important differences in the physical effort exerted in the three splicer jobs. Heavy exertion is called for upon occasion on each of the jobs, but this is insufficient to push the job over into the higher rating of D-1.5 requested by the Union. The average exertion is more properly that represented by C-.8.

13. *Factor 11. Surroundings.* The splicing activity of this job, alone, would warrant B-.4 in recognition of the dirt and grease accompanying the work. Since half the working time also is devoted to welding (which distinguishes the job from the work at New Haven and Trenton), this markedly affects the general conditions of the job. This is reflected, specifically, in the coding of the New Haven Welder's job at C-.8 under this Factor, in line with Specimens 1106 and 1095. The welding fumes, glare, and heat involved in the Joliet job therefore warrant the C-.8 coding here.

14. *Factor 12. Hazards.* All of the reference jobs—Specimens 1079, 1095, and 1106, the New Haven and Trenton Splicers, and Welder (Rope Products), (New Haven) —are assigned ratings of B-.4 on hazards. The same rating applies to the Joliet job,

which entails no hazards beyond those experienced elsewhere.

15. Several additional matters remain for comment.

16. The Union argues that the higher rate paid for this job in the Chicago Warehouse prior to its removal to Joliet requires a comparable wage here. This argument must be denied since the Board is limited to the provisions of the Manual and Section 9-D in passing on this case. Transfer of the job into the bargaining unit made necessary a job classification study of the job, and the proper rate for the job must now be that which results from application of the agreed classification procedures.

17. Since the functions of the job at Joliet include welding to an extent which makes it more than just a cable splicing job, as in the East, the classification of factors in

dispute has been on this basis. Thus, calling the job simply that of Cable Splicer is somewhat misleading.

18. Finally, the Union suggests that existence of incentives on cable splicing jobs elsewhere requires that the Joliet job be rated in accordance with actual earnings of the other jobs. Yet the existence of incentives is immaterial, so far as job classification procedures are concerned. Coding of the Joliet job can be determined only through a factor by factor analysis, with comparisons among relevant Specimen and comparable jobs.

AWARD

19. The grievance is sustained to the extent of raising Factor 5 from C-.7 to D-1.1, and Factor 11 from B-.4 to C-.8. The total classification is thus 11.5, or Job Class 12.

CI—265. Gary Sheet and Tin Mill. May 21, 1953

Herbert L. Sherman, Jr., *Assistant Chairman*
Approved by Sylvester Garrett, *Chairman*

BACKGROUND

1. This grievance requests a higher classification for the job of Bell Anneal Furnace Operator in the Sheet Mill Cold Reduction Department of Gary Sheet and Tin Mill. In dispute are factors 1, 3, 5, 6, 9 and 10, the Union contending for a total of 22.4 or Job Class 22. The Company agrees that changes have been made but asserts that Factor 5 is the only factor affected, resulting in an increase of one job class only—from Class 14 to Class 15.

2. Under the modernization program started in 1948 the number of furnaces was reduced from 80 to 32—to 20 coil furnaces, and 12 sheet furnaces. Most of the 32 furnaces were newly installed and larger than the old ones. The 12 sheet furnaces were actually old sheet furnaces which had been remodeled to the point where they were comparable to new furnaces. Although the burners on the majority of the old furnaces were centrally controlled, all the burners on the new furnaces are individually adjusted as required; but there is still a master control which regulates the total flow to all the burners.

3. The normal crew per turn consists of one Operator and two Bell Anneal Furnace Operator Helpers, one Helper usually being assigned to 12 coil furnaces and the other to 8 coil and 12 sheet furnaces.

4. Initially, the job in dispute was described and classified at Job Class 14 and issued as Specimen Example 2221. Following installation of the new annealing equipment,

the Company redescribed the job and reclassified it at Job Class 15. Since the Union agreed only with the description, the Company installed the changed job classification unilaterally—effective January 1, 1949.

DISCUSSION AND FINDINGS

5. The contentions of the parties with respect to the particular factors in dispute are as follows:

6. *Factor 1—Pre-Employment Training. Company: B-.3, Union: C-1.0.* The Union claims that a higher I.Q. is required to learn the operation of the new furnaces. Union testimony emphasized the increased amount of manual control of the burners. To this, Management replies that individual adjustment of the burners was made on some of the old sheet furnaces where some areas of the bases were hotter than others, and that no greater mentality is required to perform more of the same or a similar type of work.

The Board concludes that the rating on this Factor cannot be properly increased in the light of the evidence and the Specimen Examples for this job which consistently rate Factor 1 at B-.3.

7. *Factor 3—Mental Skill. Company: D-2.2, Union: E-2.8.* The manual control of the burners is again pointed out by the Union under this Factor. Also, it is possible, because of different size coils, that there will be two or three different cycles on the same base—each cycle at a different temperature. Such a situation calls for more adjustment of

the burners by the Operator or Helper. Normally, however, the same heating cycle and temperatures are used on a base. Sometimes on weekends two temperatures are used. Where two cycles are specified, only one will usually be employed to the advantage of one of the customers. And although heat may be reflected from one base to another, thereby requiring adjustment of the temperatures, some of the old furnaces with three bases presented the same type of problem.

Shutting down the furnaces because of gas failure and re-lighting them may be necessary on occasions. This is not a common occurrence.

The Company also notes that improvements have been installed in the control rooms which make it easier to read the meters.

On the whole, the language used in Specimen 2221 for Factor 3 still adequately describes the mental skill required for this job, i.e., "Exercise considerable judgment in setting up and operating annealing furnaces to properly anneal materials."

8. *Factor 5—Responsibility for Materials. Company: C-3.7, Union: D-8.5.* An Operator testified that it has taken as much as three hours to make one visual check on the furnaces, that he must make other checks during the turn, that he must check his Assistant's meter readings two or three times a turn, and that he must now work with closer tolerances on the coil furnaces. For these reasons the Union contends that an Operator must "use close attention for majority of turn."

As to this aspect of Factor 5, however, the language under Code C which reads as follows is particularly applicable: "Set up and operate a producing unit where cycle is long and specifications are partially obtained by mechanical control." The heating cycle of annealing may be divided into two parts. First, bringing the furnace up to proper temperature consumes about thirty hours. After lighting up (which now involves lighting all the burners individually), grievants leave the burners wide open. According to the Operators no further adjustments are then necessary during the first phase. Next comes the soaking period which consumes almost the same amount of time as the first phase. Manual control of the burners which is then required has already been noted. Upon completion of the annealing period the portable furnaces are lifted and moved to another base and the annealed product is permitted to cool.

It is agreed that "probable monetary loss" has been increased to a figure substantially in excess of $1500. An examination of the historical treatment of this Factor for the job in dispute reveals that the Operator was credited with one half a base load which may be damaged by overheating before detection less scrap value. The resulting figure was $560 for C-2.5. After changes in the annealing equipment were placed in operation by the Company, the base load was increased tenfold. By using the same convention initially employed by the parties to calculate "probable monetary loss" for this job, the result is $5600. Since everything over $1500 under Code C is given 3.7 and since Code C has already been found to be appropriate for the amount of care required, no higher rating can be attributed to Factor 5 for this job.

9. *Factor 6—Responsibility for Tools and Equipment. Company: C-1.0, Union: D-1.5.* The Union contends that Code D is warranted for this Factor since the furnaces are now larger and more manipulation of the burners is required. Also referred to are certain additions of auxiliary equipment listed under Tools and Equipment on the revised job description: explosimeter, circulating and cooling fans (which make it easier to control the temperatures), precipitrons (air cleaners), turbo-blowers, refrigerators (which keep the gas at proper temperatures), and gas dryers. Omitted from the new job description but listed on the old one are portable potentiometers; gas dryers have not been used since 1950; and the date on which the turbo-blowers were installed is not clear. In any event, this new equipment must be checked along with the furnaces and the other auxiliary equipment such as gas conditioning units.

Yet, when considered in the light of the appropriate Specimen Examples, it does not appear that these additions have so affected the degree of care required as to justify a higher coding. Probable damage being already rated as "High," no increase on this aspect of the classification is possible.

10. *Factor 9—Mental Effort. Company: C-1.0, Union: D-1.5.* The changes already described are again emphasized by grievants under this Factor. In view of the pertinent Specimen Examples, however, the coding must remain at C-1.0.

11. *Factor 10—Physical Effort. Company: B-.3, Union: C-.8.* The Union takes the position that an increase of the rating on this Factor is justified primarily because of two changes conceded by the Company. First, a basement was installed which requires the Operator or Helper to walk down a flight of steps to reset the fans. Secondly, the Operator or one of his Helpers must now climb ladders to the tops of the furnaces to adjust individual carburetors. Previously,

carburetors could be checked from the operating floor.

Estimates varied as to the frequency with which the fans must be reset. A Helper and an Operator asserted that this duty must be performed several times a turn; a management representative stated that he only found it necessary to do this once in ten days during a strike.

No agreement was reached on the average number of times per turn that the carburetors must be adjusted at the tops of the furnaces. Grievants dispute Foreman Marconi's estimate that this is only required on the average of six times a week for all turns.

In any event, a remote control to adjust the carburetor, which is designed to eliminate climbing ladders to the tops of the furnaces, has already been installed on one furnace, and other such controls have been ordered by the Company. Moreover, the Company notes that the furnaces are now located in a smaller area and that they are fewer in number, thus tending to reduce the amount of walking involved in checking.

On the whole, the present rating ascribed to this Factor must be deemed to be appropriate.

AWARD

12. The grievance is denied.

CI—266. Gary Sheet and Tin Mill. May 21, 1953

Herbert L. Sherman, Jr., *Assistant Chairman*
Approved by Sylvester Garrett, *Chairman*

BACKGROUND

1. This is a companion case to CI-265 which protested the classification values assigned to the changed job of Bell Anneal Furnace Operator at Gary Sheet and Tin Mill. Here the job of Bell Anneal Furnace Operator Helper is in dispute. Although the parties have agreed upon a revised job description, the Union objects to the ratings assigned by Management to Factors 3, 5, 6, 7 and 10.

2. This job was originally classified at Job Class 10 and issued as Specimen Example No. 2227. After the installation of the new annealing equipment described in CI-265, Management reviewed the classification ratings for this job and concluded that only Factor 5 warranted an increase. Failing to obtain the Union's agreement, it installed the changed job classification at Job Class 12 effective January 1, 1949.

3. According to the Company the job has a total point value of 11.8. The Union contends that the point value should be 19.2. The positions of the parties with respect to the Factors in dispute are as follows.

FACTOR	COMPANY POSITION	UNION POSITION
3. Mental Skill	C-1.6	D-2.2
5. Responsibility for Material	C-3.7	D-8.5
6. Responsibility for Tools and Equipment	C-Hi-1.0	D-Med.-1.5
7. Responsibility for Operations	C-1.0	D-2.0
10. Physical Effort	B-.3	C-.8

FINDINGS

4. Since the Helpers perform work similar to and assist the Operator, the evidence outlined in CI-265 as to the changes in equipment and duties is likewise applicable to this grievance. Essentially the same arguments are made by the Union to justify increases on the ratings for Factors 3, 6 and 10 which are in dispute in both cases. The Board must hold, however, that the changes have not sufficiently affected these classification ratings previously agreed upon for the Helper job to warrant higher codings. As to Factor 7—Responsibility for Operations, there is no evidence that the changes in equipment thereby changed the relationship between the Operator and the Helper. The Operator is still responsible for the Helpers and must check on their work. The coding for this Factor must therefore remain at its present level.

5. Factor 5, on the other hand, has obviously been affected by the higher "probable monetary loss." When the Helper job was initially classified, a formula was used under which the Helper was credited with one fourth a base load which may be damaged before detection less scrap value. This resulted in a dollar value of $280 for C-1.8. After the Company increased the base load by ten times pursuant to its installation of the enumerated changes in equipment, application of the same formula gives the Helper credit for $2800. Since, under the Specimen Examples, Code C is the proper coding for the degree of care required, the proper rating for this Factor is now C-3.7. This is so despite the fact that the result is to increase the Helper two job classes while the Operator job is only increased one class as noted in CI-265. Though both the Helper

and Operator are now given the same rating on Factor 5, the Board is left no alternative by virtue of the fact that 3.7 is the highest possible rating under Code C no matter how much the dollar value exceeds $1500. And the Board must be guided by the bases upon which this Factor was coded in the initial classification of the Operator and Helper jobs.

AWARD

6. The grievance is denied.

CI—202. Vandergrift Plant. February 11, 1952
Jacob Blair, *Acting Chairman*

BACKGROUND AND ISSUE

1. This grievance arises out of a change made in April, 1948, in the use of a shear in the Sheet Finishing Department.

2. Prior to this time, this shear had been used for shearing tack plate and only occasionally for shearing scrap. In April, 1948, the use of the shear for shearing tack plate was discontinued. On or about October 4, 1948, this shear was designated for the exclusive shearing of scrap into Open Hearth charging box sizes.

3. As a result of this change in the use of the shears, the Management decided that the job of Shearman, Tack Plate had been changed by one job class or more. Under Section 9-D, a new job description and evaluation was issued placing the Scrap Shearman in Job Class 4. In negotiations this was later raised to Job Class 5.

4. The issue in this case is, therefore, whether the job of Scrap Shearman was properly classified in Job Class 5. This question rests upon whether the job has been properly evaluated in terms of Factors 1, 2, 6, 7, 9 and 10.

CONTENTIONS OF THE PARTIES

5. The contentions of the parties rest upon the facts of the changed job. These are summarized in the table shown in the Findings.

FINDINGS

6. Basic to the consideration of this case, is the fact that the same shear as used for cutting tack plate is still used for shearing scrap. The differences between the parties, therefore, rest upon whether the change in the use of these shears, together with the change from tack plate to scrap, justifies the reduction in the classification given the job of Shearman, Scrap. As a consequence, the contentions raised by the Union, together with those raised by the Company, rest upon the facts of this case rather than upon any interpretation of the Agreement. The following shows the difference between the parties in the evaluation of the various factors in dispute:

FACTOR	COMPANY EVALUATION	UNION EVALUATION	BASIC DIFFERENCE INVOLVED
1	A-Base	B- .3	Company claims that shearing scrap requires a training adequate to, "operate simple machines and make simple adjustments where adjustments are limited." Union claims that since the same machine and set-ups are required, then Code B applies, which provides, "set up and operate machines or processes requiring a variety of adjustments." It also claims that Factor 1 as well as Factor 2 should not be changed from the Shearman, Tack Plate since Factors 3 and 4 remain the same.
2	A-Base	B- .4	Company maintains that operating shear for shearing scrap is a simple operation learned in less than two months. Union maintains that it is the same machine, hence, requires the same training period.

FACTOR	COMPANY EVALUATION	UNION EVALUATION	BASIC DIFFERENCE INVOLVED
6	Low B-.2	Med. C-.7	Company contends the lower value is justified since the tolerance for setting the knives is less for scrap. In addition, stops need not be set to the same tolerance. Responsibility for knives is less since there are no quality standards on shearing scrap. Union claims that the responsibility is the same as under tack plate since the tools are identical. In addition, the machine may be more seriously damaged due to shearing stickers, hence, same factor value as given Shearman, Tack Plate, is justified.
7	A-Base	C-1.0	In negotiations parties agreed to Base value for Factor 7. Company maintains that A-Base is justified since the Shearman works on a simple, highly standardized job with no other operations closely dependent. In this the Company points out that no operation is dependent upon the receipt of the bundled scrap. Union holds that the Scrap Shearman should be given the same factor value, as Scrap Shearman is responsible for operating a small or individual processing unit where continuity of production is required. Supporting this the Union claims that the department would become clogged with scrap if the Shearman did not properly maintain his operation.
9	B- .5	C-1.0	In negotiations Union agreed to .5 on this factor, raising the question only at the time of the hearing. Company holds that less mental effort is required when shearing scrap since actions taken and decisions made are limited to few possibilities and work requires only moderate degree of coordination with others. Union holds that the factor should be evaluated the same as when shearing tack plate since the piling of irregular sizes and shapes of scrap, together with the necessary handling, is equal to the mental effort required in handling tack plate.
10	C- .8	D-1.5	Company claims the Shearman handles only medium weight materials lighter than tack plate.

FACTOR	COMPANY EVALUATION	UNION EVALUATION	BASIC DIFFERENCE INVOLVED
			Union holds that bundles of scrap exceed weight of tack plate and, in addition, is more difficult to handle on the shears.

7. This case must be decided upon the facts of the job of Scrap Shearman instead of under Section 9-D. Examination of the evidence shows that the job of Scrap Shearman is one class or more below that of the Shearman Tack Plate. The Company is therefore justified under Section 9-D in issuing a new description and evaluation of the Scrap Shearman job.

8. Consideration of the evidence does not establish the Union contention that this job had been improperly placed in Class 5.

9. The Union contends that Factors 1 and 2 should remain unchanged at the B value on the grounds that Factors 3 and 4 are the same for the jobs of Scrap Shearman and Shearman Tack Plate. This overlooks the fact that both Mental and Manual Skill, as acquired abilities, are separate and distinct from Pre-Employment Training based on fixed inherited traits and Employment Training and Experience which is a function of native ability and the complexity of a given job. In this case the facts show that a Base value for Factors 1 and 2 was justified.

10. Code A of Factor 1 properly describes the Pre-Employment Training required on the Scrap Shearman job. The machine is a standard guillotine type of shear; operated by a foot treadle release. The principal adjustment required is that of changing shear knives, a job which might not be required in a period ranging from a week up to six months. In addition the operator also had to set the stops, but again infrequently and with little regard to the same tolerances required on Tack Plate. This description is properly characterized by the language under Code A providing: "Operate simple machine and make simple adjustments where adjustments are limited."

11. The requirements of the job of Scrap Shearman are also properly evaluated in Code A of Factor 2. It is not a complex job. Instead the evidence shows it is a job which can be learned in a period not exceeding two months. This is true for the operation of the shear as well as for the preparation of required reports. The job is therefore properly evaluated at A Base in Factor 2.

12. The Union request that Factor 6 be retained at the same level for the Scrap Shearman as for the Shearman Tack Plate is also denied. Basic to this is the fact on Tack Plate, the Shearman was responsible for maintaining the shear in such condition that sheets would be cut to the proper tolerance and without burrs. He does not have this responsibility on scrap. Instead, only such attention and care is required as will prevent breaking or seriously damaging the knife, or the machine. Such a situation would appear to be of an obvious type properly described under Code B as "Recognize obvious trouble and shut down routine machines . . . to prevent or minimize damage."

13. The Union claim with reference to Factor 7 is denied. Shearing tack plate involves the responsibility for maintaining production schedules. This is not required when shearing scrap. Instead, the only responsibility of the Shearman is that of properly using his own time. This condition meets the contentions raised by the Union concerning the accumulation of scrap in the department because obviously the latter would take place only when such an accumulation resulted from work beyond the normal expectation of the Shearman to remove it.

14. The Union contention with regard to Factor 9 is denied. It seems obvious that shearing scrap would involve less mental effort on the part of the Shearman than that of shearing tack plate, which work is done to relatively close tolerances.

15. The Union contention in regard to Factor 10, "Physical Effort," is denied. Factor 10 measures that level of physical effort which best describes the average degree of muscular exertion required throughout the time. It may even be granted that on occasions the weight of scrap handled may exceed that of the weight of tack plate handled at one time. But this exception does not establish the average. Instead, the scrap is considerably lighter in gauge than tack plate. The average weight of the scrap is therefore less. It is this fact upon which the case must be decided.

AWARD

16. The Union grievance is denied and it is held that the job of Scrap Shearman is properly placed in Class 5.

CI—203. **Vandergrift Plant of Irvin Works.** February 11, 1952

Jacob Blair, *Acting Chairman*

BACKGROUND FACTS

1. The background of this case, together with the contract provisions involved, is identical to that in Case No. CI-202, Grievance A-48-24. The issue is whether the job of Helper, Scrap Shearman has been properly evaluated.

2. The basic contentions of both the Union and the Company are also closely similar to that in Case CI-202, Grievance A-48-24, and are shown under the caption Findings.

FINDINGS

3. This case, like the one involving the Shearman in Case No. CI-202, Grievance A-48-24, rests upon the facts. The following table shows the principal differences between the parties in regard to the evaluation of the Shearman Helper job on the scrap shears:

FACTOR	COMPANY EVALUATION	UNION EVALUATION	BASIC DIFFERENCE INVOLVED
4	A-Base	B-.5	The Company maintains that A-Base is justified since the Helper handles only ordinary materials manually.
			The Union holds that the job should carry the same value as the Helper on tack plate, since the Helper must now position sheets of unequal sizes and different shapes on a wagon in such a manner that they can be bundled expeditiously.
7	A-Base	B-.5	The Company maintains that the Helper on the scrap shear has no responsibility for the operations beyond that expected in the proper use of his time.
			The Union maintains that scrap must be promptly disposed of to prevent accumulation in the department.
9	A-Base	B-.5	The A-Base value was agreed to during negotiations, as requiring a minimum of mental application in the performance of highly routine work.
			The Company claims this should be sustained.
			The Union claims that the mental effort in banding the scrap should be given consideration since the work is more hazardous and greater mental effort is required in properly banding the scrap together.

4. The Union request in regard to Factor 4 is denied. The work performed by the Helper does not satisfy the conditions set forth in Code B, of Factor 4. Instead, his work is primarily that of removing the sheared scrap and piling it on a wagon, using only such care as is necessary to prevent the pile from falling over, or otherwise causing some mishap. But no skill of more than a very ordinary degree is required in such an operation.

5. The Union request in regard to Factor 7, "Responsibility for Operations," is denied on the same grounds as the decision applicable to the Scrap Shearman. The evidence does not indicate that the Scrap Shearman Helper is responsible beyond the use of his own time.

6. The Union request in regard to Factor 9, "Mental Effort," is denied. The evidence is such as to show that the job is properly classified under Code A. The work done by the Helper is highly routine, using simple tools for rough work. In addition, he manually handles the product from the processing unit. In point is the fact that the Helper no longer is required to position the scrap sheet against the stops. This fact reduces materially the requirement that the Helper coordinate his work with that of the Shearman.

AWARD

7. The Union grievance with respect to Factors 4, 7 and 9 is denied and the job of Helper, Scrap Shearman is held to be properly placed in Job Class 2.

CHAPTER 13

JOB CLASSIFIED, NOT INDIVIDUAL

A fundamental principle of job classification is that "It is the job that is under consideration, and not the individuals who work on the job." The few cases in this brief chapter take note of this principle. One further award—N-100, which may be found at p. 364, is also relevant to this chapter.

USC—293. Irvin Works. April 30, 1953
Herbert L. Sherman, Jr., *Assistant to Chairman*
Approved by Sylvester Garrett, *Chairman*

BACKGROUND

1. This grievance seeks higher job classifications for the Boiler House Operators and Firemen (Stokers) in the Boiler House at Irvin Works, as the result of a number of changes effected by the Company. A claim for a higher job classification by the Coal Unloaders was withdrawn in the processing of this grievance, but Factors 2, 3, 5, 6, 7, and 10 for the Operator and Fireman jobs remain in dispute.

2. Numerous improvements, additions, and changes have taken place at the Irvin Boiler House over the years. Among the changes related in the testimony at the hearing are the following.

3. In July, 1948, a second stack—seventy-five feet taller than the original stack—was added. The Fireman or Coal Unloader must now clean fly ash from the bases of two stacks once each week, and the Operator must observe the smoke from two stacks in checking the operation of the smoke control unit—installed in 1949—at least once each turn. The smoke control unit is adjusted very infrequently and can be stopped from the floor by a button. One Operator has never adjusted it.

4. Fly ash from the stacks can be cleaned out by use of a vacuum. According to the Company it takes about two hours to clean a stack, but only 45 minutes are required of the Fireman or Coal Unloader to position the vacuum. In exceptional cases, however, the Operators testified that it may take ten or more hours. It is also possible for clinkers to clog the vacuum, and the clinkers must be dug out of the stack once a year.

5. In September, 1948, the stoker electric motor and forced draft fan electric motor on No. 3 Boiler were replaced with two steam turbines. The same changes were made on No. 4 Boiler in October of that year. Although the electric motors for the forced draft fans could be started from the operating floor, the Operator must now walk down a flight of stairs to the basement to start the forced draft turbines by turning the exhaust, steam, and drain valves. This must be done on No. 3 and 4 Boilers several times each year. However, it was always required that the Operator check his equipment in the basement before starting the forced draft fans, and it has always been necessary for the Operator to go to the cellar a couple of times every turn to ascertain whether everything was operating properly. Also, steam turbines were not new to these Operators since a similar steam turbine has been used on No. 5 Boiler from the time of its completion in 1943, and there have been steam turbines on the feed water pumps for many years. Nevertheless, the amount of greasing required of the Fireman has been increased due to installation of the steam turbines which must be greased every turn.

6. In December, 1948, a second ash pump was put into service. The ash pumps are operated by the Fireman and Coal Unloader once or twice a turn. Although the Company contends that addition of a second pump as a stand-by unit has eliminated hand shoveling of ashes in the event of pump failure, this is only partially true. If the line to the first pump becomes clogged, the other pump may continue to operate;

232

but if the sump becomes clogged, neither pump will operate.

7. During January, 1949, the Boiler House was enlarged by approximately fifty feet. New chemical storage, locker, and toilet facilities were provided. A new cellar chemical pump room was added; two chemical pumps were added to the four already in use. These pumps must be checked once or twice a turn. And the steps to the platform on which the controls for these pumps are located were removed in favor of a ladder to make room for more filters. It is necessary for the Operator to go to this platform once a month.

8. At the same time an additional reaction tank and an additional solution tank were installed. It is agreed that the two reaction tanks operate similarly although one is air operated and the other electrically operated. According to the Company both tanks are required only during the winter months when an additional test must be run on treated water every twenty-four hours. The Operators dispute the Company's estimate that only fifteen minutes are required to make the additional test. In any event, it is not disputed that each tank must be "blown down" (sludge bled off) twice a turn by the Operator. This, however, only involves turning a cock valve to 90 degrees.

9. Concurrent with the installation of the second reaction tank was the relocation of the float control valve for the first tank. It used to be more accessible at the top of the reaction tank. Now, instead of climbing steps, the Operator must climb a ladder to a new platform in the "crow's nest." He is not required to check this valve very frequently.

10. Two additional filters have been installed, one in January, 1949, and the other in March, 1949, increasing the number to six. The frequency with which filters are washed by the Fireman depends upon the steam load and seasonal conditions. At maximum winter load, it was necessary to wash two filters each turn and the same is required today.

11. In January, 1950, another feed water heater was put into operation. The two heaters preheat the water before it is pumped into the boiler tubes. The Operator must now "blow down" two feed water heaters twice a month instead of one as previously. Also during the month of January, 1950, the Company replaced three 400 G.P.M. feed water pumps with three 800 G.P.M. pumps. Of the three 400 G.P.M. pumps, two were driven by separate steam turbines and the third by an electric motor. (Two of the 800 G.P.M. pumps are likewise steam turbine driven.) The two steam turbine driven pumps were often operated "in parallel" to meet requirements, which necessitated some adjustment of the valves. Now, each 800 G.P.M. pump is capable of carrying the normal steam load of the entire Boiler House. Although "paralleling" has been virtually eliminated, the Operators emphasize that no longer do they merely lose one-half the water upon the failure of one pump. It appears, however, that less trouble has occurred with the new pumps. And an Operator familiar with the 400 G.P.M. pumps has no difficulty familiarizing himself with the 800 G.P.M. pumps.

12. During April, 1950, a larger coal hopper and a car shaker were put into service. Although it is still necessary to move the coal cars to unload all the doors, the number of times this positioning is required has been decreased by the larger coal hopper.

13. Before the car shaker was installed, the Coal Unloader had to climb into the coal car and break up the frozen coal. The car shaker, which now loosens the coal in the cars mechanically, is operated by controls which consist of four buttons installed on the operating floor of the Boiler House. Estimates varied as to the amount of time consumed in manipulating the buttons, possibly because this task is not performed solely by one member of the crew. On a visit to the plant a Laborer, who is assigned to work in the Boiler House when necessary, was observed operating the controls.

14. As a result of the elimination of hand shoveling of coal by the Coal Unloader, he was taken inside the Boiler House and given additional duties in assisting the Fireman and Operator. He helps out by blowing the soot blowers, removing ashes, and charging solution tanks. He has also been given full responsibility for cleaning the fire boxes, whereas he merely assisted the Fireman in this respect previously.

15. No. 6 Boiler was put into normal service in July, 1950. It is steam turbine driven and is similar to Nos. 3, 4, and 5 Boilers with a similar instrument panel. Its rated capacity—around 100,000 pounds of steam per hour—is greater than any of the other five Boilers. With the installation of this Boiler the steam demands are more easily met. No longer is it necessary to supplement Boiler House facilities with steam locomotives to meet peak demands as was true previously.

16. Further changes related by Union witnesses include the installation of locks on doors which must be opened by someone in the Boiler House when a bell is rung, enlargement of the coal cellar, addition of an air compressor (in 1943), addition of two

new car pullers, addition of new panel boards for meter charts, with more charts which must be changed by the Fireman, increased use of an old stand-by hot strip pump which must be checked by the Fireman or Coal Unloader once or twice a turn —consuming about ten minutes, increased amount of steam being put out, addition of new steam lines, and the installation of I. K.

Soot Blowers which clean the Boilers better so that they do not have to be cleaned as often as before. About 33 steps must now be climbed to the I. K. Soot Blowers whereas the soot could previously be blown from the operating floor.

17. The following chart shows the present ratings and the ratings proposed by the Union on the factors in dispute.

| | BOILER HOUSE OPERATOR | | STOKER FIREMAN | |
| | PRESENT | UNION | PRESENT | UNION |
FACTOR	RATING	RATING	RATING	RATING
2—Employment Training & Experience	F-2.0	G-2.4	C- .8	D-1.2
3—Mental Skill	D-2.2	E-2.8	C-1.6	D-2.2
5—Responsibility for Materials	C- .7	C-1.2	C- .5	C- .7
6—Responsibility for Tools & Equipment	C-1.0(Hi)	D-2.0(Hi)	B- .5(Hi)	C-1.0(Hi)
7—Responsibility for Operations	D-2.0	E-3.0	C-1.0	D-2.0
10—Physical Effort	B- .3	C- .8	B- .3	C- .8

DISCUSSION AND FINDINGS

18. When the initial classification for Boiler House Operator at Irvin Works was being discussed, the Company referred to Specimen 554 at 10.6 as being applicable. Although the local Union committee proposed Job Class 14, they finally agreed to Job Class 12 by referring to Specimen 550 at 11.6. No Specimen could be found that went beyond this. Nevertheless, all three Boiler House Operators who testified at the hearing asserted that they believed that a mistake was made in the original classification of the job and that they had been treated unfairly. As time passed, they became incensed all over again due to the enumerated changes effected by the Company.

19. It is clear, however, that the Board has no authority to disturb the initial classification of this job on the ground that a mistake was made. Only if the changes related above sufficiently affect the classification factors is the Board empowered to raise the job class.

20. The Union contends that the Boiler House Operator job should be increased from Class 12 to Class 16, and the Fireman job from Class 8 to Class 11. It points to classifications for the Boiler House Operator (Leader) at South Works—Worcester which is rated at Job Class 15, the Duquesne Boiler House Operator at Job Class 14, and a Boiler House Engineer at South Works (Chicago Central Operations) which is clas-

sified at Class 11 under the Salary Manual. Even if it is true that the latter job class would be much higher when converted under the manual for production jobs, the differences in the manuals and the Unions involved undermine the weight to be given to this classification. The Worcester job cannot be considered as applicable since it involves a Leader's position on the second and third turns when there is no Foreman in the Boiler House. And, after a visit to the Duquesne Boiler House, it is concluded that the classification for this Boiler House Operator cannot control the present case.

21. More appropriate for comparison are the Benchmark and Specimen jobs, two of which give the Boiler House Operator Class 12 and three of which give the job a rating of Class 11. (Incidentally, the Boiler House Operator is given Job Class 12 at eighteen or more other plants of the Corporation. A very few are rated slightly higher or lower.) For the Fireman one Specimen job is classified at Class 7, another at Class 9. But the relationship between the Operator and the Fireman at Irvin Works has remained unchanged.

22. In the light of these Specimens and Benchmarks, the Board is compelled to rule that the factor ratings for the two jobs in dispute have not been affected by the changes instituted by the Company. Even though it is clear that the Operator must climb more steps and ladders, adjust more

valves, and check more equipment, and the Fireman must also change more charts and do more greasing, the gist of the grievance is that more of the same type of work is being required. The Board, however, cannot take workload into account except as it affects the quality of the work performed.

23. At least two of the changes have relieved the Operators and Firemen to some extent, i.e., the new coal unloading equipment which made the Coal Unloader available to assist inside the Boiler House, and the I. K. Soot Blowers. Although it still takes about the same time to blow the soot when it is required, it is not necessary to do so as often as previously.

24. As to Factors 2 and 3, the new steam turbines and the additional reaction tank are similar to previously used equipment. No higher degree of mental skill or longer period of training is necessary to learn to operate this additional equipment. And the time required to learn to operate the four buttons that control the new car unloading system is not substantial.

25. With respect to Factors 5 and 6, the degree of attention has not increased. Factor 6 is already rated as Hi for Possible Damage to Equipment, and no evidence of any increase in monetary value of materials used was presented to the Board.

26. The addition of Boiler No. 6 has not increased the rating of Factor 7 since it is now easier to meet the steam demands of the plant. And although more walking and climbing are now required of the Operator and Fireman, that has not increased the degree of physical effort described under Factor 10.

27. One further comment. The employees involved in this grievance appear to be exceptionally well qualified for their jobs. It must be kept in mind, however, that it is the "occupation that is under consideration and not the individuals who work on the occupation."

AWARD

28. The grievance is denied.

USC—721. Gary Sheet and Tin Mill. September 24, 1958
Sylvester Garrett, *Chairman*

FINDINGS

1. This grievance from the Utitlties Department of Gary Sheet and Tin Mill asserts that the Boiler House Operator job (Class 12) has changed to the extent of one full job class or more and that it should be reclassified in Class 16.

2. Principal support for this grievance is found in the testimony of Boiler House Operator Leonard Woods, who spelled out various equipment changes made effective since his initial employment in this Boiler House about 10 years ago. This testimony was directed primarily to Factors 2, 6, 7, and 12, as to which the parties' positions are:

FACTOR	PRESENT CLASSIFI- CATION	PROPOSED BY THE UNION
2. Employment training and experience	F-2.0	G-2.4
6. Responsibility for tools and equipment	C-1.0	D-2.0
7. Responsibility for operations	D-2.0	E-3.0
12. Hazards	B- .4	E-2.0

3. All other factors of the job are in agreement, in line with codings under the Specimen Examples included in the January 1, 1953 Job Description and Classification Manual.

4. In 1951 a new Riley Water Tube Boiler—1,200 BHP—(125,000#/hr) was added to the Boiler House facilities, along with auxiliary equipment for feedwater treating (which doubled existing capacity), and a new pneumatic ash handling system for the new Riley Boiler as well as for two Vogt Boilers which had been operated since the job originally was described in 1944.

5. Grievance A-51-125 was filed in 1951, requesting that the Boiler House Operator be placed in Class 17 because of changed duties said to result from operation of the new equipment. The grievance was processed to Fourth Step, but not appealed to arbitration after denial on January 27, 1953.

6. The present grievance resulted from the addition, in early 1957, of one more Riley Water Tube Boiler of the same capacity as that installed in 1951. At the same time, however, six old Sterling Boilers, which had been operated for many years, were abandoned. As a result, the total number of boilers operated in the Boiler House was reduced from 10 to 5.

7. Most of the testimony of Grievant Woods related to requirements of the Operator job which have been present since its original description and classification, or since the addition of equipment in 1951. He

indicated, however, that on certain occasions the Operators have assumed responsibility for maintenance and repair, as when it was necessary to change over the economizers, or blow out the new vacuum system (installed in 1951) for ash removal when it became jammed.

8. The Boiler House Operator always has been responsible for some minor repairs. Assistant Superintendent Mullins of the Utilities Department pointed out that changing of the economizers had been a requirement of the job for many years, although occasionally it is necessary to call in maintenance when there is trouble with the damper. Also, the maintenance work cited by Woods as occasionally arising when the ash removal system clogs is not actually a requirement imposed on the Operator, but occasionally some Operators pitch in on their own initiative. These minor maintenance-type activities apparently were at least as much a part of the job when Grievance No. A-51-125 was processed, and settled in 1953, as they are today.

9. In the last analysis, this case is essentially the same as other Boiler House Operator cases previously before the Board as Cases USC-293, -343, -490, and A-697. These make plain that the Specimen Examples for Boiler House Operator are controlling in determining proper classification of this job. The fact that a Boiler House Operator at Duquesne was placed in Class 14 by the parties locally, and one at Edgar Thomson Works locally placed in Class 13, cannot govern decision by the Board, since the primary reference in job classification under the Manual is to relevant Specimen Examples. Neither the Duquesne nor Edgar Thomson Works job is a Specimen.

10. It may be worth noting that Boiler House Operator Woods apparently is a superior and highly cooperative employee. But it is the job, not the individual, which is classified under the Manual. Considerations of individual employee merit could not be taken into account without ultimately producing the type of chaotic rate structure which led the parties many years ago to launch their joint efforts to eliminate wage rate inequities.

AWARD

11. The grievance is denied.

USC—858. Fairless Works. December 28, 1959

Sylvester Garrett, *Chairman*

BACKGROUND

1. This grievance from the Rolling Division at Fairless Works claims that the job of Ingot Buggy Operator (PC 4110-4044) is improperly classified at 5.5, and that allegedly new phases of the job, attendant upon installation of a trolley phone, require that it be put in Job Class 8.

2. As originally described and classified in April of 1954, the Ingot Buggy Operator was (and is) required "To operate electric cable drawn ingot buggies, moving ingots from soaking pit building to roll table." Originally, communication to and from the soaking pit and rolling areas was handled through a public address system connecting the Pit Recorder and the pulpits of the Ingot Buggy Operator, and, using the 45-inch mill as an example, various component stations in that mill, such as the Roller, Scarfer, Shearman and Stamper. Under this system the Pit Recorder could speak to the Pit Craneman by the trolley phone, but (since the Pit Craneman was not connected into the mill P. A. system) direct communication on the P. A. system between the Ingot Buggy Operator and the Pit Craneman was not possible. The Pit Recorder would announce over the P. A. system the sequence for drawing ingots.

Then, on the trolley phone, he would tell the Pit Craneman which pits were to be drawn and the number of ingots from each pit. Drawing and rolling would then operate according to that sequence.

3. When trouble developed at the mill requiring departure from the scheduled sequence, the appropriate information would come back over the P. A. system. Then the Ingot Buggy Operator, using a signal light and a horn, would attempt to attract the attention of the Pit Craneman and inform him that something was wrong. Sometimes the Pit Craneman would discover the fact that difficulty had occurred simply by noticing that the ingots were not moving. In any event, before the Pit Craneman could discover specifically what was wrong and what he should do about it, he would have to get in touch with the Pit Recorder on the trolley phone. Only then would he learn what the change in the drawing schedule was to be. Similarly, if some difficulty occurred at the soaking pits which required a change in the scheduled order of drawing ingots, the Pit Craneman would have to contact the Pit Recorder on the trolley phone, and the latter would then broadcast the proposed change over the P. A. system to the various stations in the mill.

4. In 1955 the Ingot Buggy Operator was connected with the Pit Craneman by a trolley phone. And in 1958 additional outlets were installed, connecting the Cover Craneman into the trolley phone. The trolley phone connects also with three stations on the soaking pit floor.

5. Under the present system, made possible by these changes, if difficulty in rolling requires deviation from the schedule, the changed order comes to the Ingot Buggy Operator over the P. A. system, and he passes it on to the Pit Craneman by the trolley phone. And if a snag develops at the pits, forcing the Pit Craneman to depart from the schedule, he notifies the Ingot Buggy Operator on the trolley phone, and the latter informs the rolling mill on the P. A. system.

6. The table below shows the position of the parties on each factor:

FACTOR	PRESENT CLASSI- FICATION	UNION PRO- POSALS
1. Pre-employment training.	Base	Base
*2. Employment training and experience.	.4	.8
*3. Mental skill.	1.0	1.6
4. Manual skill.	.5	.5
5. Responsibility for materials.	B .3	B .3
6. Responsibility for tools and equipment.	B .2	B .2
*7. Responsibility for operations.	1.0	2.0
8. Responsibility for safety of others.	.4	.4
*9. Mental effort.	1.0	1.5
10. Physical effort.	.3	.3
11. Surroundings.	.4	.4
12. Hazards.	Base	Base
Total	5.5	8.0

* Factors in dispute.

7. No Specimens or comparable jobs are cited by the Union. The Union in substance contends that the Ingot Buggy Operator, because of his increased ability to communicate with operations at each end of the mill, is now coordinating the flow of steel between the soakng pits and the rolling mill. It feels that the old system was at best inefficient visual communication by which the Ingot Buggy Operator could tell the Pit Craneman when to stop and when to go, but that he could not pass on specific, verbal informa-

tion, such as now is possible since installation of the trolley phone.

8. Moreover, the Union argues that the Ingot Buggy Operator now has a greater responsibility for seeing to it that ingots are fed to the mill in the correct order. In this connection grievant pointed out that he is expected to (and on one occasion did) shut down the mill when he believes that a mistake has occurred.

9. The Company insists that there have been no changes in the content of the disputed job and that every current function is covered by the description and classification which was agreed upon in 1954. It says that in the past the Ingot Buggy Operator, by use of the signal light, notified the Pit Craneman to hold ingots in the pits, and that installation of the trolley phone simply improved the manner of communication between the two jobs.

10. The Company refers to three Specimen Example jobs and quite a few nonspecimen jobs in justification of the present classification of the job in dispute.

FINDINGS

11. An alert Ingot Buggy Operator indubitably is important to smooth and efficient rolling in this mill, and the grievant appears to be a valuable member of the production team. It is the job which is classified, however, not the individual. This record does not show that, in any real sense, the job coordinates the flow of steel from the pits to the rolling mills. Observation confirms this conclusion.

12. Addition of the trolley-phone communication in one direction to the publicaddress communication in the other has enabled the disputed job to convey more explicit information in each direction, but that function continues to be, as it was before the advent of the trolley phone, a relaying of information about a decision that has already been reached by one of the jobs at either end of the operation. In some cases, simply by observing the situation immediately outside his pulpit, the Ingot Buggy Operator is able to make the fairly obvious decision that the mill is running a little behind or ahead of the supply of ingots from the soaking pits, and in that event, a word or two to the Pit Craneman on the trolley phone will tell him to hurry up or slow down for a minute. But this much was done before the trolley phone, although not so efficiently.

13. To the extent that the Ingot Buggy Operator has a part in assuring that ingots go to the mill in proper sequence, it is no greater than that of the other production jobs and is not significantly different from what

it was before the coming of the trolley phone. The only really new incident of the Ingot Buggy Operators job is the ability to communicate verbally with the Pit Craneman. Communication with the Pit Craneman was part of the job when first established, however, as reflected by Item 5 of the Working Procedure of the original description and classification: "Communicates with Pit Craneman regarding when ingots are to be drawn."

14. No Specimen Example is cited to justify increasing any of the disputed factors. Accordingly, the grievance will be denied.

AWARD

15. The grievance is denied.

USC—587.   South Works.   November 7, 1956

Sylvester Garrett, *Chairman*

FINDINGS

1. This grievance from the Locomotive Repair Shop, Maintenance Division, South Works, asserts that the job content of Locomotive Repairman (Diesels) has changed to the extent that its classification should be increased from Class 15 to Class 16.

2. It is urged that significant changes have occurred in the equipment serviced by the Locomotive Repairman over the years since 1947, and that greater skills and knowledge now are required. The evidence does not show, however, any sufficient change in job content to require new description and classification as provided in Section 9-D. While the principal Union witness was a Locomotive Repairman with impressive background and technical qualifications, this cannot affect the description and classification of the job, as described and classified under the Inequities Program of the parties.

AWARD

3. The grievance is denied.

T—72.   Fairfield Steel Works.   April 28, 1948

Ralph T. Seward, *Chairman*

BACKGROUND FACTS

1. Some time in May, 1947, the Company installed a 96" Horizontal Boring, Drilling and Milling Machine in the machine shop at its Fairfield Steel Works, and classified this work as a Labor Grade 16 occupation.

2. On May 16, 1947, the employee working on this machine filed the following grievance:

"Request that the occupation of 96" Horizontal Boring, Drilling and Milling machine man be placed in Job Class 18, as I feel that Job Class 16 does not properly cover this occupation."

3. The differences between the parties have been narrowed down to two of the twelve basic factors determining the classification of the job. One is the element of the employment training and experience, where the Company assigned 3.2 points, while the Union is demandind 4.0. The other is the element of responsibility for tools and equipment, where the Company assigned 0.7 points, while the Union is requesting 1.0.

FINDINGS

4. It will be noted that the total difference between the parties is 1.1 points. Consequently, even if it were conceded that the Union is correct, its own evidence would not place the job at higher than Labor Grade 17, although the grievance requests Labor Grade 18. The Union offered to compromise on Labor Grade 17 in the 4th Step.

5. In attempting to justify its figure on employment training and experience, the Union has largely relied on the fact that the employee originally placed on this machine had forty some years of experience. Consequently, according to the Union, only an exceptionally well-trained employee can hold this job. This is refuted by the fact that shortly after the beginning of operations, the Company assigned to this machine on a different shift, a young man with 2½ years of experience as a machinist with the Company. No criticism of his ability to fill the job has been offered by either of the parties. This latter evidence seems to remove the principal argument of the Union on this score.

6. In view of this situation, the total difference between the Company and the Union is narrowed to .3 of a point. If this were granted to the Union, it would not be sufficient to raise the job from Labor Grade 16 to 17, let alone to 18.

7. While the Union contends that there is a greater responsibility for tools and equipment, this is set off by evidence that the machine is equipped with more automatic and safety controls than other machines, thus reducing the probability of damage.

8. It should also be pointed out that in the classification of the machinist as well as the other more important machine tool operators in this plant, the weights given to the factors involved in this dispute are identical with those proposed by the Company in this case.

9. The Union has not established that the two factors in dispute should be increased as requested, or that the total job value should be raised to Labor Grade 17 or 18. For these reasons the grievance is denied.

AWARD

10. The Board denies the grievance.

CHAPTER 14

"MORE OF THE SAME" PRINCIPLE

The volume of work of a job may obviously fluctuate. If the workload of a job is increased by the addition of more of the same kind of work, is the classification of the job affected? The cases contained in this chapter explore that question. See also Chapter 6, "Claim of No Significant Change in Job Content."

Other relevant cases reported elsewhere in this volume are: USC-293 (page 232), USC-319 (page 154), CI-247, -248 (page 157), USC-605 (page 128).

USC—626. Fairless Works. August 15, 1957
Herbert L. Sherman, Jr., *Arbitrator*
Approved by Sylvester Garrett, *Chairman*

BACKGROUND

1. This grievance arose as a result of the addition of three HNX Generators to two HNX Generators for which grievants have always been responsible. The Union claims that higher ratings are required on Factors 2, 5, 6, 7, 8 and 10 for the job of Gas Plant Tender (HNX), now in Job Class 11, in the Sheet and Tin Division at Fairless Works.

2. Protests over the classification ratings for this job have been pending in the grievance procedure a good part of the time since it was first established in July, 1953. An earlier grievance, protesting the classification of the job, was denied by Management in the Third Step of the grievance procedure on January 19, 1955. This decision was not appealed by the Union to the Fourth Step. On September 19, 1955 the present grievance, claiming that additional changes affected the classification ratings, was filed.

3. The primary function of the job in dispute is to operate gas conditioners to produce gas for both batch and continuous annealing. After the earlier grievance was settled, Management added three Westinghouse Monogas HNX Generators to the two original Surface Combustion HNX Generators. No Form G was issued by the Company because it believed that the original job description covered the operation of the three new units.

4. Grievants contend that more credit should be assigned to Factor 2—Employment Training and Experience. They emphasize that different instruction books are used in the operation of the two types of generating units, that the Westinghouse units require more frequent adjustments, that regular operators are called out when a relief man is faced with a breakdown, and that two supervisors were used to operate the gas plant during a strike. More training is necessary to operate the Westinghouse units, they claim, because the blowing of pre-mixed gas into combustion chambers may give rise to an explosion. Management concedes that workload has been increased by way of adjustment of more valves, but it contends that no significant increase in employment training or experience is required to learn to do the job.

5. Since the number of machines to be checked has been increased from two to five, production has been greatly increased, the number of charts to be checked has increased, and the building has been enlarged, the Union urges a higher rating on Factor 5 —Responsibility for Materials. The Company notes that the material produced by the Surface Combustion and Westinghouse Generators is the same and that it is used for the same purpose. Both types of units discharge into the same common header before the gas goes to batch anneal. The recording devices are also similar for both types of machines. According to the Company no higher degree of responsibility for material has been imposed upon grievants.

6. With respect to Factor 6—Responsibility for Tools and Equipment, the Union stresses the cost of the three new Westinghouse units and also the replacement cost of a catalyst if grievants fail to exercise proper care. And in connection with Factor 7—Re-

240

sponsibility for Operations, the Union emphasizes the dependence of the annealing process upon the proper operation of the gas plant. Management states that there has always been some danger of loss of equipment, such as a catalyst, but that there has been no change warranting higher ratings on Factors 6 and 7.

7. Under Factor 8—Responsibility for Safety of Others the Union points out that grievant has no assistant and that he must telephone plant protection every hour to advise them that he is all right. His building is set apart from others because of the possibility of an explosion. With respect to Factor 10—Physical Effort grievants note that they are sometimes required to use a very long wrench to turn valves, to lift 100 pound bags and drums, to walk a great deal on a concrete floor, and to use ladders to check equipment. The Company's testimony is that these conditions and duties do not constitute changes in the job.

8. Management argues that the only changes in the job are "more of the same," and that although an increase in the workload may affect grievants' incentive earnings, it does not affect the classification ratings. To support this position, the Company cites the Board's Awards in USC-605, USC-281, USC-282, USC-293 and A-499. The Union relies on descriptive language in the Classification Manual opposite the codings which it seeks.

9. The Union proposes factor value increases as follows:

FACTOR	PRESENT CLASSIFICATION		UNION PROPOSAL	
2. Employment Training and Experience	C	.8	D	1.2
5. Responsibility for Materials	D	.8	E	2.3
6. Responsibility for Tools and Equipment	C	1.0	E	3.0
7. Responsibility for Operations	D	2.0	E	3.0
8. Responsibility for Safety of Others	C	.8	D	1.2
10. Physical Effort	B	.3	C	.8

DISCUSSION AND FINDINGS

10. Addition of three more modern HNX Generators to the two HNX Generators, for which grievants were already responsible, did not affect the classification ratings on Factors 2, 5, 6, 7, 8 and 10 in the light of prior decisions of the Board and the classification ratings on the most closely related jobs. There was no addition of equipment of a different nature. The differences between the two types of units were not shown to be significant from a classification standpoint.

11. No changes except for the increased workload resulting from installation of the three new HNX Generators were disclosed by the evidence. A Gas Plant Tender job at Irvin Works, responsible for operation of four HNX Generators to produce gas for annealing, and a Gas Plant Tender job at Gary Sheet and Tin, responsible for operation of five HNX Generators to produce gas for annealing, are coded the same as the job in dispute except for Factor 11. It is the higher rating on this factor for the job under consideration which places it in Job Class 11, while the Irvin Works and Gary Sheet and Tin jobs are in Job Class 10. A Gas Plant Tender job at Vandergrift Works has duties and responsibilities which differ from those of grievants. Hence, the grievance must be denied.

AWARD

12. The grievance is denied.

USC—281, -282.   Edgar Thomson Works.   March 16, 1953

Frederick Harbison, *Arbitrator*

1. Since the issues involved are identical, the Company and the Union by agreement argued these two grievances as companion cases in the hearings. Most of the evidence introduced had specific application to the 1st engineer job.

ISSUES INVOLVED

2. These cases involve a determination of whether the content of the grievants' jobs has been increased to the extent of more than one full job class in accordance with Section 9-D of the April 22, 1947 Agreement.

BACKGROUND

3. Before 1949, the equipment in the Number 2 Power Station consisted of two turbo-blowers and their auxiliaries. The function of the turbo-blowers is to supply air under pressure to the blast furnaces. In late 1949, a third turbo-blower along with its auxiliaries was installed in the No. 2 power house. This third unit is similar to the original two units, except that it is newer, has some improved controls, and has somewhat greater blowing capacity. All these blowers, however, are of the same general type and are made by the same manufacturer. The three units are operated by the same personnel as the original two units.

4. The Union contends that the addition of the new blower should increase the job class of the 1st Engineer from 12.8 to 15.5, and the job class of the 2nd Engineer from 9.0 to 11.7.

5. The Union contends that the addition of equipment has influenced factors 2, 5, 7, 9, and 11 in both of the instant job descriptions. It rests its case on two main grounds: *first,* that the addition of equipment in itself requires a reclassification of the jobs, and *second,* that the new equipment is different from the old and thus justifies reclassification.

6. The position of the Company is that the new turbo-blower is the same as the old blowers, and that the addition of more of the same type of equipment does not influence any of the factors in either of the instant job descriptions.

7. This case requires, therefore, a determination of whether the equipment is the same, and whether the addition of more of the same type of equipment influences factors 2, 5, 7, 9, and 11 of the instant job descriptions.

FINDINGS

8. From the evidence submitted to the Board the Arbitrator finds that the new equipment is substantially the same as the old.

9. The Union contended that additional training was required for the engineers to operate the new equipment. However, it could not support this contention. It is true that the engineers who installed the new blower may have given some instructions to the grievants regarding the operation of the new equipment, but this was similar perhaps to the type of instruction an automobile dealer might give to the purchaser of a new automobile with more modern controls. For example, Mr. Henderson, a 1st Engineer (blower) testified that the operation of the

blowers was very much the same. Asked these questions by Mr. Stewart of the Company, "This new Turbo-blower is very much like any other turbo-blower, isn't it? It may be a little more modern?", Mr. Henderson replied, "Well, as to that, I would have to be honest enough to say yes." The testimony of the 2nd Engineer, Mr. McAndrew, was in the same vein. When asked by Mr. Stewart the question, "All of these units function more or less the same, do they not?", Mr. McAndrew replied, "In principle, I would say so, yes." Both Mr. McAndrew and Mr. Henderson emphasized that the effect of addition of the new blower was to increase the responsibility of the job "by a third." As Mr. McAndrew summed up, "Well, just as Mr. Henderson stated, I believe it is one-third more responsibility, completely, all the way around, such as added valves and added controls, charts, condensers, the whole complete unit is one-third more."

10. It is true that the testimony of Mr. Callahan, a maintenance man, emphasized certain differences in the equipment from a maintenance point of view. This testimony, however, is irrelevant to the operation of the equipment which is the job of the engineers.

11. For the purposes of these cases, therefore, the arbitrator finds that, as related to the jobs of 1st and 2nd engineers, the new turbo-blower is practically identical to the two older blowers, and that thus the addition of the third unit represents an addition of more of the same equipment rather than an addition of a new kind of equipment in the No. 2 Power Station. For this reason, the Arbitrator finds that there has been no change in Factor 2 of the instant job descriptions because no additional employment training or experience is necessary to operate more of the same type of equipment.

12. With respect to *Factor 5—Responsibility for Material,* the Union argues that the factor ratings on both jobs should be increased from B.3 to C.7. The material handled on these jobs is mostly air, and the responsibility of the engineers is to maintain proper vacuum and sufficient supply of air to the blast furnaces. The Arbitrator is unable to understand why the addition of the new blower would influence the responsibility of the engineers with respect to maintaining the supply of air, and he fails to find any explanation of, or support for, the contention by the Union that "Equipment on this job is considered materials." He finds, therefore, that Factor 5 is not influenced by the addition of the new blower.

13. With respect to *Factor 7—Responsibility for Operations,* the Arbitrator is unable to find any basis for a change in the

factor value. The engineers are responsible only for supplying air to the furnaces. The decision regarding the amount of air to be supplied is made by a member of the furnace crew. The addition of the third blower does not change the basic responsibility of the engineers for "operation of a medium-sized producing unit closely associated with other operations."

14. With respect to *Factor 9—Mental Effort,* the Union argues that "with added new control boards, bearing readings, oil temperature readings, etc., the visual concentration has been increased." In the case of both jobs, the Union proposes an increase from C 1.0 to D 1.5. Though there are more gauges to watch, the Arbitrator is unable to find evidence to show that the addition of the third blower would require "close mental or visual application" as described in the manual as opposed to "moderate mental or visual application" as contemplated in the existing descriptions. The witnesses for the Union did not offer any convincing testimony which would provide a sound basis for an increase in factor ratings on this score.

15. With respect to *Factor 11—Surroundings,* the Union argues that the increase in heat and noise resulting from addition of the third blower is grounds for increasing the factor value of both jobs from B.4 to C.8. When the new equipment was first installed, there appears to have been a very substantial increase in both heat and noise which would probably be sufficient to justify the contention of the Union on this score. However, recognizing this problem, the Company later insulated certain lines and pipes which apparently reduced both the heat and the noise from the blowers. Accordingly, it is doubtful whether any increase in factor values is now justifiable because of increased heat and noise.

16. The Union attempted to show in the hearings that the Company had set a precedent for an increase in classification of blowing engineer jobs when it introduced an additional blower in a similar power station at the Youngstown Works. In the Youngstown case, the job class of the 1st Engineer was increased from 13 to 14. In this case, however, the original equipment consisted of reciprocating blower engines, while the additional unit was a turbo-blower. In the settlement of this case by agreement between the Company and Union, it was specifically stated that "the addition of steam turbo-blower equipment to steam reciprocating blower engines constitutes the addition of equipment dissimilar to existing equipment and, therefore, is proper cause for a change in job content; whereas the addition of 'more of the same' ordinarily does not materially affect the job classification." Since the Arbitrator finds that the addition of the third blower in the instant grievances represents an addition of more of the same type of equipment, the Youngstown case lends support to his finding that there is no basis for a change in the classification of the jobs of the engineers involved in the instant cases.

AWARD

17. The grievances are denied.

A—499. New Haven Works. April 27, 1953

J. Orvis Keller, *Arbitrator*

BACKGROUND

1. It is the contention of the Union that in the case of two (2) Class A-19 wire-stranding machines located in the Fine Cord Sub-Section of the Stranding and Laying Section of the Rope Department at the New Haven Works of the American Steel and Wire Division, a higher job classification should be given this operation than was originally agreed upon as Operator—Stranding Machine Class A—(Plant Code 20-55) by the Joint Wage Rate Inequity Negotiating Committee, commonly known as the Cooper-Maloy Committee or the Maloy-Cooper Committee. While it was originally agreed by both the Union and the Company that all Class A stranding machines should be placed in the same job class, the Union believes that the job content in this particular operation has been increased more than one job class subsequent to the time the original classification was determined and agreed upon.

2. Specifically the Union contends that while the wording of the job description should remain essentially as originally approved for Class A stranding machines, in this specific case the classification is in error for three factors relating to job content for a total of 1.2 points determined as follows:

*Factor 2—Employment Training
        and Experience:* should be 0.8 instead of 0.4.................. .4 increase
Factor 3—Mental Skill: should be 2.2 instead of 1.6......... .... .6 increase
*Factor 5—Responsibility
        for Materials:* should be C.7 instead of 0.5.................... .2 increase

Total points increased: 1.2

DISCUSSION AND FINDINGS

3. The Company contends that the job description for all Class A stranding machines was established at New Haven as Plant Code 20-55, and that this description covers and was meant to cover all Class A stranding machines in any combination. While this job description was dated March 30, 1945, Company representatives stated and Union representatives did not deny that the approval signatures of both the Union and Company representatives were not affixed to the proper forms until late 1946 or early 1947. The Company then introduced in evidence a "Draw Off" of production run on the Class A-19 stranding machine located in the department under consideration and known as machine number 19 to show that this machine was in operation on 19 wire jobs as early as March 8, 1945.

4. The Union testified that there were separate classifications for B-7, B-19, C-7, C-13, C-19 and F-19 stranding machines and saw no reason, therefore, why A-19 machines could not have a classification separate from A-7 and A-13 machines. The Company in rebuttal contended that the very fact that different sized B, C, and F stranders had separate job classifications was ample precedent for originally considering different sized A stranders separately. The fact that the local union and management committees proceeded to draw up and sign a single description for all Class A stranders, in spite of the separate descriptions for the B, C, and F stranders, is rather conclusive evidence that the parties fully intended the description to apply to all types of "A" stranders.

5. It was further stated by Company representatives that the single job description and classification agreed to locally to cover the operation of all Class A stranders was reviewed by representatives of the Cooper-Maloy Committee prior to April 22, 1947, and was approved by them as being in line with the over-all objective of placing all jobs in their proper relationships with each other.

6. It was brought out in testimony that no request was made by the Union for a review of the findings during the period June 22, 1947, to July 6, 1947, which was the period specified by the Cooper-Maloy Committee for final questioning of job descrip-

tions and classifications in effect on April 22, 1947, when the basic agreement between the parties was executed.

7. A Company representative testified that at the Trenton plant a job description was tentatively drawn up covering A-7 and A-13 stranders, but when two A-19 stranders were put into operation, the job description and classification was changed to make the description and classification include all Class A stranders. This description and classification was agreed to by both the Union and the Company at the Trenton Plant. As was the case in New Haven, this Trenton job description and classification of Class A stranders went through the whole program of review by representatives of the Joint Wage Rate Inequity Negotiating Committee, according to a statement made by Company Counsel which was unchallenged by the Union.

8. It was mutually agreed that the Job Description and Classification entitled "Operator, Stranding Machine Class A—(Plant Code 20-55)" was in effect on April 22, 1947.

9. Section 9-D of the Agreement of April 22, 1947, states in part:

"The job description and classification for each job in effect as of the date of this Agreement shall continue in effect unless (1) Management changes the job content (requirements of the job as to the training, skill, responsibility, effort, and working conditions) to the extent of one full job class or more; (2) the job is terminated or not occupied during a period of one year; or (3) the description and classification are changed in accordance with mutual agreement of officially designated representatives of the Company and the Union."

10. The burden of proof was therefore upon the Union to show that management had changed the job content to the extent of one full job class or more. The Company pointed out that during the discussion of a grievance in the Step Four Minutes, which were introduced in evidence, the Union admitted that the installation of the two A-19 stranders did not make it necessary to make any changes in the Job Description. The job

description of Operator, Stranding Machine Class A—(Plant Code 20-55) for Factor 2, Employment Training and Experience, reads as follows:

"This job requires experience on this and related work of 3 to 6 months of continuous progress."

11. The numerical classification as shown in the Manual for Job Classification dated August 10, 1945, for this amount of experience required for a job is 0.4, and not 0.8, as contended by the Union. For this higher rating a job must require from seven to twelve months' experience. The Union had introduced as an exhibit copies of the official job descriptions and classifications for the following wire stranding machines: B-7, B-19, C-7, C-13, C-19, and F-19. In the case of the classifications of B-19, C-19 and F-19 stranding machines, the numerical rating for Factor 2 was placed at 0.8, while for the other machines this rating was 0.4, the same as the rating for Class A stranding machines. However, the job descriptions for Factor 2 in the higher rated machine were given as "7 to 12 months of continuous progress" while in the case of the B-7, C-7, C-13 and the Class A stranding machines, the description for Factor 2 reads: "3 to 6 months of continuous progress." As previously mentioned, the Union had contended that the wording of the description for A-19 stranders required no change from the wording of the Class A stranders as given in the description designated as Plant Code 20-55.

12. Since the elimination of Factor 2 from consideration in this case would reduce the total points advocated by the Union to less than one full job class, the Board would conclude that the installation of the two additional A-19 stranders did not change the job content one full job class.

13. However, the Union did not produce evidence to show that Factor 3—Mental Skill, had been changed by the introduction of the two additional A-19 stranders. No new type of equipment was added, but rather only more machines of the same kind.

14. The Union also failed to show that the installation of the two additional A-19 stranders changed Factor 5—Responsibility for Materials. The Union pointed out that some materials formerly run on the B-19 stranders (Job Class 11) were transferred to the A-19 stranders (Job Class 9) at a higher rate of production. The Company Counsel pointed out that a comparison of the classification of the B-19 stranders with the classification of the "A" stranders, based on the same product being made on both, can be of value to the position of the Union in the grievance only insofar as the Union alleges an inequity in the original classification of the one job or the other.

15. Section 9-H of the Agreement of April 22, 1947, provides as follows:

"No basis shall exist for an employee, whether paid on an incentive or nonincentive basis, to allege that a wage-rate inequity exists and no grievance on behalf of an employee alleging a wage-rate inequity shall be filed or processed during the term of this Agreement."

16. From the foregoing, the Board would conclude that the existing description and classification of the job of Operator—Stranding Machine Class A (Plant Code 22-50) is properly Job Class 9 and covers the operation of all Class A stranding machines used in any combination together.

AWARD

17. The grievance is denied.

N—251. Ellwood Works.   March 21, 1958
Clare B. McDermott, *Assistant to the Chairman*
Approved by Herbert L. Sherman, Jr., *Chairman*

FINDINGS

1. The issue in this grievance from the Accounting Department of the Ellwood Works is whether certain changes made in December of 1953 in the content of the job of (Draw Bench) Incentive Clerk require that its classification be raised from Job Class 9 to Job Class 12, under Section 9-D of the August 15, 1952 Agreement.

2. The job was first classified by agreement in 1950 in Job Class 7. In 1951 certain incentive-rating duties were added, and,

therefore, the classification was raised to Job Class 9.

3. In January of 1954 the following changes in the job were submitted to the Union representatives, retroactive to December 1953.

"Add to Item #3:

"Calculate and post the average piece length for each bale of material.

"Change the First Part of Item #4 to read as follows:

"Refers to appropriate Cold Draw Bench Operator and Gauger Incentive Applications and selects and posts to Reports of Cold Drawing, particular incentive standards and size change standards in accordance with such determining information as material size and gauge, type of material, steel grade, and operation performed." (Underlining added to indicate change.)

4. Further changes in the job were made in January of 1956, but these are not before the Board.

5. The job is now classified as D2.2 in Factor 3, and the Union contends for E2.8. Basically, the Union's position is founded upon the fact that before the change the Clerk was required to perform incentive rating as to the Benchman only, whereas since the change, he must perform incentive rating for both the Benchman and the Gauger. It is said that the mental skill required of an incumbent has increased because the number and complexity of the charts to which he must refer have increased. The Company replies that work load may very well have increased, but insists that the increase is simply more of the same kind of work.

6. Before the 1953 change the primary function of the job included, in general, weighing cold-drawn product, reporting drawbench production data, and applying Benchman incentive rates to that production by reference to the appropriate charts. After the change the primary function remained essentially the same in nature and, therefore, in the requisite degree of mental skill involved. True, the incumbent must now rate both the Benchman and the Gauger, but the necessary mental facility has not increased. The job is classified at 2.2 in Factor 3, which is the same as the classification of the comparable Incentive Clerk jobs, Specimen Examples No. 4770 and 4772. Furthermore, the classification in Factor 3 is the same as that of the two plant jobs of Pointing Incentive Clerk and (Pickling) Incentive Clerk, each of which observes and records production data and selects and applies incentive standards, as does the job in dispute. The Union's chief reference is to the job of Timekeeper (Plant Title: General Clerk—Clock Stations), which is classified 2.8 in Factor 3. It is true that that job, too, involves the application of incentive rates. The evidence indicates, however, that that classification is based upon several significant duties

in addition to incentive rating. As its title indicates, that job involves timekeeping, which includes, among other duties the correlation and reporting of exceptions to the pre-determined schedule and the rating of several production reports which are not rated by a clerk in the mill, which involve a thorough knowledge of timekeeping operations. On the whole, it must be concluded that the change in the job does not justify an increased classification in Factor 3.

7. It should be noted that the addition to the job that requires the clerk to "Calculate and post the average piece length for each bale of material" does not affect classification here. The job had several similar calculating and posting duties before the change.

8. The Factor 5 classification is C1.2, and the Union seeks E1.6. The present Factor 5 classification must be deemed correct. The changes of December, 1953, do not require a higher level of responsibility for materials than that involved in the weighing and incentive-rating duties set forth in the job description of 1951. The jobs cited by the parties that are wholly clerical in nature receive a lower point value in this Factor than does the job in dispute.

9. The objection to the classification of Factor 6 was withdrawn at the hearing.

10. Factor 7 is classified C1.0, but the Union insists that it should be D2.0. There was Union testimony to the effect that operations would be slowed by improper weighing. But it must be pointed out that the changes did not relate to weighing. The weighing functions are the same now as they were before, and thus there is no reason to change this factor, which is classified at the same level as the specimen examples and other jobs referred to by the parties.

11. Factor 9 is classified at D1.5, and the Union asks for E2.5. The evidence indicates that the changes simply added more of the same type of duties but not in such degree as to affect the quality of work performed. Therefore, they do not justify a change in the classification of this Factor, which is equal to that of the reference jobs.

12. Finally, there was some Union testimony bearing upon the classification of Factor 2. It was not of such weight, however, as to justify a change in the rating of this Factor.

AWARD

13. The grievance is denied.

USC—740. Fairless Works. November 19, 1958
Sylvester Garrett, *Chairman*

FINDINGS

1. This grievance from Central Maintenance Department, Fairless Works, asserts that the Trade and Craft job of Painter has been changed to an extent requiring increase of classification from Class 11 to Class 13.

2. During the summer of 1957 a new type paint spray gun and a portable sand blaster were added to equipment used by the Paint Shop at Fairless Works. The paint sprayer, operated hydraulically, atomizes and heats paint to minimize dripping. It supplements an older type spray gun used in the Paint Shop for some years, and eliminates much of the over-spray and fogging which occurs in using the older type spray gun. This new equipment is used rarely—about a dozen times between the summer of 1957 and hearing date.

3. The sand blaster is a portable pneumatic tool with hose and nozzle device feeding from a hopper capable of holding up to 200 pounds of sand. Its use replaces manual scraping, chipping, and sanding to prepare surfaces for painting on some work assignments. It is used by the Painters from 1% to 2% of their work time.

4. The Union urges that use of these items of equipment affect the coding of factors as follows:

FACTOR	PRESENT CLASSI- FICATION	PROPOSED CLASSI- FICATION
6—Responsibility for Tools and Equipment	B- .2 Low	C-1.0 High
7—Responsibility for Operations	A-Base	B- .5
8—Responsibility for Safety of Others	B- .4	C- .8
11—Surroundings	B- .4	C- .8

5. The Union stresses that the new equipment adds to responsibility under Factor 6 and affects responsibility for operations under Factor 7. Because of the dust arising from use of the sand blaster, it believes that Factor 8 should be increased and that the Painters are entitled to a higher coding under Factor 11 because they wear protective clothing and use a respirator while operating both the sand blaster and the new paint sprayer.

6. The new spray gun does not differ essentially from the old for purposes of coding the factors in dispute. The protective clothing and respirator used in operating the sand blasting equipment are the same as for spray painting. The original description and classification of Painter at Fairless covers use of spray gun equipment. The new sand blasting equipment is simply an additional tool which simplifies preparation of surfaces for painting where previously scrapers, chipping hammers, wire brushes, blow torches, or sandpaper may have been used.

7. Upon review of all of the evidence, these two new items of equipment provide no basis to sustain the grievance.

AWARD

8. The grievance is denied.

CI—223. Homestead Works. December 20, 1951
Frederick H. Harbison, *Acting Chairman*

BACKGROUND

1. The grievance is a request for a new description and classification of the job of Fuel Attendant at #5 Open Hearth in the Company's Homestead Works. It reads as follows:

"We, the Fuel Attendants at Open Hearth #5, request that management develop a new job description and classification in accordance with Section 9, Subsection D, of the Agreement."

The request is based upon a claim that the addition of new pumping equipment and storage capacity has changed the content of the job to the extent of more than one job class. The Union requests that any adjustments be made retroactive to the date when the disputed change in job description should have been put into effect.

2. The comparison of the "old" and "changed" job as set forth by the Union in the Third Step grievance meeting is as follows:

OLD JOB

1. Three one-half million gallon tanks containing oil and tar.
2. Operate two unloading pumps.
3. Four pumps to be installed for fuel oil pressure to 160″ Mill and 100″ Mill.

4. Care for all steam traps and oil heaters.
5. Raise and lower pressure as required. Raise and lower temperature from time to time, as required by Fuel Engineers.
6. Keep the pump house and all machinery clean and orderly at all times.
7. Oversee the unloading of all oil cars. See that all outside area is kept clean and orderly.
8. Unload and pump oil from all tank trailer trucks and keep record of same.
9. Make Shipping bills for all tank cars unloaded at pump house.
10. Plenty of trouble in cold weather with steam-traps, and oil heaters freezing up.
11. Operators pack and oil all pumps.
12. Dispensing and keeping records of Diesel fuel oil, putting Dacrol in fuel oil and keeping records of same.

CHANGED JOB (Additional Duties)

1. Two 1¼ million gallon tanks #4 and #5 containing oil and tar.
2. Pumphouse containing three electric pumps and all necessary equipment for operation of same.
3. #32 steam traps to operate and maintain.
4. Supervision of unloading tracks and tank men. Also must see that outside area is kept clean and orderly.
5. Load tank cars with tar for OH #4 from storage tanks.
6. It is approximately 1/5 mile between the old pump house and the new one, which we must make several trips per day, through all kinds of weather, crossing three railroad tracks.
7. When oil supply gets low, it is necessary to pump oil from #4 and #5 storage tanks to #1, #2 and #3 storage tanks. This means, traveling from one pump house to the other, opening several different valves for the operation of same.
8. All cars that are unloaded into #4 and #5 tanks are billed in and out by the pump house operators.
9. Strainers in pump house cleaned daily. This work is done by the operators.
10. Operators duty to operate new Foamite Station now being built for #4 and #5 oil and tar tanks.
11. Operators pack and oil all pumps.

3. The Company's position is that the new equipment added is similar to the existing old equipment. The Company alleges that the additional equipment does not create duties different from those covered in the original job description, but has had the effect of increasing the work load, thus utilizing a portion of the stand-by time of the incumbent. The Company's position is that the addition of "more of the same" equipment does not warrant a change in any of the factors in the original job description.

4. The Union alleges that changes should be made in Factors 2, 5, 6, 8, 10 and 11 and that as a consequence the new "rack-up" for the job should total 8.8 instead of 6.0 as called for in the existing job description.

5. Both sides are in agreement that the amount of new equipment added is quite substantial. Under the new set-up, the number of pieces of equipment for which the attendant is responsible has been approximately doubled. The attendant is now required to maintain pumping equipment and storage tanks at two locations (one-fifth of a mile apart) instead of at only one location.

FINDINGS

6. On the basis of analysis of the evidence submitted in the briefs and the hearing and also an observation of the job in question as well as related jobs, the Board makes the following findings:

7. (1.) With respect to Factor #2— Employment Training and Experience, the Union proposes a rating of C.8 instead of B.4 on grounds that there are (1) floating gauges on the new storage tanks, (2) the equipment in the new pump house is substantially different from the equipment in the original pump house, and (3) a new Foamite station has been added. The Board finds, on the basis of statements by one of the operators, that the new equipment is sufficiently similar to the old equipment as to not require any significant additional employment training and experience, and hence no additional rating is warranted on this score.

8. (2.) With respect to Factor 5—Responsibility for Materials, the Union proposes a rating of B.4 instead of B.3 because more material is handled and thus there is a greater possible chance of waste. The Board finds that the great increase in the volume of materials handled fully justifies the Union's contention on this score. According to an operator's statement, furthermore, there is more danger of mixing oil and tar by turning the wrong valve.

9. (3.) With respect to Factor 6—Responsibility for Tools and Equipment, the Union claims C-1.0 instead of B.3 on the grounds that there is always a chance of more damage because of additional and more complicated equipment. The Board finds that the responsibility of the operator

requires some attention and care required to recognize obvious trouble and shut down equipment. Because of the greater amount of equipment which must be watched by the operator in widely separated locations, the Board finds that a change in rating from Med. B.3 to High B.5 is appropriate. It does not feel that a C-1.0 rating is called for since the new equipment is roughly similar to the old. Comparable job descriptions provide for the C-1.0 rating only when substantially different equipment is involved.

10. (4.) With respect to Factor 8—Responsibility for Safety of Others, the Union proposes a rating of C.8 instead of A-Base. The Union pointed out that trucks are constantly coming into the area at all times. It also pointed out that the OH #5 reporting shed is in the area, and thus large numbers of people are occasionally exposed. From this the Board must conclude that the equipment in question is operated where others are occasionally exposed. It finds, however, that Factor 8 should be rated as B.4, which is similar to the rating on other fuel oil attendant and pump tender jobs where others are occasionally exposed.

11. (5.) With respect to Factor 10—Physical Effort, the Union proposes C.8 instead of B.3. The Union alleged that required physical effort is greater because of (1) strainers to pick up and clean at frequent intervals, (2) occasional climbing to top of 55-foot tanks to read or check floating gauges, (3) walking up and down stairs in two pump houses instead of one, (4) frequent walking between the two pump houses, (5) re-packing more pumps, and (6) additional occasional assistance in loading or un-loading tank cars near the new pump house. Conversation with an operator on this job confirms the fact the physical effort required has been greatly increased because of the addition of the new equipment. The change in equipment certainly calls for moderate physical exertion rather than light physical exertion. Thus, the Board agrees with the rating of C.8 proposed by the Union and for generally the same reasons as those advanced by the Union.

12. (6.) With respect to Factor 11—Surroundings, the Union proposes C.8 instead of B.4. The Union alleges that the operator is outside a great part of his time because of (1) walking between pump stations, (2) watching float gauges on new fuel tanks, (3) occasionally climbing new tanks to check gauges, and (4) assisting in loading and unloading of more tank cars and trucks. The operator who was interviewed indicated that he was required to be outside in all weather conditions a great deal more of his time as a consequence of the installation of the new equipment. He also said that he frequently had to climb on tank cars when his helper was at the other pump house. He is also exposed to oil, tar, and grease. For these reasons the Board agrees with the position taken by the Union.

AWARD

13. The content of the job of Fuel Attendant in the #5 Open Hearth has been increased a total of 1.6 job classes. The operators are entitled to an adjustment retroactive to the date when the new job description should have been put into effect.

USC—390. South Works. December 30, 1953
Herbert L. Sherman, Jr., *Assistant to Chairman*
Approved by Sylvester Garrett, *Chairman*

BACKGROUND

1. This grievance arose in the Physical Laboratory of the Metallurgical Division at South Works. Grievants, incumbents of the job known as Inspection Record Clerk, Record Clerk-Foreign Inspection, or Physical Laboratory Clerk, request that the classification of the job be raised from Job Class 10 to Job Class 11 on the ground that new duties have been added. The job description has been revised at the request of the Union. Higher ratings are sought on Factors 2, 3 and 5.

2. The present ratings on the Factors and those proposed by the Union are set forth in the table below.

FACTOR	PRESENT RATINGS	PROPOSED BY UNION
1. Pre-employment Training.	C- 1.0	C- 1.0
*2. Employment Training and Experience.	E- 1.6	F- 2.0
*3. Mental Skill.	D-2.2	E-2.8
4. Manual Skill.	B- .5	B- .5
*5. Responsibility for Material.	D- .8	D-1.1
6. Responsibility for Tools and Equipment.	B- .2	B- .2
7. Responsibility for Operations.	D-2.0	D-2.0

FACTOR	PRESENT RATINGS	PROPOSED BY UNION
8. Responsibility for Safety of Others.	A-Base	A-Base
9. Mental Effort.	D-1.5	D-1.5
10. Physical Effort.	A-Base	A-Base
11. Surroundings.	A-Base	A-Base
12. Hazards.	A-Base	A-Base
Total	9.8	11.1

* Disputed Factors

3. At the hearing the Union contended that Factor 5 should be raised at least to D-1.1. It does not rely on any particular monetary value, but asserts that the Company should negotiate in order to arrive at a mutually satisfactory figure.

4. Although other added clerical tasks which were introduced over a period of time, such as arranging for processing of special tests requested by the Steel Analyst and keeping time records on certain turns, are set forth by the Union, greatest stress is placed on the new duty of release for shipment of tested mill inspection material when test results meet ordered specifications. Previously, the incumbents of the job in dispute only handled release of foreign inspection material, i.e., material subject to inspection by customer representatives before it leaves the plant. The Inspection Record Clerk was and still is required to check all prior test information for foreign inspection material including the checking of physical test results against specifications, and he arranges for foreign inspection service. If the material fails to conform to test requirements, he refers it to higher authority in the Metallurgical Division.

5. Prior to April, 1951, mill inspection material was released through a more complicated procedure involving the Metallurgical Department and the Accounting Department. Since the former department was dissatisfied with that method, the procedure was revised and clearance of mill inspection material for shipment was made a part of the Inspection Record Clerk job. Release of material was then undertaken on all three turns and five more employees were added to the two already assigned to this job. The Shipping Clerk in the Accounting Department, however, still checks on all shipping requirements including proper clearance from the Metallurgical Department. No change was made in the classification of the Shipping Clerk job.

6. Both in the case of foreign inspection material and in the case of mill inspection material, certain forms have to be prepared and information transcribed. If the checking reveals that the product fails to meet specifications, the matter is referred to higher authority whether foreign inspection or mill inspection material is involved. The Union points out that more than one customer's name may appear on the sheet for a heat where mill inspection is involved, thus creating more opportunity for error. If the customers' specifications are different, more checking is required. Also, more checking of the tensile ranges is involved for mill inspection material, since the possibility of release for other than ordered specifications must be explored. Although grievants check several tensile ranges for mill inspection material to ascertain whether the product meets more than one range as contrasted with foreign inspection material, the method of checking is the same in both instances.

DISCUSSION AND FINDINGS

7. There is no doubt that several duties have been added to the job in dispute. The only addition that might appear to affect the classification ratings, however, is the release of mill inspection material. Nevertheless, it cannot properly be found that the procedure involved is essentially different from the function of releasing foreign inspection material for the purpose of coding Factors 2, 3 and 5. The type of checking, transcribing, and forwarding of information is fundamentally the same. Although the volume of work has increased, more employees have been assigned to the Inspection Record Clerk job to handle the greater workload.

8. Specimen 4730, an Inspection Record Clerk job in Class 9, releases material based on metallurgical and chemical test results and is similar to the job in dispute; both jobs are rated the same on Factors 2, 3 and 5. The Shipping Clerk job at South Works has higher ratings on these Factors, but the function of billing customers is emphasized in the classification as a basis for the higher ratings. No other job presented to the Board is assigned higher ratings than those presently assigned to the job in dispute. In the light of this background, the grievance must be denied.

AWARD

9. The grievance is denied.

USC—859.   Fairless Works.   July 17, 1959
Sylvester Garrett, *Chairman*

FINDINGS

1.   This grievance from the Utitlities Department at Fairless Works claims that changes in the job content of the Utilities System Operator job warrant an increase in the classification from Job Class 12 to Job Class 17. Last year, in USC-651, the Board denied a grievance protesting the ratings originally assigned to this same job.

2.   There is no testimony in the present case addressed to any particular factor rating. Nor were any comparisons made at the hearing in terms of other job descriptions and classifications.

3.   According to the Union the ratings on Factors 3, 4, 5, 6, 7, 8 and 10 should be increased. Following is a table which shows the present and the proposed ratings on these Factors:

FACTORS:	PRESENT CLASSIFI-CATION	PROPOSED CLASSIFI-CATION
3. Mental Skill	D-2.2	E-2.8
4. Manual Skill	B- .5	C-1.0
5. Responsibility for Materials	C- .5	D-1.1
6. Responsibility for Tools and Equipment	High C-1.0	High D-2.0
7. Responsibility for Operations	D-2.0	E-3.0
8. Responsibility for Safety of Others	C- .8	D-1.2
10. Physical Effort	B- .3	C- .8

4.   As noted in USC-651, grievants have always been required to inspect, service and operate utilities distribution systems equipment while making periodic rounds of the various utilities stations. Similar additional units of pump and turbine equipment have been added to their responsibilities, such as the equipment in the Open Hearth Pump House. Daily inspection must be made to determine whether certain automatic equipment is functioning properly, and a report must be filled out. Grievants were furnished with written instructions relating to the operation of the Pump House equipment, so that they would be familiar with the proper procedures if it was necessary to stop or start certain stand-by pumping equipment.

5.   Though there may be some increase in the volume of work, there is no evidence that any higher degree of skill is required or that any greater degree of responsibility has been imposed on grievants as a result of duties added since the original classification of their job.

6.   With respect to grievants' duties in connection with the unloading of oil barges, it does not appear that there has been any significant change from the standpoint of the classification ratings. This duty has been performed on an average of once a week.

7.   There is one further point that deserves comment. At the hearing there was considerable discussion concerning the truck driving duties of grievants. Most of the discussion was in terms of misunderstandings that have developed between the parties on this point. Since another grievance is pending on this matter, which was unavailable at the hearing, this problem cannot be finally resolved in this award. It is appropriate to note, however, that the Utilities System Operator's job description has always provided for driving a truck in the performance of his duties, that the Operator originally was expected to transport the Motor Inspector to various locations on some occasions, and that occasionally transporting other Repairmen in similar fashion would not affect the classification ratings of grievants' job.

AWARD

8.   The grievance is denied.

USC—960.   Clairton Works.   February 29, 1960
Sylvester Garrett, *Chairman*

BACKGROUND

1.   This grievance from the Benzene Laboratory of the Coke Works, Chemical Laboratories Department, Clairton Works, claims that the job of (Benzol) Chemical Technician should be redescribed, and its classification increased from Class 13 to 23, because of changed job content. Management denies that any significant change has occurred affecting job content and no Form G has been issued.

2.   To meet competitive pressures from

the petroleum industry affecting sale of aromatics (principally benzene, toluene, and xylene), the Company in 1958 introduced an improved method for production of light oil-derived aromatics at Clairton Coke Works. The new process required a hydrogen-producing plant (Girdler Unit) and a paraffin removal plant, commonly referred to as Udex. The new processes and units make up what is known as the B.T.X. Plant which, in the flow of processing, is located approximately at the mid-point of the process as it existed prior to activation of the new B.T.X. Plant.

3. Corollary to these process and equipment changes, a new Benzene Laboratory was built with apparatus necessary to perform additional tests needed for high grade specification products. The disputed job of (Benzol) Chemical Technician (Plant Title —Chemist Analyst Benzol) previously performed laboratory tests necessary to the old process, and was assigned the additional tests when the B.T.X. Unit went into operation.

4. The job description of the disputed job provides:

PRIMARY FUNCTION: Collects and analyzes Benzol Plant materials and products and analyzes Pyridine Plant products.

TOOLS AND EQUIPMENT: Chemical Laboratory facilities and chemicals.

MATERIALS: Light oil, light oil distillates, light oil residues, wash oil, naphthalene, intermediate products, process materials, plant effluents (water), pyridine products.

SOURCE OF SUPERVISION: Chemist-Benzol Plant.

DIRECTION EXERCISED: None.

WORKING PROCEDURE:
1. Receives samples by sample chute and by operating personnel and makes various plant control tests in Benzol plant light oil products, oils in process, process materials, plant effluents and pyridine plant products.
2. Collects samples from tanks and makes various routine analyses for control of production of all benzol products.
3. Collects samples from tanks and makes analyses on crude and refined benzol products.
4. Collects miscellaneous samples and makes miscellaneous analyses of samples as required.
5. Cleans equipment and working area as required.

6. Maintains records and reports as required.
7. Carries out safety regulations.

5. While a substantial number of new tests have been added to those previously performed, the Company holds that the changes in equipment, materials, and testing methods have not resulted in any significant change in job content. It stresses that the new tests in good part use more precise and modern laboratory equipment in order to minimize errors of human judgment. It further urges that the new tests, like the tests which always have been part of the job, involve the distillation, titration, physical testing, and colorimetric analysis of benzene, toluene, and xylene, along with processing chemicals at various stages of refinement. Thus, Management concludes that there should be no real question that the basic nature of the new tests is simply "more of the same" type of testing as always has been an integral part of the (Benzol) Chemical Technician's job.

6. The 14 old tests (which still are performed) include:

1. Specific Gravity
2. Solidifying Point (Benzene)
3. Solidifying Point (Naphthalene)
4. Acid Wash Color
5. Distillation
6. Copper Corrosion
7. Thiophene Concentration (Visual Method)
8. Flow Test
9. Moisture Content
10. Light Oil Content of Wash Oil
11. Titration
12. Resin Test
13. H_2S—SO_2 Test
14. Color

7. The additional tests include:

1. Bromine Index
2. Thiophene Content
3. H_2S Content in Hydrocarbon (Lead Acetate Test)
4. Paraffin Content (FIA) (Fluorescent Indicator Absorption)
5. Carbon Dioxide in MEA Solution (Monoethanolamine)
6. pH
7. Titration Tests—% Monoethanolamine (MEA) Total and Free Caustic Alkalinity
8. Reid Vapor Pressure
9. Doctor Test
10. % DEG (Diethylene Glycol)
11. Mercury Corrosion
12. Hydrocarbon in Lean Glycol
13. % Water in Diethylene Glycol

14. Ash Content
15. % Sediment
16. Hydrogen Sulfide in Gas (Tutweiler)
17. Total Acidity *
18. H₂S in Light Oil (Shaw)*
* These new tests were not used and are not currently being used.

8. In operating the new equipment to make the added tests, says the Company, the (Benzol) Chemical Technician follows routine operating instructions in a step-by-step manner. All critical standard solutions involved are made up by others and supplied to the Technicians. The Technician annotates his observations at the various steps from graduate markings, dial readings, color comparisons, and the like, and achieves the final test result through using simple arithmetic calculations of given formulae or by reference to standard graphs.

9. The Union notes that the new laboratory facilities were established to serve what generally is regarded as the world's largest coal chemical hydrogenation unit or light oil purification plant. To achieve the objective of producing benzene, toluene, and xylene which is virtually free of impurities, it is essential that test methods and equipment be exact. The Union stresses that the scope of the changes affecting the job is revealed in the substantial number of new tests, new products being tested, and new equipment used for purposes of performing the various tests.

10. The following tabulation shows the present factor values assigned to the job and the changes proposed by the Union in Third Step:

FACTOR	PRESENT CLASSIFI- CATION	UNION PROPOSAL
1. Pre-Employment Training	C 1.0	C 1.0
2. Employment Training & Experience	E 1.6	G 2.4
3. Mental Skill	D 2.2	E 2.8
4. Manual Skill	C 1.0	D 1.5
5. Responsibility for Materials	D 2.4	D 4.5
6. Responsibility for Tools & Equipment	C .7 Med	D 2.0 Hi
7. Responsibility for Operations	C 1.0	E 3.0
8. Responsibility for Safety of Others	A Base	E 2.0
9. Mental Effort	D 1.5	E 2.5
10. Physical Effort	B .3	B .3
11. Surroundings	B .4	B .4
12. Hazards	B .4	B .4
	12.5	22.8

11. The Union protests that the general language in the Primary Function of the current job description makes no reference to specific products from the Benzene, Toluene and Xylene Plant, and that the description of tools and equipment is simply in broad general terms, making no mention of the 16 new items of equipment which the Union claims have been added. In like vein, it emphasizes that the description of materials involved in the disputed job is in such broad general terms as to be inadequate in light of the 13 new materials which the Union asserts are now utilized in performing the job.

12. Turning to the broad general language of the Working Procedure, the Union holds that this does not reveal what (according to the Union) is required to achieve the high purity objectives and exacting testing methods followed. No mention is made, for example, of the scientific detail to be followed in using electronic chemical testing equipment.

FINDINGS

13. It would be tedious and unnecessary to detail all of the arguments and job comparisons suggested by the parties at the hearing.

14. Essentially, the Union places its greatest emphasis upon several production jobs—as, Pure Benzol Stillman (Class 17); B.T.X. Purification Operator (Class 18); and a relatively new J. and L. Class 21 job at Aliquippa (B.T.X. Refining Plant Operator)—in support of substantially increased codings for various Factors. As applied to Factors 2, 5, 6, 7 and 8, some or all of these jobs might be thought to lend support to higher codings.

15. In point of fact, of course, these operating jobs are so unlike the present, both as to duties, responsibilities and working conditions, that they do not warrant close scrutiny.

16. The present job operates in a laboratory, to perform a function which is auxiliary to, and not responsible for, production. It cannot be coded as if it were a line operating job.

17. On the other hand, the evidence reveals the disputed job now to be reasonably comparable with Specimen 4813 in Class 15. Thus the present somewhat general language of the description does not adequately reflect the true level of knowledge of

chemical principles which now is required. It should be noted, however, that the Working Procedure of Specimen 4813 is extremely detailed, and the men on the disputed job are not required to perform the same wide *variety* of duties as a man might perform, over a year or two, while working under Specimen 4813. There are other differences, such as in the promotional sequences affecting training for the two jobs, but these do not affect the point here in issue. The critical fact is that the level of skill, knowledge, and responsibility of the disputed job now is such that it reasonably may be held to require substantially the same level of knowledge of chemical principles as Specimen 4813.

18.   Surely, if the (Tar) Chemical Technician at Clairton properly is coded at 14.5 for Class 15 by reference to Specimen 4813, the new tests assigned to the disputed job more than suffice to warrant its coding now on the basis of that Specimen.

19.   The Board, therefore, finds that the disputed job has been changed to the extent of one full job class or more, for purposes of Section 9-D, and so should be redescribed and classified, with retroactive payments to incumbents as contemplated in Section 9-D. In so ruling, the Board acts on the basis of Specimen 4813, which now reflects the appropriate codings for the disputed Factors.

20.   Since Management has not issued a new description or Form G, and the parties have never focussed on the matter of proper description, the Board will not undertake itself to deal with this matter. Management should, for example, revise the description to include a more precise (even if only illustrative) specification of some of the more significant tests—even though the same type detail as in Specimen 4813 may not be necessary or desirable. Such action, of course, would be within the framework of Section 9-D and the Manual. The Board anticipates that the parties will have no difficulty with the details of the job description, in light of this decision.

AWARD

21.   The grievance is sustained to the extent indicated in the opinion.

CHAPTER 15

CODING "SKILL" FACTORS

The first four classification factors (Factor 1—Pre-Employment Training, Factor 2—Employment Training and Experience, Factor 3—Mental Skill, Factor 4—Manual Skill) are commonly called the "skill" factors. Included in this chapter are cases which discuss the coding of one or more of these factors. The figures after each docket number designate the specific "skill" factors in dispute.

Following the awards set forth in this chapter is a table of cross-references to many other cases.

A—693. 1, 2, 3, 4. Rankin Works. December 17, 1954
Herbert L. Sherman, Jr., *Arbitrator*
Approved by Sylvester Garrett, *Chairman*

BACKGROUND

1. This grievance claims that the position of Operator-Nail Machine (Wire Drawing) in the Nail Mill of the Rankin Works should be evaluated at 17.2 for Job Class 17 instead of the 10.5 for Job Class 11 assigned by the Company. The job in dispute is a #4 Glader Nail Machine with a wire drawing attachment as part of a machine assignment with other nail machines. The new nail machine was installed July 30, 1951, to replace an old German Spike Machine. The operation of the old spike machine was covered by a job description and classification for Nail Machine Operator in Job Class 11, the ratings on the Factors being the same as those assigned by the Company to the job in dispute.

2. The positions of the parties with respect to the ratings on the Factors are as follows:

FACTOR	COMPANY	UNION
1. Pre-Employment Training	B-0.3	C-1.0
2. Employment Training and Experience	D-1.2	F-2.0
3. Mental Skill	D-2.2	E-2.8
4. Manual Skill	B-0.5	C-1.0
5. Responsibility for Materials	D-1.1	C-2.5
6. Responsibility for Tools and Equipment	C-0.7 (Med)	E-2.0 (Med)
* 7. Responsibility for Operations	D-2.0	D-2.0
8. Responsibility for Safety of Others	A-Base	B-0.4
9. Mental Effort	C-1.0	D-1.5
10. Physical Effort	B-0.3	C-0.8
*11. Surroundings	C-0.8	C-0.8
*12. Hazards	B-0.4	B-0.4
Total	10.5	17.2

* There is no dispute on Factors 7, 11 and 12.

3. It was originally contemplated by Management that a number of nail machines with wire drawing attachments would be installed, and that they would be operated as a separate set. A new job description, with which the Union agrees, was drawn up to cover such a separate set of machines. In fact, no additional Glader Machines with wire drawing attachments were purchased. Instead, the one #4 Glader is operated in a

255

set with two or three Brooklyn Nail Machines.

4. A Nail Machine Operator testified that his previous experience was sufficient to enable him to operate the new nail machine, but that it took him a year to master the operation of the wire drawing attachment. Initially, he stated, he had difficulty with the coordination of this equipment. A Management witness testified that the new nail machine and wire drawing attachment have never failed to synchronize since the "bugs" were worked out of them in another area of the Mill, and that grievant's difficulties during his first year on the new set were with the Brooklyn Nail Machines with which he had no prior experience.

5. To set up the other nail machines at Rankin Works for a new order of nails, the job description requires the Operator to "replace and adjust gripper dies, cutters, hammers, etc., in nail machines to close tolerances." The Operator for the new machine must do the same thing, but he must also replace and adjust the wire drawing dies and gripper dies in the wire drawing attachment. He must adjust the connecting rod according to the size of the nail desired. In operating the wire drawing attachment, which draws wire from a bundle of rods on a flipper reel and gives the wire a "skin draft" (reduces it), the Operator must butt weld the first end of a new bundle of rods to the last end of the previous bundle, and file and grind the weld smooth. When four machines are operated in the set in which the Glader Machine falls, the Helper performs the duties of welding and grinding.

6. The Union witness stated that it took 4 to 5 hours to make a set-up on the new machine. Although he never operated the old German Spike Machine which the new Glader Machine replaced, the Union believes that the old machine could be set up in a half hour. Disputing this estimate, Management asserts that it took 1½ to 2 hours to complete the set-up of the old German Spike Machine. This machine processed two wires simultaneously, thereby producing nails in "doubles." It was necessary to set up and adjust double dies. The Company claims, as is set forth in the time allowance in the incentive standards, that it takes an average of less than two hours to set up the new equipment. This estimate is also based on observation of performance of other incumbents of the job. Management agrees, however, that a lesser time is necessary to set up the Brooklyn type nail machine. It also agrees that a scratching wire die could score a rod and that such a die would have to be adjusted, but it points out that gripper dies on other

nail machines would have to be replaced under similar circumstances.

7. The range of product produced on the Glader Machine compares favorably with the product of the German Machine, although the German Machine could make larger nails. On the Glader Machine, the same size nail may be run for as long as two months. The Glader Machine produces an average of 3 tons of product during 8 hours; the German Machine produced an average of 2½ tons. The range of tons produced in terms of sets of nail machines at Rankin Works is 2½ to 8 tons. The average for the set in which the Glader Machine falls is 5 tons.

8. There is a circuit breaker installed in connection with the new equipment which will cut off the power if there is an overload. Such a device is not installed on the other machines. Also, the rod feeds off the flipper reel through a safety lever which shuts off the machine if a snarl occurs.

9. As to the speed of the set, this set is the slowest running in the Mill. In terms of the type or design of nail machines, the Glader Machine is next to the slowest in the Mill. The Company contends that no more care and attention are necessary to prevent damage to the Glader Machine with the wire drawing attachment than for other types of nail machines. No evidence was presented to show any damage that has ever occurred to the wire drawing attachment.

10. Although the replaced German Machine was larger, the new machine including the attachment is longer. It is two feet closer to the aisle. A shed which used to be across the aisle from the machine, where the buggies are weighed, has been torn down. As a result, the Union contends that the employees performing the weighing functions are in greater danger of flying nail whiskers during the cutting of the first few nails while the guard is off the new Glader Machine and the Operator is making adjustments. The guard is off for a few minutes on an average of five times a turn. The number of employees exposed to flying whiskers has remained unchanged. The Buggy Pusher weighs on an average of 40 times a turn. According to the Company, some of the nail whiskers from the old German Machine, which also threw whiskers across the aisle where the buggies are weighed, were larger and flew farther. And even while the shed was in existence, the weighing platform itself was still in the open. Also, the guards on the other machines, though some of them do not throw whiskers towards the aisle, are off while the machines are being set up.

11. The Union witness stated that the bars, which support the guard on the new

machine, weigh about 50 pounds, the nail die block with dies 75 pounds, without dies 65 pounds, that the nail die block with dies on the ordinary nail machine weighs 10 pounds, and that the breaking bar, used in setting up the Glader Machine when the hammer is on dead center, weighs 50 pounds. According to Management testimony, the supporting bars are not lifted, but are pushed back to the lugs on the machine; the Glader die block empty is 54 pounds, with dies 65 pounds. The die block on the old German Machine was estimated as twice as heavy. Nor do the parties agree as to whether the breaking bar on the new machine weighs the same or more than the bar used on the old German Machine.

12. Management further notes that finished nails from the new machine are mechanically carried by an automatic conveyor into a buggy. On other nail machines, the finished nails fall into tote pans (weighing 40 to 50 pounds when full), which must be manually lifted and dumped into a buggy.

CONTENTIONS OF THE PARTIES

13. The Union's argument that more credit is warranted than assigned by the Company under the "skill" Factors, involving Pre-Employment Training, Employment Training and Experience, Mental Skill and Manual Skill, is based primarily upon grievant's testimony that it took a year to master the coordination of the new equipment, his testimony that it took the best part of an operating turn to make a set-up, his comparison with the bench wire drawing job at Rankin Works, and the fact that the dies must be set up to close tolerances and changed in accordance with nail specifications.

14. With respect to Factor 5—Responsibility for Materials, the Union seeks a rating of C-2.5, which calls for less care to prevent damage to materials than the D-1.1 assigned by the Company. But the Union challenges the amount of probable monetary loss. Under Factor 6—Responsibility for Equipment, the Union contends that the Operator runs a battery of high-speed machines. It points to the language of the Manual under Code E which reads:

"Sustained high degree of care and attention required (to) prevent damage to expensive equipment when responsibility is placed on the Operator and not entirely on automatic devices."

The amount of probable damage to equipment is not challenged.

15. For Factor 8—Responsibility for Safety of Others, the Union emphasizes the removal of the shed and the danger of flying whiskers to the Buggy Pushers. Under Factor 9—Mental Effort, the Union argues that close mental and visual application is required in making adjustments. With respect to Factor 10—Physical Effort, the Union stresses the weight of the tools and equipment used.

16. Finally, the Union points out that there is no Specimen job which covers the operation of a nail machine with a wire drawing attachment. It contends, therefore, that the language of the Manual must be consulted to determine the proper codings.

17. Management asserts that the operation of all types of designs of nail machines is covered by the original Benchmarks and the Specimen Example for Nail Machine Operators. To code the first four Factors for the job in dispute, the Company takes the position that the appropriate numerical value for the highest of the skills required to perform the regularly assigned duties of the job should be assigned, and that numerical values for each of the skills of a job should *not be added*.

18. To support its position, Management calls attention to Specimen 1537 for a Wire Drawer-Continuous and Specimen 1538 for a Wire Drawer-Continuous (Operator-Welder). The incumbent of the latter job performs the same duties as Specimen 1537 and, in addition, welds his own bundles by operating a welding machine, yet the two jobs are coded the same in each Factor. Also, no rating on any Factor in the classification of these two Wire Drawing Specimens, or in the classification of Specimen 1535 for a Wire Drawer-Bench, is higher than the ratings already assigned to the job in dispute, with the exception of the rating of C-.8 under Factor 10 for the Wire Drawing Specimens. Secondly, reference is made to the application of the "Spell Hand Convention" to the first four Factors for that type of job. Thirdly, the Board is directed to Specimen 2327 for a Batch Pickler Loader job, which performs the duties of Specimen 2326—a Feeder job, Specimen 2328—a Loader job, and Specimen 2329—a Catcher job. In the first four Factors, the combination job of Batch Pickler Loader is rated only as high as the highest coding for each of the other three jobs. And finally, numerous combined jobs at Rankin Works and elsewhere, in which the codings of the first four Factors were no higher than the highest codings of each of the jobs which were combined, were presented to the Board by Management as exhibits and in testimony to demonstrate the actual application of the guides furnished by the Benchmark and Specimen Example jobs.

19. Management further contends that a job of Nail Machine Operator at Joliet Works, which used a wire drawing attachment at the time it was classified, is an original Benchmark job and should be used as a guide in resolving this dispute. That job is coded exactly as Management has coded the job in dispute.

DISCUSSION AND FINDINGS

20. Although both parties refer to the classification of numerous jobs not closely related to the job in dispute, Specimen 1620 for a Nail Machine Operator and Specimen 1537 for a Wire Drawer provide the best guidance in this case for the proper interpretation of the words used in the Classification Manual. Specimen 1620, coded in all Factors precisely the same as the job in dispute, covers the operation of nail machines without limitation as to a particular design. The job of Nail Machine Operator at Rankin Works, which the Company asserts is an original Benchmark, is also coded precisely the same as the job in dispute. The job description specifically lists several types of machines: "American, Brooklyn, German Spike, Ideal, Allentown 'A'." It cannot be found that grievant's duties with respect to the #4 Glader Machine differ so markedly as to affect the classification of his job.

21. The real question to be decided is whether the addition of the wire drawing attachment provides a basis for raising the classification of the job in dispute from 10.5 to a higher job class.

22. Under the Specimen Examples, it is clear that numerical values should not be assigned to each of the skills of a job and then added. On the contrary, the highest skill required to perform the regular duties of the job is selected; the appropriate numerical value is then assigned to each of the first four Factors. Neither Specimen 1620 for a Nail Machine Operator nor Specimen 1537 for a Wire Drawer, which involves skills similar to those employed in the operation of the wire drawing attachment even though the machine wire drawing equipment has a more continuous pull, is rated on any of the "skill" Factors any higher than the ratings already assigned to those Factors for the job in dispute. The Board must, therefore, rule that the present ratings on the first four Factors of the job in question adequately reflect the necessary pre-employment training, employment training and experience, mental skill, and manual skill required to operate the equipment involved in grievant's job.

23. No evidence was presented to show that the rating for the amount of probable monetary loss should be increased under Factor 5—Responsibility for Materials. Although the Union urges that the C level, denoting a lesser degree of care and attention for materials, is warranted, the D level assigned by the Company is proper. Nor does the evidence warrant the conclusion that grievant operates a "battery of high-speed machines" for purposes of Factor 6 —Responsibility for Equipment. The present codings on these Factors must be considered as appropriate. Both of these Factors are already coded higher than the ratings found in Specimen 1537.

24. No increase in the coding of Factor 8—Responsibility for Safety of Others is justified on the basis of the removal of the shed, since it was torn down when the Buggy Pusher and Weigher jobs were combined and the Buggy Pushers, the number of which has remained unchanged, were always subject to the possibility of being hit by nail whiskers from the old German Spike Machine. The shed only protected the Weighers. The other minor changes established by the Union with respect to this Factor are not significant from the classification standpoint.

25. By application of Specimen 1620 for a Nail Machine Operator and Specimen 1537 for a Wire Drawer, Factor 9—Mental Effort is found to be properly coded at C-1.0. Under Factor 10—Physical Effort, the rating of B-.3 is appropriate. Even if the nail die blocks and bars for the new nail machine are heavier than those used on the average nail machine, the automatic conveyor which carries the finished nails to the buggy eliminates the necessity of lifting the tote pans and emptying them when they are filled. This added feature certainly compensates for whatever extra physical effort may be involved in handling the new die blocks and tools. The automatic conveyor at the end of the nail making operation likewise distinguishes grievant's duties from the duties of the Wire Drawer (Specimen 1537) who must band the finished bundles of wire and load them on trucks. It cannot be found, moreover, that average physical effort required in connection with the new equipment is significantly greater than that required to operate the old German Machine, which the new equipment replaced. The rating on Factor 10 for the Operator of the German Machine was B-.3.

AWARD

26. The grievance is denied.

A—755. 2, 3. Cyclone Waukegan Works.   **August 5, 1957**

Herbert L. Sherman, Jr., *Arbitrator*

Approved by Sylvester Garrett, *Chairman*

BACKGROUND

1.   This grievance results from a change in job content of a Belt Fabricator job (Auto. Button Weld) in the Belt Department of the Cyclone Fence Plant at Waukegan. Higher ratings are sought on Factors 2, 3, 5 and 6. The job was originally described and classified in 1950, the total point value being 9.1 for Job Class 9.

2.   The product of the job is various sizes of flat wire conveyor belt. In the fabrication and assembly of the belt the incumbent of the job (PC 02-19) has always set up, adjusted and operated a 4-Slide Machine and an automatic button weld machine. The 4-Slide Machine shapes, drills holes in and cuts to length from flat wire the pickets for the belt. The button weld machine straightens the ends of the pickets and simultaneously forms button heads on the ends of the rods inserted through the holes in the pickets. Even after the button heads have been automatically welded to the ends of the rods linking the pickets, a small amount of play is left in the rods.

3.   Prior to the change this play was eliminated by another job—a spot welder. In 1956 the Company installed a scissors-type gun welder to perform this function automatically. Under the Form G, dated December, 1956, grievant "Sets up Gun Welder by adjusting pressure, timing and position of points to weld straight rod to formed picket automatically." On this form Management also increased the rating for Factor 6—Responsibility for Tools and Equipment from B .2 to C .4.

4.   The positions of the parties with respect to the ratings on the factors in dispute are shown by the following table:

FACTORS	COMPANY		UNION	
2. Employment Training and Experience	D	1.2	E	1.6
3. Mental Skill	C	1.6	D	2.2
5. Responsibility for Materials	D	1.1	D	1.6
6. Responsibility for Tools and Equipment	C	.4 (low)	B	.5 (high)

DISCUSSION AND FINDINGS

5.   Grievant and the Company agree that learning to set up, adjust and operate the 4-Slide Machine requires more employment training and experience than does the button weld machine or the gun welder. Furthermore, there is no dispute that the 4-Slide Machine calls for more mental skill than the button weld or gun weld machines. But the Union contends that setting up, adjusting and operating all three machines warrant higher ratings on Factors 2 and 3 than the ratings presently assigned to these factors on the basis of setting up, adjusting and operating the 4-Slide Machine and the button welder alone. Management replies that the duties connected with the new gun welder can be learned within the same period of time that the duties connected with the 4-Slide Machine and the button welder are being learned.

6.   The classification principle which controls the present dispute over the appropriate ratings on Factors 2 and 3 is found in the Board's Award in A-693. It reads:

"Under the Specimen Examples, it is clear that numerical values should not be assigned to each of the skills of a job and then added. On the contrary, the highest skill required to perform the regular duties of the job is selected; the appropriate numerical value is then assigned to each of the first four Factors. . . ."

7.   Since addition of the gun welder does not require any more employment training and experience or mental skill than that required for the 4-Slide Machine or the automatic button welder, the request for higher ratings on Factors 2 and 3 must be denied.

8.   Nor is there justification for changing the rating on Factor 5—Responsibility for Materials. The probable loss at any one time is substantially unchanged. Although grievant must now inspect the finished belt periodically to make sure that the gun welder is operating properly, his original job description of 1950 always called for periodic inspections of the completed belt for size and pitch and to recognize obvious defects through the button weld operation. He now observes the results of the button welding and the gun welding at the same time. No significant change in the inspection duties of grievant has been made.

9.   The Union contends that more damaged material could be run through before

detection under the new arrangement. Pictorial exhibits, however, show that the run-out table is now longer, thus providing a longer opportunity to detect bad material. Also, though grievant states that he has not noticed any change in the speed of the operation, Management maintains that it is 10% slower since the gun welder was added.

10. With respect to Factor 6—Responsibility for Tools and Equipment, the parties are not sure as to what would happen to the parts of the new gun welder if grievant failed to make sure that the water to cool the machine was running at all times. In any event, because of the added responsibility for equipment assigned to grievant, the Company has already granted a higher coding for this Factor in the Fourth Step of the grievance procedure. On the basis of the evidence presented, no further change in the rating on this Factor is warranted.

AWARD

11. The grievance is denied.

T—289.   2, 4. Fairfield Tin Mill.   March 31, 1955
Herbert L. Sherman, Jr., *Arbitrator*
Approved by Sylvester Garrett, *Chairman*

BACKGROUND

1. This grievance seeks higher ratings on Factors 2, 4 and 8 for the new job of Oil Recoveryman in the Mechanical and Electrical Department at the Fairfield Tin Mill. The job description for this job has been jointly approved. Grievant is the only incumbent of the job.

2. Following is a table which shows the positions of the parties with respect to the ratings on the Factors:

FACTORS	COMPANY CLASSI- FICATION		UNION CLASSI- FICATION	
1. Pre-Employment Training	B	.3	B	.3
*2. Employment Training and Experience	B	.4	D	1.2
3. Mental Skill	C	1.6	C	1.6
*4. Manual Skill	B	.5	C	1.0
5. Responsibility for Materials	C	.7	C	.7
6. Responsibility for Tools and Equipment	CM	.7	CM	.7
7. Responsibility for Operation	C	1.0	C	1.0
*8. Responsibility for Safety of Others	C	.8	D	1.2
9. Mental Effort	C	1.0	C	1.0
10. Physical Effort	C	.8	C	.8
11. Surroundings	B	.4	B	.4
12. Hazards	B	.4	B	.4
Total		8.6		10.3
Job Class		9		10

* Disputed Factors

3. The Oil Recoveryman is primarily responsible for collecting, transporting and centrifuging various grades of recovered oil. He goes to units where oil is used and observes the containers in which the recovered oil is collected. He directs and is assisted by the Oil Recovery Laborer in removing full containers of oil (replacing them with empty containers), or in pumping oil from the containers into a portable tank. For collecting the oil, he operates a tractor with a wagon which has space for three containers. The oil is dumped from the containers or pumped from the portable tank into pre-heating tanks.

4. After the Oil Recoveryman adjusts the steam valves to maintain the proper temperature in the tanks, he then takes the necessary steps to operate the centrifuge machines to clean the oil. The centrifuge machine throws dirt to the wall of the machine, and separates the water and the oil. The cleaned oil is subsequently pumped into barrels. Grievant collects a sample of each grade of oil, and submits it to the laboratory for testing. When hydraulic or other oil is required by the Lubrication Specialist, grievant must blend light or heavy oil to reach the proper consistency. Viscosity charts are available to him for consultation, but grievant has had so much experience in blending that he rarely feels the need for them in determining how much oil to add. In any event, part of the "know how" in blending must be acquired by experience. The Oil Recoveryman also makes reports of oil centrifuged by grades, and reports any leaks observed in the oil lines or pumps while he is collecting the oil.

5. In addition, the Oil Recoveryman makes certain repairs and adjustments to his equipment. For example, he must replace the brass bushings for the bearings on his centrifuge machines. The bearings on the bottom are more difficult to repair than the ball bearings on the top. Other duties involve tearing down the bowl of the centrifuge machine after each run so that the three-bladed

paddle may be removed and cleaned (after which it must be properly aligned in the casing), removal of the head on the pump so that it can be cleaned, and cleaning clogged lines on his oil wagon.

CONTENTIONS

6. The Union argues that Specimen 1028 for an Oil Filter Machine Operator and Specimen 1035 for an Oiling System Operator, both of which were introduced by the Company, justify the ratings sought by the Union on the Factors in dispute. It notes that Factor 2—Employment Training and Experience for Specimen 1028 is given a rating of D 1.2. While Specimen 1035 is rated at B .4 on this Factor, it only calls for *assisting* the Millwright in making repairs, and is otherwise much more limited in scope than grievant's job.

7. A rating of C 1.0 is sought for Factor 4—Manual Skill by the Union, since the Manual under that coding reads "use several hand tools on assembly work, such as . . . simple carpentry work or pipe fittings." When operation of the tractor is added to grievant's other duties, the Union feels that a higher rating than B .5, which is allowed for "simple adjustments and repairs," is justified.

8. With respect to Factor 8—Responsibility for Safety of Others, the Union calls attention to the language under the D level in the Manual: "Operate power-driven mobile equipment in congested area." The Union also points out that grievant has no horn on his tractor to warn other employees of his presence.

9. Management cites numerous Specimen Examples in support of its position, but emphasizes Specimen 1028 in particular. It contends that Specimen 1028 is given a rating of D 1.2 on Factor 2 because incumbents, in addition to operating an oil filtering machine, must make tests of oil in transformers and switches.

10. The Company also relies on a job of Solution Tender in the Hot Strip Mill of the Fairfield Tin Mill. That job is similar to the job in dispute in that it maintains concentrations and temperatures of acid solutions in various tanks of the continuous pickling lines, and in addition, operates a tractor to transport coils and scrap. The codings on that job are identical with those proposed by the Company for the job in dispute except that the latter has a higher rating on Factor 10—Physical Effort because of the requirement of handling heavy barrels.

11. With respect to the repair duties of grievant, Management cites several Specimens for Millwright Helpers, Machinist Helpers,

Electrician Helpers and Pipefitter Helpers—all coded the same as the job in dispute on Factors 2 and 4. With respect to grievant's operation of the tractor, Management notes that Specimens for Tractor Operators are coded at B .4 in Factor 2 and at B .5 in Factor 4. For the general guidance of the Board, reference is also made to Specimen 2354 for an Electrolyte Attendant, Specimen 2077 for an Acid Tester, and Specimen 2081 for a Cleaning Solution Tester.

12. Specimens 2403 for a Loader Helper, 2446 for a Loader, 2465 for a Loader Helper and 1501 for a Charger—Pot Annealing—all rated at B .4 on Factor 8—were cited by Management to show that its proposed rating on that Factor should not be any higher. All of these jobs involve occasional use of a tractor. Also cited as involving occasional use of a tractor were Specimens 1518 for a Salt Annealer and 1519 for a Salt Annealer Helper—rated at C .8 on Factor 8.

DISCUSSION AND FINDINGS

13. Of all the Specimens cited for the Board's guidance in this case, Specimen 1028 for an Oil Filter Machine Operator is the most helpful. Both of the parties rely heavily on this Specimen Example. Although no Specimen is directly on point, Specimen 1028 is the most comparable to the job in dispute in terms of the duties performed, the material processed, and the equipment used.

14. Incumbents of both jobs are required to operate equipment which centrifuges various grades of oil. They are also required to make necessary repairs and adjustments to their equipment. Grievant performs such repairs without supervision. He does not "assist" others, as is true of the Helper Specimens and the Acid Tester in the Hot Strip Mill relied upon by the Company. Specimens 2354, 2077 and 2081, involving the processing of different types of product, do not require incumbents to make repairs at all.

15. Although the Company seeks to distinguish Specimen 1028 and to justify its rating of B .4 on Factor 2 for the job in dispute (instead of D 1.2 as found under Factor 2 for Specimen 1028) on the ground that incumbents of Specimen 1028 also make oil tests, the Board cannot adopt that position. The stated reasons for classifying the factors of Specimen 1028 do not treat that duty as requiring greater skill than the other duties. Nor do the actual ratings on the other factors closely related to Factor 2 support the Company's position. Factor 1—Pre-Employment Training, Factor 3—Mental Skill and Factor 9—Mental Effort are all coded the same as the proposals of the Company for the job in dispute. Testing of the oil is not

segregated from the duties of operating the oil filter machine and making the necessary repairs and adjustments in the classification of Specimen 1028.

16. Since the duty or duties requiring the highest skills must be selected as the basis for determining the proper ratings on the skill Factors, without adding or subtracting credit for the performance or non-performance of other duties requiring equal or lesser skills, it must be concluded that D 1.2 is the proper rating for Factor 2 for the job in dispute.

17. For the same reason, however, the rating of B .5 on Factor 4 is deemed to be appropriate. Ratings are not assigned to the various duties and then added up for a grand total. Specimen 1028 is coded at B .5 in Factor 4. The duties of that job with respect to oil reclamation and making repairs and adjustments are comparable to grievant's duties. Since operation of a tractor also calls for a rating of B .5 on Factor 4, no higher rating is justified for grievant's job.

18. For Factor 8, the rating of C .8 is proper. Although Specimen 1028 is coded at

A Base for this Factor, the incumbent of that job does not operate a tractor. On the other hand, the D level is not appropriate, since grievant does not exercise a "sustained high degree of care and attention" for the safety of others. Grievant testified that most of the areas in which he operates the tractor are not "tight." He estimated that he used the tractor on an average of 8 hours a week. The Company's estimate is 4-6 hours a week. Grievant admits that on some days he does not use the tractor at all, though he has, on a rare occasion, used it for a full turn. He does not use the tractor when checking twice a week for oil leaks, but only when he is hauling drums. In view of the evidence and the Specimens cited by the Company to support its position on this Factor, no higher rating is justified.

AWARD

19. The grievance is sustained to the extent that the rating on Factor 2 for the Oil Recoveryman job at the Fairfield Tin Mill is increased from B .4 to D 1.2.

T—494. 1, 2, 3, 4. Fairfield Tin Mill. February 16, 1959

Clare B. McDermott, *Assistant to the Chairman*
Approved by Sylvester Garrett, *Chairman*

BACKGROUND

1. This grievance from the Fairfield Tin Mill presents two questions. First, the Union contends that the new job of Wrapper (Coils) resulted from an improper combination of several other jobs, in violation of Section C-5-h of the January 1, 1953 Job Description and Classification Manual; and, second, assuming that the Company was within its rights in establishing the job as it did, the Union insists that the job should be classified higher than the 5.7 classification which was assigned to it by the Company, for Job Class 6.

2. The present codings for the job in dispute are as follows:

Factor	1	—	A Base
"	2	—	B .4
"	3	—	B 1.0
"	4	—	B .5
"	5	—	C .5
"	6	—	BM .3
"	7	—	B .5
"	8	—	C .8
"	9	—	B .5
"	10	—	C .8
"	11	—	A Base
"	12	—	B .4

3. In the Spring of 1957 the Company began shipping tin plate product in coils, and it was at that time that the Wrapper (Coils) job was installed. A typical work cycle for the Wrapper (Coils) involves the operation of a jib crane to position a wooden pallet on an up-ender. The Wrapper (Coils) then drives a ram tractor to pick up and haul coils, weighing about 12,000 pounds on the average, from various temporary storage areas and to place them on the up-ender, which fits the coil on the pallet and then turns the package so that the coil sits on the pallet. The Wrapper (Coils) then uses a fork lift tractor to remove the mounted coil from the up-ender and to place it on the floor nearby. Next the wrapping process is completed by dressing up the wrapping paper and stuffing it in the eye of the coil at one end. A cardboard doughnut is then put in place, the package is banded and labeled, and certain data are copied onto the label. Finally, the Wrapper (Coils) remounts the fork lift tractor and uses it to stack the wrapped coil near the wrapping area.

4. When the job is filled the number of men assigned to it has varied from one to twelve, depending upon the level of operations, with a four-man crew being normal.

5. While there are various other wrapper jobs in the mill, none of them were engaged

in wrapping coils, simply because product was not shipped in coil form prior to the installation of the job in dispute.

CONTENTIONS

6. The Union asserts that in establishing the Wrapper (Coils) job the Company improperly combined the functions of wrapper jobs with those of tractor operator jobs, and that this is prohibited by Section C-5-h of the January 1, 1953 Job Description and Classification Manual. It is not contended by the Union that a specific wrapper job and a specific tractor operator job have been terminated and their duties given to the Wrapper (Coils). The claim is that part of the duties of the Wrapper (Coils) job are really tractor operator duties and that the other part of the duties of the Wrapper (Coils) are inherently wrapper duties, and that the Company may not combine these functions in one job. In the Company's view the section relied upon by the Union is not relevant to the question presented.

7. On the classification question the Union argues that the Wrapper (Coils) job is essentially a tractor operator job, that by far the greater part of its duties and efforts requires the operation of one or the other of the two tractors and, therefore, that it should be coded as a tractor operator job. The Company challenges this and says that only about 20% of the work cycle of the job involves tractor operation. This means, as the Company sees it, that the job calls for only part-time tractor operation, and in justification of the coding it decided upon, the Company cites as proper references Specimen Example 2474, Wrapper, and six Specimen Examples which are said to involve part-time tractor operation and which, with one exception, are in the same or a lower Job Class than is the job in dispute.

8. The Union, on the other hand, feels that Specimen Example 1523, Stocker, Job Class 7, and numerous tractor operator jobs in the Fairfield Tin Mill in Job Class 8 are the more appropriate comparisons. The Company asserts that those are full-time or substantially full-time tractor operator jobs.

9. The Union alleges that there have been times when one or two of the men assigned to the Wrapper (Coils) job have, at Management direction, operated a tractor all or nearly all of the turn while the others on the job were used exclusively on the wrapping phase. This is said to support the Union's contention that the Company's purpose here is to get full-time tractor operation at Job Class 6 rates. The Company denies this charge and says that it happened on only two occasions when two men were told to operate the tractors because the other members of the crew were not experienced at tractor operation. Aside from these two instances, the Company insists that when certain incumbents have performed the tractor duties and others the wrapping duties it has resulted from voluntary agreements among the men. Furthermore, says the Company, the Union position ignores the fact that it may be said with equal fairness that as a result of the Company's classification of the job in Job Class 6, it is paying Job Class 6 rates for wrapping work that it would otherwise get at Job Class 4 rates.

FINDINGS

10. There is no doubt that the Company was entitled to establish the job in dispute as a new job in this case. The only serious question is the proper classification of that job.

11. The parties are in dispute as to whether tractor operation constitutes a major portion of the duties of the Wrapper (Coils). The witnesses on both sides agreed, however, that the total tractor work required to process one coil was 8 or 9 minutes. This was confirmed by the observation of the job under normal conditions for one-man operation.

12. Tractor operation frequently requires trips of about 300 feet from the wrapping area to obtain coils for wrapping. Of course, sometimes the distance traveled is longer, and often it is shorter. Approximately once each day the tractors must be taken to the pumps for fuel. This involves a trip of between 3 and 4 city blocks. In view of all the testimony and observation of the job, it must be concluded that tractor operation takes up a very substantial but not predominant portion of the Wrapper (Coils) working time.

13. The Company relies on the following Specimen Examples as proper comparisons for the tractor phase of the job in dispute: 2465, Loader Helper; 1519, Salt Annealer Helper; 2413, Sawyer Helper; 1517, Normalizer Helper; 2239, Coiler (titled a Helper job when it was originally classified); and 2123, Hooker. The job descriptions for these jobs show that they are obviously operating tractors under more limited circumstances than the present job. Specimen 2123, Hooker, involves only "occasional" tractor operation, which is also true of Specimen 1517, Normalizing Helper. These Specimens are thus distinguishable from the job in dispute.

14. Many times the Board has held that the first four factors should be coded by reference to that regularly performed duty of the job which requires the highest skill.

That is tractor operation in this case. Specimen Example 1523, which requires tractor operation as a part of its duties, is coded, on the first four factors, the same as full-time tractor operation jobs. Tractor operation was the reason given for the coding of the first four factors on that job. It appears to be the most closely related of the Specimens cited. Thus, the substantial tractor operation required of the job in dispute entitled it to the same treatment. Hence, the rating on Factor 1 should be raised from A Base to B .3, and on Factor 3 from B 1.0 to C 1.6. The codings on Factors 2 and 4, B .4 and B .5, respectively, already reflect tractor operation.

15. *Factor 5.* No job cited has a higher rating on this Factor than the C .5 presently assigned to the Wrapper (Coils).

16. *Factor 6.* It is not disputed that the tractor work required of the job in dispute is done in congested areas. The reason for coding Factor 6 at C .7 in Specimen 1523, which also operates a tractor part time, is "Moderate care in driving tractor in congested area." Similarly, the Wrapper (Coils) job is entitled to C .7 on this Factor instead of the B .3 presently assigned.

17. *Factor 7.* The present coding of .5 is the same as that for Specimen 1523. No higher rating is justified.

18. *Factor 8.* This is now coded at .8, the same as Specimen 1523. While it is true that most of the plant jobs cited by the Union are coded at 1.2, these are full-time tractor jobs. Even one of those jobs, however, Plant Code D40-105, is coded at .8, and it operates under generally the same conditions as does the tractor work of the Wrapper (Coils). Thus, .8 is not improper in light of Specimen 1523.

19. There is no evidence sufficient to justify higher ratings on Factors 9, 10, 11, or 12.

AWARD

20. The grievance is sustained in part to the extent that Factor 1 should be coded at .3, Factor 3 at 1.6, and Factor 6 at .7. The other Factors are not changed. This results in a total of 7.0 for Job Class 7. There was no impropriety in Management's action in establishing the new job in question, comprising the duties assigned.

A—865. 2. Duluth Works.   March 31, 1959
Clare B. McDermott, *Assistant to the Chairman*
Approved by Sylvester Garrett, *Chairman*

BACKGROUND

1. This grievance questions the classification of the new job of Cold Saw Operator, PC 14-09, in the Conditioning Department at Duluth Works.

2. In the past, test samples were burned off the billets in the Conditioning Department. To eliminate potential danger in burning leaded billets, it was decided early in 1956 that test samples from leaded billets should be cut rather than burned. Accordingly, the Cold Saw Operator job was described by agreement and, upon inability of the parties to agree as to classification of the job, it was installed and rated by the Company at 5.2 for Job Class 5.

3. The Union now contends that Factors 2 and 7 are coded improperly. The following table indicates the parties' respective positions:

FACTORS	UNION	COMPANY
1. Pre-Employment Training.	Base	Base
*2. Employment Training and Experience.	.4	Base
3. Mental Skill.	1.0	1.0
4. Manual Skill.	.5	.5
5. Responsibility for Materials.	B .3	B .3
6. Responsibility for Tools and Equipment.	B .2	B .2
*7. Responsibility for Operations.	.5	Base
8. Responsibility for Safety of Others.	.4	.4
9. Mental Effort.	.5	.5
10. Physical Effort.	1.5	1.5
11. Surroundings.	.4	.4
12. Hazards.	.4	.4
Total	6.1	5.2
Job Class	6	5

* Factors in dispute.

4. The Primary Function of the disputed job is "to cut billet samples for testing and cut scrap into charging box size." In-process preparation of test pieces is done by a Test Preparer, PC 12-37 (Class 4), who cuts test pieces or obtains test filings from billet samples in the hot mills. Later on, if the Metallurgical Department decides that a re-

test is necessary or if, for one reason or another, the original test was missed, the Billet Inspector, PC 14-15, is notified. If the billet to be cut is non-leaded, a piece is burned off by the Burner (Conditioning), PC 14-11, Job Class 5, and a test piece is then cut by the Test Preparer. If, on the other hand, the billet is leaded, the test piece is cut by the Cold Saw Operator. The Inspector and the Cold Saw Operator locate the place in the Conditioning Department where the billets to be cut have been stocked. The Cold Saw Operator hooks for the crane so that the billets can be moved to the work area near the saw. After the billet is positioned in the saw, the test sample is cut by a power hack saw in the length marked by the Inspector or the size is determined by eye. The Cold Saw Operator stamps the proper identification on the samples and places them in a pile nearby, where they are picked up and taken to the Metallurgical Department approximately once each day. The billets are then put back in the proper storage pile, and the Cold Saw Operator hooks for the crane in making this transfer.

5. The Cold Saw Operator also cuts scrap billets into lengths of about five or six feet so that they will fit into the scrap box.

CONTENTIONS

6. In regard to Factor 2, the Union refers to the Test Preparer in Job Class 4 at Duluth as a comparable job. Since both the Test Preparer and the job in dispute operate essentially the same kind of saws, the Union feels that the coding of .4 on that job must be applied to the Cold Saw Operator. The Company insists that other aspects of the Test Preparer indicate that it is more involved than the Cold Saw Operator.

7. On Factor 7, the Union contends that the Cold Saw Operator is entitled to credit for responsibility for operations in the sense that he cuts test samples from billets before the final authorization for shipping is given. Moreover, the Union emphasizes that the Cold Saw Operator works in conjunction with the Billet Inspector (Conditioning A) in transferring billets from the stock piles to the saw and back again. In this connection, the Union notes that other billet inspectors are assisted by a Loader Helper (Shipment), PC 16-07, and that the Loader Helper is coded at .5 in Factor 7. Therefore, the Union argues that the Cold Saw Operator is equally entitled to .5.

8. As the Company sees it, the Loader Helper is not an appropriate reference because it is part of a fairly large crew, which supplies several production units, which actually loads materials on cars for shipment.

9. The Union cites Specimen Example 3394 as support for its position on Factor 7.

FINDINGS

10. *Factor 2.* Here the Company justifies its rating of A-Base by reference to Specimens 327, Test Preparer; 646, Test Preparer; 648, Test Preparer; 3394, Cold Saw Operator; and to the non-specimen jobs of Billet Grinder (Swing), PC 14-05 at Duluth; Burner (Conditioning), PC 16-07 at Duluth; and Test Preparer, PC 50-20 at South Works, all of which are in A-Base in Factor 2. Even if it be assumed, as the Union insists, that the Billet Grinder at Duluth may not be used for purposes of comparison, because it is not currently filled, the remaining jobs referred to, particularly the Specimen Examples, seem sufficiently similar to justify the present rating.

11. The Union's sole reference here is to the Test Preparer, PC 12-37, in Job Class 4 at Duluth. That job uses substantially the same kind of saw to cut test pieces and to collect test filings as does the Cold Saw Operator. In addition, the Test Preparer may be required to operate a drill press and a grinding machine. While these duties are not performed frequently, they still are significant elements of the job. Moreover, the Test Preparer sorts billet samples by heat numbers and billet numbers in preparation for sawing or drilling. The job in dispute does not call for operation of a drill press or grinding machine, nor does it require sorting of samples. Finally, the Cold Saw Operator does not refer to a specification book for data, to be marked on the sample, (as to the tests that should be run by the laboratory), as does the Test Preparer.

12. While precision cutting to close tolerances is not required of either job, and while no extremely high degree of skill is required of the Test Preparer, it must be concluded that there are sufficient differences between the two jobs to preclude reliance upon the Test Preparer job in coding this factor for the Cold Saw Operator—particularly in view of the Specimens cited by the Company.

13. *Factor 7.* This factor presently is rated A-Base. The Union cites Specimen 3394, Cold Saw Operator, to support its .5 proposal. That is a production job, however, which after sawing the tubing, rolls it to the next operation. This seems to provide the basis for its coding at .5.

14. The Union feels that because the Cold Saw Operator cuts samples for tests which are made before the product is shipped that it, too, is entitled to .5 on responsibility for operations. The relationship seems re-

mote. It is undisputed that the samples cut by the Cold Saw Operator are taken to the laboratory only once or twice a day, and that the man who actually makes the tests works only on the day turn. It is worth noting that the Test Preparer at Duluth, which makes more and different test samples than the Cold Saw Operator (and thus might have a closer connection with the Metallurgical Department) is also in A-Base on Factor 7.

15. The main thrust of the Union's position here is that the Cold Saw Operator works with the Billet Inspector (Conditioning A) in transferring billets to and from the saw, and consequently, in the Union's view, the Cold Saw Operator is comparable to the Loader Helpers who assist other billet inspectors in transferring piles of billets and is thus entitled to the .5 rating which the Loader Helpers get. The evidence indicates, however, that the Loader Helpers work as a crew which services several producing units, one of which, the Grinders, is on incentive. Furthermore, the Loader Helpers also supply the shipping beds, and some of them help load cars.

16. The Company relies on Specimens 327, Test Preparer; 646, Test Preparer; 648, Test Preparer; and non-specimens Test Preparer, Burner (Conditioning), and Billet Grinder (Swing), all at Duluth, and the Test Preparer at South Works. All are coded at A-Base in Factor 7, and there is no evidence to warrant finding that the job in dispute is entitled to a higher rating.

AWARD

17. The grievance is denied.

T—256. 2. Fairfield Sheet Mill.   October 6, 1953
Herbert L. Sherman, Jr., *Assistant to the Chairman*
Approved by Sylvester Garrett, *Chairman*

BACKGROUND

1. This grievance involves classification of the new job of Coil Inspector in the Inspection Department at Fairfield Sheet Mill. Management rates the job at Class 10, and the Union seeks Class 12. Mutual agreement has been reached on the job description. Since no agreement was reached on the classification, the Company unilaterally installed Job Class 10 on October 27, 1952. The ratings on Factors 2, 5, 6, 8, 10 and 12 are in dispute.

2. Following is a tabulation showing the codings developed by Management and those sought by the Union:

FACTOR	COMPANY CLASSI-FICATION	UNION CLASSI-FICATION
1. Pre-Employment Training.	B- .3	B- .3
*2. Employment Training and Experience.	E-1.6	F-2.0
3. Mental Skill.	D-2.2	D-2.2
4. Manual Skill.	B- .5	B- .5
*5. Responsibility for Materials.	D-1.6	D-2.4
*6. Responsibility for Tools and Equipment.	B-.2 Low	B- .5 Hi
7. Responsibility for Operations.	C-1.0	C-1.0
*8. Responsibility for Safety of Others.	A-Base	B- .4
9. Mental Effort.	D-1.5	D-1.5
*10. Physical Effort.	B- .3	C- .8
11. Surroundings.	A-Base	A-Base
*12. Hazards.	B- .4	C- .8
Total	9.6	12.4

* Disputed Factors

DISCUSSION AND FINDINGS

3. Under *Factor 2—Employment Training and Experience* the Union emphasizes the line of promotion in the Inspection Department. It does not believe that the Company has given sufficient consideration to the necessary time spent on directly related work where the incumbent learns to detect pits, pinches, scratches, etc. A few days after agreement was reached on the job description for Coil Inspector, the parties agreed upon a line of promotion for thirteen Inspector jobs. The top seven jobs with the ratings on Factor 2 are as follows:

Head Rack Inspector—Classified by application of the Gangleader Convention
Coil Inspector E-1.6 (job in dispute)
Inspector-Secondary Product F-2.0
Jobbing Mill Inspector F-2.0 (recently abandoned)
Coating Inspector (Continuous Galvanizing) E-1.6
Shear Line Inspector (Cold Reduced) E-1.6
Shear Inspector E-1.6

4. In March, 1953 a new line of promotion was agreed upon under which the job of Head Rack Inspector was eliminated and the other six jobs listed above were placed on one line on the top rung of the ladder, all of them being in Job Class 10.

5. Specimen Examples for Inspectors relied upon by the Union, with ratings of F-2.0 under Factor 2, are 4027, 4026, 4025, 4000, 4004. Also emphasized was the fact that the Coil Inspector is a final inspection job.

6. The Company notes that Specimen 4027 is an Inspector job which has contact with customers, Specimens 4026 and 4000 are Merchant Mill Inspector jobs, Specimen 4025 apparently is required to work at different locations, and Specimen 4004 is a job which inspects axles. Although the Secondary Product Inspector and Jobbing Mill Inspector jobs at Fairfield Sheet Mill were rated at F-2.0 under Factor 2, Management calls attention to the fact that the highest rating on this Factor for Specimens 4033, 4032, 4034, 4036, and 4035—Specimens for Sheet and Tin Mill Inspectors—is E-1.6. It further argues that the line of promotion for Inspectors at Fairfield Sheet Mill cannot control this grievance.

7. The only regular incumbent of the Coil Inspector job is required to check material at the Side Trimming and Recoil Line for gauge, width, flatness, surface condition and stenciling, according to customer specifications. He checks recoiled strip for specified recoiling, banding and coil weight.

8. It is recognized that a line of promotion cannot control the classification of a job or the rating of any of the Factors. Nevertheless, it may be considered along with the rest of the evidence. Although the Company argues that the Secondary Product Inspector job is different in that it must reclassify pre-inspected rejected product for purposes of disposition, grievant fills out inspection reports showing rejects, reasons for the rejects, and recommended dispositions for the benefit of the Turn Foreman. Also, grievant should not receive a lower coding because he makes determinations as to product which has not been previously inspected. On the whole, it appears that F-2.0 is the proper coding for Factor 2.

9. The degree of attention under *Factor 5—Responsibility for Materials* is not in dispute. To determine the monetary loss for which the Inspector is given credit, a special Convention is provided. Under this Convention five percent of one turn's production for which the Inspector is responsible is multiplied by the difference between the value of the product per ton and the scrap value. In this case it means 5% X expected tonnage per turn X ($45, value

of product per turn—$15, scrap value). The only element of this formula in dispute is that of expected tonnage. The Company relies on the figure of 126.8 tons as estimated by the Engineering Department before the equipment was put into operation. The Union's calculation is based on the rated capacity of the equipment, which is 350 tons. It also notes that tonnage per turn has occasionally exceeded 167 tons, which is the breaking point between D-1.6 and D-2.4.

10. Under Code D, $250 or less is rated at 1.6. To find a probable monetary loss of greater than $250, it must be found that expected tonnage exceeds 167 tons per turn. Between October, 1952, when the job in dispute was installed, through June, 1953—the last full month for which figures are available, the average number of tons per turn for any one month exceeded 126.8 only once. For April the figure is 131.02 tons. The Union, however, emphasizes that incentive coverage has been gradually expanded, beginning in March, 1953, and that average tonnage has increased under incentive coverage. Even so, the average number of tons (including both good and rejected product) for the 10 turns during the month of June, 1953 which were worked with 100% incentive coverage, amounted to 151.9 tons per turn. Thus, it cannot properly be found, even by using the figures most favorable to grievant, that a higher rating than D-1.6 for Factor 5 is justified.

11. *Factor 6 concerns Responsibility for Tools and Equipment.* The parties agree that Code B adequately reflects the level of care and attention required. Probable damage is rated as High by the Union; the Company rates it as Low. Under the job description tools and equipment are "tape, micrometer, report forms, pencils, automatic printing machine, etc." Since the automatic printing machine has not been used, no one is certain what damage, if any, could be caused. And although the Union emphasizes that grievant uses a "flying mike," other Inspectors with no higher rating on this Factor use such a micrometer. A stop button which grievant employs to stop the line is not for the purpose of preventing damage to equipment but to product. B-.2 is the proper rating under this Factor.

12. With respect to *Factor 8—Responsibility for the Safety of Others,* all other Inspector jobs in the Inspection Department at Fairfield Sheet Mill receive a rating of A-Base. No evidence was presented which would justify a higher rating for this job. The purpose of the button to stop the line is to prevent damage to product although it could be used to prevent injury to one who was improperly too close to the line.

13. Under *Factor 10—Physical Effort* Union testimony pointed out that grievant's work station is on a platform 2½ feet above the level of the floor and that grievant must step up and down every time a coil is finished. This happens 20 to 25 times a turn. The Shear Lines also have platforms for the Inspectors. Today grievant has a chair on the platform for his use. B-.3 is the proper rating for Factor 10.

14. For *Factor 12—Hazards* B-.4 is appropriate. All Inspector jobs in the Fairfield Sheet Mill are coded at B-.4 for this Factor. Although the coil going through the line is under tension, and might fly out in case of a break, the speed of the line appears to be more of a controlling consideration. No one has ever been injured while performing the duties of the job in dispute. The work station is now in a relatively safer position today than when the job was installed.

AWARD

15. The grievance is sustained only to the extent of increasing the rating on Factor 2 for the new job of Coil Inspector from E-1.6 to F-2.0.

T—293. 1, 2. Fairfield Sheet Mill. March 31, 1955

Herbert L. Sherman, Jr., *Arbitrator*

Approved by Sylvester Garrett, *Chairman*

BACKGROUND

1. In the absence of agreement on the proper classification of the new job of Inspector (No. 2 Coating Line) at the Fairfield Sheet Mill, the Company unilaterally installed its proposed job classification of Job Class 10, effective August 4, 1953, in accordance with the terms of Section 9-D-3 of the August 15, 1952 Agreement. This grievance, protesting the classification, was filed on August 31, 1953. The job description was jointly approved.

2. The Company's classification of the job in dispute is shown by the following table:

FACTORS	CLASSIFICATION	
1. Pre-Employment Training	B	.3
2. Employment Training and Experience	E	1.6
3. Mental Skill	D	2.2
4. Manual Skill	B	.5
5. Responsibility for Materials	D	2.4
6. Responsibility for Tools and Equipment	BL	.2
7. Responsibility for Operation	C	1.0
8. Responsibility for Safety of Others	A	Base
9. Mental Effort	D	1.5
10. Physical Effort	B	.3
11. Surroundings	A	Base
12. Hazards	B	.4
Total		10.4

3. Inspector Lindsay, who is one of the grievants and is also Grievance Committeeman for the Inspection Department, believes that higher ratings are warranted on Factors 1, 2, 5, 6, 7, 8, 9 and 10. He describes the #2 Coating Line as a "major producing unit," and argues that although there is no Specimen Example directly on point, his job should be compared with Specimen 4000 for an Inspector in the Merchant Mills. The Union further asserts that the same line of reasoning should be used by the Board to raise Factor 2 to F 2.0 as was employed in T-256 involving a Coil Inspector.

4. Management contends that the most appropriate Specimen Examples to be used as guides in this case are Specimen 4035 for a Sheet Inspector, and Specimen 4033 for a Stainless Strip Inspector. It points out that these Specimens are more applicable to the present dispute than Specimen 4000 for an Inspector in the Merchant Mills, which is a different type of Mill, and where the scope of the Inspector's duties is quite different. Other Specimen Examples for Inspector jobs cited by Management are 4032, 4034, 2462, 4036, 2399 and 2389. Although Specimen 4033 is rated D 3.5 in Factor 5 while grievants' job is coded D 2.4, the Company notes that probable monetary loss for Specimen 4033 is rated higher because of the nature of the product inspected—stainless steel. In any event, the Union only disputes the level of care and attention under Factor 5.

5. Also emphasized for purposes of comparison by Management are the Inspector jobs on #1 and #3 Continuous Coating Lines at the Fairfield Sheet Mill. These jobs are coded the same as the job in dispute except for Factor 5. On this Factor the job in dispute is coded higher because of probable monetary loss of material. Grievant Lindsay distinguishes these jobs on the ground that they are only responsible for a prime piler and one reject piler, while he is responsible for a prime piler and two re-

ject pilers. Management points out, finally, that none of the Inspector jobs at the Fairfield Sheet Mill are classified higher than Job Class 10. Even the Secondary Product Inspector, which is responsible for inspection of a wide variety of rejected products, is in Job Class 10.

DISCUSSION AND FINDINGS

6. Although Grievant Lindsay testified at considerable length at the hearing as to the duties and responsibilities of his job, no useful purpose would be served by detailing them in this Award. A comparison of his duties with those of the incumbents of Specimen Example 4035 for a Sheet Inspector shows that no change in the present classification of the new job is warranted. Specimen 4035, which is in Job Class 10, does differ from the job in dispute in some respects. It appears to work more closely with the operating crew. On the other hand, there is no substantial difference in the duties of these jobs involving the operation of deflector buttons to classify the product. The Working Procedure of Specimen 4035 states "Operates deflector control in deflecting rejected sheets to master piler," and "Operates several sheet counters in counting rejected sheets *as to type of rejection.*" The Sheet Inspectors must know the exact reason for rejection of a given sheet. Although it appears that incumbents of this Specimen job only operate one deflector control, it could not be found that the addition of one deflector control would, in view of the requirements already inherent in the job, affect the job classification. Thus, the mere operation of one additional deflector button on the line by grievants cannot affect the classification of the job in dispute.

7. This finding is further supported by an examination of the Inspector jobs for the #1 and #3 Continuous Coating Lines at Fairfield Sheet Mill. The only difference between the new job and the Inspector jobs for the #1 and #3 Continuous Coating Lines which merits extended analysis is that the #2 Continuous Coating Line Inspector is responsible for three pilers instead of two pilers. Instead of one deflector button to segregate all rejects from primes, the #2 Coating Line Inspector has two deflector buttons so that product not prime may be further subdivided. Prime product goes in one piler. Another piler is used for scrap product. The third piler is used for one of three types of assorted rejects (called "rejects," "wasters," or "waste wasters"). The particular use of the third piler at any time depends on the nature of the orders of customers who are willing to take product not

acceptable to the customer for the "prime" product, but which is not scrap.

8. It cannot be concluded that the three way classification of product by use of two deflector buttons, instead of a two way classification of product into "primes" and "rejects" by operation of one deflector button, requires a higher job classification for the #2 Coating Line Inspector than that granted the #1 and #3 Coating Line Inspectors for the following reasons. There is no such thing as a "perfect" sheet. To know what is a prime sheet, any Sheet Inspector must be aware of the different degrees of imperfections. The #1 and #3 Continuous Coating Line Inspectors must have the same basic knowledge, training and skills as the #2 Coating Line Inspectors to know whether a given sheet is defective. The #1 and #3 Coating Line Inspectors must also fill out the same kind of report as the #2 Coating Line Inspector, showing a breakdown of the *number of rejects under the various reasons* for the rejects.

9. Nor do the other contentions of the Union provide any basis for increasing the classification ratings for the job in dispute. All three Coating Lines at the Fairfield Sheet Mill are "continuous." No distinction can be made on that basis. The speed of the #3 Line was observed on a plant visit to be even greater than the speed of the #2 Line. While grievants' unit was running at a speed of 200 feet a minute, the #3 Line was running at a speed of 250 feet a minute.

10. No Sheet Mill Inspector job at the Fairfield Sheet Mill is coded higher than the D level for Responsibility for Materials. Nor is any Specimen Example Inspector job coded higher than the D level on Factor 5. The job in dispute has already been classified by the Company in the D level on this Factor.

11. Nor does the list of tools and equipment outlined by Grievant Lindsay, including the automatic printing machine, provide any basis for increasing the rating of Factor 6—Responsibility for Tools and Equipment.

12. To the extent that the reasoning of the Board in T-256 in raising Factor 2 to F 2.0 for a Coil Inspector, was based on the line of promotion formerly followed in the Inspection Department, that Award does not help the Union in this case. On the contrary, since the Continuous Galvanizing Coating Inspector job was listed lower than the Coil Inspector in the line of promotion, among the jobs rated at E 1.6 on Factor 2, this line of reasoning supports a rating of E 1.6 on Factor 2 for the job in dispute.

13. With respect to Grievant Lindsay's contention that higher ratings are in order because he also performs part of the job of

a Secondary Product Inspector, it must be noted that the Secondary Product Inspector examines many types of rejected product for reclassification. His material is not limited to the product from one line. The Secondary Product Inspector also reinspects some of the product of the #2 Line. Although product not prime but acceptable to some other customer may be sent directly to that other customer, the Secondary Product Inspector does reinspect scrap and some primes—when there are defects not discoverable by grievants due to failure of equipment—coming off the #2 Line. Thus, grievants do not perform all the duties of a Secondary Product Inspector even with respect to their own Line. Moreover, the fact that the Secondary Product Inspector reinspects all rejected product coming off the #1 and #3 Lines does not disclose a significant difference between those two lines

and the #2 Line. Prime product is normally sent directly to the customer for all three lines.

14. One more point. The Board does not find that the fact that the #2 Continuous Coating Line is also equipped to run aluminum coated sheets, in addition to galvanized sheets, warrants a higher classification for the Inspector job. Although the #1 and #3 Lines are similarly equipped, it does appear that this change was made subsequent to the installation of the Inspector jobs for those lines. Nevertheless, only two test runs have been made with aluminum coated sheets on the #2 Line since August, 1953, and the evidence fails to show how inspection of such product differs materially from inspection of galvanized sheets.

AWARD

15. The grievance is denied.

T—294. 1, 2. Fairfield Sheet Mill. March 31, 1955
Herbert L. Sherman, Jr., *Arbitrator*
Approved by Sylvester Garrett, *Chairman*

BACKGROUND

1. This grievance protests the classification of the new job of Inspector (No. 4 C. R. Shear) in the Inspection Department at the Fairfield Sheet Mill. The job description was jointly approved by the parties, but the Union continued to dispute the classification of Factors 1, 2, 5, 6, 8, 9 and 10. The Company's classification, which was installed unilaterally in accordance with Section 9-D-3 of the Agreement, is shown by the following table:

FACTORS	CLASSIFI-CATION	
*1. Pre-Employment Training	B	.3
*2. Employment Training and Experience	E	1.6
3. Mental Skill	D	2.2
4. Manual Skill	B	.5
*5. Responsibility for Materials	D	1.6
*6. Responsibility for Tools and Equipment	BL	.2
7. Responsibility for Operation	C	1.0
*8. Responsibility for Safety of Others	A	Base
*9. Mental Effort	D	1.5
*10. Physical Effort	B	.3
11. Surroundings	A	Base
12. Hazards	B	.4
Total		9.6

* Disputed Factors

2. Grievants are primarily responsible for making a sheet by sheet inspection of materials processed through the No. 4 Shear Line for surface imperfections, and to check materials for proper gauge, size and finish according to specifications. Management has classified this job the same as the Inspector (No. 2 Coating Line) job, except for Factor 5 where the latter job has a higher rating because of estimated cost of probable damage to materials. The total job class is, nevertheless, the same.

FINDINGS

3. The parties agree that the testimony and arguments presented in Case T-293 should also be considered in this case. The main issue presented for determination is practically identical.

4. A comparison of the duties of the job in dispute with those of incumbents of Specimen 4035 (which is even more applicable to this case than to the facts of T-293) shows that no change in the present classification is warranted. Additional support for this conclusion is found in the fact that the job in dispute performs essentially the same duties as incumbents of the job of Inspector (No. 1 C. R. Shear Line) at the Fairfield Sheet Mill. The classification ratings of the new job and of the Inspector job at the No. 1 C.R. Shear Line are identical. The principal distinction between these two jobs

is the distinction between the #2 Coating Line Inspector job and the #1 and #3 Coating Line Inspector jobs discussed in Award T-293. More concretely, grievants are responsible for classifying product into primes, assorted rejects, and scrap by use of three pilers, while Inspectors at the No. 1 C.R. Shear Line classify product into primes and rejects by use of two pilers. On the basis of the reasoning in Award T-293, the Board finds that the operation of one additional deflector button affords no basis for increasing the classification ratings on the job in dispute.

5. Nor does the Board find any other classification question presented in this case not already covered in Award T-293. The Board must, therefore, deny the grievance.

AWARD

6. The grievance is denied.

Following is a table of all the other cases decided by the Board of Arbitration which involve disputes specifically on the coding of one or more of the first four classification factors. For each case the docket number is listed, the specific "skill" factors in dispute are noted, and the page in this volume where the case can be found is cited.

CHAPTER 16

RATING "RESPONSIBILITY" FACTORS

The "responsibility" factors are Factor 5—Responsibility for Materials, Factor 6—Responsibility for Tools and Equipment, Factor 7—Responsibility for Operations, and Factor 8—Responsibility for Safety of Others. Included in this chapter are cases which discuss the coding of one or more of these factors. The figures after each docket number designate the specific "responsibility" factors in dispute.

Following the awards set forth in this chapter is a table of cross references to many other cases.

A—668. 5, 6, 7. Joliet Works. March 31, 1954
Herbert L. Sherman, Jr., *Arbitrator*
Approved by Sylvester Garrett, *Chairman*

BACKGROUND

1. This grievance requests a higher classification for the job of Roll Builder, in Job Class 10, in the Roll Shop at the Joliet Works on the basis of certain changes which have taken place. Grievants' primary function consists of servicing the Rod Mills by changing bearings on rolls, testing and adjusting roll bearing assemblies, and repairing or replacing couplings. Although the parties have signed the changed job description, they do not agree on the effect of these changes on Factors 5, 6 and 7.

2. The Union proposals, which would result in a total classification of 13.3 for the job, and the present values assigned to these factors are as follows:

FACTOR	PRESENT VALUES	UNION PROPOSALS
5. Responsibility for Materials	C-1.2	D-3.5
6. Responsibility for Equipment	C- .4	C- .7
7. Responsibility for Operations	C-1.0	D-2.0

DISCUSSION AND FINDINGS

3. The Union contends that the Roll Builder should receive a higher rating than the Roll Turner job on Factor 5—Responsibility for Materials. It relies on wage increases and higher prices which have made the materials more costly, the introduction of a new type of coupling, and the addition of a Porto Power Unit in 1948, to remove and replace the bearings.

4. It is clear, however, that the actual fluctuating cost of materials cannot determine the proper level of "Probable monetary loss" for classification purposes, since the Classification Manual requires that the codings for the value of materials be consistent with the benchmark and specimen example jobs. And the change from the solid type coupling to the gear type coupling had been so far completed at the time that the job in dispute was classified that it cannot now serve as a basis to affect the classification. The change was started in October of 1945, and was completed for all of the finishing stands in the #1 and #2 Rod Mills by December 1, 1945. The change to the gear type coupling for the stands in the #3 Rod Mill came about at a later date.

5. With respect to the types of bearings and rollnecks used, no significant change has taken place. Although an SKF type bearing, which goes on a tapered rollneck, was added in 1949, both straight and tapered Timken rollnecks and bearings were used at the time that the job was classified.

6. The Porto Power Unit is a portable, electrically operated hydraulic pump which weighs 100 pounds and stands twenty inches high. The ram is inserted in a threaded center hole in the rollneck, the valve is turned on, and the bearing assembly is removed. The Unit can be operated to exert a pressure of 10,000 pounds per square inch. The Union notes that this is more pressure than could be exerted previously by use of a sledge hammer in removing the bearings,

and argues that a greater damage could result to the rolls and bearings. For example, a chunk could be knocked off the roll. There is also Union testimony that since the introduction of the Porto Power Unit damage to rolls, couplings, and cones (tapered sleeves inside the bearings) has been discovered after their installation in the Mill, including six cracked cones since the first of this year. Of these six cones, however, five of them had served their assigned time in the Mill, thus showing that a cracked cone does not necessarily render the bearing and roll inoperative. And although the Union stresses damage that may result from an overheated bearing, it is agreed that a cracked cone, which may be caused by pushing them too far on the taper with the Porto Power Unit, is only one of many reasons why a bearing may become overheated and freeze on the rollneck. Overheating and freezing of the bearing may be caused by insufficient grease, a cracked roller, a cracked outer race, insufficient clearance in the bearing, spalling of the metal, etc.

7. The Company does not dispute the Union's claim that such cracks in cones have come about since the Porto Power Unit was installed in 1948. Nevertheless, it does hold that the records clearly show that *overall* damage to the materials of the job has not increased but that, on the contrary, the possibility of damage has been decreased by the elimination of most of the sledging. Management emphasizes that there has been no damage to a roll or bearing in the removal of bearings since the Unit was placed in operation. On the other hand, under the old system of sledging, rolls were sometimes so damaged in removing the bearings, particularly the roll collars, that it was necessary to scrap them.

8. Using Specimen Example 1296 for a Roll Builder and Specimen 1728 for a Roll Assemblyman as guides, both of which receive a rating of C-.7 for Factor 5, the Board finds that C-1.2 adequately reflects the requirements of the job in dispute with respect to responsibility for materials. Any increase in responsibility in this regard does not so exceed the credit already assigned to this factor to warrant a higher rating.

9. For the purposes of coding Factor 6—Responsibility for Equipment, the Board finds that two pieces of equipment have been added to the job in dispute: The Porto Power Unit and a gas torch. No damage has ever occurred to the Porto Power Unit, except that a hose was broken when it was first installed. Nor is there any evidence to show how it might be damaged. The Union appears to make the argument that the new equipment, added to the hydraulic press and other tools included in the original job, must be considered as cumulative, thus justifying a higher rating on probable damage. It does not dispute the "C" level of care. The Board finds that the probable damage "at any one time," as specified in the Classification Manual, does not warrant a higher rating than C-.4. This is likewise applicable to the introduction of the gas torch in 1952, which is used on an average of less than once a turn to "sweat" the flinger rings on the shoulders of the rolls. In fact, a Welder, who uses welding and burning equipment, only receives a rating of B-.2 in Factor 6.

10. The Union holds that the coding on Factor 7—Responsibility for Operations should be increased from C-1.0 to D-2.0 because two finishing stands have been added to #1 and #2 Rod Mills, the speeds of the Mills have been increased, grievants must give estimates to the Roll Turners as to the length of time it will take to prepare the rolls, and the incumbent on the night turn lacks supervision by a Foreman. It is clear, however, that the latter two reasons advanced by the Union cannot affect the classification since they do not represent changes from the time that the job was classified. Nor can the addition of two stands or the increase in the speeds of the Mills warrant a higher rating. The relevant Specimen Examples do not provide any basis for making distinctions founded on the number of stands or the speed of the Mills served.

11. Consequently, the grievance must be denied.

AWARD

12. The grievance is denied.

USC—371. 5, 7. Irvin Works. December 18, 1953
Herbert L. Sherman, Jr., *Assistant to the Chairman*
Approved by Sylvester Garrett, *Chairman*

BACKGROUND FACTS

1. In this grievance the two incumbents of the Water Cooler Repairman job at Irvin Works request that their job description be revised and that the classification be raised from 11.6 to 17.3. Although the Union called the Board's attention to evidence under Factors 4, 6 and 8 insofar as such evi-

dence also bears on other Factors, higher ratings are sought specifically on Factors 2, 3, 5, 7, 10 and 11. Other contentions listed in the original grievance had been dropped by the time of the hearing.

2. Since the job was classified in 1946, the number of air conditioning and refrigerating units and the number of drinking fountains have been increased. New air conditioning and refrigerating units have been installed, some of the older units have been scrapped or stored, and some have been relocated. Smaller capacity units have been replaced by those of larger capacity. They also embrace a larger area of operation. For example, in the General Mill Office two 60-ton air conditioning units were placed in the basement in 1949, replacing several units of greatly reduced capacity. In 1948 two 20-ton units replaced three 3-ton and one 5-ton units (which were moved to other locations) in the Engineering Department on the third floor of the General Office Building. In November, 1947, and April, 1948, 15-ton refrigerating units replaced 10-ton units in Nos. 1, 2 and 3 NX Units (Box Annealing). A Union Exhibit lists a total of fifteen new equipment installations since the job was classified.

3. From December, 1946, through September, 1950, two Water Cooler Repairmen and one Helper were assigned to such repair work. Since September, 1950, to the present, an additional Water Cooler Repairman Helper has also been assigned to the force.

CONTENTIONS

4. The following tabulation shows the present ratings on Factors 2, 3, 5, 7, 10 and 11 and the ratings urged upon the Board by the Union to raise the total point value to 17.3:

FACTOR	PRESENT RATING	UNION'S PROPOSED RATING
2. Employment Training and Experience.	G-2.4	H-3.2
3. Mental Skill.	D-2.2	E-2.8
5. Responsibility for Material.	C- .7	C-3.1
7. Responsibility for Operations	C-1.0	D-2.0
10. Physical Effort.	B- .3	C- .8
11. Surroundings	B- .4	C- .8

5. The Union seeks higher ratings on Factors 2 and 3 on the ground that larger and more complex air conditioning equip-

ment must now be serviced. The new installation in the Mill Office is emphasized with its differences in capacity control through cylinder unloading, its evaporative condensers, its anti-freeze controls interlocked with temperature controls, and its pneumatic control system. Company testimony pointed out the similarities between the Mill Office installation and air conditioning units which existed at the time the job was classified. Management asserts that the fundamental principles with which grievants must be familiar have remained unchanged even though more modern equipment is now used.

6. Grievant Reed testified that he has done much home reading to increase his knowledge in this field, that he has helped to train the other employees who work with him, and that he believes that he is more competent than necessary to fulfill the requirements of the job.

7. Particular stress is placed by the Union on the requirement that grievants "rebuild" units on occasion, such as two of the three compressors in the hospital air conditioning units. Absence of the word "rebuild" in the job description is emphasized. The Union cites an arbitration award to the effect that "install and rebuild" are different from "repair and maintain." On one occasion, grievant was asked to draw a detailed sketch in connection with a change in wiring. To the claim that "rebuilding" requires a change in the present description and classification, the Company's answer is twofold. First, it is argued that the present job description encompasses the requirement in the Primary Function which reads "Inspect, repair, replace, install, adjust, and maintain water coolers, air conditioning units and refrigeration systems in use throughout the plant" and in Item 4 of the Working Procedure which reads "Dismantle, repair, replace, install, adjust, maintain and re-assemble equipment, including items, such as compressors, crankshafts, valves, pistons, copper tubing, motors, belts, pulleys, switches, etc." And secondly, an exhibit was introduced to show that Grievant Reed filed a grievance as far back as 1944 alleging that his duties involved "rebuilding compressors, rebuilding condensing water regulators," and "rebuilding bubbler valves."

8. Though the job description requires incumbents to "read and interpret blueprints," grievants assert that the blueprints are now more complicated. An additional claim that grievants supervise craftsmen is denied by the Company which only agrees that assistance is rendered at times. To the further Union contention that grievants are now required to repair "systems" instead of "units," Management points to the item of

the Working Procedure which states "Answer emergency calls for repairs or adjustments to units and systems."

9. Under Factor 5 the degree of attention and care is not disputed, but the Union seeks a higher rating based upon probable monetary loss. Greater probable damage to the larger units is cited. Management replies that the Specimen Example ratings for this type of equipment must be followed despite an increase in the over-all value of the equipment worked by grievants unless there is a basic change in the nature of the equipment.

10. With respect to Factor 7, Union testimony brought out the installation of new galvanizing lines which require the use of refrigeration equipment to maintain low temperatures in induction heating capacitors for continuity of galvanizing operations. The Company holds that repair work on refrigeration equipment associated with producing units was performed at the time the job was classified, such as repairs on units with the DX and NX Gas Machines used in connection with the Annealing operation. It also considers that the refrigerating units in the #1 Galvanizing Line basement are very similar to refrigerating units which were removed from the NX Units in 1947 and 1948.

11. Under Factor 10 the Union points to 150 pound pumps, motors, oxygen and acetylene tanks, which must be carried up five flights of Mill Office steps. The use of ladders is also noted. Management states that the flights are half-story flights of steps, and that the average degree of muscular exertion required throughout the turn has not changed appreciably. The type of compressed gas containers most frequently handled are those containing freon. They weigh 205 pounds. The average number of tanks of freon consumed during 1950-1952 was 1½ tanks per month.

12. The Union claim for a higher rating on Factor 11 is based upon the addition of equipment in congested quarters. Although reference was made to protective clothing such as goggles and gloves, it seems that this is nothing new to the job. Management denies any change in the average working conditions of the job.

DISCUSSION AND FINDINGS

13. The job in dispute was initially classified by reference to Specimen Example 925 for a Water Cooler Repairman. An examination of this Specimen Example and the pattern of similar non-Specimen jobs leads to the conclusion that the evidence in this case does not warrant higher ratings on Factors 2, 3, 5, 7, 10 and 11 for the Water Cooler Repairman job at Irvin Works.

14. Specimen Example 925 receives precisely the same ratings on Factors 2, 3, 5, 7, 10 and 11 as those assigned to the job in dispute. The only Water Cooler Repairman job presented to the Board which is assigned higher ratings on any of these Factors is located at Gary Sheet and Tin Mill. Even this job has the same ratings on Factors 7, 10, and 11. Although higher ratings are found for Factors 2, 3 and 5, there was testimony that this job was classified partially on the basis that it requires the making of repair parts. In any event, all other Water Cooler Repairman jobs called to the Board's attention, including such jobs at Edgar Thomson Works, South Works, Clairton Works, Duquesne Works, and Homestead Works, receive exactly the same ratings on Factors 2, 3, 5, 7, 10 and 11 as those presently assigned to the job under consideration. Although the evidence discloses that the Company has instituted some changes at Irvin Works along with an increase in the volume of work, they do not impose requirements which sufficiently go beyond the present ratings on these Factors to justify higher codings.

AWARD

15. The grievance is denied.

N—236. 5. Lorain Works. November 23, 1955

Sylvester Garrett, *Chairman*

FINDINGS

1. This grievance asserts that the job of Shipper-Checker, Shipping Department, Lorain Works, is improperly classified in Factor 5—Responsibility for Materials.

2. The parties agree that Factor 5 is properly coded at the D level. Their difference relates only to the cost of probable loss resulting from error. The Company has set the figure at "up to and including $250" with a numerical coding of 1.6. The Union feels that the cost figure should be "up to and including $500" for a numerical coding of 2.4.

3. The Shipper-Checker job was established in July, 1951, to check truck loadings. In most respects the job is the same as Car-Checker in the Warehouse save that the latter checks loading of railroad cars as well as trucks. The Car-Checker is in Class 11, while the Shipper-Checker at present is in Class 10. All codings of Shipper-Checker are identical

with those of Car-Checker save Factor 5.

4. The evidence leaves no doubt that ordinarily the cost of correcting errors in rail shipments will exceed substantially the cost of correcting similar errors in truck shipments. While there does not appear to be any directly comparable Specimen job, the Company cites: (a) Specimen 4614 (Job Class 7) coded C-.7 under Factor 5; (b) Specimen 4618 (Job Class 7) coded C-.7 in Factor 5; (c) Specimen 2459 (Job Class 7) coded at C-.7 under Factor 5; and (d) Specimen 668 (Job Class 10) coded at C-.7 under Factor 5. These are sufficiently relevant in terms of job duties to confirm that the disputed coding here is not too low.

5. The evidence includes also jobs from Columbia-Geneva, Central Operations, and the Wire Divisions showing difference in coding of Factor 5 for checking truck shipments in comparison with rail shipments. In all such instances, checking of truck shipments is coded lower under Factor 5 than is checking of rail shipments.

6. A timeliness issue raised by the Company need not be passed upon, since grievance could not be sustained in any event.

AWARD

7. The grievance is denied.

COL—76. 5. Pittsburg Works. March 20, 1957
Sylvester Garrett, *Chairman*

FINDINGS

1. In this grievance the Union seeks a coding of D 2.4 under Factor 5 for the new job of Classifier, Electro-Tinning, No. 2 Line, Pittsburg Works.

2. The evidence indicates that all similar jobs in the Corporation are coded at D 1.6 under this Factor. The Company has assigned this coding to the disputed job. The Union believes that under Section 12.b (3) of the Manual, (Page 45), the monetary loss to be considered in application of Factor 5 is 5% of an *actual* turn's production. The Company stresses that Section C, paragraph 5.e of the Manual (Page 36), clearly states that classification of each job must take into account the kinds of work performed and the surrounding circumstances "when the employee on the job is performing at normal pace."

3. Since no comparable job is shown to be coded at more than D 1.6 in any event, there is no basis for the Board to code Factor 5 higher than D 1.6 in this case. The speeds and tonnages on the No. 2 Line are not out of line with those of the other Lines throughout the Corporation where the Classifier job is utilized.

AWARD

4. The grievance is denied.

T—442. 5. Fairfield Tin Mill. June 28, 1957
Sylvester Garrett, *Chairman*

FINDINGS

1. This case involves an issue between the parties as to the proper method of determining codings under Factor 5 for Strip Inspector (Temper Mills) and Strip Inspector (Tandem Mills).

2. The parties agree that the coding of D-3.5 (which has been assigned by the Company) is correct for each job under Factor 5, but the Union objects to the method by which the Company determined "one turn's production" for purposes of Section C-12-b-3 (p. 45) of the Manual. For this purpose the Company relied upon its own interpretation of Section C-5-e (p. 36) of the Manual, stating that classification of each job shall take into account the kinds of work performed and the surrounding circumstances when the employee on the job is performing at "normal pace." The Union disagrees with the Company's interpretation of this phrase.

3. Even if the Union's point of view were found correct, the end result still would be the coding already assigned by the Company. Since there thus is no real issue as to coding under this Factor, it would be premature to pass on the issue raised by the Union. As in Case COL-76, there is no occasion to embrace either the Union's contention, or the method followed by the Company in its underlying calculations, as long as the end result is right in either event.

AWARD

4. The grievance is denied.

USC—383. 5, 6, 7, 8. Homestead District Works. December 30, 1953

Herbert L. Sherman, Jr., *Assistant to the Chairman*

Approved by Sylvester Garrett, *Chairman*

BACKGROUND

1. Two grievances are involved in this case. The first requests a new description and a higher classification for the job of Floorman—Rolls and Sleeves in the Heat Treating Department at Homestead Works; the second grievance requests a new description and a higher classification for the job of Floorman Helper—Rolls and Sleeves at the same location. These jobs are presently classified in Job Class 12 and Job Class 6 respectively.

2. The present ratings on the Factors and those sought by the Union for the two jobs are shown by the following tables.

FLOORMAN

FACTOR	PRESENT RATING	PROPOSED BY UNION
*1. Pre-employment Training.	B- .3	C-1.0
*2. Employment Training and Experience.	C- .8	D-1.2
*3. Mental Skill.	C-1.6	D-2.2
4. Manual Skill.	B- .5	B- .5
5. Responsibility for Material.	C-2.5	C-2.5
*6. Responsibility for Tools and Equipment.	C-1.0 Hi	D-1.5 Med
*7. Responsibility for Operations.	C-1.0	D-2.0
*8. Responsibility for Safety of Others.	B- .4	C- .8
*9. Mental Effort.	C-1.0	D-1.5
10. Physical Effort.	C- .8	C- .8
11. Surroundings.	C- .8	C- .8
12. Hazards.	C- .8	C- .8
Total	11.5	15.6

* Higher ratings sought by Union

FLOORMAN HELPER

FACTOR	PRESENT RATING	PROPOSED BY UNION
*1. Pre-employment Training.	A-Base	B- .3
*2. Employment Training and Experience.	B- .4	C- .8
*3. Mental Skill.	B-1.0	C-1.6
4. Manual Skill.	B- .5	B- .5
*5. Responsibility for Material.	B- .3	C-2.5
*6. Responsibility for Tools and Equipment.	A-Base	C-1.0 Hi
*7. Responsibility for Operations.	B- .5	C-1.0
8. Responsibility for Safety of Others.	B- .4	B- .4
*9. Mental Effort.	B- .5	C-1.0
10. Physical Effort.	C- .8	C- .8
11. Surroundings.	C- .8	C- .8
12. Hazards.	C- .8	C- .8
Total	6.0	11.5

* Higher ratings sought by Union

3. In addition, the Company claims that the ratings on Factors 11 and 12 for both jobs should be reduced from C-.8 to B-.4 as the result of changed conditions. Management's reason for failing to decrease these ratings unilaterally is that it would not have effected a change of a full job class.

4. Primarily it was the introduction of the new draw-back treatment which gave rise to these two grievances. The other processing duties of grievants are essentially the same today as before the filing of the grievances. Protective material is applied to the roll or sleeve, which is heated and then hardened by water quenching. After the roll or sleeve is subjected to the spraying operation, it is transferred to the water tank. The next operation is to remove the product from the water tank by means of an overhead crane and chain slings which are attached to the product. The latter function, however, is not performed by grievants.

5. The product was previously deposited by crane in one of four oil draw-back tanks, which were open, gas-fired tanks. To light the gas in the burners under the tanks, grievants merely inserted a piece of lighted waste. During the heating cycle grievants were required to control the temperature of the oil by frequent regulation of the gas valves which turned the various gas jets on and off. In addition, the oil temperatures were recorded on a heating card at least once each hour per tank. At the completion of the cycle the Floorman or Floorman Helper manually stripped the protective covering from the product and hand cleaned the entire surface.

6. However, in place of the four oil draw-back tanks, six draw-back ovens were installed. The ovens are gas fired and semi-automatically controlled. To light the ovens,

grievants must check the valves to make certain they are in proper position. Grievants then throw in the main fan switches and push the buttons to start the combustion air fan, the recirculating fan, and the draft fan. The next step is to open the gate valve for the main and pilot burners. The safety toggle switch on the operating control panel must be pushed to the "on" position. Unused gas which may have leaked into the oven during the shut-down period is purged for three minutes. Then two lights should indicate that the oven is in a safe condition to proceed with the lighting process. Next a starter button is pushed until a red light indicates that the pilot burner is ignited. The air pressure is adjusted, and the gas safety shut-off valve is opened. After grievants have completed these steps, the ovens are ready to be fired. The automatic temperature control brings the oven up to the desired temperature as set by the proper program control cam which must be selected by grievants and placed on the program control device prior to pushing the appropriate button on the control board located at the rear of the ovens.

7. These are the high points of the nine step instructions issued to grievants to guide them in lighting the ovens. Also issued were four step instructions for shutting down the furnaces along with numerous tips for locating trouble if the oven fails to light or goes off during the heating cycle.

8. Some of the draw-back cycles are of a longer duration than can be regulated by the continuous cam operation. In these cases, grievants maintain the temperatures beyond the cam controlled period by use of an electric clock or by their watches. Over an eighty hour cycle of heating, approximately eighteen hours are devoted to manual control of the furnaces. In addition, the cams must be reset if the ovens go off during an electrical storm.

9. After the furnace is lighted, the panel doors are raised by the Floorman or the Helper. The oven is loaded by grievants who operate a six-wheeled jeep which inserts a two level supporting carriage. The product is placed on the buggy by the overhead crane. If the buggy is dry, a hazard to the jeep operator exists in that the rolls may be shoved back over the jeep as the carriage is being pushed into the ovens. Also, spalls ranging from the size of a penny to an estimated eighty-five pounds may blow off the rolls. Grievants testified that they are now subjected to greater hazards in this respect since their duties require that they work closer to the product while it is being inserted or removed.

10. Grievants operate the jeep not only to push and pull the buggy but also to drive outside the building in order to obtain asbestos or to haul salvaged tin for storage. Such duties take grievants into areas where other people are working.

11. Other new or revised duties with respect to which testimony was presented involve maintenance of oil levels on cleaning devices installed with the ovens (use of natural gas in the meantime instead of by-product gas has eliminated this duty); changing charts on recorders and marking the number of rolls; making up sleeve pans; salvage and storage of tin used for protective covering (this is easily accomplished since the rolls are dry when they come from the ovens); and accounting for time distribution at the end of each turn.

DISCUSSION AND FINDINGS

12. No Benchmark or Specimen Example for a Floorman or Floorman Helper as such was presented for the Board's consideration. However, Specimens 671, 1518, 382, 810, 3304, 3364, 3354, 664, 2227, 255, 1516, and 2223 for Carburizer Operators, Annealer Operators, Normalizer Operators, and Furnace Operators, were brought to the Board's attention.

13. An examination of these Specimen Examples reveals that none of them is coded higher than B-.3 in Factor 1. On the other hand, ratings on Factor 2 vary from .8 to 1.2, and ratings on Factor 3 from 1.6 to 2.2. Although none of these Specimens contains precisely the over-all job content of the Floorman job at Homestead Works, the Board finds, using these Specimen Examples as guides, that Factor 2 for the Floorman job in dispute is more appropriately coded at D-1.2 and Factor 3 at D-2.2. Factor 1 remains at B-.3.

14. With respect to Factor 6—Responsibility for Tools and Equipment, only one of the above Specimens has a rating higher than C-1.0. In any event, Factor 6 for the Homestead Floorman job is already rated "Hi" on probable damage and no evidence was introduced to justify a conclusion that a higher degree of attention is required to prevent damage to the ovens. The Manual states that the "C" level is appropriate to cover attention to prevent damage to light mobile equipment, such as tractors and trucks. Likewise, the "C" level is warranted for care and attention to prevent damage to the jeep.

15. The rating on Factor 7—Responsibility for Operations must remain at C-1.0. The same type of product is being processed to the same receiving units. The relationship of the Floorman job to other departments has not changed.

16. Factor 8—Responsibility for the

Safety of Others should now be coded at C-.8. Not only are most of the Specimens above rated at C-.8 for this Factor but the Manual also indicates that C-.8 should be accorded the job in dispute in view of the various purposes for which the jeep is used. Under the "C" level the Manual refers to operation of "power-driven mobile equipment where others are exposed but probability of accident is low."

17. It cannot properly be found that a higher rating than C-1.0 for Factor 9—Mental Effort is justified. Although new equipment is now in operation, the average degree of concentration and attention required of grievants throughout the turn is no greater. Constant checking of the temperature of the oil in the draw-back tanks was required prior to February, 1949, and frequent regulation of the gas jets was necessary.

18. The Board finds that the ratings on Factors 11 and 12 should remain unchanged. It cannot be found that the conditions taken as a whole are so substantially changed as to warrant a decrease in the ratings of these Factors. Although grievants are not exposed to the oil and gas fumes which previously emanated from the oil tanks, they are still exposed to the same significant degree of wetness in the other processing steps. Also, the heat in the summer due to the proximity of the ovens must be taken into account. And grievants are subjected to the odor of raw gas when the warning signals on the ovens fail to work.

19. The following language is found in the present classification of Factor 12 for the Floorman job: "Exposed to severe injury from spalls from treated rolls; works with hot product and inflammable liquids in open vessels." Although the fire hazard has been considerably decreased by the elimination of the oil tanks, reference has already been made to the testimony indicating the increased hazard from spalls and the danger of a roll being pushed up over the fender of the jeep.

20. For the Floorman Helper job higher ratings are sought by the Union on Factors

1, 2, 3, 5, 6, 7 and 9. Management believes that the ratings on Factors 11 and 12 should be reduced.

21. Although Specimen 1519 for a Salt Annealer Helper, Specimen 705 for an Annealer Helper, and Specimen 1517 for a Normalizer Helper were presented to the Board for its consideration, it is clear from the testimony on both sides that, prior to the filing of these two grievances in February, 1949, the incumbents of the Floorman and the Helper jobs worked together as a team, and that the relationship has not been changed by the introduction of new methods, duties, and equipment. In the light of the discussion and findings in connection with the Floorman job, the Board likewise finds that the ratings on Factors 1, 6, 7, 9, 11 and 12 for the Helper job should remain the same.

22. Factor 2 is increased to C-.8 and Factor 3 to C-1.6 as the result of new duties and methods, requiring a longer period of training and a higher degree of mental skill. The rating on Factor 5—Responsibility for Materials remains the same since the Floorman job is given this responsibility and the relationship between the two jobs has not substantially changed. The only testimony concerning probable damage to product as the result of failure to notice the signal lights on the ovens promptly was that it might take longer to treat the product.

23. Under the findings of the Board new descriptions and classifications are in order for both jobs in dispute. The classification of the Floorman job is increased to 12.9 because of the impact of the changes on Factors 2, 3 and 8, and the Helper job classification is increased to 7.0. Retroactive compensation shall be made to February 17, 1949, the date the grievances were filed.

AWARD

24. Both grievances are sustained. New job descriptions are in order. The Floorman job is raised to Class 13, the Floorman Helper job to Class 7. Retroactive compensation shall be made to the date of filing of the grievances.

A—869. 5, 7. Joliet Works. April 20, 1959
Sylvester Garrett, *Chairman*

BACKGROUND

1. This case challenges classification of the job of Warehouseman (Merch. Prod. Whse.), PC 44-33, in the Warehouse Finishing Department at Joliet Works. The job was classified by the Company at 10.2, for Job Class 10. The Union insists that Factors 5,

7, and 11 were incorrectly coded.

2. Prior to 1957, stocking and restocking of wire products in the Main Warehouse were handled by a Piler Groupleader (Class 5) and by several Wire Products Pilers (Whse.), PC 44-25 (Class 3). Management dissatisfaction with Warehouse operations

led to a reorganization in 1957, one phase of which involved creation of the Warehouseman (Merch. Prod. Whse.) job by addition of duties to the Piler Groupleader job. In general, the Warehouseman (Merch. Prod. Whse.) was given more responsibility than the old Groupleader for the warehousing of merchant products, and operation of material-handling equipment was made a part of the job.

3. The primary function of the Warehouseman is to "Plan, direct and maintain warehousing of Merchant Products in the Warehouse and other storage areas and to operate materials handling equipment in storage areas."

4. For the most part, material is brought into the Warehouse for storage by Transportation Department employees, and material is taken out of the Warehouse for shipment by shipping crews. The stocking and restocking of merchant products within the Warehouse are done by the Warehouseman (Merch. Prod. Whse.) and by the Wire Products Piler (Whse.).

5. Outside storage of fence posts is provided at two areas. The posts are loaded and unloaded to and from cars by the shipping crews, but the rearranging and cleaning up of the outdoor post-storage areas and the handling of broken bundles of posts were done in the past by the Piler Groupleader and the Wire Products Pilers (Whse.) and are done now by the Warehouseman (Merch. Prod. Whse.) and the wire Products Pilers (Whse.).

6. The following table shows the respective proposals for each factor:

FACTOR	UNION	COMPANY
1. Pre-Employment Training	.3	.3
2. Employment Training and Experience	1.2	1.2
3. Mental Skill	2.2	2.2
4. Manual Skill	.5	.5
*5. Responsibility for Material	D1.6	D.8
6. Responsibility for Tools and Equipment	C.7	C.7
*7. Responsibility for Operations	2.0	1.0
8. Responsibility for Safety of Others	.8	.8
9. Mental Effort	1.5	1.5
10. Physical Effort	.8	.8
*11. Surroundings	.4	Base
12. Hazard	.4	.4

* Factors in dispute.

CONTENTIONS

7. In relation to *Factor 5,* the Union relies upon the Joliet job of Shipper, PC 44-11 (Class 11), arguing that the Warehouseman's responsibility for materials is the same as that of the Shipper and, therefore, that the Warehouseman, too, should be rated at D 1.6 rather than D .8.

8. The Company contends that the appropriate reference is Specimen 4547, Warehouseman (Class 9), coded at D .8 in Factor 5. Mistakes by the Warehouseman in stocking material in the Warehouse, in the Company's view, will cause some loss by requiring that the misplaced product be located and rehandled. On the other hand, mistakes by the shipper in loading material improperly or by loading the wrong kind or the wrong amount, it is argued, will cause a much greater loss, not only in damaging product or requiring the rehandling of material but also may necessitate rerouting the car. The Company insists that this alleged difference between the Warehouseman and the Shipper finds support in the different codings of Factor 5 in Specimens 4547 and 4548, the former being, in the Company's judgment, the proper reference on this factor for the Warehouseman and the latter the pertinent Specimen for a Shipper job.

9. With regard to *Factor 7,* the Union sees the Warehouseman job as leading the Wire Products Pilers (Whse.) in much the same manner as did the old Piler Groupleader job. Therefore, it feels that application of the groupleader convention is required in Factor 7 of the Warehouseman job and calls for coding at 2.0.

10. The Company replies that the groupleader convention necessarily was applied in coding Factor 7 of the old Piler Groupleader (Class 5) so that it would be classified two job classes higher than the basic job, which was in Class 3. With the advent of the Warehouseman in Job Class 10, the Company feels that the groupleader convention is not applicable since the Warehouseman is classified higher than two job classes above the basic job, which remains in Job Class 3. Specimen 4547, Warehouseman, is cited to support the present 1.0 coding of Factor 7.

11. The presentation as to *Factor 11* is such that the Board believes it unsound to attempt final disposition of this Factor now. Accordingly, the various contentions as to this Factor are set forth under "Findings" below, together with explanation of the necessity for returning this issue to the parties for full analysis in the grievance procedure.

FINDINGS

12. *Factor 5.* The present rating is D .8, and the Union seeks D 1.6. Granted that greater responsibility has been imposed upon the Warehouseman than was imposed upon the old job of Piler Groupleader, that increased responsibility has been given recognition in the present coding of Factor 5. Specimen 4547, Warehouseman, seems closely comparable on this factor, and is coded at D .8. The doubtful validity of the Union's reliance on the non-Specimen Shipper job is revealed by a comparison with Specimens 4547 and 4548. The latter is coded at D 1.6, but this is because of its loading functions, which are not called for by the disputed job or by Specimen 4547. The evidence does not support any increase in this factor.

13. *Factor 7.* This is now coded 1.0, and the Union demands application of the groupleader convention, for 2.0, simply because the job which is directed by the Warehouseman is rated at Base in Factor 7. The Warehouseman is in Job Class 10, while the Wire Products Piler is in Job Class 3. In the light of Specimen 4547, the record supplies no foundation for increasing the coding of Factor 7.

14. At the hearing the Union, over the Company's objection, argued for a higher rating on Factor 10, and the Company retaliated by suggesting a lower coding of Factor 4. The record does not furnish any significant support for either position.

15. *Factor 11.* The Union argues that much more outdoor work now is required of the Warehouseman than was required of the Piler Groupleader and Pilers. It says that when the Piler Groupleader was established in 1946 no outside work was required of that job but that outdoor time gradually built up over the years to a substantial level, all of which is said to require a .4 coding of Factor 11. The Union cited an instance, occurring shortly after the Warehouseman job became operative, when the Warehouseman and several Wire Products Pilers (Whse.) spent about eight straight weeks outside rearranging fence posts. Other occasions were said to have included two weeks of outdoor work and at times it was alleged that the men worked outside all day.

16. According to the Company, no more than about 5% of the Warehouseman's time is spent out of doors, because the loading and unloading of posts to and from cars are done by the shipping crews.

17. The Union agrees that loading and unloading are handled by the shipping crews, but contends that, in addition, most of the rearranging of posts was also done in the

past by the shipping crews but has now become a routine part of the Warehouseman's job, and that this accounts for the claimed increase in outdoor work of the latter. The Union also asserts that the former Piler Groupleader got around to clearing up the storage yards only when he could find some free time and that the areas were very untidy, whereas now the Warehouseman's greater control of warehousing functions gives him more opportunity to look after the fence posts. The Warehouseman, as the Union sees it, spends more time outside than do the shipping crews. It is said that the Warehouseman may have to go outside to handle lumber and pallets and that the shipping crews do not deal with these items, and also that the Warehouseman must take tractors to Scott Street.

18. The Union refers to the Joliet job of Tractor Operator (Hyster), coded in April 1953 at .4 in Factor 11, which is said to require about the same amount of outdoor work as is required of the Warehouseman. Since this job was created after the description and classification of the original Shipping and Warehouse jobs at Joliet, the Union believes it to be the most valid comparison for purposes of Factor 11 today.

19. The Company's position is that the outside work of the Warehouseman is no greater than that of the Piler Groupleader, who is said to have worked outdoors in the storage yards since 1946. It holds that the outside work constitutes such a small percentage of the Warehouseman's time that it does not support more than Base in the coding of Factor 11. The Company feels that the shipping crews and the car blockers are outside under all weather conditions much more than the Warehouseman, and since the former jobs are coded at Base, the latter is entitled to no more. In the Company's view the Union's reliance upon the Tractor Operator (Hyster) is misplaced, since that job was established and classified primarily to function out of doors. The Company says that the post-storage areas are now much more orderly than in the past; that post inventory is now much lower; that some indoor racks have been installed; that improved bundling methods have cut down the number of broken bundles; that cargo lumber need not be handled now; and that all of those factors have necessarily reduced the outside work of the Warehouseman. The Union replies that there may well be more outside work for handling fewer posts, but in any event, it denies that post inventory is down.

20. The Company alleges that the one instance of a sustained period of outside work, shortly after the Warehouseman job

became effective, was necessary to implement the improved stocking plan and that since that initial effort no extensive outside work has been necessary. Thus it holds that under normal conditions, now prevailing, the required outdoor work of the disputed job is too insignificant to be given weight.

21. Late in the hearing the Union produced affidavits from three men now working as Warehousemen, stating in effect that at least 25% to 30% of their total working time involved outdoor work. This evidence, if accurate, might well be highly significant in dealing with the problem under Factor 11. It was not, however, presented or considered in the grievance procedure.

22. It would be an abuse of the grievance procedure, and a disservice to both parties, for the Board to give weight to such evidence without full exploration by the parties. On the other hand, the Board's obligation to code disputed jobs properly, on the basis of the available facts, is plain under Section 9-D and the January 1, 1953 Manual.

23. To attempt to resolve the conflict on the basis of plant inspection of the job and work areas, at this juncture, also might leave much to be desired since the very nature of the outdoor work makes it uncertain that any representative amount might occur in the course of a plant visit of limited duration.

24. Therefore the issue as to Factor 11 will be returned to the parties for further consideration in the grievance procedure in light of their practical knowledge of plant conditions, the claims of the Warehousemen, and the elimination of all other disputed Factors by this decision.

AWARD

25. The grievance is denied as to Factors 5 and 7. As to Factor 11, it is remanded to the grievance procedure for further consideration.

USC—652. 6, 7. Fairless Works. May 29, 1958

Herbert L. Sherman, Jr., *Chairman*

BACKGROUND

1. In this case from Fairless Works the Union asserts that the job of Utilities Dispatcher in the Utilities Department has been improperly classified, under Section 9-D of the August 3, 1956 Agreement, in Factors 2, 3, 6, 7 and 9.

2. Fairless Works has been engaged in the process of centralizing the control, operation and distribution of the various utilities by placing meters and controls for outlying stations in the main power house. These improvements resulted in the establishment of the Utilities Dispatcher job, effective October 7, 1956, and also the job of Utility System Operator involved in Case USC-651.

3. The job description for the job in dispute shows that the duties go well beyond any of the other "Utilities" jobs cited for the Board. It reads as follows:

PRIMARY FUNCTION: Control distribution of supplies of electricity, fuel oil, gas, water, etc., to various consuming activities according to requirements and available supply.

TOOLS AND EQUIPMENT: Manual and supervisory controls for 132 K.V., 69 K.V., 13.8 K.V., 2400 Volt, etc., distribution systems, and operating equipment, sub-station and gas mixing equipment, gas mains, fuel oil, water and fuel lines and equipment, vehicle, instruments, electrical testing equipment, office machines and communication equipment, hand tools, etc.

MATERIALS: Electricity, gas, oxygen, steam, oil, water, compressed air, etc.

SOURCE OF SUPERVISION: Turn Foreman—Utilities Dispatching.

DIRECTION EXERCISED: Utilities System Operator and on occasion Motor Inspector.

WORKING PROCEDURE:

1. Plans and controls the operation of utilities equipment in distributing supplies of electricity, gas, fuel oil, water, oxygen, steam, compressed air, etc., to various consuming activities according to requirements and available supply.

2. Records meter readings and makes out utilities operations charts.

3. Records switching and relay operations, abnormal conditions, plant operations, and utilities systems data in log book.

4. Notifies Turn Foreman of abnormal conditions affecting the distribution of utilities; performs corrective operations quickly and accurately with correct interpretation of signals received and proper procedure to follow.

5. Makes charts and graphs, and analyses same to determine economical and efficient usage of utilities as directed.

6. Maintains utilities consumption rate to insure continuous plant operation and sets utilities alarm devices to indicate abnormal consumption.

7. Synchronizes generators and 69 K.V. system with Utility Co. and removes generators from line.

8. Places mill holds on the consumption of utilities so as not to invoke penalties from the Utility Co. as directed.

9. Regulates generators to conform with

power demands and availability of fuels and steam as directed.

10. Sets and adjusts tie-line controls to assure proper use of purchased and generated electric power and fuels.

11. Checks panels, changes charts on graphic meters, replaces indicating lights and makes supervisory master checks for any disagreement.

12. Participates in phases of the Utilities Department directly or as directed by the Turn Foreman such as assisting in the accounting distribution of utilities, making consumption predictions, arranging for extra capacity from the Utility Co., etc.

13. Receives trouble calls from substations or other utility stations, traces or directs the tracing of trouble and directs or performs repairs, adjustments and installations as necessary.

14. Receives requests for switching protection, including operational or relay trip testing, plan procedure, and takes necessary action and precautions.

15. Adjusts or directs the adjustment of generator excitation or taps on transformers to maintain proper reactive power exchange with Utility Co.

16. Keeps working area clean and orderly.

17. Observes safety regulations.

4. A Switchboard Tender job, in Job Class 16, operated a switchboard under the old system at Fairless to supply electricity to plant operating units. Management recognized, however, that the Utilities Dispatcher job involves considerably greater skill and responsibility. It assigned higher ratings to Factors 2, 4, 5 and 7, thereby placing the Utilities Dispatcher job in Job Class 19. Since no agreement was reached on the classification, it was unilaterally installed on January 10, 1957. The present grievance was filed on January 18, 1957.

5. The following table shows the ratings presently assigned to the Factors for the job in dispute and the ratings sought by the Union:

FACTORS	COMPANY	UNION
1. Pre-Employment Training	C- 1.0	C- 1.0
*2. Employment Training and Experience	H-3.2*	J -4.0*
*3. Mental Skill	E-2.8*	F-3.5*
4. Manual Skill	C- 1.0	C- 1.0
5. Responsibility for Materials	D-1.1	D-1.1
*6. Responsibility for Tools and Equipment	D-2.0*	E-3.0*
*7. Responsibility for Operations	F-4.0*	G-5.0*
8. Responsibility for Safety of Others	D-1.2	D-1.2
*9. Mental Effort	D-1.5*	E-2.5*
10. Physical Effort	B- .3	B- .3
11. Surroundings	A-Base	A-Base
12. Hazards	C- .8	C- .8
Total	18.9	23.4

* Factors in dispute.

6. The Union, relying particularly on a Duquesne Switchboard Tender job rated at E-3.0 in Factor 6, stresses the fact that grievants have a great deal of responsibility and that they must exercise discretion in performing the numerous duties listed in the working procedure of their job description. The Union asserts also that the Utilities Dispatcher has less Management supervision and less help than were available to the Switchboard Tender. At one time one foreman was present with the Switchboard Tender most of the time and another foreman was in and out of the control room. The present supervision consists of a Turn Foreman—Utilities Dispatching who is only present at the main power station about half the time. And the Utility System Operator is outside the main power house the vast majority of the time.

7. Management points out that as the men have become more proficient, less supervision has been required. The amount of supervision for the Switchboard Tender was reduced a number of months before the present job was established.

8. For purposes of comparison and contrast the Company cites Specimen Examples 541 and 542 for First Power Engineers, Specimen 543 for a Motor Room Tender, and Specimen 562 for a Substation Tender. Plant jobs cited are the original Switchboard Tender job at Fairless, and Switchboard Tender and Utilities Dispatcher jobs at Clairton, Duquesne, Edgar Thomson, Gary Sheet and Tin, Gary Steel, Homestead, Irvin Works, and Youngstown. Some of these positions are non-exempt salaried jobs.

9. Management asserts that grievants' duties with respect to electricity are the same as those performed by the Fairless Switchboard Tender job, and that no higher ratings than those presently assigned are warranted. It states that the Duquesne Switchboard Tender job, rated at Class 19, controls and switches electrical power for U. S. Steel plants throughout the Monongahela Valley area.

DISCUSSION AND FINDINGS

10. There is no job cited for the Board which is exactly the same as the job in dispute. Those which are closest and which provide the best guidance are Specimen Ex amples 541 and 542 for First Power Engineers and the Duquesne Switchboard Tender job.

11. On Factor 2 Specimen 541 is rated the same as the job in dispute, Specimen 542 and the Duquesne job are given lower ratings. On Factor 3 Specimen 541 and the Duquesne job are coded the same as the job in dispute, while Specimen 542 receives a lower rating. On Factor 7 Specimens 541 and 542 are coded lower than the job in dispute; the Duquesne job is coded at the same level as the job in dispute. On Factor 9 Specimen 541 and the Duquesne job are rated the same as the job in dispute, while Specimen 542 is given a lower rating.

12. There is no valid basis for increasing the present ratings on Factors 2, 3, 7 and 9 for the job in dispute. The same conclusion, however, cannot be reached as to Factor 6. Grievants have significantly greater responsibility for their equipment than that assigned to the old Switchboard Tender at Fairless. The degree of care and attention which grievants must now exercise for their equipment is more similar to that required in the Duquesne job, which is rated at E-3.0 on this Factor. The same rating is appropriate on Factor 6 for the job in dispute.

AWARD

13. The grievance is sustained to the extent that the rating on Factor 6—Responsibility for Tools and Equipment is raised from D-2.0 to E-3.0, thereby placing the job of Utilities Dispatcher in Job Class 20. Retroactive compensation shall be paid to grievants in accordance with Section 9-D-3 of the Agreement.

T—395. 6, 8. Ore Mines & Quarries. June 13, 1956

Herbert L. Sherman, Jr., *Arbitrator*

Approved by Sylvester Garrett, *Chairman*

BACKGROUND

1. By stipulaton of the parties this case is before the Board under the July 1, 1954 Agreement which covers T.C.I. Ore Mines and Quarries. In T-328 the Board settled preliminary issues as to whether the Company eliminated the three jobs of Crusher Laborer, Scrap Picker and Feeder, and Chute Attendant at the Ore Conditioning Plant when the Plant was remodeled in 1954. The remaining issues involve classification of the two new jobs of Conditioning Operator and Assistant Conditioning Operator.

2. The Conditioning Operator, by manipulating controls on the panel in his control room and occasionally at other locations in the plant, controls the flow of ore from the rotary dump and the reclaiming hopper through the various feeders, crushers, discharge chutes, screens, and conveyor belts to the silos. He is responsible for the physical examination of equipment to ascertain whether it is functioning properly. From his control room he also checks the equipment for proper operation by means of lights, speed indicators, etc. on his control panel, and by telephone. It is his responsibility to notify the Rotary Dump Operator when to start and stop the dumping operation. He regulates the heat for screening efficiency,

adjusts the flow of ore over the screens, makes written reports, and occasionally assists in making repairs.

3. While the Conditioning Operator spends most of his time in his control room, the Assistant Conditioning Operator keeps a continuous check, with the help of a Crusher Laborer, on the operation of the equipment by making periodic inspection rounds during the turn. Many of the duties and responsibilities of the Operator and Assistant overlap. The Conditioning Operator gives the Assistant general instructions, such as when to light the gas burners under the screens. The Assistant reports the condition of the equipment to the Operator. He is also responsible for unstopping chutes, bins and crushers. In performing these duties and cleaning up the machinery and ore conditioning plant in general, the Assistant directs a crew of laborers. He notifies the Conditioning Operator when choke-ups have been cleared and the equipment is ready to be started. He removes tramp iron from the conveyor belts when they are stopped by the metal detector, and starts the belts when the tramp iron has been removed. When necessary, he operates selector switches, reversing switches and safety switches. And he relieves the Conditioning Operator and Rotary Dump Operator for personal reasons.

CONTENTIONS OF THE PARTIES

4. The job descriptions as finally revised are not in dispute. Following is a table which shows the classification ratings assigned by the Company and those sought by the Union:

| | CONDITIONING OPERATOR | | ASSISTANT CONDITIONING OPERATOR | |
FACTOR	COMPANY	UNION	COMPANY	UNION
1. Pre-Employment Training.	*B.3	C1.0	*B.3	C1.0
2. Employment Training & Experience.	*E1.6	G2.4	*D1.2	F2.0
3. Mental Skill.	D2.2	D2.2	C1.6	C1.6
4. Manual Skill.	B.5	B.5	*B.5	C1.0
5. Responsibility for Materials.	C1.8	C1.8	C.7	C.7
6. Responsibility for Tools & Equipment.	*CM.7	EH3.0	*CM.7	EH3.0
7. Responsibility for Operations.	F4.0	F4.0	E3.0	E3.0
8. Responsibility for Safety of Others.	*B.4	D1.2	*B.4	D1.2
9. Mental Effort.	D1.5	D1.5	C1.0	C1.0
10. Physical Effort.	*B.3	C.8	*C.8	D1.5
11. Surroundings.	C.8	C.8	C.8	C.8
12. Hazards.	*B.4	D1.2	*B.4	D1.2
	14.5	20.4	11.4	18.0

* Company ratings disputed by Union

5. Since the Assistant Conditioning Operator relieves the Conditioning Operator, the Union contends that the Assistant should receive the same higher codings on Factors 1, 3, 8 and 12 that it seeks for the Operator job.

6. For purposes of coding Factor 1—Pre-Employment Training on both jobs, the Union relies on that part of the descriptive language under Code C of the Manual which refers to operation of a complex production unit. The Union contends that the Operator manipulates the equipment to separate the grades of ore and that this in turn results in controlling the size, shape, analysis or physical property of the product.

7. Management refers to the descriptive language under Code B which reads: "Perform work of a nonrepetitive or semirepetitive nature where judgment is required to obtain results." It denies that the job determines size, shape, analysis or physical property of the product. Although the job may adjust the flow of product over the screens when a red light appears on the control panel, it does not determine the size of the screen opening to be used. The sizing and shaping equipment is fixed. Nor, urges the Company, is this job any more apt to mix product at the tail end of a run of ore from one mine with the head end of ore from another mine than is the Rotary Dump Operator, coded at B.3 in Factor 1. Management believes that the Sinter Operator, who operates sinter machines and other equipment from a control board, the Blender-Ore, and the Control Room Operator (all coded at B.3) provide a better comparison on this Factor than the job of Head Miner, coded at C1.0 and cited by the Union.

8. On Factor 2—Employment Training and Experience the Union seeks a higher rating for the Conditioning Operator on the basis of the number of jobs with which he must be familiar. He is responsible for direction of eight jobs. The Head Miner, coded at G2.4, is again cited as a comparable job. Like the Company the Union believes that the rating for the Assistant on this Factor should be one degree lower than that assigned to the Operator. The Union also relies on the fact that the Assistant assumed some of the duties of the Assigned Labor Leader job.

9. Management distinguishes the Head Miner job on the basis of the different duties performed, and cites the job of Sinter Operator—coded at the same level as the Assistant on this Factor, the Operator being coded one level higher. Although the Company denies that the number of jobs directed controls the coding of this Factor, it notes that the Assigned Labor Leader at the time of classification directed such jobs as Car Droppers, Loading Operator, Tractor Loader Operator, Truck Driver, Car Unloader, Fuel Plant Operator, Feeder Crusher, Scrap Picker and Feeder, Slate Picker, Chute At-

tendant, Surge Bin Watcher, Crusher Laborer and Laborer. Yet the Conditioning Operator, who directs fewer jobs than the Assigned Labor Leader is now given the same rating on Factor 2 as the Assigned Labor Leader.

10. An increase in the rating on Factor 4—Manual Skill is requested only for the Assistant. Management calls attention to the fact that the tools and equipment for the Operator and the Assistant are the same, and argues that use of such by the Assistant does not require any higher degree of muscular ability or dexterity.

11. A higher rating on Factor 6—Responsibility for Tools and Equipment is sought for the two jobs primarily on the basis of possible damage to belts which may become ripped or pulled off the rollers, and possible damage to shafts and motors. On this Factor the Union cites the job of Hoist Engineer, coded at EH3.0, as a comparable job. The Company argues that damage to a hoist and tipple is more likely from inattention by a Hoist Engineer than is damage to individual parts of the conditioning equipment which may occur at one time through the fault of the Conditioning Operator. Management cites the jobs of Sinter Operator, Control Room Operator, and Blender-Ore, all coded at CM.7 in this Factor, as comparable, since they control similar moving equipment by means of a control panel.

12. The Union stresses grievants' Responsibility for Safety of Others under Factor 8. It asserts that a higher rating than B.4 is warranted for the degree of care which they must exercise for the safety of the crew under their supervision. At the start of the shift the Assistant assigns two to eight laborers to various parts of the plant. Danger to the crew while cleaning out crushers, chutes and other equipment is noted. Failure of the Assistant to notify an Electrician to "tag out" equipment may result in the starting of equipment which could result in serious harm to members of the crew and to craftsmen. Negligence of either the Operator or Assistant could cause the equipment to be put into operation before the crew is in a safe place.

13. Reference is also made by the Union to the possibility of explosives that may come in on the belts with the ore. Management replies that the remodeling of the plant did not increase the frequency or likelihood of dynamite coming in on the belts. It asserts that the Union's request for the same coding —D1.2—as that assigned to the Head Miner on this Factor is not justified, since the Head Miner regularly works with explosives.

14. With respect to the Union contention that the Assistant should be coded at D1.5 on Factor 10—Physical Effort because he uses heavy hand tools to clean out the crusher, the Company cites such jobs as Crusher Laborer and Laborer which use bars to unstop chutes. These jobs are coded at C.8 on this Factor—the same as the Assistant. Since the Operator spends so much time in the control room, though he may use a bar on occasion to help clean out a crusher, Management believes that B.3 is appropriate for this job. Considering the average degree of muscular exertion required of the Operator, it cites such jobs as Control Room Operator and Assigned Labor Leader, coded at B.3 on this Factor.

15. For Factor 12—Hazards the Union again refers to the possibility of explosives coming in on the belts as the basis for a higher coding on these two jobs. The Company repeats that there is no greater likelihood of that happening now than before the remodeling of the plant. It also stresses that no jointly approved job classification in the Ore Conditioning Plant has been assigned D1.2 in this Factor.

DISCUSSION AND FINDINGS

16. Of the seven Benchmark jobs at the Ore Conditioning Plant, the top rated jobs are: Millwright—Class 14, Sinter Operator —Class 14, Blender-Ore—Class 12, Control Room Operator—Class 8, and Rotary Dump Operator—Class 8. The Conditioning Operator, in Class 15, is now the highest rated job at the Ore Conditioning Plant.

17. After consideration of the evidence submitted at this hearing, arguments made under the Classification Manual, and observations made upon a plant visit, the Board makes the following analysis.

18. With respect to Factor—1 Pre-Employment Training and Factor 2—Employment Training and Experience, the present codings for the Operator and Assistant jobs are as high or higher than the codings on any of the Benchmark jobs at the Ore Conditioning Plant except the Millwright. Grievants' duties do not qualify under the descriptive language of Code C of the Manual for Factor 1, as it has been applied by the parties. Grievants do not perform tradesman's duties like those of a Millwright or Machinist. Nor do they plan and direct complex work details of the nature credited to the head Miner job. The equipment under their control is fixed insofar as openings determining size and shape of product are concerned. No adjustments in the openings are made by grievants to control the size and shape of product. For Factor 2 no job presented to the Board with duties similar to those of the Conditioning Operator receives a higher rating than that now assigned to the Conditioning Operator. And

the Union agrees that there should be one degree difference in the coding on this Factor for the Assistant. It must be found, in the light of analysis and comparison of all the jobs presented to the Board, that no proper basis exists for increasing the present ratings on Factors 1 and 2 for the jobs in dispute. No regularly performed duty of either of these jobs justifies higher codings than those now assigned to these Factors.

19. B.5 is the proper rating on Factor 4 for the Assistant Conditioning Operator. This job is not entitled to a higher rating for Manual Skill than the Conditioning Operator.

20. Factor 6—Responsibility for Tools and Equipment is properly coded. Comparable Benchmark jobs which control similar types of equipment by a control panel are all coded at CM.7 on this Factor.

21. C.8 is the more appropriate rating for the two jobs in dispute on Factor 8— Responsibility for the Safety of Others. To the extent that negligence by incumbents of either job could cause equipment to be started at a time when employees under their supervision would be endangered, the degree of care required of grievants is similar to that of the Benchmark job of Control Room Operator, coded at C.8 on this Factor. Other responsibilities in connection with directing the crew in cleaning up the plant and unstopping chokes are similar to those of the Assigned Labor Leader, also coded at C.8 on Factor 8. By rating the two jobs in dispute at B.4 on this Factor, Management has recognized that grievants have a higher degree of responsibility for safety of others than the Sinter Operator, coded at A Base. On the other hand, the classification pattern for jobs in the Ore Conditioning Plant shows that a coding of D1.2, on the basis of explosives occasionally coming in on the belts with the ore, is not warranted.

22. The Assistant job is properly coded at C.8 on Factor 10—Physical Effort, the same as that assigned to the Crusher Laborer and Laborer jobs. Since the average degree of physical effort of the Conditioning Operator is substantially less than that of the Assistant, B.3 is the appropriate rating for his job on this Factor. Nor does the evidence justify, in the light of the classification pattern established by numerous jobs in the Ore Conditioning Plant, any higher rating than B.4 on Factor 12—Hazards.

AWARDS

23. The grievance is sustained only to the extent that the rating on Factor 8—Responsibility for Safety of Others is raised from B.4 to C.8 for the Conditioning Operator and for the Assistant Conditioning Operator. The total point value of the Conditioning Operator job is raised from 14.5 to 14.9. The total point value of the Assistant Conditioning Operator job is raised from 11.4 to 11.8, thereby placing the job in Job Class 12.

COL—57. 6, 7. Pittsburg Works. October 10, 1951

Sylvester Garrett, *Chairman*

BACKGROUND

1. In connection with commencement of operations at the new Sheet and Tin Mill at the Pittsburg Works, Plant Job No. 74110, Classifier, Electro-Tinning, was established and the parties agreed on the job's description on February 10, 1950. Subsequent meetings to classify the job did not produce agreement, however, and the job was installed unilaterally on February 17, 1950 in accordance with Section 9-D-3 of the April 22, 1947 Agreement. The present grievance was filed shortly thereafter.

2. The primary duties of the Classifier are to inspect tinplate produced on the Electrolytic Tinning Line and to deflect defective tinplate into mender or salvage pilers.

3. The Electrolytic Tinning Line serves to uncoil steel strip, coat the strip with tin, shear the strip into sheets and pile the sheets into production units of bundles or lifts. The crew is supervised by the Electro-Tinning Turn Foreman, and technically does not include the Classifier, who is supervised by the Classification Turn Foreman. The crew consists of an Operator who directs the crew and operates the line, a Feeder who charges strip coils into the entering end of the line, a Finisher who sets the shears and roller levelers, a Piler who attends the prime pilers at the exit end of the line and a Helper who assists in the operation of the three pilers.

4. The exit end of the line is designed to permit segregation of the sheets into three different pilers: prime, mender and salvage. Tinplate collected in the prime piler is normally packed and shipped directly to the customer without further inspection for quality. Tinplate collected in the mender and salvage pilers is later reinspected, mechanically or manually.

5. At the hearing the parties were in disagreement as to the classification credit to be assigned the subject job on three fac-

tors: Factors 1, 6 and 7. As to Factors 1 and 6 the Company assigned a coding of A-Base; and as to Factor 7 it assigned a coding of B-.5. The Union requests a coding of B-.3 for Factor 1, B-Low-.2 for Factor 6, and C-1 for Factor 7. The Company's classification places the job in Class 6.9; whereas the Union's classification, as developed at the hearing, would place the job in Class 7.9.

CONTENTIONS OF THE PARTIES

6. As to Factor 1, the Union contends that the job should be compared with a similar job at the Irvin Works, Plant title Assorter Electro-Tinning; Standard Code 0804; Plant Code 5354-217. The Irvin Job is coded B-.3 in Factor 1, and has been classified by the parties in Job Class 7.5.

7. The Union urges, moreover, that the subject job requires the Operator to use judgment in the performance of work which is of a non-repetitive or semi-repetitive nature where judgment is required to obtain results. Finally, it is urged that the reports which are filed by this Operator at the end of each turn are of such a nature as to come within the descriptive language under Factor Level B in the Inequities Program.

8. Management argues that the degree of intelligence required in this position is no more than that necessary to recognize a patent defect when it appears, and to perform a simple operation of pushing a button to divert sheets which are not of prime quality. In the Company's view, the subject job is closely comparable to the job, Classifier, Hot Dip Tinning, Plant Code 73510. In addition, the Company relies on Specimen Job No. 2380, Assorter—Tin Finishing and Shipping. It urges that no comparison properly may be made to the Irvin Works job cited by the Union on the ground that the operations in the two plants differ. If a comparison is to be made with non-specimen jobs in other plants, however, the Company contends that a similar job exists also at the Gary Plant. The Gary job is in Job Class 5.1 and is coded A-Base in Factor 1.

9. As to Factor 6, the Union contends that the Classifier, in the proper performance of the duties of the subject job, is responsible for prevention of damage to the production line. Such damage can occur when a cobble takes place at either the No. 2 or No. 3 piler. If the line is not shut down promptly, the sheets pile up at the cobble, and upon occasion have cut the conveyors and also have cut electric wiring leading to magnets used to hold the sheets in place. When such a breakdown occurs, operations may be shut down for as much as half

an hour. Under these circumstances, the Union contends that a coding of B-Low-.2 is necessary to give due recognition to the responsibility of the position under Factor 6.

10. The Company relies in large part on the fact that under coding A for Factor 6, the Inequities Manual makes specific reference to Assorter-Tinplate as a position properly coded at A-Base. It is also urged that the subject job does not often shut down the line, and that it is the primary responsibility of other employees along the line to avoid cobbles which would require shutdowns.

11. As to Factor 7, the Union urges that the Classifier functions as part of the crew of the Electrolytic line, and that the Piler is coded at C-1 under Factor 7. The Irvin Classifier job is coded at C-1, and the Union believes that the subject job is entitled to similar treatment.

12. The Company's position as to Factor 7 is that the Classifier already is given a coding of B-.5 for working as a member of a crew on a production unit performing work in coordination with other members of the crew. Moreover, the Piler plays a more important role in maintaining the flow of operations than does the Classifier, and is entitled to a higher coding under this factor for this reason.

13. The Company directs attention to four plant jobs to support its position. These are Plant Job No. 73510, Classifier—Hot Dip Tinning; No. 73612, Classifier—Reclassification and Counting Line; No. 73013, Hand Classifier—Black Plate; and No. 74515, Hand Classifier—Tin Plate. The latter two jobs require manual classification and have been given an A-Base coding under Factor 7; whereas the first two jobs perform machine line classification and have been given a B-.5 coding. It is the Company's position that the Classifier on the Electrolytic line should not receive a higher coding under Factor 7 than that which has been assigned the two other machine line type of classification jobs in the plant.

FINDINGS

14. At the outset it should be stated that the present grievance cannot be determined by the Arbitrator on the basis of comparison with either the Irvin or Gary Classifier positions on which the parties have relied to some extent in their presentation. It is plain that significant elements affecting the classification of jobs will vary from plant to plant, even though the jobs have similar titles and perform generally similar operations. Without an opportunity to observe all such jobs closely, or receive evidence from persons

familiar with the manner in which such jobs were classified, it would be impractical for the Arbitrator to rely on them in determining the proper classification of a job of the same title in some other plant.

15. Since the parties have classified all but an extremely small number of jobs in the Pittsburg Works to their mutual satisfaction, the Arbitrator believes that the most practical and significant reference in determining the present grievance is to those jobs in the Pittsburg Works which are most closely similar in regard to the Factors which are in dispute here.

16. This is not to say that the descriptions and classifications of non-specimen jobs in other plants are irrelevant. There is no doubt as to their value in suggesting bases of comparison and distinction between the subject job and other jobs in the Pittsburg Works to which reference has been made by the parties.

17. *Factor 1:* Management cites three specimen jobs and four plant jobs as indicating that a coding of A-Base is proper for the subject job under Factor 1. The three specimen jobs all involve manual sorting— either of black plate or tinplate. Of the Plant Jobs, No. 73013 manually inspects and classifies black plate sheets, and No. 74515 manually inspects and classifies tinplate. The functions of the other two plant jobs are more nearly similar to the functions of the subject job. Job No. 73510, Classifier, Hot Dip Tinning, inspects and classifies tinplate as it comes off a cross conveyor, and operates push button controls to divert menders or waste to the proper pilers. Job No. 73612 reclassifies both Hot Dip and Electro-Tinning tinplate as it passes by on a conveyor with push button controlled diverter gates.

18. All of these Classifier jobs are engaged essentially in the same process as is the subject job and at first blush it would seem clear enough that a similar coding under Factor 1 would be proper for Job No. 74110. As possible bases for distinction, however, are the facts (a) the subject job entails inspection of tinplate which is moving at a speed of up to 685 feet, and (b) the subject job calls for preparation of a production report.

19. As to speed, it appears that the Hot Dip Conveyor, which may carry sheets side by side, operates at approximately 400 inches per minute, so that the speed of decision in classifying does not appear to be the same for Job No. 73510 as in the case of the subject job. Likewise, the conveyor operated by Job No. 73612 for reclassifying purposes is substantially slower than the electrolytic tinning line. If the inference is correct that the speed of the particular line is commensurate with the speed of decision or judgment necessary to classify tinplate on such line, then it would appear that the subject job is entitled to more than an A-Base coding under Factor 1.

20. It appears, however, that the defects in electrolytic tinplate normally run through a series of sheets, rather than occurring in individual sheets, and may be visually detected by the Classifier as the tinplate passes a point some 30 feet ahead of the Classifier's working position. Moreover, about 94 percent of the plate from the electrolytic line is prime product. This is in marked contrast to the tinplate which is reclassified by Job No. 73612, all of which has been inspected previously and found not to be prime plate. No precise measurement of the type or speed of judgment required is possible, as between the subject job and Jobs 73612 and 73510, yet it seems reasonably clear from all the evidence that the native intelligence necessary to handle the subject job is not demonstrably greater than that necessary in filling the other two jobs.

21. Insofar as the reports prepared by this subject job are concerned, these are simple in form and indicate only major types of defects in the tinplate experienced during the turn. In like manner, Job No. 73510 makes out delay reports on the Hot Dip Reclassification line, and there does not appear to be a significant difference between the two jobs in this respect.

22. *Factor 6:* The evidence is clear that the subject job is responsible on some occasions for prevention of damage to the production line. When a cobble occurs at either of the Diverter Gates, the Classifier is in a good position to observe the difficulty and shut down the line promptly. If such action is not taken, the cobble can build up a jam of sheets which may sever electric wiring essential to the operation, or cut the conveyor belt itself. The Company in recent months has taken steps to protect the electric wiring from being cut by the piling up of tinplate at Diverter Gate 2 and 3. Counsel for the Company agreed, however, that this corrective action is not to be considered in decision of the present case, since taken after all material facts in the present grievance had been considered by the parties under the grievance procedure. The Piler, Electrolytic Line, No. 73913, is coded B-Low-.2 under Factor 6, and so is the Helper, Electrolytic Line, No. 73915. Moreover, both the Classifier, Hot Dip, No. 73510, and the Classifier, Reclassification and Counting Line, No. 73612 have been coded B-Low-.2. The evidence supports a similar coding for the subject job, in accordance with the Union's request.

23. *Factor 7:* The case for coding the subject job at C-1.0 in Factor 7, rather than at B-.5, is based on the coding of the similar job at the Irvin Plant, and on the fact that the Piler, Electrolytic Line, No. 73913, is coded C-1.0 in this Factor. The Piler, however, is responsible for the continuous operation of the Piler so as to permit uninterrupted operation of the line. While it is true that the Classifier occasionally may be called upon to shut down the line to prevent damage which would entail a delay in operations, and contributes indirectly in other ways to the smooth flow of operations, this does not appear to be true to a sufficient extent to justify a coding of more than B-.5 under Factor 7. Thus, the job of Helper on the Electrolytic Tinning line, which is included in the production crew, is coded B-.5 under Factor 7.

24. In view of the evidence, the subject job appears fairly comparable to Job No. 73510, on the Hot Dip line in regard to Factor 7. Job No. 73510 is coded B-.5. Under all the evidence, therefore, the coding of B-.5 for this factor is found to be proper.

AWARD

25. The grievance is sustained in part. Job No. 74110 is coded B-Low-.2 under Factor 6. In all other respects the grievance is denied.

USC—342. 6, 7. Gary Steel Works. July 24, 1953
Sylvester Garrett, *Chairman*

BACKGROUND

1. This grievance involves classification of the new job of Pump Tender in the Turbo Blower Boiler House at Gary Steel Works. Management rates the job at Class 9, and the Union seeks Class 11. The description having been agreed upon, the Company installed Job Class 9 on February 5, 1950, effective August 28, 1949.

2. Following is a tabulation showing the codings developed by Management and those sought by the Union:

FACTOR	COMPANY CLASSIFICATION	UNION CLASSIFICATION
1. Pre-employment Training	B- .3	B- .3
*2. Employment Training and Experience	D-1.2	E-1.6
3. Mental Skill	C-1.6	C-1.6
4. Manual Skill	B- .5	B- .5
5. Responsibility for Materials	C- .5	C- .5
*6. Responsibility for Tools and Equipment	C-1.0 Hi	D-1.5 Med.
*7. Responsibility for Operations	C-1.0	D-2.0
8. Responsibility for Safety of Others	B- .4	B- .4
9. Mental Effort	C-1.0	C-1.0
10. Physical Effort	B- .3	B- .3
*11. Surroundings	B- .4	C- .8
12. Hazards	B- .4	B- .4
Total	8.6	10.9

* Disputed Factors

DISCUSSION AND FINDINGS

3. At Gary Steel there are nine Boiler Houses. The Pump Tender jobs in five of these were classified and issued as Specimen Examples. Three of these Specimen Examples for Pump Tenders were placed in Job Class 7 (Pump Tender for #4 Boiler House —Spec. 576, Pump Tender for No. 1, 3, and 4 Open Hearth Waste Heat Boilers—Spec. 578, Pump Tender for #1 Benzol Boilers— Spec. 577); one in Job Class 8 (Pump Tender for #5 Open Hearth Waste Heat Boiler—Spec. 572); and one in Job Class 10 (Engineer 2nd for #5 Power Station—Spec. 559).

4. It will be noted that only Specimen 559 has a higher classification than the Class 9 installed by Management for the job in dispute. This is due to higher ratings on Factors 2 and 7.

5. Factor 2 of Specimen 559 is given a rating of E-1.6. The other Specimen Pump Tender jobs have been given B-.4 for this Factor. Even Specimens 557, 558, and 566 for Pump Station Operators have only received D-1.2 for this Factor. A rating of D-1.2 for the job in dispute must be considered as appropriate in view of this pattern. Although both the present job and Specimen 559 require training in the operation of pumps and auxiliary equipment, this cannot be controlling because of the definite pattern in the other Specimens and the other evidence presented on this issue.

6. For Factor 6, a rating of C-1.0 is proper. The Company rates the *amount* of "probable damage" higher than the Union does, the Company's evaluation being C-1.0 *Hi* and the Union's request being D-1.5 *Med*. Thus, the only aspect which the Union is disputing is *the level of care and attention* required to prevent damage to tools

and equipment. None of the applicable Specimen Examples (including Specimen 559) presented to the Board give this Factor a higher rating than C-1.0. The degree of care and attention required of the job in dispute in checking pressure gauges, etc., does not so exceed the requirements of these Specimen Examples as to justify a higher coding.

7. Equipment under the control of grievants consists of 4 feed water pumps, 1 make-up pump, 3 induced fans, 3 forced fans, 3 ventilating fans, 1 roof washer pump, 3 fuel oil pumps, 7 water treating pumps, 2 air compressors, and feed water heaters. Although the Specimen jobs referred to above are not responsible for fans in addition to numerous pumps, they do encompass other types of equipment not under the control of grievants. The forced and induced draft fans are automatically controlled.

8. Factor 7—Responsibility for Operations is coded at C-1.0 by the Company. The Union, relying on Specimen 559 and other Specimens claimed to be comparable to the job in dispute with respect to this Factor, asserts that D-2.0 is proper.

9. Both the present job and the Helper —Pump Tender (Fuel and Oil), function in the basement of the Boiler House. The Helper job here is quite comparable to the Helper job at #5 Power Station. Management argues that the Second Engineer at #5 Power Station is given a higher rating than the other Specimen Pump Tenders because he must be prepared to relieve the Engineer Turbine. It is common, however, to find that an incumbent of a job is expected to fill in temporarily on a higher rated job. This distinction cannot be considered a fair basis for denying grievants a rating of D-2.0 on Factor 7, particularly in that under Factor 7 of both classification sheets occurs the identical language, "Responsible for operation of all pumps and auxiliary equipment."

10. The Company also contends that the Boiler House Operator is given D-2.0 for Factor 7 and that the Pump Tender under his direction should not receive as high a rating. Nevertheless, the Pump Tender and his Helper perform their duties in the basement while the Operator and the Fireman are normally on the operating floor. Although the overall directional responsibility of the Operator may be somewhat greater than that of the Pump Tender, it does not necessarily follow, and has not been demonstrated, that the difference is so great that the two jobs must receive different ratings on this Factor.

11. On the whole, a rating of D-2.0 on Factor 7 is considered as proper for the job in dispute.

12. As to Factor 11—Surroundings, all of the applicable Specimen Examples presented to the Board evaluate this Factor at B-.4 or lower. Although it is clear that grievants are exposed to a fair amount of heat and noise, especially while taking readings when standing next to the Turbines, a higher coding for the job in dispute cannot properly be granted in view of the ratings on Surroundings for other jobs in this Boiler House. The surrounding conditions are not out of line.

13. In this case both the Union and Company rely in part on certain non-Specimen jobs elsewhere than Gary, which are claimed to be similar to the job in dispute. The Board has not attempted any extensive comparison in view of the substantial number of Specimen Examples available for analysis.

AWARD

14. The grievance is sustained to the extent that the new job of Pump Tender is classified at Job Class 10, effective August 28, 1949.

COL—60. 7. Pittsburg Works.   September 10, 1951
Sylvester Garrett, *Acting Chairman*

BACKGROUND

1. Effective May 16, 1950, a new job, "Repairman, Roads No. 14525" was established in the Maintenance Department at the Pittsburg Works, in order to operate newly acquired road repair equipment.
2. In accordance with the April 22, 1947 Agreement, the Company developed a description of the new job which was approved by the Grievance Committee. The parties' subsequent efforts to classify the job did not produce agreement as to Factor 7, "Re-

sponsibility for Operations." The Company coded Factor 7 as A-Base, whereas the Union requested a coding of C-1.0. In the absence of agreement on classification, the Company installed the job unilaterally, effective May 16, 1950, in accordance with Section 9-D-3 of the April 22, 1947 Agreement.

3. The Union contends that the subject job should be coded C-1 in Factor 7, because it has "full responsibility for directing the work of a large group of laborers."

FINDINGS

4. The Repairman, Roads No. 14525, operates an oil spreader in repairing roads, under the supervision of the Labor Foreman. One, and occasionally, two Laborers are assigned to assist him. The Road Repair operation includes preparation of the patch area by removal of loose materials, excavating to subgrade, tamping the subgrade, adding and tamping the patch materials, spreading the oil binder and adding topping.

5. The Union brief asserts that the Repairman, Roads is responsible for directing a large group of Laborers, but the evidence at the hearing did not warrant this conclusion. The Repairman, Roads has not directed more than two Laborers in the past, from time to time, and the job description provides only that he shall work with a crew of one, or ocassionally two Laborers.

6. While there are no jobs in the plant closely similar to the subject job, there are a number of other jobs which the parties have classified in which the incumbent is required to direct one or two Helpers upon occasion. Of these, the jobs of Operator, Jack Hammer—Hot Work, No. 14510; Operator Concrete Breaker, No. 14511; Track Walker, No. 14514; Gardener, No. 14534; Washer, Checker, No. 44122; Scrap Baller, No. 70817; and Dunnage Saw Operator, No. 79913, all have been coded by agreement of the parties at A-Base under Factor 7. Against these is the job Operator, Cement Mixer, No. 14512, which has been coded at B-.5 under Factor 7. The Cement Mixer job is dintinguished from the subject job in the requirement that the Cement Mixer directs laborers in the loading of correct amounts of each component material into the concrete mixer.

7. In view of all the evidence, it is found that the requirements of the subject job are such that the coding of A-Base under Factor 7 is proper.

AWARD

8. The grievance is denied.

COL—61. 7. Pittsburg Works. September 10, 1951
Sylvester Garrett, *Acting Chairman*

FINDINGS

1. In January, 1950, a new job, "Repairman, Floors, Job No. 14524," was established at the Pittsburg Works. The primary function of the Floor Repairman is to repair wood block flooring. One or two laborers may be assigned to assist him by the Labor Foreman from time to time, depending upon the amount of work involved. The parties quickly reached agreement on the description of the new job, but were unable to agree as to its classification because of a difference of opinion as to Factor 7, "Responsibility for Operations."

2. The Company has assigned the subject job a coding of A-Base in Factor 7, whereas the Union alleges that the job should be coded at B-.5 in Factor 7.

3. At the hearing, the Union took the position the present grievance was based on the same considerations as were presented in Case No. COL-60, and that the case should be governed by the decision in Case COL-60. Under the circumstances, the findings and award in that case are controlling.

AWARD

4. The grievance is denied.

COL—68. 7. Pittsburg Works. October 27, 1953
Sylvester Garrett, *Chairman*

FINDINGS

1. This case involves the single issue of what coding is required under Factor 7—Responsibility for Operations, for the new job of First Helper in the Open Hearth of Defense Plant Corporation facility, Plancor #516, located adjacent to the Pittsburg Works and operated by the Company under lease commencing August, 1950. Only retroactivity is involved, since the job no longer is operating.

2. The Company has assigned a coding of E-3.0, while the Union seeks F-4.0. The Company codings totaled 20.2, or Job Class 20.

3. There are three relevant Specimen jobs derived from Columbia-Geneva operations: #217, First Helper, #1 Shop, Pittsburg, coded at E-3.0; #218, First Helper, #2 Shop, Pittsburg, coded at F-4.0; and #219, First Helper, #1 Shop, Torrance, coded at F-4.0.

4. Other Specimens cited include #173, #174, #9220, #804, and #807. The first three of these receive F-4.0 under Factor 7.

The other two, Nos. 804 and 807, are maintenance Department jobs, operating Foundry Furnaces. No. 804 is coded E-3.0, and No. 807 is coded D-2.0, under Factor 7.

5. Under Factor 7 the Manual sets forth First Helper—O.H. as the illustrative job justifying code F-4.0. In view of this some kind of affirmative showing would seem to be required to justify holding that the present disputed job is sufficiently different from the typical First Helper job to warrant a coding of less than F-4.0.

6. The Company believes three factors establish such a difference: (a) the disputed job operates only a 40-ton furnace, (b) the steel produced is not the "primary" source of steel for any of the plants using the ingots, and (c) the Melter Foreman can give the disputed job closer supervision than ordinarily is true in Open Hearths, because only two furnaces are under his supervision.

7. As to size of furnace, Specimen 217, coded at 3.0, operates a 25-ton furnace, while Specimen 219, coded at 4.0, operates a 58-ton furnace. If furnace size alone were the controlling consideration, the disputed job at the 40-ton level, would fall roughly mid-way between the two most relevant Specimens.

8. But there is nothing in the Manual or Specimens to suggest the propriety of any mathematical formula, based on furnace size, for coding under Factor 7. The Union stresses that F-4.0 codings have been assigned for Specimens operating from 58-ton to vastly larger size furnaces. It cites in particular also a non-Specimen job, at Worcester Works of the Wire Division operating a 36-ton furnace and coded at F-4.0. As a matter of logic, at least, it would seem apparent that the relative heat time, and the various techniques used in the respective operations could in some cases be at least as important, to coding under Factor 7, as furnace size standing alone.

9. The Union sought to minimize the significance of Specimen 217 on the ground that this job operated a Foundry Open Hearth, and hence—like Specimens 804 and 807—was inapplicable in coding a job operating a basic Open Hearth producing steel for a variety of subsequent operations.

10. While it is true that Specimen 217 was in the Foundry Department, it is equally true that it operated a basic Open Hearth Furnace in the regular course of production at Pittsburg Works. Hence this Specimen is fully relevant to the present dispute. An apparent difference between 217 and the present job, however, is that the former operated the Charging Machine, whereas the present job does not.

11. Specimen 217, moreover, is the only Specimen coding Factor 7 at less than 4.0. The Foundry in which Specimen 217 formerly operated no longer is in use, and shortly will be dismantled. These facilities were small enough so that the First Helper also operated the Charging Machine. The D.P.C. facilities are considerably more modern, and ingots there produced were used at Geneva and Torrance as well as Pittsburg. They are of such a nature as to require a Charging Machine Operator in addition to the First Helper.

12. On the whole, the coding of the disputed job at 4.0 under Factor 7 seems proper in view of the express language of the Manual, and the fact that the only relevant Specimen coded less than 4.0 is #217, which operated significantly smaller, obsolescent facilities not like other Open Hearths.

AWARD

13. The grievance is sustained. The disputed job is coded at 21.2, Job Class 21, retroactive to the date the disputed classification was put into effect.

A—724. 7. Cyclone Waukegan Works. March 29, 1956

Sylvester Garrett, *Chairman*

FINDINGS

1. This grievance disputes coding of Factors 7 and 10 of a changed job of Truck Driver, P. C. 08-15 (Class 8) in the Yard Department at Waukegan (Cyclone) Works.

2. Prior to the change the primary function of the job was to "operate light truck, with or without trailer, to transport miscellaneous small loads within and without the plant." The Working Procedure, entailing operation of a Willys Jeepster, included:

"Receives orders from foreman and/or turn foreman.
"Picks up and removes rubbish from plant to dump.
"Loads truck or attached trailer with naphtha, other types of material.
"Hauls Naphtha, other types of material to proper destination and unloads.
"Grades and fills in road either with truck, or by hand.
"Picks up and hauls scrap wood to wood pile, unloads.

"Plows and shovels snow from roads and sidewalks during season with truck or by hand.

"Fills truck with gasoline and oil as necessary.

"Performs minor lubrication tasks on truck, trailer or truck equipment.

"Periodically has truck and trailer serviced by maintenance department.

"Makes out own daily time distribution.

"Observes all safety rules."

3. Around March 1, 1954, the Company assigned to the Truck Driver operation of a small wheeled tractor with a scoop type loader and small snow plow which could be attached to the front end. The purpose of the new equipment was to facilitate performance of the above listed duties where appropriate, and the Truck Driver also continued to operate the Willys Jeepster as needed.

4. After various discussions, the Company increased coding of Factor 11 from .4 to .8, but concluded that no justification existed for increases in Factors 7 and 10. The positions of the parties in the grievance procedure essentially was as indicated in Table A below.

5. At the hearing the Union also cited 16 Specimen Tractor Operator jobs coded at C-1.0 in Factor 7, while the Company stressed Specimens 1646 and 1647 for Truck Drivers. The Company did not agree that Tractor jobs provided a proper comparison, but pointed out that Specimens 317, 980, 2119 and 2319 (all Tractor Operators) were coded A-Base under Factor 7.

6. The evidence as to Factor 7 indicates that the coding of A-Base is justified under Specimens 841, 851, 1646 and 1647, which are the most appropriate references. The Tractor Operator Specimens are inapplicable because of significant differences in function, such as servicing processing or shipping units. While the Tractor Operator (Payloader) job at Waukegan (P. C. 70-07) is coded at C-1.0 under Factor 7, this clearly is because the job entails close coordination with maintenance crews. This type coordination is not involved in the disputed job.

7. The evidence also provides no basis to find significant change in physical effort under Factor 10 because of the new equipment.

AWARD

8. The grievance is denied.

TABLE A

		FACTORS											
		1	2	3	4	5	6	7	8	9	10	11	12	Total
08-15	Truck Driver (Original Classification)	.3	.4	1.6	.5	C.7	C.7	—	1.2	1.0	.8	.4	.4	8.0
08-15	Co. Proposal	.3	.4	1.6	.5	C.7	C.7	—	1.2	1.0	.8 **	.8	.4	8.4 *
08-15	Union Proposal (Step 4)	.3	.4	1.6	.5	C.7	C.7	1.0	1.2	1.0	1.5	.8	.4	10.1

Specimens relied on by Company

		1	2	3	4	5	6	7	8	9	10	11	12	Total
Spec. 841	Truck Driver	.3	.4	1.6	.5	C.7	C.7	—	1.2	1.0	.8	.4	.4	8.0

Tools and Equipment: 1-1½ to 7 ton stake trucks. 2-4 ton dump trucks, tank, panel, box trucks, etc.

		1	2	3	4	5	6	7	8	9	10	11	12	Total
Spec. 851	Truck Driver	.3	.4	1.6	.5	C.7	C.7	—	1.2	1.0	.3	.4	.4	7.5

Tools and Equipment: Sedan, station wagon, light truck, (heavy truck) ambulance, fire truck, on occasion.

Job relied on by Union

		1	2	3	4	5	6	7	8	9	10	11	12	Total
70-07	Tractor Operator (Pay Loader)	.3	.4	1.6	.5	B.3	C.7	*** 1.0	.8	1.0	.3	.8	.4	8.1

COL—38.   8. **Pittsburg Works.**   September 7, 1951

Sylvester Garrett, *Acting Chairman*

BACKGROUND

1. When the Sheet and Tin Mill at the Pittsburg Works commenced operations in 1948, a number of new jobs were established including that of Operator, Tractor (Loading), Plant Job No. 77714 in the Sheet and Finishing Warehouse Department. The principal function of this job is to operate an articulated loading tractor as well as a fork tractor in loading finished material into freight cars. Miscellaneous tractor duties also are performed in transporting materials to and from Pickling and Galvanizing Departments and carrying supplies in the Sheet Finishing Department.

2. The parties promptly adopted a description of the subject job, but failed to reach agreement as to its classification, and the present grievance was filed on September 8, 1948. The grievance originally was directed to the classification of eighteen jobs in the Sheet and Tin Mill, but agreement ultimately was reached as to all such jobs except that here discussed.

3. It is only with respect to Factor 8—Responsibility for the Safety of Others, that the parties are in disagreement in coding the subject job: Management has assigned a coding of C-.8 for this factor, while the Union seeks a coding of D-1.2. Management's evaluation of the position places it in Job Class 8.4.

POSITION OF THE PARTIES

4. A. *Position of the Union.* The Union holds that the Tractor Operator (Loading) works in a congested area, requiring a sustained high degree of attention and care to prevent injury to others. It stresses that warehouses normally are used for storage and shipping purposes with only a few men involved in performing these functions. In the Pittsburg Plant, however, finishing and other processes are carried on in the Sheet Finishing and Warehouse Department. The Union lists the following operations and personnel as within the area serviced by the subject job:

Bundling Table	2 men
Corrugater	4 men
Ungerer Leveler	4 men
Hookers & Helpers	4 men
Shears	2 men
Sheet Wrappers	4 men or more
Checkers	2 men
Laborers	2 men
Shipper	1 man

In addition, from time to time, office personnel, maintenance men, galvanizing and pickling crews, salvage crews, truck drivers, sheet wrappers and lift splitters are present in the department. The Union estimates that approximately twenty-five men normally work in the area in which the subject job operates.

5. The Union also stresses that the subject job services three sub-departments while other tractor jobs in the plant, which are coded C.8 in Factor 8, service only one sub-department or unit. It would create an inequity, in the Union's view, to code the subject job with jobs that service only one or two units in a particular sub-department in a restricted area, when the subject job works in the three sub-department bays where numerous processing units and employees are involved.

6. Finally, the Union contends that the duties of the present job make it analogous to Specimen Job No. 2432, which is coded D-1.2 in Factor 8.

7. B. *Contentions of the Company.* The activities of the subject job are carried on in the Sheet Finishing Warehouse, which is a new, well lighted building. The warehouse and shipping platform areas have wide, marked passageways with relatively few individuals employed there. The Pickling and Galvanizing unit, occasionally serviced by the subject job, is located nearby, and does not involve congested locations where many employees are engaged in other activities. Much of the area within which the subject job works is the same as that for Plant Job No. 76519, which has an accepted classification of C.8 for Factor 8.

8. A review of all tractor jobs in the plant shows that only nine jobs out of a total of twenty-eight have received a coding higher than C.8 for Factor 8. In each instance these jobs operate in congested areas, or under conditions where a large number of employees are exposed, requiring a sustained high degree of attention and care to prevent injury to others.

9. In addition to the subject job, there are three other tractor jobs in the Sheet Finishing Department: Plant Job No. 76520, Plant Job No. 77116 and Plant Job No. 76519, all of which are coded C.8 in Factor 8. This indicates substantial agreement between the Company and the Union as regards the lack of congestion in the depart-

ment, and the care necessary to prevent injury to others while operating tractors in various areas in the Sheet Finishing Department.

FINDINGS

10. A total of four tractor jobs operate in the Sheet Finishing Department: No. 76520 (Ram Tractor), No. 77116 (Ram Tractor), No. 76519 (Ross Carrier), and the subject job. Of these, the first three named have been coded C-.8 in Factor 8, by agreement of the parties.

11. Insofar as the carloading activities of the subject job are concerned, visual inspection at the plant indicates clearly that the subject job is properly coded at C-.8, in Factor 8. Much of the area in which the subject job performs these activities is identical with the area in which Job No. 76519 operates (i.e., the Ross Carrier). Operation of the Ross Carrier calls for at least as high a degree of care in regard to the safety of other persons, as does performance of the subject job.

12. In performing miscellaneous tractor duties, however, the subject job ranges over a wider area than other tractor jobs in the Sheet Finishing Department. Most of this additional area is not congested, and operating a fork truck through such area would

not warrant a higher coding than C-.8 in Factor 8. During a small portion of each shift, however, the subject job transports pig zinc, skimmings, banding strips, and other supplies used in the galvanizing process. This work does bring the fork truck into a portion of the plant in which a greater number of employees are working than would be the case generally throughout the warehouse. The servicing of the galvanizing process takes only a small fraction of the fork truck operator's time each shift, however. On the basis of comparison with two tractor jobs operating in connection with Black Plate Salvage, and Hot Dip Tinning which were observed at the plant, it is clear that these jobs operate in considerably more congested areas than the subject job. These two jobs are coded D-1.2 under Factor 8 and require an appreciably higher degree of care and attention by the operator to avoid injury to others. It would appear improper to code the subject job at the same level under Factor 8 as these jobs are coded. Rather, a coding similar to that of the other tractor jobs in the Sheet and Finishing Warehouse is sound under all of the evidence.

AWARD

13. The grievance is denied.

A—754. 8. Cyclone Waukegan Works. August 5, 1957

Herbert L. Sherman, Jr., *Arbitrator*
Approved by Sylvester Garrett, *Chairman*

BACKGROUND

1. In this case the Union claims that the changed job of Hooker, in the Yards and Receiving Department of the Cyclone Fence plant at Waukegan, requires a higher rating on Factor 8—Responsibility for the Safety of Others. The job was originally described and classified in 1949, the codings totaling 6.1 for Job Class 6. At that time Factor 8 was rated at B.5. Although the parties recognize that no such rating is found for Factor 8 in the Classification Manual, it is agreed that this error does not affect the present dispute.

2. On April 15, 1956 Management issued a Form G. To Tools and Equipment a "Pinch Bar" was added. And the Working Procedure of the job description was changed by adding "Makes up pipe lifts requiring the handling of pipe manually and/or by means of a pinch bar." It also appears that shortly after the job was described and classified, a new crane with a different boom was installed to remove the pipe lifts. When the Form G was issued, the rating on Factor 10

—Physical Effort was increased from C.8 to D1.5. The present grievance seeks a rating of C.8 on Factor 8.

3. Issuance of the Form G was prompted by a substantial increase in the proportion of cut-to-length pipe received from the National Tube Division, compared to the amount of random-length pipe received. The amount of cut-to-length pipe increased from 10% or less to about 60% of the total pipe shipments, but no change took place in the over-all number of pipe lifts always prepared and unloaded from the railroad cars by grievants.

4. This increase in the proportion of cut-to-length pipe called for a considerably greater amount of physical effort by grievants. Cut-to-length pipe, normally segregated by lengths, has always arrived loose in the railroad cars, thus requiring more manhandling in the preparation of these lifts than is usually involved in the preparation of random-length pipe lifts. Random-length pipe usually arrives already tied with black wire, making it easier to prepare the lift. In all

cases, however, the pipe is tied in bundles of appropriate size by the two Hookers in the crew, using No. 6 galvanized wire. In the case of bundles already tied with black wire, grievants replace the ties with galvanized wire so that the pipe will not become stained while in the storage area.

5. After the bundles have been made up, grievants hook and unhook for the Hyster Operator as the bundles are removed to storage areas or platform trucks. Although grievants have other loading and unloading duties, about one half of their time is devoted to unloading pipe from railroad cars.

DISCUSSION AND FINDINGS

6. Since there has been no change in the job affecting the coding of Factor 8, the grievance must be denied.

7. No change was effected in the manner in which lifts are prepared, the types of lifts to be hooked and unhooked, or in the total number of lifts to be unloaded and piled, by the increase in the proportion of loose pipe received. There was no change in the frequency or identity of persons who might be exposed to danger by grievants, or in the types of hazards which grievants might create as to others. Even if bundling of cut-to-length pipe were considered as a new duty, it should be noted that Specimen Examples 3206, 3213, 3216 and 3219 for Bundlers of **pipe and Bundler Helpers are all coded at** B.4 in Factor 8.

8. After the lifts are made up, there is no difference in the hooking, unhooking and piling of cut-to-length pipe and lifts of random-length pipe. There has been no significant change in the hooking duties of grievants since their job was described and classified. Therefore, the 21 Specimen Examples for various types of Hooker jobs cited by the Union, most of which are coded at C.8 on Factor 8 (though some are coded at B.4 and one at A Base), can provide no basis for increasing the rating on Factor 8 for the job in dispute. The same is true of Specimen Example 3074 for a Crane Follower, where Factor 8 is coded on the basis of the incumbent's hooking duties.

AWARD

9. The grievance is denied.

T—528. 8. Rail Transportation. January 9, 1959
Sylvester Garrett, *Chairman*

BACKGROUND

1. This grievance protests classification of the job of Tractor Operator (L40-415), a new job at the T.C.I. Rail Transportation Works, at Pratt City, made effective July 8, 1957. The Job Description states the job is: "To operate tractor in handling various materials in and about Pratt Shops."

2. The Job Description is mutually agreed, but the Union contends that Factor 8, Responsibility for Safety of Others, should be coded D1.2 instead of C.8. It asserts that the tractor operates in a congested area not only when it is in and about the Car Shops, but also when it travels in the general area to which it is assigned. The Union particularly feels that the Car Shops area places upon a Tractor Operator an unusually high degree of responsibility for the safety of the car repairmen who are working in, on and under railroad cars and who may step out into the path of the tractor as it carries materials for this repair work.

3. The Union argues that neither C.8 nor D1.2 in the Manual contemplates part-time operations of mobile equipment in congested areas. It cites as Specimens in point, 682, 1647, 2385, 2386, and 2391.

4. The Company agrees that the Car Shops area is congested, but argues that less than 25% of a Tractor Operator's time is spent in this area, with the balance spent in areas which are not congested, with few employees about. It supports the C.8 rating for Factor 8 by citing Specimens 317, 980, 1105, 1201, 1595, 1596, 1646, 1736, 2123, 2234, 2291, 2382, 2390, 2403, 2413 and 2464.

FINDINGS

5. The present tractor is a Pay Loader— a four-wheeled, gas driven vehicle. Its width is about 6 feet, and on the front is located a shallow bucket which is the same width as the tractor. The bucket can be raised and lowered. When car wheels are carried, the wheel axle is suspended by a hook which is permanently attached to the underside of the bucket. The tractor also is used to transport rubbish and scrap from the Car Shop to dump areas, to carry car parts to a storage area, and occasionally to go back and forth to the Carpenter Shop from the Car Shop with lumber. The tractor enters no other building except the Car Shop.

6. The Shop area was estimated to cover 8 to 10 acres and is enclosed by a wire fence. The trash dump and Carpenter Shop, how-

ever, are outside the fence at the west and east ends, respectively. Within the Shop area about 150 workers are employed.

7. The Car Shop is the largest structure and in near proximity are the Boiler Shop, Forge Shop, Pipe Shop, and Fab Shop. While transporting materials the tractor follows paths between and around these buildings and crosses eleven railroad tracks. It was stated that there was no movement of cars or engines on these tracks in the daytime.

8. The Union asserts that the entire area in which the tractor operates is a congested area, but a plant visitation did not substantiate this claim. It is true that some workers were moving about the area, but it was observed that these were few in number and only ordinary caution is required to be exercised by the Tractor Operator.

9. Considerable observation was made at the Car Shop, which the parties mutually agreed is a congested area.

10. The building is substantial in size and contains two sections, not separated by a physical partition, termed the "heavy side" and the "light side." Six parallel railroad tracks lead into and through the Shop. Each track is separated by a path about 12 feet wide. Three of these tracks serve the "light side" and on these three tracks are spotted railroad cars in, on, and under which car repairmen are working.

11. The Tractor Operator services only the "light side" of the Shop. Since the tractor itself has a width of 6 feet and the load it carries sometimes juts out laterally to the extent of an additional 3 or 4 feet, the clearance afforded is meager in relation to the 12-foot area between the parallel tracks on which the spotted cars are in process of repair. It was also noted that the tractor, when required to cross one of the three tracks, had to make a 90° turn between the cars which were uncoupled to make a path for the tractor to cross the track. So little room was afforded as to require the loaded tractor to go forward and then reverse several times in order to negotiate the 90° turn. Over and above the customary noises which exist in a working area of this nature, the constant din of riveters' hammers was a major distraction. Regardless of the degree of safety consciousness exercised by the car repairmen, the possibility of their coming out from between or under the cars is great. It is evident that the Tractor Operator has a grave responsibility for the safety of these workers. It was testified that an average of

5 or 6 trips were made daily by the Tractor Operator transporting car wheels, etc. into the Car Shop. It was stated approximately 41 men were employed on the "light side" of the Car Shop.

12. There is considerable conflict between the Union's and Company's testimony regarding the approximate time the Tractor Operator spends in the Car Shop. The Union asserts 75% of his time is spent there, while the Company contends it does not exceed 25%.

13. The Company's position is that the percentage of work done in the Car Shop is so small as to bring it within the category of a part-time situation in a congested area. Its Specimens, cited above, which were coded no higher than C.8, form the basis of their conclusion in this respect. It interprets "part-time" as being a percentage-wise matter.

14. The Union replies that the Company's citations, in the main, pertain to jobs which encompass other duties in addition to operating mobile equipment. It cites Specimens 2386, 1681 and 1565 as examples of full-time operators coded at D1.2 but who are only present in congested areas part of the time. Also relevant are Specimens 1529, 1647, and 1733, particularly the latter.

15. The Company argues that the departments involved in the above Specimens are congested to begin with, whereas in the instant case the congested area is only a part-time factor. A company witness believed that a Tractor Operator must work in a congested area about 50% or more of the time for the Union's cited Specimens to be properly applicable.

16. Although there is wide difference in the opposing testimony relative to the amount of time the Tractor Operator spends in the Car Shop, the issue primarily must be considered on a practical basis in light of the plant inspection. The Tractor Operator is subjected to considerable responsibility for the safety of others due to the physical surroundings in which he operates in the Car Shop. This responsibility exists during a sufficiently substantial portion of the typical turn, as a regular, recurring part of the work, to warrant a D1.2 coding for Factor 8.

AWARD

17. The grievance is sustained. Factor 8 of the job in dispute is coded at D1.2, effective July 8, 1957. Thus the total point value is 8.7 or Job Class 9.

Following is a table of all the other cases decided by the Board of Arbitration which involve disputes specifically on the coding of one or more of the "responsibility" factors. For each case the docket number is listed, the specific "responsibility" factors in dispute are noted, and the page in this volume where the case can be found is cited.

CHAPTER 17

CODING "EFFORT" FACTORS

Cases in this chapter involve the coding of Factor 9—Mental Effort and Factor 10 —Physical Effort. The figures after each docket number designate the specific "effort" factors in dispute.

Following the awards set forth in this chapter is a table of cross references to many other cases.

USC—879. 9. Fairless Works. January 13, 1960
Sylvester Garrett, *Chairman*

BACKGROUND

1. This case challenges classification of the changed job of Safety Equipment Repairman (P.C. 2030-7562) in the Blast Furnace Department at Fairless Works.

2. The job was described and classified by agreement in 1955 at 4.5, for Job Class 5. Its Primary Function then read "To inspect, adjust, repair and test gas detection, and protection and rescue equipment." In fact the job was required also to make tests for the presence of toxic gases and explosive mixtures at various locations. Apparently by oversight, the gas-testing duties were omitted from the original description and were given no weight in the original classification.

3. A grievance was filed, and in March of 1957 the description was changed by addition of the underlined language as follows:

"To inspect, adjust, repair and test gas detection, protection, *alarm* and rescue equipment. *Tests various locations for presence of toxic gases.*"

Consequently, the classification was raised from 4.5 to 6.4, for Job Class 6.

4. The table below shows the classification details.

FACTOR	ORIGINAL CLASSIFI-CATION	CHANGED CLASSIFI-CATION	UNION POSITION
1	—	.3*	.3
2	.4	.4*	.8
3	1.0	1.6	1.6
4	.5	.5*	1.0
5	.4	.4	.4
6	.2	.3	.3
7	—	.5	.5
8	.4	.8*	1.2
9	.5	.5*	1.0
10	.3	.3	.3
11	.4	.4*	.8
12	.4	.4*	.8
Total	4.5	6.4	9.0

* Factors in dispute.

5. The Union contends that more and more duties have been added to the Safety Equipment Repairman job so that it is now quite similar to Specimen Example 974, Repairman (Respirators), which is in Job Class 9. In support of its Factor 9 argument, the Union also relies upon a non-specimen job of Safety Inspector (Gas) at Gary Steel Works (Class 6) rated at 1.0 in Factor 9.

6. The Company insists that the only question properly before the Board is whether appropriate weight was given to the addition of gas-testing duties to the job when the classification was raised from 4.5 to 6.4. Reference is made to four Specimen Examples and to three non-specimen jobs, each of which runs tests for the presence of toxic gases.

FINDINGS

7. Specimen Example 974, Repairman (Respirators) (Job Class 9), cited by the Union, makes no gas tests and its repair duties are more extensive (and of greater complexity) than the repair functions of the disputed job. Specimen 974 inspects, maintains, and repairs all the gas detection and resuscitation equipment at Gary Steel Works, Gary Sheet and Tin, Joliet Works, Tubular

Alloy Steel, and the City of Gary. It handles all in-plant repairs on the equipment involved; if a particular repair job is too difficult for Specimen 974, the equipment is sent back to the manufacturer for correction. On the other hand, the disputed job inspects, adjusts, and makes the more minor repairs on the gas equipment in the Blast Furnace Department; major in-plant repairs are handled by Instrument Repairmen at the Maintenance Shop. Observation of the Safety Equipment Repairman job shows that it is not essentially similar to Specimen 974.

8. The Union places great weight on the non-specimen job of Safety Inspector (Gas) (Job Class 6), at Gary Steel Works. The disputed job is, however, presently rated as high as, or higher than, that job on every Factor except Factor 9. The Safety Equipment Repairman is rated at .5 in Factor 9, and the Gary job is at 1.0. Both jobs make the same kind of gas tests with substantially the same kind of equipment, but this is only one of the several duties of the instant job, while the Gary job does nothing but make gas tests, through the entire Gary plant. Thus, in the language of the Job Description and Classification Manual, ". . . the average degree of concentration and attention required throughout the turn" by the gas-testing duties of the disputed job are substantially less than that of the Gary job, and this explains the difference in the rating of the two jobs on Mental Effort. While there was some argument as to the time spent making gas tests on the disputed job, examination of the available records (made by incumbent) reveals that performance of this duty does not consume a dominant portion of the incumbent's time on the job. In this respect therefore the job differs significantly, for purposes of Factor 9, from the jobs at Gary Works devoted exclusively to testing for gas.

AWARD

9. The grievance is denied.

COL—69. 9. Pittsburg Works. October 27, 1953
Sylvester Garrett, *Chairman*

FINDINGS

1. This case involves classification of the new job of Solution Maker, Job No. 08518 at Pittsburg Works.

2. The parties are in disagreement as to coding of six Factors, as follows:

3. The total of codings assigned by the Company is 9.5, or Job Class 10. The Union codings total 13.4, Job Class 13.

4. The parties have referred to nine Specimen jobs, involving various types of chemical work, as relevant to proper coding of the Factors in dispute here. These Speci-

FACTOR	#1	#2	#3	#5	#9	#11
Company coding	B- .3	D-1.2	D-2.2	C-1.2	D-1.5	A-Base
Union coding	C-1.0	F-2.0	E-2.8	D-1.6	E-2.5	B-.4

mens, and their respective codings under the Factors here in dispute, are:—

5. Of the nine Specimens only #4817 involves the preparation of standard chemical

FACTOR	#1	#2	#3	#5	#9	#11
#4810—Chemist (Leader)	1.0	2.0	2.8	D-2.4	2.5	.4
#4811—Chemist (Phos. & Sulf.)	1.0	2.0	2.8	D-2.4	2.5	.4
#4813—Chemist	1.0	2.0	2.8	D-2.4	2.5	.4
#4817—Chemist (Std. Soln. & Stock)	1.0	2.0	2.8	D-1.6	2.5	.4
#4812—Chemist (Comb. Carb.)	.3	1.2	1.6	D-1.6	1.5	.4
#4814—Chemist—(Sil. & Mangan.)	.3	.8	1.6	C-1.2	1.0	.4
#4815—Chemist—Open H. Contr.	1.0	1.2	2.2	D-2.4	1.5	.4
#4816—Chemist—Phos. & Sulf.	.3	.8	1.6	C-1.2	1.0	.4
#4818—Chemist—Blast Fce. Iron	.3	1.2	1.6	D-1.6	1.5	.4

solutions for testing purposes. Since the preparation and standardization of such solutions is the primary and essential function of the job here in dispute, Specimen #4817 prima facie represents the logical reference for guidance in coding of the disputed job.

6. The Union rests its case substantially on Specimen 4817, and asks comparable

codings on all Factors in dispute. In addition it cites a similarly coded Solution Maker job from Gary Sheet & Tin, which is not a Specimen.

7. The Company believes Specimen #4817 is not properly applicable. It infers that Specimen 4817 involves a chemical "analyst" type of job, while the Company regards the job here in dispute as a "Technician" job. In fact, of the nine Specimens listed above, the Company believes that the first four are "analyst" type jobs, and the last five "technician" type.

8. Such an attempted distinction cannot be given weight in the absence of evidence to establish that Specimen 4817 actually is substantially different from the disputed job. No such evidence has been presented.

9. It is significant also that the Manual for "Fringe" jobs, which is here applicable, lends express support to the Union position as to Factors 3, 5, and 9. Under each of these Factors the words "standardize chemical laboratory solutions" is used to describe a type of duty or responsibility requiring the coding requested here by the Union. This language describes the essence of the disputed job.

10. Finally, an analysis of the working procedures of the Specimens particularly relied upon by the Company reveals that the functions performed are of a considerably more limited nature than in the disputed job, which involves preparation of nearly fifty different types of chemical solutions.

The Board can find no basis in the evidence to justify a failure to apply the codings of Specimen 4817.

AWARD

11. The grievance is sustained. Solution Maker, Job #08518 is coded at 13.4, or Job Class 13, retroactive to the date upon which the disputed classification was put into effect.

A—729. 9. Duluth Works. February 4, 1957
John R. Coleman, *Assistant to the Chairman*
Approved by Sylvester Garrett, *Chairman*

BACKGROUND

1. The installation of fence-post galvanizing equipment at Duluth in the spring of 1954 led to the establishment of five new jobs on operating turns and one new job, that of Furnaceman, PC 22-59, on nonoperating turns. The proper rate for this latter job is in dispute here. The Company proposes Job Class 8, the same as for the operating turn job of Cleaner from which men are currently assigned one turn in four to the Furnaceman job. The Union seeks Job Class 9, claiming that Factors 2 and 9 should be assigned points more nearly comparable to those given the operating turn job of Fence Post Galvanizing Operator.

DISCUSSION AND FINDINGS

2. The primary issue here is the comparability of the job of Furnaceman with that of Fence Post Galvanizing Operator on the operating turns. The Union cites the Duluth examples of Heater in the Merchant Mill, Furnace Operator on the Rod Mill, and Heater on the Soaking Pits in support of the view that practice is to pay the same rates on operating and nonoperating turns where the work is comparable. The Company does not dispute this but argues that the Furnaceman's job is not strictly comparable with that of Fence Post Galvanizing Operator, and that it is a distinct job for which a description has been mutually agreed upon.

3. Job Classification summaries for the two jobs, together with the Union's request for the Furnaceman job, are as follows:

		FACTORS												TOTAL CLASSI-FICATION	CLASS
		1	2	3	4	5	6	7	8	9	10	11	12		
PLANT CODE	PLANT JOB TITLE														
DUL 22-59	Furnaceman (Fence Post Galvanizing)														
	Company Proposal	.3	.4	1.6	.5	B.3	C.7	1.0	.4	.5	.3	.8	.8	7.6	8
	Union Demand	.3	.8	1.6	.5	B.3	C.7	1.0	.4	1.0	.3	.8	.8	8.5	9
DUL 22-55	Fence Post Galvanizing Operator	.3	1.6	2.2	.5	C.7	C.7	2.0	.4	1.0	.8	.8	.8	11.8	12

4. Inspection of the two job descriptions, plus testimony in the hearings, tend to confirm the view that the jobs involve different levels of training and experience and of mental effort. The Operator's primary function is "to operate continuous fence post galvanizing unit including control of cleaning and fluxing materials, temperature and strength." The Furnaceman's primary function is "to maintain proper temperatures in spelter, acid, rinse, and flux tanks during down turns." Thus, the Furnaceman is doing only part of the job done on production turns by the Operator and he is doing it without the extra pressures and responsibilities associated with a production turn.

5. It is true that both jobs carry major responsibilities for maintaining proper temperatures for the galvanizing unit. But this is a more critical task on the operating turns where improper coating of posts would result from serious departures from prescribed temperatures and where visual inspection of the finished posts by Operator and Galvanize Post Bander is as important as reading of the unit's gauges in determining whether or not temperatures are correct. The Furnaceman is expected to have temperatures at the right level at the end of the down turn, but there is apparently sufficient leeway left at the start of the operating turn before posts actually move through the galvanizing unit to allow the Operator to make minor corrections necessary to avoid poor galvanizing.

6. Added to his greater responsibilities in maintaining temperatures, the Operator has duties involving correct volume and pressure on water sprays and air rings, the arranging of galvanized posts in the roller line kick-off cradle, removal of the post submerging mechanism at the end of an operating turn, and, with the Bander, inspection of posts for surface and camber.

7. These differences in the jobs of Furnaceman and Operator need to be contrasted with the jobs cited by the Union in support of its argument that down and operating turns pay the same for Heaters and Furnaceman elsewhere at Duluth. On these other jobs, the Heaters or Furnacemen in question are doing essentially the same job on both types of turns. They do not assume the role of chief operator on the working turn, and thus their situations are not really analogous to what the Union is claiming for the two jobs in the galvanizing unit.

8. For the galvanizing unit alone, the Union has accepted job descriptions which make it clear that there are two distinct jobs involved. These two jobs have certain characteristics in common, as witness Company and Union agreement on the same points for Factors 1, 4, 6, 8, 11 and 12. But, on Factors 3, 5, 7 and 10, the Union has already agreed to lower points for the Furnaceman's job than are assigned to the Operator's job. The principle of differences in the jobs is thus established. It only remains to be seen what difference, if any, prevails on Factors 2 and 9.

9. The Company has stated that the training period required for a man to reach proficiency on the Furnaceman's job is amply provided for in the B-.4 rating originally assigned to the job for Factor 2. No testimony was developed to contradict this claim. Certainly the extra duties and extra care involved in the Operator's job will require considerably more months of continuous progress than is true of the Furnaceman. It seems appropriate, therefore, that the job in question carry the B-.4 rating already assigned to it.

10. A similar situation prevails on Factor 9. The mental application associated with the Operator's job is greater than that of the Furnaceman's assignment because of the Operator's special problems in checking on the quality of the actual galvanizing coating and the extra tasks rising out of the maintenance of a production flow. The fact that wrong temperatures are, within limits, correctible on the down turn without loss distinguishes this turn from the operating periods when wrong temperatures mean poor product. This justifies a difference in the Factor 9 ratings, and the B-.5 assigned to the Furnaceman's job by the Company seems warranted.

AWARD

11. The grievance is denied. The job of Furnaceman is correctly classified at 7.6 with a Job Class of 8.

T—67. 9. Fairfield Tin Mill. July 26, 1948
Ralph T. Seward, *Chairman*

BACKGROUND FACTS

1. On January 5, 1947, certain new occupations were established in the Tin House Department of the Company's Fairfield Tin Mill. Among these was the job of operating the so-called "Dexter Feeders," a machine which combines the functions of the "pickler" and "tinning stack." Whereas in the older "Poole Feeder" operation, the sheets were first pickled, then delivered to the tinning stacks in a "bosh," and there fed manu-

ally into the tinning pot, the Dexter Feeder receives a pile of sheets before they have been pickled, picks the sheets up, one by one, by the use of vacuum cups, and feeds them automatically into rolls which deliver them into a pickling solution and thence to the tinning pot. Each operator works two Dexter stacks.

2. On May 6, 1947, the Company presented to the Union a proposed job description for the job of "Feeder Operator (working 2 Dexter stacks)." It also proposed that this job be classified in Job Class 7. The Union declined to approve the description and contested the proposed classification, claiming that the job properly belonged in Job Class 8. In accordance with Section 9-D-3 of the April 22, 1947 Agreement, the Company thereupon installed the classification and the Union brought the present grievance.

3. Though the job description was not approved by the Union, its accuracy has not been challenged in this case. The only question is whether the job belongs in Job Class 7 or in Job Class 8 under the classification rules and principles established by the May 8, 1946 Agreement.

4. The parties are in disagreement only as to Job Classification Factors 1, 2, 6, 9 and 11. These factors and the points assigned to them by the Company and Union respectively are:

JOB CLASSI- FICATION FACTOR	POINTS ASSIGNED COMPANY	UNION
1. Pre-employment Training	A-Base	B-0.3
2. Employment Training and Experience	B-0.4	C-0.8
6. Responsibility for Tools and Equipment	B-0.3	C-0.7
9. Mental Effort	B-0.5	C-1.0
11. Surroundings	B-0.4	C-0.8

5. With regard to the remaining Job Classication Factors, the parties are in agreement. The points assigned by the parties to these factors total 5.0. It should be noted that the points assigned by the Company to the disputed factors total 1.6, while those assigned by the Union to these factors total 3.6. In the opinion of the Company, then, proper evaluation of the job should give it a rating of 6.6. Since according to the Manual for Job Classification, the final class for a job is to be determined by the use of the closest whole number, this is just enough to place it in Job Class 7. The Union's evaluation, which results in a rating of 8.6, should technically lead to a claim for Job Class 9. The

Union made clear at the hearing, however, that it was contending only for Job Class 8.

FINDINGS

6. The Board finds from the evidence presented at the hearing and obtained during an investigation at the plant, that the job of "Feeder Operator (working 2 Dexter stacks)" is properly classified in Job Class 7 and that the grievance must be denied.

7. Considering first the factor of *Pre-Employment Training,* the Union contends that the judgment required of the Dexter Feeder Operator in eliminating the mixing of plates, maintaining the solution in the pickling unit at the proper level, adding new pig tin, and lubricating and adjusting the Feeder, is such as to justify a rating of B-0.3. The Board does not agree. To prevent the mixing of plates the operator is required merely to check the tag which accompanies the pile of plates to see if there has been any change in size. Thereafter he merely writes his stack number, the date and the turn on the back of the tag and attaches it to the finished sheets that have been tinned. This clearly comes under the heading "make out simple reports such as crane reports and production cards" which, according to the Classification Manual, calls for only a "Base" rating. It appears from the Board's investigation of the job, moreover, that the matter of keeping the solution at the proper level and adding new pig tin is closely supervised and requires little independent judgment. As to lubrication, the operator is required only to keep the lubricator on the air pump and vacuum full of oil. The adjustments required are simple and limited. No substantial basis exists for the Union's claim for a B-0.3 rating under this factor. The "Base" rating applied by the Company is approved.

8. In regard to Factor 2, the question is whether it requires from three to six months or from seven to twelve months to become proficient as a Dexter Feeder Operator working two stacks. We see nothing in the operation which could possibly require seven months to learn. Maximum production was reached on these machines within a few days after they were placed in operation. It is true that all the operators who were assigned to the Dexter Feeders had had previous experience on the Poole Feeders. On that basis, we discount as unproven the Company's claim that the job can be learned in a week or less. It appears to us, nevertheless, that an estimate of three months to learn the job is liberal and that the Union's claim that seven months is required is utterly without foundation. The rating of B-0.4 is approved.

9. Under the heading *Responsibility for*

Tools and Equipment the Company has rated the Dexter Feeder at B-0.3. The Union asks for a rating of C-0.7. The latter is the agreed rating of the Stack Mechanic, who has responsibility for an entire unit of ten stacks. We do not believe that the Feeder Operators, who are responsible for only two stacks, can possibly qualify for this rating. Nevertheless, there does appear to be some possibility of damage to rolls if the plates are not properly positioned in the machine. The necessity of watching for cobbles, doubles, stickers and so forth on two machines at the same time justifies a higher rating than the B-0.3 rating applied by the Company. We hold that the proper rating should be B-0.5.

10. As to Factor 9, *Mental Effort,* we note that the Job Classification Manual lists a B-0.5 job as calling for "Light mental or visual application . . . for performing work where there is some variety, but actions to be taken and decisions made are limited to few possibilities." We believe that this accurately describes the degree of concentration required of the Dexter Feeder Operators. The C-1.0 rating for which the Union argues, on the other hand, calls for "Moderate mental or visual application . . . for performing manual work, machine operations, set-ups, inspection and adjustments which require frequent decisions to detect and adjust for variance from proper operation." In no sense, does the Dexter Feeder job meet this latter standard. We note again, moreover, that the Union is here asking that the Feeder Operators receive the same rating as the Stack Mechanic whose responsibility is far greater and who must exercise that responsibility with regard to ten stacks as compared to the Feeder Operator's two. The Union's claim on this point is clearly without merit. The B-0.5 rating applied by the Company is approved.

11. As to Factor 11, *Surroundings,* finally, the Board finds that the B-0.4 rating imposed by the Company is correct. This is the same grade which the parties have agreed should apply to the other jobs which exist in connection with the operation of the Dexter Feeders such as the Stack Mechanic, the Unit Operator and the Head Unit Operator. According to the Manual, that grade applies to work which requires "exposure to wetness and some fumes and smoke." The C-0.8 grade for which the Union is arguing has been applied by agreement to the Poole Feeder Operators who work in such continual wetness that they must constantly wear rubber boots, rubber aprons and rubber hand pads. The Poole Feeder is required to lift the plates manually out of a water-filled bosh, the water necessarily draining down over his body and his work place. The C-0.8 grade which is applicable to work requiring exposure "to considerable wetness, acids, fumes, dust or glare necessitating the wearing of protective clothing or devices" is properly applicable to the Poole Feeder's job. It has no application to the Dexter Feeder operation in which there is comparable little wetness, the fumes are minor and the Operator does not have to wear protective clothing.

12. We find accordingly that the ratings proposed by the Company are correct for all factors except that of *Responsibility for Tools and Equipment.* The correction of this factor as above indicated should raise the point rating of the job from 6.6 to 6.8. As this is still within the point range equivalent to Job Class 7, the request of the Union for a higher classification must be denied.

AWARD

13. The grievance is denied.

USC—453. 9. McDonald Works. March 30, 1956
Donald A. Crawford, *Arbitrator*
Approved by Sylvester Garrett, *Chairman*

FINDINGS

1. The Union claim, that the new job of Wheeler has been improperly classified, is upheld in part. The disputed factor ratings, Mental Skill and Mental Effort have each been under-rated one degree, but the Responsibility for the Safety of Others has been properly rated.

2. The Wheeler is a three wheel, gas powered wheelbarrow, weighing 500 lbs. with a capacity of 1500 lbs., used to transport material, supplies and debris in Mc-Donald Mills, Youngstown District Works.

There are no relevant benchmark jobs. The work was formerly done by a laborer with a wheelbarrow. The classification of a somewhat similar job, Operator, Floor Sweeper, has been twice arbitrated (T-288,A-557). It is a gas driven sweeper which the Operator drives through aisles. The agreed upon Mental Skill rating of the Sweeper job is B-1.0, Mental Effort rating, B-.5, and Responsibility for Safety of Others is rated B-.4 at T.C.I. and Central Operations, but C-.8 at American Steel and Wire.

3. The Mental Skill requirements of

the Wheeler job—adjusting the clutch, gas feed, brake, dump lever in operating the Wheeler and recognizing obvious defects—are a step above those required on a labor job (no varied, adjustment of controls) and comparable to those involved in operating the Sweeper. Similarly, the Mental Effort—the concentration required in operating the Wheeler, adjusting controls, as the Operator goes through the mills and shops, loads and dumps—is a step higher than that required on a Labor job and comparable to that required on the Sweeper job. Pushing and dumping a wheelbarrow does not involve the simultaneous adjustment of controls.

4. The Responsibility for Safety of Others, however, is not a degree greater than that of the Labor job. The Wheeler operates in congested areas with a load up to 1500 lbs., including such things as shear knives, grease barrels, brasses, guides. With a wheelbarrow, the load is much lighter, the control easier, stopping quicker, some congested ares are avoided, no mechanical controls are involved. These considerations make the possibility of injury to others somewhat greater with the Wheeler than with the wheelbarrow.

5. This consideration must be weighed against the fact that the parties, in evaluating the specimen jobs, have given only a C-.8 Factor 8 rating (Responsibility for Safety of Others) to such jobs as the operation of hi-lift trucks in congested areas (1592, 1757, 1646, 1595), the operation of crane trucks in mill areas (1200-1209) and the operation of a Krane Kar tractor in the Weld Shop (1105). Clearly, the operation of the Wheeler in a congested area does not require nearly the same care to prevent injury to others. The proper Factor 8 rating, therefore, falls at the B-.4 level which is given to labor jobs where the laborer works with others and may injure them in handling tools or materials. As noted, the Sweeper job is rated at both B-.4 and C-.8 on this factor, but here the agreed upon Central Operations rating should control.

AWARD

6. The grievance is sustained in part. The Wheeler job, McDonald Mills, Youngstown District Works, shall be rated B-1.0 on Factor 3, B-.4 on Factor 8, and B-.5 on Factor 9, resulting in a total value of 4.2 for Job Class 4. The awarded classification should be made effective June 21, 1953.

T—301.   10. Ensley Steel Works.   March 31, 1955
Herbert L. Sherman, Jr., *Arbitrator*
Approved by Sylvester Garrett, *Chairman*

BACKGROUND

1. This grievance requests the Board to find that the old job of Checker Cleaner and the new job of Checker Layer at Ensley Steel Works should be combined into one job—comparable to Specimen Example 1001 for a Furnace Repairman-Checker at Job Class 6. In the event that the Board does not make such a finding, the Union then asserts that Factors 10 and 11 of the new job of Checker Layer should be coded the same as Specimen 1001.

2. Prior to 1951 Laborers in Job Class 2 cleaned out the checker chambers and the flues at the Ensley Open Hearth. Following this operation, four of the gang, abstracted as Bricklayer Helpers at Job Class 3, were assigned the task of replacing the checker bricks.

3. During the 1951 Review Program the job of Checker Cleaner at Job Class 4 was established in the Yard Department by mutual agreemnt of the parties. Thus, the job which formerly cleaned out the checker chambers and flues at the Job Class 2 rate was advanced two job classes. This meant that the employees who continued to lay the checker bricks as Bricklayer Helpers at Job Class 3, instead of receiving the rate for one *more* job class than that assigned to the job which removed the checkers, were actually receiving one job class *less* than the Checker Cleaners.

4. About this same time the old job description of Brickmason Helper was replaced by the "standard" job description for a Bricklayer Helper. In April, 1953, Grievance 151-1176 was filed by certain employees who had been abstracted as Bricklayer Helpers while laying checker brick. This grievance asserted that laying checker brick was not in the Bricklayer Helper job description, and requested the Bricklayer rate of pay when such duty was performed. In the Fourth Step of the grievance procedure, the following decision was rendered on July 28, 1953:

"In order to settle this grievance, the Company is willing to discontinue requiring Brickmason Helpers to perform the work of replacing checker brick in Open Hearth Checker Chambers. *A new job will be established by the Company to cover this function.* This settlement is made without prejudice to the position of either party to this case." (Emphasis added.)

5. As a result of this settlement of Grievance 151-1176, the new job of Checker Layer was described and classified by the Company. Although the description was jointly approved, the Union did not agree with the classification. Management, therefore, installed its proposed Job Class 4 unilaterally on November 1, 1953, in accordance with Section 9-D(3) of the Agreement. The grievance protesting the classification was filed in the First Step on November 24, 1953.

6. Other than the ratings on Factors 10 and 11, the proposed ratings for the new job are the same as those for Specimen 1001 which is responsible for both the removal of the checkers and the laying of the checkers. Management contends that C .8 should be assigned to the new job on Factor 10—Physical Effort, rather than D 1.5, because grievants only lay checker bricks; they do not, as Checker Layers, remove the checker bricks with bars and sledges. For Factor 11—Surroundings, the Company argues that C .8, instead of D 1.6, is the proper rating, since the intense heat of the checker chambers has been reduced during the two to three days while the checker bricks are being removed and the flues cleaned.

DISCUSSION AND FINDINGS

7. The Board finds that Management had the right to establish the new job of Checker Layer, separate and distinct from the job of Checker Cleaner. This conclusion naturally flows from the mutual agreement of the parties during the 1951 Review Program to establish the separate job of Checker Cleaner, and also from the terms of the 1953 settlement of the Bricklayer Helpers' grievance.

8. The Board cannot agree, however, that the average degree of physical effort and surroundings of the new job differ so materially from the average physical effort and surroundings of Specimen 1001 as to warrant lower ratings than those assigned this Specimen Example on Factors 10 and 11. Although grievants do not remove *and* lay checker bricks as required of incumbents of Specimen 1001, it must be remembered that the Checker Layer job is not a full-time job. Grievants are only abstracted as Checker Layers for that part of the turn or week when they are laying checker bricks. For that period of time D 1.5 is the more appropriate rating for Factor 10 and

D 1.6 is the more appropriate rating for Factor 11. Other periods of time, when grievants are working as laborers, cannot be considered in determining the average working conditions for the job in dispute.

9. Under the reason for classification of Factor 10 for Specimen 1001, several duties are listed. Among them is "Lays checker brick . . ." For the period of time in which that duty is being performed, it calls for a rating of D 1.5 on Factor 10. Also, although Management argues that bars and sledges are only used by the Checker Cleaner job and not the Checker Layer job, it seems clear that the latter job is required on some occasions to use heavy tools.

10. When only a partial rebuild job is in process, additional cleaning may be necessary, particularly when laying checkers at the side wall and the dividing wall of the chamber, before the new checkers may be placed in their proper positions. The necessity for use of heavy tools may thus arise even after grievants have undertaken their checker laying duties. It is reasonable to infer that grievants are not suddenly abstracted on the Checker Cleaner job when these instances occur.

11. It should also be noted that a bottom block for the first layer in the chamber weighs 45 pounds, while the ordinary checkers weigh 17 pounds. Although a Bricklayer handles both heavier and lighter type bricks, more appropriate guidance is furnished in this case by Specimen 1001.

12. With respect to Factor 11—Surroundings, again the Board must conclude that deviation from Specimen 1001 is not warranted. Even though the intensity of the heat in the checker chamber has diminished somewhat while the bricks are being removed, the difference in grievants' average surroundings for the period in which they are abstracted as Checker Layers is not so substantial as to require a lower rating than that assigned to Factor 11 for the Specimen Example. The chambers are still very hot, dirty and dusty while the checkers are being laid. Grievants, who are exposed to these conditions for extended periods, use leather hand pads over their gloves, and wear goggles and an extra pair of pants. They also spell each other, because of the disagreeable conditions, every 15 to 25 minutes. Except for two openings, grievants are enclosed within the four walls of the checker chambers. When only a partial rebuild job is performed, the old checker bricks are still hot.

13. Although Management points out that fans are placed in front of the chambers for a period before the furnace is taken

off and that a steam jet has been installed to pull air through the checkers, these additions would also help to improve the conditions of the Checker Cleaners. They do not provide any distinction between the surroundings of the Checker Cleaners and those of the Checker Layers. The Checker Cleaner job is coded at D 1.5 in Factor 10 and D 1.6 in Factor 11.

14. Since the Board concludes that the new job of Checker Layer should be coded at D 1.5 on Factor 10 and D 1.6 on Factor 11, the total point value is raised from 4.1 to 5.6. Grievants are, therefore, entitled to retroactive compensation to November 1, 1953.

AWARD

15. The grievance is sustained to the extent that Factor 10 is coded at D 1.5 and Factor 11 at D 1.6 for the new job of Checker Layer.

USC—651. 10. Fairless Works. May 29, 1958

Herbert L. Sherman, Jr., *Chairman*

BACKGROUND

1. This grievance from Fairless Works protests, under Section 9-D of the August 3, 1956 Agreement, the Job Class 12 presently assigned to the job of Utility System Operator in the Utilities Department.

2. Fairless Works has been engaged in the process of centralizing the control, operation and distribution of the various utilities by placing meters and controls for outlying stations in the main power house. About the same time that the Utilities Dispatcher job involved in USC-652 was established, the Utility System Operator job was also developed. The job in dispute performs some of the duties performed under the old system by such jobs as Switchboard Tender Helper, Gas Producer, Mixing Station Operator and Pump Tender (Auxiliaries Equipment).

3. In addition to assisting in the operation of controls on the central switchboard at the main power station, grievants make periodic rounds of the outlying utilities stations under the direction of a Turn Foreman and the Utilities Dispatcher. Grievants inspect, service and operate utilities distribution systems equipment at the gas mixing station, fuel stations and electrical substations. Routine preventive **maintenance is** performed. If the Utility System Operator is confronted with repairs of a major nature, a Motor Inspector is assigned to make them. Grievants also keep records and change charts.

4. The following table shows the present ratings on the Factors for the job in dispute and the ratings sought by the Union:

FACTORS	PRESENT CLASSIFICATION	PROPOSED CLASSIFICATION
1. Pre-Employment Training	C-1.0	C-1.0
* 2. Employment Training and Experience	E-1.6*	F-2.0*
3. Mental Skill	D-2.2	D-2.2
4. Manual Skill	B- .5	B- .5
* 5. Responsibility for Materials	C- .5*	D- .8*
* 6. Responsibility for Tools and Equipment	C-1.0*	D-2.0*
7. Responsibility for Operations	D-2.0	D-2.0
8. Responsibility for Safety of Others	C- .8	C- .8
9. Mental Effort	C-1.0	C-1.0
*10. Physical Effort	B- .3*	C- .8*
11. Surroundings	B- .4	B- .4
*12. Hazards	C- .8*	E-2.0*
Total	12.1	15.5
Job Class	12	16

* Factors in dispute.

5. The Union also questioned the rating on Factor 8 at the hearing because of an alleged change in the use of a truck. It appears, however, that another grievance is pending, which protests alleged changes in the job since the present classification was installed in January, 1957. No ruling will be made with respect to this Factor in this case.

6. The Union seeks a higher rating on Factor 2 because it believes that it would take 30 months or more to become proficient in the various duties of the job. Particular reference is made to the fact that grievants relieve the Utilities Dispatcher when necessary. Management points out that the Switchboard Tender Helper also did the same thing for the Switchboard Tender under the old system.

7. According to the Union grievants work to close tolerances, thereby justifying a higher rating on Factor 5. And the rating on Factor 6 should be increased, says the Union, because improper operation of the equipment could cause great damage.

8. The Union holds that the rating on Factor 10 should be increased because griev-

ants carry ground cables of 30 to 100 pounds, climb towers to put grounds on wires, and perform such duties of the Fuel Unloader as opening and closing heavy valves for the oil barges when he is not present. The Fuel Unloader job has been coded at C- .8 on this Factor. Management agrees that an incumbent of the job may spend up to a couple of hours on the first turn in grounding wires to prepare for daylight maintenance. But there is less work of this nature for incumbents of the job on other turns, and the coding on Factor 10 is based on average physical effort. With respect to the unloading of oil barges, grievants may devote from one and one half to three hours per barge. Over a period of eighteen months the job in dispute was assigned to unloading an average of less than four barges per month.

9. For a higher rating on Factor 12 the Union points to the fact that grievants work around high tension wires, and an Electrician (Lineman) receives a rating of E-2.0 on this Factor. The Company notes that other jobs, coded at C- .8 on this Factor, are also occasionally exposed to high voltage electricity when making grounds with high voltage wires.

DISCUSSION AND FINDINGS

10. The following Specimen Examples are the closest to the job in dispute: Specimen 561—Gas Producer (Job Class 10), Specimen 562—Sub-Station Tender (Job Class 10), and Acetylene Line Repairman (Job Class 8). As a further basis for comparison, the following Fairless jobs are in point: Switchboard Tender Helper (Job Class 10), Gas Producer (Job Class 11), Mixing Station Operator (Job Class 11) and Pump Tender (Auxiliaries Equipment) (Job Class 8).

11. All of the above jobs are coded lower in Factor 2 than the job in dispute, except for the Mixing Station Operator

which is coded the same as the job in dispute. There is no valid basis for assigning a higher rating than the E-1.6 now assigned to this Factor. The Fairless Fuel Unloader job is rated at C- .8 on Factor 2.

12. With respect to Factor 5, probable monetary loss is not in dispute. Of the jobs cited above all are coded at the "B" level in Factor 5 except for the two Gas Producer jobs (the Fairless job and Specimen 561), which are rated at the "C" level. It must be concluded that the "C" level is appropriate for the job in dispute.

13. Probable damage under Factor 6 has already been rated as "High." Most of the jobs cited above are coded in the "C" level—the same as the job in dispute. None is coded higher. The Fuel Unloader job is rated at B- .3 on both Factors 5 and 6. There is no evidence in the record which would justify a higher rating on Factor 6 than that presently assigned to the job in dispute.

14. On Factor 10 all of the jobs cited above are coded at B- .3 except for Specimen 562 for a Sub-Station Tender (rated at A Base) and the Fairless Fuel Unloader (rated at C- .8). B- .3 best describes the average degree of muscular exertion required for the job in dispute.

15. On Factor 12 an Electrician Lineman receives a rating of E-2.0 because of "Frequent exposure to a hazard where failure to exercise extreme care and judgment might cause an accident which would result in total disability or a fatality." Most of the jobs cited above are rated at B- .4 on this Factor. None is coded higher than C- .8. Two of the jobs are sometimes required to make grounds and are coded at C- .8. This rating must also be deemed appropriate for the job in dispute.

AWARD

16. The grievance is denied.

USC—275. 10. Johnstown Works. May 25, 1953
J. Orvis Keller, *Arbitrator*

BACKGROUND

1. In 1949 the Plant Management at Johnstown decided to create a new job with the standard title of Record File Clerk and the plant title of Mill Clerk (Time Keeper) in the Service Bureau of the Accounting Department. Under date of September 30, 1949, there was agreement between the Union and Company as to the job description for this newly created job. The Company prepared

a job classification and presented it to the Union for approval. As no agreement could be reached between the two parties on the job classification, it was installed by the Company on November 13, 1950, under the provisions of Section 9-D-3 of the Agreement of April 22, 1947.

2. The Union requests a change in both the Job Description and the Job Classification on the grounds that Factors 5, 7 and 10 had not been properly considered when

the job was classified by the Company, and that the Job Classification has never been agreed to by the Union. The Union also requests that the award be retroactive to the date when the disputed job classification was put into effect by the Company. The Union further alleges that the Company has added duties to the job since the description and classification were put into effect, and that the Company has therefore violated the provisions of Section 9-D of the 1947 Agreement by not presenting a new job description and classification to the Union.

3. The original position of the Union as set forth in its brief contends that the following factors had not been properly considered when the job was originally classified:

	UNION POSITION	POINT DIFFERENCE
Factor 5—Responsibility for Materials: Company classification C.5	should have been C 1.2	.7
Factor 7—Responsibility for Operations: Company classification B.5	should have been C 1.0	.5
Factor 10—Physical Effort: Company classification B.3	should have been C .8	.5
	Total Difference	1.7

4. The Company submits that this grievance should be dismissed by the Board for the reason that the factor valuations which it has selected for the three factors under dispute, namely factors 5, 7 and 10 are correct. Furthermore the Company denies that it has violated the provisions of Section 9-D of the 1947 Agreement and contends on the other hand that it has properly followed the provisions of Section 9-D-3 when it placed the job description and job classification of the disputed job, Record File Clerk, into effect on November 13, 1950.

DISCUSSION AND FINDINGS

5. During the hearings it was admitted by the Union that the job description for the job in question, Record File Clerk (Plant Code 9130-409) was agreed to by the Union, the date thereon being September 30, 1949. It was admitted by the Company that the Union did not and has not agreed to any classification of the job submitted by the Company. Accordingly, the Company on November 13, 1950, installed the job classification under Section 9-D-3 of 1947 Agreement which contains the following statement:

"If Management and the grievance committee are unable to agree upon the description and classification, Management shall install the proposed classification, and the standard hourly wage scale rate for the job class to which the job is thus assigned shall apply in accordance with the provisions of Subsection B of this Section. The employee or employees affected may at any time within 30 days file a grievance alleging that the job is improperly classified under the job description and classification procedure of May 8, 1946, Agreement between the parties hereto***"

6. The Union contended that the Company had changed the job content (requirements of the job as to the training, skill, responsibility, effort, and working conditions) to the extent of more than one full job class and that the Company had therefore violated the provisions of Section 9-D in not presenting a new job description and classification for the job to the Union Grievance Committee for approval. The Union presented in evidence exhibit material purporting to show the changes in the job content.

7. Without admitting that the alleged changes as shown in the exhibit were valid, the Company contended that such items would not change the original job classification to the slightest extent, and that it was unnecessary for the Company to present a new job description and classification unless the changes were made in the job content to the extent of one full job class or more. The Company read into the hearings portions of Section 9-D of the April 22, 1947, Agreement as follows:

"The job description and classification for each job in effect as of the date of this Agreement shall continue in effect unless (1) Management changes the job content (requirements of the job as to the training, skill, responsibility, effort, and working conditions) to the extent of one full job class or more;***"

"When and if from time to time the Company, at its discretion, establishes a new job or changes the job content (requirements of the job as to training, skill, responsibility, effort, and working conditions) of an existing job to the extent of one full job class or more, a new job description and classification for the new or changed job shall be established in accordance with the following procedure:***"

8. Through testimony by the plant industrial engineer the Company explained how the original classification had been determined from the Manual insofar as factor 10 was concerned and how the original classification had been determined for factors 5 and 7 from a Supplement to a Memorandum of Understanding between the Union and the Company made on May 1, 1950. This Supplement was introduced as Exhibit material by the Company, and contained additional definitions and interpretations for application of the Production and Maintenance Manual to clerical and technical jobs unclassified as of March 9, 1950. No evidence or testimony was introduced by either party relative to other factors, and the Board finds by implication, therefore, that no other factors were in dispute in this instant grievance.

9. The job description of Record File Clerk (Plant Code 9130-409) for Factor 5—Responsibility for Materials, reads as follows:

"Close attention part of time to catalogue, file, bundle, label records consigned to central storage areas. Error would result in inaccurate records. Estimated Cost up to $50.00."

In applying the Supplement for this factor the directions state:

"If the reports, schedules, etc., have no direct relationship for determining the sequence of production, grade or character of product or payment of money, the replacement or correction cost of such reports, schedules, drawings, data, etc., shall be considered as the probable monetary loss."

10. Since testimony was introduced to show that the records concerned with the job of Record File Clerk are for the most part historical in nature, although not necessarily obsolete, but in most cases they have been used to the extent that they will be needed in current operations, the value of $50.00 would seem fair and the Board would

hold that the classification of B.3 was correct. There were no items among the alleged job changes claimed by the Union that would change this rating.

11. The job description of Record File Clerk (Plant Code 9130-409) for Factor 7—Responsibility for Operations, reads as follows:

"Catalogues and file records requiring some coordination with all plant departments."

12. In applying the Supplement for this factor there is a bench mark job known as File Clerk which is classified as Code A and given the Base in the numerical classification. Because the job of Record File Clerk required certain determinations and some coordination with all plant departments the Company gave this job the higher Code of B.5. The Board finds that Code B is the proper determination and does not see how the alleged items of changed content would effect this numerical classification.

13. The job description of Record File Clerk (Plant Code 9130-409) for Factor 10—Physical Effort, reads as follows:

"Manually handles bundles of stationery to and from storage."

14. For this factor the Manual is used, and in applying the Manual the instructions read:

"Consider the muscular exertion required by the job for the performance of a fair day's work. Select that level which best describes the average degree of muscular exertion required throughout the turn."

15. Again Code A—(Minimum physical exertion) might have been used, but the Company selected Code B—(Light physical exertion) because the job duties required varying degrees of muscular effort from time to time beyond the usual clerical type of job, and the Company felt that the average condition permitted the higher classification B-.3. Again the Board finds this to be a sound determination for this factor and does not see how the items in the alleged job changes would increase the factor of physical effort.

16. Comparisons were made with four other jobs somewhat similar in nature to the Record File Clerk (Plant Code 9130-409). These were the Specimen 4806 File Clerk, a bench mark job, the Johnstown MA-0030-Counterman (Plant Code 9120-453, 461), the South Works (Chicago) MT-0350 Custodian (Files and Vaults) (Plant Code 9129-903) and the Homestead MT-

0150 Record File Clerk (Plant Code 9131-119).

17. For Factor 5—Responsibility for Materials all of these four jobs received Code A Base except the Johnstown Counterman, which was given the Code C.5 the same as the job in this instant grievance Record File Clerk (Plant Code 9130-409).

18. For Factor 7—Responsibility for Operations the Record File Clerk (Plant Code 9130-409) was the only one to receive the .5, as all the other four were given only Base.

19. For Factor 10—Physical Effort—both Record File Clerk jobs were given the .3 value while File Clerk, the bench mark job, was given the base rating. The Johnstown Counterman and the South Works Custodian (Files and Vaults) were both given the next higher rating to the Record File Clerk of C.8 which is what the Union contends should be given the Record File Clerk (Plant Code 9130-409). It was shown from the job descriptions that the former two jobs require greater physical effort. Code C of Factor 10 reads as follows:

"C. Moderate physical exertion. Handle medium weight materials. Use a variety of medium sized hand tools for performing tradesman's work. Climb and work from ladders. Operate heavy controls and valves. Use light sledge."

20. The job description for the Johnstown Counterman states that the Counterman assists in loading, unloading and disbursing structural shapes, sheets, strips, plates, bars, etc. Trackwork parts and appendages, mine and industrial car parts, paints, oils, waste, nails, bolts, etc. Directs crane movement with hand signals when moving materials with crane. Opens boxes and crates, unloads trays, and stores the material in bins, on shelves or on the floor. Hooks and unhooks for O.E.T. crane to load and unload railroad cars, trucks, trays, etc., and transport to bins or storage. Makes necessary hitch with chain or cable around the material to be moved and follows crane and unhooks the lift. Moves material manually in transfer wagons.

21. The Custodian (Files and Vaults) uses among other items an electric elevator, a hand truck, hammer and nails, screwdrivers and wood screws, packs his materials into wooden cases for storing instead of into paper boxes.

22. The Record File Clerk uses paper boxes according to the testimony at the hearing. The Custodian (Files and Vaults) also positions the wooden cases in proper case number order using a hand truck, and is required to open and nail shut wooden cases as may be required.

23. The Board, therefore, finds that the physical effort required of the Counterman and the Custodian (Files and Vaults) is somewhat greater than that required of the Record File Clerk (Plant Code 9130-409).

24. From the foregoing, the Board finds that the present classification for Record File Clerk (Plant Code 9130-409) of Job Class 5 is correct.

AWARD

25. The grievance is denied.

CI—230. 10. Gary Steel Works.   March 15, 1951

Donald Crawford, *Acting Chairman*

BACKGROUND FACTS

1. This grievance arose in the Maintenance Construction Division of the Carnegie-Illinois Steel Corporation, and involves the appropriate classification of a new job titled "Craneman (Truck 15-20 Ton)," Plant Code No. 8120-175. The Company placed the 15-20 ton truck mounted crane in operation in May, 1948, and the disputed classification in effect on January 21, 1949. The Union contends that the job evaluates at Job Class 11 with 11.3 points instead of Job Class 10, with 10.4 points as Management has rated it. This disagreement has narrowed to a difference in judgment over Factor 2, Employment Training and Experience, and Factor 10, Physical Effort. Concerning the first of these factors, the Union rates the job at 1.2 instead of Management's .8; and regarding the second, .8 instead of .3.

2. The Union bases its argument primarily on a comparison of the 15-20 ton truck mounted crane operator's job with that of caterpillar crane operator (8120-165). The Company objects to this comparison because on truck mounted cranes, the craneman operates the crane only, and the truck is driven by a truck driver, while on the caterpillar crane, the operator is responsible for the mobile portion of the machine as well as the crane, and because the caterpillar crane is considerably larger and more difficult to control. Therefore, Management made its comparison with the 4 and 10 ton truck mounted crane operators'

jobs with allowances for differences between them.

3. The Union points out that the caterpillar crane frequently is hauled to location on a trailer, thus making it comparable to the truck mounted crane, and that on the job the truck mounted crane operator has to direct the truck operator, which is as difficult as the crawler crane operator's responsibility for moving the crane himself.

FINDINGS

4. Evaluation of the evidence and the detailed presentation of the general contentions outlined above, led the Board to these findings:

5. (1.) *Factor 2—Employment Training and Experience.* The Board finds that the job of Craneman (Truck—15-20 tons) can be learned in less than one year, and so the Company's evaluation of C (.8) requiring from 7 to 12 months of continuous progress to become proficient, is proper. The Board considers that the learning time required for the caterpillar crane job is greater because of the additional knowledge required in (a) moving the crane, with particular reference

to the operations of loading the caterpillar crane onto a trailer involving precise use of levers and know-how to avoid turning the crane over, and handling the crane in field terrain; (b) operating the additional mechanisms required in starting the larger engine with its gasoline starting engine, and in transferring the crane between travel and crane operation.

6. (2.) *Factor 10—Physical Effort.* The Board finds that the "B" level of physical effort, common light physical exertion, is the correct evaluation, and therefore on this factor, the .3 rating is proper. As regards the comparison with the caterpillar crane, the Board considers that the physical effort required of that operator is greater because of the heavier equipment, levers, materials, and tools handled, particularly in changing between crane operation and travel and changing buckets.

7. We hold, accordingly, that the evaluation of Management concerning the disputed factors is the more correct evaluation.

AWARD

8. The grievance is denied.

USC—476, -477, -478, -490.   10. Ohio Works, Youngstown District.   June 24, 1955
Donald A. Crawford, *Arbitrator*
Approved by Sylvester Garrett, *Chairman*

FINDINGS

1. This award includes four cases (USC-490, 476, 477, 478) involving four jobs in the new No. 10 Boiler House at Youngstown. The Union considers the jobs of Boiler Operator, Pump Tender, Water Treater and Pump Tender Helper undervalued.

2. The Board, pursuant to the Labor Agreements between the parties, has been governed by the parties' own application of the agreed upon job evaluation system as shown by Specimen Boiler House job ratings, and the Board's prior application of the job evaluation system to disputed jobs in the new Boiler House at Gary. In order to make sure that these different Boiler Houses and jobs were properly compared to the Youngstown No. 10 Boiler House jobs, all of these Boiler Houses were inspected.

3. The plant visits demonstrated that the purpose and function of the Boiler House Operator and Pump Tender jobs were similar in all of these houses. Since no significant difference in job content exists, the Youngstown No. 10 Boiler House Operator and Pump Tender jobs cannot be increased in point ratings.

4. The Youngstown Water Treater job

cannot be increased in any of the three disputed factor ratings because (1) if Mental Skill rating is increased, it becomes rated equal to the Boiler House Operator job which requires knowledge of the operation of the entire No. 10 Boiler House and its crew; (2) the Water Treater job is one which essentially requires working alone and requires little care to avoid injury to others, so that the Safety Factor rating cannot be increased; and (3) the Water Treater job is comparable in exposure to the Pump Station Operator job (Youngstown), which was rated .4 by the parties.

5. Since the noise has been removed from No. 10 House, and since a C-1 rating for Factor 11 for the period it was there would have no effect on the classification of any of the four jobs, no useful purpose is served by judging it.

6. The No. 10 Boiler House Pump Tender Helper is underrated. Factor 10, Physical Effort, is increased to .8, and Factor 11, Surroundings, is increased to .8. This yields a total coding of 5.5 points, or Job Class 6. The physical effort required on the Helper job is equal to that of the Water Treater job (rated .8) and the surroundings are com-

parable to those of the Pump Station Operator Helper (Youngstown), and the Boiler Cleaner, No. 10 Boiler House, both of which are rated .8.

N—148. 10. Lorain Works. April 25, 1952.
Jacob J. Blair, *Acting Chairman*

BACKGROUND FACTS

1. This grievance arises out of a change made in the job of the Bell Driller.
2. Sometime in the latter part of 1948 or early 1949, production of bedstead tubing was discontinued. This eliminated the need for about thirty sizes of bells. Upon this change taking place in the content of the Bell Driller's occupation, the Company then added certain duties, among these being the cleaning and stacking of air bars, the preparation of rough inventory reports on bell blocks, the hauling of bells from a warehouse to the Bell Driller's place of work and performing miscellaneous errands for the foreman.
3. The Union alleges that the additions changed the classification by one class or more, thus justifying a redescription and reevaluation of the job of Bell Driller.
4. The issue in this case is therefore whether the changes in the job content of the Bell Driller did result in the change in the job by one class or more.

CONTRACT PROVISIONS INVOLVED

5. This case requires an application of Section 9-D, which provides:

"The job description and classification for each job in effect as of the date of this Agreement shall continue in effect unless (1) Management changes the job content (requirements of the job as to the training, skill, responsibility, effort, and working conditions) to the extent of one full job class or more; (2) the job is terminated or not occupied during a period of one year; or (3) the description and classification are changed in accordance with mutual agreement of officially designated representatives of the Company and the Union."

CONTENTIONS OF THE PARTIES

6. Involved in this case is a question of whether the changes in the job content have affected Factors 3, 5, 10 and 11, since it was agreed at the hearing that these were the only factors in dispute. A summary of the positions taken by each of the parties is shown under Findings in tabular form.

FINDINGS

7. This case must be decided upon the facts of the changes in the job content of the Bell Driller, since such facts are determinative as to the rights of the parties under Section 9-D of the Agreement.
8. The principal differences and contentions of the parties are shown in the table below:

FACTOR	COMPANY EVALUATION	UNION EVALUATION	BASIC DIFFERENCES INVOLVED
3	B-1.0	C-1.6	The Company maintains that all changes made were comprehended in the original description and classification.
			The Union maintains that the preparation of reports and inspection justify a higher evaluation.
5	B- .3	C-1.2	The Company contends that responsibility for materials is based upon the possible damage to materials worked on by the operator and does not go to the materials processed by the device worked upon by the operator, such as the air bar.
			The Union maintains that poor cleaning or inspection or processing of the bells or air bars could do damage to product amounting to $250, thus justifying Code C.
10	B- .3	C- .8	The Company maintains that the average degree of muscular exertion required throughout the turn has not been changed as a result of requiring the Bell Driller to transport bells from the yard.
			The Union maintains that at times more than one trip for a daylight turn is required, and that when such work is performed the degree of physical effort is increased, justifying Code C.

FACTOR	COMPANY EVALU- ATION	UNION EVALU- ATION	BASIC DIFFERENCES INVOLVED
11	A-Base	B- .4	The Company maintains that the degree describing the average working conditions for the job has not been changed by storing the bells in the yard. In this they point out that much of the area is covered, thus protecting the operator from the weather.
			The Union contends that the average condition has been changed by requiring the Bell Driller to go outdoors to secure the bells.

9. From the evidence it seems clear that all of the duties added to the Bell Driller's job are, so far as Factor 3 is concerned, fully comprehended in the original job description and evaluation. The reports now required on the air bars and bell blocks are very similar to those previously required under the original job description. Likewise, the inspection function applicable to the air bars does not exceed that required on bells. It is held, therefore, that the changed job is properly evaluated in Factor 3 at Code B.

10. No justification is found for changing the Company evaluation of Factor 5. Among the conditions expressed in Factor B is that the measure of responsibility is based upon materials, "actually worked on." It further provides that, "On attendant jobs only the material handled . . . is to be considered as material for the job." Accordingly this requires that responsibility for materials be based in this case upon the value of the air bars, and not upon the value of the product in which the air bar is used for processing. The value of the air bar does not exceed $50.00. Hence, the present evaluation is proper.

11. The evidence does justify the Union request in regard to Factor 10. Sometime late in 1948 or the early part of 1949, the Bell Driller was assigned the regular task of transporting the bells from the storage yard some two to three hundred yards from his place of work. Moreover, he is also required to transport by hand, bell blocks weighing about thirty pounds each. In addition, it was admitted that during freezing weather a sledge was required to break the bells apart. These conditions properly fall under Code C, "Moderate physical exertion." The factor evaluation is therefore changed from B- .3 to C- .8.

12. The evidence, based not only on that submitted at the hearing but, even more, upon that gathered as a result of an inspection of the Bell Driller's job and related jobs, establishes that the Union contention with respect to Factor 11 must be denied. True, the Bell Driller is now required to go out of doors to secure his materials. But this factor was found to also be present in a number of other jobs evaluated at A-Base. This is true, for example, in the Central Station Attendant Repairman's job, the Utility Man, the Repairman—Valve, the Utility Room Attendant, and General Labor at the furnaces. It is also to be noted that on all but the last job, this condition of working both inside and outside is specifically noted in the job classification. Even on the last job, that of General Labor, the description of occasional duties indicates that this employee performs some of his work out-of-doors. Careful consideration of the work presently required of the Bell Driller shows that it does not differ materially in regard to Factor 11 than is found on the jobs previously mentioned. Since these jobs are classified as A-Base in Factor 11, it must be held that the Company has properly classified the Bell Driller.

AWARD

13. Under the Grievance, Factor 10 is increased from B.3 to C.8. The total change in job content amounts to only .5 of a job class. Under Section 9-D the job must change to the extent of one full job class or more before the Company is required to establish a new description and classification. Accordingly, since the change is less than one full job class, the Union request is denied.

Following is a table of all the other cases decided by the Board of Arbitration which involve disputes specifically over the coding of "effort" factors. For each case the docket number is listed, the specific "effort" factors in dispute are noted, and the page in this volume where the case can be found is cited.

CHAPTER 18

RATING "SURROUNDINGS" AND "HAZARDS"

The title of this chapter embraces Factor 11—Surroundings and Factor 12—Hazards. Included in this chapter are cases which discuss the coding of one or both of these factors. The figures after each docket number designate whether Factor 11 or Factor 12, or both, are in dispute.

Following the awards set forth in this chapter is a table of cross references to many other cases.

USC—352.   11, 12.   Edgar Thomson Works.   October 30, 1953
Herbert L. Sherman, Jr., *Assistant to the Chairman*
Approved by Sylvester Garrett, *Chairman*

BACKGROUND

1. In this grievance the Scrap Burners of the Open Hearth Department at Edgar Thomson Works seek a new job description and a higher classification. The Union asserts that the ratings on Factors 1, 5, 6, 11 and 12 have been affected by changes instituted by Management to the extent of increasing the classification from Job Class 6 to Job Class 8.

2. Union testimony was presented to support its claim that nineteen duties have been added to the job since it was classified. An increase in the amount of hot and hazardous work was particularly emphasized. Grievants testified that some of them spend 90% of their time on such work. It was further stated that some of the work now assigned to grievants was performed in large part at the time of classification by members of the Pit Crew with a rating of D-1.6 on Factor 11. It was also asserted that an Ingot Shipper receives C-.8 on Factor 12, though he is only required to make a few trips to the Open Hearth Pits.

3. Management contends that the grievance is untimely since many of the duties listed were added to the job in 1948 or 1949 and the grievance was not filed until October, 1951. Nevertheless, there was testimony that some of the changes relied upon by the Union took place around the date that the grievance was filed, and it is clear that many of the changes were put into effect gradually. In any event, the Company holds that some of the duties were already performed at the time that the job was classified and that the others are comprehended by the present job description and classification.

4. Between 1947 and 1951 the Scrap Burner force for a 24-hour period was increased from 6 or 7 men to an average of 15 or 20 Burners.

5. The nineteen duties listed by the Union, with Management's comments, are as follows:

(1.) Burns skulls from ladles.

Company: although most of the skulls were pulled from the ladles by Steel Pourers or members of the Pit Crew prior to 1948, this duty was occasionally performed by Scrap Burners. As the number of skulls and the number of Scrap Burners increased, more rough burning of skulls was assigned to Scrap Burners.

(2.) Burns chestnuts from castings at rear of furnace while furnace is operating.

Company: this is normally the duty of the Second Helper. Only when he is too busy are grievants assigned to rough burning of these chestnuts. Starting in 1948, Burners were asked to perform this duty.

(3.) Burns scrap from ladle trunions.

Company: it would be against Company policy to burn scrap from trunions. If scrap should become welded to the trunions, the Maintenance Department would chisel it off. Rough burning around ladles has always been a duty of the job.

(4.) Burns bolts from and assembles steel runners.

Company: burning bolts and scrap from steel runners was always a duty of the job. Replacement of the steel runner is not one of grievants' duties.

(5.) Burns scrap from steel runner at rear of furnace while furnace is operating.

Company: this duty is not new and is listed in Item 2 of the Working Procedure. (Grievants emphasize, however, that burning is now performed while the furnace is in operation.)

(6.) Burns scrap from angle which holds platform at rear of furnace, while furnace is operating.

Company: normally this is the duty of the Second Helper. As the number of Scrap Burners has increased, they have been asked to do it more often but with the help of a spellhand. It consists only of rough cutting.

(7.) Burns bolts from tap-hole castings.

Company: this duty, though first required of the Burners in 1949, merely consists of burning off four nuts when the furnace is down for repairs or is checked back. It does not affect the classification.

(8.) Trims ingots at pouring platform.

Company: burning of scrap around ingot moulds has always been a duty of the job. (Grievants admit trimming cold ingots in the Mould Conditioning Yard previously, but claim that trimming ingots at the pouring platform was gradually assigned to them only after a Steel Pourer was burned to death while performing this duty about 1949.)

(9.) Burns end wall and front wall supports from furnace while furnace is hot.

Company: this duty only involves rough cutting; it was gradually assigned to the Burners during 1948 and 1949 as the force increased.

(10.) Burns plates for Bricklayers.

Company: this duty only requires the burning of notches in plates and is rough burning; it was added to the work of the Scrap Burners during 1948 and 1949 as the force increased.

(11.) Burns scrap from ladle nozzle welds.

Company: this rough burning duty occurs about once a month.

(12.) Burns scrap from front flush buggy and motor underneath the furnace.

Company: it is true that scrap is burned off the frame of the buggy—the fenders, etc., but there is a shield around the motor. This is rough burning.

(13.) Burns scrap from rails on spills in front of furnace and front flush.

Company: only rough burning is involved.

(14.) Burns scrap from mould buggy couplings and wheels.

Company: this does not happen too often and, in any event, does not affect the classification.

(15.) Burns section out of bottom of thimble (cinder ladle) to remove "frozen metal," when this fails, burns thimble in half.

Company: the Scrap Burner usually burns a hole in the skull out in the Cinder Yard so that a weight can be dropped down to knock the skull out.

(16.) Burns tap holes.

Company: this duty was performed by Scrap Burners when the job was classified.

(17.) Burns holes in crust of hot metal in ladles so metal can be poured before becoming entirely solidified.

Company: this is a task rarely performed.

(18.) Works under furnace while metal is in furnace.

Company: grievants are not required to work under the furnace while metal is in it.

(19.) Trims lip on hot metal mixer while heat is on.

Company: this duty is performed rarely, such as after a strike. It consists only of rough burning.

6. Following is a tabulation showing the present classification ratings and those sought by the Union:

FACTOR	PRESENT CLASSI-FICATION	PROPOSED CLASSI-FICATION
*1. Pre-employment Training.	A-Base	B-.3
2. Employment Training and Experience.	B-.4	B-.4
3. Mental Skill.	B-1.0	B-1.0
4. Manual Skill.	B-.5	B-.5
*5. Responsibility for Materials.	A-Base	C-.7

FACTOR	PRESENT CLASSI- FICATION	PROPOSED CLASSI- FICATION
*6. Responsibility for Tools and Equipment.	B-.2 Low	B-.3 Med.
7. Responsibility for Operations.	B-.5	B-.5
8. Responsibility for Safety of Others.	B-.4	B-.4
9. Mental Effort.	B-.5	B-.5
10. Physical Effort.	C-.8	C-.8
*11. Surroundings.	C-.8	D-1.6
*12. Hazards.	B-.4	C-.8
Total	5.5	7.8

* Disputed Factors.

DISCUSSION AND FINDINGS

7. The primary function of the Scrap Burner as stated in the present job description is to "perform all burning operations for the Open Hearth Department which comes under labor." The Working Procedure reads as follows:

1. Burn scrap off stopper rods.
2. Burn scrap from steel runners.
3. Burn scrap from slag spouts.
4. Burn to charging box size all scrap in the stock house, open hearth pit and under the furnaces.
5. Burn off and recover ring from iron spouts on open hearth floor.
6. Does any other burning in the Open Hearth Department which comes under labor.
7. Responsible for transporting burning equipment to job.
8. Burn scrap from C & D Hot Top Castings.
9. Burn scrap off Bessemer moulds.

8. All types of rough burning by hand torch or oxygen lance in the Open Hearth Department are already encompassed by this job description. It has not been demonstrated that greater mentality is now required to learn to perform the types of burning assigned. Specimens 319 (Billet Mill Burner), 1101 (Maintenance Burner), 1103 (Scrap Burner), 3180 (Seamless Finishing Burner), 3166 (Tube Burner), 1099 (Maintenance Burner), and 1100 (Maintenance Burner) are coded at A-Base under Factor 1—Pre-Employment Training. Two Scrap Burner jobs at Duquesne, one at Johnstown, one at Gary Steel, and two at Homestead receive A-Base for this Factor. Only one Scrap Burner job presented to the Board is given a higher rating. The Operating Burner at Homestead is given higher ratings than the job in dispute on Factors 1, 3, 5 and 12. That job, however, is required to repair and change furnace doors, frames, spouts, safety equipment and furnace aprons in addition to numerous scrap burning duties. A-Base must still be considered as appropriate under Factor 1 for the Edgar Thomson Scrap Burner job.

9. With respect to Factor 5—Responsibility for Materials, the job in dispute was originally coded in A-Base. Since that time grievants have been required to work on added and different equipment which involves responsibility more comparable to the Specimen and non-Specimen jobs with a rating of B-.3 on this Factor. All of the Specimens referred to previously are rated at B-.3 for this Factor except Specimens 3180 and 3166 which are coded at C-.5 because of the requirement to cut pipe to specifications. Specimen 1103 allows liberal tolerances in rough cutting of rejected product, yet is coded at B-.3 for Factor 5. The same rating is justified for the Edgar Thomson Scrap Burner job. A Johnstown and a Duquesne Scrap Burner job receive B-.3 on this Factor. The two Homestead and the Gary Steel Scrap Burner jobs which are given A-Base work on more limited types of materials with less care required.

10. For purposes of Factor 6—Responsibility for Tools and Equipment, the Board finds that no change has taken place to warrant a higher coding than B-.2. The Union does not dispute the B level; it seeks a rating of B-.3. Greater probable damage to the tools and equipment, which have remained the same, has not been demonstrated.

11. Under Factor 11—Surroundings Union testimony emphasizes the requirement that some of the incumbents perform various burning duties around the furnaces while exposed to considerable heat. The Company points out that when the Scrap Burner is at times exposed to intense heat, a spellhand is provided, and that the job description, which specifically refers to burning in the Open Hearth pits and around the furnaces, makes no distinction as to whether or not the furnace is operating. One of the most disagreeable hot tasks mentioned by grievants is that of burning scrap from C and D Hot Top Castings, but this also is specifically listed in the job description. Apparently, however, it was formerly done in a more secluded area.

12. Nevertheless, the job as a whole must be evaluated. One of the incumbents works almost all the time in the stock house; the rest work all over the Open Hearth including the Mould Yard and Cinder Yard. Although some of the incumbents are assigned fairly consistently to the area around the furnaces,

many others are rotated throughout the various areas. All of the Specimens and all of the non-Specimen jobs discussed above receive C-.8 for this Factor except for two Specimens with the lower rating of B-.4. Though grievants undeniably work under unpleasant conditions, such surroundings are recognized in the present rating of Factor 11 at C-.8. The average heat condition for the job as a whole is not comparable to that experienced by a Soaking Pit Craneman.

13. As to Factor 12—Hazards, the added duties do not require grievants to work under any greater danger of injury than was contemplated by the initial classification at B-.4. There is no limitation in the job description on the particular area in the Open Hearth Department where the incumbents may be required to perform their burning duties. Although Union witnesses testified

that they now work under the furnaces when there is metal in them, the General Foreman stated that they are not required to do so; and if they are under the furnaces at such time, they are there "of their own accord." All seven Specimens cited above plus all the non-Specimen jobs with the exception of the Homestead job noted in the discussion of Factor 1 receive B-.4 for this Factor. The hazards for the job in dispute as a whole do not warrant a higher rating than the B-.4 presently assigned.

AWARD

14. The grievance is sustained only to the extent of raising Factor 5 for the job of Scrap Burner from A-Base to B-.3. The job class remains the same.

COL—72. 11. Pittsburg Works. March 29, 1955

Sylvester Garrett, *Chairman*

BACKGROUND

1. This grievance involves coding of three Factors of the new job of Craneman, Continuous Coating, Sheet Finishing Department, Pittsburg Works.

2. The disputed job operates a 20-ton capacity overhead travelling crane as follows:

"Operates crane controls to perform the following types of operations:

Unload coils from transfer car and place in storage area or on entry ramp of Continuous Coating line; load coils from storage area to entry ramp.

Transports lifts of prime galvanized sheets from prime conveyor to storage or transfer conveyor, and lifts of secondary product from secondary conveyor to prime conveyor for weighing, then to storage or transfer conveyor.

Uses magnet to clear scrap from entry end of line.

Assembles lifts of prime or secondary product for shipping; transports to storage areas or to trucks for shipment.

Occasionally makes lifts from storage to transfer conveyor.

Transports empty and loaded scrap boxes as directed.

Transports chemicals and supplies to various locations on line as directed.

Lifts floor hatches and handles material to and from basement as directed.

Makes lifts as required for Continuous Coating line maintenance.

Removes and replaces firebrick covers at annealing unit during strip breaks or inspection.

Remove skimmings containers from pot floor to main floor in coating line area.

Performs drossing using balanced drossing spoon.

Occasionally makes lifts for Coil Slitting and Sheet Side Trim & Recoil lines.

Makes all lifts as directed, within the travel and capacity of the crane.

Regularly lubricates crane and inspects cables and brakes; maintains good housekeeping in cab.

At beginning of each turn Craneman will raise hooks slowly to check limit switches; if either of the switches are inoperative he shall report condition."

3. The codings assigned by the parties are:

FACTOR	COMPANY CODING	UNION CODING
1	B- .3	Same
2	B- .4	C- .8
3	C-1.6	Same
4	B- .5	Same
5	C $100-.7	C $250-1.2
6	C Med-.7	Same
7	C-1.0	Same
8	C-1.2	Same
9	C-1.0	Same
10	B- .3	Same
11	A-Base	B- .4
12	A-Base	Same
Total Class	7.7	9.0
Job Class	8	9

4. The crane operated by the disputed job services the Continuous Coating line, which uncoils steel strip, anneals the strip, coats it with zinc, shears it into sheets and piles the sheets into lifts. The work is performed in a new building, part of the Sheet and Tin Mill.

5. The craneman normally operates Crane #958, overhead travelling crane with hoist capacity of 20 tons and span of 116 feet. The craneman may use auxiliary equipment such as "C"—hook, slings, chains, sheet lifter, magnet, cables, drossing spoon, oil can, grease gun and rags. When Crane #958 is temporarily out of service, standby crane #572 is used. This is an Alliance end cab overhead travelling crane with hoist capacity of 10 tons and span of 116 feet.

6. Regularly, the craneman moves coils to the entry end of the Coating line and removes finished sheets from the exit end of the line. He uses the crane to clear scrap away from the line, assemble coated sheets for storage and truck loading, and handle scrap boxes, chemicals and supplies.

7. There are other duties which are not performed each turn, which are greatly stressed here by the Union. These include drossing the coating pot, handling sink and scrubber rolls and removing the rigging. These operations may be performed only once a week.

8. There are no Specimen jobs, as such, for overhead cranes servicing Continuous Coating lines. However, the Company cites Specimen Job Nos. 2074, Craneman Service Crew, and 2075 Craneman Line Crew pertaining to overhead electrical cranes making production and maintenance lifts to serve a continuous line, in these instances a Continuous Pickling line.

9. The Union cites Specimens 2104, 2107, 2006, 2257, 2258, 1721, 1722, 2032 and 2033. Of these, seven—Nos. 2104, 2107, 2006, 2257, 2258, 1721, and 1722—service major producing units such as Tandem Mills, Hot Strip Mills, Temper Mills, and Rod Mills. All seven handle work rolls and roll changes. The coding of Factor 5 in four of these seven jobs refers specifically to the handling of roll changes (Nos. 2104, 2006, 1721, and 1722). The working procedure of the other three (Nos. 2107, 2257, and 2258) leaves no doubt that the handling of work rolls and roll changes are a significant—if not major—function of these jobs.

FINDINGS

10. In view of the evidence and plant observation, it appears that Specimens 2074 and 2075, cited by the Company, present more appropriate references on Factors 2

and 5 than the Specimens cited by the Union. Since no work rolls are handled by the disputed job (save rarely, *after* use in the galvanizing line), the Specimens do not support the classification of Factors 2 and 5 sought by the Union.

11. There was considerable discussion by the parties of various other crane jobs—in Classes 8, 9 and 10—which service facilities in the same building as the disputed job, or in adjacent buildings. There is room for difference of opinion as to what inferences may be drawn from these comparisons for purposes of coding the present job. This fact may have contributed to inability of the parties to settle this case short of arbitration. But there is no preponderant support in the agreed Craneman classification at Pittsburg Works for the codings of Factors 2 and 5 sought by the Union here. In any event, there can be little question of the necessity for applying the Specimens, even though they do not involve operations identical to the present job.

12. The Board therefore finds the present codings of Factors 2 and 5 to be proper on the basis of the Specimen jobs.

13. On Factor 11, the Specimens are less helpful, since the basis for a B-.4 coding stressed by the Union includes both diesel truck fumes, and fumes from galvanizing pots in the adjacent "culvert line" in the same building. Truck shipments are made directly out of the area serviced by this crane and numerous trucks may pass through, or park in, the plant during regular operations. There has been difficulty inducing the truck drivers to cut off the diesels while parking in the plant. This has been a source of friction in the plant for the past two years. On several occasions, the fumes have induced Management to test the air at the crane cab level for carbon monoxide concentration, but this was found to be well below the point of danger to human life.

14. The precise nature of this adverse condition was not revealed when this operation was inspected: there were little fumes at the time because of favorable weather conditions, relatively light movement of diesel trucks, and the fact that only narrow sheets (relatively) were being processed in the adjacent galvanizing pots. The latter are serviced in part by a forced draft hood to draw off fumes. This operates successfully save when large sheets are processed, which cause fumes to ascend outside the effective draft area of the hood.

15. The crane job servicing the adjacent sheet galvanizing or "culvert" line was coded at C-.8 originally, but the Company since has reduced this to B-.4—for its own records at

least—because of elimination of one culvert line and a batch pickler. The Union has not concurred in this change, nor has any definite issue thereon as to proper classification been presented in the grievance procedure, in view of the provisions of Section 9-D.

16. Under the evidence, and in view of plant conditions, it seems not to have been uncommon for performance of the disputed job to involve appreciable exposure either to diesel fumes, or to pot fumes, or to both. Such exposure may be for substantial periods, even though not consistent. As the

coding of Factor 11 of Specimen 2074 recognizes, a B-.4 coding does not necessarily require constant exposure to adverse surroundings. On the whole record, therefore, such a coding seems appropriate for Factor 11 in this case.

AWARD

17. The grievance is sustained in part only: No change is warranted in present codings of Factors 2 and 5; a coding of B-.4 under Factor 11 is proper.

USC—343. 11. Gary Steel Works. July 24, 1953
Sylvester Garrett, *Chairman*

BACKGROUND

1. This grievance involves classification of the new job of Boiler House Operator in the new Turbo Blower Boiler House at Gary Steel Works. The Boiler House is equipped with three modern boilers which can be gas or oil fired, and converted from one fuel to the other by automatic controls.

2. Mutual agreement has been reached on the job description. Since no agreement was reached on the classification, Management unilaterally installed Job Class 12 on February 5, 1950, effective August 28, 1949. The Union, seeking Job Class 15, disputes the ratings on Factors 2, 5, 6, 7, 8 and 11.

3. The following tabulation shows the respective positions of the parties:

FACTOR	COMPANY CLASSIFICATION	UNION CLASSIFICATION
1. Pre-Employment Training	B-.3	B-.3
*2. Employment Training and Experience	F-2.0	G-2.4
3. Mental Skill	D-2.2	D-2.2
4. Manual Skill	B-.5	B-.5
*5. Responsibility for Materials	C-.7	D-1.1
*6. Responsibility for Tools and Equipment	C-1.0 Hi	E-2.0 Med.
*7. Responsibility for Operations	D-2.0	E-3.0
*8. Responsibility for Safety of Others	C-.8	D-1.2
9. Mental Effort	C-1.0	C-1.0
10. Physical Effort	B-.3	B-.3
*11. Surroundings	B-.4	C-.8
12. Hazards	B-.4	B-.4
Total	11.6	15.2

* Disputed Factors

DISCUSSION AND FINDINGS

4. The Operator jobs in five of nine Boiler Houses at Gary Steel Works were classified and issued as Specimen Examples. Two of the five were placed in Class 12: Specimen 550—Operator for #4 Boiler House; Specimen 552—Operator for #2 Benzol Boiler House. The other three were placed in Class 11: Specimen 554—Boiler House Operator for the Axle Mill; Specimen 555—Operator for #1 Benzol Boiler House; Specimen 556—Operator for #2 Blast Furnace Boiler House.

5. The Company relies on these Specimens to support its proposed Job Class 12. Grievants assert that they were led to believe, when assigned to the job, that the classification would be higher than Class 12. Misleading remarks of such a nature are indeed unfortunate, and should be avoided. If such remarks were made, however, they cannot affect the proper job classification since that is a matter controlled by the guideposts erected by the parties for uniform application throughout the bargaining unit.

6. Under *Factor 2—Employment Training and Experience* Union testimony emphasizes differences between the Turbo Blower Boiler House and #4 Boiler House. The new Boiler House has Pressure Reducing Valves, usually on automatic, and temperature reducing devices. There are various combinations of controls and a P.R.V. panel board. There are eleven controls on one panel board for one boiler. At #4 Boiler House there are fewer controls on a panel

board but there are eleven boilers as compared to the three in the Boiler House in dispute. Also, the #4 Boiler House Operator is not required to blow soot as grievant. Moreover, an employee with 19 years' experience in the Power and Fuel Department, having worked from the bottom to First Engineer, testified that he was informed by Superintendent Schmidt that it would take six months to teach him the job of Operator at the Turbo Blower House.

7. The Company points out that the incumbent of the Operator job at #4 Boiler House must also know how to use coke breeze, according to his job description, in addition to oil and gas while grievants are only required to be familiar with the use of oil and gas. The Turbo Blower Boiler House consists of a smaller area, and is equipped with automatic controls for firing. Specimens 222 and 223 for Heaters are cited to show that automatic controls make acquisition of knowledge concerning the use of fuels less important.

8. It is agreed, however, that the automatic controls sometimes fail to operate properly. For example, there has been trouble with the air flow regulator when there is a fuel change. Grievants must then give the fuel more air manually by turning knobs on the panel board. And when the Bailey meters, air flow and gas flow regulators are being recalibrated, some controls must be operated manually.

9. An examination of the Specimen Examples for Boiler House Operators reveals that none receives as high a rating on Factor 2 as the F-2.0 presently assigned to the job in dispute except Specimen 550 for the #4 Boiler House which also receives F-2.0. It cannot be held that the greater number of comparable controls at the Turbo Blower Boiler House sufficiently increases the learning period to acquire the necessary understanding of the principles of steam production and the equipment involved to justify a higher coding than F-2.0.

10. Materials under *Factor 5—Responsibility for Materials* for the Operator job are air, oil, gas and water. The same is true for #4 Boiler House Operator except that coal and coke breeze may be used (they have not been used in recent years). While the #4 Operator must make manual adjustments for eleven boilers, automatic controls at the Turbo Blower Boiler House reduce the possibility of wasting fuels. Of course, the gauges on the panels for the boilers may not be accurate. Integrator, pressure and temperature readings must be recorded every hour, and load conditions must be reported to the Load Dispatcher.

11. None of the Specimen Examples for Boiler House Operators and none of the non-Specimen jobs presented to the Board rate Factor 5 higher than C-.7. In the light of this pattern and the evidence before the Board, C-.7 is held to be appropriate for this Factor.

12. With respect to *Factor 6—Responsibility for Tools and Equipment,* one of the grievants testified that his equipment is more expensive than that found in other Boiler Houses. Greater pressures are given as the reason for the greater probability of damage. The Company agrees that probable damage is "High" in its proposed rating of C-1.0, while the Union merely claims that probable damage is "Medium." The issue then boils down to the level of attention and care required to protect the equipment from damage.

13. Grievants assert that they have more items of equipment to look after. Desuperheating pumps and other auxiliary equipment are listed as falling under their control though not found at #4 Boiler House. Nonreturn valves must be opened and closed at least every six months at the new Turbo House by the Operator. At #4 Boiler House a Fan Tender cares for the non-return valves.

14. However, it cannot be held that the added responsibility for this auxiliary equipment justifies a rating higher than C-1.0. All Specimen Examples for the Operator have received C-1.0 on this factor. In fact, all non-Specimen jobs presented to the Board, except one at Duquesne, have been given C-1.0. It should be noted that the closer arrangement of controls and panel boards in the new Boiler House makes them easier to attend than at #4 Boiler House.

15. Under *Factor 7—Responsibility for Operations* the Union stresses the various operations supplied with steam and the important function of the P.R.V.'s in lowering the pressure from 650 pounds to 250 pounds. One of the grievants stated that he cannot afford to lose a boiler since there are only three under his command, whereas there are eleven boilers at #4 Boiler House. The difficulty with this contention is that the Specimen Examples do not distinguish between the number of boilers for purposes of rating this Factor. Nor do they distinguish the supplying of steam for power generation, air blowing or mill operation.

16. About the same amount of steam is produced at #4 Boiler House as the new Boiler House. At the former the Operator directs a Fireman (Oil or Gas), Water Tender, Pump Tender, Handyman, Pump Tender (Fuel Oil), Fan Tender, Oiler and Greaser, Boiler Cleaner, a Laborer, and a Janitor. At the Turbo Blower Boiler House the Operator is responsible for direction of a Fireman (Oil

or Gas), Pump Tender, a Pump Tender (Fuel Oil), and 3 Laborers. He is under supervision of a Foreman whose responsibility is principally confined to the Turbo Blower Boiler House. On the other hand, the Foreman for #4 Boiler House has responsibilities extending to other locations. A higher rating than D-2.0 for this Factor cannot be justified, since this is the precise rating accorded this Factor by all of the Specimen Examples for Boiler House Operators. The vast majority of the non-Specimen Operator jobs have also received this figure.

17. *Factor 8—Responsibility for the Safety of Others:* It was testified that fuel cutback safety devices to prevent excess use of gas are only operating automatically within limits. The Operator, however, can accomplish manually what these devices would do automatically. It was also argued that there is greater danger to others than at #4 Boiler House or at #2 Benzol Boiler House because these Houses are not situated as close to other units which might be destroyed or caused to blow up. The Union claims that the language under Code D which reads "responsible for flow of electric power or steam or the operation of high pressure vessels where others are exposed to accidents" is applicable to the job in dispute because of the danger of asphyxiation.

18. On the surface this argument appears plausible. An analysis of the coding of other Boiler House Operator jobs, however, shows that three of the Specimens have received B-.4 for this Factor and two of them have received C-.8. None of the thirty non-Specimen Operator jobs presented to the Board received higher than C-.8. No distinction seems to have been made between Boiler Houses situated close to other units and those that are not. In view of the established pattern and the evidence before the Board, C-.8 must be deemed to be the appropriate rating for this Factor.

19. With respect to *Factor 11—Surroundings,* grievants emphasize that three Pressure Reducing Valves are in operation all the time and that they make a great deal of noise. The system is parallel to the concrete operating floor which the Union believes accounts for reverberations. The temperature is at least 15 degrees higher in the Boiler House than outside. There is no window ventilation except for one window recently installed, and, according to grievants, the large ventilating fans do not help much though they have recently been improved. Electric lights are necessary for the operating floor.

20. Grievants are also subjected to noise from the Turbo Blowers adjacent to the Boiler House with no separating wall, and the exhaust snorts from #2 Blowing Engine on the other side of a thin wall. Earplugs have been approved by the Safety Department. Management has had studies conducted to determine methods of reducing noise. Enclosing one of the Pressure Reducing Valves with glass wool is now being tried experimentally in accordance with Management's effort to reduce the amount of noise insofar as practicable.

21. Two Company witnesses believe that the subject job is not exposed to any more heat than the Operator at #4 Boiler House, and one witness stated that the noise in his opinion was no worse than the noise in the basement of #5 Boiler House. Though the intensity of the noise in both places may be about the same, grievant's job is subjected to more of a variety of noises and some at a fairly high pitch.

22. All Specimen Boiler House Operators receive B-.4 on this Factor. All such non-Specimen jobs presented to the Board, except two given A Base, receive B-.4. None are rated higher.

23. It is clear that grievants are subjected to a considerable amount of unpleasant noise from the Pressure Reducing Valves located a couple of levels above the operating floor where the Operator spends most of his time. To grant the C-.8 requested by the Union, however, would be to place grievants in the same coding as that for Nail Machine Operators. Relatively speaking, the noise is not so intense as to justify that high a coding. Nor can the heat in the new Boiler House be considered as out of line with #1 Benzol Boiler House where Specimen 555 Operator works, the latter job also being subject to much dirtier conditions than are grievants.

AWARD

24. The grievance is denied.

USC—742   11. Fairless Works.   November 26, 1958

· Sylvester Garrett, *Chairman*

FINDINGS

1.   This grievance requests higher classification for the job of Burner in the General Services Department, Fairless Works.

2.   The disputed job was established in 1957. It involves the burning of slag and fused steel from floors and walls of soaking pits by powder-burning lances. The Company rates the job at 5.8 for Job Class 6.

3.   The grievance initially claimed Factors 1, 8, 9 and 11 were not properly classified. In Step 4, however, the Union stated that Factor 11—Surroundings—was the only one in dispute. The Company rates Factor 11 at D 1.6, whereas the Union feels it should be E 3.0 with a resultant 7.2 coding.

4.   The Union points to Specimens 331 and 332, for Bottom Makers, as comparable jobs, with Factor 11 rated E 3.0. It further cites Specimens 18, 20, 35, 38, 66, 3025, 3060, 3061, 3062, and 3065 as rated E 3.0 in Factor 11 because incumbents are exposed to extreme heat. It believes the Burner is exposed to a similar degree of heat during performance of his duties.

5.   When soaking pits are renovated, the first operation is the removal of debris, and this task is performed by Furnace Repairman (Plant Code 4020). This first operation is not begun until approximately 48 hours after the soaking pit gas is off and the heat has been substantially dissipated. Since the Burner begins his work after the Furnace Repairman is finished, it is obvious that he is subjected to less heat radiation than the Furnace Repairman, who is coded at D 1.6 in Factor 11.

6.   The Company also cites Specimen 1001—Furnace Repairman-Checker, in the Open Hearth, rated at D 1.6 in Factor 11, as comparable to the Burner job. The Company feels that the heat to which the job incumbent in Specimen 1001 is exposed is as great or greater than that experienced by the Burner.

7.   Since this job entails working in the Soaking Pits only after the Furnace Repairmen (Plant Code 4020) have finished their work in the same pits, it is plain that the disputed job cannot be rated higher than the Furnace Repairman in Factor 11. The D 1.6 coding also is supported by Specimen 1001. The Specimens cited by the Union do not apply, since they entail close exposure to live heat.

AWARD

8.   The grievance is denied.

USC—532.   11, 12. Ohio Works.   December 12, 1955

Sylvester Garrett, *Chairman*

BACKGROUND

1.   As the result of certain changes in the job of Carbometerman in the Metallurgical Department of the Ohio Works in the Youngstown District, made effective June 15, 1954, the Union seeks a redescription of the job and higher classification ratings on Factors 6, 8, 10, 11 and 12. Essentially, this dispute, as developed at the hearing, involves the effect on these classification ratings of the new duties which are required in the taking of Open Hearth bath temperatures with an immersion-type thermocouple. The job of Carbometerman was originally described and classified in Job Class 7 (total point value of 6.7) in February, 1951, with the following primary functions:

(1.) Make carbon determinations from samples of Open Hearth heats by means of a carbometer instrument.

(2.) Measure Checker Chamber temperatures by means of an optical pyrometer, and estimate slag basicity by visual examination of slag patties.

2.   To reflect the changes in the job, the Company made the following deletions and additions to the job description by use of Form G.

PRIMARY FUNCTIONS:

(Second Sentence) *Should Read:* Measures Open Hearth bath temperature by means of an immersion thermocouple.

Instead of: Measures checker chamber temperature by means of an optical pyrometer, and estimates slag basicity by visual examination of slag patties.

TOOLS AND EQUIPMENT:

Add: Thermocouples, recorder, graphite and silicon tips, plugs.

Delete: Optical pyrometer.

MATERIAL:

Add: All grades of Open Hearth steel.

Delete: Slag samples.

WORKING PROCEDURE:

(Seventh Paragraph) *Delete:* Collects, identifies and interprets slag patties. Determines slag characteristics by visual examination in comparison with slag patty charts of known lime-silicon ratio and iron-oxide contents.

(Eighth Paragraph) *Add:* Makes temperature measurements by means of an immersion thermocouple of Open Hearth bath.

Change thermocouple tips.

Delete: Makes temperature measurements by means of an optical pyrometer of Open Hearth furnace checker-brick in gas and air regenerated chambers on a predetermined schedule by furnace.

3.   Under Tools and Equipment the word "buggy" should also have been inserted, since a three-wheeled buggy is used by grievants to transport the thermocouples from location to location. And, although the duty of determining the slag characteristics of slag patties has been eliminated from the job, grievants must still occasionally *collect* slag patties for laboratory analysis.

4.   That part of the job which involves the making of carbon determinations has remained unchanged. Each man continues to take an average of eight carbometer readings per turn. In addition, under normal 14 furnace operations, each of the two Carbometermen, who work on each turn, is responsible for obtaining bath temperatures on seven furnaces. Approximately eight good temperature readings, on the average, are taken by each man per turn. Occasional additional readings are sometimes necessary because of faulty thermocouples. Because of the wide fluctuation of the amount of time spent per turn on the various duties involved in taking bath temperatures, it is not possible to determine the exact proportion of the turn devoted to such duties. Nevertheless, from all the evidence available, it appears that on the average each incumbent of the job spends approximately one fourth of his working time in the performance of these tasks.

5.   Five thermocouples are normally carried on the three-wheeled, rubber-tired buggy, which is used to transport the thermocouples from furnace to furnace. The buggy is pushed by the Carbometerman along a three feet wide walkway used by other employees. Each thermocouple is approximately 12 feet long, 3 inches in diameter, and weighs about 50 pounds. They extend in front of the buggy as it is pushed along the walkway. Often the tips are still hot from the previous temperature readings.

6.   On reaching the area where he will be required to take a temperature reading, the Carbometerman removes a thermocouple from the buggy and plugs it into a stationary junction box. After a couple of minutes he lifts the thermocouple and inserts one end through the wicket hole in the Open Hearth furnace door. While the thermocouple is immersed in the bath, the Carbometerman is standing about a foot away from the furnace door. His back is to the door while he is watching for the red light on the instrument panel, which will signify that the temperature has been recorded. The thermocouple remains in the bath for less than a minute. When the red light appears, the thermocouple is extracted from the bath. The First Helper, with a specially designed hook to hold up the hot end, assists in laying it on the floor. Sometimes the First Helper chips off hot slag which has gathered around the end immersed in the bath. The Carbometerman then places the thermocouple back on the rack on the buggy.

CONTENTIONS OF THE PARTIES

FACTOR 6—RESPONSIBILITY FOR TOOLS AND EQUIPMENT

Company   B .2   Union   C .7

7.   The Union contends that extreme care must be exercised in transporting the thermocouples along the pathway between the charging machine and the locomotive, and in taking a temperature measurement with a thermocouple. Possible damage to the platinum wires is emphasized by the Union. It stresses that among the operating instructions issued on October 13, 1954, the following sentence is inserted under Immersion Procedure:

"Extreme care must be exercised in handling the thermocouple to prevent breakage of graphite sleeves or thermocouple wires."

The Union notes that a Thermocouple Maker job, whose Materials include thermocouples, usually receives a coding at the "C" level on Factor 5—Responsibility for Materials.

8.   Management denies that extreme care must be exercised in the handling of a thermocouple in the sense that the words are used in the Classification Manual. It asserts that the words used in the operating instruction merely constitute a general description of the way that the Chief Metallurgist wanted his men to perform the job, and cannot control the classification rating. It also denies that the classification level on Factor 5 for a Thermocouple Maker job may properly be transposed to establish a "C" level rating on Factor 6 for the job in dispute. Several Specimen Examples are cited to show that a job which uses an item as Tools

and Equipment may have a different rating on Factor 6 from the rating on Factor 5 given to the job which makes the same item.

9. The Company recognizes that some care and attention are required in handling a thermocouple. But it feels that there is no greater possibility of damaging a thermocouple than there was of damaging the optical pyrometer which was previously used to take Checker Chamber temperatures.

10. As to probable amount of damage to a thermocouple resulting from lack of care, Company testimony is that the current value of a thermocouple is $150—$100 for the platinum wire and $50 for the rest. If the wire is damaged from the heat, normally only six to eight inches on the end—out of ten to eleven feet—are lost. If the thermocouple is dropped, the usual extent of the damage is a broken graphite sleeve. On the other hand, the optical pyrometer, which was formerly carried around by use of a leather shoulder strap by incumbents of the job, cost $280.

FACTOR 8—RESPONSIBILITY FOR SAFETY OF OTHERS

Company A Base   Union B .4

11. The Union stresses the danger to other employees in the pathway along which the buggy is pushed by the Carbometerman. Also stressed is the fact that the Carbometerman must be careful not to injure the various First Helpers who aid him in extracting the thermocouple from the bath after the temperature is recorded.

12. Management refers to the descriptive language in the Manual under A Base for this Factor, which reads

> "performs work exposing one other person such as Helper where the likelihood and probable seriousness of accident is small."

It also points out that Carbometermen have worked with various First Helpers in the past in obtaining carbon samples.

FACTOR 10—PHYSICAL EFFORT

Company B .3   Union C .8

13. According to the Union considerable physical exertion is now required of the job in pushing the buggy with the five thermocouples on it, in lifting a thermocouple to insert it through the wicket hole, and in extracting it with slag on the end. The fact that a thermocouple is heavier than the optical pyrometer is also noted. The Company denies that the added duties merit an increase in the rating on this Factor.

FACTOR 11—SURROUNDINGS

Company B .4   Union C .8

14. The Union contends that C .8 is justified on this Factor on the grounds that the Carbometerman is exposed to the glare of the heat through the wicket hole, and that he is exposed to the heat around the furnace door when the thermocouple is immersed. On the other hand, the Company takes the position that the heat around the furnace door is no greater than the heat around the Checker Chambers when the readings were taken by the optical pyrometer. According to temperature measurements made by the Company the temperature at the Checker Chamber was 104 degrees and the temperature next to the furnace door was 109 degrees. Also emphasized is the fact that the furnace door is *closed* when the thermocouple reading is taken. Management asserts that the Carbometerman job is not entitled to the same rating on this Factor as the First Helper who is regularly exposed to extreme heat with one or more furnace doors open.

FACTOR 12—HAZARDS

Company B .4   Union C .8

15. The Union asserts that a Carbometerman is exposed to severe and possibly fatal burns from molten metal. A final temperature measurement is required just prior to the tapping of a heat. According to the Union it is at this point that a heat is most likely to break out on the floor of the Open Hearth and engulf the Carbometerman as he is taking the final measurement. And while the thermocouple is immersed in the bath, the Carbometerman is standing with his back to the furnace, watching for the red signal on the control board. At this time he could also be injured by a passing charging machine. Or he could be injured if another employee accidentally leaned on the control which raises the furnace door, thereby raising the door while the thermocouple is in the wicket hole and in turn lifting the Carbometerman off the floor as he is holding the end of the thermocouple. And although the Company states that there has always been a rule requiring incumbents of this job to wear protective clothing, the Union claims that the rule was not rigidly enforced until the new duties were added to the job.

16. Union witnesses testified that on October 8, 1955, a temperature measurement was made at 1:43 p.m., and that the heat for that furnace broke out on the floor at 1:45 p.m. This incident is cited as an example of the hazards to which the Carbometerman is subjected, in addition to the

hazards from the charging machine, dolomite car, hot metal streetcar and overhead crane.

17. The Company contends that the hazards of the job have not increased. It argues that the Carbometerman is not exposed to molten metal splashes like the Process Observer job, which receives C .8 in this Factor. The latter job is exposed to molten metal splashes on the pouring platform while a heat is being poured and also when working behind the furnace when the heat is being tapped, while the Carbometerman works in front of the furnace at a time when the heat is ready for tapping and is less active. The Company believes that a heat breakout is less likely at this time. It states that heats only break out at tap time about three or four times a year, and normally there is some warning.

18. With respect to all of the Factors in dispute, Management believes that the present codings are consistent with the ratings on numerous Specimen and non-Specimen jobs which it cites. Among these are Specimen 4520 for a Carbometerman in the Open Hearth, Specimen 2357 for a Temperature Recorder in a Tin Mill, Specimen 2235 for a Thermocouple Repairman, and numerous non-Specimen Thermocouple Maker and Carbometerman jobs. The Union claims that all these jobs are distinguishable from the job in dispute, and that at other plants the First Helper in the Open Hearth takes bath temperature readings with immersion thermocouples.

DISCUSSION AND FINDINGS

19. At the outset it should be noted that no job directly on point with the job in dispute was presented to the Board for its consideration. All jobs submitted to the Board are clearly distinguishable from the job in question. The Specimen Example closest to the job in dispute is Number 4520 for a Carbometerman. But that job appears to spend most of the time in the plant office making carbon determinations and identifying steel and slag test samples. It does not take temperature measurements with an immersion thermocouple.

20. A Thermocouple Maker job at the Homestead Works is the only job presented to the Board which includes among its regular duties the taking of Open Hearth bath temperatures with an immersion thermocouple. Most of the duties of this job involve the repair and assembly of thermocouples. Immersion thermocouples are listed under Materials for this job, but they are not listed under Tools and Equipment. Incumbents are not required to make carbon determinations

or to spend time on the Open Hearth floor collecting carbon samples. Nor do they transport thermocouples by use of a buggy. In any event, the classification of this one non-Specimen job can hardly be considered as establishing a pattern which would control the classification ratings for the job in dispute.

21. In this case the best course available to the Board is to consider the changed duties of the Carbometerman job in the light of the Manual, the closest Specimen Example, and the old duties of the job. Specific findings on the Factors in dispute are now in order.

22. Factor 6—Responsibility for Tools and Equipment is presently coded at the "B" level. It is already recognized that some care and attention (as specified in the Manual for Code B) are required to prevent damage to the buggy and the thermocouples. No longer are grievants responsible for the care of an optical pyrometer, for which the "B" level was granted. It should also be noted that today when a temperature reading is taken, which is the point at which the greatest amount of total loss is apt to occur to the platinum wire (the most expensive item), only one thermocouple is being used. That this is the point at which the greatest care must be exercised is evident from the operating instruction upon which the Union relies. Yet even at this point the greatest amount of probable damage to the thermocouple would not normally exceed the amount of damage which might have resulted if there had been a failure to exercise due care in the handling of the optical pyrometer.

23. The Board finds that the new duties do not warrant a higher rating than B .2 on this Factor. The language in the operating instruction of October 13, 1954, cannot control the proper classification rating. Nor can the ratings on Factor 5—Responsibility for Materials for Thermocouple Maker jobs be transposed to Factor 6 for this job. As has already been indicated, the Thermocouple Maker jobs presented in the Company's exhibit are essentially different from the job in dispute.

24. Factor 8—Responsibility for Safety of Others should be coded at B .4. Although the duties listed on the original job description, such as the taking of Checker Chamber temperatures, did not involve any responsibility for safety of others, it is clear that such responsibility is involved under the new duties. When the Carbometerman pushes the buggy along the walkway, other employees could be burned by the hot tip of a recently used thermocouple if proper care were not exercised by the Carbometerman. On a plant

visit by a representative of the Board, craftsmen of various types were observed walking up and down the pathway. The Carbometerman also had to halt his buggy while a Second Helper completed a task he was performing in the pathway. It should be noted further that the Carbometerman works with different First Helpers when the thermocouples are being extracted from the baths. Since precisely the same procedure is not always followed, the fact that different First Helpers may be assisting the Carbometerman increases the degree of care which must be exercised to avoid injuring the various First Helpers with hot thermocouples.

25. It is true that the Carbometerman is not performing these duties throughout the turn, but he is engaged in such duties for a substantial portion of the turn. B .4 is justified by analogy to "occasional crane hooking" referred to in Code B, as distinguished from "ordinary crane hooking," for which Code C is proper under this Factor.

26. The rating on Factor 10—Physical Effort should remain unchanged. On the average only light physical exertion is involved even with the added duties. It is not difficult to push the buggy on the fairly smooth walkway. The fact that a thermocouple is lifted several times a turn to insert it through the wicket hole and is extracted shortly thereafter does not justify a higher rating. And the Carbometerman is aided in the extraction of the thermocouple from the bath.

27. Factor 11—Surroundings is properly coded at B .4. Even though the representative of the Board who visited the operation feels that the heat and glare of the Open Hearth furnace doors are greater than that at the Checker Chambers where the temperature readings were taken by an optical pyrometer (contrary to the claim of Management), the average surroundings of the job have not changed so substantially as to fall in the class of those jobs coded at C .8

in this Factor. No interpolation between point levels is permitted by the Classification Manual.

28. Factor 12—Hazards should be coded at C .8. Specimen 4520 for a Carbometerman, who works primarily in a plant office, is coded at A Base in Factor 11—Surroundings, but at B .4 in Factor 12—Hazards because some tasks are performed on the Open Hearth floor. This Specimen Example shows that, if the hazards are sufficiently grave to warrant a higher coding in Factor 12, the fact that the exposure to the hazards is for the same period of time as that in which the incumbents are also exposed to disagreeable surroundings will not necessarily limit the coding on Factor 12 to the same level as that granted on Factor 11. B .4 is already recognized as appropriate for Factor 11 for the job in dispute, and the hazards of this job are of the type which call for a rating of C .8 on Factor 12. The hazards already outlined are definitely greater under the new duties than those to which incumbents were exposed in taking Checker Chamber temperatures. In the latter case the principal danger was only that fumes might blow out of the Checker Chamber if a brick were removed at the wrong time.

29. Hence, Factor 8 should be coded at B .4 and Factor 12 at C .8. However, since the total increase in points is .8—less than a full job class, the job class of the job in dispute remains unchanged.

AWARD

30. The grievance is sustained only to the extent that the Board finds that the new duties have resulted in an increase of the rating on Factor 8—Responsibility for Safety of Others from A Base to B .4, and the rating on Factor 12—Hazards from B .4 to C .8. There is no change in job class.

USC—575.   11, 12. Johnstown Works.   July 6, 1956
Herbert L. Sherman, Jr., *Arbitrator*
Approved by Sylvester Garrett, *Chairman*

BACKGROUND

1. This grievance arose in the Electric Steel Foundry at Johnstown Works. It claims that the job of Casting Cleaner (Grit), formerly titled Shot Blaster in Job Class 6, was improperly classified in Job Class 4 after its duties were changed basically from manual blasting to machine shot blasting due to changes in equipment and method of operation.

2. Prior to December of 1954 the cleaning of castings in the Electric Steel Foundry was completely performed by manual shot blasting as follows:

3. The Shot Blaster, wearing protective clothing, entered a steel-enclosed room approximately 12' square by 7' high and manually cleaned all castings by directing a stream of shot, impelled by compressed air, through a hose at the surface of steel castings in order to remove the adhering scale

and sand, and to impart an even finish to the casting. The castings were cleaned by working from the outer edge to the center. The Operator would blast the castings on the outer edge, roll the castings over manually using a pry bar, blast the bottom edge, step on the manually rotated table at floor level and manually blast the second row of castings. This process was continued until all castings were cleaned with an even finish. After the castings were cleaned, the table was rotated manually 180°, and the cleaned castings would be on the outside of the enclosed room with the uncleaned castings on the other half of the table remaining inside the room. The Operator duplicated the cleaning process on the inside, while the Hooker on the outside unloaded the cleaned castings and reloaded the portion of the table on the outside of the steel-enclosed room.

4. In December of 1954 the Company decided to change the method of cleaning castings from manual blasting to automatic machine blasting. The old steel-enclosed room was removed and a Pangborn Roto-Blast Machine was installed along with a Gantry-type crane. This new installation eliminated well over 90% of manual cleaning by the Operator and is performed as follows:

5. The Operator loads the casting table with the aid of the push-button controlled crane, rotates the table by 180° and starts blasting by pressing the various control buttons. While the castings inside the machine are being blasted automatically by centrifugally impelled shot with the auxiliary table rotating automatically, the Operator loads the portion of the table on the outside. At the completion of the controlled cycle time, the Operator rotates the table automatically 180° and starts the cleaning process for the uncleaned castings. He then unloads the cleaned casting with the crane and reloads the portion of the table on the outside with castings to be blasted. Occasionally, certain castings may require manual blasting; the Operator, in such cases, puts on protective clothing, enters the enclosure of the machine and manually blasts these castings as done under the previous method.

6. Due to these changes in equipment and method of operation the job of Casting Cleaner (Grit) was described and classified in Job Class 4, effective December 17, 1954. At the hearing the Union protested the ratings on Factor 7, 8, 11 and 12.

7. The following table shows a factor-by-factor comparison of the original classification of the job, the present classification, and the classification requested by the Union:

FACTOR	ORIGINAL	PRESENT	REQUESTED
1. Pre-Employment Training	A-Base	A-Base	A-Base
2. Employment Training & Experience	A-Base	A-Base	A-Base
3. Mental Skill	B-1.0	B-1.0	B-1.0
4. Manual Skill	B- .5	B- .5	B- .5
5. Responsibility for Materials	A-Base	B- .3	B- .3
6. Responsibility for Tools & Equipment	B- .2	B- .2	B- .2
*7. Responsibility for Operations	A-Base	A-Base	B- .5
*8. Responsibility for Safety of Others	A-Base	A-Base	B- .4
9. Mental Effort	B- .5	B- .5	B- .5
10. Physical Effort	D-1.5	C- .8	C- .8
*11. Surroundings	D-1.6	B- .4	C- .8
*12. Hazards	C- .8	B- .4	C- .8
Total Classification	6.1	4.1	5.8
Job Class	6	4	6

* Factors in dispute

DISCUSSION AND FINDINGS

8. None of the eighteen Shot Blaster or Sand Blaster jobs, ranging from Job Class 5 to Job Class 8, which were submitted to the Board by the Company, is exactly comparable with the job in dispute. Neither is the job of Casting Cleaner (Grit), in Job Class 3, in the Iron Foundry at Johnstown Works. Nevertheless, these jobs have been considered by the Board, to the extent that they are applicable, in arriving at a decision in this case.

9. With respect to Factor 7—Responsibility for Operations, there has been no significant change in the job in dispute to warrant a higher rating. The relationship of grievants' job to other operations is essentially the same as before the changes were instituted.

10. On the other hand, the changes in

the job definitely require a higher rating on Factor 8—Responsibility for Safety of Others. Grievants not only operate a Gantry-type crane to load the table with uncleaned castings brought to their working area by the magnet of an overhead crane, but they also use their crane to convey cleaned castings to the other end of their working area. There the castings are piled next to the burning tables. Numerous trips are made each turn to this end of the working area by grievants. Improper operation of their crane could cause a cleaned casting to swing against Burners and Floggers who walk through this part of grievants' working area, or even against Burners while they are working at the ends of their tables. Improper hooking of a cleaned casting could also cause it to fall against these other employees while the piece is being transported by grievants. And improper stacking of cleaned castings at the far end of the working area could cause them to fall against the legs of Burners working at the ends of their burning tables. Although the possibility of injury to employees using the walkway beside the Roto-Blast Machine is fairly remote, there is the further possibility that grievants might injure, through improper hooking and improper operation of their crane, the Hooker who sometimes follows the overhead crane into grievants' working area.

11. In the light of these circumstances, the Union request for a rating of B .4 on this Factor under the Classification Manual must be granted. Although Management believes that the Casting Cleaner job in the Johnstown Iron Foundry is comparable with respect to the crane operation duties of grievants, that job is distinguishable. It operates a post crane in a smaller area in order to load a grit blast machine. This post crane, observed on a plant visit, is only powered to go up and down, while grievants operate a Gantry-type crane through six controls on a bar. Not only do they operate controls for up and down movements, but there are also controls for moving the crane in any one of four directions. More attention and care to prevent injury to others in the immediate area are required of grievants than is required of the Operator of the post crane in the Iron Foundry.

12. The present ratings on Factor 11—Surroundings and Factor 12—Hazards are appropriate. Only on fairly rare occasions are grievants now required to perform manual blasting inside the machine. The Union recognizes a change in the surroundings of the job, but protests a reduction in the rating from D 1.6 to B .4. According to the Company a rating of A Base would be justified on Factor 11 if grievants spent all of their time outside the machine. Only because occasional manual touch-up blasting is required is the job rated at B .4 on this Factor. And insofar as the Union relies on routine crane hooking as a basis for increasing the rating on Factor 12, the descriptive language under B .4 for this Factor already recognizes that duty. Other evidence and arguments have been considered by the Board, but they do not justify disturbing the present ratings on these Factors. The average surroundings and hazards of the job are reflected in the present codings.

13. Since the proper rating of B .4 on Factor 8 places the job in Job Class 5, grievants are entitled to retroactive compensation, under Section 9-D-3 of the Agreement, to 30 days prior to January 19, 1955—the date on which the grievance was filed.

AWARD

14. The grievance is sustained to the extent that the rating on Factor 8—Responsibility for Safety of Others is increased from A Base to B .4, thereby placing the job of Casting Cleaner (Grit) in Job Class 5.

USC—514. 11, 12. South Works. June 16, 1955
Donald A. Crawford, *Arbitrator*
Approved by Sylvester Garrett, *Chairman*

BACKGROUND

1. This grievance requests the advancement of the job of Furnace Rebuild Recorder, presently in Job Class 7, one full job class or more. Both parties agree that certain changes have been made in this job. These changes were recorded in a Form G, issued by Management on December 21, 1953. The Union claims that the changes are of such a character as to warrant higher ratings on Factors 7, 11 and 12. The Management contends that these changes do not affect the classification of the job to the extent of one full class or more.

2. The duties which have been added to this job are as follows: (1) rubber stamping time cards; (2) preparing daily report of men working; (3) assisting in transcribing and posting Foreman's safety contacts; (4) posting incentive pay factors on bulletin boards; (5) answering telephone and relaying messages.

3. In addition to these changes in duties, which are listed in Form G, the Union contends that Furnace Rebuild Recorders now have to go into the field to get information which previously was brought to the office by the Foreman. The Union argues that these changes warrant an increase in rating under Factor 7, Responsibility for Operations.

4. This job was formerly performed on a day turn basis only, but is now performed on all shifts. This fact, the Union argues further, warrants an increase in the values given for Factors 11 and 12, Surroundings and Hazards.

DISCUSSION AND FINDINGS

5. (1.) *Factor 7.* There is testimony for the Union that the 2 additional duties of rubber stamping time cards and transcribing and posting Foreman's safety contacts formerly were performed by the Foreman. It's not clear from the testimony whether it is also claimed that the function of preparing daily reports of men working (referred to in the Union's brief as preparing "crew sheets") was performed by the Foreman. In any event, it is implied that the transfer of these duties to the Furnace Rebuild Recorder amounts to his assuming responsibilities formerly discharged by a Foreman.

6. In contradiction of this, there is ample testimony for the Company, not disproved by the Union, that the essential information for the performance of these (two) functions is supplied to the Furnace Rebuild Recorder by the Foreman. The Recorder's actual functions in these connections are of a clerical nature (such as stamping, posting, etc.) altogether comparable in complexity and responsibility to other clerical duties always performed in this job.

7. As regards the preparation of the daily report of men working, the testimony (Transcript, pp. 33-36) demonstrates that all of the information contained in this report is supplied either verbally by the Foreman, from pre-printed forms, from the time cards, or from observations that the Recorder is required to make in the course of those regular duties which are not in controversy. His function in this case also is one of posting.

8. In the matter of posting incentive pay factors to bulletin boards, the testimony demonstrates that all that is involved is the simple act of operating a door and attaching a sheet of paper to the board. This cannot conceivably modify the job in any way.

9. Testimony by the Company states that all of these duties are performed in numerous specimen jobs which are classified in Job Class 7 or lower.

10. On the subject of answering the telephone, there is confusion in the testimony as to whether this is in fact an added duty, or whether it has always been performed but had not been recorded in the job descriptions previously. It seems to be demonstrated that there has always been some use of the telephone (see, for example, Union testimony, lines 21-25, p. 2, transcript), and the only question which can be in doubt is whether any relaying of messages not previously involved is now required. However, assuming that there is now more relaying of messages, the fact is that the Recorder is not required to make any determinations of proper responses to telephone inquiries, but only to forward messages. Accordingly, there is no significant element of additional responsibility involved.

11. So far as going into the field is concerned, the original job description establishes that this has always been required of the Furnace Rebuild Recorder. Testimony establishes that gathering data in the field was performed by Foremen only when the Recorder's job was limited to the first shift. Foremen brought this data to the office for the use of the Recorder in preparing reports covering the second and third shifts. For his reports covering the shift on which he worked, the Recorder obtained his own data from the field. This is what is now done on each shift; the fundamental character of the job—observing field operations and recording data—has not changed.

12. In addition to the arguments discussed above, the Union cites the decision in Case No. USC-296 as favorable precedent for the present case. In this cited case, however, there were added duties of a kind qualitatively different from the former functions of the job, which is not true in the present case. These added duties created a rather clearly seen increase in Responsibility for Materials.

13. *Factors 11 and 12:* The Union's claim in this connection is that because the job is now performed on an around-the-clock basis, the Furnace Rebuild Recorder must go into the field at night. This, it is argued, increases the hazard inherent in the job.

14. The Union's argument relative to this point adds up to the contention that artificial lighting is more hazard-producing than natural light. There is conflicting testimony on the extent to which there is adequate natural light during daylight hours and, therefore, on the extent to which conditions at night could be less satisfactory. There is no convincing showing by the Union that there are in fact greater hazards at night. But, in any event, the controlling consideration on this point is that the parties

recognize a compensable difference between night and day work only through payment of shift differentials, and not in their application of job classification procedures.

15. Insofar as the Union contention regarding Factor 11 and Factor 12 is based on field work, the controlling consideration is that the job, when performed on a day shift basis only, required close to half a turn in the Open Hearth and Soaking Pit area, and this ratio has not changed significantly (trs. pp. 49-50). Hence, the original evaluation presumably rated this condition, and, in any event, there has been no significant change.

AWARD

16. The grievance is denied.

T—292. 12. Fairfield Tin Mill. March 31, 1955

Herbert L. Sherman, Jr., *Arbitrator*

Approved by Sylvester Garrett, *Chairman*

BACKGROUND

1. In this case the Union seeks a higher job class for the job of Maintenance Spares Attendant in the Tractor Department of the Fairfield Tin Mill. This grievance was filed after the issuance of an Exhibit G by the Company, dated May 7, 1953 and issued in June of that year, to reflect certain changes in the established job of Tool and Parts Attendant.

2. The job description of that job, which was established as a new job in Job Class 7 for physically handicapped employees in September, 1950, was revised in May, 1953, to note (1) a change in the title from Tool and Parts Attendant to Maintenance Spares Attendant, (2) a change in the Subdivision from Electrical Service and Inspection to Tractor Department, (3) a change in the Tools and Equipment by deleting "Tool grinder" (which grievants never had) and by adding "brake lining machine, spark plug cleaning machine, vise, clamps," and (4) a change in the duties from "Makes minor repairs to tools as directed" to "Makes minor repairs to tools *and parts* as directed."

The Working Procedure, with the additional words "and parts," reads as follows:

(1.) Receives general instructions regarding parts and tools.

(2.) Receives and checks incoming parts, storing them in proper bins. Notifies Tractor Maintenance Foreman of any damage to parts or shortage in shipment.

(3.) Issues parts in exchange for parts removed from tractor, making reports accordingly.

(4.) Issues special tools to Tractor Department employees in exchange for tool checks. Returns tool checks when tools are returned.

(5.) Inspects and checks tools before issuing them and after they are returned. Notifies Tractor Maintenance Foreman and/or Gangleader (Repairman-Tractors) of any damaged or defective tools, or of any tools not returned during turn.

(6.) Keeps record of all parts issued and on hand, and records tractor number for which parts are issued.

(7.) Makes list of parts to be ordered on approval of Tractor Maintenance Foreman.

(8.) Assists in taking inventory of parts, etc., as directed.

(9.) Makes minor repairs to tools and parts as directed.

(10.) Keeps Tool and Parts Room and all tools and parts in a clean and orderly manner.

3. Although the initial dispute in this case turned on whether grievants were always required to repair parts, it was finally agreed that the Board should consider this as a new duty. There is no question, however, that grievants always did *tear down* certain tractor parts in order to salvage the good pieces. The issue before the Board is whether the added requirement of repairing these parts affects the classification of the job in dispute.

4. Examples of the types of repairs on tractor parts emphasized by grievants in their testimony, which consumes from 25% to 50% of the turn, are as follows:

(1.) Relining brake shoes. The rivets in the old brake shoe lining are punched out. A piece of asbestos lining is cut by grievants with a chisel or hack saw. The new brake lining machine is then used to drill six to ten holes, to "brad in" the new rivets, and to rub smooth the new lining with a sand paper buffer. Since October 17, 1953, the job in dispute has operated only on the day turn and the only remaining incumbent has not relined brake shoes. This duty is not required of him because he has an artificial leg and the machine involves operation of a foot pedal.

(2.) Filing contact tips. The tips are placed in a vise and are manually filed down with a 12 or 8 inch file. The amount of the filing depends on the extent of the burn on the tips.

(3.) Building up reversing blocks. Triangular wooden blocks are placed in a vise; a screw driver is then used to attach the fingers with wood screws. Tips are installed on the fingers so that contact may be made with the electrical juice.

(4.) Building up collector rings. Collector rings convey electrical juice from one part of a tractor to another part. Grievants build them up by riveting brass rings on fiber rings in the proper places with a hammer and a small anvil. The finished rings are rubbed smooth by the sand paper buffer on the brake lining machines.

(5.) Building up grid resistors. Copper and insulating washers are installed in the proper places on a grid, and the wires are checked for the proper amount of resistance. A sample piece is available to guide grievants.

5. Other related repair work consists of building up hoist controller assemblies and travel controller blocks by the use of small hand tools and various small parts. The added duties were previously performed by Tractor Repairmen. Tool repairs, always performed by grievants, involve such duties as removing the end from a hydraulic jack and blowing the trash out of the air hose, fixing ratchets by inserting new screws, and replacing handles. Pneumatic tools are sent to the Machine Shop for repairs.

CONTENTIONS OF THE PARTIES

6. The Union argues that some of the new duties require a knowledge of electricity. It points out that one grievant had studied electricity, one had previously worked with electricians, and one grievant swapped repairs of electrical parts for brake lining duties with which he was more familiar.

7. For these reasons the Union seeks higher ratings on Factors 1, 2, 3 and 9. Because of the necessity for grievants to file, rivet, hammer, and use wrenches and screw drivers in the course of making the enumerated repairs, the Union believes that higher ratings on Factors 4 and 10 are justified. It stresses that grievants had to acquire additional hand tools after they were required to repair parts.

8. The coding for Factor 5 is affected, the Union urges, because the brake shoes and other parts of a tractor could be damaged through lack of care in making repairs. With respect to Factor 6, the Union argues that the brake lining machine and the spark plug cleaning machine (which has never

been used) could be injured through lack of attention.

9. Since a tractor may be waiting for parts, the Union believes that the coding on Factor 7 should be raised. A higher rating is sought on Factor 8 because of the possibility that a tractor with a defectively repaired part might injure others.

10. There is no dispute on Factor 11, but the Union contends that the rating on Factor 12 is affected because grievants are subject to severe bruises, cuts, and fractures in the course of making repairs.

11. The following jobs are called to the Board's attention by the Union as being similar in job content to the job in dispute. Specimen 969 for a Repairman (Air Tools) in Job Class 11; a Maintenance Spares Attendant job in Job Class 9 at Fairfield Steel Works; 5 Tool Repairman jobs, ranging from Job Class 10 to Job Class 12, at Fairfield Steel Works; 2 Tool Repairman jobs, in Job Class 11 and 12 respectively, at Ensley Steel Works; a Mechanical Repairman job in Job Class 11 at Ensley Steel Works; a Repairman (Air Tools) job in Job Class 11 at the Fairfield Tin Mill; and a Maintenance Spares Attendant (Gen.) job in Job Class 9 at Gary Steel Works.

12. Management contends that these jobs are not comparable to the job in dispute. It distinguishes the Union exhibits as follows. The Maintenance Spares Attendant at Fairfield Steel Works works with grinders, emery wheels, calipers and dies. The reasons for the classification ratings emphasize the duties of grinding and sharpening cutters, tappers and other tools. With the exception of one of the Tool Repairman jobs at Ensley (which works with a turret lathe, drill press, and tool and cutter grinder), the Tool Repairman jobs cited by the Union repair pneumatic tools, a duty which calls for application of Specimen 969 for a Repairman (Air Tools). This is also true of the Repairman (Air Tools) at the Fairfield Tin Mill, which is classified in line with Specimen 969. The Mechanical Repairman job cited by the Union repairs and maintains all types of rigging equipment. And finally, the reasons for classification of the Gary Maintenance Spares Attendant job, which is responsible for "Mechanical and electrical repair parts and assemblies and supplies located in several widely separated locations in the Coke Plant Div.," emphasize that the incumbents must have the ability to make substitution of materials when conditions warrant.

13. The Company characterizes the added duties of the job in dispute as "minor repairs on parts." It points out that grievants always did tear down these parts to salvage good pieces. Reassembling these parts, Man-

agement asserts, requires the same basic skills.

14. Specimen Examples relied upon by Management for purposes of comparison are Specimen 4559 for a Storeroom Attendant (Job Class 8), Specimen 4560 for a Storeroom Attendant (Job Class 7), and Specimen 931 for a Toolman (Line Gang) (Job Class 4). These are the Specimens used as a guide when the job in dispute was initially classified in 1950. The first two of these jobs are primarily responsible for receiving and distributing supplies. Specimen 4559 is coded the same as the job in dispute on the first three Factors. Specimen 931, in addition to distributing and collecting tools, performs minor repairs and assembly work, such as replacing sledge handles, grinding chisels and drills, insulating tools, and assembling new light fixtures, conduit sections, and sockets. The tools and equipment of this job include a hammer, screw driver, wrenches, files, soldering iron, taps and dies, drill press, and abrasive wheel. Factors 4 and 10 are coded the same as the job in dispute.

15. Also cited by the Company is Specimen 1040 (Job Class 6) for a Repairman Tools, which is a job responsible for assisting in the maintenance and ordering of supplies for three different areas, and for making minor repairs to power driven tools. That job is coded at B .5 for Factor 4. Further Specimen Examples called to the Board's attention are Specimen 1034 for a Millwright Helper, Specimen 984 for a Machinist Helper, Specimen 929 for an Electrician Helper (Wire), and a Specimen 930 for an Electrician Helper (Armature Winder). All of these Specimens are coded at B .5 in Factor 4, yet they contemplate that minor repair work may be performed without supervision.

DISCUSSION AND FINDINGS

16. The following table shows the present ratings assigned to the job in dispute, and the ratings sought by the Union in the Fourth Step of the grievance procedure.

FACTORS	PRESENT CLASSI- FICATION		UNION CLASSI- FICATION	
1. Pre-Employment Training	B	.3	C	1.0
2. Employment Training and Experience	D	1.2	D	1.2
3. Mental Skill	C	1.6	D	2.2
4. Manual Skill	B	.5	D	1.5
5. Responsibility for Materials	C	1.2	C	1.2
6. Responsibility for Tools and Equipment	BL	.2	CL	.4
7. Responsibility for Operation	A	Base	C	1.0
8. Responsibility for Safety of Others	A	Base	B	.4
9. Mental Effort	D	1.5	D	1.5
10. Physical Effort	B	.3	D	1.5
11. Surroundings	A	Base	A	Base
12. Hazards	A	Base	B	.4
Total		6.8		12.3
Job Class		7		12

17. Using the Specimen Examples cited as guides in this case to evaluate the effect of the changes in the job in dispute, the Board finds that no higher ratings are warranted on the "skill" Factors—the first four Factors. The repair duties required of grievants do not require more mentality, training or mental skill than the extensive storeroom duties which constitute the primary function of the job. The first three Factors are already coded as high as the highest ratings on these Factors for Specimens 4559 and 4560 for Storeroom Attendants.

18. Specimen 4559 is coded at A Base for Factor 4—Manual Skill and Specimen 4560 is coded at B .5 (since that job also uses hand tools and operates a power saw). The job in dispute is already given credit of B .5 for the use of light hand tools in making minor repairs and adjustments. Certainly, grievants do not perform repair duties comparable to those outlined in Specimen 969 for a Repairman (Air Tools). That job, similar to many of the plant jobs called to the Board's attention, disassembles, repairs, assembles and tests different types of pneumatic hand tools. Such tools in the Tractor Repair Shop are not repaired by grievants but are sent to the Machine Shop. Nor are the tools with which grievants perform repairs comparable to the tools of the Repairman (Air Tools). Grievants admit that the brake lining machine is simple to operate.

19. Factor 5—Responsibility for Materials is already coded at C 1.2. Possible damage, through lack of attention, to brake shoes and other tractor parts actually worked on cannot justify a higher coding. Nor is the rating on Factor 6—Responsibility for Tools and Equipment affected by the additional duties. Jobs cited for the Board, which work with tools and equipment subject to greater damage than a brake lining machine through lack of care and attention, receive no higher rating on this Factor.

20. No change in the job has taken place to require a higher rating on Factor 7—Re-

sponsibility for Operations. Specimens 4559 and 4560, cited above, and Specimen 931 which repairs tools for maintenance men, are all coded the same as the job in dispute on this Factor.

21. The rating on Factor 8—Responsibility for the Safety of Others must remain the same. Grievants rotate their shifts when all are working. Only one Attendant is on duty in the Tool and Parts Room at one time. No one is directly exposed to injury through an act of negligence by grievants.

22. The additional duties do not require any change in the rating on Factor 10—Physical Effort. Code B calls for the manual use of light hand tools. Specimens 931 and 1040 require similar physical effort in making repairs. Both are coded at B .3 on this Factor. Incidentally, Specimen 969 for a Repairman (Air Tools), relied upon by the Union, is also coded at B .3 on this Factor.

23. Factor 12—Hazards is presently coded at A Base. As a result of the repair work, now required, the probability of injury to grievants has been increased. Certainly there is more probability of mashed fingers in the course of making the repairs outlined by grievants than is involved in the performance of the storeroom functions. The operation of the buffer on the brake lining machine also exposes grievants to additional hazards. Specimens 931 and 1040 receive a coding of B .4 on this Factor. The same is true of Specimens 4559 and 4560. Considering all of the evidence in the light of these Specimen Examples, the Board concludes that Factor 12 for the job in dispute should be coded at B .4.

AWARD

24. The grievance is sustained only to the extent of increasing the rating on Factor 12 from A Base to B .4.

T—526.   12. Fairfield Wire Works.   October 24, 1958

Sylvester Garrett, *Chairman*

BACKGROUND

1. This grievance from Fairfield Wire Works claims that successive changes in content of the Weigher (Nail Mill) job require raising the present 7.4 coding to 8.7.

2. The following table shows the positions of the parties:

	PRESENT	UNION PROPOSAL
1. Pre-employment Training	B-0.3	B-0.3
2. Employment Training and Experience	C-0.8	C-0.8
3. Mental Skill	C-1.6	C-1.6
4. Manual Skill	A-Base	A-Base
*5. Responsibility for Materials	C-1.2	C-1.8
*6. Responsibility for Tools and Equipment	BL-0.2	BH-0.5
7. Responsibility for Operations	C-1.0	G-1.0
8. Responsibility for Safety of Others	A-Base	A-Base
9. Mental Effort	D-1.5	D-1.5
10. Physical Effort	A-Base	A-Base
11. Surroundings	C-0.8	C-0.8
*12. Hazards	A-Base	B-0.4
Total	7.4	8.7

* Factors in dispute.

3. The Union contends that since the Weigher now must accompany a Tractor Operator to the box warehouse, unlock the door, verify the items removed by the latter, on a requisition form, and relock the door, there is additional responsibility for materials warranting increase under Factor 5 to C-1.8 rather than the present C-1.2.

4. On Factor 6 the Union points out that the Weigher now has additional responsibility of an adding machine; therefore, the proper coding for this Factor should be BH-0.5 rather than BL-0.2.

5. Finally, the Union feels that Factor 12—Hazards, should be coded B-0.4 rather than A-Base. It calls attention to the Weigher's exposure to "flying whiskers" emanating from the nail machines, while enroute to and from the box warehouse. A similar hazard is said to be present when the Weigher goes on the mill floor to check operation of two sets of machines each turn. It is emphasized that these latter checks are made twice a turn since there are actually two different production shifts which overlap the turn worked by the Weigher.

6. Company witnesses emphasized that coding of Factor 5 at C-1.2 is appropriate, and cited comparable codings in Specimens 4555, 4559, 4560, 4561 and 4594. These Specimens entail receipt, disbursement and maintenance of records in storehouse jobs and the highest coding in Factor 5 is C-1.2, as in the instant case. The Company also noted that the Weigher is not responsible for any material stored in the box ware-

house, nor for soap stored in a separate locked enclosure in the box warehouse. It also was pointed out that the Weigher actually does not have a key to the separate enclosure for soap storage. The Company asserts that the Weigher's sole duty in accompanying the Tractor Operator to the box storehouse, when stock items are removed by the latter, is to check the number of boxes the Tractor Operator withdraws so as to maintain a more accurate inventory record than before.

7. As to Factor 6, the Company stresses that addition of an adding machine does not increase responsibility under this Factor an appreciable extent over the major existing responsibility of the Weigher for the weighing scales. The Company notes that the Manual states that "the degree of responsibility is determined by the probability and the cost of damage which might occur at any one time" and there was no real likelihood that damage to the scale and adding machine could occur simultaneously. The Company stresses the similar BL-0.2 classification in 32 Specimen Jobs involving use of an adding machine, citing particularly Nos. 4689, 4692, 4706, 4707, 4709, 4723, 4724.

8. As to Factor 12—Hazards, the Company notes that the Union's claim for B-0.4, based on need for the Weigher to go to the box warehouse with the Tractor Operator and to enter the mill to check the machine in operation, at best involves about 30 minutes per turn. This amount of time is about the same as was required formerly when the Weigher had to check badge numbers of employees at the machines—which latter requirement now is abandoned. The former badge-checking entailed at least the same exposure to flying whiskers as now exists in checking the two sets of machines each turn and in trips to the box warehouse.

9. On this score the Company cites Specimens 4544, 4545, 4546, 4550, 4551, coded at A-Base under Factor 12. It holds these to be more appropriate references than Specimens 1620 and 1628 (at B.4) cited by the Union.

FINDINGS

10. The disputed job originally was classified July 3, 1946. Subsequently, on March 2, September 1 and October 1, 1955, the Job Description was amended with respect to the following: (1) under Primary Function the incumbent was relieved of responsibility for checking badge numbers of all men working in the Nail Mill during a turn; (2) an adding machine was included under Tools and Equipment; (3) under Materials

was added boxes, liners, tops, bottoms, requisition forms and Control for Verification forms; (4) under Working Procedure was added the posting of weight numbers to the Control for Verification form and identifying the turn on the weight ticket, obtains weight tickets and Control for Verification forms to Weigher (Galvanizing) and, when applicable, searches for missing buggies of nails; records on Delay and Gauge Change Report the number of nail and staple machines operating on each turn; records weights of nails or staples cut for special orders, calculates balance due on each order and delivers cards to set on which nails or staples were produced; when requested by Tractor Operator goes to box warehouse, unlocks door, fills out requisition showing stock removed by Tractor Operator, locks door and returns to his weighing station and sends requisition to Cost Division.

11. The significant changes in the working procedure involve discontinuance of checking badge numbers, addition of the adding machine, and going to the box warehouse and checking operation of the Nail machines during each turn.

12. While the Union in the Grievance Procedure took the position that the Weigher had assumed greater responsibility for materials in that he was now required to check out boxes from the warehouse, they produced no evidence to support this contention. It appears, in fact, that the Weigher's duties in checking out material to the Tractor Operator are related solely to inventory control and involve no responsibility for shortages.

13. The Union pointed out that Factor 6 now should reflect the fact that the Weigher was responsible for the care of an adding machine as well as the scales. The Company called attention to the extreme improbability that damage would befall both the scale and the adding machine *at the same time,* as specified in the Manual. It cited a substantial number of Specimen Examples where two pieces of equipment were involved, such as a typewriter and an adding machine, and in all such examples Factor 6 was weighted no higher than the instant BL.2. There is no basis here to support a higher coding.

14. With respect to Hazards, the only substantial issue is the asserted exposure to "flying whiskers," but the Union's cited Specimens (1620 and 1628) are for Nail Machine Operators and Helpers. These relate to duties which require men to be constantly in close proximity to the nail machines. The Weigher is not required to leave the aisles between the machines and

walks down them only for a small portion of the turn.

15. Under the evidence, therefore, there is no support for ratings higher than those already in effect for the Factors in dispute.

AWARD

16. The grievance is denied.

USC—540, -541. 12. Fairless Works. July 6, 1956
Sylvester Garrett, *Chairman*

BACKGROUND

1. These two cases, arising in the 80″ Hot Strip Mill of the Rolling Division at Fairless Works, involve claims that the jobs of Roll Hand (Job Class 9) and Roll Hand Helper (Job Class 6) have not been properly classified.

2. The rolls on Hot Strip Mills must be changed frequently to produce strip steel of proper quality. Other Strip Mills in Central Operations operate on a continuous basis for 15 or more turns per week. There is a set up turn preceding the cycle of operating turns when all necessary roll changes are made by the Mill and/or Maintenance Crews. Rolls are then changed as necessary during the cycle of operating turns by the Mill Crew working on the turn when the roll change is required.

3. At Fairless Works the 80″ Hot Strip Mill operates on an intermittent basis and runs only one turn in each 24-hour period. When this Mill started operations in July, 1953, the work of changing rolls was done by the Mill Crews and Mill Crew rates were paid. Early in 1954, however, Management decided, in order to increase operating efficiency and to satisfy complaints of excessive overtime, that a separate roll changing crew of two Roll Hands and two Roll Hand Helpers should be established. For a short period employees assigned to the roll changing crew were paid Mill Crew rates.

4. After the jobs in dispute had been checked, job descriptions were mutually approved by the parties. As reflected in the job descriptions, the Roll Hand, assisted by the Roll Hand Helper, removes, cleans and replaces various parts from the scalebreakers and the roughing and finishing stands. The parts include rolls, guides, water lines and water sprays. Care must be exercised by the crew not to scratch the rolls when they are being replaced and adjusted. Ends of the rolls are painted by the crew, and the mill is prepared for the start of operations. Every other week grievants work 8 a.m. to 4 p.m.; on the alternate weeks they work from midnight to 8 a.m. On the daylight turns they report to an operating Turn Foreman or a Maintenance Foreman. On night turns a Maintenance Foreman is in charge of their department.

5. Although Fairless is the only plant which operates a Hot Strip Mill one turn each 24 hours and makes roll changes on the down turn preceding each rolling turn by a separate roll changing crew, there are numerous Roll Builder, Roll Hand and Helper jobs in the Corporation that perform essentially the same work in changing rolls for other types of Mills, and in building up spare roll stands. Approximately fifty such jobs were introduced at the hearing by the Company and Union.

6. Following is a table which shows the present ratings on the Roll Hand job and those proposed by the Union. No specific Factor ratings for the Helper job are disputed by the Union, but a substantially higher job class is sought.

FACTOR	PRESENT RATINGS FOR ROLL HAND		RATINGS PROPOSED BY UNION	
*1. Pre-employment training	B	.3	C	1.0
*2. Employment training and experience	D	1.2	G	2.4
*3. Mental Skill	C	1.6	E	2.8
*4. Manual Skill	B	.5	C	1.0
*5. Responsibility for materials	C	.7	C	2.5
*6. Responsibility for tools and equipment	B	.2	C	1.0
*7. Responsibility for operations	C	1.0	D	2.0
*8. Responsibility for safety of others	B	.4	C	.8
9. Mental Effort	C	1.0	C	1.0
10. Physical effort	C	.8	C	.8
11. Surroundings	B	.4	B	.4
*12. Hazards	B	.4	C	.8
Total		8.5		16.5

* Factors in dispute.

DISCUSSION AND FINDINGS

The original grievances in these cases requested payment of Mill Crew rates to grievants by reference to such jobs as Roller, Assistant Roller and Finisher. These jobs, however, go so far beyond the duties of grievants that they cannot be considered as similar to the jobs in dispute.

8. *Roll Hand:* Of the numerous jobs presented to the Board to be used as guides in determining the proper classification ratings for the Roll Hand job, two stressed by the Union are clearly inapplicable. One is a Roll Assembly Man job, in Job Class 12, in the #10-10" Shape Mill at McDonald Works; the other is a Guide Setter job, in Job Class 14, at Edgar Thomson Works. Classification ratings on the McDonald Works job were arbitrated in Case USC-270. That job is a combination Roll Builder and Guide Setter job. It makes *final* adjustments on guides and rolls, while the job in dispute has no such responsibility. The Mill Crew makes the final adjustments. Moreover, although the Board raised the Job Class of the McDonald Works job from 11 to 12 in USC-270, Job Class 14 Guide Setter jobs were distinguished on the ground that they were engaged in production operations as an integral part of the operating crews. Likewise, the Edgar Thomson Guide Setter job relied on by the Union in this case is distinguishable in that it is apparently part of the operating crew. It performs duties at the Finishing Rolls of the #2 Mill while the Mill is in operation. Grievants' duties are limited to those of a preparatory nature.

9. The remaining thirty jobs presented by the parties to aid the Board in classifying the Roll Hand job in dispute form the basis for the following analysis. This group of jobs includes Specimen 249—a Roll Hand in Job Class 7, Specimen 4114—a Gang Leader Roll Hand (who directs Specimen 249) in Job Class 9, Specimen 420—a Roll Builder in Job Class 8, and Specimen 1728—a Roll Assembly Man in Job Class 8.

10. For the first four Factors, the "skill" Factors, the ratings on these thirty Roll Hand or Roll Builder jobs are the same or lower than the present codings on the disputed job with a few exceptions. An Irvin Works Roll Builder job, the Primary Function of which is "To direct and perform repair and maintenance work on roll trains and associated equipment," is coded at E 1.6 on Factor 2. A Roll Builder job at South Works of the Wire Division, which makes mill repairs on the #4 Rod Mill, receives a rating of C 1.0 on Factor 4. And several Roll Builder jobs at the McDonald Mills of Youngstown District are coded at C 1.0 on Factor 4. Close adjustment of guides and rolls is emphasized in the reason for classification of Factor 4 on these Youngstown jobs.

11. In any event, the Board must conclude that the first four Factors of the Roll Hand job in dispute are coded consistently with the appropriate Specimen Example jobs and the predominant patterns which have been developed by the parties in applying the Specimens to similar local plant jobs. The evidence does not warrant higher ratings on these Factors.

12. With respect to Factor 5—Responsibility for Materials, none of the thirty jobs considered in this analysis is coded higher than the C .7 now assigned to the job in dispute. There is no basis for assigning a higher rating on this Factor. Factor 6—Responsibility for Tools and Equipment, is also properly coded. Only one of the thirty jobs noted above is coded higher than B .2. That job, a Roll Builder at South Works of the Wire Division, is rated at C .7 on Factor 6 because of possible damage to rolls, even though rolls are not listed as part of the equipment of the job.

13. No higher rating than the C 1.0 now assigned to Factor 7—Responsibility for Operations for the Roll Hand job in dispute is warranted. Specimens 249, 420 and 1728 are coded at C 1.0 on this Factor. Specimen 4114 receives a rating of E 3.0 on the basis of the Gang Leader Convention. Of the thirty Roll Hand or Roll Builder jobs considered in this analysis, twenty-six are coded no higher than C 1.0. Although a Roll Builder job at Irvin Works and one at South Works of the Wire Division, which are responsible for making mill repairs on large producing units, and a Roll Builder job at Homestead Works, which directs a crew of three or more mill rigger helpers, are coded at D 2.0 on this Factor, the pertinent Specimen Examples and the classification pattern of the numerous related plant jobs indicate that C 1.0 is the proper rating on Factor 7 for the job in dispute.

14. Factor 8—Responsibility for Safety of Others is properly coded at B .4. Twenty-one of the thirty Roll Hand or Roll Builder jobs under consideration, including four Specimen Examples and three other Roll Builder jobs at Fairless Works, receive B .4 on this Factor. With respect to grievants' responsibility for directing a crane when changing the rolls, this duty is also found in Specimen 1728 for a Roll Assembly Man who directs others assisting in making roll changes. Specimen 1728 is coded at B .4 on Factor 8. And Specimens 249, 4114 and 420 all receive B .4 on Factor 8 on the basis of crane hooking in connection with building up roll stands. The Board finds that the job in dispute has been properly coded on Factor 8.

15. The Union's proposed ratings on Factors 9, 10 and 11 are the same as those now assigned.

16. Factor 12—Hazards is the most troublesome. About half of the jobs presented to the Board are rated at B .4 on this Factor, the other half at C .8. Of the four Specimen Examples cited above two are rated at B .4 and two at C .8. Incumbents of all four of these Specimens are exposed to hazards of crane hooking. From the reasons given for classification of this Factor on Specimens 249 and 4114, it appears that C .8 was assigned because of duties performed around moving machinery. But grievants do not perform their duties around moving machinery. Hence, on the basis of the most closely related Specimen Examples, the Board concludes that Factor 12 for the job in dispute should be coded at B .4.

17. One final word. It was brought out at the hearing that Management had made a proposal to settle this case prior to Arbitration. This offer, however, was refused by the Union. In any event, an offer of compromise in the grievance procedure cannot prejudice the rights of the parties before the Board.

18. *Roll Hand Helper:* The Roll Hand Helper assists the Roll Hand in changing rolls and allied equipment on the 80″ Hot Strip Mill. Working under the direction of the Roll Hand, the Helper performs many of the same duties. The Helper, however, does not direct the crane in the removal of the rolls. That duty is performed by a Roll Hand.

19. Only the Company introduced related jobs at the hearing for the Board's guidance in reaching a decision on the classification of this job. Of these 19 related jobs, submitted for comparative purposes, one is in Job Class 4, nine are in Job Class 5, five are in Job Class 6, and four in Job Class 7. A Roll Builder Helper in the 10″ Bar Mill at Fairless Works is in Job Class 6—the same as the job in dispute.

20. The four jobs cited by the Company in Job Class 7 are distinguishable. Specimen 249 is for a Roll Hand who adjusts rolls during mill operation and who works around moving machinery. Specimen 458 is not a Helper job; it is a Mill Rigger job which directs Specimen 459—a Mill Rigger Helper in Job Class 5. Specimen 237 directs a Craneman in changing rolls and is not closely supervised. It also assists on the mill train in removing cobbles. And finally a Roll Builder Helper job at Edgar Thomson Works is coded identically with Specimen 237. Both of these jobs, according to the reason for classification of Factor 3—Mental Skill, are "not closely supervised."

21. After careful consideration of all the evidence, observations made upon a plant visit, and a comparison of similar jobs under each of the Factors, the Board concludes that the present classification of the Roll Hand Helper job in dispute is appropriate.

AWARD

22. The grievances are denied.

USC—567.   12. Vandergrift Plant of Irvin Works.   June 4, 1956

Herbert L. Sherman, Jr., *Arbitrator*

Approved by Sylvester Garrett, *Chairman*

FINDINGS

1. This grievance involves classification of the new job of Gas Plant Tender in the Maintenance Department at the Vandergrift Plant of the Irvin Works. At the hearing it was agreed that a stenographic report of the arbitration proceedings would be waived.

2. After installation of Job Class 11 for the job in dispute on May 5, 1955, and prior to the hearing, Management changed the job content of the job. A revised job description was then mutually approved by the parties. As the result of the change in duties, the Company raised the Job Class from 11 to 12. It also agreed that retroactive compensation would be paid to May 5, 1955. At this time a companion grievance, involving classification of the Gas Plant Tender Assistant Job, was settled on a mutually acceptable basis, and was withdrawn from arbitration.

3. Although the Union continues to press its claim, in the present case, for higher ratings on Factor 5—Responsibility for Materials (now coded at D .8) and Factor 12—Hazards (now coded at B .4), the Board finds that higher ratings are not warranted under the Classification Manual. On the basis of a comparison of Specimen Example jobs and also jobs with similar functions and job content in other plants of the Company, the present ratings on these Factors must be found to be appropriate.

AWARD

4. The grievance is denied.

Following is a table of all the other cases decided by the Board of Arbitration which involve disputes specifically over the coding of Factors 11 and 12. For each case the docket number is listed, notations are made as to whether Factor 11, Factor 12, or both, are in dispute, and the page in this volume where the case can be found is cited.

CHAPTER 19

ABSENCE OF OTHER COMPARABLE JOBS

It is possible that a job may be created which is so unique that there is no similar Specimen Example or non-Specimen Example job available for comparison. The few cases in this chapter show how these problems have been handled.

T—290. Ensley Steel Works. March 31, 1955
Herbert L. Sherman, Jr., *Arbitrator*
Approved by Sylvester Garrett, *Chairman*

BACKGROUND

1. This grievance, filed in the First Step on March 21, 1953, protests the job classification of the newly established job of Driller-Blaster in the Shops Department, Ensley Steel Works. Job Class 7 was installed unilaterally by the Company, effective February 22, 1953, agreement having been reached with the Union only on the job description. The job in dispute is not a full-time job. When not working on this job, grievant is usually paid as a Brickmason Helper at Job Class 3.

2. The primary function of the new job is to perform drilling and carbon dioxide blasting of slag accumulations, mostly at the Open Hearth so that the tractor shovel operator can remove the slag from the slag pockets. The source of supervision for the new job is the Foreman of the Brickmasons. Grievant directs and is assisted by Bricklayer Helpers or Laborers in the performance of his duties, including the knocking in of the bulkheads, the preparation of the drilling area and the setting up of the drill. The rotary drill weighs 275 pounds, the tripod 200 pounds. About 4 set-ups are made per turn. About 15 blasts are set off. Since the drill can only be set up to a height of five feet, scaffolding erected by Carpenters must be used when slag accumulations reach a greater height.

3. Grievant must drill holes in the slag so that the cardox shells may be inserted. He must check the hardness of the slag to determine how many holes and how many shells are needed, and how high the slag will be lifted. One to four shells are used. The proper locations must be selected, so that the "shots" will do the most good. The holes must also be carefully selected so that the raised slag will not pull the false wall in such a way as to shake up the main wall and the roof of the slag pocket. Since the false walls in the deeper parts of the pocket are thinner, having been burned out from the intense heat, even more judicious selection of locations for the holes is required. Heavy timbers or sheet iron must be placed on top of the charge in such an area in order to prevent damage to the furnace.

4. After removing the drill and other equipment to a safe place, grievant obtains his cardox shells, lead wire, blasting machine and galvonometer. A cardox shell is about four feet long and weighs eighteen pounds. It consists of a casing with carbon dioxide gas which is exploded by an electrical charge. The weights of the shells are checked on a scale. The shells are inserted in the holes and the wires are connected. Various tests must be made on the equipment to make sure that it is in good working order.

5. Grievant next blows the siren for three minutes to warn others of the impending blast, and stations his helpers in strategic places to warn anybody passing by. When the area is clear, he connects the lead wires to the blasting machine and pushes down the plunger to set off the blast.

6. After the blast he disconnects the lead wires from the blasting machine and salvages the used shells for recharging. If a shell has failed to "shoot," he removes the shell and "bleeds it off" by opening the gas valve. Removal of such a shell from the hole and decharging it are necessary because of the possibility that the heat from the slag could cause it to explode.

7. Management points out, however, that carbon dioxide blasting procedures are safer than dynamite blasting. While caps and dynamite may not be carried by the same employee at the same time at T.C.I., grievant could safely carry all of his blasting equipment in the same box. Also, the danger of an inadvertent explosion of a cardox shell is not as great as that with dynamite. Cardox shells may be handled in a rough manner.

8. While performing his duties, grievant is exposed to the noise from the drill, dust from the checkers, heat from the slag, and steam from the water poured in the holes.

DISCUSSION AND FINDINGS

9. There is no Specimen Example under the January 1, 1953 Classification Manual closely related to the job in dispute. Management has classified this job by reference to the Ensley job of Driller, whose primary function is to drill rock or concrete by use of a pneumatic or steam drill. Blasting, however, is not listed among the duties in the job description.

10. The Union challenges the proposed classification ratings on all twelve of the Factors for the Driller-Blaster job. It relies on a Dynamiter job at Homestead Steel Works, a Blaster job at National Works, and a Construction Repairman job at Ensley Works. It also points to a Specimen Example for a Blaster in Job Class 10 at the Oliver Ore Mines. Management notes, however, that different Benchmarks and a different Manual are used at the Oliver Ore Mines.

11. The Homestead job is distinguishable because it blasts with dynamite. The National Works job not only blasts with dynamite, but it also performs such duties in connection with a wide range of construction, rebuilding and repair work. And the Ensley Construction Repairman, in Job Class 12, is primarily a gang leader of 8 to 20

men on major construction or repair work. Only occasional blasting is performed by this job.

12. The Company further argues that Factors 7, 8 and 11 of the job in dispute are coded properly in view of the Board's holdings in a prior case concerning the classification of a Tractor Shovel Operator job. The latter job works under substantially the same surroundings in removing slag from slag pockets. The Board there assigned the same ratings to Factors 7, 8 and 11 as the Company now assigns to the job in dispute. It should be noted, however, that the Tractor Shovel Operator job is not responsible for direction of others like the new job, nor is it responsible for the safety of others in conducting blasting operations.

13. The following tables show the Company and Union positions with respect to the classification ratings for the job in dispute. In addition, these tables show the ratings on the jobs most closely related to the job in dispute. And finally, the last column lists the ratings which the Board concludes are most appropriate for the Driller-Blaster job at Ensley Works. These conclusions are based upon the evidence submitted to the Board, observations made upon a plant visit, the contentions of the parties, and a careful comparison and contrast of the duties of the job in dispute with the duties of the jobs listed in the tables of attached Appendix A. No useful purpose would be served by a twelve Factor discussion and analysis of the similarities and differences which exist between the Driller-Blaster job and the other jobs considered.

AWARD

14. The grievance is sustained. The Driller-Blaster job is properly classified at Job Class 10. Retroactive compensation shall date from February 22, 1953.

APPENDIX A

FACTOR	COMPANY CLASSI-FICATION	UNION CLASSI-FICATION	DRILLER AT ENSLEY (PLANT CODE) (811 290)	DYNAMITER AT HOMESTEAD (PLANT CODE) (2168)	BLASTER AT NATIONAL (PLANT CODE) (5837)	BOARD'S FINDINGS FOR JOB IN DISPUTE
1. Pre-Employment Training	A Base	B .3	A Base	B .3	C 1.0	B .3
2. Employment Training and Experience	B .4	D 1.2	A Base	C .8	F 2.0	C .8
3. Mental Skill	B 1.0	C 1.6	A Base	D 2.2	E 2.8	C 1.6
4. Manual Skill	B .5	C 1.0	B .5	B .5	B .5	B .5

FACTOR	COMPANY CLASSIFICATION	UNION CLASSIFICATION	DRILLER AT ENSLEY (PLANT CODE) (811 290)	DYNAMITER AT HOMESTEAD (PLANT CODE) (2168)	BLASTER AT NATIONAL (PLANT CODE) (5837)	BOARD'S FINDINGS FOR JOB IN DISPUTE
5. Responsibility for Materials	B .3	C .7	A Base	C .5	C 3.7	C .7
6. Responsibility for Tools and Equipment	B .2	C .7	B .2	D 1.5	B .2	B .2
7. Responsibility for Operation	B .5	C 1.0	A Base	C 1.0	C 1.0	C 1.0
8. Responsibility for Safety of Others	C .8	E 2.0	B .4	C .8	E 2.0	D 1.2
9. Mental Effort	B .5	C 1.0	B .5	C 1.0	D 1.5	C 1.0
10. Physical Effort	C .8	D 1.5	D 1.5	C .8	C .8	C .8
11. Surroundings	C .8	D 1.6	C .8	C .8	C .8	C .8
12. Hazards	C .8	E 2.0	B .4	E 2.0	E 2.0	D 1.2
Total	6.6	14.6	4.3	12.2	18.3	10.1
Job Class	7	15	4	12	18	10

T—239. Fairfield Steel Works. April 24, 1953
Sylvester Garrett, *Chairman*

BACKGROUND

1. The issue in this case is whether in reclassification of the job of Scrubber Operator in the Benzol Department of the Coke Plant at Fairfield Steel Works the rating under Factor 11—Surroundings—should have been C-.8, instead of B.4.

2. Late in 1950 the Company installed new automatic naphthalene flotation recovery equipment at the Coke Plant. Under Section 9-D of the April 22, 1947, Agreement, the Company developed a revised description and classification of Scrubber Operator to reflect the changes in the job which resulted from use of the new equipment. The old classification of the job was in Class 9; the classification proposed by the Company was 10.3, or Class 10.

3. There is no dispute as to the job description, or as to the proper rating under all of the Factors save 11. As to this the Union asserts that the proper coding should be C-.8 —"exposed to considerable wetness and fumes necessitating wearing of protective clothing." Prior to installation of the new equipment this factor was coded at B.4 based on the parties' mutual belief that the surroundings were properly described by the language in the Manual: "Inside and outside. Exposed to considerable fumes." The Company holds that the coding of B.4 must be retained since there has been no significant change in conditions affecting surroundings.

FINDINGS

4. There are no Benchmark or Specimen jobs which might fairly be considered as of more than general or remote significance in passing on the present case.

5. Prior to installation of the new flotation recovery equipment, water from the coolers flowed over a series of baffles on which the naphthalene collected, and the Scrubber Operator was required to go outside during his turn to rake the naphthalene off the baffles with a long wooden-handled rake. The naphthalene then went over into a pit where it was melted and then pumped to a storage tank by the Scrubber Operator. Formerly, the melting operation was performed once every 24 hours. The new naphthalene flotation recovery equipment includes a number of paddle wheels installed in flotation cells. These are operated electrically to skim the naphthalene from the surface of the water into flumes which lead into a similar pit where the naphthalene is melted. With the new automatic recovery equipment, the naphthalene is melted twice during a 24 hour period, once on the afternoon turn and once on the night turn.

6. Both before and after the change in equipment it was necessary for Scrubber Operators to spend a considerable portion of time outdoors. The Operator always went outside to check the scrubbers, oil tanks, pumps, and storage tanks. He always has been exposed to naphthalene fumes when

naphthalene was being melted. In fact, the record leaves no doubt that there has been no substantial change in the surroundings of the job merely as a result of the change in equipment, and method of recovering naphthalene. The over-all time outdoors, and exposure to fumes and wetness, is not significantly different today from what it was before the change.

7. One further word. The Union has emphasized that while the grievance was pending, Management agreed to issue a rainsuit (raincoat, rainhat, and boots) to each Scrubber Operator. This action did not result from a change in conditions or exposure to weather, but from a decision to provide bet-

ter protection from inclement weather that existed previously. For some years a single slicker was available for use by all of the men who were assigned to the job on the three shifts. Boots were added later. The General Superintendent in January, 1952, agreed to issue separate rainsuits because the men objected to everybody wearing the same protective clothing.

8. In view of the foregoing, the Board finds that B.4 is the proper coding under Factor 11 for the Scrubber Operator job.

AWARD

9. The grievance is denied.

USC—326.   Edgar Thomson Works.   April 30, 1953
Herbert L. Sherman, Jr., *Assistant to Chairman*
Approved by Sylvester Garrett, *Chairman*

BACKGROUND

1. This grievance involves the proper classification ratings on eight of the twelve factors for the newly created position of Vermin Exterminator at Edgar Thomson Works. Although the Job Description was mutually agreed upon in August, 1951, the classification values remained in dispute. Subsequently, Management unilaterally installed its proposed Job Class 4 for the position, effective September 2, 1951, in accordance with the provisions of Section 9-D-3 of the April 22, 1947 Agreement. The grievance was filed within 30 days, the Union contending for Job Class 9.

2. In February, 1949, a Sanitation seniority unit was created in the Plant Protection Department and all Janitors were transferred to this unit. Previously, each department had its own Janitors—all in Job Class 1—under the control of the department superintendent. Extermination duties performed by the Janitors were so infrequent that they were not even mentioned on the job descriptions. Only commercial preparations were used when extermination was required.

3. It was later determined that in the interest of efficiency and economy, all vermin extermination should be assigned to one individual, all Janitor supplies should be issued from Sanitation headquarters rather than being stocked at the Main Storeroom, and all cleaning of toilet facilities with organic cleaner should be delegated to one individual. These miscellaneous duties were, therefore, incorporated under the new job title of Vermin Exterminator.

4. The following tabulation indicates the positions of the parties as to the proper values for the twelve factors:

FACTOR	COMPANY POSITION	UNION POSITION
1	B-.3	B-.3
2	B-.4	C-.8
3	B-1.0	D-2.2
4	A-Base	B-.5
5	A-Base	C-.5
6	A-Base	C-Low-.4
7	A-Base	C-1.0
8	A-Base	B-.4
9	B-.5	B-.5
10	B-.3	B-.3
11	B-.4	C-.8
12	C-.8	C-.8
Total	3.7 (Job Class 4)	8.5 (Job Class 9)

DISCUSSION AND FINDINGS

5. There is no dispute on the classification values for Factors 1, 9, 10, and 12. The other eight Factors will be discussed in chronological order.

6. *Factor 2—Employment Training and Experience:* The occupant of the job should be sufficiently familiar with his duties to perform satisfactory work by the end of six months. Dispensing supplies to the Janitors is a relatively simple process; the records kept are not complicated. And although the Union argues that it takes longer than six months to become acquainted with all places where extermination is required, the evidence is clear that the general areas which must be treated are designated daily by supervisory personnel. Furthermore, the Vermin Exterminator does receive general instructions on methods of extermination and the type of

location where rats, mice, roaches, and silver-fish are likely to be found. Six months experience should be ample training for the incumbent to perform the duties of the job properly. B-.4 is therefore the appropriate rating for this Factor.

7. *Factor 3—Mental Skill:* The Union claims that D-2.2 is warranted for this Factor on the basis that considerable judgment is required in the preparation and application of poisons and in dispensing supplies to employees. The Company, asserting that the tasks involved are of a routine nature, believes that B-1.0 is proper.

However, the language which best describes the mental ability required to perform the primary duties of this job (preparation and application of various types of raticides and insecticides) is found under Code C-1.6—"Perform semi-routine job involving some variety of detail and requiring judgment." Although the disbursement of janitorial supplies is a rather routine duty, this task is only performed one day of the week. The major portion of the grievant's time is devoted to vermin extermination. In determining the precise method which should be followed to achieve results on any given job in such a large plant, judgment must be exercised. More than minor changes in routine are involved. The details will vary as to the exact location of the vermin, the type of bait to be used, the amount of bait needed, and the proper areas in which to place the poison. The occupant of the job must also be able to plan his work in such a way that it will not interfere with operations in occupied areas.

Nevertheless, the judgment required of the job cannot properly be characterized as "considerable." The degree of mental skill necessary to *prepare* the various poisons is not high. Commercial preparations, such as Dolge ant dust, mice seed, and rat biscuits, are used for the most part. Although the Vermin Exterminator must prepare his own mixture of roach powder, the ratio of Pyrethrum, Sodium Fluoride, and flour is fairly well standardized.

8. *Factor 4—Manual Skill:* No appreciable amount of dexterity is necessary for the adequate performance of the duties in question. Once the appropriate decisions have been made with respect to a particular extermination project, the physical skill required to carry them out is relatively insignificant. Manual handling of the sanitary supplies, cleaning of the urinals, making minor repairs to such articles as buckets, and changing the filters in air conditioning units likewise do not call for particular physical ability. Thus, this Factor is properly coded at A-Base.

9. *Factor 5—Responsibility for Materials:* A-Base is the proper rating for this Factor. The poisons and cleaners employed are difficult to damage and have a very low value. The same is true of the supplies handed out to the Janitors once a week, such as paper towels, soap, and toilet paper.

10. *Factor 6—Responsibility for Tools and Equipment:* The tools used by the Vermin Exterminator are largely simple hand tools. Damage to wrenches, hammers, and a respirator is not likely. The Union's position that moderate attention must be exercised to prevent damage to toilet facilities from use of organic acid cannot be sustained since the toilets are made of porcelain which is not harmed by the use of organic acid in the cleaner. A-Base is therefore the appropriate rating for this Factor.

11. *Factor 7—Responsibility for Operations:* Although the Vermin Exterminator in a sense operates his own individual unit in exterminating rodents, etc., he is neither required to maintain a particular pace to assure continuity of production nor to direct the work of others. He is under the direction of the Sanitary Supervisor and has little responsibility beyond use of his own time. This Factor is properly coded at A-Base.

12. *Factor 8—Responsibility for Safety of Others:* According to the Company, this Factor should be coded at A-Base since the materials with which the Vermin Exterminator works are not injurious if used properly. The Union denies that grievant works only in areas where others are seldom exposed and argues that a rating of B-.4 for this Factor is proper.

In any event it is clear that in cleaning the toilet facilities with organic acid the Vermin Exterminator must exercise caution lest he carelessly spill some where employees are likely to come in contact with it. Otherwise, burns and irritations could result to the employees using the lavatory facilities. Grievant himself is provided with goggles and rubber gloves to clean the toilet facilities with organic acid—a task for which he is given the sole responsibility. On one occasion he ruined his clothing when he carelessly splashed some acid on himself.

When engaged in application of the roach powder by means of a hand type bulb duster, the Exterminator tries to avoid places where employees keep their lunches. He often warns the supervisor of the area to caution the employees to remain clear of the places dusted. There have been occasions when employees have been requested to remove their belongings from lockers so that the bases of the lockers could be dusted with the poison without danger of creating unhealthful conditions. Shower rooms have been treated similarly to eliminate roaches and waterbugs.

On the whole, it appears that B-.4 is the more appropriate rating for this Factor, requiring ordinary care and attention to prevent injury to others who are occasionally exposed to possible hazards which may be created by the negligence of the Vermin Exterminator.

13. *Factor 11—Surroundings:* Although the incumbent of the job in question is exposed to some wetness, acid, and dust, it is not so substantial as to warrant a C-.8 coding. Despite the fact that care must be exercised when cleaning the lavatory facilities with organic acid, such facilities are cleaned in this manner but once a month. This is the only occasion when protective devices (goggles and gloves) are actually used by the incumbent. The language under B-.4 best describes the over-all working conditions of this job.

14. The sum of the proper numerical classifications for the Factors in dispute plus the ratings on the four Factors not in dispute total up to 4.7. The job of Vermin Exterminator is therefore classified at Job Class 5, retroactive to September 2, 1951— the date when the disputed classification was put into effect.

AWARD

15. The grievance is sustained to the extent that the new job of Vermin Exterminator is classified at Job Class 5, effective September 2, 1951.

A—557. New Haven Works. April 29, 1953
Sylvester Garrett, *Chairman*

BACKGROUND

1. This grievance involves classification of a new job of Floor Sweeper Operator, installed at the New Haven Works in April, 1951, at Job Class 5. Although the parties have agreed upon the job description, the Union disputes the Company's ratings on classification factors 1, 2, 3, and 9.

2. The new Floor Sweeper consists of a power driven mobile vacuum sweeper which weighs less than 1000 pounds and has a six-horse power gasoline motor. It has a two-way pedal type clutch, steering wheel, accelerator, brake, levers that control the rotary brush, and a vacuum which sucks up the dirt and dust. Its maximum speed is six miles per hour, controlled by a governor.

3. According to the Union, the Floor Sweeper Operator should be compared favorably with a Tractor Operator as to the factors in dispute which would raise the present classification to Job Class 6. Thirty-two Tractor Operator jobs, classified in Class 8 or 9, were listed by the Union. The Company contends that the duties of the job only warrant a total of 4.6 points, or Job Class 5. It relies in part on classifications of Floor Sweeper Operator jobs at the Cyclone and Cuyahoga Works which are identical with the job in dispute and are in Class 5.

4. The Company views this new equipment as a vacuum cleaner with an attachment for driving it, doing the work formerly performed by Laborers in sweeping-up.

5. The evidence and contentions with respect to the particular factors in dispute are as follows:

6. *Factor 1. Pre-Employment Training.*

Company: A-Base   Union: B-.3

The Union argues that the Floor Sweeper Operator operates "powered mobile equipment servicing a number of units" and performs a variety of tasks to the same extent as a Tractor Operator normally does. The language of the manual upon which the Company relies is "operate powered mobile equipment performing simple tasks where little judgment is required." It was testified that the Sweeper only operates his machine in the aisles, the other areas being swept by hand.

7. *Factor 2. Employment Training and Experience.*

Company: A-Base   Union: B-.4

The Union asserts that the same amount of experience is required of a Floor Sweeper Operator as that required of a Tractor Operator. A Union witness testified that a Floor Sweeper Operator with seniority may bump a Tractor Operator. A Company witness noted that a Tractor Operator must know where particular equipment is located, what load is safe, and how to raise and lower loads. The Sweeper performs only the function of picking up dirt into a container which need only be emptied when full.

8. *Factor 3. Mental Skill.*

Company: B-1.0   Union: C-1.6

The Union contends that there is no proper language under Code B which describes the duties of the job in dispute. According to Union testimony the Operator must use judgment in determining which aisles to clean at a given time depending upon traffic congestion, the number of times he goes through a department in a day, and the route he will follow. Also he must follow the lines of the aisles.

The Company witness distinguished the Tractor Operator's job in that the Tractor Operator must maneuver into position with materials carried on his equipment, not confining himself to the aisles; the equipment and loads of the Tractor Operator average 5 to 20 thousand pounds; the Tractors oft-times damage walls in minor collisions whereas the Sweepers do not; and the Tractor Operator must consider whether his load is safe and he must follow some sort of schedule.

9. *Factor 9. Mental Effort.*

Company: B-.5 Union: C-1.0

The Union refers to that language under Code C which reads as follows: "Operates cranes and tractors in congested areas . . ." The Company witness testified that the Tractor Operator does not follow the same pattern, his routine varies. But the Sweeper follows the aisles and goes over the same spots every day. Also the speed of the Sweeper is slower; it has a one-cylinder motor.

10. The Union also relied heavily on the fact that in one instance a Tractor Operator walks beside his Tractor, which runs about three miles per hour and pulls a buggy. This Tractor is operated by handle and weighs less than one thousand pounds. Therefore, the Union urges that the Floor Sweeper Operator should be given the same ratings on the factors in dispute as the Operator of this walk-type Tractor.

DISCUSSION AND FINDINGS

11. The Tractor Operators in Job Class 8 or 9 relied on by the Union as a basis for comparison with the Floor Sweeper Operator usually transport material from one place to another. They pull, push or lift materials. The equipment is usually heavier than the Floor Sweeper. A Tractor ordinarily operates at a higher speed. Judgment is required in the positioning of materials. For these and related reasons, the jobs of Tractor Operator and Floor Sweeper Operator cannot be equated so as to warrant the same ratings on the factors in dispute.

12. Although the walk-type Tractor is a simple piece of equipment, which would seem to be reasonably comparable to the Floor Sweeper, no new job description was prepared for the Operator of this Tractor when this walk-type equipment was added about 1950 or 1951. The job description and classification for this Tractor Operator were agreed upon long before this walk-type Tractor was put into operation. Under the original and unchanged description, he continues to operate an electric battery-type Tractor about ten percent of the time.

13. Under all the evidence, a comparison with Tractor Operator jobs does not justify a higher level than is presently ascribed to the four disputed factors in the Floor Sweeper Operator job.

AWARD

14. The grievance is denied.

USC—270. Youngstown District Works. May 21, 1953

Herbert L. Sherman, Jr., *Assistant Chairman*
Approved by Sylvester Garrett, *Chairman*

BACKGROUND

1. The issue in this grievance is the proper classification for the newly created job of Roll Assembly Man on #10-10" Shape Mill at McDonald Works, Youngstown District. Grievants protest Job Class 11 assigned by Management and request that the job be placed in Class 14.

2. Sometime in 1950 Management decided to discontinue the jobs of Roll Builder and Guide Setter on #10-10" Shape Mill, both in Job Class 9. This was accomplished upon the simultaneous establishment of the new position of Roll Assembly Man, effective September 17, 1950. Although the parties have agreed upon the job description, the ratings on Factors 2, 5, 6, 7 and 8 remain in dispute.

3. Under the new arrangement, two men per turn (four turns) were assigned to the Roll Assembly Man position instead of one per turn (four turns) assigned as Roll Builder and one man on day turn only as Guide Setter. This resulted in eight men working as Roll Assembly Man as compared with five men working as Roll Builders and Guide Setter. (Helpers were often assigned, however, to the Roll Builder.) A few new duties were added to those previously performed on the Roll Builder and Guide Setter jobs.

4. According to the Union the Roll Assembly Man on #10-10" Shape Mill should be classified with the same point values as those assigned to the Guide Setter on #7-12" Hoop Mill, the Guide Setter on #12-12" Strip Mill, and the Guide Setter on the

#17-10″ Bar Mill, each with a total point value of 13.6. Seven of the twelve factors in the Roll Assembly Man classification have been coded by the Company the same as those for the three Guide Setter jobs. The Union believes that the other five factors should likewise be coded the same as for the Guide Setter jobs.

5. The Company, asserting that most of the duties now performed by the Roll Assembly Man were previously performed on the two abandoned jobs, relies primarily on the classifications for these two jobs and also, for certain factors, Specimen Example No. 1728 which classifies a Roll Assembly Man at Job Class 8.

6. The following tabulation presents the positions of the parties with respect to the factors in dispute.

FACTOR	COMPANY POSITION	UNION POSITION
2. Employment Training and Experience	D-1.2	E-1.6
5. Responsibility for Materials	C- .7	D-1.1
6. Responsibility for Tools and Equipment	Low C- .4	Hi C-1.0
7. Responsibility for Operations	D-2.0	E-3.0
8. Responsibility for Safety of Others	B- .4	C- .8

DISCUSSION AND FINDINGS

7. At the outset it should be noted that none of the jobs relied on by the parties, although presenting important bases for comparison, can be considered as controlling the ratings on all factors in the instant case. An important difference between the three Guide Setter jobs and the Roll Assembly Man position exists in the fact that the Guide Setters are an integral part of the operating crews on their respective mills and are responsible for specific phases of the operations. For example, such a Guide Setter adjusts the guides and changes the rolls "on the line." They are engaged in production operations while the work of the Roll Assembly Man is essentially of a preparatory nature. He changes rolls, rebuilds roll housings, makes final adjustments to guides, before the Mill is put into operation, keeps guides properly stored, orders replacements, and keeps records of guides and rolls. His work station is off to the side of the operating crew.

8. On the other hand, Specimen Example

No. 1728 clearly contemplates the performance of more limited duties (as has been recognized by the Company) than those set forth in the job description for the job in dispute. The same is true of the abandoned jobs of Roll Builder and Guide Setter on #10-10″ Shape Mill.

9. For both the Roll Builder and Guide Setter jobs, Factor 2 was rated at D-1.2. Not only must the Roll Assembly Man perform the duties of these two former jobs but his job description also requires him to set the guides in the housing, finish grind the guides, and make final adjustments in accordance with blueprints to the rolls and guides before the first trial bar is sent through. It is agreed that it is easier to set and adjust the guides on the three Mills relied on by the Union than on #10 Mill. The new job description also indicates more responsibility for decision making than was true under the previous jobs. Just as the Company has recognized the increased amount of mental skill over the abandoned jobs on #10 Mill in its proposed rating of Factor 3, the Board likewise concludes that additional training is now required which justifies a coding of E-1.6 for Factor 2.

10. As to Factor 5, the parties are not in dispute with respect to "probably monetary loss" but only with regard to the amount of care required, the Union contending for Code D-1.1 and the Company pointing to Code C-.7. Stress is placed by the Company on Specimen No. 1728 which gives this Factor a rating of C-.7. It is clear, however, that although "Materials" are essentially the same for both Specimen No. 1728 and the job in question, the duties performed by the incumbents with respect to the "Materials" are not the same. This has been recognized in the coding of other Factors and is confirmed by a comparison of the two job descriptions. The duties of the job in dispute are more comprehensive, requiring attention for greater part of the turn. Factor 5 for the Roll Assembly Man job, on the whole, is more properly rated at D-1.1.

11. No question is raised under Factor 6 as to the degree of attention and care required for tools and equipment. Both parties assert that Code C is applicable. In view of the agreed upon listing under Tools and Equipment in the job description, i.e., calipers, rule, flashlight, grinders, templates, cables, chains, wrenches, sledges, file, hammer, and inventory records, it cannot properly be held that "Cost of damage" is other than "Low." It should be noted that rolls, guides, etc. are not equipment but materials for purposes of this job.

12. On Factor 7, the Roll Builder and Guide Setter jobs were rated at C-1.0. The

Company has classified this Factor for the new job at D-2.0. Since the Finisher, Strander, and Strander (Planisher) on #10-10″ Shape Mill are given D-2.0 for Responsibility for Operations, it would be inappropriate to grant a higher rating for the crew which is not directly in the producing line and where a superior degree of responsibility cannot be demonstrated.

13.　Factor 8—Responsibility for Safety of Others has been rated by the Company at B-.4. The former Guide Setter on #10 Mill was given A Base and the Roll Builder B-.4. Union witnesses emphasized the crane hooking involved in the new job, but this duty is one that is normally performed by a Roll Builder. Specimen Examples 420 and 1296 for Roll Builders rate this Factor at B-.4, a coding which must be deemed to be proper also for the job in dispute.

14.　Since the Board concludes that Factors 2 and 5 should be coded at E-1.6 and D-1.1 respectively, the present total point value of 10.8 is thereby increased to 11.6 for Job Class 12. Grievants are accordingly entitled to retroactive compensation to the date of installation of the new job.

AWARD

15.　The grievance is sustained to the extent that the new job of Roll Assembly Man is classified at Job Class 12, effective September 17, 1950.

CHAPTER 20

TRADE OR CRAFT AND ASSIGNED MAINTENANCE JOBS

Special problems exist in connection with trade or craft and assigned maintenance jobs. The January 1, 1953 Job Description and Classification Manual recognizes special rules for these jobs, as distinguished from production jobs.

For each trade or craft job there are three applicable standard hourly wage rates—a standard rate, an intermediate rate and a starting rate. Section A in this chapter presents cases dealing with the problem as to which of these rates an incumbent of a trade or craft job should receive. The last two cases in this section consider the related question of whether incumbents of a given job are entitled to any rate of a trade or craft job, as distinguished from the rate of pay for some other job such as a Helper or an assigned maintenance position. Section B then goes on to present cases involving claims that certain employees should have been slotted into higher ranking assigned maintenance jobs. And finally, in Section C of this chapter, several cases dealing with assignment of duties among trade or craft and assigned maintenance jobs are set forth.

Other cases involving particular trade or craft and assigned maintenance jobs may be found by consulting the Index of Disputes by Job Titles.

SECTION A. SLOTTING AND ADVANCEMENT IN TRADE OR CRAFT JOBS

A—249. Duluth Works. July 8, 1949.
Ralph T. Seward, *Chairman*

BACKGROUND FACTS

1. The six grievants whose cases have been combined in the present proceeding are all employed as Journeymen Machinists in the Wire Mill Machine Shop at the Company's Duluth Works. Subsequent to January 4, 1944, but prior to February 9, 1947, they had each been classified as an "A," or top rated Machinist. On the latter date, when the new schedule of trade or craft rates was made effective pursuant to the Agreement of January 13, 1947, they were assigned to the starting rate. In their grievances, they contend that they should have been assigned to the standard rate.

2. It appears that the reason the Company assigned these employees to the starting rate is the fact that they were unable to operate vertical or horizontal boring mills. It further appears that there are no vertical or horizontal boring mills in the Wire Mill Machine Shop and that the grievants do not need to know how to operate such machines in order to complete satisfactorily the work required of them in that Shop. Three vertical and three horizontal boring mills are in use in the General Machine Shop at the Duluth Works, however, and substantially all of the Machinists in that Shop are assigned to work on them from time to time.

3. The contractual rules governing the classification of trade or craft jobs and the assignment of Journeymen to the starting, intermediate or standard rates for such jobs are set forth in Section 1 of the Agreement of April 15, 1946. Insofar as is here applicable, that Section provides that:

"(a) The term 'trade or craft jobs' shall be understood to mean the following journeyman jobs:

. . . .
(9) Machinist
. . . .

"(b) Such of the foregoing trade or craft jobs as are **required in each plant** shall be described and classified in accordance with procedures of the October 23, 1945 Intra-Plant Wage Rate Inequities Agreement. These descriptions shall reflect the scope of duties which a fully qualified journeyman may be called upon to perform in **the plant,** and the classifications shall reflect the job's requirements as to training, skill, responsibility, effort and working conditions.

"(c) For each job classification thus developed for a trade or craft job there shall be established three hourly wage rates, such rates to include: (1) a 'standard rate' equal to the plant standard hourly wage scale rate for the respective job class of the job; (2) an 'intermediate rate' at a level two job classes below the 'standard rate'; and (3) a 'starting rate' at a level four job classes below the 'standard rate.'

"(d) With exception of trade or craft journeymen who prior to January 4, 1944 were paid at or above the highest prevailing journeyman rate of the respective trade or craft, each employee in the plant regularly performing the described work of a journeyman in a given trade or craft and each employee subsequently hired as a journeyman shall be assigned either to the established starting rate, intermediate rate or standard rate classification of the respective trade or craft, which assignment shall be on the basis of each individual employee's qualifications and ability in relation to requirements of the job under consideration. Trade or craft journeymen who prior to January 4, 1944 were paid at or above the highest prevailing journeyman rate of the respective trade or craft in the plant shall be assigned to the established standard rate classification of the respective trade or craft.

". . . . .

"(j) The determination of employee qualifications and ability shall be made by management, subject to review in the grievance procedure of the March 13, 1945 Agreement of any right either party may have under the March 13, 1945 Agreement as amended from time to time." (Boldface supplied.)

4. The Company maintains that its action with respect to the grievants has been in full compliance with these contractual provisions. Referring to Section 1(b) above, it notes that vertical and horizontal boring are among the "duties" which a fully qualified journeyman must perform "in the plant"; i.e., at the Duluth Works. Under Section 1(d), it had the task of assigning the grievants to the starting, intermediate or standard rate on the basis of their "qualifications and ability in relation to requirements of the job under consideration." The "duties" referred to in Section 1(b), taken together, comprise the "job under consideration" referred to in Section 1(d).

5. Under the April 15, 1946 Agreement, then, the grievants' "job requirements" include not only their normal assignments in the Wire Mill Machine Shop but also such duties as are expected of fully qualified Machinists in the General Machine Shop and elsewhere in the Duluth Works. As they are

unable to perform two of such basic duties, the Company concludes, they are not entitled to the standard rate.

6. The Union denies that it was ever the parties' intention, in negotiating the April 15, 1946 Agreement, that the qualifications and ability of journeymen should be judged upon the basis of work which they are not normally required to perform. The "requirements of the job under consideration," in relation to which the ability of these grievants was to be judged, were the requirements of their work in the Wire Mill Machine Shop. For years Management had considered them fully qualified to perform this work and in consequence had paid them the "A" rate. To lower them from the top rate because they cannot operate machines which have never even existed in their shop, the Union holds, is to misapprehend the intention of the parties, misapply the April 15, 1946 Agreement, and create rather than remove inequities.

FINDINGS

7. The classification of trade and craftsmen presents a number of problems which do not arise in classifying the ordinary types of position rated jobs. The latter tend to be stable in location, function and content; by observing what an employee is required to do on one day, one can be reasonably sure what he will be doing on other days; the objective, moreover, is clearly to classify the job and not the man. As the parties recognized in Section 1 of the April 15, 1946 Agreement, however, the requirements of trade and craft jobs may vary widely from day to day, from task to task and from location to location. Journeymen in the trades and crafts have traditionally been expected to possess a wide range of special skills upon which Management may call for the performance of any work in which such skill is required. Their "job" cannot fairly be classified upon the basis of their actual assignments on any day or series of days; one must consider also the nature and scope of their potential assignments. In a real sense, Management is paying them not only for their work but for their skill; the assignment of a standard rate Machinist for several days to a simple lathe operation, for example, would not affect his rate, because he is being paid for his readiness and ability to perform complicated operations on many other types of machine tools if such should be assigned to him.

8. The parties have recognized, therefore, that in dealing with the trades and crafts under the Inequity Program they must classify not only the job but the man upon the basis of his skill. For each trade and craft job, they have established three rates—stand-

ard, intermediate and starting—and have provided in Section 1(d) for the assignment of trade and craft employees into one or the other of these rates upon the basis of "each individual employee's qualifications and ability in relation to requirements of the job under consideration."

9. What, however, did the parties mean by "the job under consideration"? Conceding that the "requirements" of the job include potential as well as actual assignments, with respect to what unit of the Company's operations are we to determine what assignments are potential? Were the parties concerned with the potential assignments of the individual himself? With those of the craftsmen in his department? In his mill? In the entire plant? Or throughout all the plants of the Company? This is the central question in this case.

10. It is clear that no matter which of these various alternatives the parties chose, the results might seem equitable from one point of view and inequitable from another. To the extent that they narrowed the unit and gave primary weight to a journeyman's ability to perform the work to which he is normally assigned—work which is frequently specialized and which may sometimes be limited to a simple type of operation—they might appear to be unjust to employees of broader skill and a more complete knowledge of their craft. To the extent that they widened the unit and placed their main emphasis upon an employee's full mastery of his trade, they might appear to be penalizing employees in specialized jobs or departments who had little opportunity to develop or retain broad skill.

11. It is not for us to tell the parties how we think they should have resolved this dilemma. Our only proper concern is with the way in which they did resolve it in the Agreement of April 15, 1946. We find from a reading of that Agreement that the parties adopted the **plant** as the unit in which the "requirements of the job under consideration" are to be determined. Section 1(b) requires the description and classification of trade or craft **jobs** and provides that the descriptions "shall reflect the scope of duties which a fully qualified journeyman may be called upon to perform **in the plant."** The so-called "grandfather clause" in the same sub-section provides for the assignment to the standard rate of journeymen who, prior to January 4, 1944, were paid at or above the highest prevailing rate of the trade or craft **"in the plant."** Section 1, in its entirety, is to be distinguished from Section 2, which deals with Assigned Maintenance Jobs, in that this latter section expressly adopts "the assigned area" as the basic unit in which to measure job content. The absence of such restrictive language in Section 1 underscores the parties' agreement that the content of trade and craft jobs is to be determined with reference to the entire plant.

12. The "plant" in this case is the Duluth Works. It is clear from the evidence that work requiring both vertical and horizontal boring is regularly performed in the General Machine Shop at this Works. The operation of vertical and horizontal boring mills, thus, is a part of the "duties which a fully qualified journeyman may be called upon to perform" in that plant. The grievants are admittedly unable to perform this operation. Judged upon the basis of their "qualifications and ability in relation to requirements of the job under consideration," they clearly are not entitled to the standard rate.

AWARD

13. The grievances are denied.

A—250. Duluth Works. July 11, 1949

Ralph T. Seward, *Chairman*

BACKGROUND FACTS

1. These grievances are brought by four employees in the General Machine Shop of the Company's Duluth Works. Prior to February 9, 1947, Grievant Bianco had been rated as an "A," or top rate, Machinist while Grievants Martin, Lundgren and Galleberg had been rated as "B" Machinists. On the latter date, pursuant to the Agreement of January 13, 1947, the old rates and classifications for trade and craft jobs were superseded by new rates and classifications. The grievants were each assigned to the starting rate. In these grievances they contend that they should have been assigned to the intermediate rate.

2. The basis upon which the grievants were assigned to the newly established "starting" rate for the Machinist classification may be summarized as follows. In the absence of any agreement between the Company and the Union as to the guideposts or standards which should be used in slotting trade and craft employees into the starting, intermediate and standard rate classifications, the Company adopted and applied its own criteria. Under the system which it developed, each trade and craft job was broken

down into a series of "factors of ability," each "factor" representing a task or type of operation which a fully qualified journeyman should be able to perform. The "factors of ability" for the Machinist classification are: 1) lathe work; 2) milling; 3) vertical boring; 4) horizontal boring; 5) shaping; 6) planing; 7) radial drill press work; 8) bench, floor and field work; and 9) layout work.

3. Each of these factors was further analyzed and broken down into the individual elements of skill involved (e.g. "set up," "select, sharpen and obtain proper contours on cutting tools," "adjust cutting tools and operate machine tools at an efficient rate," etc.) and the principle adopted that in order to be considered "fully skilled" in any basic factor an employee must be able to perform satisfactorily all of the elements applicable to that factor.

4. In addition to the "factors of ability," the Company listed the general "trade knowledge" required of all trade and craft journeymen (i.e. shop calculations, blueprint reading and special "trade information").

5. In slotting trade and craft journeymen, the Company applied these criteria according to the following formula:

"STANDARD RATE CLASSIFICATION
—Full skill in all of the basic factors of ability and full skill in knowledge requirements.

"INTERMEDIATE RATE CLASSIFICATION—Full skill in all but one of the basic factors of ability and full skill in all knowledge requirements.

"STARTING RATE CLASSIFICATION
—Full skill in all but two of the basic factors of ability and full skill in all of the knowledge requirements."

6. The Company had originally proposed to the Union that the skill of each journeyman in the various "factors of ability" should be measured by a series of tests. The parties decided, however, that it would be more practical to have the employees rated, in the first instance, by their foreman and supervisors. Thereafter, if disputes arose over the rating of any individuals, performance tests might be provided.

7. The four grievants, when rated by their supervisors, were each judged to be deficient in more than one of the "factors of ability" and in one or more of the "Trade Knowledge Requirements." Grievant Martin was held to be less than fully skilled in Vertical Boring, Horizontal Boring, and Layout Work; Grievant Bianco, in Lathe Work, Milling and Vertical Boring; Grievant Lundgren in Milling, Bench, Floor and Field

Work and Layout Work; Grievant Galleberg in Milling and Layout Work. All four were considered deficient in their knowledge of shop calculations and all but Bianco, in "Trade Informaton." They were therefore assigned to the starting rate.

8. When the present grievances were filed protesting these assignments, the Foreman, in his 1st Step answer offered to each grievant an opportunity to demonstrate his ability through a series of performance tests. The employees declined this offer, and in the later stages of the grievance machinery the Union took the position that in view of the past experience of the grievants and their previous ratings as "A" or "B" Machinists it did not see why a fresh test was necessary.

9. Before the Board the Union amplified its stand by contending, in substance, that the fact that the Company for many years had rated the grievants in the highest or next to the highest Machinist rate classifications was in itself a conclusive demonstration of their ability. It pointed out that it had never agreed to the standards and formula devised by the Company for the slotting of trade and craft journeymen, and stated that neither those standards nor the Company's unilateral judgment of an employee's ability, was binding upon it.

10. The Company, in reply, notes that Section 1(j) of the April 15, 1946 Agreement provides that:

"The determination of employee qualifications and ability shall be made by management, subject to review in the grievance procedure of the March 13, 1945 Agreement of any right either party may have under the March 13, 1945 Agreement as amended from time to time."

Under this language, it claims, the guideposts established by the Company for the classification of journeymen may not be questioned in the grievance procedure. The only question which these grievants may properly present to the Board, in the Company's opinion, is whether or not these standards have been properly and fairly applied to them.

11. On the latter point, the Company asserts that its Machine Shop Supervision has applied its standards uniformly to all employees according to the supervisor's best judgment of their individual ability. It acknowledges the possibility that here and there the supervisors may have erred, but points out that where errors were suspected, the affected employees were offered an opportunity to demonstrate their ability through performance tests. In view of the fact that these grievants have declined to take advantage of this opportunity, the Company says,

the foreman's judgment remains as the sole basis for determining their ability. No evidence before the Board casts doubt upon the accuracy or fairness of the foreman's rating of these grievants. In the opinion of the Company, therefore, the grievance should be denied.

FINDINGS

12. At the outset we must reject the Union's contention that the fact that these grievants had been classified as "A" or "B" Machinists prior to February 9, 1947, was in itself enough to entitle them at least to the intermediate rate. This contention is nothing more nor less than an attempt to read another "grandfather clause" into Section 1(d) of the April 15, 1946 Agreement. That Section provides:

"With exception of trade or craft journeymen who prior to January 4, 1944 were paid at or above the highest prevailing journeyman rate of the respective trade or craft, each employee in the plant regularly performing the described work of a journeyman in a given trade or craft and each employee subsequently hired as a journeyman shall be assigned either to the established starting rate, intermediate rate or standard rate classification of the respective trade or craft, which assignment shall be on the basis of each individual employee's qualifications and ability in relation to requirements of the job under consideration. Trade or craft journeymen who prior to January 4, 1944 were paid at or above the highest prevailing journeymen rate of the respective trade or craft in the plant shall be assigned to the established standard rate classification of the respective trade or craft."

13. It is clear that under this language the only employees who are entitled to be classified upon the basis of their prior rating and regardless of their present ability are "trade or craft journeymen who prior to January 4, 1944 were paid at or above the highest prevailing journeyman rate of the respective trade or craft in the plant." All other journeymen must be classified "on the basis of each individual employee's qualifications and ability in relation to requirements of the job under consideration." None of the grievants was paid the "A" rate prior to January 4, 1944. Their rating prior to the reclassification of February 9, 1947, therefore, is immaterial, and they are entitled only to be fairly classified on the basis of their "qualifications and ability."

14. On the other hand, we cannot accept the Company's contention that the guideposts and criteria for the slotting of trade and craft journeymen which it has unilaterally established are sacrosanct and not subject to challenge before this Board. The statement in Section 9-K-2 of the April 22, 1947 Agreement that the parties, *"through the Joint Wage Rate Inequity Negotiating Committee* will complete the program of the May 8, 1946 Agreement . . . including the tasks of developing . . . the guideposts for assigning trade and craft journeymen to the respective starting, intermediate, or standard rates,"* is a clear indication of the parties' belief that the official and binding yardsticks should be established by agreement and not by the unilateral action of either side. No indication to the contrary is contained in any of the earlier inequity agreements. Section 1 (j) of the April 15, 1946 Agreement (quoted above) upon which the Company relies, merely means that as a matter of practical procedure Management must take the initiative in slotting journeymen, subject to the review of its actions in the grievance procedure. In carrying out its obligations under this provision, the Company had every right to develop a set of uniform criteria for the guidance of its supervision; indeed, had it not done so, the program might well have created more confusion and inequity than it removed. But this does not mean that its criteria are beyond criticism or challenge, or are binding upon this Board.

15. The only standards which this Board can properly accept as controlling are those laid down in the agreements over which we have jurisdiction. The system of guideposts —of "ability factors," "elements of skill," etc.—which the Company has developed for the classification of its journeymen Machinists has not been incorporated in these agreements either directly or by reference. Whatever may be its virtues or its faults, we cannot ourselves be bound by it.

16. Neither, on the other hand, may we properly establish our own standards or guideposts. We cannot perform for the parties a function which they have expressly reserved for themselves. We cannot make the parties' agreements for them; no more can we give binding effect to the assertions of either side as to what such an agreement ought to provide.

17. How, then, can we rule on the instant case? Management, upon the basis of its own standards and the judgment of its supervisors, has determined that—"on the basis of each employee's qualifications and ability in relation to requirements of the job under consideration"—these grievants should be assigned to the starting Machinist rate. The grievants, supported by the Union,

claim that they deserve assignment to the intermediate rate. How can we uphold either Management or the grievants without establishing and applying our own system of standards, in excess of our jurisdiction and in defiance of the parties' injunction that the Board shall not "add to, detract from, or alter in any way" the provisions of the Agreement?

18. We believe that the answer lies in the provisions of Section 2-B of the existing basic Agreement, at least insofar as concerns the period subsequent to its execution. The methods used by Management in classifying the journeymen in a given plant clearly constituted a "detailed application of the subject matter" of the wage provisions of that Agreement and of the provisions of the Wage Inequity Agreements which were incorporated by reference in Section 9-B-4. *As applied in practice,* therefore, the rules of classification used by the Company in slotting journeymen at the Duluth Works constitute a "local working condition" in effect at the Duluth Works. Under Section 2-B-3, employees are entitled to have the same criteria standards and testing methods applied to them that were applied to other employees.

19. In ruling upon these grievances, then, we must be guided not by the system of standards as it appears on paper in the Company's manual but by the manner in which that system was in fact applied at Duluth. We must examine not only the bases upon which the grievants were classified, but also the bases upon which other employees were classified who in fact were assigned to the intermediate rate. If our examination reveals that the grievants were rated in the same manner and according to the same criteria as other employees, similarly situated, their complaint must be held to be without

merit. If, on the other hand, they were the victims of special discriminatory treatment they are clearly entitled to redress—to the benefits of the same "local working condition" which other employees enjoyed.

20. We have therefore requested and received from the parties evidence upon this point. Our examination of the evidence regarding the classification of the five employees who in fact were assigned to the intermediate rate reveals nothing on which we could base a finding of discrimination or special treatment. So far as we can judge from the records and comments of the parties, the Machine Shop supervision applied to these five employees the same standards which were applied to the grievants. In the opinion of supervision, the successful five measured up to those standards; the grievants did not. It is true that the Union, on the basis of the information supplied to it by other employees in the Machine Shop, states that certain of the five had never been seen to operate one or two of the machines on which supervision rated them as proficient. This statement, in itself, however, would not support a finding that these employees were in fact not capable of operating these machines or that supervision had applied its standards less rigidly to them than to the grievants. And apart from these few statements, no evidence has been presented which might throw doubt on the fairness with which Machine Shop supervision has rated these employees.

21. We hold, accordingly, that the grievants have failed to show that they were entitled to be classified as Intermediate Rate Machinists and that the grievances must be denied.

AWARD

22. The grievances are denied.

A—252. Duluth Works.   July 8, 1949
Ralph T. Seward, *Chairman*

BACKGROUND FACTS

1. Pursuant to the Wage Inequity reclassification of February 9, 1947, the six grievants in this case were assigned to the starting rate of the Welder classification. When they protested this assignment, they were given a "performance assignment" as a test of their abilities. The test consisted of welding together two pieces of six-inch extra-heavy pipe by the electric arc method and two other pieces of the same size by the gas torch method.

2. All of the grievants passed the electric arc test. All failed the gas torch assignment.

3. In the instant grievance the employees claim that the test was unfair and improper. They also claimed before the Board that their original assignment was erroneous and that they should have been assigned to the standard rate.

FINDINGS

4. The latter claim is based on the fact that acetylene welding is not part of the work normally performed by these grievants and that they should have been judged solely on the basis of their abilities in arc welding. The Board rejects this contention. As we

explained in Case No. A-249, the Agreement of April 15, 1946 provides that craftsmen are to be rated "on the basis of each individual employee's qualifications and ability in relation to requirements of the job under consideration." The "job" includes in its scope those "duties which a fully qualified journeyman may be called upon to perform *in the plant."* Journeyman Welders at the Duluth Works are unquestionably called on to do acetylene welding from time to time. The Company had a right—both in its initial judgment and in the later test—to base its rating of the grievants upon their abilities as gas welders as well as electric welders.

5. The second issue concerns the fairness of the performance assignment. The grievants complain not only of the nature of the test but of the manner in which it was given. Instead of being told merely to weld certain sizes of pipe by the gas torch method, they were told *how* they should do the work. According to the grievants, they were restricted in the size and type of rod they could use, were not allowed to "tack," were told how many passes they might make, etc. The Union claims that certain of these instructions were erroneous in themselves and could not possibly have resulted in a successful weld. It points out further that under the job description a Welder is required to have the knowledge and ability to judge for himself *how* a given welding operation could be performed and a test which prevented the grievants from using their own knowledge of their trade was unfair from the outset.

6. In Case No. A-250, the Board considered the question of its jurisdiction to review the standards and tests used by the Company in classifying trade and craftsmen. We held

that though the Company's standards in themselves were not binding upon the Union, the Board did not have jurisdiction to establish alternative standards. Where the Company, *in practice,* had established a uniform system of judging and rating the abilities of craft journeymen in a plant, we held that the methods used in that plant constituted a "local working condition" within the meaning of Section 2-B of the present basic Agreement and had to be applied without discrimination to all similarly situated journeymen in that plant.

7. The instant test, however, clearly could not constitute a "local working condition." It has no necessary validity or invalidity under the Agreement. The Board could neither approve the test nor disapprove it, without establishing, in this instance, a "guidepost" for the rating of trade or craft journeymen. In Section 9-K-2 of the basic Agreement the parties have expressly placed the power to establish such guideposts in the hands of the Joint Wage Rate Inequity Negotiating Committee. The Board may not usurp that power.

8. We hold, accordingly, that the Board is without jurisdiction to determine the fairness or unfairness of the performance assignment here at issue and that the grievance must be dismissed. This action is without prejudice to the rights of either side before the Joint Wage Rate Inequity Negotiating Committee.

AWARD

9. The grievance is dismissed without prejudice to the rights of either side before the Joint Wage Rate Inequity Negotiating Committee.

USC—451. I. Clairton Works. September 16, 1955
Sylvester Garrett, *Chairman*

BACKGROUND

1. In this grievance eight Instrument Repairmen in the Special Engineering Section, Power and Fuel Department, Clairton Works, claim that on May 28, 1950, they should have been slotted as Standard Rate Instrument Repairman rather than Starting Rate.

2. Prior to May 28, 1950, the job of Instrument Repairman did not exist under this name at Clairton. The typical work of an Instrument Repairman prior to this date was performed at Clairton by grievants as salaried employees under the title of Service Men.

3. In the course of the Inequities Program, this job did not receive definitive treat-

ment until 1950, since it was in the Salaried Unit. On April 26, 1950, the parties executed a local agreement as follows:

"At a conference held in the office of Assistant General Superintendent at 10:30 a.m., Wednesday, April 26, 1950, the following understanding with respect to the occupation of Instrument Repairman was mutually accepted:

"1. The salary rated position of Service Man is within the scope of a trade or craft job and is therefore to be described and classified in accordance with procedures currently applied to journeyman jobs.

"2. Negotiations to resolve the description and classification of Instrument

Repairman will be the responsibility of the joint Production and Maintenance Management Wage Rate Inequity Committee.

"3. At the time mutual agreement is reached regarding the description and classification of the Instrument Repairman occupation, management will proceed to change the incumbents of the Service Man position from a salary method of pay to an hourly basis of pay, thereby removing them from the Salary Workers bargaining Unit, Local #3018, and placing these employees in the Production and Maintenance Workers Bargaining Unit, Local #1557.

"4. Representatives of Local #1557 will determine to which plant unit the Instrument Repairman belongs and will notify in writing the Superintendent of Industrial Relations of their decision."

Thereafter the local Wage Rate Inequity Committee adopted the standard Instrument Repairman job description and classification to cover the work previously performed by the Service Men. (They added five items, to the standard working procedure, covering various subsidiary functions of the job at Clairton, but none is relevant here.)

4. Once the foregoing steps had been taken, the only remaining step to complete the Inequities Program as to incumbents of the erstwhile Service Man job was to slot them into the 3 rate levels for Instrument Repairman, in accordance with the practices at Clairton Works for initial slotting of trade and craftsmen. At this point, the Company judged qualifications of the Service Men on the basis of a requirement that they be able to install, maintain and repair electrical relays as well as integrating, indicating and recording instruments which measured electrical quantities. Requirements for working with devices controlling the flow and measurement of electrical current were set forth as to Instrument Repairmen in the Company's classification manual, to which the Union never agreed. The Company's Manual provides tests to determine qualifications for repair of devices *to measure and control the flow of electrical current,* apparently on the basis of the fact that the standard Instrument Repairman description, Working Procedure, Item 3, states:

"Dismantles, cleans, inspects, repairs or replaces parts, calibrates tests and adjusts any type of integrating, indicating or graphic electrical instruments, pressure

and flow meters, combustion control equipment, relays, regulators, timing devices, pyrometers, etc."

While the Primary Function of the job reads:

"To install, repair, calibrate, test and adjust any type of integrating, indicating, or graphic electrical or mechanical instrument."

5. This type of work never was performed by Service Men at Clairton Works. For at least 21 years prior to this grievance, installation and repair of such electrical measurement and control instruments at Clairton has been handled by men in the Electrician-Wireman job. The Union does not agree with the Company's interpretation of Item 3 of the Working Procedure. It believes that the use of the term "electrical" in the job description is designed only to describe the type of power used in operating the measurement and control devices serviced by men in this job.

6. Assuming this type work reasonably is comprehended by the Instrument Repairman description, it also would fall under the description of Electrician-Wireman, Specimen #921. The situation in May, 1950 thus was: (1) this type of work with electrical flow measurement and control instruments long had been performed by Electricians-Wiremen, (2) such work never had been performed by Service Men at Clairton, (3) such work fell within the scope of working procedure of Journeyman Electrician (Wireman) and always had been performed by an Electrician-Wireman at Clairton.

7. The fact that the Serviceman and the Instrument Repairman trade or craft job were the same, and that a new job had not been created, was reflected in the Company's action treating the two highest paid employees (assigned as Serviceman) under the "grandfather clause." This automatically entitled these two to the standard rate classification of the Instrument Repairman trade or craft job. They were paid retroactively to January 4, 1944 on the basis of the "grandfather clause."

FINDINGS

8. This case involves a problem of slotting as an incident of the parties Joint Wage Rate Inequity Program. The difficulty here traces to the fact that the parties did not determine that the salaried job of Service Man was the same as Instrument Repairman until more than three years after other Journeymen had been slotted at Clairton as an inci-

dent of installation of the Standard Hourly Wage Rate structure.

9. In 1946 and 1947 craftsmen (other than those covered by the "grandfathers clause"—Section 1(d) of the April 15, 1946 Agreement) first were slotted by the Company following discussions with the local Wage Rate Inequity Committee. Since the Union protested that too few employees were slotted at Intermediate and Standard, the Company took a "second look." This entailed further discussion with Union representatives, and a substantial number of employees were slotted into higher rates than originally.

10. The only question properly before the Board in the present case, is whether slotting of the grievants conformed with the requirements of the April 22, 1947 Agreement. The parties never agreed upon the guideposts for slotting contemplated under Section 9-K-2 of the April 22, 1947 Agreement. There is no agreed program applicable here.

11. The same type problem has arisen often enough, however, for relatively clear principles to emerge for present application. In Case A-249 the Board stated:

"The parties have recognized, therefore, that in dealing with the trades and crafts under the Inequity Program they must classify not only the *job* but the *man* upon the basis of his *skill*. For each trade and craft job, they have established three rates —standard, intermediate, and starting— and have provided in Section 1(d) for the assignment of trade and craft employees into one or the other of these rates upon the basis of 'each individual employee's qualifications and ability in relation to requirements of the job under consideration.'

"What, however, did the parties mean by 'the job under consideration'? Conceding that the 'requirements' of the job include potential as well as actual assignments, with respect to what unit of the Company's operations are we to determine what assignments are potential? Were the parties concerned with the potential assignments of the individual himself? With those of the craftsmen in his department? In his mill? In the entire plant? Or throughout all the plants of the Company? This is the central question in this case.

"It is clear that no matter which of these various alternatives the parties chose, the results might seem equitable from one point of view and inequitable from another. To the extent that they narrowed the unit and gave primary weight to a journeyman's ability to perform the work to which he is normally assigned—work which is frequently specialized and which may sometimes be limited to a simple type of operation—they might appear to be unjust to employees of broader skill and a more complete knowledge of their craft. To the extent that they widened the unit and placed their main emphasis upon an employee's full mastery of his trade, they might appear to be penalizing employees in specialized jobs or departments who had little opportunity to develop or retain broad skill.

"It is not for us to tell the parties how we think they *should* have resolved this dilemma. Our only proper concern is with the way in which they *did* resolve it in the Agreement of April 15, 1946. We find from a reading of that Agreement that the parties adopted the *plant* as the unit in which the 'requirements of the job under consideration' are to be determined. Section 1(b) requires the description and classification of trade or craft *jobs* and provides that the description 'shall reflect the scope of duties which a fully qualified journeyman may be called upon to perform *in the plant.*' The so-called 'grandfather clause' in the same sub-section provides for the assignment to the standard rate of journeymen who, prior to January 4, 1944, were paid at or above the highest prevailing rate of the trade or craft *'in the plant.*' Section 1, in its entirety, is to be distinguished from Section 2, which deals with Assigned Maintenance Jobs, in that this latter section expressly adopts 'the assigned area' as the basic unit in which to measure job content. The absence of such restrictive language in Section 1 underscores the parties' agreement that the content of trade and craft jobs is to be determined with reference to the entire plant."

12. In the related case of A-250, the Board further stated:

"On the other hand, we cannot accept the Company's contention that the guideposts and criteria for the slotting of trade and craft journeyman which it has unilaterally established are sacrosanct and not subject to challenge before this Board. The statement in Section 9-K-2 of the April 22, 1947 Agreement that the parties, *'through the Joint Wage Rate Inequity Negotiating Committee* will complete the program of the May 8, 1946 Agreement . . . including the tasks of developing . . . the guideposts for assigning trade and craft journeymen to the respective starting, intermediate or standard rates,'* is a clear indication of the parties' belief that the official and binding yardsticks should be established by agreement and not by the unilateral action of either side. No indicaton to the contrary is contained in any of the earlier inequity agreements. Section 1(j) of the April 15, 1946 Agreement (quoted above) upon which the Company relies, merely means that as a matter of practical procedure Management must take the initiative in slotting journeymen, subject to the review of its actions in the grievance procedure. In carrying out its obligations under this provision, the Company had every right to develop a set of uniform criteria for the guidance of its supervision; indeed, had it not done so, the program might well have created more confusion and inequity than it removed. But this does not mean that its criteria are beyond criticism or challenge, or are binding upon this Board.

"The only standards which this Board can properly accept as controlling are those laid down in the agreements over which we have jurisdiction. The system of guideposts—of 'ability factors,' 'elements of skill,' etc.—which the Company has developed for the classification of its journeymen Machinists has not been incorporated in these agreements either directly or by reference. Whatever may be its virtues or its faults, we cannot ourselves be bound by it.

"Neither, on the other hand, may we properly establish our own standards or guideposts. We cannot perform for the parties a function which they have expressly reserved for themselves. We cannot make the parties' agreements for them; no more can we give binding effect to the assertions of either side as to what such an agreement ought to provide.

"How, then, can we rule on the instant case? Management, upon the basis of its own standards and the judgment of its supervisors, has determined that—'on the basis of each employee's qualifications and ability in relation to requirements of the job under consideration'—these grievants should be assigned to the starting Machinist rate. The grievants, supported by the Union, claim that they deserve assignment to the intermediate rate. How can we uphold either Management or the grievants without establishing and applying our own system of standards, in excess of our jurisdiction and in defiance of the parties' injunction that the Board shall not 'add to, detract from, or alter in any way' the provisions of the Agreement?

"We believe that the answer lies in the provisions of Section 2-B of the existing basic Agreement, at least insofar as concerns the period subsequent to its execution. The methods used by Management in classifying the journeymen in a given plant clearly constituted a 'detailed application of the subject matter' of the wage provisions of that Agreement and of the provisions of the Wage Inequity Agreements which were incorporated by reference in Section 9-B-4. *As applied in practice,* therefore, the rules of classification used by the Company in slotting journeymen at the Duluth Works constitute a 'local working condition' in effect at the Duluth Works. Under Section 2-B-3, employees are entitled to have the same criteria standards and testing methods applied to them that were applied to other employees.

"In ruling upon these grievances, then, we must be guided not by the system of standards as it appears on paper in the Company's manual but by the manner in which that system was in fact applied at Duluth. We must examine not only the bases upon which the grievants were classified, but also the bases upon which other employees were classified who in fact were assigned to the intermediate rate. If our examination reveals that the grievants were rated in the same manner and according to the same criteria as other employees, similarly situated, their complaint must be held to be without merit. If, on the other hand, they were the victims of special discriminatory treatment they are clearly entitled to redress—to the benefits of the same 'local working condition' which other employees enjoyed."

13. More recently, in Case G-24, the principles enunciated in A-249 and -250 were elaborated and applied.

14. For purposes of the present case, the important principles of A-249 and -250 are (1) slotting of trade and craft employees must be done on the basis of the skills and duties required of the particular craft *in the particular plant,* and (2) all journeymen are entitled under Section 2-B to have the same criteria, standards, and testing methods applied in their slotting under the Inequities Program as were applied in slotting of other journeymen in the same plant as an incident of installation of the Standard Hourly Wage Rate structure.

15. The first of these principles stems from the April 15, 1946 Inequities Agreement which states that trade and craft job descriptions should reflect the scope of duties which a fully qualified journeyman might be

called upon to perform "in the plant." The January 1, 1953 Job Description and Classification Manual again emphasizes that . . . "the job description of a trade or craft job is required to reflect the scope of duties which a fully qualified journeyman may be called upon to perform *in the plant . . ."*

16. It may be that this principle would not apply here if Instrument Repairman were an entirely new job at Clairton Works. The Company seems to have proceeded in part on this basis. Yet the evidence leaves no doubt that the job of Serviceman simply was given its proper label of Instrument Repairman and placed in the proper bargaining unit as an application of the Inequities Program—however belated. In particular, the application of the "grandfather clause" recognized that the incumbents of the Serviceman job were in effect performing the trade or craft duties of the Instrument Repairman.

17. The Board here must look to substance, not to form. A negotiated change of a job from salaried to hourly pay basis or vice versa, does not necessarily and for all purposes produce an entirely new job. This already has found recognition in at least two earlier Board decisions; compare, Cases T-200 and G-29.

18. The April 26, 1950 local agreement on its face deals with the occupation of Instrument Repairman, and leaves no doubt that the parties recognized the salaried job of Serviceman to be in substance the same job. The first numbered paragraph states that the Serviceman job *"is within the scope"* of a trade or craft job. The agreement then provides that after the parties have agreed upon description and classification of Instrument Repairman the incumbents of the Serviceman job thereafter will be paid on an hourly basis rather than salary.

19. Nothing here suggests creation of a new job. Essentially the parties agreed to move the Servicemen to the P&M unit and thereafter designate them as Instrument Repairmen. There was no occasion in 1950 for either party to believe they were creating a new job, and their joint conduct in handling the job (as, slotting of "grandfathers" and making retroactive payments under the Inequities Program) indicates that they did not believe they had created a new job from scratch.

20. The grievants therefore were entitled, in accordance with the principles recognized in A-249, A-250, CI-115, CI-119, CI-145, USC-419, and G-24, to have their qualifications for initial slotting purposes determined on the basis of duties which had been performed in Clairton Works by incumbents of the Serviceman job. The Company thus

was not entitled to disqualify all incumbents of the Serviceman job for slotting at Intermediate or Standard Rate because of inability to perform a function never previously performed by Servicemen, but performed by Electricians-Wiremen.

21. The remaining question is whether each of the eight grievants was entitled on May 28, 1950 to be slotted either at Standard or Intermediate Rate rather than Starting. The Union evidence is to the effect that:

(1.) In all other cases of initial slotting of trade and craftsmen under the Inequities Program the matter was discussed and negotiated locally,

(2.) In no other instance were all incumbents initially slotted at Starting Rate,

(3.) In all other instances, the slotting included a "second look" when the Union protested that too few men had been placed on the Standard and Intermediate Rates,

(4.) In no other instance of initial slotting were trade and craftsmen at Clairton required to take "representative job assignment" tests, while grievants were told that if they were dissatisfied with their slotting they could take such tests to prove full qualifications.

22. While the Company believes that grievants were accorded the same treatment as other trade and craftsmen in slotting under the Inequities Program, the evidence does not support this view.

23. These observations do not lead automatically to the conclusion that all grievants —on this record—should have been slotted at Standard Rate on May 28, 1950. Rather the situation here is akin to that in G-24, where the Board stated:

"In the present case, however, the Board does not believe the evidence presented is sufficiently clear to permit precise application of the principles first announced in Case A-250. This difficulty seems to have arisen because the parties have not yet focused their attention clearly on the crucial matter of ascertaining whether there was *discrimination* against the grievants when the manner in which they were slotted is compared with the manner in which other craft and tradesmen were slotted. In the Company belief, there appears the following:

" 'The actual rating of each employee was the responsibility of his supervisor and the over-all program was directed with respect to procedure by the Industrial Engineers to insure uniformity. It is only natural that several situations would develop where an employee or group of employees who were assigned by their foreman to other than the standard rate would feel that their qualifications and ability were not fairly judged by their foreman. As a result of discussions in such cases, certain employees were reclassified into higher brackets. However, in all cases where the foreman and the employee could not reach agreement with regard to this initial classification, tests were offered to resolve these differences of opinion.' (Underscoring added).

"These items are mentioned not for the purpose of suggesting that Pruitt did not slot grievants fairly in comparison with the slotting of other trade and craftsmen in the plant. On the other hand, these facts do demonstrate that the Board cannot determine accurately how these men fared in comparison with other trade and craftsmen who were given higher classifications *after discussion with their foremen* and without the requirement that they undergo performance or written tests.

"In fairness to the grievants, particularly since four other men since have been given the standard rate for Welder in the Open Hearth, it seems essential that the parties review all of the available data as to exactly how other trade and craftsmen were slotted in 1948. The grievance will be returned to the parties for this purpose. If this further review does not result in settlement of all cases presented in the griev-

ance, any remaining issue may be returned to the Board. In resubmitting any such unsettled portion of the case, of course, it will be the responsibility of the Union to substantiate any claim of discrimination in accordance with the principles set forth in Cases A-249 and A-250." (Underscoring added.)

24. In closing, it appears that Management's position was influenced by a belief that it is entitled to assign Instrument Repairman to perform this kind of work at its discretion in the exercise of the rights recognized in Section 3 of the Agreement. It does not appear, however, that such a question properly is before the Board. Nothing here said is intended to pass on any potential issue of Management authority to assign various duties to incumbents of either of two craft jobs provided that the trade or craft job in each instance reasonably may be considered to include performance of the same or similar duties. The Board here passes only on the slotting issue in effectuation of the Inequities Program, in accordance with Case A-250.

AWARD

25. This case is returned to the parties for further consideration in the grievance procedure as indicated in the opinion. If the parties do not settle the case within 90 days of this Award, and do not agree to an extension of such 90-day period, the case may be returned to the Board by the Union for final disposition.

USC—451. II. Clairton Works. July 13, 1956
Sylvester Garrett, *Chairman*

FINDINGS

1. In an Award dated September 16, 1955, this case was returned to the parties for settlement in the grievance procedure. Since this did not produce agreement, the case now is before the Board once more.
2. The critical issue is whether on May 28, 1950, the grievants were entitled to be slotted as Standard Rate Instrument Repairmen, under the Inequities Program, and in accordance with the parties' local agreement of April 26, 1950.
3. The problem of classifying the salaried job of Serviceman had been pending for years under the Inequities Program. The April 26, 1950, local agreement recognized it to be within the scope of the trade and craft job of Instrument Repairman, in the P. and M. bargaining unit, and contemplated

slotting of grievants in the same manner as other journeymen.
4. In light of earlier Board decisions, the September 16, 1955, Award held that grievants had been slotted improperly at the Starting Rate because they were found deficient only in duties never performed by Instrument Repairmen (formerly Servicemen) at Clairton Works. Further review of the evidence leaves no doubt that, but for the inclusion of this type duty in the scope of testing, all grievants would have been slotted at Standard Rate on May 28, 1950.

AWARD

5. Grievants were entitled to be slotted at the Instrument Repairman Standard Rate on May 28, 1950.

USC—451.   III.   Clairton Works.   June 18, 1957
Sylvester Garrett, *Chairman*

FINDINGS

1.   This represents the final phase of a case which has been the subject of two earlier Awards.

2.   The problem of classifying the salaried job of Serviceman at Clairton was pending for several years after 1947 under the Inequities Program. An April 26, 1950, local agreement recognized the job to be within the scope of the trade and craft job of Instrument Repairman, in the P. and M. bargaining unit, and contemplated slotting of grievants in the same manner as other journeymen. The September 16, 1955, Award in this case held that grievants had been slotted improperly at the Starting Rate because they were found deficient only in duties never performed by Instrument Repairmen (formerly Servicemen) at Clairton Works. The remaining question is whether they were entitled to retroactivity in the same manner as other employees under the Inequities Program. The Company holds that they are not so entitled, and that the Board lacks authority to so award.

3.   The Company position essentially is that the problem of retroactivity here is but a phase of the Inequities Program, as to which the Board has no authority. But it is clear that the parties in their April 26, 1950, local agreement, contemplated that the Serviceman job belonged in the P. and M. unit, and thus was subject to the provsions of Section 9-B-4 of the April 22, 1947 Agreement, including its reference to the May 8,

1946 Agreement. The existence of this local agreement, therefore, removes any doubt concerning the Board's authority. Indeed the Company itself has applied the local agreement to slot grievants (at Starting Rate) and in some instances to compensate them retroactively to January 1, 1944, in the usual manner. The only question now is whether grievants should have been so compensated at Standard rather than Starting Rate. On the basis of the record made, this question must be answered in the affirmative, and the following dates are found to be appropriate for the respective grievants: John J. Toth, March 6, 1946; William D. Nagy, July 29, 1946; William E. Kuskie, January 1, 1944 to April 7, 1945, and August 19, 1946 to May 27, 1950; Matthew L. Verlich, January 4, 1944 to March 29, 1944, and December 31, 1945 to May 27, 1950; Edgar J. Thompson, January 1, 1944; Kent C. Scott, August 13, 1944; Thad Dragoski, May 20, 1945; John B. Harding, March 6, 1948.

4.   While the Union believes that earlier dates should be set for Scott (January 1, 1944), Dragoski (September, 1944) and Harding (February, 1948), because they claim to have started work as Instrument Repairmen on these dates, there is no affirmative evidence to support these claims.

AWARD

5.   The grievants are awarded retroactivity as set forth above.

CI—150.   Johnstown-Lorain Works.   November 2, 1950
Donald A. Crawford, *Acting Chairman*

BACKGROUND

1.   Since early in 1946, B. Nicodemus and R. McGregor have been seeking reclassification from the job of Moulder Helper to that of Moulder (Starting Rate). Both men have been employed as Moulder Helpers for approximately seven and one-half years in the Lorain Foundry. At present, and during almost all of this period of employment, they have worked as members of the Roll Moulding Unit, which normally is composed of three Moulders and nine Moulder Helpers. Both men can, and do perform the manual tasks of the Moulder working on roll moulding in this department. Neither man has the Moulder's responsibility for the quality of the crew's work, nor the instruction of Helpers. Neither man can do, nor does, the full scope of the craft job. McGregor can do

more of the other kind of moulding than Nicodemus can.

UNION POSITION

2.   (1.) Both men have been doing Moulder's work for 50% or more of their time for a period of years.

(2.) Both men have been seeking reclassification since early 1946; have received encouragement from supervision; but have not been promoted.

COMPANY POSITION

3.   (1.) Management has no need for additional Moulders on this crew. So irrespective of the question of ability, no vacancy exists, and Management cannot be compelled to create Moulder jobs for these men.

(2.) Neither man is qualified to perform,

nor performs, the craft duties of Hand Moulders.

(a) On their present jobs, neither man exercises supervision over, nor instructs Helpers. Moreover, admittedly since 1947, at least one Moulder has been on the job to instruct or check the work of Nicodemus and McGregor if they have needed assistance.

(b) Neither man can fulfill the requirements of the craft occupation since there are other types of moulds they cannot make.

(c) During the job evaluation program, their jobs were evaluated and by joint agreement of Union and Management were classified as Moulder Helper.

FINDINGS

4. The problem in this case is that both Nicodemus and McGregor are superior workers who are thoroughly familiar with the roll moulding done in this department because of their ability and long years on the job. Either can and does do the manual duties of the Moulder's job in this type of moulding. Under these circumstances, they both perform more than the requirements of the Moulder Helper's position.

5. Against these facts are the considerations that neither man *is required* to do Moulder's work; neither has the Moulder's responsibility for quality of the moulds nor instruction of Helpers; and neither can perform the full requirements of the craft occupation.

6. Under the Inequities Program completed by the Company and Union in 1947, all jobs have been rated and classified, including a special group of craft occupations. Since the adoption of this plan, inequities can no longer be alleged and a worker receives the rate of the job he is required to perform. Accordingly, in this crew a man is either a Moulder or a Helper and there are no in-between rates.

7. By agreement, craft occupations (Moulder is one) have been created with "starting," "intermediate," and "standard"

rates. Individually rated jobs for this kind of work have been abolished, and the worker has to be a Journeyman to qualify for the craft job and rates, irrespective of how much of his skill is utilized on a specific assignment.

8. In reference to Nicodemus and McGregor, neither man can perform all of the duties of the Journeyman Moulder. McGregor, presumably the more experienced, stated that he could make some of the other moulds and some he could not. Moreover, under the Inequities Program, each employee regularly performing craft work was assigned to the starting, intermediate or standard rate of his craft. Nicodemus and McGregor have been performing substantially the same work, at least since 1946, and yet both were designated as Helpers. It is doubtful that either can qualify for the starting rate of Moulder.

9. But assuming that each can qualify as Moulders, the Company is not employing them as Moulders. Considering only the work of the Roll Moulding Crew to which they are assigned, neither Nicodemus nor McGregor discharges the directional duties, nor have they the quality responsibility that the three Moulders on the Roll Moulding Crew are given, nor are they required to perform the full manual duties of the Moulders. Therefore they are not assigned and do not perform the full duties of the craft job even on the Roll Moulding Crew.

10. In view of the foregoing, the Board cannot concur with the Union and order the classification of these men at the Moulder's starting rate. True, a very substantial amount of the time, they do the *manual* tasks of the Moulder on the Roll Moulding Crew and do them on their own. But they are not *assigned* nor *required* to assume the Moulder's responsibilities on the Roll Moulding Crew. Since the Inequities Program eliminated the in-between rate and established Journeyman requirements for craft work, and since these men are not required to perform the full scope of Moulder's work on roll moulding, the Board can neither increase their rate, nor direct their reclassification to Moulder's starting rate.

AWARD

11. The grievance is denied.

N—100.   Lorain Works.   October 14, 1948
Ralph T. Seward, *Chairman*

BACKGROUND FACTS

1. Prior to February 2, 1947, William W. Warner and Michael Polutnik were employed at the Company's Lorain Works as

Electrical Repairmen, Classes 1-A and 1 respectively. On that date, pursuant to the Wage Inequity Reclassification Program, their jobs were placed in the "Motor Inspector" classification. In these grievances they claim that this classification was improper and that their work entitled them to be classified as "Electrician (Wireman)." They ask that they be reclassified accordingly, effective February 2, 1947. They ask in addition that their retroactive pay under Section 4-D of the May 8, 1947 Agreement, as amended, be computed upon the assumption that "the newly established applicable rate of pay" is the rate of the "Electrician (Wireman)" classification rather than that of the "Motor Inspector" classification.

2. The Union contends that both Warner and Polutnik are exceptionally competent electricians, fully capable of performing all the duties of an "Electrician (Wireman)." That the Company has consistently recognized their competence is indicated by the fact that they have both served, from time to time, as relief foremen, and on such occasions have sometimes had Wiremen working under them. Each has frequently been assigned to installation or repair work of exceptional complexity. Upon several occasions since 1944 they have been assigned to work involving the installation of new equipment which is commonly considered to be Wireman's work. The Union notes, moreover, that the work which they were doing, both before and after February 2, 1947 is covered by the "Electrician (Wireman)" negotiated job description. Referring to the "Primary Function" of the "Electrician (Wireman)" job as outlined in that description, the Union asserts that both grievants have consistently been required "to inspect, repair, and install, and wire all electrical apparatus, devices and circuits, of any voltage" in their assigned area. Referring to the "Working Procedure" of an "Electrician (Wireman)" as set forth in the job description, the Union asserts that the grievants from day to day perform all of the operations specified.

3. The Union notes finally that on September 3, 1947, while these grievances were still under discussion in the grievance procedure, both grievants were transferred to the "Electrician (Wireman)" classification. The Company thus recognized that their ability and their work entitled them to the classification. The Union regards the action of the Company in postponing their reclassification until September of 1947 as an effort to avoid the payment of the full retroactive pay to which the grievants were entitled.

4. The Company does not dispute the exceptional ability of both men. It points out, however, that it is required by its agreements with the Union to classify *jobs*, not *men*. The work which the grievants were doing at the time of the reclassification was essentially the maintenance and repair of existing elec-

trical equipment in their assigned area, and was covered completely by the "Motor Inspector" classification. Their reclassification on September 3, 1947 resulted from their transfer from the Pipe Mill Maintenance Department to the Construction Gang, and their consequent assignment to work involving new construction and major installations and repairs, as opposed to the maintenance work which they had formerly been doing.

5. The Company concedes that the negotiated job description for the "Electrician (Wireman)" classification applies to much of the work which they had been doing as Electrical Repairmen at the Pipe Mill. It points out, however, that the negotiated job description for the "Motor Inspector" classification also covers this same work. To establish its case, the Company asserts, the Union must show not only that the work of the grievants *was* covered by the language of the "Electrician (Wireman)" job description, but that it was *not* covered by the "Motor Inspector" job description. This, it asserts, the Union has failed to do.

FINDINGS

6. In approaching this case we must discount at the outset the admitted facts with regard to the ability of the grievants. Their ability, which the Company concedes, is irrelevant to the issues presented in this case. We are concerned only with the question of whether the work which they were doing at the time of the general reclassification properly fell within the scope of the "Motor Inspector" or the "Electrician (Wireman)" classification.

7. The determination of this issue is complicated by the fact that the negotiated job descriptions overlap. As both parties recognized at the hearing, language can be found in both descriptions which would seem to apply to the normal day to day work which these employees were required to perform. For example the grievants were called upon from time to time to repair faulty wiring on the switch boards which control various items of equipment in the Pipe Mill. If one refers to the "Motor Inspector" job description, one finds that this work is clearly within the "Primary Function" of the "Motor Inspector" classification, which is, in part: "To inspect, repair, replace, install, adjust and maintain all electrical equipment in a major producing unit or assigned area." It is also within the stated "Primary Function" of the "Electrician (Wireman)" classification which, as has been noted above, is: "To inspect, repair, and install, and wire all electrical apparatus, devices and circuits, of any voltage in the plant or assigned area." Under

the "Working Procedure" section of the "Motor Inspector" job description this switchboard rewiring job could be covered by the following language:

"Receives instructions covering the scheduled and emergency repair, installation, and inspector work to be done . . . When faulty operation is observed or pointed out by operating crews, diagnose trouble using testing equipment or own judgment based on general knowledge of electrical principles. Determines the best way of making repairs to minimize interruption of production. Advises when immediate shutdown of equipment is necessary to minimize damage or when temporarily continued operation will have no harmful effect. Interpret and analyze drawings and wiring diagrams to locate and trace electrical circuits to determine material and replacement needs, and to select a logical approach to 'trouble shooting' and repair problems . . . Makes either temporary or permanent repairs as required to equipment such as main motor drives, generators, control panels, relays, interlocking control systems, electronic devices and circuit breakers . . ."

8. Under the "Working Procedure" section of the "Electrician (Wireman)" job description, however, we find the following language which is equally applicable:

"Receives wiring diagrams, specifications, and instructions covering the scheduled and emergency repair, installation and inspection work to be done . . . Analyzes all types of drawings and wiring diagrams to locate and install circuits and equipment to determine material or replacement needs and to select a logical approach to 'trouble shooting' and repair problems. Plans details of working procedure to effect the most logical approach to the job. Considers all safety precautions and the proper isolation of circuits to cause a minimum of interference to operations . . . Locates sources of trouble of any type of electrical equipment by tracing and testing circuits and inspecting for faulty operation. Dismantles, inspects, repairs, adjusts or replaces faulty parts and wiring on motors, generators, power distribution and control panels, circuit breakers, rectifiers, electronic devices, etc. Reassembles, tests and adjusts equipment for safe and proper operation . . . Installs conduit, fittings, switches, controls and fixtures, and wires and connects all types of electrical equipment as required for new installations or replacement of facilities . . ."

9. The same could be said of almost any of the electrical maintenance work which the grievants customarily performed in the Pipe Mill and would likewise be true of a large proportion of the work performed by recognized "Wiremen" in connection with new installations or "major" repairs.

10. As one might expect, this overlapping of the negotiated job descriptions reflects an overlapping of the jobs themselves. Many of the individual operations performed by "Wiremen" in the course of their work as members of the Construction Gang are very similar to operations performed by "Motor Inspectors" as part of their work of maintaining electrical equipment in their assigned area. Employees in both classifications must be thoroughly familiar with the principles and practice of electrical wiring; both must read wiring diagrams; both must be able to diagnose trouble and work out adequate methods of repair; both make use of the same tools and materials; both are required to install equipment; and both are assigned from time to time to the repair of equipment which has already been installed.

11. The fact remains, nevertheless, that the parties themselves, by agreement, have placed these jobs in two separate classifications; have negotiated two separate, though similar, job descriptions; have rated the two jobs differently with respect to certain of the job classification factors, and in consequence, have placed the "Motor Inspector" job in Job Class 14 and the "Electrician (Wireman)" job in Job Class 16. Though they are now in disagreement, they nevertheless must, in their negotiations, have agreed that the two jobs were substantially different and have understood the difference. Our inquiry then cannot properly be limited to the mere mechanical application of separate phases in the job description. We must look rather at the jobs as a whole and ascertain the essential function of each in the carrying on of plant operations.

12. The essential function of the "Motor Inspector" job is that of maintenance—to keep the equipment in their assigned area in good working order. That function is reflected in the fact that they are part of the Maintenance Department and work under the supervision of the Turn Foreman in their assigned area. It is further reflected in the fact that the job was considered an "assigned maintenance job" within the meaning of Section 2 of the April 15, 1946 Agreement, and was given one of the classification titles established by paragraph A. of that section. In this connection, we note that the Union has not questioned the appropriateness of the Pipe Mill as an "assigned area" and therefore the Board need not pass on this issue.

13. The essential function of the "Electrician (Wireman)" job at this plant is that of new construction or the installation of new equipment. The "Wiremen" in the Construction Gang have no assigned area; they have no responsibility for day to day inspection or the making of routine repairs. They work, not under the Turn Foreman in a production area, but under their own Wireman Foreman. Significantly their work was classified as a "Repair and Maintenance Trade or Craft" job under Section 1 of the April 15, 1946 Agreement, and their job description reflects duties which they may be required to perform, not merely in an assigned area but throughout the entire plant.

14. This basic difference in function cannot be obscured by the fact that "Motor Inspectors" may sometimes be called upon to install new parts or to perform repairs which are comparable in complexity to the work involved in new construction. Neither can it be obscured by the fact that the "Wiremen" in the Construction Gang are sometimes called in to aid in a major repair. The basic long-run distinction between the parts which are played by the two classifications still remains.

15. The parties have agreed that in spite of the similarity of much of the work which is performed by the employees in the two classifications, the "Wireman's" work requires greater employment training and experience, greater mental skill, a greater degree of responsibility for tools and equipment, and a greater degree of responsibility for the safety of others. The "Motor Inspectors," on the other hand, have greater responsibility for the continuity of operations and a somewhat more important obligation to prevent loss through damage to processed material. By agreeing to these differences in the rating of the jobs, the parties recognized the long-run differences between work which is primarily concerned with construction and work primarily concerned with day to day repair.

16. The essential question in this case, therefore, is whether or not the grievants at the time of their reclassification were regularly performing the function assigned by the parties to the "Motor Inspector" classification or that assigned to the "Electrician (Wireman)" classification. On that issue the decision must clearly be for the Company. The grievants were working in the daylight "bull gang" in the Maintenance Department at the Pipe Mill. They were working under the direction of the Turn Foreman. The "bull gang" it is true, appears to have been assigned to the more important repairs which were necessary in the Pipe Mill. Among the Electricians in the "bull gang," prior to the reclassification, the grievants received a somewhat higher personal rate because they were assigned to the more complicated repair work in the Seamless Mill. Nevertheless, the basic function of the grievants as well as that of the other Electrical Repairmen in the Maintenance Crew was that of maintaining the equipment in the Pipe Mill in good repair. The Union has not established that they were regularly assigned, as were the "Wiremen," to construction or the installation of major items of new equipment.

17. We find accordingly that these grievances must be denied.

AWARD

18. The grievances are denied.

SECTION B.   SLOTTING IN ASSIGNED MAINTENANCE JOBS

CI—185, -186, -187, -188, -189, -190, -191.   Gary Steel Works.   January 16, 1951
Sidney L. Cahn, *Acting Chairman*

AWARD

1. In the analysis of these cases, several elements emerge which appear to be common to each grievance. In an effort to reduce the length of each award, these common elements will be discussed and principles established, which, when applied to each grievance, will be controlling.

2. (1) *History:* These grievances involve employees of the Gary Steel Works of the Carnegie-Illinois Steel Corporation.

3. During the course of the preparation of the Wage Rate Inequity Program, the parties, by agreement, described and classified the jobs in the plant.

4. On February 9, 1947, the new classifications and applicable wage rates were installed. In the course of preparation of the program and during review of certain classifications, the parties recognized a problem concerning certain jobs theretofore entitled "Machinists." Previous to the installation of the Program, this title had been used in a broad and loose sense to include various mechanical and repairman jobs, but the title, after the installation of the Program, was no longer descriptive of the actual job content of the repairman jobs.

5. On April 15, 1948, agreement was finally reached to classify certain of these

"Machinist" jobs as the occupation of Mechanical Repairman in Job Class 16. Management proceeded to assign to these occupations, the personnel who it considered were entitled to the Job Class 16 rate and paid them the retroactive payment due under the Inequity Agreements. The grievances herein arose from Management's alleged failure to "slot" certain employees into Job Class 16 who the Union claims, either then or subsequently, had performed the work covered by the new description. Where the parties agreed on the classification of Repairman, Mechanical, Floor, Job Class 12, Management slotted certain of these individuals into that classification. Where the parties did not agree upon the establishment of a job description for Mechanical Repairman, Class 12, the individuals were not changed from Machinists, Class 12, despite the admitted fact that the men were not machinists. Subsequently in two departments the parties agreed to the establishment of a new job, Repairman, Mechanical, Floor, Job Class 12, and agreed upon the description. In those two departments, the aggrieved were changed from Machinists to Repairmen, Mechanical, Floor, Job Class 12. For purposes of brevity the jobs in dispute will hereinafter be referred to as Machinist, Repairman, Job Class 12, and Repairman, Job Class 16.

6. (2) *The Broad Issue:* There appears to be tacit agreement between the parties that the "machinists," i.e., the grievants and those actually slotted in to Job Class 16, were not, before the Inequity Program, and are not now, machinists in fact even though they may have been or still are classified as such.

7. The parties appear to be in joint agreement (as disclosed by Board representatives of the parties) that one of the purposes of the Inequity Program was to enable them to classify employees into job classifications most nearly conforming to their actual job content. The issue then resolves itself into a question of determining (1) whether Management (in those cases where Repairmen, Class 12 descriptions have not been agreed upon) has properly classified the grievants into classifications most nearly conforming to the employees' actual job content; (2) in the other cases, whether Management has properly classified the individuals.

8. (3) *The Effect of Prior Coding as Machinists:* As already indicated, prior to the Inequity Program, the grievants, along with others subsequently slotted into Job Class 16, were known as and carried the title of "Machinists."

9. It was contended in effect that, as some of these "Machinists" had been slotted into Job Class 16, such act was some proof

of the fact that all men originally carrying the "Machinist" title were similarly entitled to be slotted into Job Class 16. The Board disagrees with this contention. Nothing was disclosed, by agreement or otherwise, which would enable the Board affirmatively to make such a finding.

10. So long as employees are assigned to perform certain work, with its concomitant duties and responsibilities, substantial performance of such duties and responsibilities requires that the employees be classified and paid for such work and responsibility, despite any assigned job title. The job title as such, past, present or future, does not carry any weight, for a job title is nothing more than a name and an aid in locating a particular job. It is not now nor can it ever be used as a substitute for a job description or an explanation of the actual job content.

11. The record disclosed that historically and actually no weight is to be attached nor is there any significance to the fact that these men were originally coded as Machinists.

12. (4) *The Question Concerning Experience and Ability to Perform Job Class 16 Work:* Management contended that as the grievants herein had neither the necessary experience nor ability to perform Job Class 16 work, it would be improper for the Board to classify them as Job Class 16 men.

13. Under the terms of the Inequity Program (contract dated April 15, 1946), it would appear that the factors of experience and ability properly to perform the work are necessary only to what are known as journeymen "trade or craft jobs," and are not factors in "assigned maintenance" jobs. The Class 16 jobs herein involved are "assigned maintenance" and not "craft" jobs.

14. If an employee has been assigned to an "assigned maintenance" job and performs it, whether he has ability or not (i.e., comparison of ability with others in the same job), and whether he is or is not performing it as satisfactorily as others, is unimportant. Once assigned to the job, Management must pay the contractually designated rate, so long as the work is performed in a manner sufficient to preclude a claim of inefficiency and incompetence. The Board is of the opinion that relative or individual experience and ability is immaterial in a determination of the issues in these cases. Whether the grievants have less, the same, or a greater experience and ability when assigned to the work than some other employees in Job Class 16 has no bearing.

15. (5) *The Alleged Agreement of May (April) 2, 1948:* The Union claimed that an understanding had been reached with Management on May 2, 1948 (also referred to as April, 1948), wherein Management agreed

that all employees performing work similar to that required for Job Class 16 would be slotted into that classification. Management emphatically denied the existence of any such agreement.

16. A thorough study of the testimony fails to disclose evidence sufficient to warrant a finding that such agreement had in fact been executed. Under the circumstances, no weight can be attached to this claim.

17. (6) *Concerning the Claim that the Grievants must be Requested to Perform Job Class 16 Work as Distinguished from the Voluntary Assumption of such Work:* From the evidence in several of the cases, it appeared that a number of the grievants had voluntarily assumed performance of considerable part of the work either actually performed by Class 16 men or as set forth in the Job Class 16 description. Such evidence may have been introduced by the Union either for the purpose of disclosing the grievants' ability to perform or for the purpose of creating what may loosely be termed an "estoppel," i.e., if Management accepted such work it should be required to pay for it.

18. Section 2a of the April 15, 1946 Agreement defined "assigned maintenance jobs" to mean "all jobs (other than craft jobs)—in which employees *are assigned* (emphasis supplied) to operating and service units—."

19. It is contractually clear, therefore, that employees, to become entitled to the Job Class 16 rate, must actually be assigned by Management to the work "within the assigned area." The same requirement is set forth in Section 2d and 2e involving assigned maintenance jobs of a general mechanical repair nature.

20. Therefore, it appears clear to the Board that unless the grievants were specifically assigned to perform Class 16 work, there was no contractual obligation to pay for it. Management should not be required to pay for Class 16 work if an employee voluntarily and without Management's consent, express or implied, performs work of a Class 16 nature. But the assignment to Job Class 16 work as such need not be in express words. It is sufficient if an employee is requested to perform work normally and regularly assigned to and performed by Job Class 16 employees.

21. (7) *The Issue Concerning "Similarity" of Work and the Contention that Employees must Perform "the Full Scope" of the Job Class 16 Requirements before becoming Eligible for the Job Class 16 Rate:* Management contended that before any one of the grievants could be held entitled to Job Class 16, it was necessary for him to show that he could perform the full scope of the

job requirements as set forth in the Job Class 16 description.

22. The Union maintained that (1) with the possible exception of "major or complex" work (which occurred very rarely and infrequently), Class 12 and Class 16 men performed the same kind of work, and (2) the men in both job classes worked interchangeably on the same work, and (3) in any event substantial performance of Job Class 16 work was sufficient to meet all requirements. To sustain these contentions, the Union, in the Machine Shop cases, generally attempted to compare the duties of the grievants with other employees who had been classified into Job Class 16, and in the other cases, i.e., Locomotive, Power & Fuel, the Union generally attempted to show that the grievants substantially performed the job requirements as set forth in the job description for Job Class 16.

23. In almost all instances the *duties* of 12 and 16 Repairmen not only overlapped to a considerable extent, but in a principal part of all work assigned and performed, they worked either interchangeably or alone on the same operations. The essential difference between the two grades does not appear to be the work performed.

24. The "major" or "complex" work assigned to the Job Class 16 employee occurred so infrequently as to make that factor relatively unimportant to a determination of the issue, particularly when one considers the fact that sometimes even a Job Class 12 man *alone* was assigned to such work.

25. The record conciusively discloses that the actual work performed by Class 12 and Class 16 men, with the possible exception of the rarely performed "major" or "complex" work, is similar if not identical, and Management itself has not at all times required performance of the "full scope of the Job Class 16 requirements."

26. The Board concludes that such work itself cannot be considered as the sole test in ascertaining whether or not the grievants are entitled to the relief sought. If, however, all other elements herein discussed are favorable to the grievant's claim, then the question of whether the grievant is and has been substantially performing the same type of Grade 16 work as required of others in his department becomes important.

27. (8) *Concerning the Claim that an Employee, to be Entitled to a Job Class 16 Classification, must Supervise and Direct the Work of Other Employees:* The record discloses that in practically all of the instant grievances, the question of supervision and the amount thereof is, for all practical purposes, relatively unimportant. The degree of

supervision, in those cases where it does exist, appears to be extremely flexible even in "major" or "complex" work. Grade 16 men will be paid their regular Grade 16 rate whether they do or do not supervise others. Similarly with the Grade 12 men. Frequently when both work together, either one will, in effect, supervise the work of and instruct the other. Just as frequently, when a Grade 12 man works alone, it will be without direct supervision. In other cases the Grade 12 man will, in turn, work with and supervise a crew of lower grade men.

28. Management indirectly raised one other point which requires some discussion. Subsequent to the setting up of the Job Class 16 classification and immediately prior to the slotting of the men into that classification, neither group of men, 12 nor 16, had been required to supervise each other. But once the Job Class 16 description was agreed upon and the required number of men slotted into such class, then, and from that time on, contends Management, it was necessary for the grievants and others who aspired to that job, to fulfill the Job Class 16 requirements concerning supervision of others. Therefore, contends Management, the grievants' claim, lacking this agreed-upon requirement, must be denied.

29. The Union, however, contended that the instant claims must be considered retroactively, at least to the period immediately prior to the agreement as to the Job Class 16 description, at which time none of the men, grievants and those who were later slotted into the jobs, had ever been required to supervise others. If this be so, argues the Union, why the discrimination between both groups? The Union claims that as the grievants' requests are retroactive in nature, the Job Class 16 description is not and should not be considered applicable.

30. To sustain its contention, the Union points to the alleged agreement of May 2, 1948 (See Item #5 herein), wherein it is alleged that the parties had agreed to slot all machinists into Job Class 16 and claims, therefore, that the requirement concerning "supervision" is inapplicable. Management points to the April 15, 1946 contract which grants to it the sole right to determine the number of men to be assigned to this grade irrespective of the existence or nonexistence of the element of "supervision." In view of the finding that the Union's proof of this alleged agreement of May 2, 1948 was insufficient, any rights which the Union might have must flow not from the May agreement nor from an alleged violation by Management of the exercise of its contractual right to determine the number to be assigned to Job Class 16, but from some factor occur-

ring subsequent to the exercise of that right by Management. The moment that conclusion is conceded, it must follow that as the Job Class 16 description was already in effect, then in order for a grievant successfully to claim a Class 16 classification, he must show that he presently fulfills and in the past has fulfilled, the requirement concerning supervision.

31. The view taken herein, however, that the question of supervision is relatively unimportant in these particular cases, sufficiently disposes of all these contentions whether considered retroactively or not, for it was undenied that the actual job content, including "supervision," had not changed over the years.

32. (9) *The Effect of Section 2j of the April 15, 1946 Agreement:* Management claimed that by virtue of this section, it retained the sole right to determine the number of employees originally to be assigned to the Class 16 jobs in question and that the Board, unless it violated the contract, was precluded from rendering an award in favor of the grievants.

33. Apparently this clause was incorporated into the contract specifically to prevent the Union from claiming, when the new assigned maintenance jobs were set up, that more men should be assigned to the higher rated job than was deemed necessary by Management.

34. In the opinion of the Board, however, the contractual limitation, designed to prevent such a claim, can have no future effect once the jobs have been set up and men assigned to perform the work. If, subsequently, other men are assigned to and perform the work with its concomitant responsibility, they must be paid for it and this provision (Section 2j) cannot then be utilized to prevent reclassification and payment of the contractual rate. In other words, the clause is effective as a statement of Management's prerogative in the setting up of Class 16 jobs, but cannot thereafter be deemed to act as a bar and prevent men who have been specifically assigned to and are performing the work of Job Class 16 from being classified and paid as such.

35. The Union claimed that under the Inequity Program, Management was required to treat all employees in Job Class 16 and not others. But this argument, retroactive as it must be, flies in the face of the specific provision of Section 2j, which gives Management the sole right to determine the number of men required.

36. The Union's other claim that this clause (Section 2j) does not grant Management the right to differentiate in payment to men who perform the same work is ade-

quately disposed of by the statements here-inabove contained.

37. (10) *The Issue Concerning "Responsibility:"* Management contended that to determine the real difference between the two classifications, one must look to the relative responsibility of each. As Management views it, even assuming that all other factors might lead to reclassification, two factors, i.e., actual assignment to Job Class 16 work and responsibility for the work itself, are determinative.

38. In the Board's opinion the real difference between the two job classifications lies, not solely in the current work performed by the employee at any given time, but also in the comparative responsibilities of the men to the completed job and the difference in the scope of their duties. Though the 12 and 16 men may for the most part perform the same work, work hand-in-hand with each other, may or may not supervise others, or be supervised and directed, ultimately, only the 16 man is responsible for all work performed by both. He is the person who, in the final analysis is able to diagnose major trouble, make procedural decisions, perform and be responsible for all the work, including the "major" or "complex."

39. The factor of "responsibility" as all others must be considered retroactively: that is, have the grievants since the creation of the Class 16 job and the slotting of men into that classification, been held responsible for the work to be performed whether minor, major or complex.

40. The Union indirectly maintained that the element of "responsibility" must be disregarded because immediately prior to the original assignment of men into the new grade Job Class 16, none of the men, grievants or others, were, in the sense here used, held "responsible" for the work as such.

41. But this claim appears contrary to the actual facts which disclosed that at the time of reclassification, Management slotted into Job Class 16 only those employees it believed had been responsible for the completion of the job as such.

42. Though the description for Job Class 16 indicates the differences herein enumerated, the essential distinguishing factor, responsibility, was graphically illustrated by one of the grievants who, subsequent to the filing of his grievance, signed a job posting for Job Class 16 and was actually reclassified. In answer to counsel's question, this employee, who only sought retroactive pay to the time he was reclassified, testified that the sole difference between the Job Class 16 work he was performing and the work he performed previous to reclassification was the factor of responsibility. As he put it, "Well, the other work, you didn't have no responsibility, you repaired the machines. When you get the 16 work, we got the responsibility."

43. To ascertain whether or not Management, by any action on its part, had imposed on, or assigned to, any one of the grievants this element of responsibility, was one of the main functions assumed by the Board. The records were carefully scrutinized for any and all such evidence as well as similarity of work, etc., to determine whether the claim should be granted.

CONCLUSION

44. Other points, not here discussed, were propounded by the parties, evaluated and found wanting.

45. To determine each grievance, the Board duly considered all the elements herein analyzed in relation to the evidence introduced by the parties and, if all were favorable to the grievant, the claim was granted.

GRIEVANCE NO. A-48-107, CASE NO. CI-185
GEORGE BURRESON

46. Though all other elements would appear favorable to Burreson's claim, the proof concerning the element of "responsibility" discloses that Burreson does not maintain nor has he been assigned that degree of responsibility which would warrant a finding in his favor. Claim denied.

GRIEVANCE NO. A-48-108, CASE NO. CI-186,
THEODORE A. BENNETT

47. On March 27, 1950, Bennett was reclassified as Repairman Mechanical (Air Compressors and Pumps) Job Class 16.

48. The one question, therefore, is whether Bennett should have been reclassified prior to that time, i.e., whether he is entitled to retroactive pay.

49. Here again the sole criterion is "responsibility," for all other factors, i.e., job content, etc., would appear to require an affirmative finding.

50. The record discloses, however, that prior to Bennett's reclassification, he worked with at least one and sometimes two Class 16 men. The Board is convinced that during the period prior to Bennett's reclassification in March, 1950, it was the Class 16 man and not Bennett who was held responsible by Management for the proper performance of the work. Thus, the element of responsibility was lacking from Bennett's job content prior to March of 1950. This lack is sufficient to deny the claim.

GRIEVANCE NO. A-48-109, CASE NO. CI-187,
WILLIAM WICSEK

51. Here two elements are involved, assignment and responsibility. The record discloses that Wicsek works, and has worked alone, and thus, apparently, has full responsibility for the work assigned him, which is within the scope of the job content for Job Class 16. The Board finds that over the years Wicsek has been assigned to and has been performing practically the same kind of work generally performed by Class 16 men. The alleged "complex" work which Management claimed Wicsek has not performed and which claim Wicsek denied, has been performed so very infrequently by anyone, Class 16 men or otherwise, as to render it inappropriate for use as a norm. The grievant is held entitled to the reclassification and rate of Repairman Mechanical (Machine Tools), Job Class 16, with retroactive back pay in accordance with provisions of the Inequity Agreements.

LOUIS KOCH

52. Here the determinative factor is one of assignment. The evidence is conclusive that Koch has not been assigned to and, therefore, does not perform, a substantial part of the work generally performed by Repairman Mechanical (Machine Tools), Job Class 16. The grievance is denied.

GRIEVANCE NO. A-48-113, CASE NO. CI-188,
OBREN BOKICH

53. Here the issued turned upon the question of Management's assignment of Job Class 16 work to Bokich. The evidence satisfies the Board that Bokich has been assigned to and has been performing the job content of Job Class 16, with the exception of setting the valves. The testimony discloses, however, that in Job Class 16, only one man, Herman Scott, is able to set valves. The Board, therefore, must dismiss as a factor the grievant's inability to set valves. It is obvious that none of the Job Class 16 men, with the exception of Scott, could qualify even under a strict interpretation of the job description. The grievant is held entitled to the classification and rate of Locomotive Repairman (Steam and Diesel), Job Class 16, with retroactive back pay in accordance with the provisions of the Inequity Agreements.

GRIEVANCE NO. A-48-115, CASE NO. CI-189,
LOUIS BOTTOS

54. Subsequent to the filing of his grievance and on March 21, 1949, Bottos signed a job posting for the position of Auto Mechanic, Job Class 14. At the hearing Bottos stated that he desired to retain the Auto Mechanic's job, but at the rate of Repairman Mechanical (Pumps and Turbines), Job Class 16, the classification for which he grieved. Actually then, all Bottos seeks is retroactive pay beginning with the time he claims he should have been classified in Job Class 16, up to March 21, 1949, when he accepted the job of Auto Mechanic.

55. The evidence discloses that during the period in question, Bottos was not assigned to, nor did he perform a substantial part of the required duties of Repairman Mechanical (Pumps and Turbines), nor was he responsible for such work. The grievance is denied.

GEORGE MACAULAY

56. Subsequent to the filing of his grievance, and on September 21, 1948, MacAulay signed a job posting for the job of Repairman Mechanical (Pumps and Turbines), Job Class 16, the same job for which he had grieved. On October 3, 1948, MacAulay was assigned to the job. On October 25, 1948, three weeks after his assignment and at his own request, MacAulay was removed from the Class 16 job and returned to his former job.

57. At the hearing MacAulay disclosed that he objected to the Job Class 16 assignment because of the dusty conditions under which he had to work, and for this reason had requested a return to his old job. The only question which must be resolved is whether his "old job" is similar to and should have been classified in the same manner as the existing Class 16 job.

58. An examination of the record discloses a number of facts which require denial of this grievance. One, because it is somewhat indicative of the others, is here set forth. MacAulay, at one point in his testimony, stated that he is and has been performing the same work as two other men who had been classified in Job Class 16, Pumps and Turbines. After making known the fact that in October, 1948 he had been assigned to the same Class 16 job (Pumps and Turbines) as the two men, and that later, at his request, he had been transferred to his former job, MacAulay admitted that while "that job (Class 16) on Pumps and Turbines was desirable to the two men," he wanted "to get away from the dust—"

59. Thus, despite MacAulay's first statement that he was performing the same work as the other two Class 16 men, his final statements clearly disclose that the "work surroundings" and the "work" of the two Class 16 men in Pumps and Turbines, differ considerably from the "work surroundings" and "work" he is performing in his old job.

The Board thus must conclude that Mac-Aulay is not and has not, with the exception of the short period in October, 1948, been substantially performing the same type of work as is required of other Class 16 men in his department. The grievance is denied.

GRIEVANCE NO. A-48-116, CASE NO. CI-190, ELZA E. CAMPBELL, EDWARD E. WESLEY, LORAL L. YOHE, MORECE A. SIMMS

60. During the course of the hearing, the parties stipulated that the discussion and testimony introduced with reference to Campbell should be considered as applicable to Wesley, Yohe and Simms, except that Yohe and Simms "have not been paid by the Company the rate of Job Class 16 for any work and Mr. Wesley has."

61. Though it appeared that the grievants and Job Class 16 men have performed the same kind of work, the major issue involved the question of relative ability to execute the work requirements of Job Class 16. As heretofore ruled, the question of relative ability to perform the work is unimportant in a noncraft job. However, the testimony disclosed that though the grievant Campbell was assigned to perform substantially the same work as one Bragg, the Class 16 man, it was Bragg to a greater extent than the grievant who was held "responsible" for the work, simple or complex.

62. Thus, under the principles herein outlined, it would appear questionable whether the grievants were entitled to awards in their favor. The grievance would have been denied had it not been for one other controlling factor.

63. As the parties are in accord that these grievants are not now, nor have they ever been "Machinists," and as the parties have failed to agree upon a job description for these employees which would more accurately describe their job content, it becomes the duty of the Board, despite the questionable absence of one or two of the elements here found essential, to classify these employees into job classifications most nearly conforming to their actual job content, i.e., the existing Job Class 16.

64. The grievances of Campbell, Wesley, Yohe and Simms are granted. They are entitled to the classification and rate of Repairman Mechanical (Floor and Field) Blast Furnace, Job Class 16, with retroactive back pay in accordance with provisions of the Inequity Agreements.

GRIEVANCE NO. A-48-119, CASE NO. CI-191, J. F. FYDRYCH, M. YENCO, A. MODRAK, J. TAIT, C. KIEFER

65. *Re: J. Tait.* This case, perhaps as much as any other, clearly discloses the overlapping of and similarity between the job duties of both classifications.

66. Tait stated, and Management agreed, that on innumerable occasions he has worked as, and been paid a rate for, Job Class 16. He testified that at other times, while performing the same work, he received only the rate for Job Class 12. Tait admitted that at these times, when the work was complex, he frequently worked with a foreman or a Job Class 16 man, who was available and apparently responsible for the work.

67. Tait's foreman, however, testified that Tait had been assigned to, and had assumed, the responsibility for a fair part of the complex work. From July, 1948 to July, 1950, Tait had been assigned to and been held responsible for 73 turns of Job Class 16 work. Payment for other turns had been inadvertently omitted.

68. The Board finds that although Tait's "responsibility" is not fully the equivalent of a Job Class 16 Employee, it is nevertheless considerably greater than that of the Job Class 12 man. The grievant is held entitled to the classification and rate of Repairman Mechanical (Utilities), Job Class 16, with retroactive back pay in accordance with the provisions of the Inequity Agreements, less the turns for which he was actually paid the rate of Job Class 16.

69. *Re: A. Modrak.* The parties stipulated that all the testimony introduced in the Tait case shall be deemed to apply to Modrak. Under the circumstances, the grievant is held entitled to the classification and rate of Repairman Mechanical (Utilities), Job Class 16, with retroactive back pay in accordance with the provisions of the Inequity Agreements, less the turns, if any, for which he was paid the rate of Job Class 16.

70. *Re: M. Yenco.* Yenco's own testimony highlighted the essential element of responsibility when an employee is assigned to Job Class 16. He stated that on the rare occasions when he worked as a Job Class 16 man, "I take the gang on the job just like a boss—you have the responsibility for everything—." But when he is on Job Class 12, though he may do the same work, he "works as a member of the gang," obviously without the responsibility for the work performed. Because he is rarely called upon to assume responsibility as such, his case differs radically from that of Tait. The claim will be denied.

71. *Re: J. F. Fydrych.* The evidence was wholly insufficient to warrant a finding that Fydrych is or was entitled to the classification of Repairman Mechanical (Utilities). The claim is denied.

72. *Re: C. Kiefer.* Subsequent to the

filing of his grievance, and since November 14, 1948, Kiefer has been assigned to the job of Repairman Mechanical (Utilities), Job Class 16. The only issue is whether Kiefer is entitled to retroactive pay for the period prior to his assignment to Job Class 16.

73. Kiefer admitted that prior to November, 1948, he performed work "pretty near the same as I am doing now," but that the actual difference involved the degree of responsibility for the work performed. As he phrased it, "Well, the other work you didn't have no responsibility, we just repaired the machines. When you get the 16 rate we got the responsibility." Decided on the principles hereinabove set forth, the claim must be denied.

N—95. Lorain Works. June 22, 1948
Ralph T. Seward, *Chairman*

BACKGROUND FACTS

1. Maurice Hiser, the grievant, is presently employed as a Repairman-Mechanical, assigned to maintenance and repair work at the Blooming Mill, Soaking Pit area in the Company's Lorain Works. In this grievance he claims that his job is improperly classified and should be changed to the classification of Millwright.

2. Hiser works on the 3-11 turn. The repair and maintenance work on the Soaking Pits during the day turn is performed by a crew consisting of a Millwright, 2 Repairman-Mechanical and several Helpers. The Union claims that Hiser's work and responsibility on the 3-11 turn is essentially the same as that of the day turn Millwright— that in effect, Hiser relieves the day turn Millwright. There is no justification, the Union contends, for classifying a job in one manner on the day turn and in another manner on the afternoon turn. The negotiated job description for the Repairman-Mechanical classification, moreover, provides that a Repairman-Mechanical shall "work with a Millwright" on major or complex work and that the source of supervision includes not only a Foreman, but a "Millwright or Specialized Repairman." Hiser, the Union notes, works with a helper. He neither works with nor is directed by a Millwright or "Specialized Repairman." Clearly then, the Union argues, the description does not apply to his job and he is entitled to the Millwright classification.

3. The Company denies that Hiser's job is the same as that of the day turn Millwright. It concedes that the duties of Millwrights and Repairman-Mechanical customarily overlap—that there may be substantial periods of time when the Millwright is doing work which might just as well have been performed by Repairman-Mechanical or a Millwright Helper. This possibility is inherent in all assigned maintenance jobs. The parties expressly recognized in Section 2 of the Agreement of April 15, 1946, that the requirements of assigned maintenance jobs, and the duties which assigned maintenance employees are called upon to perform from day to day, may vary widely. To discover the real difference between the Millwright and Repairman-Mechanical classifications, one must look, not at the actual activities of the employees on any given day or days, but at the comparative responsibility of the two jobs and at the difference in the scope of their potential duties. During a period when only minor repairs are necessary, the actual work of the Repairman-Mechanical may be identical with that of the Millwright. Should major or complex repairs become necessary, however, the difference in their work will at once become apparent. It will be the Millwright who will be called upon to diagnose the trouble, make the repairs, see that tools and materials are secured and give immediate direction to the work. The Repairman-Mechanical would work on the job with the Millwright, it is true, but he would be working under the Millwright's direction and would not have the responsibility for planning the job and carrying it through.

4. Only one Millwright, the Company contends, is necessary at the Blooming Mill Soaking Pits, and he need be there only during the day turn. It is during that turn that most of the major repair work is done. Originally, indeed, all maintenance repair was done on that turn. A Repairman-Mechanical was assigned to the afternoon turn only because the Soaking Pit area was too small to permit more than a few men to work on the repairing of doors at the same time. In the Company's opinion, however, the job is still that of Repairman-Mechanical even though it is performed on a different turn. Hiser does not have the responsibility for directing other Repairmen-Mechanical, for the long-term ordering of materials, or for the general planning of the maintenance repair work in the Soaking Pit area. Though he does not "work with a Millwright," he also does not perform "major or complex" repair jobs such as are referred to

in the job description. Under the circumstances, the Company argues, Hiser's classification should be found to be correct and his grievance denied.

FINDINGS

5. The Board finds that the grievant, Hiser, is in fact performing the work of a Millwright and is entitled to a Millwright classification and pay. It is true that little, if any, of the actual repair work which he performs could properly be called "major" or "complex" within the meaning of Repairman-Mechanical job description. That Hiser does not "work with a Millwright" on this work is not therefore decisive. The crucial factor in distinguishing between a Millwright and a Repairman-Mechanical is not the actual maintenance operation which employees in either classification perform at any one time or even over long periods of time, but is the element of responsibility. Our award in this case is based upon a finding that Hiser is exercising responsibility above and beyond that of a Repairman-Mechanical, and approaching that of his counterpart on the day turn who is already classified as a Millwright.

6. The importance of this factor of responsibility may be seen in the job descriptions themselves. Both descriptions refer in general terms to the same types of maintenance and repair work. The difference is that a Millwright is expected to perform all types of repair work which arise in his assigned area with or without the assistance of other Millwrights and—save for such direction as may be given by his foreman—on his own responsibility. The Repairman-Mechanical, on the other hand, is expected to work alone only on "routine" work; on "major" or "complex" work, he is expected to work with and under the direction of a Millwright.

7. The job description for Repairman-Mechanical, moreover, makes no reference to the diagnosis of trouble or the planning of repairs. The Millwright description, on the other hand, places great emphasis upon these functions. In the second paragraph under the heading "Work Procedure" it states that a Millwright—

"Inspects mill equipment for defects such as misalignment, wear, insufficient lubrication, etc. Determines the best way of making repairs to minimize interruption of production. Advises when immediate shut down of equipment is necessary to minimize damage or when temporarily continued operation will have no harmful effect."

8. The Board finds that Hiser is performing functions that are covered by this language in the Millwright job description and which are not covered by the Repairman-Mechanical job description. Neither Hiser nor the day turn Millwright have any set routine for the inspection of soaking pit equipment, yet both do inspect that equipment from time to time. In case of a breakdown on the second turn, Hiser examines the situation and advises either an immediate shut down or temporarily continued operation, just as the Millwright does on the day turn. In the normal course of his job, when there is a breakdown on the second turn, Hiser looks into it and determines whether immediate repairs can be made without interrupting production.

9. It is true that the day turn Millwright exercises the responsibility for the long term ordering of materials, and that Hiser is not asked to perform this function. From time to time, however, Hiser does order the materials that are necessary for emergency repairs on his turn. That he does not do long term ordering, in the opinion of the Board, does not discount the fact that his responsibilities are greater than those called for by the Repairman-Mechanical job description.

10. It is also true that the day turn Millwright directs the work of two Repairmen-Mechanical and two Helpers, while Hiser is assisted only by a Helper. This fact may indeed indicate that Hiser's actual working responsibility is less than that of the day turn Millwright. It appears to the Board, nevertheless, that it is greater than that called for by the Repairman-Mechanical job description.

11. The Company places great emphasis upon its claim that the day turn Millwright instructs Hiser in the work which he is to perform, leaving him notes or giving him oral instructions at the time of the change in shifts. The facts revealed by the Board's investigation of this case do not support this claim. On routine days there is frequently no communication between the two men whatsoever. When important repairs are under way, the day turn Millwright will inform Hiser of the existing state of the work, and of the further operations needed. These communications, however, are only those which normally would have to take place when one workman relieves another on a repair job. There is no evidence that the day turn Millwright is in any sense directing Hiser's work or could properly be held accountable for it.

12. The Board finds that the work performed by Hiser and the day turn Millwright is of substantially the same type and

degree of difficulty, and that, though Hiser's responsibility is not in all respects the equivalent of that exercised by the day turn Millwright, it is nevertheless greater than that contemplated by the Repairman-Mechanical job description. We hold, accordingly, that Hiser is entitled to the classification and rate of a Millwright with back pay to the date on which the grievance was filed.

AWARD

13. The grievant is held entitled to the classification and rate of Millwright with back pay to the date on which the grievance was filed.

DISSENTING OPINION

14. In my opinion the majority has not properly evaluated the facts in connection with the basic fundamental involved in this case. At the outset there are three phases contained in this issue which should be made clear.

15. First, it should be understood that the question of Hiser's individual ability is immaterial in the issue before us. Whether Hiser, the grievant, has less ability, the same ability, or greater ability than some other employee has no bearing on a proper decision.

16. Second, it must be understood that job descriptions and classifications have been agreed upon by duly authorized representatives of the Company and the Union. This Board has no jurisdiction to alter such agreements in any way. In fact the Labor Agreement provides specifically in Section 9-D that the job descriptions and classifications in effect shall continue in effect (providing there is no change in the job content) except as such changes are made in accordance with mutual agreement of the officially designated representatives of the parties. Such descriptions and classifications represent standards which are to be compared with the work of any given employee who claims he is not receiving the proper and established rate of pay for the work performed.

17. Third, the only question which this Board had to determine is whether Hiser is being paid the correct rate of pay for the work performed. To determine this question the Board is required to compare the work performed by Hiser with the standard agreed upon as embodied in the job description which the Company has applied to determine Hiser's classification. Should the Board find as a matter of fact that Hiser is not being required to perform work beyond that comprehended by the standard applied by

the Company, the Board must deny the grievance. In case the Board should find that Hiser is being required to perform work beyond that comprehended by that standard, it would be necessary for the Board to determine as to whether there is some other standard agreed to by the parties that properly may be compared with the work being required of Hiser, in order to determine his proper classification and likewise the rate of pay he should receive. For example, Hiser claims that the standard that should be applied is the one which has been agreed upon by the parties for determining the work of the Millwright.

18. An analysis of these three phases indicates first, that no consideration is to be given Hiser as an individual. Determinations made on this case should depend entirely upon the assigned work performed as determined for the job under the job description.

19. As for the second phase, no further consideration is required as there have been no changes in the job, therefore permitting application of the standard contained in the job description as such standards are now in effect.

20. With reference to the third phase, Subsection 2-E of the April 15, 1946 Agreement (which Agreement is controlling regarding the standards, methods and procedures to be used in classifying employees to determine the applicable rate of pay) provides that assigned maintenance jobs of a general mechanical repair nature which involve a lower job content than a Millwright's job as defined in Paragraph D, Subsection 2 shall be identified as Repairman-Mechanical jobs. The standards for determining whether an employee is performing Millwright work set forth in Subsection 2-D is the full scope of job content involved in the inspection, repair, replacement, installation, adjustment and maintenance of all mechanical equipment in major producing departments such as Open Hearths and Rolling Mills.

21. Thus, the parties indicated clearly that the standard to determine whether certain assigned maintenance work is that of Repairman-Mechanical is made up of two factors. First the Repairman-Mechanical job description and classification is the primary factor. The second factor is to determine whether the work is of a lower job content than that involved in the Millwright job in the particular major producing department and/or the assigned area involved. As applied to this case, the above simply means that to determine whether Hiser has been paid the proper rate of pay, the work required of him is to be compared with the standard agreed upon between the parties,

which standard the Company has applied to him, namely, Repairman-Mechanical Rolling Mill. If everything he is doing is comprehended by the job description for Repairman-Mechanical Rolling Mill and if, in addition, he is not performing the full content of a Millwright job as the Millwright job is found to exist in the Rolling Mill and/or assigned area, it must follow that the Company has applied the correct job description and assigned him to a proper classification under which he would be properly paid.

22. Applying the above reasoning, we find that the claim in this grievance must be determined in accordance with one or the other of the following:

(A) That Hiser is being required to perform work which exceeds that comprehended by the Repairman-Mechanical standard in the following particulars (specify items that he is being required to do which are both, [1] not included in the Repairman-Mechanical description and classification that has been applied to him by the Company, and [2] that which is contained in the job content of "Millwright" employees in the Rolling Mill Department). Such finding would conclude that the work performed by Hiser is comprehended only by the standard agreed to between the Company and the Union in the form of a Millwright description and classification, to the extent that such general description and classification is applicable in the Rolling Mill Department and/or assigned area, and therefore Hiser is to be paid the Millwright rate.

or (B) The work that is being required of Hiser does not exceed that included within the standard represented by Repairman-Mechanical Rolling Mills description and classification as above explained or modified.

23. It is clear from the evidence that the determination "B" above is here applicable. The Award is improperly based on a comparison of a day-turn Millwright job with that of the work performed by the grievant as a Mechanical-Repairman. The day-turn Millwright job here referred to has been so

classified only because the occupant filling that particular Millwright assignment regularly supervises two or three Mechanical-Repairmen (Helpers, etc.). Hiser does not regularly supervise other Mechanical-Repairmen.

24. Under the prescribed and agreed to method of classification the application of the standard job description was required in every case within the areas in which the employees were assigned to work. In the area here involved there are employed more than twenty Millwrights. All such Millwrights are assigned to the Blooming Mills and assigned area excepting the one-day-turn Millwright assigned to the Soaking Pits—which is the particular occupation considered by the majority to be involved. The application of the standards to such employees must be made to cover the "assigned area," namely, the Blooming Mills and Soaking Pits and the area surrounding these operations.

25. Had proper consideration been given to the application of the standards as defined under the job descriptions, it would have been quite evident that the day-turn Millwright assigned to the Soaking Pits performed such work and had such responsibilities as to provide a very minimum round of duties applicable to the Millwright job description. Further, the work performed by the grievant is clearly such work as is found in the standards set forth in the Repairman-Mechanical job description. In this instance we find the work performed and the duties outlined to be definitely such as may be defined properly as routine work. There is no major or complex work in the location where the grievant performs his work, namely, the Soaking Pits. The job description of the Repairman-Mechanical indicates a definite requirement that such incumbents are expected to work alone on routine work. This was the full extent of the grievant's activities.

26. This arbitrator would have denied the grievance on the basis of the grievant's proper classification when full consideration is given to the work performed and such activities compared to those outlined under the Repairman-Mechanical job description.

Walter Kelly, *Companies' Member*

A—223, -224, -225, -226. Waukegan Works. July 29, 1949
Ralph T. Seward, *Chairman*

BACKGROUND FACTS

1. Prior to the "Wage Inequity" reclassification of February 9, 1947, the four grievants in these combined cases were classified as "Millwrights C" in the Wire Mill at the

Company's Waukegan Works. Three of them, Robert O. Etchell, Ray Beauchamp and Leonard Anderson, were reclassified on that date as "Millwright Helpers." The fourth, Charles Paavilainen, was placed in the "Oiler—Maintenence" classification, which is in the same job class as "Millwright Helper" and carries the same standard hourly rate. All of the grievants claim that they should have been reclassified as "Millwrights" and ask that their classification be corrected and that they be made whole for the wages lost.

2. Since the filing of the original grievance, the status of all four grievants has changed. Etchell was promoted to the Millwright classification in May, 1947 and quit his employment with the Company in October of the same year. Beauchamp quit in the spring of 1947. Anderson was promoted to the Millwright classification in the spring of 1948. Paavilainen has also been working as a Millwright since 1948, replacing a Millwright who has been on leave of absence.

3. Two hearings have been held on this case. At the first, the Union presented little specific evidence regarding the work which the grievants had been doing but confined itself to the general allegation that they worked largely on their own, doing repair work similar to that performed by the Millwrights in their respective departments, and that since they were not "helping" these Millwrights they should not be classified as "Helpers."

4. The Company's evidence at the first hearing may be summarized briefly as follows. At the time of the reclassification, each of the four grievants was normally assigned to routine oiling and machine maintenance in one of the departments of the Wire Mill; Etchell in the Dry Drawing Department; Anderson in the Galvanizing and Stranding Department; and Beauchamp and Paavilainen in the Wet Drawing Department. One or more Millwrights were also assigned to these departments. The bulk of the repair work in the finishing end of the Wire Mill consisted of simple machine adjustments and the replacement of easily accessible parts— jobs which the Company characterized as "minor repairs." On such tasks, the grievants customarily worked alone, as did the Millwrights who were assigned to the same areas. "Major repairs" were customarily taken care of over the weekend by Millwrights and Helpers assigned to the "general maintenance" crew. When such repairs were necessary during the week, one of the grievants might work on it, but only as an assistant to a Millwright.

5. The Company conceded that for days at a time there might be little difference between the specific tasks performed by the grievants on the one hand, and the Millwrights on the other. In the Company's opinion, however, there was a marked difference in the responsibility which went with the two types of jobs. The Millwrights were held responsible for the condition of the machines in their assigned area; inspected them, diagnosed the source and nature of any serious trouble, decided whether and when a machine should be shut down, and performed the more difficult repairs either alone or with the assistance of a "Helper." The grievants normally had no such responsibility. On one or more occasions, it is true, each of the four grievants had taken over the duties of their respective Millwrights when the latter were absent or on vacation. On such occasions, though their actual work might not be substantially different, they were considered to have a Millwright's responsibility and were therefore paid the Millwright's rate.

6. Following the close of the first hearing, the Board referred this case back to the parties for the submission of further evidence with regard to the actual work performed by the grievants. As Etchell and Beauchamp, in the meantime, had left their employment with the Company, the additional evidence submitted at the second hearing concerned only Anderson and Paavilainen.

7. It appears from this evidence that at the time the grievance was filed Anderson normally devoted the greater portion of his time to oiling. He had, however, performed all of the types of machine repair which were required in the Galvanizing and Stranding Department except two: (1) "Install trunion bearings and line up a drum on a Stranding Machine"; and (2) "Remove take-up frame reducer and line up same." The first operation seems to be done quite often; the second is most infrequent. Since his promotion to the Millwright classification, Anderson has done the first, but still has not performed the second.

8. Paavilainen, at the time of the grievance, also spent most of his time in oiling (in fact, as we have noted, he was classified as "Oiler-Maintenance"). He had done considerable repair work, however, and was assigned to an increasing variety of this work in 1947 and 1948. The Union submitted a list of the different repair jobs Paavilainen had performed by himself during December, 1947 and early January, 1948. The Company contended that these jobs were all "minor," but conceded that they were typical of the repair jobs customarily required in the Wet Drawing Department. The Company listed three jobs which Paavilainen had not performed prior to the filing of the grievance. (I.E., (1) "pull out frame, line up main shafting drums, etc., on old style 8″ equipment"; (2) "line up block spindle and bearing on 22″ coarse wet wire frame"; and (3) "line up 8″ tinning take-up frame block spindle.") Certain of this work he has since

performed, but only as an assistant to the Millwright in his department.

FINDINGS

9. Section 2(d) of the Agreement of April 15, 1946 provides that:

"Assigned maintenance jobs of a general mechanical repair nature which reflect the full scope of job content (requirements as to training, skill, responsibility, effort and working conditions) involved in the inspection, repair, replacement, installation, adjustment and maintenance of all mechanical equipment in major producing departments such as open hearths and rolling mills shall be described, classified and identified as 'Millwright' jobs, and helping jobs in such areas of assigned work shall be described, classified and identified as 'Millwright Helper' jobs."

10. Representatives of the Company stated on the record that the Finishing Department (including Wet Wire Drawing, Bundling, Galvanizing and Stranding) was a "major producing department" within the meaning of this section. The Dry Drawing Department is the other "major producing department" in the Wire Mill. The question before us, then, is whether, at the time of the reclassification of February 9, 1947, the grievants were performing work which "reflected the full scope of job content . . . involved in the inspection, repair, replacement, installation, adjustment and maintenance of all mechanical equipment" in the Finishing Department.

11. With regard to Mr. Etchell and Mr. Beauchamp, the Union has clearly failed to establish its case. The Board found at the conclusion of the first hearing that the evidence submitted by the Union up to that point was inadequate and gave the Board no clear or certain idea of the work performed by any of the four grievants. No additional evidence with regard to Etchell and Beauchamp's work has been submitted. We find, accordingly, that their grievance must be denied.

12. With regard to Anderson and Paavilainen, the Union has submitted considerable additional evidence concerning the nature of the repair work they were performing. In our opinion, the effect of this evidence is to demonstrate conclusively what the Company, in any case, concedes: That few complex or "major" repair jobs were necessary in the Finishing; that Anderson and Paavilainen did all types of "minor" repair work that arose in their assigned areas; that most of the repair jobs performed by the Millwrights in

those areas were "minor"; and that for days at a time both the grievants and the Millwrights were doing the same type of repair work.

13. This evidence, however, is not sufficient to support the Union's case. It overlooks entirely the element of responsibility—an element of prime importance in the Millwright classification. An employee receives the Millwright classification and rate, not because he is constantly working at major and complex repairs, but because he is available and has the ability to make such repairs if the need arises. Under his Foreman, he is responsible for the condition of the machines in his assigned area. If things go well, complex repair jobs may rarely be necessary and he will be able to devote his time to minor repair work, inspection and even lubrication. His responsibility continues, none the less. It is his job, insofar as is possible, to see that things do not go wrong; to prevent the need for major repairs which will tie up the machines and stop production; and in the event that a major repair becomes necessary, to perform it efficiently and effectively.

14. The Union has not shown that at the time of the reclassification or during the period prior to their promotion, either Anderson or Paavilainen exercised this responsibility. Management did not require them to assume a Millwright's *responsibility* for the maintenance of the equipments in their areas. They did not exercise such responsibility. They did the oiling and the minor repair jobs they were asked to do and they assisted the regular Millwrights on such major repairs as were required. That is all that the evidence shows, and it is insufficient to support a claim for the Millwright rate.

15. This case may appropriately be compared with our decision in Case No. N-95, in which we upheld the claim of an employee who was classified as a Repairman-Mechanical that he should be classified as a Millwright. We found in that case that the grievant, who worked by himself during the 3-11 turn, was doing essentially the same type of repair jobs as the Millwright who worked the 7-11 turn. We noted that little if any of the repair work which either performed could properly be called "major" or "complex" within the meaning of the job descriptions. We pointed out, however, that "the crucial factor in distinguishing between a Millwright and a Repairman-Mechanical is not the actual maintenance operations which employees in either classification perform at any one time or even over long periods of time, but is the element of responsibility." We found that the grievant, working on a turn *by himself,* was in fact exercising a degree of responsibility for the condition of

the equipment on that turn which entitled him to the Millwright classification.

16. We cannot make such a finding here. Neither Anderson nor Paavilainen worked alone in their assigned areas, except when the regular Millwrights were absent from work. On such occasions, they properly received the Millwright rate, for they were exercising a Millwright's responsibility. By the same token they were not entitled to that classification and rate when the Millwrights were present and the grievants had responsibility only for the successful completion of the individual repair jobs to which they were assigned.

AWARD

17. The grievances are denied. (Union member of Board dissented without opinion.)

SECTION C. ASSIGNMENT OF DUTIES

N—209. Lorain Works. December 31, 1953
Sylvester Garrett, *Chairman*

BACKGROUND

1. This grievance protests the failure to call out a Pipefitter and Pipefitter Helper to perform certain work on the 11:00 p.m. to 7:00 a.m. turn on April 6, 1953.

2. On the weekend of April 5 and 6, 1953, the Company installed a siphon with a six-inch discharge line in the Mandrel Mill sump pit of No. 4 Seamless Mill. Installation of the new siphon and line was started on the 7:00 a.m. turn, Sunday, April 5 and completed on the 3:00 p.m.-11:00 turn. When this phase of the installation was completed, however, a section of four-inch discharge line (which had been removed for installation of the new six-inch line) still required replacement when the 11:00 p.m. turn commenced on April 6. This replacement required cutting a short length of pipe to add to the four-inch line, so as to pass it over the six-inch line, bolting a flange in place on one end of the pipe, and welding the flange and pipe in place.

3. When the 11:00 p.m. turn started, Mechanical Turn Foreman Horne discussed with the assigned maintenance crew the best means of handling the various jobs on hand. The assigned maintenance crew in No. 4 Seamless Mill includes both a Pipefitter and a Millwright. On this particular turn there was an important job to be done which required a Pipefitter. If he assigned the Pipefitter to this job, Horne thus was faced with the problem of how to handle the 4" discharge line. The Millwright present then suggested that he might handle this minor job, so as to free the Pipefitter to work on the other more important job. This arrangement was satisfactory to both the Pipefitter on the shift and the Millwright, who proceeded to complete the discharge line work. In so doing he worked with a Welder. His main functions in the operation included cutting the pipe and bolting the flange. The entire operation apparently consumed several hours, the precise time being in dispute.

4. Grievants are the Pipefitter and Pipefitter Helper who initially started the siphon installation on the 7:00 a.m. turn. They believe they should have been called out for an overtime shift at 11:00 p.m. Sunday to complete the job, on the ground that the work in question is Pipefitters' work rather than Millwrights' work.

5. During consideration of the grievance the Union took the position that work on four-inch pipe was clearly Pipefitters' work and not Milliwrights' work. The Company denies the existence of any clear and fixed line of demarcation between Pipefitter and Millwright work involving handling of pipe. It points to the agreed job description of Millwright which refers to pipe work. Under the working procedure of Millwright, reference is made to use of a pipe threading machine and the tools and equipment include burning equipment such as the Millwright used in the present instance. Under Factor 3 of the Millwright classification reference is made to the use of considerable judgment in "cutting and fitting pipe and in adjusting valves, etc."

FINDINGS

6. The Union recognizes that the job descriptions of, and functions normally performed by, Millwrights and Pipefitters overlap to some extent. Millwrights for many years have done work with pipe. Nonetheless, the Union contends that work with pipe of this size (4 inches) should have been assigned to Pipefitters rather than to Millwrights.

7. The evidence does not support the existence of any practice or understanding to this effect. Actually, considerable flexibility has been practiced for years in assigning work cutting and fitting pipe among various craft jobs, the duties of which require work

with pipe from time to time. It is clear that normally this work would have been assigned to a Pipefitter rather than a Millwright, except for the special circumstances which arose. In the present instance the work performed did not require the full or specialized skill of the Pipefitter, and fell within the scope of pipe cutting and fitting contemplated under the Millwright description. Finally, the Board cannot assume that, had

Management decided to use a Pipefitter, the grievants would have been entitled to assignment to the work on this given shift. No basis appears on which grievants were entitled to insist upon being called out for such an overtime assignment.

AWARD

8.   The grievance is denied.

USC—530.   Fairless Works.   November 7, 1955
Sylvester Garrett, *Chairman*

BACKGROUND

1.   The two grievances from the Utilities Department of Fairless Works, protest assignment of simple pipe fitting type duties to Pump and Turbine Repairman.

2.   Pump and Turbine Repairmen are in Class 15 at Fairless Works, while Pipe Fitters are in Class 13. No Pipe Fitters have protested assignment of the disputed simple pipe fitting duties to Pump and Turbine Repairmen.

3.   The grievances were precipitated on November 8, 1954, when Grievance Committeeman O'Keefe was directed to install additional drain lines in the Powerhouse. The particular job consisted of installing 5 pieces of pipe of 1¼" diameter varying in length from 2½' to 6½', the installation of 5 elbows, and 1 piece of ¾" pipe 3' long. This was to provide a simple drain, under no pressure, exhausting from an Air Ejector into a floor level drain—bypassing water into the floor level drain rather than into the After Cooler. (There is some confusion as to whether the entire job was not done first by O'Keefe with ¾" pipe rather than 1¼" pipe, but this is not material.) Subsequently, O'Keefe was assigned to install similar drains in 3 or 4 other locations.

4.   O'Keefe's objection to performance of these duties stems from his belief that the parties have an agreement that this type of pipe fitting work does not fall within the scope of the Pump and Turbine Repairman job.

5.   Item 10 of the Working Procedure of the job states:

"Removes and replaces existing piping on machinery to be repaired. Performs simple pipe fitting." (Underscoring added.)

The Union holds that the words "simple pipe fitting" cannot be deemed to include installation of new piping as here required of O'Keefe. The Company stresses that around 25% of the work of Pump and Turbine Re-

pairmen involves pipe work and pipe repairs, including replacement of bad fittings, valves, and simple pipe fitting. It believes the only reasonable meaning to be given to such a term as "simple pipe fitting" would include the disputed assignments.

6.   The Pump and Turbine Repairman job description was agreed upon at a meeting on March 11, 1954. The Union representatives who participated in the meeting feel that the Company representatives accepted the Union's definition of "simple pipe fitting" to include only:

1. Replacement of bad fittings such as elbows, unions, pipe couplings, etc.;
2. Replacement of bad valves;
3. Repair of leakage in the center of the line where the work involved would simply be cutting and rethreading existing pipe and coupling the two segments.

7.   Even though the Company suggested language of "simple pipe fitting" appears in Item 10 of the Working Procedure, rather than just the three items listed above, the Union representatives believe that there was agreement that "simple pipe fitting" would have the same meaning and no other meaning than the three specific items.

8.   The Company representatives in the meeting deny that any such agreement was made. They assert that the parties were unable to agree upon a practical over-all definition of the term "simple pipe fitting," and hence used the words without further elaboration.

FINDINGS

9.   Since the disputed work involved no blueprints, no pressure, straight lines, no complex fittings, and was of modest over-all proportions, it appears to fall within common usage of the term simple pipe fitting in the mills.

10.   Under the Inequities Program both parties have recognized that the function of

the job description is to provide only the basis upon which to classify the job accurately. They also have recognized that (1) the inherent nature of assigned maintenance work (such as here involved) is such that the job content requirements may vary from day to day within any given assigned area, and (2) employees engaged in performance of assigned maintenance work may be called upon to perform varying duties in discharging the responsibilities of their assignments.

11. In the present instance, however, the newness of Fairless Works apparently injected an unusual element into the discussions of the parties at the time of the description of the various jobs. Without the long history of operation which characterized most other plants where the Inequities Program was put into effect, Fairless was characterized by a considerable amount of confusion as to who did what, and under which jobs.

12. Here the Union feels that the parties' discussions on March 11, 1954, were not merely for the purpose of describing the job as an incident of classification, but also were for the purpose of determining exactly what assignments should be given to incumbents of the job in the future and what assignments never could be made.

13. The problem presented here is by no means unique at Fairless. The parties there found it desirable to establish a joint committee known as the "Job Overlap Committee" in order to work out difficulties of this sort which arose through the plant with considerable frequency. The present grievances were among those considered by the Job Overlap Committee in an unsuccessful effort to evolve an agreement concerning the term "simple pipe fitting."

14. There is no occasion to question the good faith of the representatives of either party who participated in the meeting of March 11, 1954. It is easily possible that each came away from the meeting convinced that the other party had agreed with it. It now appears, however, that there was no agreement that the term "simple pipe fitting" would include only the three items specified by the Union, and also was intended to embody a commitment that all pipe fitting assignments would be thus limited. Where the testimony of the men at the meeting is in direct conflict, the Board naturally must give great weight to the fact that the only writing which evolved from the meeting is the agreed description itself. This uses the term "simple pipe fitting" without the limitations pressed by the Union. This on its face reflects lack of agreement as urged by the Union.

15. This conclusion is strengthened by the fact that for some months prior to March 11, 1954, the Pump and Turbine Repairmen (then listed as Millwrights) had been called upon to perform work of the same type as involved here. Foreman Hunziker described three instances prior to March 11, 1954, in which simple pipe fitting work was performed going beyond the limited items relied upon by the Union. Grievance Committeeman O'Keefe apparently objected in most or all of these instances, yet this does not detract from their significance as background for the meeting of March 11, 1954. It is significant that, against this background, there is nothing in the job description to indicate that such work does not fall within the term "simple pipe fitting."

16. The Union spokesman has urged that the legal canon of construction known as the "ejusdem generis rule" should be applied to the interpretation of Item 10 of the Working Procedure. Under this analysis the sentence "performs simple pipe fitting" would have no broader meaning than the first sentence of Item 10, namely, "removes and replaces existing piping on machinery to be repaired." There are many reasons why the Board cannot adopt this type approach to construction of job descriptions, most important of which is that such an approach would be inconsistent with the mutual objectives of the parties. Since the phrase "simple pipe fitting" is included separately from the "removes and replaces" phrase, and on its face has a broader meaning, the Board finds no appropriate basis for limiting it in the manner suggested. Neither the parties nor the Board as yet have adopted a formalistic approach to interpretation and application of job descriptions, in view of the manner in which they were prepared and their limited function under the Agreements of the parties.

AWARD

17. The grievances are denied.

N—210.   Lorain Works.   December 31, 1953
Sylvester Garrett, *Chairman*

BACKGROUND

1.   This grievance protests the failure to call out men in the Diesel Garage Maintenance Department, Lorain Works, to handle repairs to a diesel shovel on Sunday, February 8, 1953.

2.   On the morning in question, the diesel shovel was involved in an accident which damaged the radiator to the point of requiring replacement. This job was assigned to the Shovel Operator, Job Class 12, immediately after the accident. Grievants include both Automotive Mechanics and Automotive Mechanics' Helpers, in Job Classes 14 and 6, respectively, who contend that they should have been called out to perform this work.

3.   In completing the repair in question, the Shovel Operator worked with a Millwright, Job Class 14, and a Helper.

4.   The job description of Diesel Shovel Operator under "Occasional Duties" includes "aid Diesel Mechanic in making repairs to shovel" and "make minor repairs to shovel." Under Factor 12 of the Diesel Shovel Operator classification states: "make repairs to shovel and assist on engineer repairs."

5.   The job description of Auto Mechanic under "Primary Function" reads: "to make all necessary repairs, adjustments and installations to all diesel and gasoline powered equipment used throughout the plant." Under "Working Procedures" the description includes, "makes necessary repairs to equipment in field as required."

6.   Under "Primary Function" the Millwright job description provides, "To inspect, repair, replace, install, adjust and maintain all mechanical equipment in a major producing unit or assigned area." Under "Working Procedure" the Millwright description includes: "Dismantles, cleans, repairs, replaces, installs, maintains, assembles and lubricates mechanical equipment," and further, "Works with repair crews as directed on emergency breakdowns."

7.   Owing to the gradual increase in diesel units used throughout the plant, the Diesel Garage was established in the Maintenance Department in February, 1950. The Diesel Garage functions as a service to the operating departments of Lorain Works in connection with diesel equipment such as the Diesel Shovel. It operates regularly 13 turns per week with three men in the Automotive Mechanic classification covering these shifts and also handling repairs on call-out basis. At the start of each turn, the Diesel Garage

Foreman reviews the requests for services of Automotive Mechanics which have been made by various operating departments and determines how to lay out the work.

8.   In this case, the Union relies primarily on the broad language of the Automotive Mechanic job description to assert that *all necessary repairs* to diesel powered equipment throughout the plant must be made by Auto Mechanics. It also cites various prior instances when Auto Mechanics were called upon to handle repairs of no greater magnitude than involved in the present case, including replacement of radiators.

9.   The Company contends that the job description of Automotive Mechanic was not intended and cannot be construed to give an exclusive right to Automotive Mechanics to make all necessary repairs to diesel equipment. Such, in fact, has not been the practice over the years. In February, 1950, the three Auto Mechanics then assigned to the Diesel Garage asked Foreman Long just what kind of diesel repairs they would be called upon to handle in working out of the garage. Long advised them that in general, all work in connection with hydraulic clutches, main engines, lighting plants and starting engines on the diesel equipment would be handled by the Automotive Mechanics. There was no protest made at the time that this was an unreasonable or improper allocation of diesel repair work to the Automotive Mechanics.

FINDINGS

10.   It is clear that the Auto Mechanics over the years have not been given an exclusive right, or "franchise," to handle all necessary repairs to diesel powered equipment throughout the plant. Many such repairs have long been handled by employees in the various operating departments, including the Shovel Operator involved in this case. The Diesel Garage was set-up to service operating departments upon request, and not to take over all diesel equipment repair work. It is agreed that the skill of an Automotive Mechanic is not required to change a radiator on a diesel shovel.

11.   While some radiator replacements in the past have been handled by Auto Mechanics, in other instances the identical repair has been handled by the Shovel Operator with other employees. There is no established practice which could apply in the present case. The applicable job descriptions were not intended to, nor do they, provide any clear guidance as to which of the various jobs, which might handle such repairs, is

entitled to handle all such repairs as a matter of exclusive right.

N—234. Lorain Works. September 15, 1955
Sylvester Garrett, *Chairman*

FINDINGS

1. This grievance protests change in work assignments of Electrician-Wireman Serrano, Electrical Repairs Division, Maintenance Department, Lorain Works.

2. Grievant completed apprentice training as Electrician-Wireman on August 1, 1949, and was assigned to duties in the Telephone and Meter Department seniority unit. For about five years, at least, these duties consisted for the most part of service work on meters, electric wiring, pyrometers, various testing devices, and other miscellaneous electrical jobs.

3. These work assignments preponderantly were the same as duties performed by Instrument Repairmen, for which there was no apprentice training program until 1950. There is a substantial overlap of duties of Electrician-Wiremen and Instrument Repairmen at Lorain Works. Both jobs are Class 16 and the main difference between them at Lorain Works appears to be that the Wiremen's duties comprehend generally those of the Instrument Repairmen, along with other duties. The less inclusive duties of the Instrument Repairmen relate more specifically to work on meters.

4. On July 23, 1954, grievant was assigned with other Wiremen to complete a construction job in the Pipe Mill area where Wiremen were urgently needed. Since then he has been assigned to various other jobs throughout the plant as Wireman. This change in the nature of work assignments has not affected grievant's seniority status. He continues in the Telephone and Meter seniority unit.

AWARD

12. The grievance is denied.

5. In protesting the change in nature of his work assignments, grievant primarily is concerned that this change may prejudice his opportunity to promote to Electrical Technician (Class 20) or to Electronic Repairman (Class 18). Originally he feared that he no longer would be eligible to bid for these two jobs. Apparently he checked this with Superintendent Butler and was told, erroneously, that as Wireman he would not be eligible to bid. This misconception was corrected at the hearing. Grievant also feels that other men, working on the assignments he handled prior to July 23, 1954, ultimately may acquire greater knowledge in these specialized areas and thus acquire relatively greater ability for promotion to the two higher rated jobs.

6. Grievant is a well qualified Wireman, and has been utilized to instruct Instrument Repairman apprentices. Superintendent Butler agrees that Serrano could qualify as Instrument Repairman even though not so slotted. Both Superintendent Butler and General Foreman Terry deny that grievant's opportunity to promote either to Electrical Technician or to Electronic Repairman is prejudiced by the change in his assigned duties.

7. No provision of the July 1, 1954 Agreement, or of any local agreement, appears to have been violated under the evidence in this case.

AWARD

8. The grievance is denied.

N—235. Lorain Works. November 23, 1955
Sylvester Garrett, *Chairman*

BACKGROUND

1. This grievance protests assignment of electrical welding to Welders in the Fuels and Power Department of Lorain Works. It is filed on behalf of Welders in the Welding Division of the Maintenance Department.

2. For many years a small number of Welders have been employed in the Fuels and Power Department. The bulk of welding at Lorain Works long has been performed by Welders in the Maintenance Department, who now number more than 100.

3. The Welders in Fuels and Power, as well as in the Maintenance Department, work under the standard craft description of Welder, with Primary Function of—"performs all kinds of welding, brazing and cutting of any type of metal using gas and electric welding equipment."

4. Prior to January 11, 1955, electric welding was not done by the Welders in Fuels and Power Department. Instead Welders were called from the Maintenance Department to bring along an electric welding machine and perform this type welding.

5. Since it was necessary to bring the electric welding machine a substantial distance whenever electric welding was required in Fuels and Power, a good deal of inefficiency was involved. To eliminate this the Fuels and Power Department acquired an electric welding machine and placed it in operation January 11, 1955. Fuels and Power Welders then were assigned to perform electric welding in the Fuels and Power Department, using the new equipment.

6. Shortly before there had been a reduction in force of Welders in the Maintenance Department. Perhaps because of this, the new method of handling electric welding in Fuels and Power was protested by the grievance as a threat to the job security of the Central Maintenance Welders. The Union urges that performance of electric welding by Fuels and Power Welders violates an established local working condition and infringes upon seniority rights of the Central Maintenance Welders.

7. In support of the view that a local working condition prevents assignment of this type welding to the Fuels and Power Department Welders, the Grievance Committeeman testified that in slotting Welders in 1947, it was understood that they did not have to perform all functions of the job in order to receive Intermediate or Standard rate. It is felt that this understanding requires that such men not be assigned after 1947, to performance of these duties, even though they may be at Intermediate or Standard rate.

8. While Fuels and Power Welders are in a separate seniority unit from Central Maintenance Welders, there is no provision of any local seniority agreement covering the present problem.

FINDINGS

9. The performance of electric welding is included in the standard craft description of Welder at Lorain Works. It was largely because of lack of equipment in the Fuels and Power Department that the Central Maintenance Welders were called in from time to time to perform electric welding there prior to January 11, 1955.

10. There is no doubt that Journeyman Welders were slotted in 1947 at Intermediate or Standard rate even though not capable of performing all aspects of welding work under the standard description. But this was not intended to preclude training and assignment of the Welders to perform different types of welding within the craft than they performed at the time of slotting. The evidence does not reveal any agreement to prevent such training and assignment.

AWARD

11. The grievance is denied.

N—241. Lorain Works. June 7, 1956
Sylvester Garrett, *Chairman*

FINDINGS

1. Motor Inspector Vasu protests in this grievance that he was required to perform simple rigging duties in changing a motor on the roof of No. 4 Seamless Mill at Lorain Works.

2. As the case has developed, the only question is whether the protested rigging work was in the category of "simple rigging" such as clearly contemplated in the Motor Inspector's Job Description. The evidence requires that this question be answered in the affirmative because of the nature of the work itself. It also appears that the same motor change which gave rise to this grievance was performed on five earlier occasions. The first occasion antedated permanent removal of a weather hood which complicated the job, and Riggers were used with a number of other employees. On the four subsequent occasions after the weather hood had been removed, no Riggers were used, and Motor Inspectors performed such simple rigging duties as were required. This is what was done in the present case, but it was grievant's first assignment to handle this specific motor change.

3. The Union stresses that one or more Foremen were present throughout most of the work by Vasu on this assignment and infers that this was because Management believed the grievant needed help in performing rigging duties. The record indicates that grievant demurred from the outset when directed to perform the assignment, and it seems clear the Foremen were present to make sure that the work proceeded without untoward incident or unnecessary delay.

AWARD

4. The grievance is denied.

A—747. Donora Plant. March 29, 1957
Sylvester Garrett, *Chairman*

FINDINGS

1. In this grievance various Machinists in the Electric Weld Machine Shop at Donora Steel and Wire Works contend that they should not be assigned duties which they believe more properly should be assigned to Electricians.

2. The disputed duties involve minor electrical aspects of the maintenance and repair of production equipment in the Electric Weld Department. From 1936 to February 1947, these duties were performed by Mechanics in the Electric Weld Machine Shop, who were slotted as Machinists upon installation of the Standard Hourly Wage Scale. While the disputed duties, over the years, were performed by various Mechanics up to February 1947, in later years most of this type of maintenance was handled particularly by Machinists Carlson and Listopad in addition to their other work as Machinists. After retirement of Carlson on March 31, 1955, the work which he performed was assigned to other Machinists. Four months later it became necessary to go to 3 turn operation of the Machine Shop so that still other Machinists were required to handle this particular type of repair duty.

3. While the Union does not here challenge the general principles recognized and elaborated in Cases A-249, USC-418, USC-419, and USC-451, concerning the scope of craft job duties in particular plants, it holds that at Donora Carlson and Listopad were not really Machinists, but should have been slotted in 1947 into some other job classification. On this basis it reasons that the duties in which Carlson and Listopad became specialized were not truly within the scope of the Machinist job at Donora.

4. The undoubted performance of the disputed duties by various Machinists in the Electric Weld Shop at Donora extending at least as far back as 1936 leaves no basis to sustain this grievance.

AWARD

5. The grievance is denied.

CI—228. Gary Steel Works. June 29, 1951
Sidney L. Cahn, *Acting Chairman*

BACKGROUND

1. By this grievance, a Motor Inspector Helper, objects to Management requiring him to assist in painting a small store room used for electrical spare parts.

2. The agreed upon job description for Motor Inspector Helper does not, by express terms, make any provision for such work as painting. The description, however, does contain the following printed form (as distinguished from the typewritten contents): "The above statement reflects the general details considered necessary to describe the principal functions of the job identified, and shall not be construed as a detailed description of all of the work requirements that may be inherent in the job."

3. The major contention raised by Management is that its requirement, concerning the rough painting of this store room by the Motor Inspector Helper, is an *inherent* part of his job, while the Union maintains that the contrary is true.

FINDINGS

4. The word "inherent" in its generally accepted meaning refers to "an attribute to a subject"; something "naturally pertaining to a subject"; an "intrinsic part" of something else.

5. The evidence disclosed that Management employs craftsmen whose sole duty is that of painting, either by hand or machine. It would appear that the duty of painting the store room would naturally be part of the Painter's work and not that of a Motor Inspector Helper. But the record also discloses that Motor Inspector Helpers at this plant paint switches, motor shells, switch boards, etc. In addition there has been a practice whereby the maintenance gang, as a part of good housekeeping, have always painted their shack. On this premise Management claimed that painting is an inherent part of the Motor Inspector Helper's job. While such work, as the painting of switch boards, etc. (or the shack, for good housekeeping purposes) is an inherent part of a Motor Inspector's duties, being part of the maintenance of the equipment upon which he works, the painting of shelves in a store room, sub-store room or storage place should not be considered in the same light. One is an inherent, i.e., an intrinsic part of his regular job while the other is not. Should Management be desirous of obtaining such work as part of the duties, it should provide a new job developing a suit-

able job description for classification.

6. It was undenied that the painting of the shanty or shelves takes no more than a few hours of work per month. Ordinarily the maxim "de minimis non curat lex" (the law does not concern itself with trifles) would be considered as applicable even to an arbitration proceeding and certainly as between mature and experienced Union and Management negotiators. Were it not for the possibility that this action of Management, if approved, might be considered as permission to extend the job content of an individual, the grievance might well have been denied on the de minimis theory.

7. In situations of this character it is preferable that the parties have a definite line of demarcation in what is properly inherent and what is not. It is the opinion of this Board that the continuation of the past practice of having the Millwright gang take care of its own quarters is proper. However such painting of the Millwright shack should end with this action and not be extended to cover storage space such as the shelves of the substore room herein involved.

AWARD

8. The grievance is granted.

CHAPTER 21

GROUPLEADERS

The January 1, 1953 Job Description and Classification Manual gives special treatment to Groupleader jobs. The first four cases in this chapter (USC-790, USC-373, T-463, A-753) are concerned with the classification of Groupleader jobs, while the next five cases (T-461, USC-616, A-666, USC-413, T-140) deal with elimination of Groupleaders. The award in A-406, which may be found on p. 12, is also relevant to this chapter.

USC—790. Gary Steel Works. September 26, 1958
Sylvester Garrett, *Chairman*

FINDINGS

1. This grievance from the Coke Plant of Gary Steel Works claims that since combination of the Job Class 1 and Job Class 2 Standard Hourly Wage Scale rates into one common rate as of August 3, 1956, the grievant has been improperly compensated at Job Class 3 for performing the job of Janitor (Groupleader).

2. The Union holds that since Janitors (Class 1) now are paid the same rate as Class 2 jobs, the Janitor (Groupleader) should be in Class 4 in accordance with Section C-10 (p. 40) of the January 1, 1953, Job Description and Classification Manual.

3. The Janitor (Groupleader) originally was classified in Job Class 3 by application of the Groupleader convention in conformance with the Job Description and Classification Manual. There is no claim of change of job content to the extent of one full job class since original description and classification.

4. In support of the grievance, however, the Union cites Sections 1 and 2, and Section 9-H and -I of the August 3, 1956, Agreement, asserting that historically a Groupleader has received a rate of pay at least two job classes higher than the highest rate received by employees working under his direction. It feels that since the standard hourly wage rates for Job Class 1 and Job Class 2 are now the same, it constitutes an obsolete practice under Section 9-I to continue payment of the Janitor (Groupleader) at Class 3 rather than Class 4. Thus, it would have the Board correct this "error" by virtue of Section 9-H.

5. Section 9-D includes:

"The job description and classification for each job in effect as of the date of this Agreement shall continue in effect unless (1) Management changes the job content (requirements of the job as to the training, skill, responsibility, effort, and working conditions) to the extent of one full job class or more; (2) the job is terminated or not occupied during a period of one year; or (3) the description and classification are changed in accordance with mutual agreement of officially designated representatives of the Company and the Union."

6. These are the only conditions specified in the Agreement that permit a job classification that is in effect to be changed or eliminated. None of these conditions are present in the instant case nor does the Union allege them to be.

7. The basic job for classification of the Groupleader job here is Janitor, classified A-Base in Factor 7, and with a total classification of .7 for Job Class 1. Thus, the correct classification for Janitor (Groupleader) was and is D-2.0 in Factor 7, with a total classification of 2.7 for Job Class 3.

8. Section E, Paragraph 1 of the January 1, 1953, Job Description and Classification Manual states:

"1. The descriptions and classifications of jobs, determined in accordance with the foregoing Sections of this manual, apply to assign each job to its appropriate job class. The basic labor agreement in effect establishes the standard hourly wage scale

388

rate for each job class and sets forth provisions to enable application of the established standard hourly wage scale rate to the employee who performs the respective job . . ."

9. The August 3, 1956, Agreement states in Section 9-B-1:

"1. The standard hourly wage scale rate for each job class shall be the standard hourly wage rate for all jobs classified within such job class . . ."

10. The fact that the Standard Hourly Wage Scale established under Section 9 of the August 3, 1956, Basic Labor Agreement combined Job Classes 0, 1 and 2 into a common rate does not change the agreed job class of the respective jobs, but rather provides the proper hourly rate of pay to be applied to each such job class.

AWARD

11. The grievance is denied.

USC—373. Youngstown District Works.   March 31, 1954
Herbert L. Sherman, Jr., *Arbitrator*
Approved by Sylvester Garrett, *Chairman*

BACKGROUND

1. This grievance requests a higher job classification for the job of Gangleader Scale Repairman in the Maintenance Department at the McDonald Works. Grievant is the sole incumbent. Prior to 1948, grievant's job was labeled Foreman Scale Repair. With that designation grievant performed certain functions which he no longer performs, such as attending Management meetings and visiting the plant of a customer on Company business. Under the Management Alignment program the Union was advised in 1948 that the position would be considered as being in the bargaining unit. A job description was drawn up, but it was not accepted by the Union. At the insistence of grievant and the Union the description was revised several times. By the time of the hearing agreement had been reached on a comprehensive and detailed listing of the duties.

2. On October 1, 1952, Management installed Job Class 13 unilaterally, in accordance with the August 22, 1952 Letter of Understanding from John A. Stephens to the late Philip Murray. Since the primary function of the job requires grievant to direct a crew of Scale Repairmen and Scale Repairmen Helpers in the inspection and repair of scales, overhead doors and tag machines, the job was classified by use of the Gangleader Convention. This resulted in Job Class 13, two job classes higher than that for Scale Repairman which was classified by agreement of the parties in Job Class 11. The Union continued to contend that grievant also supervised craftsmen, such as Boilermakers, Machinists, Carpenters and Blacksmiths, and that his job should be placed in Job Class 18 by application of the Gangleader Convention to the highest rated of these craft jobs. It was pointed out by the Union that at one time the Scale Repair

Gangleader job at Ohio Works was classified as a Machinist Gangleader, even though the incumbent was not a fully qualified journeyman in that craft. To this the Company replies that grievant could not direct these jobs in their craft work since, as he admits, he is not a qualified journeyman in any of these crafts, and that a misapplication of the Gangleader Convention at one location cannot properly serve as a basis for misapplying the Convention at other locations.

3. At the hearing the Union frankly adopted a different approach. By considering the classification on a factor by factor basis, the Union now agrees with the present ratings on Factors 10, 11 and 12, but seeks higher ratings on the other nine Factors. The present ratings and those sought by the Union are set forth in the following table:

FACTOR	PRESENT RATING	UNION PROPOSAL
*1. Pre-Employment Training	B- .3	C-1.0
*2. Employment Training and Experience	E-1.6	H-3.2
*3. Mental Skill	D-2.2	E-2.8
*4. Manual Skill	C-1.0	E-2.0
*5. Responsibility for Materials	C-1.2	E-3.2
*6. Responsibility for Tools and Equipment	B- .2	C- .7
*7. Responsibility for Operation	E-3.0	C-1.0
*8. Responsibility for Safety of Others	B- .4	C- .8
*9. Mental Effort	C-1.0	E-2.5
10. Physical Effort	C- .8	C- .8

FACTOR	PRESENT RATING	UNION PROPOSAL
11. Surroundings	B- .4	B- .4
12. Hazards	B- .4	B- .4
Total	12.5	18.8

* Disputed Factors

DISCUSSION AND FINDINGS

4. The Union's proposed ratings on the Factors are based in large part upon language in the Manual under the respective codings which refers to tradesmen's work, particularly where the Benchmark job of Machinist is cited as a guide. In fact, the proposed ratings on all Factors except Factor 7 are the same or higher than those assigned to a Machinist Gangleader. In addition, the Union used Toolmaker and Instrument Repairman job classifications at McDonald as guides in adopting its present position. The Board finds, however, that these jobs call for higher skills than are involved in the inspection, maintenance and repair of scales, overhead doors, and tag and stencil machines.

5. Grievant does not pretend to be a qualified Machinist, Blacksmith, Carpenter, Boilermaker or Motor Inspector. Although he occasionally works with Boilermakers, Motor Inspectors or American Bridge Company repairmen on overhead door installations, and repairs when craft work is necessary, he is only required to "direct" them in the sense of telling them what must be repaired, showing them where the repairs are to be made, and checking the results to assure proper operation. It is not disputed that at times he informs craftsmen as to his needs, but he is not required to instruct them in the actual craft work being performed.

6. The fact that grievant's repair work is not limited to scales but extends to overhead doors and tag machines is not significant. This is similar to the Homestead Inspector-Scale Gangleader job which is responsible not only for direction of the crew on scale repairs but also for the repair of plant elevators. Grievant directed his crew of Scale Repairman and Scale Repairman Helper in their work on overhead doors and tag machines when those two jobs were classified as Job Class 11 and Job Class 5 respectively. Such work was not considered as requiring more skill or responsibility than was already necessary for scale repairs, and there has been no change in these duties since those two jobs were classified.

7. Although there is voluminous evidence in the record to show the duties which have been performed by grievant, it is clear that these duties fall in one of five categories: (1) those duties which grievant performed when he was considered a foreman, but which are no longer performed by him; (2) those duties which are expressly set forth in both the Gangleader and the Scale Repairman job description; (3) those duties which the Gangleader job description states are performed by the Gangleader and the Scale Repairman (and which have been performed by both jobs since 1946), but which are not expressly set forth in the Scale Repairman job description; (4) those duties which are not performed by the Scale Repairman, but which literally fall under the definition of a Gangleader; (5) and other duties which are not performed by the Scale Repairman, but which are closely related to the duties already noted.

8. The question before the Board is whether it is appropriate to apply the Gangleader Convention to grievant's job. Those duties falling in categories (2), (3) and (4) would clearly lead to an affirmative answer. Duties falling in the first category are irrelevant. With respect to the third category of duties, it should be noted that the Specimen Examples show that the language in a Gangleader's job description does not always set forth the duties to the same extent as is found in the job description of the highest rated job which is led, but that fact has not precluded application of the Gangleader Convention.

9. Grievant's duties which are covered by the definition of a Gangleader include planning a routine schedule of inspection for the crew, direction of the crew in making repairs on scales and doors, maintaining a supply of spare parts on hand, and requisitioning new parts to be used in the repair work. The estimated cost of a part is noted on the requisition.

10. Of the duties falling in the last category, the Union points out that the job description requires grievant to check the causes of customers' complaints concerning irregular weights at the request of the operating departments. This duty, of course, ties in closely with the primary duty of directing the crew in the inspection and repair of the scales. As to the statement in the job description that the incumbent makes and tempers scale bearings, it appears that this is a minor function no longer performed since the small gas heating furnace which grievant once used is no longer in operation.

11. The only duty of this job which is difficult to evaluate concerns the require-

ment that grievant make reports on damage to equipment under his jurisdiction, including a statement of the cause of the damage and an estimate of the cost of repairs which have been made. However, grievant is given some of this basic information by other departments, and this duty is limited to his specific equipment. Since it is not a major function of the job in dispute, the Board cannot fairly find that it provides a basis for disregarding the Gangleader Convention and adopting a coding which would place this job higher than two job classes beyond the Scale Repairman job in Job Class 11.

AWARD

12. The grievance is denied.

T—463.   Fairfield Tin Mill.   March 21, 1958

Herbert L. Sherman, Jr., *Chairman*

BACKGROUND

1. This grievance asserts that substantial changes in the jobs of Stocker Groupleader (Supplies) and Stocker (Supplies) in the Tinning Operations Department of the Fairfield Tin Mill have not been properly recognized in the classification codings. The present ratings on Factors 5, 8 and 9 for both jobs are protested under Section 9-D of July 1, 1954 Agreement.

2. As a result of a shift in customer demand in recent years away from hot dip tin plate to electrolytic coated tin plate, the need for servicing the operation of hot dip tin stacks has declined. One of the service functions for maintaining hot dip tin stacks is the "burn-off" operation. By this operation badly worn or defective tin machines, feeders, catchers, and heating elements, which must be dismantled or repaired, are heated in a furnace in order to remove accumulated tin, burnt oil, flux and other materials.

3. Prior to 1954 a "burn-off" furnace was primarily operated by the jobs of Burn-Off Furnace Operator and Burn-Off Furnace Helper. Other duties connected with the dismantling of tin stack equipment, such as the removal of bolts and nuts by burning with an oxy-acetylene torch, were performed by the job of Burner.

4. Installation of the new No. 4 Electrolytic Tinning Line required removal of the "burn-off" furnace building in 1954. Since the volume of "burn-off" work was also reduced, this work was transferred to the Scruff House. The duties of a Burn-Off Furnace Operator were assigned to the job of Dross Refining Operator, and the duties of a Burn-Off Furnace Helper were assigned to the job of Solution Tender. The Burn-Off Furnace Operator and Burn-Off Furnace Helper jobs were cancelled.

5. New job descriptions and classifications were prepared for the Dross Refining Operator and the Solution Tender, and also for the Stocker and Stocker Groupleader. The Dross Refining Operator and Solution Tender jobs were each raised one job class. Responsibility for supervising these jobs, and the requirement that grievants perform some of the "torch" work formerly performed by a Burner, were added to the existing duties of the Stocker and Stocker Groupleader jobs by the following language:

> "Directs and works with crew in the dismantling and burning off of tin machines, feeders and catchers, and uses oxy-acetylene torch to heat or burn off parts prior to dismantling."

6. Furthermore, "Operates tractor to transport tin machines, feeders, catchers, and parts to and from Machine Shop and Scruff House" was added to the Stocker job.

7. The Stocker job was raised from Job Class 9 to Job Class 10 and the Groupleader job from Job Class 11 to Job Class 12 by the Company's increasing the ratings on Factors 2, 5, 10 and 11. The new rates were made effective August 7, 1954; the grievance was filed on August 17, 1954.

8. At the request of the Union in the grievance procedure the Stocker Groupleader job description was further expanded to reflect other duties performed by incumbents of that job. These include spotting cars for unloading, making out truck tallies and hauling orders, checking loaded and incoming materials and supplies, and signing a receipt for materials delivered by truck. Management takes the position that such duties do not affect the classification of the Groupleader job. In any event, the parties agree that the new job descriptions presented to the Board are correct.

9. The following table shows the *present* ratings assigned by the Company to the Factors for the two jobs in dispute, and the ratings sought by the Union:

	STOCKER		GROUPLEADER	
	PRESENT	UNION	PRESENT	UNION
1. Pre-employment Training.	B .3	B .3	B .3	B .3
2. Employment Training and Experience.	D1.2	D1.2	D1.2	D1.2
3. Mental Skill.	C1.6	C1.6	C1.6	C1.6
4. Manual Skill.	B .5	B .5	B .5	B .5
*5. Responsibility for Materials.	C1.2	C2.5	C1.2	C2.5
6. Responsibility for Tools and Equipment.	CM .7	CM .7	CM .7	CM .7
7. Responsibility for Operations.	C1.0	C1.0	E3.0	E3.0
*8. Responsibility for Safety of Others.	B .4	D1.2	B .4	D1.2
*9. Mental Effort.	C1.0	D1.5	C1.0	D1.5
10. Physical Effort.	C .8	C .8	C .8	C .8
11. Surroundings.	C .8	C .8	C .8	C .8
12. Hazards.	C .8	C .8	C .8	C .8
Total	10.3	12.9	12.3	14.9
Job Class	10	13	12	15

* Factors in dispute.

10. Prior to the changes of 1954 the total point value of the Stocker job was 8.6, the total point value of the Groupleader job was 10.6.

DISCUSSION AND FINDINGS

11. The Union emphasizes both the new duties and also duties always performed by the two jobs in dispute in claiming higher ratings on Factors 5, 8 and 9. And since incumbents of the Stocker job perform almost the same duties as the Stocker Groupleader, the Union believes that the Stocker should be designated as a Groupleader.

12. The relationship between these two jobs, however, has not changed since 1946. Both in 1946 and in the first Review Program of 1947 the parties did not consider the Stocker as a Groupleader. The job was classified on its own, and the classification was signed both in 1946 and in 1947 by top representatives of the Union.

13. That the Stocker Groupleader is in fact a Groupleader is not disputed. He continues to direct the Stocker and other members of his crew.

14. Thus, the proper approach in this case is to determine the proper ratings for this basic job of Stocker, and then apply the Groupleader Convention for the Stocker Groupleader job.

15. The Company has already raised the rating on Factor 5—Responsibility for Materials from B.8 to C1.2. This coding is higher than that assigned on this Factor to the Burn-Off Furnace Operator, the Burn-Off Furnace Helper or the Burner jobs. Management assigned this rating to the Stocker job because of the possibility of damaging tin machine rolls through im-

proper use of the oxy-acetylene torch. Placing Factor 5 for the Stocker job in the "C" level of care and attention makes it consistent with the "C" level assigned to the Burn-Off Furnace Operator and Burn-Off Furnace Helper jobs on this Factor. Credit for probable monetary loss in the amount of $250 remained unchanged since this level was already higher than the monetary loss level for the Burn-Off Furnace Operator and Burn-Off Furnace Helper jobs. The Company also points out that the rating of C1.2 on this Factor is the same as that for Specimen Example 960, a Car Repairman who uses a torch to burn steel from ingot buggy draw-heads, wheels and deck plates. No evidence was presented to justify a higher rating on this Factor for the Stocker job.

16. For Factor 8—Responsibility for Safety of Others the present rating is B.4. The Union calls attention to the fact that Specimen Example 2110 for a Tractor Operator is coded at D1.2 for this Factor. Management points out that the following Specimen Examples sometimes operate a tractor and are rated at B.4 on Factor 8: 2239—Coiler, 2403—Car Blocker, 2120—Coil Feeder, 1501—Charger, 2079—Hooker, 2465—Loader Helper, and 2446—Loader.

17. The Stocker job has always operated a tractor in delivering supplies, but the parties are not sure as to how much tractor work was performed when this job was initially described and classified. Witnesses for both parties, however, testified that the amount of tractor work for grievants has increased since the original classification. Grievants must use the tractors more frequently, they must travel longer distances and through different areas. The Stocker spends about 25% of his time operating trac-

tors. While transporting, by tractor, tin machines and other equipment to and from the Machine Shop and Scruff House, grievants must travel through some areas which are fairly congested. The Company agrees that grievants must also make deliveries to an additional operating line. It states, however, that this fact should be ignored because this addition, though made long before the last Fourth Step Meeting, was made after the grievance was filed. It also notes that deliveries to some other areas have decreased.

18. The Board finds that tractor operation is neither an occasional or incidental function, nor the primary function, of the Stocker job. Considering the amount of tractor operation work and the nature of the areas through which grievants must travel, the Board concludes, in the light of the Specimen Examples, that C.8 is the more appropriate rating on Factor 8.

19. Factor 9—Mental Effort is properly coded at C1.0. No evidence or argument was presented which requires a higher rating.

20. For the Stocker Groupleader job the coding is automatic under the Groupleader Convention. The Classification Manual provides in Paragraph C-10-b:

"For purposes of classifying the group leader job, use the same classifications as those for the basic job in Factors 1, 2, 3, 4, 5, 6, 8, 9, 10, 11, and 12 of Paragraph 4 of this Section, and in Factor 7 use two levels higher than that of the basic job . . ."

21. Since the rating of C.8 on Factor 8, in addition to the other increased ratings assigned by the Company, raises the total point value of the Stocker job from 8.6 to 10.7, and the total point value of the Groupleader job from 10.6 to 12.7, the Stocker job is placed in Job Class 11 and the Groupleader job in Job Class 13.

AWARD

22. The grievance is sustained to the extent that Factor 8—Responsibility for Safety of Others should be coded at C.8, thereby placing the Stocker job in Job Class 11 and the Stocker Groupleader job in Job Class 13.

A—753. Cyclone Waukegan Works. December 20, 1957
Sylvester Garrett, *Chairman*

BACKGROUND

1. This grievance from the Cyclone Fence Plant at Waukegan claims failure properly to pay R. O'Brien as a Group Leader.

2. Prior to September 30, 1954, Grievant was a Tool Maker—Group Leader (Class 20) in the Machine Shop. He worked 3:00 p.m. to 11:00 p.m. and was responsible for directing four to a dozen or more other employees including a Tool Maker in Class 18.

3. Early in 1953, three Tool Makers working day shift in the Machine Shop filed a grievance claiming that their work actually was the same as performed in another job in Class 20. This grievance was settled in Fourth Step, September 30, 1954, on the basis that the work of the three grievants was that of Mechanical Equipment Developer (Class 20). In considering this grievance of the three men, both parties were aware that four other employees also were performing work of the same general nature, save that the present grievant (O'Brien) and a day shift employee (Wilder) were carried as Group Leaders.

4. The Fourth Step Minutes covering the September 30, 1954 grievance settlement state:—

"In accord with the Standard Title Program, the job of Tool Die Maker, Code 8-30, will henceforth be known as Mechanical Equipment Developer, Code 09-30.

"The making of dies or tools is part of the craft job of Tool Maker, Code 8-31. Only when employees with the proper skills are assigned by Management to perform such functions as designing machines or when they perform work requiring a knowledge and technique to perfect mechanical movements and work with the Mechanical and Engineering Departments in the design and construction of new production machines, dies, etc., are they entitled to the rate of the single-purpose job, Mechanical Equipment Developer, Code 09-30.

"Stanley Gregorian, Arthur Dahlin, Charles F. Bruce, George B. Wilder, Robert O'Brien, Sulo H. Waaramaki, and Walter Repkow will be classified and paid retroactive to July 1, 1953, as Mechanical Equipment Developer, Code 09-30. It is agreed that this classification is the proper classification for the work performed by the above named individuals during this period and the direction exercised by any of the above is contemplated in the description and classification of job code 09-30. The assignment of the above individuals to this work at this time does not in any way bar the Division from assigning such work to an engineering or like department and assigning only those employees in the P & M bargaining unit, as Management may require, to perform work it deems necessary. It is agreed that the assignment of these employees at this time does not establish the number of employees to be assigned to this work, but future assignments will be in accord with Management's discretion as to the work to be performed.

"Although Walter Repkow, Sulo H. Waaramaki, George B. Wilder, and Robert O'Brien were not grievants and, therefore not entitled to any retroactive adjustment, Management will waive this defense for this grievance and this grievance alone." (Underscoring added)

5. Neither O'Brien nor Wilder signed grievance CYF-W-26. Since the settlement eliminated the two job class differential which he had enjoyed over other employees, Grievant protested to his Foreman, who said he would see what he could do. Several subsequent conversations with the Foreman produced no more substantial results, and the present grievance ultimately was filed.

6. Grievant continued after September 30, 1954, to perform the same duties which he had performed prior to that date. The Union now sees no valid basis for failing to pay him as a Mechanical Equipment Developer—Group Leader (Class 22). It asserts that the true nature and extent of O'Brien's and Wilder's directional duties were not adequately considered by the parties in the September 30, 1954 meeting on Grievance CYF-W-26.

7. The Company feels that the present grievance is an effort to re-open the September 30, 1954 settlement in CYF-W-26. It stresses that the earlier settlement was specific in stating that whatever direction of other employees was exercised by O'Brien and Wilder was within the scope of the job of Mechanical Equipment Developer.

8. The Company emphasizes also that there must be judgment exercised in determining whether, and how, a particular job shall be treated under the Manual. It feels that the September 30, 1954 settlement constitutes a mutually agreed exercise of such judgment.

FINDINGS

9. The description and classification of jobs involves exercise of judgment by the parties. Here the parties in 1954 did not describe and classify any Group Leader job based on the Mechanical Equipment Developer position, although aware of the relevant circumstances then existing. The grievance now seeks recognition of such a job by the Board, based on duties performed by O'Brien.

10. The parties in their September 30, 1954 settlement agreed that the duties of Mechanical Equipment Developer included whatever directional responsibilities previously had been performed by Wilder on day shift and O'Brien on afternoon shift. Apparently the unique nature of the work of the Mechanical Equipment Developers in Class 20 raised a question as to whether the Group Leader concept properly fitted the situation. In their September 30, 1954 settlement the parties locally concluded that it did not, and the record here provides no basis for the Board to set aside this joint determination.

AWARD

11. The grievance is denied.

T—461. Fairfield Steel Works. January 31, 1958

Herbert L. Sherman, Jr., *Chairman*

BACKGROUND

1. In this grievance W. W. Gober protests discontinuance of his assignment to the "Fitter Groupleader" job on the 3-11 turn at the Fabricating Shop of the Fairfield Steel Works. For many years prior to February 15, 1957 Gober had worked on this job, which was known as "Sub-Foreman" in earlier days. The duties of the job are clearly of the planning and directional type.

2. The Union contends that Management's action was capricious because there was no change in underlying conditions, that this Groupleader job is not of the conventional type because the working procedure does not read the same as a basic job, that the job description for this job constitutes an agreement that this job belongs in the bargaining unit, that the Union's status as bargaining representative is being undermined,

that the Board's Award in T-140, relied on by the Company, is distinguishable because in that case grievants had never actually performed gangleading duties, and that other Arbitrators have sustained the Union position. The Union also points out that Gober has voted in NLRB elections. For these reasons it asserts that Sections 2-A, 2-B, 9-D and 13 of the August 3, 1956 Agreement and the Classification Manual have been violated.

3. Management notes that changes in supervision in the Fabricating Department were made pursuant to an over-all study. Six supervisors were added to this department, two to the Fab Shop. One Foreman was added to the day shift for the Fab Shop; another Foreman and a Fitter Groupleader were retained for that shift on which 125 employees worked. Because Management personnel had been required to stay over on the 3-11 shift in the past and had been called out in the evening to the Fab Shop, the Company decided to assign a Turn Foreman to that Shop for the 3-11 shift. Previously, Gober had no direct supervision, although a Welder Foreman was available as required. Since there were only 21 employees in the Fab Shop at this time, Management decided to dispense with the services of a Groupleader on that shift and to have the directional and planning duties assumed by the Foreman. The new Foreman was also assigned a number of Management functions never performed by Gober. In accordance with his seniority Gober was offered the Groupleader job on the day shift, but at his request he was retained on the evening shift as a Fitter 1st.

4. The Company denies that its action was arbitrary. It notes that other Arbitrators have disagreed in their rulings on the issue presented by this case, but that, in any event, the Board has had occasion to pass on this question in prior cases. Moreover, it holds that the job description for the job in dispute does not constitute an agreement that the job will always be filled.

FINDINGS

5. At the bottom of the job description for the Fitter Groupleader job, the following is found:

USC—616. South Works. June 18, 1957
Sylvester Garrett, *Chairman*

FINDINGS

1. This grievance from the Foundry and Pattern Shop Department of South Works protests discontinuance of the assignment of

"Basic Job for Application of Group Leader Conventions.
Fitter (676-655) Classification 15.1.
Factor 7 C-1.0."

6. The classification codings for this job are the same as those for Fitter (1st), except for Factor 7 where the Groupleader Convention was applied. Hence, it is clear that the parties have treated this job as a Groupleader job.

7. Whether Management is required to continue utilizing the services of an employee in a Groupleader capacity is not a novel question for the Board. In Case A-666 the Board said:

"Cases T-140 and USC-413 recognize that direction of the working force is a Management function, and that it rests in Management discretion whether—at any given time—it desires to utilize the services of employees in Gang Leader capacity. On February 17, 1953, Management made plain that it would not thereafter utilize the services of a Machinist—Group Leader in connection with auto repair work. The Board cannot reverse this determination, which is a proper exercise of Management discretion in direction of the working force."

8. A few months ago the Board decided USC-616, in which substantially the same arguments were made as in this case. There the Board quoted the above language from A-666 and stated:

"The Union suggests that the January 1, 1956 Manual requires the Board to adopt a different rule in this case. But Cases T-140, USC-413 and A-666 were decided on the basis of Agreements of the parties which for all practical purposes were the same as those now in effect. General language from opinions of other Arbitrators in different bargaining relationships often does not provide a reliable guide to interpretation of agreements between the present parties."

9. Thus, the present grievance must be denied.

AWARD

10. The grievance is denied.

James Nelson as Ingot Mould Finishing Groupleader.
2. In 1940 Nelson was designated Foreman and thereafter directed up to 40 em-

ployees in conditioning moulds. Under the Management Alignment program in 1949, however, Nelson's title was changed from Foreman to Groupleader while he continued to perform the same duties until the reorganization in 1956, which gave rise to this grievance.

3. Under the reorganization Foreman Valles was transferred to the mould finishing area to assume part of the duties and responsibilities of General Foreman Strieby, as well as the directional duties performed by Nelson as Groupleader. Nelson's job as Groupleader was terminated and he was assigned to the Chipper job. There is no issue raised as to Nelson's competence and reliability in performing his directional duties from 1940 to 1956.

4. The Union feels that all of the directional duties performed by Nelson as Gangleader still are performed by Foreman Valles and that it therefore was improper to terminate his assignment as Groupleader. It believes that Management's action infringes upon Nelson's seniority rights as well as Section 9-D and undermines the Union's status as bargaining representative by removing a job from the bargaining unit. It cites various decisions of other Arbitrators to support this view.

5. It is clear that Foreman Valles is not simply performing Nelson's former job under a Foreman label. Valles handles important supervisory duties not handled by Nelson, and does not perform non-supervisory duties which Nelson performed. While all the work Nelson once did is being performed either by Valles or by other employees, the result stems directly from Management's decision that reorganization of its supervisory force was required.

6. The Union does not question the basis of this decision, or suggest it to be capricious. In Case A-666 the Board stated:—

"Cases T-140 and USC-413 recognize that direction of the working force is a Management function, and that it rests in Management discretion whether—at any given time—it desires to utilize the services of employees in Gangleader capacity. On February 17, 1953, Management made plain that it would not thereafter utilize the services of a Machinist—Groupleader in connection with auto repair work. The Board cannot reverse this determination, which is a proper exercise of Management discretion in direction of the working force."

7. The Union suggests that the January 1, 1953 Manual requires the Board to adopt a different rule in this case. But Cases T-140, USC-413 and A-666 were decided on the basis of Agreements of the parties which for all practical purposes were the same as those now in effect. General language from opinions of other Arbitrators in different bargaining relationships often does not provide a reliable guide to interpretation of agreements between the present parties.

AWARD

8. The grievance is denied.

A—666. Joliet Works. June 10, 1954
Sylvester Garrett, *Chairman*

BACKGROUND

1. This grievance requests (a) retroactive compensation for grievant for work performed as Machinist—Group Leader in the Auto Repair Shop of Joliet Works, and (b) that the job of Machinist—Group Leader be declared to exist in the Auto Repair Shop, and filled as such.

2. The roots of this grievance in part lie in the manner in which the parties dealt with description and classification of several jobs involving repair and maintenance of combustion engine-powered vehicles and equipment at Joliet Works. When the standard hourly wage scale first was installed at Joliet on February 9, 1947, certain automotive repair work handled by Anton Tadey ostensibly was described and classified as the work of Machinist—Group Leader (Job Class 18).

3. This treatment of Tadey's work for classification purposes was agreed upon by the parties despite the fact that they had developed a job description and classification for a job of Automotive Mechanic (Class 14), seemingly to cover the duties of Tadey. But when Tadey was shown the description of Automotive Mechanic by Grievance Committee Chairman Stewart, Tadey pointed out that it did not cover certain important portions of his work. When the Union then questioned whether the description properly was applicable to Tadey, the parties finally settled the matter by agreeing that Tadey would be called a Machinist—Group Leader (Job Class 18), and paid as such.

4. The working procedures outlined in the two descriptions of Automotive Mechanic and Machinist—Group Leader are fundamentally different. This is partially

indicated by the primary function in the respective descriptions: (a) Automotive Mechanic—"Inspect, overhaul and at all times maintain and keep in repair all types of trucks, automobiles, tractors and diesel locomotive crane," and (b) Machinist—Group Leader—"To perform Machinist work and direct maintenance crew regularly on specific assignments. To lay out work, set up and operate machine tools, and perform any dismantling, fitting or assembly work required for plant maintenance or construction."

5. The fact seems to be that neither of the two descriptions were fully, or accurately, descriptive of the work done by Tadey as an individual. While the Auto Mechanic description may come closer to defining the work done by Tadey, nonetheless he carried certain responsibilities which reasonably could be deemed to embody a leading function. According to the Union's undisputed evidence, a group of Riggers, Millwrights, Machinists and Laborers was assigned to work under Tadey's direction, whenever he handled a locomotive crane repair. In addition, the evidence reveals that on big diesel repair jobs, Tadey had one or two other men working under his direction. Grievance Committeeman Schweizer agreed that this kind of job was not very frequent, even though one came along at periodical intervals.

6. In July, 1951, a Machinist Helper (Mitok) was assigned to the Auto Repair Shop to work with Tadey. At the request of the Union, however, Mitok later was slotted into the Automotive Mechanic job on December 23, 1951, and raised to the Class 14 rate.

7. Payment of Tadey as Group Leader continued until November 11, 1952, when he was transferred out of the Auto Repair Shop to handle the installation and operation of a newly acquired diesel locomotive crane. At this time grievant Pavnica, Standard Rate Machinist (Class 16) was transferred into the Auto Repair Shop to take over the work done by Tadey. Pavnica was paid only Job Class 16, however.

8. On December 21, 1952, Tadey was reassigned to the Auto Repair Shop and Pavnica returned to the Machine Shop. On January 2, 1953, Tadey quit working for the Company, and Pavnica was reassigned to the Auto Repair Shop. Again he was paid only the Class 16 rate, and the present grievance resulted.

9. Allegedly on the basis of a decline in volume of repair work, Pavnico was relieved from duty on February 13, 1953, the day following the filing of his grievance, and returned to the Machine Shop. Later a

notice of job opening for a second Automotive Mechanic in Job Class 14 was posted, and was filled April 6, 1953. Since that time all work in the Auto Repair Shop has been handled by two employees slotted into the job of Automotive Mechanic. The Machinist—Group Leader classification has not been utilized in the Auto Repair Shop since April 6, 1953.

10. In the First Step answer to the present grievance, Foreman Meyer stated, "Management has determined not to fill the job Gang Leader—Machinist that formerly had been in use in the Auto Repair Shop." There is no showing that Management at any time prior to the First Step answer on February 17, 1953, told grievant or others that the Machinist—Group Leader duties were not to be performed in the Auto Repair Shop thereafter.

FINDINGS

11. Cases T-140 and USC-413 recognize that direction of the working force is a Management function, and that it rests in Management discretion whether—at any given time—it desires to utilize the services of employees in Gang Leader capacity. On February 17, 1953, Management made plain that it would not thereafter utilize the services of a Machinist—Group Leader in connection with auto repair work. The Board cannot reverse this determination, which is a proper exercise of Management discretion in direction of the working force.

12. But the record is barren of any showing that Management had reached such a decision, or communicated it to grievant, at any time prior to February 17, 1953. There is nothing to suggest that grievant did not perform the full scope of the duties performed by Tadey as Machinist—Group Leader during the time grievant served in the Auto Repair Shop. Hence, grievant was entitled to assume that he not only took over Tadey's duties, but also the rate applicable to those duties. Grievant should be made whole for loss of earnings sustained by failure to pay him at the Class 18 rate during the period he served in the Auto Repair Shop up to February 17, 1953.

13. The Union stressed its view at the hearing that work formerly done by Tadey, and now done by two men in the Automotive Mechanic position, requires "a higher type of skill" than contemplated under the description and classification of Automotive Mechanic. The present Decision deals only with the elimination of the Machinist—Group Leader job in the Auto Repair Shop, and the rate which should have been paid to Pavnica. No opinion is expressed, therefore, on whether the elimination of Machinist—

Group Leader produced a significant change in job content of the Automotive Mechanic position, within the meaning of Section 9-D.

AWARD

14. The grievance is sustained in part only. Grievant Pavnica shall be made whole for loss of earnings suffered as a result of failure to pay him at the Machinist—Group Leader rate for the work he performed in the Machine Shop between November 11, 1952, and February 17, 1953. In other respects the grievance is denied. No opinion is expressed as to possible change in job content of the Automotive Mechanic position subsequent to February 17, 1953.

USC—413. Youngstown District Works. March 31, 1954

Sylvester Garrett, *Chairman*

BACKGROUND

1. This grievance comes from the Mechanical and Electrical Maintenance Shops, Ohio Works, and Maintenance Shops Department, McDonald Mills, of the Youngstown District Works. It presents an issue as to Management authority to eliminate Gang Leaders, as well as claims by 18 grievants that they should be reinstated as Gang Leaders, and paid retroactively to the date they were demoted from Gang Leader positions in February, 1952.

2. For many years prior to 1952 substantial numbers of employees were used in Gang Leader capacity at both McDonald Mills and Ohio Works. Some men labelled as "Gang Leaders" actually performed supervisory duties. This situation produced a grievance late in 1950 which protested that Gang Leaders in fact were acting as supervisory employees and asking that they either be relieved of supervisory duties or given a special rate. This grievance reached the Third Step and led to a careful study by Management of the utilization of Gang Leaders both at McDonald Mills and Ohio Works. Management finally became convinced that a number of the Gang Leaders should be placed in supervisory positions, and that others were no longer needed as Gang Leaders and could be returned to the Standard Rate of the job which they had been assigned to lead.

3. About January 15, 1952, the Grievance Committee of the Youngstown District Works was notified that the Maintenance Shops would be reorganized with some Gang Leaders eliminated and others designated as members of Management.

4. The McDonald Maintenance Shops' reorganization was effected February 1, 1952. Of 15 Gang Leaders, 5 were promoted to supervision and 10 demoted to the applicable standard hourly rate. The Ohio Works Mechanical and Electrical Maintenance Shops' reorganization went into effect February 16, 1952, and approximately 60 Gang Leaders were eliminated by promoting 35 to supervisory jobs and demoting 25.

5. In effecting the reorganization, each demoted Gang Leader was interviewed by his Department Superintendent and told that he was no longer to serve in a Gang Leader Capacity. The grievants are 18 of the 35 demoted Gang Leaders.

6. While the elimination of Gang Leader positions in the Maintenance Shops was discussed with Union representatives several times before the reorganization was effected, no complaint was registered by the Union until this grievance was filed on November 26, 1952.

7. The Union protests the demotion of the Gang Leaders as a violation of Section 2-B-3, and requests restoration of Gang Leader status to all demoted Gang Leaders. In this regard it relies on the long-standing practice of using men as Gang Leaders, and holds this to be an established local working condition within the meaning of Section 2-B.

8. The Union also urges that the former Gang Leaders in fact have continued to function in the same manner as in the past when they were paid as Gang Leaders. Thus, under Section 9-B-3 and 9-B-4, the Union requests that the men be paid for the Gang Leader rate. The Union presented evidence as to six grievants calculated to establish that they were performing their work today in the same manner as before February, 1952, when they were recognized as in the Gang Leader status.

9. Management stresses that the present grievance was not filed until November 26, 1952, even though the principal events complained of transpired in February, 1952.

10. As to Section 2-B-3, the Company relies on Board Decisions in Cases T-140 and CI-257, indicating that Management retains discretion to direct the working force and particularly to determine whether to utilize the services of employees in a Gang Leader capacity.

11. Finally, with respect to the six grievants whom the Union contends continued to perform substantially the same duties as prior to February, 1952, the Company introduced evidence calculated to show that none of the men in fact continued to per-

form Gang Leader duties subsequent to February, 1952.

FINDINGS

12. Insofar as this grievance seeks to protest Management's discontinuance of use of Gang Leaders as a violation of Section 2-B-3, it would be untimely. But even on the merits the Union argument as to application of 2-B-3 in this type situation could not prevail in view of the Board's Decision in Case T-140. Accordingly, this aspect of the grievance will be dismissed.

13. As to the specific grievants who claim to have continued to function in Gang Leader capacity since February, 1952, a question involving the integrity of the agreed rate structure is presented. If the men are in fact performing Gang Leader duties, with Management's knowledge and consent, the failure to pay them the proper rate violates 9-B-3 and 9-B-4, and constitutes an error in wage payment within the scope of 9-I. The defense of untimeliness cannot be effective as long as the alleged violation continues, even though the failure to file a timely grievance will affect retroactivity of any adjustment in rate which may be required under Section 9. Hence the Board must consider the cases of six grievants on their merits from the time of filing the grievance.

14. Before considering the evidence as to the six grievants, however, a preliminary word is in order. Each man plainly was told by higher supervision in February, 1952, that he no longer should function as a "Gang Leader." Ordinarily one would suppose that this would be the end of the matter and that no grievant, having been so instructed, thereafter legitimately could claim to have served in fact in Gang Leader capacity. The evidence is quite clear, however, that some of the grievants did later perform as Gang Leaders at the express direction of their immediate supervisors (and perhaps without the knowledge of higher supervision).

15. This anomalous situation is perhaps best understandable in light of the fact that prior to February, 1952, many of the "Gang Leaders" actually functioned in the same manner as supervisors, and should not have been in hourly-rated positions at all. Thus, in February, 1952, some supervisors and employees, alike, labored under a false impression as to what actually constituted service as a Gang Leader.

16. This misunderstanding on the part of some has continued up to the present, as appeared in testimony of witnesses of both parties at the hearing. For example, General Foreman Kroll—whose testimony is particularly significant as to grievants Kellgren,

Protich and Evans—was not familiar with the Gang Leader description, and testified that he instructed Protich as to his Gang Leader duties on the basis of "past practice." The evidence leaves no doubt that Protich was something more than a mere Gang Leader prior to February, 1952, since he assigned work to, and directed, crews of from 20 to 50 men, and lined up the materials for use in the various jobs performed under his direction.

17. In these circumstances the Board is obliged to review the evidence as to each grievant to ascertain what duties he performed after February, 1952. If such duties in a given instance were of Gang Leader nature, and were performed at the direction of—or with the full knowledge and consent of—a responsible member of Management, then the particular grievant is entitled to pay at the applicable Gang Leader rate. But where a man volunteers to function as a Gang Leader without the authorization or consent of Management, he is not entitled to receive the Gang Leader rate. As Case T-140 indicates, it is within the discretion of Management as to whether it wishes at any time to utilize the services of employees as Gang Leaders in directing the working force.

18. Roy Mountford has been employed in the Electrical Department of McDonald Works for 28 years. He was promoted to Gang Leader in 1947, and worked in that capacity until February 1, 1952, when he was demoted to Armature Winder. Prior to February, 1952, Mountford spent approximately 50% of his time doing field work involving armature winding. In handling such assignments he normally had another Armature Winder working with him, and occasionally still other employees. In seven months prior to the hearing, Mountford had done no field work. During the period from February 1, 1952 until seven months prior to the hearing he estimated that he had spent approximately 25% of his time on field assignments. During such assignments he normally did not have more than one other man working with him.

19. While it is clear that Mountford received the Gang Leader rate at all times prior to February, 1952, the only apparent basis for this was his field work when he and another employee or two were outside the Electrical Shop. In view of the nature of this field work it is apparent that Management can, if it elects, have it handled without use of a Gang Leader. The evidence does not establish that Mountford in fact has functioned as a Gang Leader, within the proper meaning of that term, since February, 1952.

20. *John Goddard* has been employed

in the Electrical Department of McDonald Works for 30 years. He served as Assistant Foreman from 1942 until 1947, when his title was changed to "Gang Leader" without change of duties. He received $.20 per hour more than the rate of the highest job which he led, instead of the $.10 differential called for by the true Gange Leader status. He was demoted to Armature Winder on February 1, 1952, with a $.20 reduction in wage rate. While the Union contends that Goddard's work after February 1, 1952, continued to be the same as before, this is not supported by Goddard's own testimony. After February 1, 1952, he was put on armature winding, but was given other miscellaneous assignments by Foreman Brauer from time to time in order to give him an opportunity to adjust to the work gradually. In addition he continued to give advice and information to newly promoted Foremen, and was generally helpful to them in performance of their supervisory duties. The advice and information which he gives to green supervisors is not required of him, and does not provide the basis for payment of a Gang Leader rate.

21. *Lorain Morris* has served 13 years in the Carpenter Shop at McDonald Works. He was promoted to Gang Leader in January, 1951, and served as such until February 1, 1952, when he was demoted to standard rate Carpenter. Prior to his demotion about 50% of Morris' gang-leading duties were performed in connection with the fabrication and erection of concrete forms. He handled the blueprints on the form jobs, and used them to direct other Carpenters in the shop, when the panels were made, and was in charge of erecting some large forms at the job site.

22. Morris testified that Superintendent Bentz told him in February, 1952, that the Gang Leader jobs were being abolished and that he would have to work thereafter at the standard rate for Carpenter. After a few months, according to Morris, his immediate Foreman—Scott—nonetheless resumed giving him direction of a crew of four or five men in fabrication and erection of heavy concrete forms. He flatly stated that he had run every form job in the months before the hearing just as he had prior to February, 1952.

23. Morris admitted that he has not prepared estimates on jobs since February, 1952, has not assigned other men to various jobs, and has not directed more than one crew at a time since that date, as he did before. Since these duties are supervisory and do not fall within the proper scope of Gang Leader duties, their elimination after

February, 1952, would appear irrelevant to the issue here.

24. Foreman Scott testified that after February, 1952, he gave Morris work assignments only as a standard rate Carpenter. But he agreed that he had never reviewed the description of a Gang Leader-Carpenter, and was basing his knowledge of the requirements of Gang Leader *on what he had seen Morris do previously* as a "Gang Leader."

25. Scott guessed that Morris spent about 25% of his time working on concrete forms. He went on to testify as follows:

"Q: But the general practice is for the same group of Carpenters who made the paneling to go out and install it?

"A: I'd say, if it is possible, yes.

"Q: And isn't it true if there is a question about the preparation of the paneling, and their setting up, the men generally go to Morris with their questions?

"A: Not always, no. Just as I said, Mr. Morris isn't there all the time. Somebody has got to answer their questions, that would be me." (Underscoring added)

Foreman Scott also stated that he was absent from the Carpenter Shop about 75% of his time, checking on field work.

26. While the matter is not free from doubt, the evidence establishes that Morris has continued to perform as Gang Leader in connection with concrete form jobs since February, 1952. The actual duties he has performed in this connection have been performed at least with the knowledge and consent of Foreman Scott, if not at his specific direction. This situation has arisen because of Scott's unfamiliarity with the actual requirements of gangleading. Apparently he has assumed that the supervisory functions which Morris performed prior to February, 1952—going beyond the actual requirements of gangleading—provided the only basis on which a Gang Leader rate was required.

27. Morris is entitled to be made whole for loss of earnings suffered from the failure to pay him the Gang Leader rate, retroactive to the date of the grievance, for all time spent leading other employees in the fabrication and erection of concrete forms. If the Company's records do not provide the necessary detail in this regard, the parties can agree as to the amount of time thus spent by Morris. Failing agreement, the matter may be returned to the Board.

28. *Oscar Kellgren* has been employed in the Machine Shop of Ohio Works for 31 years. He was promoted to Machinist Gang Leader about 1940, and continued as such

until February 16, 1952, when he was informed that he would no longer be required to act as Gang Leader. For a few weeks following February 16, 1952, Kellgren may not have performed the same kind of duties as he had in the past. Since that time, however, and up to the hearing, Kellgren has been performing duties partaking of supervision, as in the past, and certainly exercising at least as much authority in directing employees as is normally the case for a Gang Leader. Kellgren works with and directs two or three other Machinists (called "Fitters") who fabricate and assemble equipment for the Rolling Mills. Kellgren has a desk and a file of blueprints, and each week is given a list of projects which are to be carried out by the men working in his group handling the Machine Shop jobs for the Rolling Mill. General Foreman Kroll agreed that Kellgren continues to direct the men in his gang "more or less" in the same manner as before February, 1952. Kellgren has been offered a supervisory position, but prefers to work under the title and rate of Gang Leader. There is no doubt that the duties assigned him by Management entitle him to the Gang Leader rate, retroactive to the date of filing the grievance.

29. *James Evans* has 40 years' experience as a Machinist, and is in the same situation as Kellgren in the Machine Shop at Ohio Works. Whereas Kellgren is responsible for Rolling Mill jobs in the Machine Shop, Evans directs the men working on Electrical Department jobs. Evans did not testify, but Kellgren and another Union witness gave an adequate description of his duties, which was not challenged by any Company witness. There is no doubt that Evans is entitled to a retroactive adjustment based on the applicable Gang Leader rate, because of the duties assigned him by the Company, retroactive to the date of the grievance.

30. *George Protich* has worked in the Machine Shop of Ohio Works for 18 years. He was promoted to Machinist Gang Leader in 1948, and demoted February 16, 1952. While serving as "Gang Leader," Protich was assigned to work in the Casting Yard area, used by the Machine Shop to work on and assemble equipment for various operating units. Normally as many as 20 men worked in the Casting Yard, with Protich in charge. At times he was in charge of as many as 50.

31. Shortly after February 16, 1952,

Protich was given a special assignment as a "Coordinator" on a Blast Furnace rebuild job, in the course of which he served in more or less of a supervisory capacity. This in part was for the purpose of providing higher supervision an opportunity to observe his capacity as a potential member of Management. He was paid the Machinist rate and worked 12 hours a day, 6 days a week. After completing the "Coordinator" assignment Protich, for the most part, served at his old work station in the Casting Yard, and performed the same duties as before February, 1952. In so doing he acted at the direction of Foreman Peck, who told him to carry on pretty much as he had in the past. From this point on, his regular crew included 16 men. After the Third Step meeting in this case, Protich was interviewed by Superintendent Round and again told that he should not serve in a Gang Leader capacity. Rather than continue in the anomalous position of being told by his Superintendent not to serve in a "Gang Leader" capacity while being directed by his Foreman to perform Gang Leader duties, Protich requested a transfer into the Machine Shop. This was granted and he has worked there since, without performing any Gang Leader work. Retroactive payment to Protich of the difference between the Machinist and Gang Leader rate is due for the period from the date of the grievance up to his transfer into the Machine Shop proper.

AWARD

32. The grievance is sustained in part only. The claim that a practice exists, within the meaning of Section 2-B-3, which precludes Management from eliminating Gang Leader positions in Youngstown District Works, is dismissed. The claims that Roy Mountford and John Goddard in fact have been required to perform Gang Leader duties, without payment of the Gang Leader rate, are denied. The claims that Lorain Morris, George Protich, Oscar Kellgren, and James Evans in fact have been required to perform Gang Leader duties are sustained to the extent indicated in the accompanying Opinion. They shall be made whole as specified in the Opinion, and paid the appropriate Gang Leader rate hereafter whenever called upon to perform Gang Leader duties in accordance with the applicable job description and classification.

T—140. Fairfield Steel Works. December 31, 1953

Sylvester Garrett, *Chairman*

BACKGROUND

1. In this grievance two employees in the By-product Coke Department of Fairfield Steel Works protest the Company's action on August 5, 1948, in reducing their rate of pay from that of Gangleader (Carpenter) to that of Carpenter.

2. Grievant Rutledge testified that from 1941 until August 5, 1948, he was designated as a "Lead" Carpenter. As "Lead" Carpenter he received a rate above that of regular Carpenters. The two grievants, plus a third man, were the only Carpenters in Fairfield Steel Works who enjoyed the designation and rate of "Lead" Carpenter during this period. A complement of about 40 Carpenters was maintained at Fairfield Steel Works.

3. At no time between 1941 and August 5, 1948, did the grievants actually perform "lead" functions in the sense of directing a crew of Carpenters. Thus it is remarkable that for more than a year after institution of the standard hourly wage scale grievants were paid the Gangleader rate.

4. The Union spokesman at the hearing indicated that this anomolous situation had its roots in a widespread reaction of consternation among employees at TCI during 1946 over the prospect of substantial reductions in their rates which they believed would flow from installation of a standard hourly wage scale upon completion of the Inequities Program as to hourly rates. As a result a delegation representing TCI employees protested to top officials of the Union. A meeting between Union and Corporation officials, with local Union and TCI representatives present, then was held in Pittsburgh. At this time a TCI official assured the protesting employees that he would see that they did not suffer adversely from institution of the new standard hourly wage rate structure. Thereafter men who had been carried as "Lead" workers in various craft jobs were labelled as "Gangleaders" by the Company and paid as such from the time the standard hourly rate structure was installed up to 1948.

5. While the Union's background explanation was not substantiated by testimony the Company spokesman took issue only with specific aspects of the recital. For example, it was denied that any actual agreement was reached between Management and Union representatives at any level that the "Lead" employees in 1946 and early 1947 would be designated as Gangleaders and assured of receiving the Gangleader rate irrespective of functions performed.

FINDINGS

6. The actual duties performed by grievants never were the subject of description and classification as such. Grievant was not consulted about the duties of his position, nor did he see any Carpenter or Gangleader job description during development of the Inequities Program. The Carpenter job is a craft job as to which the parties recognized that the precise day-to-day functions, performed by men qualified as Carpenters, would not affect their receiving the appropriate rate as Journeymen. Similarly the Gangleader classification was not developed on the basis of description of the duties of particular employees. Rather, the test of whether a man is entitled to a Gangleader rate rests solely upon whether at a given time he directs the work of other employees in a crew.

7. The conventions of the parties covering Maintenance Group Leaders provide in part:—

"The functions of Maintenance Group Leaders are generally defined as follows:

"Performs and directs the work of Craft or Trade Jobs classified as standard jobs or performs and directs the work of jobs classified as position-rated jobs. Such direction consists of generally determining 'On-the-job' working procedure and delegating work assignments.

"Has recourse to supervision on labor decisions affecting the course of work."

8. From this it is clear that whether a man performs as Group Leader depends exclusively *on the duties assigned to him by Management* in regard to direction of other employees.

9. It is undenied that grievants were contacted by supervision prior to the reduction in their rate on August 5, 1948. This was for the purpose of advising them of the change in their rate and the reason for it. During the conversations the job description of Carpenter was reviewed with grievants, and they agreed that this description actually covered their work. Grievants also agreed that they did not lead other Carpenters and were not performing as Gangleaders. On one later occasion—covering a number of shifts in the Fall of 1949—grievant Rutledge actually was assigned to lead a gang of Carpenters and was paid the Gangleader rate for this period.

10. These circumstances conveyed to

grievants Management's decision that they were not to function as Gangleaders except as specifically directed thereafter, and that they would not receive the Gangleader rate unless they actually performed Gangleader duties.

11. The direction of the working force is a Management function. It rests in the discretion of Management whether—at any given time—it desires to utilize the services of employees in a Gangleader capacity.

12. The Board cannot direct that particular men be used as Gangleaders when Management has decided that no gangleading function is to be performed. Hence, it would seem clear that the Board cannot grant the present grievance.

13. While the Union seems to urge that the grievants must be paid as Gangleaders for the indefinite future, no matter what work they do, any claimed agreement to this effect made prior to April 22, 1947, would be unenforceable by the Board since it would plainly conflict with Section 9-B-3 of the April 22, 1947, Agreement. Hence it would be stricken down by Section 9-J.

AWARD

14. The grievance is denied.

CHAPTER 22

LEARNERS

The only award of the Board of Arbitration which discusses the status of Learners is set forth in this chapter. This case not only notes a distinction between Learner and other jobs, but it also recognizes that there may be more than one type of Learner situation.

A—735. Worcester Works. December 14, 1956

Herbert L. Sherman, Jr., *Arbitrator*

Approved by Sylvester Garrett, *Chairman*

BACKGROUND

1. In this case the Union contends that grievant, while he was assigned as a Learner on the Drop Forge in the Rail Bond Department at Worcester Works, should have been considered an Operator and paid incentive earnings under the pre-1947 incentive plan applicable to the Drop Forge Operator job, whenever his production exceeded his Learner rate. Otherwise, according to the Union, grievant was entitled to the applicable Learner rate under Section 9-B-1-(c) of the July 1, 1954 Agreement.

2. Among the jobs in the Rail Bond Department for which the parties have established a schedule of Learner rates is the job of Drop Forge Operator in Job Class 13. The schedule for this job consists of three Learner periods of 520 hours each. As prescribed by Section 9-B-1-(c), the respective rates for these stages are Job Class 7, Job Class 9 and Job Class 11. While grievant was still in the first Learner period, his production of a particular product on a couple of days was such that, if he was entitled to earnings under the incentive plan applicable to an Operator, his incentive earnings would have been higher than the Job Class 7 Learner rate which he was actually paid.

CONTENTIONS OF THE PARTIES

3. At the hearing the Union contended that, under Sections 9-F-2 and 3 of the Agreement, grievant was entitled to incentive earnings *as an Operator* on the days in question. This was the position adopted by the Union when Management offered to show that grievant, in his status *as a Learner,* was not entitled to earnings under the Operator's incentive plan. When given further opportunity to explore this issue, the parties mutually declared their agreement that the Board should decide the case on the basis of the position adopted by the Union.

4. To support its contention that grievant was an Operator rather than a Learner on those days when his production exceeded the Learner rate of pay, the Union stresses that grievant was working alone on the drop forge equipment. Hence, the Union believes that he is entitled to incentive earnings for those days under Section 9-F-3-(a), which reads:

"Each employee while compensated under an existing incentive plan in effect on April 22, 1947, shall receive for the applicable single or multiple number of eight-hour turns in effect as of January 13, 1947, the highest of the following:

"a. The total earnings under such plan;"

5. Although Management agrees that grievant was working alone while learning the Drop Forge Operator job, it denies that he should be considered an Operator for the days in question. It argues that the present case involves the very type of Learner situation contemplated by Section 9-B-1-(c) (incorporated into the April 22, 1947 Agreement on May 1, 1950, and carried forward into the July 1, 1954 Agreement), as distinguished from the "extra man" Learner type situation contemplated by Section 9-B-1-(d).

6. The Company asserts that the purpose of the Amendments of May 1, 1950, was to replace completely the old Learner rate practices under the various types of Learner programs then in effect. Although prior to May 1, 1950, some Learners at Worcester Works,

404

operating under learning programs with many variations from the Learner program prescribed in Sections 9-B-1-(c) and (d), were paid incentive earnings of an Operator, the Company stresses that there is no instance at Worcester Works since the adoption of the May 1, 1950 Amendments where Learners have been paid Operator incentive earnings. This has been true whether the Learner was of the type contemplated by Section 9-B-1-(c) or Section 9-B-1-(d).

7. Moreover, the Company declares that even if a practice did exist prior to May, 1950, to pay either the old Learner rate or earnings under the old incentive, whichever was the higher, continuation of such a practice would have required its continuance as an entity. And this would have been inconsistent with the new Learner stages and rates under Section 9-B-1-(c).

8. Furthermore, Management contends that the Learner and the Operator positions are separate jobs and that if grievant is to be considered an Operator for purposes of the incentive plan applicable to an Operator, then the whole plan must apply. That would mean that the Standard Hourly Wage Rate for an Operator—Job Class 13—would be the daily minimum guarantee, and the Company could not pay Learner rates. Thus, the Company urges, the Union position would render meaningless the schedule of Learner rates provided for in Section 9-B-1-(c) and also Section 9-B-6. According to the Company, grievant is only entitled to the rates of pay specified in these Sections of the Agreement.

9. Management argues that a Learner does not become an Operator simply because his production may occasionally exceed his Learner rate. In fact, that is not unusual when a Learner approaches the end of a Learner period. Also, a Learner may exceed his Learner rate while producing some product, though he has not mastered production of other products.

FINDINGS

10. In accordance with the declared wishes of the parties, the Board's decision in this case is limited to a determination as to whether grievant was entitled to incentive earnings as an Operator whenever his production exceeded his Learner rate. Thus the question of whether the incentive actually contemplated payment of incentive earnings to Learners, as distinct from regular Operators—as to which the evidence is not entirely clear—need not be decided.

11. That grievant was assigned as a Learner for the Drop Forge Operator job is not disputed. While learning to become an Operator under the learning program prescribed in the Agreement, grievant was clearly not an Operator. There is nothing in the Sections of the Agreement cited to show that he should be considered an Operator. Nor can he be viewed as an Operator simply because he was working alone on the Drop Forge equipment. A comparison of Section 9-B-1-(c) with Section 9-B-1-(d) indicates that this type of Learner situation was contemplated by the parties. Hence, grievant was not entitled to compensation as an Operator under Section 9-F of the Agreement.

AWARD

12. The grievance is denied.

INDEX OF DISPUTES BY JOB TITLES

The figure in parentheses following each docket number shows the page number in this volume where that case may be found.

INDEX

The figure in parentheses following each docket number shows the page number in this volume where that case may be found.

VOLUME OF WORK
Effect on job classification, see Ch. 14.
WAGE RATE INEQUITY
See Error.
WORKLOAD
Effect on assignment of duties, CI-257 (64).

Effect on job classification, see Ch. 14. Also USC-293 (232).
Relationship to performance standards, CI-257 (64).
WORKING CONDITIONS
See Surroundings and Hazards.